D1453805

The Politics of Progress

Hiram Caton

The Politics of Progress

The Origins and Development of the Commercial Republic, 1600–1835

University of Florida Press / Gainesville

University Presses of Florida is the central agency for scholarly publishing of the State of Florida's university system, producing books selected for publication by the faculty editorial committees of Florida's nine public universities: Florida A&M University (Tallahassee), Florida Atlantic University (Boca Raton), Florida International University (Miami), Florida State University (Tallahassee), University of Central Florida (Orlando), University of Florida (Gainesville), University of North Florida (Jacksonville), University of South Florida (Tampa), and University of West Florida (Pensacola).

Library of Congress Cataloging-in-Publication Data

Caton, Hiram.
    The politics of progress.

    Bibliography: p.
    Includes index.
    1. World politics—To 1900.   2. Political science—History.   1. Title.
D217.C33   1987   909   86–30886
ISBN 0–8130–0847–6
(alk. paper)

Printed in the U.S.A. on acid-free paper

To D. F.

Aut inveniam viam aut faciam.

contents

acknowledgments

THE LONG duration of this project and the range of the subjects covered have caused me to enlist the assistance of many colleagues and institutions. I gratefully acknowledge my appreciation to all, but confine express notice to the main collaborators.

The project commenced during an appointment in the History of Ideas Unit, Research School of Social Sciences, Australian National University. My investigations were quickened by a succession of visiting fellows: Shlomo Avenari, C. B. MacPherson, Sir Isaiah Berlin, J. G. A. Pocock, Frank Manuel, Walter Kaufmann, and Peter Munz. Discussions with them and the seminar series led by Eugene Kamenka were essential to maintaining equilibrium with a project that often, in that early phase, threatened to degenerate into an idiosyncratic philosophical statement.

In 1979 the Department of Government at Harvard University provided me an opportunity to tap the unique resources of that institution. I owe the boon principally to Harvey C. Mansfield, Jr. He and his talented postgraduate students made the period of my appointment rich in collegial exchange. At that time I also received from economic historian David Landes a bibliographic pointer and a conceptual suggestion that proved to be vital.

The long gestation came to term during the year of my fellowship at the National Humanities Center in North Carolina. The amenities, support staff, environment, and resources of the center are beyond praise, so I leave it at that. It was among the Carolina pines that I dragooned a profound scholar into many conversations ranging over the back side and front side of modern history. I refer to that irrepressible and beautiful curmudgeon J. H. Hexter.

For an abundance of research grants I wish to thank the Australian Research Grants Committee and Griffith University's University Research Grants Committee and School of Humanities Research Sub-Committee. The library staff at Griffith and at the University of Queensland indulged my inordinate appetite for research materials. The Australian National Library furnished noncirculating materials without which the project could not have been completed.

The grid of behavioral biology that furnishes the framework of the present study was unapproachable without patient helpers and friends. S. A. Barnett, formerly head of zoology at the Australian National University, was the first to assist an aroused seeker. I gratefully acknowledge his assistance. Derek Freeman inspired confidence that the thing could be done. Over the years I have come to realize that his tenacity, learning, courage, and integrity merit the highest admiration. Another companion is E. O. Wilson, who, in a marathon conversation at the Harvard Museum of Comparative Zoology, showed me the view from the summits of untrammeled intelligence. His generous encouragement and gentle advice spurred the beast in the last phase of the project.

The scholarship of J. G. A. Pocock has been my model of contemporary intellectual history. My encounter with this uncommon human being commenced in 1973, when we discoursed of the equidistance of all times from eternity while walking the Australian bush. I was subsequently to be among the many who benefit from his measureless capacity to encourage and assist. If I took a different path out of the bush, it is because I have set sight on new scholarly modes and orders where time is measured by evolutionary reckoning.

Many have commented on portions of the manuscript: David Shi, Paul A. Rahe, Donald Winch, Isaac Kramnick, W. W. Rostow, Charles P. Kindleberger, E. O. Wilson, George V. Taylor, Tilo Schabert. Robert Eden's response to each chapter as it was written was an invaluable seismograph. As referee J. G. A. Pocock read every word and wrote copious comments that have greatly improved the final version. Finally, to my colleagues at Griffith I am indebted for establishing a social environment conducive to the release of certain behaviors usually excluded from academic life. They created a rare ethological observation post, and at the same time instructed the historian by giving a flashback to the *mentalité* common in universities prior to their subjugation by Big Science.

introduction

THE PRESENT volume is a study of polytechnic rationality under the aspect of the political program with which it was most intimately identified, here called the politics of progress. I have undertaken to describe its origins and successive legitimations, its main transformations, and its notable achievements. I have also been attentive to its limitations, liabilities, and defeats.

The commercial republic mentioned in the subtitle refers to the regime typically favored by exponents of progress. The term is drawn from the vocabulary of preindustrial politics. Writers of the last century were more comfortable with *liberalism, democracy,* and *capitalism.* I have settled on the older usage because it dominated until about 1800, when the influence of Adam Smith brought *the liberal system* into currency.

The termination of this study in 1835, with an account of the polarization of labor and capital in Great Britain, is a temporary resting point. A more satisfactory periodization would carry the story forward to 1914. I intend to cover this period in another volume.

Since the historiography of progress is a legacy of "Whig history," the orientation of my study may in some measure be characterized by reference to that tradition. Whig history is more aptly called liberal history. Its monuments are the *Cambridge Modern History* (1902–12), published under the editorship of Lord Acton, and the *Histoire de France* (1910), edited by Ernest Lavisse. The presiding concept of liberal historiography was the idea of universal, scientific history promoted by Leopold Ranke during his prolific career as scholar and teacher. Acton was among Ranke's many students, and we find him writing in the introduction to the *Cambridge Modern History* that the eight-volume study assumed "as a scientific hypothesis, a progress in human affairs." Cambridge history exhibited progress as the gradual transformation of public opinion and institutions by enlightened thought directed to large ends. The narrative was constructed from the vantage point of public and usually political events, which were treated as the intersection of thought, action, and institutions. Its successor, the *New Cambridge Modern History*, reviews European history in its political, economic, religious, social, scientific, industrial, colonial, and populational aspects. I refer the reader to it for the larger historiographic panorama envisaged by the present study.

Although history of high standard continues to be written on the basis of Acton's suppositions, liberal historiography has for some time stood accused of many sins. The revolt began at Cambridge with Herbert Butterfield's denunciation, *The Whig Interpretation of History* (1931). Butterfield lamented the tendency to read events of the past in the light of the present. His preferred alternative was a contextualization process that his colleague R. G. Collingwood called "reenactment," a method not substantially different from Dilthey's historical method and Weberian *Verstehen*. The point was that description or evaluation of events in light of knowledge not available to actors distorted history "as it actually happened." Although this rebuttal acquired great prestige, it is not an effective criticism of scientific history. The method held that the opinions of historical actors were simply more data requiring test and evaluation; they are in no way probative of events. Thus the struggles of the Reformation were not to be explained in terms of perceptions of Jesuits or Calvinists, and persecutions of witches were assumed to be due to causes other than witchcraft. In positing a cumulative historical science, the liberal historians accepted the implication that present historical knowledge was more advanced than the historical knowledge of the previous generation, so that the present necessarily sat in judgment on the past.[1]

If Butterfield did not provide good reasons for abandoning the project of scientific history, there were nevertheless telling points to be made. By 1930, the fundamental meaning postulate of liberal history that the course of European civilization exhibited moral progress was not credible. While a few, notably E. H. Carr, continued to write of the

1. Lord Acton, "Inaugural Lecture on the Study of History," in *Essays in the Liberal Interpretation of History*, ed. William H. McNeill (Chicago: University of Chicago Press, 1967), 356. See also Lionel Kochan, *Acton on History* (Port Washington: Kennikat Press, 1954), 125–35.

events of the iron decades as if progress could be discerned in them, Lewis Namier's reduction of the contest of ideas to struggles for personal power seemed truer to the lessons of the day.

Loss of faith in progress involved more than loss of morale; it implied that the basic causes of social change had not been correctly identified. It was in that ambience that the chief flaw of scientific history was to be found. Liberal historians did not conceive scientific history as an integrative discipline operating with principles drawn from other social sciences; nor did they believe that such a synthesis of principles was necessary. Believing that history was autonomous, they held that the arrangement of authenticated events in narrational sequence disposed of causal questions. They therefore made no use of the sociological intuition that neither intentional human agency nor the *Zeitgeist* is the main cause of the progress of society.[2] Herbert Spencer put the sociologists' case against narrative history when he said: "Until you have got a true theory of humanity, you cannot interpret history; and when you have got a true theory of humanity *you do not want history*."[3] However Comte and Marx differed from Spencer in other things, they shared his low estimate of the epistemic value of narrative, with its focus on action and event.

Historians today largely agree that narrative methods are insufficient to the epistemic requirements of historical science. But this is not perceived as an embarrassment because they no longer pretend to historical science. That retrenchment was paralleled by the retrenchment of sociology from the grand aspirations of the system-builders. When the social sciences were shaped into their modern form by Durkheim, Weber, Marshall, and Boas, evolutionary concepts were demoted to minor position. The decay of Comtean and Spencerian sociology left only Marxism, thrown into prominence by the Russian Revolution, as contender for the master science crown. Liberal social scientists no longer aspired to it. J. B. Bury wrote the epitaph of that aspiration among historians by transferring the progress concept from historiographic method to history of ideas.

2. For a description of this development, see Georg G. Iggers, "The Crisis of the Conventional Conception of Scientific History," in *New Directions in European Historiography* (Middletown, Conn.: Wesleyan University Press, 1975), 27–35. This is not to deny that historians often *assumed* underlying economic or other causes of events; the point is that these causes were not integrated with narrative. Thus Acton held that historical method was only "the reduplication of common sense" ("Inaugural Lecture," 338).

3. Herbert Spencer, *The Study of Sociology* (London: Williams and Norgate, 1873), 31.

The resources to break this deadlock have been quietly assembled during the past two decades. Advances in prehistory, evolutionary biology, experimental psychology, and other fields presently furnish the foundations necessary for a resumption of the universal history project. We may now identify just where evolutionary sociology went astray, rectify that error, and construct a scientific heuristic for the composition of narrative history of progress as a history of polytechnic rationality.

To introduce the heuristic assumed in the present study, I will examine the evolutionary sociology of Herbert Spencer. Spencer founded the progress of society on the "law of progress" supposedly inherent to all natural processes, namely, the tendency of homogeneity to develop toward heterogeneity and complexity.[4] Applied to Homo sapiens, the law certified as natural the development of society from the initial hunter-gatherer condition to tribes, chiefdoms, and political societies; and it did good service in inspiring many apt descriptions of the increasing complexity of institutions. The developmental mechanism was this. Spencer postulated a behavioral constant—a competitive endeavor of individuals to improve their condition. By emphasizing that competition occurred in conditions of resource scarcity, he constructed a struggle for existence as the dynamic of development. Struggle was supposed to eliminate the unfit, i.e. those ill-adapted to each successive stage of social evolution. The survivors were thus better adapted; repetition of this process eventually shaped the behavior of populations to ever more complex organizations. This was not a Darwinian scenario of natural selection operating on individuals through institutions, because adaptation was conceived as having a strong learning component that was heritable. The heritability of acquired behavior enabled Spencer to conceive behavior as the dependent variable of institutional structure.[5]

This notion, which he shared with most nineteenth-century sociologists, he used to solve two problems. The first may be called the humanity puzzle. Europeans in contact with hundreds of diverse cultures, and colliding often enough with their own newly obsolescent past, urgently needed a sorting system. Spencer's copious sociological, ethnographic, and psychological descriptions labeled everything and assigned it a rung on the great ladder of social evolution. Savages sorted out as the living fossils of what advanced populations had originally been. Ancient stag-

4. Herbert Spencer, "Progress: Its Law and Cause," in *On Social Evolution*, ed. J. D. Y. Peel (Chicago: University of Chicago Press, 1972), 33–34.
5. This formulation bypasses Spencer's methodological individualism, which derives social effects from aggregate individual interaction. The bypass is justified by the circumstance that once individual interaction generates institutions, they become formative of behavior. See *The Study of Sociology*, chap. 3.

nant civilizations (China and India) had failed to develop beyond the military despotism of aristocracies terminated in Europe by the advent of the commercial epoch, and so on. The second problem solved by Spencer's system was the direction of social evolution. The tendency as displayed in the tableau of millennia was the replacement of force and will in human relations by cooperation to reasonable ends. This tendency was to culminate in the "ultimate man," a eusocial being whose private needs were fully reconciled with public goods.[6] Abrasive competition would disappear from social interaction, and the ultimate man would live in harmony with himself and others.

The flaw in the system, as T. H. Huxley pointed out, was the Lamarckian assumption that behavior is the dependent variable of social institutions. Spencer could not relinquish the assumption without abandoning his entire concept of human progress.[7] Today, Lamarckian inheritance is excluded by the theory upon which the edifice of molecular biology is erected. A new concept of progress must accordingly be premised upon the *conservation of behaviors* on the historical time scale, that is, their resistance to extinction or creation by institutional change. Huxley recognized that relinquishing Lamarckian inheritance imposed the stupendous paradox that civilized Europeans differed from savages only in the superficial habits acquired in each individual's lifetime. Since the science of behavior lay in the future, he had no way of dealing with the paradox. That future is our present, and we may accordingly dispose of it.

Animal behavior evolves along the axes of phylogenetic inheritance and adaptation to habitat. In social species, social structure is principally a function of reproduction and resource exploitation. The social structure of our species is the family and kinship system, with its two-track option for polygamy and monogamy (owing to incomplete evolution from anthropoid polygamy). The dynamics of human social structure is described by a cost-benefit calculus of reproductive strategies evolved under the constraint of scarce resources. The application of this calculus to a wide range of species and to varieties of human family systems brings a host of disparate phenomena under a single set of principles and satisfactorily explains incest avoidance, kin alliance, the pair bond, matrilineal and patrilineal descent, dowry and bride price, female claustration, infanticide, celibacy and vagabondage, isolated occurrences of polyandry, male dominance ("patriarchy"), and monogamy.[8]

6. Herbert Spencer, *The Principles of Sociology* (London: Williams and Norgate, 1897), 3: 601.
7. Derek Freeman, "The Evolutionary Theories of Charles Darwin and Herbert Spencer," *Current Anthropology* 15 (1974): 216–18.
8. R. D. Alexander, "Evolution of Social Behavior," *Annual Review of Ecological*

Once these determinations are made, we may identify invariant behaviors as, roughly speaking, those incident to social structure and social dynamics. An appreciation of their invariance may be obtained by considering their antiquity. The genus Homo is about 3 million years old; Homo sapiens arose about 300,000 B.P. and modern man dates to 50,000 B.P. If we assume that the pair bond evolved concurrently with the enlargement of the brain of Homo erectus, then the social structure of our species is about 1.5 million years old. That structure evolved as the nomadic hunter band, comprised of twenty-five to fifty persons. Homo occupied the hunter-gatherer habitat until 10,000 B.P., when settlements were established in the Fertile Crescent, followed 4,000 years later by political societies. On entering political association, the species began to occupy a new habitat of its own devising. It was a watershed

---

Systems 5 (1974): 325–83; R. D. Alexander et al., "Sexual Dimorphisms and Breeding Systems in Pinnipeds, Ungulates, Primates, and Humans," in *Evolutionary Biology and Human Social Behavior,* ed. N. Chagnon and W. Irons (North Scituate, Mass.: Duxbury, 1979), 402–35; R. Axelrod and W. D. Hamilton, "The Evolution of Cooperation," *Science* 211 (1981): 1390–96; M. Dickermann, "The Ecology of Mating Systems in Hypergynous Dowry Societies," *Social Science Information* 18 (1979): 163–95; M. Dickermann, "Female Infanticide, Reproductive Strategies, and Social Stratification: A Preliminary Mode," in *Evolutionary Biology and Human Social Behavior,* ed. Chagnon and Irons; W. D. Hamilton, "The Genetical Evolution of Social Behavior," *Journal of Theoretical Biology* 7 (1964): 1–52; W. D. Hamilton, "Selection of Selfish and Altruistic Behavior in Some Extreme Models," in *Man and Beast: Comparative Social Behavior,* ed. J. F. Eisenberg and W. D. Dillon (Washington: Smithsonian Institution Press, 1971); J. Hartung, "Natural Selection and the Inheritance of Wealth," *Current Anthropology* 17 (1976): 607–22; J. A. Kurland, "Paternity, Mother's Brother, and Human Sociality," in *Evolutionary Biology and Human Social Behavior,* ed. Chagnon and Irons; Vernon Reynolds, "Ethology of Social Change," in *The Explanation of Cultural Change: Models in Prehistory,* ed. Colin Renfrew (London: Duckworth, 1973), 467–78; A. Suzuki, "The Origin of Hominid Hunting: A Primatological Perspective," in *Socioecology and Psychology of Primates,* ed. R. H. Tuttle (The Hague: Mouton, 1975), 259–78; Donald Symonds, *The Evolution of Human Sexuality* (Oxford: Oxford University Press, 1979); S. Washburn and C. Lancaster, "The Evolution of Hunting," in *Man the Hunter,* ed. R. Lee and I. De Vore (Chicago: Aldine Press, 1968), 293–303; Robert L. Trivers, "Parent-Offspring Conflict," *American Zoologist* 14 (1974): 249–64; Pierre van den Berghe and David Barash, "Inclusive Fitness and Family Structure," *American Anthropologist* 79 (1977): 809–23; E. O. Wilson, *Sociobiology: The New Synthesis* (Cambridge: Harvard University Press, 1975), and *Comparative Social Theory* (Ann Arbor: Tanner Foundation, 1980).

event, recognized as such by historians, who conventionally date the beginning of history from it. However, the conventional chronology is purely honorific and it creates the impression that the civilized past is the solid and interesting part of the human past. The new chronology exhibits a more balanced picture. Civilized existence occupies only 0.004 percent of the time elapsed since the rise of Homo erectus; most human beings had no direct share in civilization until very recently. As for the industrial phase, it represents a trifling 0.0001 percent of that elapsed time. The figures suggest that the experiment with the new habitat has not run long enough to warrant certainty of its permanence.

The new chronology of human history indicates that the commencement of the phase of progress dates from the construction and occupation of the urban habitat. To generate a framework for the composition of historical narratives of events of this phase, we need a description of the structure and dynamics of political association. In the present state of knowledge, two factors stand out as distinctive dynamical properties. One is exponential growth of technological and social complexity, the other the emergence of institutions. Let us look at growth.

The Anatolian settlement of Jarmo (9000 B.P.) contained four species of domesticated animals and permanent dwellings for about 200 persons. There was no pottery, no metal goods, and no evidence of status differentiation. Four millennia later, the Uruk culture of Mesopotamia was in possession of many of the arts, techniques, and institutions that were to remain the staple of civilization until industrialization. These included the plough, the sail, the cart, pottery, metallurgy, irrigation, writing, fortified cities of 50,000 inhabitants, monumental architecture, trade, social classes, law, administration, armies, and kingship.[9] The explosive precocity exhibited in this contrast suggests that the toolmaker's big brain was and remains a fundamental dynamical force of politically organized society. But why was the explosiveness, or exponential expansiveness, of polytechnic intelligence not manifest sooner? The institutional setting required to free its powers had been missing.

The formation of institutions was a feat comparable to inventing the wheel. Hunters had no institutions. They had none, first, because they

9. Georges Roux, *Ancient Iraq* (London: Penguin, 1980); J. E. Pfeiffer, *The Emergence of Society: A Prehistory of the Establishment* (New York: McGraw-Hill, 1977); Colin Renfrew, ed., *The Explanation of Cultural Change: Models in Prehistory* (Boston: M.I.T. Press, 1975); W. Oswatt, *Habitat and Technology* (New York: Holt, Rinehart and Winston, 1973). It is important to note that Homo sapiens, who emerged 50,000 B.P., was a much more adept artificer than his predecessor, Neanderthal. See Charles Lumsden and E. O. Wilson, *Promethean Fire* (Cambridge: Harvard University Press, 1983).

aggregated in numbers too small for the institutional scale and, second, because they interacted face-to-face, on a footing of ritualized equality (among adult males). Institutions, by contrast, subordinate face-to-face interaction to formalized information and command channels linking the building blocks of an organizational pyramid.

These two differences enable us to distinguish social structure and dynamics from political structure and dynamics. Social structure is the kinship system and its dynamics is the reproductive cost-benefit economy. Reproductive costs dominate the economy because they constitute by far the largest proportion of the band's total energy investment. Exchanges of goods and assistance accordingly flow through the channels of kinship established by spouse exchange.[10] Gainers in exchange acquire status, usually as male elders. The fact that kin alliance and exchange are seen to continue in every known political society corroborates the hypothesis that behaviors incident to social structure do not change on the historical time scale. However, in political society, kin alliance and exchange are supplemented by another exchange system comprised of institutions controlling the generation and distribution of public goods.

Public goods are an increment of wealth, safety, or advantage obtainable only through institutional organization. Law and defense are public goods in political communities, but not among hunters. Among the latter, defense is a function of kin association, while kin reciprocities are largely regulated by custom, the equivalent of law. Public goods are the economic component of the urban habitat. Institutions are artifacts of a particular kind—social technologies—engineered to produce public goods. They constitute the political component of the urban habitat. Political structure, comprised of public goods and institutions, piggybacks on social structure by diverting a portion of total energy output from the channels of kin reciprocity into channels of institutionally controlled production and distribution. There is probably a threshold for the proportion and kind of energy diversion required if political structure is to jell. At the other end of the scale, there are probably effects of diminishing returns. Political power should be expected to increase in

10. In addition to the titles on family systems cited in note 8, see particularly Uri Almagor, "Gerontocracy, Polygymy, and Scarce Resources," in *Sex and Age as Principles of Social Differentiation,* ed. J. S. La Fontaine (New York: Academic Press, 1978), 139–58; P. L. van den Berghe, *Age and Sex in Human Societies: A Biosocial Perspective* (Belmont: Wadsworth, 1973), and *Human Family Systems* (New York: Elsevier, 1979); Peter A. Corning, *The Synergism Hypothesis: A Theory of Progressive Evolution* (New York: McGraw-Hill, 1983).

proportion to the efficiency of production and distribution of public goods and also with the increase of the proportion of total output channeled through institutions.

This description of the cost-benefit dynamics of political societies corresponds to the observed performance of historical states. With few exceptions they have been dominated by military aristocracies leagued with priesthoods, which apportioned the largest share of public goods to themselves.[11] All aristocracies and most priesthoods were nepotistic institutions channeling the distribution of public goods significantly into familial benefit. This circumstance set a ceiling to their power and territorial extent. The modern state emerged from aristocratic feudalism by substantially increasing the proportion of public goods distributed through public institutions. One means to this end was the enhancement of distribution through market exchange, which was achieved by entrenching financial and legal institutions designed to facilitate trade. Another measure was the diminution of the share of public goods controlled by the clergy. The program to this effect was initiated by the German emperors in the protracted struggle with the Papacy. The present study identifies that struggle as the power and legitimacy contest whose consequence was the emergence of the consolidated secular state.

The mechanisms of progress are not completely described without remarking the unique productive power of institutions. I previously noted the explosion of technological innovation that occurred between 9000 B.P. and 5000 B.P. The explosion was concurrent with increasing artisan specialization, division of labor, and coordination of activities, that is, with the entrenchment of institutions. Institutions were part of the exponential growth of social complexity, but they were also its chief enabling cause. To indicate this in a clear way, let us consider an important political institution: disciplined force.

The behavioral basis of military institutions exists among hunters, although the institutions themselves do not. The warrior is a defender of himself and his folk against predators, including other men outside the kin group. Within the group, he enacts dominance behaviors common among sexually competing vertebrate species. The competition is mitigated in man by the pair bond, which promotes monogamy, but more importantly by the male bond, which unites the hunters to share risks and spoils. Risk-taking is reproductively cost-efficient, since the warrior who perishes aiding his kin may be confident that his offspring will re-

11. John Kautsky, *The Politics of Aristocratic Empires* (Chapel Hill: University of North Carolina Press, 1982).

ceive care and that his genes will be spread by surviving sibs. But it will not pay to put himself frequently or flagrantly at risk.[12] Lethal intergroup conflict reflects this reproductive fitness calculus. Hunters are not a disciplined force. They act spontaneously and as loosely associated groups under the titular headship of an elder. The numbers in which they aggregate are small because they have no means of forming alliances. Their main tactic is the ambush, which is the preferred mode of lethal conflict because it minimizes risk to attackers. Open confrontations between assembled groups usually take the form of ritualized exchanges of bluster, insult, and spears. Fatalities are infrequent and wounds are few.[13]

Such conflict is not warfare, which is found only among chiefdoms and political societies. Military discipline aims in the first instance at the control of force by creating units responsive to command. A military unit can take to the field and stay there indefinitely. It can be combined into numbers limited only by supply and communications. It can march twenty miles, cross a river, fight, regroup, and fight again. The destruction it can wreak, and the terror it can inspire, are quite beyond anything hunters can imagine. Richelieu, with an army of 8,000, inflicted one million deaths on civilian populations during the Thirty Years' War. Great Britain held the Indian subcontinent with ten regiments and a fleet. Such spectacular effects are the typical performance of politically organized peoples.

The effects are achieved without any alteration of the hunter's behavioral repertory. The secret lies in resequencing individual behavior, and in combining individual action to create group action, using no other resources than those already existing in the human material. Warriors are made into soldiers by detaching hunter solidarity from the diluting influences of family and by redirecting the evolutionary function of band solidarity to the public goods of political society. Such manipulative techniques are based on the same craftsman intuition that pervades the proto-technologies of early states. In both cases prodigious effects were achieved by recombining naturally occurring materials and forces. The wheel is nothing more than a mechanical optimization of momentum by reduction of friction. It creates no new quantum of natural force. Yet its effect is to increase exponentially the disposable power of those who

12. W. D. Hamilton, "Selection of Selfish and Altruistic Behavior in Some Extreme Models."

13. I. Eibl-Eibesfeldt, *The Biology of Peace and War* (London: Thames and Hudson, 1979); R. Gardner and K. G. Heider, *Gardens of War: Life and Death in the New Guinea Stone Age* (New York, 1968); Napoleon Chagnon, *Yanamamö, The Fierce People* (New York: Holt, Rinehart, and Winston, 1968).

possess the technology. The simple insight that natural processes, including human nature, may by deft manipulation be made to multiply their uncultivated yield, is the cornerstone of capitalization, of political organization, and of progress. It is the achievement of man's polytechnic rationality.

This framework enables us to establish a definite relation between historical narrative and evolutionary process. Homo sapiens has two histories. One is his natural history as an evolved primate species exploiting a variety of environments thanks to his fabricative precocity. The second history commenced when the clever animal constructed the urban habitat. Our narrative is accordingly a story of the works and deeds of polytechnic rationality, inclusive of its multifaceted relations with other human propensities, behaviors, and conditions. In this scenario the disjunction of action and event from underlying causes does not occur, because historical orthogenesis ("progress") is nothing else than the cumulative aggregate effect of institutional action. Man's second history, in other words, is the story of the extension of technical control over the artificial habitat.

The story is political because the habitat is political. Marx conceived the political struggle to be, in the last instance, reason's endeavor to subdue nature, including refractory human nature. True human history, he believed, would commence after the "realm of necessity" was conquered. The evolutionary framework pictures the relationship differently. The commencement of man's second history does not terminate natural history. The two are concurrent, and can only be so, because political association is piggybacked on the species' social structure by the artifice of social engineering. This circumstance means that civilized men simultaneously occupy two distinct temporal dimensions, the linear time of natural history (birth, copulation, death), and the representational time peculiar to the urban habitat. Urban life requires constant use of time representations in order to synchronize complex activities. Calendars, sundials, and astronomy were among the early techniques of time-reckoning. But in synchronizing action to the requirements of the artificial habitat, urban life forfeited synchronization with the linear time of natural history. This circumstance became the source of the enduring "discontent" with civilization, which I style the noncontemporaneity of man with himself. The malaise has apparently been perceived in all civilizations, for none lacks a mythology of yearning for the golden age and the simple life. In the Western tradition, this literature embraces some of the peak achievements of the moral intellect. Jeremiah called worldly Israel back to righteousness. Plato surveyed the folly of Greek politics from the luminous peaks of his communist utopia.

St. Augustine catalogued a millennium of empire, vainglory, and slaughter. In modern times this literary genre attracted writers of great eloquence, but it remained a secondary tradition until the severe conflicts of the present century turned it into a major voice. Man's noncontemporaneity with himself is plainly exhibited in the anguished or vehement rejection of certain requisites of modern life and the nostalgia for a golden age, past or future.[14] The values espoused in this literature correspond remarkably well to certain values of hunters—the simple life, face-to-face interaction, community, sharing, solidarity—and some authors, such as Rousseau, dated the commencement of alienated life to the origin of property and the state.

Since the literature of rejection of civilization comprises the chief written expression of opposition to the politics of progress, it must necessarily figure in our narrative. Indeed, it lies in the foreground of the polemics of advocates of progress, for whom opposition to tradition and authority—residues of the past noncontemporaneous with the present—was an ingredient of their institutional innovation. The two great cultural residues of the past were scholastic philosophy and the biblical tradition. While Protestantism is in some quarters believed to be a major mover of progress, that is not the view taken here. Protestantism revived primitive Christianity and beyond that the models of the Old Testament. The soteriology of salvation through faith placed a premium on the ecstasis of conversion, whose political forms were the concept of the godly commonwealth and the millenarian vision of a world transformation in an eschatological future. The theory of progressive politics, anchored in the teachings of Thomas Hobbes and John Locke, assailed these notions as superstition. Hobbes denied the possibility of converting temporal power to the ends of the heavenly city. He reduced all possible conversions to one—the transition from the savage state of nature to political society. Once this watershed was crossed, he maintained, there was no turning back. The alternative was not brotherliness and charity but chaos and civil war. His main teachings consistently endorse the values of civilization and denigrate the values of conversion. Cosmopolitanism was endorsed by the equality doctrine, which denies the distinction between the virtuous and the wicked required by moral suasion. His biblical commentary asserted that the Kingdom of God terminated when Israel established kingship. Religious experiences of conversion and rapture he styled hallucinations of the brain. The anthropology of competitive egos sanctioned diversity and excluded community. The natural rights doctrine endorsed upward

14. C. J. Erasmus, *In Search of the Common Good: Utopian Experiments Past and Future* (New York: Free Press, 1977).

mobility and armed individuals against sectarian demands for conformity. All this was contextualized in a mechanistic cosmology that excluded agencies of unnatural causation. It was the ultimate in karma doctrines.

The religious interpretation of modern origins is indicative of the low visibility, to historians and sociologists alike, of the causal efficacy of polytechnic rationality. This may be due in some measure to want of affinity between scholarship and technology; but it also reflects the values of weighty traditions. None of the world religions valorizes man's technical capacity; all glory is to moral heroes of cosmic dramas. While *techné* became a theme of Greco-Roman mythology and speculation, no scholar of antiquity composed a study of commerce, finance, administration, or the mechanical arts. Such objects were deemed unworthy of the gentlemen to whom intellectuals of antiquity addressed their learning. Not until the Renaissance did scholars begin to appreciate art and the artful as a theme of civilization. Their aesthetic appreciation was raised to a new plateau when mingled with science, yielding, by mid-seventeenth century, the first polytechnic conception of the gentleman as "experimental philosopher."

The historical impact of polytechnic reason is indirectly acknowledged by the interpretations of modernity that conceive its agency as capitalizing work. But its autonomous and autocatalytic properties are misrecognized when capitalizing work is derived from theological anxiety or class advantage. While on the present interpretation Marx's analysis is superior to Weber's, both miss the mark in two respects. They share—with Spencer—the belief that the causes of great social change must involve the agency of large numbers of people. My heuristic of the exponential enhancement of aggregate effects by institutional organization disposes of the appearances that make that belief seem reasonable.

Second, both believed that human reason swam in the stream of religious or social motivation. In recent years, a bulky literature in philosophy of science and intellectual history has grown up supportive of the sociology of knowledge implied by their view. When read as an autobiographical statement of intellectuals in this century, that interpretation reflects the experience of recruitment to ideologies. While that experience is undoubtedly an important datum, it does not support the global conclusions drawn from it. Regardless of what individual scientists have believed, science and technology in the age of ideology have continued to be "value-neutral," that is, true to the values inherent to those enterprises. The lesson of the experience is the opposite of the one offered, since every ruling ideology has been compelled, by the conditions of national power, to nurture science, while every attempt to subject its conceptual structure to ideology has failed. As historiography, the sociology of knowledge is equally unhappy. From its inception modern science was cosmopolitan. Its cadres were recruited across religious, national, and class lines. The self-consciousness of these cadres, as expressed in records subsequently to be examined, matched these facts. They espoused the values of liberty and intellectual independence, explicitly rejecting the traditional values of authority and personal loyalty. The derivation of these values from Protestantism and social class is achieved by arbitrarily identifying the values of a small, religiously and socially heterogeneous cadre of scientists with the values of the great mass of Protestants or the bourgeoisie.

The prominence of sociological historiography today suggested that something more than abundant citation was required to produce a lively impression of the values of polytechnic rationality. I have chosen the expedient that seemed best calibrated to the enormous diversity of the material—authorial imitation. I have deployed the allure of epic, the goad of wit, the malice of irony, the ecstasis of Eureka, the plodding determination of work, the sublimity of contemplation, the élan of innovation, the impudence of iconoclasm, and the serenity of the long view in an attempt to convey the prodigious variety of value and feeling present in one segment of the history of polytechnic rationality. In a word, my historiography is consciously graphic.

Some may complain that it is also partisan. That it certainly is, for I have written from the polytechnic point of view. But the complaint is without consequence if there is no value-neutral position for the composition of history. The authorial voice of scholarly impartiality, which I also use, is certainly not impartial, for it can render only average experience and familiar ideas. While average experience is by no means to be despised—it is the firm earth of the present study—it is not the whole of the human spirit.

I would caution, however, that the partisanship of this study is a heuristic. It is not the vehicle of the author's philosophy and it does not serve any ideology. This should be clear from the periodization, which places the congeries of attitudes, opinions, and philosophies examined in a definite past. Specifically, the Hobbes-Locke political philosophy, which I identify as the first stage of political science, lost its contemporaneity with the modern world about a century ago. Intellectually it has been superseded by evolutionary biopolitics. Similar observations apply to the Hobbesian position on religion and theology, which remain to be thought through from the new perspective. I hope that important task will be assisted by the canvass of scientific atheism and humanist superstition presented here.

chapter 1

Three Manifestos

EUROPE at midpoint in the eighteenth century was in some ways like a developing region of the late twentieth. Its largely peasant population was illiterate, devout, tied to station and place by a long chain of social distinctions. The great cities did not equal the size of Augustan Rome— Paris held about 750,000 inhabitants, London 675,000. Their water supplies were unreliable and their sanitation facilities insufficient to prevent disease and offensive odors. Most roads challenged endurance during the months of good weather and were often impassable at other seasons. Power was supplied by wind, water, and animals, especially the human animal. Everything was handmade. Craftsmen entered their trade through the apprentice system under the authority of masters, who controlled the guilds. Their exquisite workmanship, now prizes of the rich or of museums, must have been labors of love, for wages were low. Daily activity began at sunrise and for most people finished soon after sunset. Only scientists and fashionable gentlemen with pocket watches counted time in units smaller than the hour. Life was synchronized by the rhythms of weather, work, and worship rather than by the abstract schedule of the time-measuring machine. Bread riots occurred intermittently in bureaucracy-choked France, under the slogan of "just price," a notion drawn from ecclesiastical ethics. Nearly everywhere the clergy controlled educational institutions and often manned them as well. If reports of the Jesuit mission to China are credible, a mandarin visiting Europe at that time would have thought it a somewhat disorderly realm, a little backward in taste and deficient in public works.

But mingled in these textures of life there was a quality of a different kind. Had our hypothetical mandarin listened to the talk in the salons of France, or questioned a Dutch financier on commerce and agriculture, or sought explanations from a chemist in his laboratory, he would have detected an uncanny regular rhythm unknown in China and only newly born in Europe: the ticking of the clock-universe.

A stroll down London's Ludgate Street, commonly called "Sir Isaac Newton's Head" after a large sign that hung there, would have brought him among the shops of a dozen opticians and instrument makers whose devices were used to measure the world machine. The mandarin might have purchased many finely tooled precision instruments unknown among China's best engineers: spectacles, telescopes, microscopes, thermometers, hydrometers, hydrostatic balances, theodolites, and a whole line of surveying instruments, pumps of all kinds for use by chemists, even an aquatic microscope, not to mention prisms and magic lanterns for amusement and instruction.

And the ticking was discernible in the most unlikely places—*Gentleman's Magazine,* for example. Each issue reported daily barometric pressure, temperature, and births and deaths for the city of London, set out in neat tabular form, and likewise the prices of stocks and commodities. A typical issue prints an illustrated description of a diving boat and a communication from the celebrated Swiss mathematician Euler concerning Russian exploration of the northern seas in search of a passage to Hudson Bay. A report on the French Academy's latest inspection of inventions turns up a new method of cleaning fabrics in textile manufacture, a formula for converting turf to coal, a new odometer, a new method for drawing wire, a new reel for use in silk manufacture superior by a factor of ten to the English method. A report from the Midlands describes water-powered bellows built on scientific principles. Another describes a pyrometer so sensitive that it registers heat from the human body. A description of a new method of preventing suicide is followed by a critical article on Richardson's *Clarissa,* while Admiral Vernon's broadside against the British maritime service is reprinted: "Our fleets, which are defrauded by injustice, are first manned by violence and maintained by cruelty."[1]

The European's penchant for measuring and improving everything would have seemed to the mandarin symptomatic of a strange restlessness. And the savant's belief that he had not gotten to the bottom of a phenomenon until he had found a "mechanism" would have struck him as bizarre, all contrary to his views about yin and yang. Yet only a cen-

1. *Gentleman's Magazine* 19 (1749): passim.

tury later, the merest day by Chinese reckoning, the bizarre idea had penetrated or stormed every aspect of European life—and not only Europe, as the Chinese learned to their dismay.

What were the causes of that vast transformation? How did it happen that the grandiose Crystal Palace Exhibition of 1851 drew scientific and industrial exhibits from every European nation while other, more ancient civilizations had nothing of the kind to show? Despite diversity of outlook and nationality, commentators of the day agreed that the cause of the Exhibition was progress. The educated and common man alike said that steamships, vulcanized rubber, anesthesia and vaccination, even new weapons were progress. Progress meant "cause" in the double sense of "the standard to which the enlightened repair" and "the grand transforming power." That cause, in both senses, was rationality, inventive genius, science. Thus the *Edinburgh Review* (1851) commented on the Crystal Palace Exhibition:

> To seize the living scroll of human progress, inscribed with every successive conquest of man's intellect, filled with each discovery in the constructive arts, embellished with each plastic grace of figured surface or of moulded form, and unroll this before the eyes of men, the whole stream of history furnishing its contingent,—placing Archimedes, Arkwright, Davy, Jacquard, Watt, and Stephenson side by side,—leaving the instructive lesson to be learned that always lies in the knowledge and example of great things done;—this is, indeed, no mean design, no infelicitous conception. It is only by such a cosmical comparison of the known agencies of science and art that we can gradually rise to a knowledge of the varied gifts and powers of Nature, or our own control over them: hereby alone can we hope with Faust,
>
> . . . to see the secret rings,
>   Whose grasp the universe engirds;
> May know the force that works in things,—
>   Not the mere sound that breathes in words.
>
> As a nation, we cannot claim the distinction of having originated this great lever of industrial progress; but we have at least given to the world the two philosophers, Bacon and Newton, who first lent direction and force to the stream of industrial science; we have been the first to give the widest possible base to that watch-tower of international progress, which seeks the promotion of the physical well-being of man, and the extinction of the meaner jealousies of commerce.

These remarks, which occurred in one of the vital transmission belts between the Victorian intelligentsia and the public, reproduced the consensus of the day: The agency of progress is successive "conquests" by men of outstanding intellect. The conquests activate "no mean design, no infelicitous conception"—the improvement of the human condition by knowledge and control over the powers of nature. Interpreters differed about details, some very important, but they agreed that progress was the inner tendency of history toward ever more enlightened society. Thus Auguste Comte declared that "ideas rule the world" and harnessed all history to three stages of mental development. His English admirer, J. S. Mill, subscribed to this "law of progress" and asserted in *A System of Logic* that "the state of the speculative faculties . . . essentially determines the moral and political state of the community" (605). This being so, the science of society was inseparable from the explanation of its progression; hence, "a philosophy of history is generally admitted to be at once the verification and the initial form of the philosophy of the progress of society" (607).

The reading of the history of the human species as a story of progress was not the foible of men attempting to interpret unprecedented technical and social change. Nineteenth-century writers were heirs to the concept of progress disseminated a century previously, well before the astounding wave of change broke across Europe. The historiography of the philosophes described progress and the mind's march to certitude as its effective entry into human affairs in the office of guiding light and directing agency. Baconians that they were, reason implied foresight, and the potency of reason implied conscious effort to set progress in motion: it implied a politics of progress.

The decades of the mid-eighteenth century were awash in tracts that diffused that politics. In 1749, Charles Baron de Montesquieu, president of the Parlement of Bordeaux, published *The Spirit of the Laws,* in which he assessed the conditions favorable to that new goal, the commercial republic. The book itself was a fine commercial success, enjoying many printings and translations for more than five decades. Across the channel, David Hume advertised the same goal in his cheerful, urbane prose, with results nearly as brilliant. The Cartesian physician La Mettrie published *Man a Machine* (1748), which so scandalized the clergy that he sought and found refuge in the court of the philosopher-king Frederick the Great. Nor was it all words. In England, Viscount Folkestone founded the Society for the Encouragement of Arts and Manufactures (1754), while Scottish universities began that funding of the sciences that was soon to put them in the forefront of chemistry and medicine. The commercial city of Hamburg opened Europe's first polytechnic secondary school. Engineering was assiduously cultivated in France's École des ponts et chaussées, while provincial scientific academies added their weight to the encouragement of science.

The *Encyclopedia*

Such was the environment into which Denis Diderot and Jean d'Alembert launched, in 1751, that grand manifesto of progress, *The Encyclopedia, or Rational Dictionary of the Sciences, Arts, and Trades*. Despite their youth, they were prominent in the fashionable circles of Paris. D'Alembert had written a landmark treatise on mechanics, while Diderot had published several important philosophical works, particularly *Letter on the Blind*, for which he was jailed. In 1747 Diderot discussed with the Paris publisher Le Breton the prospects of issuing a translation of Ephraim Chambers's *Cyclopedia*. That plan quickly developed into the idea of a new comprehensive encyclopedia, with Diderot and d'Alembert as editors. A prospectus was circulated in 1750 and netted 2,000 subscribers. By the appearance of the third volume (1754), the number of subscribers had doubled, and Diderot had begun what became twenty years of editing twenty-eight folio volumes, which grossed the contented Le Breton over 4 million livres.[2] Months after the appearance of the first volume, a syndicate of English publishers issued the Preliminary Discourse in translation and announced a plan to translate the whole into English. Though a licensing agreement was reached with Le Breton in 1752, the plan foundered under the cascade of French eloquence.[3] Nevertheless, the work was celebrated throughout Europe and America as the grand synthesis of Enlightenment thought.

The cosmopolitan orientation of the *Encyclopedia* was reflected in the distinguished group of contributors from the professions, from commerce, finance, and manufacture, from the clergy, and from academic ranks. The breadth of the contributors was matched by the encyclopedists' conception of the diversity of their audience, which extended, as Jacques Proust noted, "from the academician to the craftsman."[4] For the *Encyclopedia*—or, more precisely, Diderot—vigorously executed the

2. The completed *Encyclopédie* ran to thirty-five volumes, including eleven volumes of illustrations. After Diderot's resignation from the editorship, Panckoucke continued the editing until all volumes were completed in 1780. A new edition, begun in 1788, eventually ran to 166 volumes, completed in 1832. For a résumé of the publication history, see John Lough, *The Encyclopédie*, 17–38.

3. Arthur Wilson, *Diderot*, 150.

4. Jacques Proust, *Diderot et l'Encyclopédie*, 203.

Baconian program of improving trades and manufacture by joining them with the appropriate sciences. Diderot supervised the *Encyclopedia's* comprehensive description of more than one hundred trades and manufactures, illustrated by thousands of engravings of tools, fabrication processes, machines, and workshops.

It is not surprising that the *Encyclopedia* fell afoul of censorship, as it did twice, despite Malesherbes' discriminating administration of antiquated law and Le Breton's editing of his own editors. Publication was suspended in 1759 when the *Encyclopedia* was cited, with a number of other books, as tending "to destroy royal authority and . . . [insinuate] irreligion and unbelief";[5] and in 1770 the press run of three volumes was confiscated by royal agents. Although the Jesuits were probably right to complain that the *Encyclopedia* was "the most formidable machine ever set up against religion,"[6] the bookshops of Paris were glutted in those days with fast-selling rationalist tracts. Censors might dam a stream but not a torrent. Malesherbes declared the futility of the censorship law in a memoir on the eve of the Revolution: "There are some books that even today lack express permission, but which are sold in shops, hawked in the streets, and announced in publishers' catalogues because everyone knows that it is useless and even ridiculous to try to oppose it."[7]

The Progress of the Mind

In the Preliminary Discourse, d'Alembert evoked a panorama of the progress of the arts and sciences and explained its bearing on the work at hand. As subscribers would have expected, he proclaimed the *Encyclopedia* an advocate of a thing called "true philosophy," newly discovered in the "century of light" by a few illustrious minds—Bacon, Descartes,

---

5. J.-P. Belin, *Le commerce des livres prohibés*, 44. For assessments of the willful impiety of the *Encyclopédie* as estimated at that time, see Lough, *The Encyclopédie*, 91ff., 102ff., 120ff., 150ff., 204ff.

6. Wilson, *Diderot*, 158.

7. Belin, *Le commerce des livres prohibés*, 33. See Wilson, *Diderot*, 161–72, for further details of censorship and harassment. On the circulation of atheist, materialist, and Deist manuscripts between 1700 and 1750, see Ira O. Wade, *The Clandestine Organization and Diffusion of Philosophic Ideas in France*. One reason why the censorship law was unenforceable in any uniform way was that many censors approved books by their friends—or even approved books as a sort of mockery of the system, as when one censor approved publication of the Koran as containing "nothing against the Catholic faith, nor contrary to good morals" (Belin, *Le commerce des livres prohibés*, 22).

Galileo, Kepler, Huygens, Locke, Newton, and some half-dozen others are inscribed on his honor roll. Despite some differences among them, upon which he remarked, d'Alembert represented their work as a unified collaborative endeavor based on a common standard, "reason." In the past, philosophical reason had spawned argumentative pedagogues and sectarian strife. "True philosophy" terminated that turmoil by discovering the actual powers of the mind and setting them to work as polytechnic rationality. This, for the encyclopedists, was among the most important events in human history; indeed it was the event-series from which historical science was to be dated, since objective knowledge of human affairs had been unattainable before the method of clearing the mind of prejudice was known. One fruit of the renovation of historiography was a view of the history of the human species as an advance from primitive conditions. The process was said to be irreversible, and the encyclopedists confidently expected it to accelerate now that the hidden agency of advance, polytechnic rationality, was understood in its manifold applications, from the manual arts to engineering and science, from the arts of government and peace to the refinements of the polite arts.[8]

The conceptual machinery d'Alembert used to launch these tidings was the debate about the relative merits of ancients and moderns (*la querelle des anciens et des modernes*). The binary terms of the debate were not adequate to the expansive views of the *Encyclopedia*'s historiography, but it was a handy introduction to them. The debate, conducted in France and England between 1680 and 1710 by literati, enjoyed a high profile. The question at issue was whether classical models of literary forms, fine arts, and moral conduct retained their authority or whether moderns had broken new aesthetic ground and surpassed the ancients in refinement, proportion, and virtuosity. This literary set-to was, how-

---

8. See the articles under the headings Agriculture, Art, Authorité politique, Barbarie, Chasse, Chronologie sacré, Commerce, Contrat, Droit naturel, Egyptiens, Espèce humain, État de nature, État morale, Famille, Gouvernement, Honneur, Industrie, Legislateur, Propriété, Raison, Sociabilité, Tolérance. The historiography of the *Encyclopedia* was the "four-stage theory" of man's development from hunter-gatherer existence ("the state of nature") through agriculture to commerce. There appear to be no recent studies of this theme, but see René Hubert, *Les sciences sociales dan l'Encyclopédie*, especially part 2. The four-stage theory was enunciated independently by A. R. J. Turgot in two writings of 1751, in particular the *Tableau philosophique des progrès sur l'histoire universelle*. Ronald Meek's *Social Science and the Ignoble Savage* describes the development of the four-stage theory among Scottish writers with but brief references to France and none to the *Encyclopedia*.

ever, only one event in a more extensive debate about the value of ancient models in philosophy, science, and politics. Machiavelli had said that the moderns equaled or surpassed the ancients in everything except *virtù* and statecraft, and this deficiency he attempted to remedy with his new science of politics. Bacon, calling on Machiavelli, and Descartes, following both, also invoked the distinction. Descartes, like his contemporaries Hobbes and Galileo, laid it down that the moderns had definitively surpassed the ancients in philosophy and science, since moderns had at last succeeded where the ancients only attempted to discover "true philosophy."[9] The significance of this achievement was that old models lost their authority, and one could, in Machiavelli's phrase, "rely entirely on oneself."

D'Alembert's treatment of ancients and moderns integrates this extensive background. The initial moderns were the Italian artists of "the first century of light," the sixteenth century.[10] The renaissance of the arts he does not allow to be mere imitation of classical taste and artistic technique. Insofar as the Renaissance was a restoration, the thing restored was not models but the sensibility that the Greeks called "imitation of nature" (*mimesis*) (*Encyclopédie*, 1: xi). In the fine arts, nature is imitated through the capacity to reproduce in imagination an alert receptivity to direct, striking sense experience. The revival of sculpture, mastery of form, composition, perspective, and light and shadow were all aspects of the lively Italian mimetic capacity.

The same sensibility brought to the sciences results in "empiricism" and rejection of erudition. "The universe and reflection," d'Alembert wrote,

> are the first book of true philosophy, and the ancients undoubtedly studied it. It is necessary to do as they did. But study of their works cannot substitute for this study, since they have mostly been de-

9. This is the message of the *Discourse,* especially the concluding part 6. The message is restated in the preface to the *Principles of Philosophy* and in the preface to the *Passions of the Soul.* Reception of the message is strongly registered in Diderot's *Encyclopédie* article, Cartésianisme, as well as in "Éloge de René Descartes," the prize essay of the Académie Française in 1765 (reprinted in *Œuvres complètes de Descartes,* ed. Victor Cousin, 1: 3–80). For more recent assessments of the message, see Richard Kennington, "René Descartes"; H. Caton, *The Origin of Subjectivity: An Essay on Descartes,* 3–9, 63ff.; David R. Lachterman, "Descartes and the Philosophy of History"; and H. Caton, "Tory History of Ideas."

10. Diderot and d'Alembert, *Encyclopédie, ou dictionnaire raisoné des sciences, des arts, et des métiers,* 1: xxii.

stroyed. . . . Scholasticism, which comprised all purported science in the centuries of ignorance, was very harmful to the progress of philosophy in this first century of light. (1: xxiii)

Classical philosophy was revived only in the sense that the moderns recovered the ancients' *directness toward nature*. The recovery met such resounding success that in natural philosophy and even politics the ancients had nothing to teach the moderns but errors (1: xxiii).

The significance of this double action of moderns in renewing and surpassing the ancients unfolds more fully when we look to the reasons why the natural relation to nature required a restoration at all. How could so "natural" a thing have been lost? In deference to the censor, d'Alembert posed this question obliquely and answered it by implication. The natural relation to nature, he said, was suppressed by "prejudice," "superstition," "ridiculous veneration for antiquity," and "authority" that blinded men in the "centuries of ignorance" (1: xiv, xii–xiii, xxxii–iii). The era intermediate between Greco-Roman antiquity and modernity was the Christian era; and the words *prejudice* and *superstition* were code words among the philosophes for *religion*. It was easy for d'Alembert's readers to notice that the Judeo-Christian religion was also "ancient." By consulting the relevant articles on this tradition, the reader finds that Judaism had no literature apart from the Bible, that it forbade sculpture, painting, and theater *because* they were mimetic arts congenial to the polytheism of their gentile enemies. Judaism was also hostile to science. What it offered was faith in the Unseen God of Israel. Men believed not their eyes but their consciences; they saw what authority told them to see. "Mosaic philosophy," as the encyclopedists called it, was the monument of a people "stupid, superstitious, xenophobic, ignorant of the study of physics, incapable of taking account of natural causes."[11]

This strong language of predatory reason on the prowl did not surface in the Preliminary Discourse, where d'Alembert played with im-

11. The quotation comes from Chevalier de Jaucourt's *Encyclopédie* article, Médicine. See also Peinture, Sculpture, and Statues, on the prohibition upon representation of human and animal forms. Israel was a polemical target for the encyclopedists because the valorization of its history by a millennium of theological influence had severely distorted ancient history. They endeavored to restore proportion by giving extensive attention to the ancient civilizations of the Mediterranean basin, China, India, and Mesoamerica. Israel was held to be a barbaric derivative from the advanced civilizations of Egypt and Babylon. See Juifs, Egyptiens, Philosophie mosaïque, Barbarie, Prophétie.

plications and insinuations. He said enough to alert readers that contemporary survivals of ancient barbarism were the occasion for the contemporary collision between ancients and moderns. Ecclesiastical authorities, he declared, had a "very real interest in opposing the advance of philosophy" and were attempting to suppress "this liberty so necessary to [it]" (*Encyclopédie,* 1: xxiv). After alluding to the "theological despotism" that disgraced Galileo, he wrote (heedless of chronology): "While ill-instructed or ill-intentioned adversaries openly made war on philosophy, she took refuge, so to speak, in the works of some great men, who, renouncing the dangerous ambition of ripping the blindfolds from the eyes of their contemporaries, prepared from afar, in shadows and silence, the light which ought to be explained to the world little by little and by insensible degrees. At the head of these illustrious personages stands the immortal Lord Chancellor of England, Francis Bacon" (1: xxiv).

On this showing, the social milieu of the seventeenth century was not especially hospitable to true philosophy. It is a good bet that whoever complains of being invaded is shooting back and calling it self-defense. Certainly in Jonathan Swift's satire of the ancients-and-moderns quarrel, the moderns return fire. And d'Alembert left little doubt about how matters stood: Judeo-Christian religion depends on authority; but true philosophy is incompatible with authority, as light is incompatible with darkness. The antithesis suggests that the Enlightenment critique of authority, superstition, and prejudice was an assault on religion intended to pave the way for the empire of reason.

That under prodding from "the party of humanity" the clergy reluctantly scaled down their claims on public affairs is well known.[12] That innumerable tracts on natural religion, rationalist arguments for religious toleration, and attacks on superstition were a major factor in that change is also plain to see. The suggestion of the Preliminary Discourse was that such effects derived from the circumstance that "true philosophy" was secular to the core and that what A. D. White called the "warfare of science with theology" was an ingredient of the politics of prog-

---

12. See Peter Gay, *The Party of Enlightenment: Essays in the French Enlightenment,* and Alan Kors's very illuminating *D'Holbach's Coterie: An Enlightenment in Paris,* for descriptions of the membership and operations of the progressive faction in France. A valuable earlier study is J.-P. Belin's *La mouvement philosophique de 1748 à 1789. Étude sur la diffusion idées des philosophes à Paris d'après les documents concernant l'histoire de la librairie.* Belin's sources (memoirs, literary histories, official records of the censorship office) reveal the underground network linking the *gens de lettres* in their overt and covert struggle with the *ancien régime.*

ress from the beginning. The advent of "true philosophy" would in that case certainly mark a turning point in history.

This was the considered view of Comte, who estimated that the critical component of positive philosophy had caused "the greatest revolution, intellectual and social, that the human race could undergo at any period of its careers."[13] Critical enlightenment had demolished not only the hold of institutionalized moral constraints over individuals but also the legitimacy of limiting intellectual freedom by requirements of political subordination. Comte expressed inconsistent views about how this delegitimation occurred. According to his theory of endogenous change, enlightenment propaganda was continuous with the spirit of rebellion manifest in the Protestant theology of conscience, which developed into the irreligion of enlightenment individualism. But then, noticing that Protestant sects prohibited and persecuted free inquiry, he traced enlightenment criticism to an exogenous cause—positive science (woefully misunderstood, as Comte believed).[14] The second of these opinions corresponds to the views of the encyclopedists about their own intentions and their relation to milieu. A statement of that relationship is contained in Diderot's *Encyclopedia* article "Encyclopedia."

Enlightenment Propaganda and Politic Religion

With his usual verve and theatrical sense, Diderot declared that the *Encyclopedia* was intended to promote the "general education of mankind"

13. Auguste Comte, *The Positive Philosophy of Auguste Comte*, 2: 253.
14. For the endogenous case, see ibid., 2: 45, 259, 268, 278, 345; for the exogenous case, ibid., 2: 269–70, 277, 279, 288, 297ff., 345. Comte's view of the Enlightenment as a Christian heresy was probably suggested by the Catholic apologist Joseph de Maistre, whom Comte cited with approval. Comte's view has been advanced by numerous clergymen and laymen writing on progress over the past four decades, e.g. Reinhold Niebuhr, Christopher Dawson, John Baillie, Karl Löwith, Eric Voegelin, Emil Brunner, Paul Tillich, and Thomas Molnar. This literature was summarized by the skeptical Warren Wagar in "Modern Views of the Origins of the Idea of Progress." In *The History of the Idea of Progress*, Robert Nisbet threads a middle course between the religious and secular origins of progress, allowing influences from both sides. One ought also mention Hermann Ley's eight-volume *Geschichte der Aufklärung und Atheismus* (Berlin: Hahn, 1966–80). Despite the formulaic Marxism in which Ley has cast his study, he frequently recognizes that the Enlightenment was a force independent of religion, class, and nation.

and as such was part of the riptide of "our philosophical age" that had already effected and would continue to effect a "revolution . . . in the minds of men and in national character."[15] The age was more "enlightened" than the previous century for several reasons. The battle against Scholasticism and for the new science had been won among thinking men. Aristotle and Ptolemy were defended only in universities, whereas men of fertile intellect affirmed the mechanistic universe and daily augmented knowledge. Among that same class of men—the philosophes—new political science was likewise unchallenged. The age was philosophical thanks to this unanimity among the intelligentsia. But the intelligentsia were a fraction of the literate population, who were in various degrees of affiliation with the new philosophy in its struggle against the old ways of thinking. Apart from objections by the censor, it was not possible to "rip the blindfolds" from this all-important middle group without confounding them. They had to remove the blindfolds themselves, as much or as little as they wanted, depending on how much truth they could endure. The *Encyclopedia* mediated this process of self-enlightenment, and at the same time humored the censors, by its system of cross-references of articles. The enlightened view on religion or miracles, for example, was not to be found in the articles on these subjects, but in the cross-referenced articles. Those secondary articles "confront one theory with a contrary one, they show how some principles conflict with others; they attack, undermine, and secretly overthrow certain ridiculous opinions which no one would dare to oppose openly. When the author is impartial, they always have the double function of confirming and confuting, of disturbing and of reconciling" (6: 642). Continuing in this cheerful vein, Diderot wrote:

> There should be great scope for ingenuity and an infinite advantage for the authors in this latter sort of cross-reference. From them the work as a whole should acquire an inner force and a secret efficacy, *whose silent results will necessarily be felt with the passage of time.* Whenever a national prejudice seems to merit respect, for instance, it will be necessary, in the article devoted to it, to discuss it respectfully and to surround it with a halo of probability and attractiveness. But by giving cross-references to articles where solid principles serve as the foundation for diametrically opposed truths, we

15. *Encyclopédie*, 6: 636. For an outstanding résumé of the character of the revolution that Diderot made in his own mind, see Tilo Schabert, "Diderot," in Arno Baruzzi's *Aufklärung und Materialismus im Frankreich des 18. Jahrhunderts,* 99–131.

shall be able to throw down the whole edifice of mud and scatter
the idle heap of dust. This method of putting men on the right
path works very promptly upon good minds, and it operates infalli-
bly, without the least undesirable effect, secretly and unobtrusively,
upon all minds. This is the way to lead people, by a series of tacit
deductions, to the most daring conclusions.[16]

To indicate that a touch of sporting malice was not wanting in this *jeu
de guerre,* Diderot commented on the ironical "eulogies" scattered
through the *Encyclopedia:* "One can aim irony secretly against certain
ridiculous customs in the same way that the philosophical reference is
directed against certain prejudices. It frequently affords a delicate and
amusing way to pay back an insult without even seeming to put oneself
on the defensive, and it offers an excellent means of snatching the masks
from the faces of certain grave persons" (6: 642).

All this may leave us breathless and a little giddy. What a combination
of hypocrisy and candor, of *humanité* and aggression! What is more remarkable, the system of confirming and confuting statements was put to

---

16. Ibid. Diderot was practicing the method of "exoteric writing," the history of
which is reviewed in the articles Cabale and Exotérique. In his *Outline of an
Historical View of the Progress of the Human Mind,* Condorcet drew attention
to this technique of writing and described it as "caressing prejudice, the
more easily to strangle it . . . sometimes soothing the enemies of reason by
pretending not to desire more than partial toleration in religion and partial
freedom in politics." John Adams's gloss on Condorcet's comment noted
that "This new philosophy was, by its own account, as insidious, fraudulent,
and cruel as the old policy of priests, nobles, and kings" (quoted from
Zoltan Haraszti, *John Adams and the Prophets of Progress,* 254). The clergyman
and progress enthusiast Joseph Priestley likewise endorsed the idea of gradual enlightenment: "The present silent propagation of truth may be compared to those causes in nature which lie dormant for a time, but which in
proper circumstances act with the greatest violence. We are, as it were, laying
gunpowder, grain by grain, under the old building of error and superstition,
which a single spark may hereafter inflame, so as to produce an instantane-
ous explosion, in consequence of which that edifice . . . may be overturned
in a moment, and so effectually that the same foundation can never be built
upon again."
A great deal has been written lately on the decipherment of intended
meaning from express statement. See particularly L. G. Crocker, "The Problem of Truth and Falsehood in the Age of Enlightenment," *Journal of the History of Ideas* 14 (1953): 575–603, and Peter France, *Rhetoric and Truth in
France: Descartes to Diderot.* The classic work on the subject is Leo Strauss's
Persecution and the Art of Writing.

work in the Preliminary Discourse. After mentioning ecclesiastical attacks on philosophy and science, d'Alembert stated, with an air of casual self-evidence, his view of the correct relation between philosophy and religion. Theology should tend to faith and morals, where its judgment is sovereign for the people as well as for philosophers, since reason has no access to revealed doctrine. On the other hand, theology should excuse itself from pronouncements on the planetary system, the antipodes, or other matters that fall under the scrutiny of reason. When reason and revelation remain within their separate spheres of competence, he implied, all is well (1: xxiii–iv.)

This conceit is a "confirming" statement. It carries a prima facie plausibility, mainly because d'Alembert appeared to be so content with it. But reflection on other assertions in the Preliminary Discourse, not to mention the body of the *Encyclopedia*, brings the "confuting" statements to light. D'Alembert did not explain why philosophers should or would accept *any* beliefs on faith, even though the need for an explanation was urgent owing to his repeated assertions that philosophy rejects all authority. Or again, belief in miracles implies a world order in which they can occur. Yet miracles are impossible in the mechanistic nature of Newton. But without miracles, it is impossible to believe in the Incarnation and Resurrection of Christ, as Newton's Socinianism testifies. Yet in that event, the gospel as preached by St. Paul falls to pieces. If one attempts to pick up the pieces by interpreting the Incarnation as a figure of moral truths, the collision between religion and philosophy is transferred to another sphere, since philosophy possesses also a moral and political teaching independent of revealed faith: the ethics of the Sermon on the Mount will not square with the ethics of Spinoza.[17]

The *Encyclopedia* view on the diffusion of enlightenment flows from its general philosophical outlook. Unlike static Scholastic philosophy, true philosophy is expansionist and dynamic—it accumulates knowledge. At the same time, it diffuses knowledge from an initially small center to an ever-widening audience that should ultimately embrace "mankind." According to its historiography of the "progress of the mind," initially this process occurred in a haphazard, undirected manner, interrupted by calamitous collapse of civilizations that plunged men back into darkness. But this changed in the seventeenth century when a small band of courageous men undertook the *conscious direction of this process*—"the general education of mankind." From that point for-

17. Irreligion among the philosophes has been assessed by many scholars. Alan Kors identifies six hard-core atheists: Diderot, d'Holbach, Naigeon, Helvetius, Roux, and Saint-Lambert (*D'Holbach's Coterie*, 41–63).

ward, the progress of the mind was held to be irreversible because the new philosophy, being true, was not open to reasonable doubt or refutation, and therefore provided reliable principles for action. As for new barbarian invasions, the response was gunpowder. This was why the advent of the new philosophy was thought to mark an unprecedented turn in human affairs.

The encyclopedists' propaganda was predicated upon the cumulative character of enlightenment about religion. In their view, which echoed the Deism of Spinoza and Locke, religion belongs to the primitive stages of human development, based as it is on ignorance of causes, disordered imagination, and the want of individual self-sufficiency that must be made good by moral authority.[18] D'Alembert's philosophical age was a milieu that had been significantly altered by the propaganda of the "first century of light." It was possible to state the truths of the new philosophy more boldly, and in greater detail, than in the previous century.[19] Diderot witnessed this rapid change of opinion in his own lifetime. By the 1780s, he dared to publish, under his own name, openly atheistic tracts. When the English chemist and Unitarian Joseph Priestley visited France in that period, the philosophes were astonished to learn that he took faith seriously, while Priestley was appalled to discover that he was not expected to. The anecdote illustrates how literally the philosophes believed that the progress of science implied the demise of religion.

The policy of enlightenment by degrees was thought to accelerate by geometrical progression, which actually happened in France until the Revolution. The policy was controlled by Machiavelli's idea of "politic religion." The *Encyclopedia* says that some political men and prelates "secretly believe that religion is only a means to political advantage and public order," while those who believe it in good faith "always come to grief." Although Diderot spurned this idea, it nevertheless was Machiavelli's vehicle for "insinuating that those who mingle in public affairs

18. See the articles under Juif and Philosophie mosaïque, and numerous articles on pagan deities.
19. The *Encyclopedia* appeared during a phase of religious and political upheaval that periodically afflicted France between the bull *Unigenitus* (1713) and 1789. From 1749 to 1753 matters were so serious that the annualist d'Argenson wrote that "all the orders are discontent. The situation has become inflammable; a riot could become a revolt, and a revolt a *total revolution*, where veritable tribunes of the people, of committees and communes, will be elected, and the king and ministers will be deprived of their excessive power to harm." See Felix Rocquain, *L'esprit révolutionnaire avant la révolution*, 142–48.

should take care to seem religious, while privately rejecting all superstition." The "confirming" statements of the *Encyclopedia* simulate the credulity of the day, which is promptly doubted by the confuting statements. D'Alembert's reconciling statement on the relation between philosophy and religion is an outstanding instance of politic religion. He conceded to faith enough to save appearances, but reserved to philosophy everything of substance. It was a nice piece of revenge that the peace terms he offered were first proposed by Galileo in his *Letter to the Grand Duchess Christina* and were subsequently elaborated by Spinoza in his *Tractatus theologico-politicus,* whose very title, detractors said, "stank of the devil." It is part of the finesse of d'Alembert's reconciling statement that he did not inscribe Spinoza's name on the honor roll of great reformers. He was, with Machiavelli and Hobbes, too closely associated with "atheistical doctrine." But in the *Encyclopedia* his heroic deeds are celebrated. Spinoza's method of historical criticism of the Bible introduced rationalism into the study of ancient authorities. That was the ultimate affront to religion: faith is not competent even to interpret the documents of faith. Purged of superstitious readings, and interrogated under the discipline of philology, the Bible appears as a compilation written over many centuries about the tribal God of Israel.

The Founders

The Preliminary Discourse singled out Francis Bacon and René Descartes as the two great innovators among the many men of the seventeenth century who contributed to the discovery of true philosophy.

Their entitlement to the place of honor was not based on the volume or importance of the scientific truths they discovered. Compared with Harvey or Huygens, they were inept experimenters. Bacon incessantly urged the method of induction, but it was Kepler who carried it out with brilliant results. Descartes advocated the method of geometric deduction from first principles, yet his own deductions were inferior to those of Galileo, Pascal, and Huygens. Bacon was a stranger to the basic insight of modern science, the quantification of force and motion, and in that respect lagged behind his contemporaries in Italy and Holland. Descartes nourished that insight as an obsession, yet his results were modest compared with others' and his world system did not survive Newton's criticism.

D'Alembert drew indulgent attention to these flaws in the Illustrious and suggested that their right to foremost place derived from an achievement of a different kind. These two were able to "see comprehensively" and to animate others with a sense of their vision. Of Bacon he wrote: "Considering the sound and extended views of this great man, the multitude of things to which he applied his mind, the vigor of his style, which unites the most sublime images with the most rigorous precision, one may regard him as the most lofty, the most universal, and the most eloquent of philosophers" (1: xxiv). The point appears to be that Bacon not only overcame in himself the decadent learning of his day, but also, thanks to his clarity and eloquence, he was able to stir others with a vivid sense of the futility of the old learning and the vitality of the new (1: xxiv). Bacon was a "methodologist"—he was able to "show the way." And similarly Descartes, "whose method alone would make him immortal" (1: xxvi). Their office was to be teachers of mankind, as Rousseau phrased it.

In singling out Bacon and Descartes, d'Alembert engaged in the uncompletable task of reevaluating and reassessing traditions, separating the gold from the dross. As it happened, the Enlightenment tradition more or less concurred in his judgment, even if Locke later seemed to some more pertinent than Bacon, and Spinoza more consistent than Descartes. D'Alembert's criterion, we have seen, was not that these two men were necessarily more profound or penetrating than others but that their writings possess that "inner force and secret efficacy" to put men into the mind of true philosophy. The achievement was precious because the new philosophy effected a "revolution" of the human mind. To carry that revolution through, the founders had to make a clean break with the received learning and its mental habits. They also had to comprehend and foresee the measure of man newly conceived as "master" of a mechanistic world.

Some scholars scarcely credit this claim. Whereas the founders' innovation and new beginning required a sharp, conscious break with received beliefs and milieu, some scholars insist on a social and superstitious origin of modern enlightenment. D'Alembert's roll of honor rendered a judgment on this line of thought. Renaissance enthusiasm for magic and alchemy, its Hermetic philosophy, Paracelsians, Agrippas, Cardanos, Rosicrucians, humanists, and Cambridge Platonists were excluded without a word of acknowledgment. The skepticism of Montaigne and Bayle merited only a subdued nod, while Bruno and Campanella, whose persecution d'Alembert might have flung into the teeth of his opposition, did not rate even honorable mention. Pascal, the first of the new philosophers to experience the terror of the mechanistic universe, was commended as a "prodigy of sagacity and penetration," while the termination of his scientific activity by prayers was regretted. Nowhere did d'Alembert hint that Calvinist or Lutheran theology supported philosophic freedom of inquiry, since Protestants no less than Catholics insisted on doctrinal conformity.

The select company in which Bacon and Descartes were placed thus throws further light on their significance as founders. D'Alembert affirmed that these men established authentic rationalism uncompromised by alchemical bypaths, superstition, Protestant enthusiasm, millenarian hokum, or loss of nerve. This significance was not lost on the Jesuits, who doggedly refused to allow works of Bacon, Descartes, and other exponents of the new philosophy to be taught in French universities. Their *Journal des Trévoux* set upon the first volume of the *Encyclopedia* as an "insidious attempt to undermine the throne and overthrow religion and morals." Attitudes at Oxford and Cambridge, which dozed in the torpor of ecclesiastical domination, were about the same. It was unthinkable that the leading lights of the day, Gibbon and Hume, might be invited to take up an appointment. Another century was to pass before chemistry and physics became part of the curriculum and before the obsolescence of classical philosophy was acknowledged.

Bacon's New Beginning

By word and deed the *Encyclopedia* honored Bacon for having opened a wholly new way to mankind, encapsulated in his slogan, "the conquest of nature for the relief of man's estate." The *Encyclopedia*'s exacting description of the arts and trades was intended to hasten the implementation of Bacon's vision of systematic linkage between science and the trades, or "manufacture," to create what by 1800 was called "technology."

The encyclopedists were not the first to raise Bacon's standard. The Académie royale des sciences had for forty years collected material for its own massive *description des arts,* which the encyclopedists forestalled. In 1732 Fontenelle and Corneille published their *Dictionnaire des arts,* though its scale was modest compared to Diderot's grandiose scheme. The Royal Society of London was composed of experimentalists and gentlemen pledged by the Charter to "perfect the sciences, improve manufacture, and invent useful arts." And Descartes, one of Bacon's important recruits, sounded the call when he wrote in the *Discourse on Method* (1637):

> But as soon as I acquired some general notions of physics . . . and observed to what point they might lead us, . . . I believed that I could not keep them concealed without greatly sinning against the law which obliges us to procure . . . the general good of all men.

For they made me see that it is possible to attain knowledge very useful in life, and that, instead of the speculative philosophy taught in the Schools, we may find a practical philosophy by means of which we may know the force and action of fire, water, air, the stars, heavens and all other bodies that environ us as distinctly as we know the crafts of our artisans, and we can in the same way employ them in all those uses to which they are adapted, and thus render ourselves masters and possessors of nature. This is not only to be desired for the invention of an infinity of arts which enable us to enjoy without any pain the fruits of the earth and all the good things which are found there, but also principally because it brings about the preservation of health, which is without doubt the chief blessing and foundation of all other blessings of this life.[20]

A politics of such colossal expansionism is not likely to be conceived, and certainly could not be propagated, in a decadent age. Bacon was born into an England quickened from many sides to activity. It is typical of his thinking that he attributed the liveliness of his times to the consequences of three inventions: the compass, the printing press, and gunpowder.

Elizabethans lived by the compass. Between 1545 and 1620, the number of English ships weighing over 100 tons increased tenfold.[21] In 1584 Walter Raleigh founded the first English plantation in America, and in 1588 Drake defeated the rival Spanish fleet in the English Channel. Productivity in a number of industries, including mining and textiles, rose sharply, providing goods for England's increasing trade.

Important though they are, these growth indices do not quite capture the poetry of the compass. The title page of *The Great Instauration* depicts a ship passing beyond the Pillars of Hercules, the traditional limits for navigators until Columbus's bold transgression. Bacon, who often compared himself with Columbus, made the sailor's proud cry, "Plus ultra!" ("Beyond the Pillars!"), his motto. Infected by his excitement, the Royal Society and Leibniz used the motto to signify the intoxicat-

20. Descartes, *Œuvres philosophiques*, 1: 634. A more expansive and aggressive statement of the utility of science is presented in the Letters Prefatory to *The Passions of the Soul*. Ferdinand Alquié, editor of the *Œuvres philosophiques*, unfortunately omitted them from his edition. They have never been included in any English or German translation of Descartes' works. This interesting selectivity is discussed in my "Descartes' Anonymous Writings: A Recapitulation," where Descartes' authorship of these letters is also established.

21. Paolo Rossi, *Francis Bacon*, 9.

ing vista of new worlds to conquer and the possibilities of unlimited expansion.

Columbus's deed was a fitting metaphor for the discovery of a new intellectual continent because the compass and courage, like the telescope, vindicated the power of reason against an ecclesiastical Nay by proving the existence of the antipodes. The theory of the antipodes was part of Greco-Roman natural philosophy, which held that the earth was spherical and that the southern continent was inhabited. The theory was inconsistent with Scripture, which gives no account of sons of Adam inhabiting the antipodes, nor the Gospel being preached there, although the Epistle to the Romans declares that "their line is gone out through all the earth, and their words to the end of the world." Such texts were used by St. Augustine to prove that the antipodes could not exist. When the antipodean heresy revived in the eighth century, it was condemned by Pope Zachary as "perverse and iniquitous." This was how matters stood when Columbus declared his purpose in Spain and Portugal, where bishops reminded him severely of the old heresy. His triumphant return from the Indies did not alter thinking in Rome. In 1493 and again in 1506, popes issued bulls, based on ecclesiastical geography, meant to settle disputes between Spain and Portugal over claims in the new world. Even Magellan's circumnavigation of the earth in 1519, and later Drake's, did not end clerical obstinance, although by that time other perplexing challenges to dogma had arisen: the Copernican theory and the origin of numerous species of animals found in the antipodes.[22]

The vindication of reason and ocular evidence in the antipodes controversy was the sign to thoughtful men of Bacon's day that dogmatic theology entrenched superstition and depraved reason.[23] Rather than consulting nature with a sound eye about questions of fact, dogmatics demonstrated by appeal to authoritative texts. The intention was not to instruct the mind or augment knowledge, but to uphold an opinion. The faithful were required to see what they were told to see; or not to see what they plainly did. That the "empire of faith over the sense"[24] was a fundamental article of religion was understood by those subtlest knights of faith, the Jesuits. In his *Rules for Thinking With the Church*, St. Ignatius penned that infamous charter of obscurantism: "That we may be altogether of the same mind and in conformity with the Church herself, if she shall have defined anything to be black which to our eyes

22. A. D. White, *A History of the Warfare of Science with Theology in Christendom*, I: 102–10.
23. *Great Instauration*, bk. 1, §89. (All references are to the Spedding, Ellis, and Heath edition of *The Works of Francis Bacon*.)
24. Ibid.

appears to be white, we ought in like manner to pronounce it to be black" (Rule 13).[25] This was the Jesuit way of bringing "every understanding in captivity to Christ."

Dispelling such thralldom to authority required a momentous "revolution of the mind" that reassessed the powers of reason and above all diagnosed the reasons for its susceptibility to so vast a degradation. Bacon's critique of the susceptibility of the mind to "idols" or vain fancy was directed against the "centuries of ignorance"; it defined negatively the coherence of his reaffirmation of the evidence of sense and reflection as the only reliable instruments of knowledge.

But, as d'Alembert pointed out, the malice of some clergymen compelled Bacon to carry out his renovation in the darkness and shadows, "from afar." One large shadow he cast over his work was the claim that it harmonized with the Scriptures. Such is the claim of every heretic conscious and unconscious. His adoption of the provocative "plus ultra" motto hinted at how the claim was to be evaluated. He threw out a stronger hint by centering his romance, *The New Atlantis,* around the antipodes problem. The Christian seafarers cast up on this island continent marvel that their charitable and scientifically advanced hosts are Christians. The governor "solves" the scriptural problem of their conversion by telling a suitably miraculous story. It seems that St. Bartholomew put the Bible in a bottle and cast it into the sea; the currents carried it from the Mediterranean to New Atlantis, where it arrived under the sign of the Cross. The credulous Europeans greedily swallow the story without reflecting on their hosts' express statements that they do not necessarily tell strangers the truth.[26] In any case, the Antipodeans do not interpret the Scriptures as the Europeans do, nor are they weighed down by gross superstitions. They interpret the Scriptures in light of the wisdom of King Solamona, who reigned 300 years before Christ, and who determined the end of knowledge to be "enlarging the bounds of Human Empire, to the effecting of all things possible."[27] Thanks to this wisdom, the Antipodeans increase their knowledge while the remainder of the world is overtaken by sloth and ignorance.

25. Although Ignatius's sharp formulation was perhaps unprecedented in theology, the idea he expressed was canonically formulated by St. Thomas in his "handmaiden" dictum, according to which "whatsoever is encountered in the other sciences which is incompatible with the truth [of church doctrine] should be completely condemned as false" (*Summa theologica,* Ia, I.6).
26. *Works of Francis Bacon,* 6: 385.
27. On the antipodes controversy as an illustration of the hostility of religion to science, see *Great Instauration,* bk. 1, §89.

The Great Instauration

Little wonder that Bacon impressed the encyclopedists as a prodigy. Among contemporaries only Montaigne rivaled his intimate knowledge of the classics, though he divided his time between politics and study. His revaluation of that heritage was endorsed by the subsequent development of natural philosophy. His nimble intellect pondered atoms and poetry with equal facility, and his mastery of English prose was precocious at a time when Shakespeare, Marlowe, Jonson, and Raleigh set the standards of English style. His physician, William Harvey, said that Bacon wrote philosophy "like a Lord Chancellor." His capacity to write of philosophers in the same manner no doubt figured in the success he enjoyed among his countrymen shortly after his death. Eloquence made his innovations palatable despite his rejection of regnant doctrines, an achievement all the more singular because Galileo and Descartes—no mean talents—failed among their countrymen in the same attempt.

The title of his chief work, *The Great Instauration,* signified the resolve "to try [philosophy] anew upon a better plan, and to commence a *total reconstruction of the sciences, arts, and all human knowledge,* raised upon proper foundations. And this, though in the project and understanding it may seem a thing infinite and beyond the powers of man, yet when it comes to be dealt with is found to be sound and sober." [28] His conception of the endeavor as a *renewal* supplied reasons for despair and for hope. Despair, because the project could prosper only by overcoming the inveterate prejudices of an old culture built on the errors and failures of the first attempt. Moreover, the antiquity of that culture created dangers for the innovator, who confronted "a troublesome adversary"—superstition and "the blind and immoderate zeal of religion" (bk. 1, § 89). There were no allies in universities, where such a one was considered forward and a rebel: "And if one or two have the boldness to use any liberty of judgment," Bacon wrote in one of his caustic attacks on Oxford and Cambridge, "they must undertake the task all by themselves; they can have no advantage from the company of others. And if they can endure this also, they will find their industry and largeness of mind no slight hindrance to their fortune. For the studies of men in those places are confined and as it were imprisoned in the writings of certain authors, from whom if any man dissent he is straightway arraigned as a turbulent person and an innovator" (bk. 1, §90; §113).

---

28. Ibid., proemium. In §81 of this work, the end of philosophy is said to be to "endow life with new discoveries and powers." See also "Orpheus," in *De sapientia veterum.*

Yet Bacon subdued as "vain apprehensions" his despair about intellectual isolation and the magnitude of his critical task because he found stronger reasons for hope. Moderns have the advantage over the ancients that they are more "ancient" than the ancients; that is, they may carry out the renewal of philosophy informed of the wrong turns previously taken in the search for knowledge. Bacon used this paradoxical formulation to turn the tables on veneration of antiquity, arguing that classical philosophy arose in the childhood of man and stammers like a child. But it was more than a debating point. The historical perspective on the failure of classical philosophy became constitutive for a new event series in the history of the mind's development.

This is apparent in his critique of the theoretical or contemplative orientation of classical philosophy as the collection point of all the weaknesses and liabilities of the mind. Its contemplative character accounts for ancient philosophy's immersion in "frivolous disputes and verbosities," for its impotence to advance learning by accumulating knowledge, its division into sects and schools, its susceptibility to superstition, its inconclusive preoccupation with logic and first principles, its remoteness from action and want of "fruits."

Such is the asperity of Bacon's graceful invective, especially against Plato and Aristotle, that a contemporary editor would probably return his manuscripts with the comment, "too negative." While profaning exalted names helped debunk the prestige of antiquity, Bacon's thought about theory was substantive. His idea was that reason or sense, or both together, are impotent before nature unless equipped with artificial "helps." Reason alone has no access to the principles of things; and of the unaided senses Bacon said, approving the skeptics, "that only the errors are here," since nature is far more subtle than sense discriminations (bk. 1, §§10, 41, 50). As words are based on sense experience, to theorize from discourse, as Plato and Aristotle did, compounds the errors of sense with errors of understanding. The needful thing is a "wholly new relation between sense and understanding," which purges both of their liabilities while setting their effective powers to work.

These strictures apply equally to the Renaissance naturalists, with whom Bacon would not combine despite their rebelliousness against Scholasticism. He took them to task for their magical, astrological, and alchemical confusions, which implied ruptures of universal natural causation.[29] An equally important objection to Paracelsus, Cardano, and

29. After canvassing Bacon's use of "magic," Paolo Rossi concluded that the natural magic he approved was of a piece with material, causally determined nature, while the magic he condemned was the something-from-nothing

the rest was their "superstition." Superstitious philosophy, the invention of Plato or Pythagoras, mingled divinity with natural philosophy, producing the bastard offspring "heretical religion and fabulous philosophy."[30] Bacon urged that theology and metaphysics be kept distinct from natural philosophy; and this he asserted at a time when not more than two or three men would have understood the cardinal importance to science of uprooting this ancient tendency to mingle theology with natural philosophy. "The master of superstition," Bacon wrote, "is the people," who are envious and weak; and philosophers who discourse of divine mysteries or the frame of the world either pander to vulgar opinion or are themselves its victims.[31] In either case, it must be rejected. Yet a rupture with tradition so abrupt is not easily carried through; and Bacon, to justify it before the tribunal of the clergy, maintained that his way heightened the merit of faith: "the more discordant therefore and incredible the Divine mystery is, the more honour is shown to God in believing it, and the nobler is the victory of faith."[32] One must look twice at this dazzling passage to see that it means the more irrational, the better. There is patristic authority for this view in the works of Tertullian, an opponent of philosophical theology. Tertullian had stated it more succinctly: "Credo quia absurdum."

The violence of Bacon's critique was due partly to his attempt to rehabilitate the materialism of the pre-Socratic philosophers, which Plato and Aristotle did so much to discredit. Bacon undertook to renew materialism, knowing in advance the spiritual objections of Plato and Christian theology, as well as the logical objections of Aristotle to the elimination of "formal" and "final" causes. His response to Aristotle is contained in the details of his call for a new relation between sense and understanding. Aristotle used these faculties "naked" and without artificial helps. When understanding is allowed to follow its natural bent

---

error associated with the term today (*Francis Bacon*, II, 35). Margery Purver drew the same conclusion from her study of Bacon's natural philosophy (*The Royal Society*, 20–59). That he used the term *natural magic* at all is probably due to his acute political sense and rhetorical gifts. In the preface to *De sapientia veterum* and in "Cassandra," he emphasized the need for popular images to convey philosophical sense. "Magic," so understood, is an icon of the power of the new science to "superinduce effects on bodies." By appropriating the term *magic* to his philosophy, Bacon could hope to arouse the followers of Cardano, Paracelsus, and Agrippa, whose natural magic he rejected as animistic, to follow his own new path.

30. "Prometheus," in *De sapientia veterum*.
31. "Of Superstition," in *Essays*. See also "Orpheus," in *De sapientia veterum*.
32. *The Advancement of Learning*, bk. 9, chap. 1.

without restraint, it courses toward the vain belief that system, logic, and abstractions, because they make a fine engine for refutation, are able to establish the truth. This is the basic illusion of "contemplation" and "theory." He was untroubled by theoretical objections against materialism because he was certain that the truth of first principles cannot be established by logical argument. This does not mean that the investigation of first principles is to be abandoned, but that the *status* of the investigation changes: understanding provides *hypotheses* for experimental investigation.[33] The materialist hypothesis was recommended by the circumstance that it concentrated investigation on material and efficient causality, and by the related fact that the sciences had made no progress under the long domination of Aristotle's teleological causal scheme.

Bacon's insight into the hypothetical character of principles has not been generally recognized. In this matter he was well ahead of Galileo, Kepler, Leibniz, and even Newton, who were ambiguous about this decisive question perhaps owing to their enchantment by mathematics. But for an experimentalist like Boyle, who struggled with the mysteries of chemistry, Bacon's methodology was in this point obviously right.

Upon rejecting contemplation Bacon set forth a new concept of truth not found in any ancient source. The concept had to meet two conditions. It had to be tailored to the efficient causality of a material world, but in such a way as to short-circuit theorizing world-explanations. It also had to cope systematically with the fact that the senses are not reliable guides to things, since most natural effects are indiscernible to sense experience. The senses need an "artificial help" that will yield systematic access to all of nature. This aid is the experiment, the formula for whose use is that "experiment judges of effects, and the senses judge of experiment." Combining this with the ban on contemplation yields the concept of truth as knowledge of effects as revealed by experiment. Knowledge is always particular, and generalizations are reached through induction. As a result of this redesign of the natural relation between sense and understanding, the fabric and design of science changes. Baconians have no finished theory of the frame of the world, but they do have effective knowledge of particulars. And they have a *research* science whose proper work is to increase knowledge without limits through numerous collaborators over many generations. For the first time, natural philosophy becomes a progressive, expansionist social institution.

Bacon emphasized that the guiding light of this new truth concept was the mechanical arts, especially those dealing with "violent and mechanical motion," which is the "foundation of practical operations" and

33. *Great Instauration*, bk. 1, §126.

the "life and soul [*sic*] of artillery, engines, and the whole business of mechanics."[34] No doubt this is the sort of thing apt to strike the fancy of a lord chancellor schooled in Machiavelli and keen on political expansion. But beyond that consideration, the mechanical arts provide an analogy to science, for the arts possess knowledge of effective causes. That knowledge of course is largely knowledge of fabrication processes, which is not the same as knowledge of natural processes. Nevertheless, it is an analogy to science in the Baconian mold. By observation, experiment, and induction, the artisan learns something of nature's way, and succeeds in "superinducing effects on bodies" by *imitating* a natural process. Science must imitate nature in the same way; it must "enter nature's workshop" and "build in human understanding a true model of the world."[35] The formula for imitation of nature (*mimesis*) is that "nature to be commanded must be obeyed." The scientific means of imitating nature—which is not at all incompatible with "torturing" it—is the experiment, understood on analogy to the artisan's fabrication processes and engines. Experiments too superinduce effects on bodies by segregating or composing bodies in natural processes, especially those too swift or minute for direct sense observation. The arts and sciences thus operate with the common notion of "effects demonstrated in things," which the sciences take as their truth criterion.[36]

If this analysis is correct, the view that Bacon identified truth with utility must be rejected. Such an identification, in itself vague to the point of uselessness, could not provide a foundation for science.[37] In the

34. *Works of Francis Bacon*, 5: 433, 435.
35. *Great Instauration*, bk. 1, §120; also §§121, 124. Bacon's best statement on philosophy as *mimesis* is *De sapientia veterum*, "Erichthonius."
36. The Royal Society's motto, "Nullius in verba," was meant to convey just this thought (Thomas Sprat, *History of the Royal Society*, 29, 111ff., 331ff.). William Gilbert, whom Bacon seems not to mention but who was admired by Galileo and Descartes, wrote in *De magnate* (1600) that his work was dedicated "not to lettered clowns, grammaticists, sophists, spouters, but to you alone, true philosophers, ingenious minds, who not only in books but in things themselves look for knowledge."
37. Bacon's editors Spedding and Ellis seem to have begun this misunderstanding in their footnote to par. CXXIV of the *Novum organum* on the phrase "Itaque ipsissimae res sunt (in hoc genere) veritas et utilitas." Spedding admits that to construe *ipsissimae* to mean that truth and utility are the "same things" does not square with Bacon's grammar, and that the phrase actually asserts that "the things themselves are truth and utility." But he believed that in that case, an *et* should appear before *veritas*. This objection is not grammatical but stylistic, and Bacon as a prose stylist set standards. Why then prefer an admittedly ungrammatical construction to a doubtful stylistic infelicity? Charles Webster (*The Great Instauration*, 336–37), after observing

foregoing discussion, the utility of the arts and sciences does not feature at all. Yet Bacon assuredly advertised the utility of the sciences as the "fruit" of the endeavor he advocated. For this reason especially we must press this analysis a little further.

Bacon harbored no illusions about the character of artisans. He complained that they work to recipes handed down for generations and that they show little inclination to improve their methods, let alone to understand the natural processes involved in fabrication techniques. The great majority, in other words, possess only a sort of cook's skill.[38] A hundred and fifty years later, Diderot found the same characteristics in the artisans of France, from which he concluded that to improve the arts one must first improve artisans. Even so, there is the exceptional artisan whose knowledge or luck or both enable him to invent new arts or to improve those existing. This type—call him an engineer—embodies elements on which Bacon modeled the future natural philosopher. The principal difference is that whereas the engineer is interested in "fruits," or some useful artifact, the natural philosopher's special concern is with "experiments of light." The new philosophy espouses both types of experiment thanks to their unification under a single truth concept of *effects demonstrated in things*. The future engineer and the philosopher will resemble one another: the latter must soil his hands and mind with things mechanical, otherwise he cannot experiment; and the engineer must raise his sights above the narrow confines of utility to instruct himself in natural philosophy. The distinction between "fruit" and "light" marks a distinction between the arts and science according to their principal function. But since they are affiliated by a single truth concept, the concept of a technological science is established. Bacon was therefore able to prophesy, and give it to man as a hope, that not only would the arts be improved and new ones invented, to mankind's infinite benefit, but that new arts would be invented by "clusters and myriads."

The Conquest of Nature as Great Politics

Bacon formulated his technological concept of truth in the booming pronouncement that "human knowledge and human power meet in one; for where the cause is not known, the effect cannot be produced."[39] Knowledge bestows power because knowledge is of the effective causes

---

that Bacon's distinction between experiments of light and experiments of fruit implies that truth and utility are not the same, falls back on this doubtful translation in order to enroll Bacon in the lists of social pragmatists.

38. *Great Instauration,* bk. i, §99.
39. Ibid., §3.

of things. We heirs of the Baconian legacy, persuaded that power aplenty may be obtained, are rather apt to wonder what to do with it all. Does the command of so much power suit man's nature? How are human nature and human ends to be construed, now that natural ends are banished from science? How did Bacon conceive the being who is to command nature in action? What is the relation between power and its use?

Although the conquest of nature as Bacon advertised it is patently political, he is not often credited with having thought much about it. No one, of course, misses the point that the use of power is to improve the human condition, according to the catch-cry, "the conquest of nature for the relief of man's estate." As we shall see presently, Bacon did not assume that his contemporaries were aware of the need for relief, or that it was necessarily a good thing. No small part of his discrediting models from the past was meant to open minds to a wholly new conception of the future. Yet some commentators believe that Bacon derived his sense of the human significance of power from Christian morality, especially from the spirit of charity and "pity for the condition of mankind," as he once put it. Whatever he may have thought about this legitimation of his project,[40] it certainly was important for the recruitment of a following. The evidence accumulated by Charles Webster suggests that some Baconian enthusiasts during the Commonwealth period understood the new philosophy as benevolent and utopian.[41] The Hartlibs, Oldenburgs, and Mersennes—those organizers and bag men of the budding scientific fraternity—conceived the relief of man's estate as an endorsement of their good intentions and an illumination of the way. On a somewhat different plane, Descartes quickly broadcast this justification of science, transformed into the notion of *humanité* as the secular ethic that dominated the European intelligentsia by 1750.

While the historical significance of this interpretation is manifest, the linkage between power and goodness is riddled with difficulties, the most apparent being that the link is wholly contingent. Of this Bacon was aware. At the conclusion of the *New Organon*, he noted the objection that the arts may be abused, and answered that all earthly goods

40. To James I, Bacon declared that he did not say all he believed: "I have also been my own Index Expurgatorius, that it [*De augmentis scientiarum*] may be read in all places. For since my end of putting it into Latin was to have it read everywhere, it had been an absurd contradiction to free it in language and pen it up in the matter" (*Works*, 7: 436; see also 1: 698, on speaking to the "envious and malignant vulgar"). Consider also Bacon's epigram "Infirmarum virtutum apud vulgus laus est, mediarum admiratio, superarum sensus nullus."

41. See below, chap. 4.

may be abused. This is hardly adequate, since his proposal for unprecedented increase in human power opened the door to unheard-of abuses.
He distracted attention from this thought by hurrying to a magisterial
command: "only let the human race recover that right over nature
which belongs to it by divine bequest, and let power be given it; the
exercise thereof will be governed by sound reason and true religion."[42]
In *The Wisdom of the Ancients,* the Baconian writing most widely read in
seventeenth-century England, he returned to the problem in a more
thorough but scarcely more reassuring way. This work teaches in para-
bles by interpreting nearly three dozen ancient myths. The remarks on
Daedalus the mechanic, who signifies the arts, style him "a man of the
greatest genius but of very bad character" because of his indifference to
moral ends. Himself the jealous murderer of a rival artisan, he did not
scruple to serve depraved and unlawful ends; whence the laws often
condemn and persecute the arts, but vainly, because men hanker after
their illicit uses. Bacon closes his trenchant observations with the surmise that the moral neutrality of the arts may be controlled by contempt
for their vanity.

The theme is continued in the parable of the myth of Prometheus,
but again inconclusively. Prometheus is the image of foresight, or as
Bacon also says, human nature. The special office of foresight is to endow men with the arts. Most of Bacon's remarks on this myth repeat his
familiar advocacy of the arts and exhortations to improve them. He
warms particularly to festivities and games in honor of Prometheus,
where men would try their strength in contests, which by "competition,
emulation and good fortune" would bring them to a new pitch of excellence. But their moral neutrality is underscored when Bacon repeats the
familiar demand that the arts and sciences be kept apart from religious
mysteries, including, for all one can tell, the mysterious theological virtue of charity. As for the cares and worries that foresight creates, the
remedy is the "gift of wisdom," especially "fortitude and constancy of
mind," given Prometheus by Hercules.

Bacon concluded his interpretation of the Prometheus myth on a provocative note. He suggested that a particular image in the fable might
adumbrate "God the Word hastening in the frail vessel of the flesh to
redeem the human race. But I purposely refrain myself from all licence
of speculation in this kind, lest per adventure I bring strange fire to the
altar of the Lord." This may well be accounted Bacon's final word on the
control of science by religion. Fire is the symbol of Prometheus, who is
in turn the emblem of Baconian philosophy. By refraining from laying

---

42. *Great Instauration,* bk. I, §129.

his fire on the altar of the Lord, he indicated by parable what he thought about the religious solution to the moral neutrality of the arts, disowning in advance the millenarianism of sectaries, which interpreted the relief of man's estate in terms of the prophesied thousand-year reign of Christ.

The suggestion that earthly power would serve charity assumes an improbable harmony between antithetical attitudes. In a second set of statements on the ends of power, hardly noticed today, Bacon dropped the unconvincing appeal to charity and related power to the end it typically seeks in human life, greatness. In these statements, power is eulogized in phrases that often soar to the heights of Bacon's surpassing eloquence. "My purpose," he wrote in the *New Organon*, "is to try whether I cannot in fact lay more firmly the foundations, and extend more widely the limits, of the power and greatness of man." Again, the end of philosophy is "to endow life with new discoveries and powers" or "to command nature in action."[43] At the conclusion of the *New Organon*, he indicated the character of the followers he hoped to recruit by delivering a rousing oration praising his way as worthy of men whose ambition is the highest. After reviewing two kinds of ambition, and stating their limits, he unveiled in a skyrocket of sparkling prose the grandest design of all: "But if a man endeavour to establish and extend the power and dominion of the human race itself over the universe, his ambition (if ambition it can be called) is without doubt both a more wholesome thing and a more noble than the other two." Ambition in such Gargantuan excess does indeed need another name. Hope of dominion over the universe bugles an assault on Mount Olympus to overthrow the kingdom of God.[44]

That power and greatness integrally link science with life is apparent in Bacon's moral philosophy. The link is forged in the first instance by his methodological requirement of unified science, which demands that all inquiry search for the effective truth of efficient causes. In moral and political matters, that requirement amounts to applying Machiavelli's injunction to study "what men do, not what they ought to do."[45]

43. Ibid., §116.
44. That Bacon escaped accusations of irreligion despite his flagrant Titanism is a testimony to the taste for the sublime that permeated the politics and religion of his times. Justification by faith and predestination are doctrines that could not work for meek and feeble types; Jesuitism is the pitch of spiritual energy. The Conquistadores, the generals and kings, the Dutch nation, the Papacy were tough and cruel as only flourishing men can be. Bacon's remark that "the inexorable necessity there is in matter to sustain itself, and not to turn and dissolve into nothing" might stand as a description of his age.
45. *Works of Francis Bacon*, 5: 17.

Bacon set out the results of his study in an analysis of "activity." He claimed that activity is preferred to hedonism because the pleasures of sense are limited, by comparison with activity, in the "novelty and variety they can afford." Elaborating on this assertion, he wrote: "In enterprises, pursuits and purposes of life there is much variety; whereof men are sensible with pleasures in their inceptions, progressions, rests, recoils, reintegrations, approaches and attaining to ends" (*Works,* 5: 11). Bacon distinguished activity, or the active good, from two states of passive good—preserving and perfecting oneself. Epicureanism and other contemplative ideals of antiquity, which aimed at tranquillity, were passive, and Bacon censured them for seeking "in all things to make men's minds too uniform and harmonical" (5: 14). He traced this preference to the circumstances of their lives, which were withdrawn from affairs. In view of his emphatic commitment to action, it is no surprise to find the active good, wherein men seek "to multiply and spread themselves," praised above the other two; indeed, activity is that in virtue of which man bears resemblance to the divine (5: 12). It is all the more curious to note that the good sought by Christianity falls outside this classification altogether; for the classification refers only to the good of individuals, whereas Christianity elevates, as no other religion, sect, or law has, "the good which is [common] and depresses the good which is private and particular" (5: 7). Bacon declined to discuss the public good, judging that it would be presumptuous in a book addressed to the king of Britain. But he didn't need to, since he reproduced Machiavelli's reasoning about how seeking one's private good through activity draws men into public affairs. The argument, with a characteristic Baconian twist, is this. One ought not believe that active men act for the common good, despite the fact that they often confer public benefits. They do not act for the public, but for the sake of their "own power and greatness; as plainly appears when this kind of active good strikes on a subject contrary to the good of society. For that gigantean state of mind . . . possesses the troublers of the world . . . who are bent on having all men happy or unhappy as they are their friends or enemies, and would shape the world according to their own humours" (5: 12).[46] These are the motives that actuate ambitious men—men like Bacon himself, who seemed to his contemporaries "too arrogant in mind and manner, too incessant in his suit for place, and too precipitous in his political undertakings."[47]

46. Ibid., 12. This political type is studied in his *History of the Reign of Henry VII* and in his vignettes of Julius and Augustus Caesar. These works, together with his actions as lord chancellor, show that Bacon was bent on empire for England. His imperial designs are embraced in Sprat's *History of the Royal Society.* See below, chap. 4.
47. F. H. Anderson, *The Philosophy of Francis Bacon,* 4.

In luminous brush strokes of candor, Bacon styled that ambition "true theomachy" (struggle of the gods). No activity could be more gigantean, nor more perfectly link power with greatness, than dominion over the universe. By playing on the medium of ancient fables, Bacon projected a renewed assault on the Olympian gods, who preside over law and convention and piety, by the Titans, whose standard is nature. His proclamation of "the kingdom of man" in this sense as the object of power was Bacon's final answer to Platonic spirituality. Plato compelled ambitious men to choose between philosophy and politics, between the raptures of contemplation and the appetite for action. Platonic philosophers could enter politics only by giving wise counsel, but had fools for an audience. If knowledge and power meet in one, all is changed. The theoretical man has become practical; or better, his practice embraces the whole domain of thought and action. As the man of comprehensive knowledge and comprehensive power, he will be "understood" by men of high political ambition. They can strike bargains and form alliances, and in that way introduce a wholly new politics. Its popular selling point may be charity, self-interest, or humanitarianism. But the moving spirits think of such goals as subordinate and contingent means to human greatness.

Bacon's relative lack of concern about the moral ends of power followed naturally from his subordination of all ends to greatness. The perils of the kingdom of man, which he clearly saw, had less force with him than the imperious necessity to sweep aside the past to make way for a new order of things. The weakness of philosophy till that time was for him unendurable. He scorned its impotence, he was even a little ashamed of it, as a man captivated by the charm of power would be.[48] In perhaps his most severe indictment of the ancients he chided their inability to purge their philosophy of superstition and the countless indignities of superstition. Rather than upholding its original promise to shelter freedom of thought, it became the "handmaid" of vulgar opinion. Thanks to his intimate knowledge of the classics, Bacon knew that this objection went to the vitals of ancient philosophy: reproaches of error it could assimilate to its own advantage, but the reproach of vulgarity was deadly.

The reproach was aimed especially at Plato. In the *Symposium,* Plato toyed with the idea of an assault on Mount Olympus by the Titans, that

48. Bacon thought that Greek philosophy suffered from a "lack of spiritedness and the mediocrity and slightness of the tasks which human industry has set itself" (*Great Instauration,* bk. 1, §87). A man who judges Greek philosophy to be decadent must be very spirited indeed.

is, the replacement of religion by the truth. In his mock-up of the battle, the Titans are defeated by the people and their gods, partly because their knowledge of nature is deficient. Bacon solved the Titans' problem. He increased their strength and number, and discovered a means for splitting the opposition. To see how his stratagem works, we must look briefly at the context.

In a discussion of the causes of atheism, he listed divisions of religion, the scandal of priests, scoffing, religious cruelty, learning, and prosperous times. So many causes so active in that time must have buoyed the spirits of the faithless and troubled men of faith. In a discussion of superstition, he contrasted zealotry unfavorably with atheism, which "leaves a man to sense, to philosophy, to natural piety, to laws, to reputation." Whereas the superstitious "trouble governments," atheists are civil and eschew sedition, at least from vain fancies. This clearly suggests that a society of atheists would compare favorably with traditional societies. Bacon underscored the drift of that suggestion by approving, in conspicuous places, Epicurus's dictum that "there is no impiety in refusing to believe in the gods of the vulgar; the impiety is in believing of the gods what the vulgar believe."[49] The vulgar believe that the gods are more powerful than men and that they are provident to those who fear them. Bacon taught on the contrary that only Prometheus or man is provident, and that by pursuing the new philosophy, he would reap infinite benefits by "relying only on [his] own strength." As for the gods, the "panic terror" of superstition is replaced by fearlessness, since the gods do not concern themselves with human affairs.[50]

Here then is the stratagem that divides and conquers. Hope of benefit will lure the people to support the new science. Every benefit conferred is a new proof of man's providence and mute testimony to the indifference of the gods. As d'Alembert indicated, Bacon's project enlightens the people "little by little," since their neglect of the gods will increase with their prosperity. We must recall, too, that prosperity is not a pas-

49. "Of Atheism," in *Essays;* also, "Of Superstition."
50. "Pan," in *De sapientia veterum.* See the discussion of religious cruelty and atheism in "Advertisement Touching a Holy War"; "Diomedes," in *De sapientia veterum;* and various other places. Bacon did some urbane scoffing himself in his *Apothegms.* As for learning and atheism, he held that philosophy, particularly materialist natural philosophy, leads to atheism, as he shows by quoting the opinions of ancient materialists on religion. Bacon was acquainted with a materialist interpretation of mind; see bk. 2, chap. 13, of *Advancement of Learning.* It is instructive to note that the notion presented there is the thinking-being concept subsequently taken over by Descartes.

sive affair of receiving benefits; it includes active participation in the technological science that augments human power, which in that way will spread to the people pride and confidence in human greatness. The plan is ingenious and strong: the whole human race is called to greatness by actively making the world over to "their own wish," in that way driving the gods from Mount Olympus and inaugurating the kingdom of man.

Bacon estimated that the "greatest obstacle by far" to the progress of science and to new undertakings was that "men despair and think things impossible."[51] Believing that the world ebbs and flows, blight following prosperity as the wheel of the world turns through its cyclic rotations, they do not hope for a new order of things. Bacon invented an apparatus for jamming the cosmic fatality, registering the consequences in artful portrayals of a wholly new perspective on time and man.[52] The past is squalor and impotence; the future a ladder of promise and possibility. The future is governed by the most ambitious politics ever conceived, a politics for the progressive transformation of heaven and earth. Subsequent thinkers found in Bacon the germ of the idea that a wholly new politics of liberty was possible if the appetite for "perfecting oneself" were harnessed to commercial and manufacturing instruments for increasing prosperity.

51. *Great Instauration,* bk. 1, §92; also §97: "There is no hope except in a new birth of science."

52. There have been "only three revolutions and periods of learning," each of about 200 years' duration: among the Greeks, the Romans, and finally the nations of Europe. All other times were "wastes and deserts" and "unprosperous" (ibid., bk. 1, §78). This historiography contradicts his often-cited derivation of the arts and sciences from the Hebrews, especially Moses and Solomon, and it rectifies that plainly untenable assertion. It also agrees with the history of learning in the New Atlantis, where King Solamona, who founded the sciences, lived hundreds of years before the Bible miraculously floated to the shores of his kingdom. Bacon's longest treatment of the relation between "active science" and biblical wisdom is contained in the unpublished *Valerius terminus,* written about 1603 as a sketch of what became the *Advancement of Learning.* Its thrust is to legitimate science against religious doubts, which implies that the Bible lays a presumption *against* science. Those of Bacon's readers who were not religiously inclined doubtless agreed with him in those passages that assert his endeavor to be without precedent, and one in which all authorities are dismissed for the sake of relying exclusively on one's own strength (ibid., bk. 1, §§122–29). Charles Webster's discussion of *Valerius terminus* explains how Oxford Puritans interpreted this text (first published in 1734) as evidence of the "religious foundation" of Bacon's philosophy (*Great Instauration: Science, Medicine, and Reform,* 22–23).

Bacon's thoughts were fixed too much on greatness to hit upon that "bourgeois" embodiment of his project. In Parliament he welcomed the union of England and Scotland for its benefits of "surety and greatness," commending the new united Britain as one of the greatest monarchies in history, which would still "grow and spread." In his emphatic endorsement of political expansionism he agreed with Machiavelli that the measure of greatness was not size or trade, but valor and military *virtù*. These counsels had little effect with the cautious king he served, who preferred ambassadors to commanders and mercenaries to militia. Nor did Bacon's many attempts to win King James to patronage of the new science come to anything, not even the endowment of a few lectureships. Even Bacon's proposals for simplifying administration seemed to that sluggish monarch a thing too rash.

Bacon lived as he wrote, in the grand manner, luxuriating in things beautiful, graceful, and strong. At the peak of his career his retinue included 150 domestic servants to serve his five estates, which were maintained by an annual budget of £12,000. But the means were not always honest. Charges of corruption were brought, and Bacon fell from grace on admitting before the House of Lords to guilt on twenty-eight counts of corruption. It was in keeping with his character to deny that accepting the bribes swayed his judgment: it was beneath his dignity to favor those who thought they could purchase his favors. Through the years of disgrace, Bacon, an aristocrat to the marrow and thoroughly corrupt, held his head aloft, the more to deserve the admiration of posterity.

An Overview

When the seventeenth century began, consensus about what natural philosophy was or what truths it taught had broken down. In some ways the ferment resembled the agitated excitement and distress of Europe's first encounter with natural philosophy five centuries earlier. Until then, Aristotle and Euclid were names vaguely known to a few. Monks had spun the spiderwebs of theology mainly from the writings of St. Augustine, who knew little of natural philosophy. Then suddenly from Arabic and Greek, the sciences were there to be studied, and not one of the new authorities was Christian. The task of assimilation was hard, its success by no means assured. Roger Bacon, William of Ockham, Abelard, and Marsilius of Padua struck off in directions deemed dangerous to faith. In 1277, at the behest of Pope John XXI, Bishop Tempier anathematized 219 philosophical propositions taught at the University of Paris; among them were several dozen defended by Thomas Aquinas. But Thomas's amalgamation of Nature and Grace (or of "Aristotle and the Bible," as Descartes wittily dubbed it) papered over the conflict by pious phrases. In 1325 Bishop Tempier's decree was revoked. Meanwhile, the modest intake of philosophy and mathematics was a leaven to fertile minds who formed a small but potent extra-ecclesiastical culture from which later innovations took their beginning.

The conflict between these two cultures was clearly visible in 1600. There was a new astronomy and a new anatomy, neither welcome to the clergy, since the first menaced ecclesiastical meteorology while the second snapped the "indestructible bone." The meteorology of the church doctors, including St. Thomas and Albertus Magnus, held that comets, among other "sublunary" phenomena, were portents of divine wrath and calamity. "From the Turk and the comet," the learned were wont to pray with the superstitious, "good Lord deliver us." Comets that streaked across European skies in 1531, 1539, 1556, 1577, and 1618 incited guilt feelings throughout Christendom and inspired clergymen to fulminations against the few astronomers who observed events free from panic terror. The redoubtable Kepler, who later just managed to save his mother from burning as a witch, announced with Tycho Brahe the sober truth that comets were not meteorological phenomena at all.

Anatomy was put on the path to science by Andreas Vesalius, professor of medicine in Padua, whose *De humani corporis fabrica* appeared the same year (1543) as Copernicus's revolutionary work. Vesalius offended the learned by preferring nature to Galen, the received authority in medicine. He studied human anatomy as Galen had—by dissection of human corpses. But if his methods broke new paths in medicine, they outraged his contemporaries, who, invoking the authority of St. Augustine, condemned dissection as "abhorrent to Christians." And no wonder. By examining nature rather than books, by believing his eyes rather than received authority, Vesalius confounded belief in the indestructible bone theologians supposed necessary for the resurrection of the body. He escaped the revenge of the reverend fathers while serving as physician to Charles V, but subsequently died in mysterious circumstances. His former colleague at Padua, Michael Servetus, another dissector, was burned in Geneva by the very religious Calvin, who would have liked to burn Copernicus too.

A new astronomy and anatomy, then, were testily available to inquirers in 1600. So were solid geometry and algebra. A few mathematicians of a practical bent pondered isolated theorems of mechanics. Finally, a sophisticated experimental methodology, developed in Bologna and Padua around medicine, was making its way across Europe through students like William Harvey.

Before the century closed, the scene was wholly transformed. The Scholastics and their ecclesiastical sciences had been trounced on the field of combat and driven inside the Gothic walls of universities. Outside, among the informed public and the experimentalists, there was no doubt that natural science did at last exist. The virtuoso performance in the century of light was Isaac Newton's synthesis of rational mechanics, published as *The Mathematical Principles of Natural Philosophy* in 1687. True to its title, this work laid down principles that would endure for two centuries. It expounded a system of mechanics, inclusive of statics and dynamics. It was, so to speak, a science of machines—a thing very useful at the beginnings of a mechanical civilization.

Newton's achievements were the highest peak in a lofty range. Optics and hydrology advanced apace after they were given mathematical formulations. Anatomy extended to knowledge of capillary action and to the first stages of histology. The velocity of light was measured, planetary masses calculated, and the law of gases discovered. Chemistry sported atomic theory and experimental methods, although chemical analysis was still primitive. Numerous new instruments and gauges increased the precision of results, or opened new areas of micro- and macro-observation. Description, analysis, and experimental ingenuity attained a new order of exactitude and finesse. Analytic geometry, the calculus, and probability theory placed in human hands undreamt-of powers of calculation, including the first calculating machines designed by Pascal and Leibniz. Spin-offs from these sciences to cartography, navigation, ballistics, and other applied sciences were numerous.

The significance of these discoveries to those who made them is not rendered by the observation that in the century of light more new knowledge was accumulated than in the previous 300,000 years of man's existence. That fact could be appreciated only at the end, when all the results were in, whereas the creators of modern science were acutely aware of its significance from the beginning. The two great manifestos interpreting the significance of science, *The Great Instauration* and the *Discourse on Method,* were published in 1619 and 1637, respectively. Not the volume of results but the quality and character of the new science was what made it seem to mark the advent of a new epoch of human history.

The *Discourse on Method for the Right Conduct of One's Reason and for Seeking Truth in the Sciences* bears the stamp of Baconian thought. Like Bacon, Descartes used skepticism to chasten pretended knowledge. He used Bacon's phrases to designate his task as "showing a new way" and as establishing "firm foundations" for science. He rejected all received authorities and even the very idea of authority. He concurred in Bacon's critique of classical philosophy, and agreed that the remedy established a new relation between sense and understanding. He also avowed that knowledge is power and that the conquest of nature is a natural outcome of the new science. The title of the *Discourse* that Descartes scrapped just prior to publication pointed insistently at that proud goal. It was to be called *Project for a Universal Science that is able to Elevate our Nature to the Highest Degree of Perfection.*

But Bacon had no conception of a mathematical physics. His discussions of the Copernican theory show his uneasiness about mathematics in science. He realized that number and measure were important applications of mathematics, particularly in mechanics and astronomy. Yet he mistrusted astronomy because he thought it impossible to decide between Copernicus and competing theories, such as Tycho Brahe's; and he seems to have believed that the heliocentric planetary system was too paradoxical. Also, he adopted a guarded attitude toward mathematics because it seemed to him a ready vehicle for Pythagorean or Platonic metaphysics.

His suspicion kept him a stranger to the basic scientific achievement of the century of light. Mathematical physics did not come about merely by applying mathematics, as one might apply geometry to measuring acreage of fields. It required the quantification of motion, and generally the mathematization of nature, which Descartes expressed in the hyperbolic boast that he had "reduced" physics to mathematics. The boast expressed the insight (to be precise, the confidence) that all motions of matter, notwithstanding the infinite diversity of things as we experience them, may be expressed as algebraic quantities in Euclidean space.

This hunch revolutionized natural philosophy by equipping it with the awesome generality of geometry. Just as the geometer proves properties of plane and solid figures without ambiguity or exceptions, so the new physicist demonstrated the properties of all bodies. Yet this generality was not obtained by a return to speculative abstractions, since its truths were the concrete truths of the levers and pulleys of the world—of force, mass, acceleration, momentum, speed, equilibria, pressures. Thanks to its concreteness, the new science was able to enter vigorously on the experimental path. Bacon advocated experimentation, but lacked specific conceptions needed to devise fruitful experiment; he thus fell back on collections of data or "natural histories" to provide the material for ideas. This is not the spirit of mathematical physics, which always begins with an idea about accessible phenomena: the compression of fluids, centripetal force, the oscillation of a pendulum. In this too the new science imitated geometry. Regardless of how complex his investigations may become, the geometer's subject matter is always accessible and before him.

Seeing nature quantitatively in Euclidean space is a very special way of looking at things—one that requires a "new relation between sense and understanding." To recognize that the action of a piston compressing a fluid in a cylinder is analogous to a lever with unequal arms, and to perceive, as Pascal did, "in this new machine that invariable regularity which occurs in all the old ones, such as the lever, the pulley, the endless screw, etc., namely, the distances vary inversely as the forces"—such a manner of discerning things was a new power on this earth. Mathematical conceptuality seemed to carry the mind directly to the inner workings of nature, where efficient causality was a matter of exact ratios and proportions of forces acting through bodies. Those forces and motions could be calculated with precision, as in a simple algebraic problem. But experience, or the unaided senses, were not up to that precision. To rectify their deficiency, the new scientists, from the beginning, devised more accurate or completely new measuring devices. The determined Tycho Brahe resolved to draw up new tables of the stars that would reduce the margin of observational error from ten minutes of arc, which Copernicus thought an inaccessible ideal, to four seconds of arc. To achieve that accuracy, he had a quadrant made with a radius of nineteen feet, while his sextant measured fourteen feet. His prodigiously accurate tables were indispensable to Kepler and Newton. The new scientists also devised a plethora of new concepts, today called "idealizations," to bring complexity within manageable proportions. Thus we hear of perfect vacuums, rigid and elastic bodies, the wave propagation of light, mass points, uniform acceleration and other notions that, though lacking a strict counterpart in experience, may well exist in nature.

The Human Significance of Science

In the evening of his life, after enduring many years of ecclesiastical impertinence and incomprehension, Galileo declared that the new science would prosper only if "men's minds are first made over." Though he had been ambushed and slandered by envious mediocrities like Father Scheiner, Galileo could console himself that he had planted his seed in able disciples. While under house arrest in Florence, the stream of visitors from abroad reminded him that he was not forgotten beyond the Alps, where for decades his writings astonished the best minds in Europe. One of those visitors, John Milton, returned to England to compose a passionate defense of freedom of speech, the *Areopagitica.* Perhaps too a friend told him the widely circulated story that when he recanted before the Inquisition, he exclaimed under his breath, "But it moves!" The story would have pleased the proud spirit of the aging philosopher. And he must have experienced quiet triumph when the reports began to come in that the Inquisition, far from removing a scandal to faith, had made itself notorious. We can imagine this lover of poetry and of the poetry of life wondering whether the Holy Congregation had played well the fool's part in this reenactment of the trial of Socrates. And what of his own part? Had recanting been wiser than defiance? How it mortified him to bow to that assembly of hypocrites! Perhaps in those moments of bitterness he read from the *Decameron* or the *Divine Comedy* to refresh himself with reminders of how wise men endure in these contests. With calmness returned his certainty that defiance would have ruined the cause of science in Italy and maybe Europe. Then, feeble and nearly blind, he began dictating his posthumous vindication, the *Dialogue concerning the Two New Sciences.*[53]

Galileo probably did not know that in France and England two men of genius and ambition silently followed his saga while preparing themselves through a long apprenticeship to take up his cause and their own.[54] There was much to ponder. The conceptual design of the new philosophy had to be mastered, corrected, extended. The means of its propagation, of "making over men's minds," had to be thought through with the utmost care. Some remedy or prophylaxis against that debauched state of mind, the empire of faith over the senses, had to be found. But at last Descartes and Hobbes spoke; and those with eyes for it, like Henry More and Pascal and Leibniz, saw that they had devised a terrible retribution for superstition. Descartes, emphasizing the positive, called it "the liberation of the mind from prejudice."

Descartes was a master of the prose that makes over men's minds. His style is clear and spare; dignified yet intimate, toned by a naïveté that one does not quite believe. His attitudes and feelings are understated in fine-grained nuance, lest strangers approach the cautious narrator too closely. He was adept with the telling phrase, and skilled in polite aristocratic deference that on second look turns out to be mockery. Full of pranks, he delighted in drawing brazen paradox across his reader's path while treating it deadpan as the most ordinary thing in the world; or again, he could evoke voices from the blue that insinuated unthinkable things to receptive readers. A good judge of audience taste, he excelled in beautifying what it thought repulsive and exposing the warts on its icons, but without seeming to. And he was fortunate in the choice of

53. This reconstruction of Galileo's assessment of his struggle was advanced by de Santillana in *The Crime of Galileo,* 201–6, 322 ff. The parallel with Socrates was of course vivid to the humanists involved in the case (ibid., 198).

54. Hobbes met Galileo on his Italian journey in 1635. Whether Descartes visited Galileo on his Italian journey is not known. News of scientific developments in France and northern Europe reached Galileo through Mersenne and Peiresc. Mersenne was privy to Descartes' Copernican views.

themes he used to introduce his chosen audience—the man or woman of "good sense"—to philosophy. One was skepticism, deployed to display the critical spirit and to exercise readers in incredulity and the detection of illusions. The other theme, disastrous unless handled by a master, was himself. The story of the *Discourse*, he said, is "a history of my mind," offered as an example that others may imitate. The story in outline is this. Descartes told of his upbringing and education at the Jesuit college of La Flèche to indicate the character of the "prejudices" and false beliefs on which he was "nourished since infancy." Then, by narrating his itinerary through stages of doubt, the discovery of a method, and scientific investigation, he showed how he emancipated himself from prejudice, and how others might as well. The *Encyclopedia* says of this didactic device that it was "in large measure responsible for the revolution of which this philosopher is the author."[55]

The *Discourse* purports to offer an active, worldly philosophy to active men and women. The bait is the mentality of the philosopher, dressed in its most attractive colors. The aspect of this mentality most difficult to popularize, yet the most necessary, was the critical, skeptical spirit. Without it his readers could not learn to think for themselves. But in his milieu, the critical spirit carried through consistently meant intellectual isolation and such severe detachment from received opinions that an accurate picture would frighten beginners and scandalize censors. The difficulty was managed by adroit representation. Descartes set up an imagery of isolation in the reader's line of sight, while tucking its reasons in shadowed corners. He depicted *his* isolation, but by taking the reader into confidence, assuaged fears of solitude. Best of all, the *Discourse* concludes with a call to collaborative endeavor in a grand scheme that sets generous souls in opposition to mean-spirited clergymen.

Readers more keen on ridding themselves of prejudice than fearful of solitude soon learn how to assemble the complete picture from the foreground imagery and the shadowed hard edges. Beginning with the depiction of the philosopher relying entirely on his own strength, the reader notices details: Descartes never sought advice and declined what was gratuitously offered; he repudiated the received learning and set out on a high-risk enterprise to build everything anew, by himself, from scratch; he impudently designated his own thinking the "first principle" of philosophy; he credited nothing not evident to his own mind; he never prayed for divine assistance or offered thanksgiving when he succeeded, although God's "immensity" was said to provide an opportune

---

55. *Encyclopédie*, 6: 415. The narrative structure of the *Discourse* is more extensively treated in my *Origin of Subjectivity*, 30–39, 60–65.

"foundation" for science; his Stoic morals extinguished all trace of humility and guilt, while lofty pride fairly crackled in every sentence. And as if that weren't temerity enough, Descartes had his own private opinion that the world was a machine.

Readers who reflected on this itinerary were astonished by the picture that emerged. Classical and ecclesiastical learning are swept away completely. Magic, alchemy, and astrology are thrown out on their ear. The world is as perspicuous and unmysterious as a clock: comets come from outer space bearing no messages from Jehovah; all bones can be fractured; a human corpse is a rusting machine, nothing more; the universe is infinite (the opinion for which Bruno was burned); the planetary system is Copernican; in the whole expanse of the universe there are no miracles, not one; belief in resurrection is for the "weak-minded" while the "strong-minded" itch to master and possess nature; Scholasticism is decadence usurping the name of philosophy, which Descartes challenges to mortal combat. Such views define philosophic isolation and independence of thought: the break with received opinion is clean, sharp, radical. The past is a smoking ruin, and a new era dawns.

The tally sheet of early reactions to Cartesian philosophy registers its vast innovation. Pascal, introduced to Descartes as a lad, was carried by his genius into the inner sanctum of Cartesian philosophy, only to discover that the "God of Abraham, Isaac, and Jacob" was nowhere to be found in it. Henry More, the magus of Cambridge philosophy, was an early, enthusiastic follower who believed Cartesian metaphysics provided a basis for a reforming Protestant philosophy. But as he examined the system more exactly, he recoiled in shock from the materialism and atheism he discerned in it. Gilbert Voët, the leading Calvinist theologian of Holland, staked his reputation in a protracted, acrimonious fight to halt the progress of Cartesianism in Dutch universities by accusing Descartes of covertly teaching atheism. Leibniz called Cartesian philosophy the "ante-chamber to the true," but warned that it taught "the most dangerous of all doctrines" (that matter assumes all forms) and that in his metaphysics Descartes had "played with those grand words, the existence of God and the immortality of the soul." Spinoza, an avowed Cartesian universally execrated by the clergy as the worst of atheists, was said by Leibniz to teach "only extreme Cartesianism." Another avowed Cartesian, the Oratorian priest Malebranche, repudiated Scholasticism, championed mechanistic philosophy, and interpreted the Bible in odd ways. When the mortal remains of Descartes were returned from Stockholm to Paris in 1662, a prominent Jesuit remarked, "The enemy is within the gate." And indeed he was, if we may believe what d'Alembert wrote in the Preliminary Discourse:

Descartes dared to show . . . good minds how to shake off the yoke of scholasticism, of opinion, of authority, in a word, prejudice and barbarism; and by this revolt, whose fruits we reap today, philosophy received from him a service perhaps more difficult to render than all those rendered by his illustrious successors. One may regard him as a chief of the conspirators who had the courage to raise the banner against arbitrary and despotic power, and who prepared a brilliant revolution by laying the foundations for a government more just and happy than any seen established.[56]

Heliocentrism and Egocentrism

Contemporary efforts to understand the *mentalité* of the seventeenth-century revolution in thought must overcome the difficulties we experience grappling with its egocentric orientation, coming as we do from an intellectual climate consciously gregarious and socially oriented. The individualism of modern political theory, to be discussed later, has long since been replaced in the social sciences by Social Man—man understood as determined even in his private desires by an all-embracing social environment. Similarly, the Cartesian principle of individual consciousness has for some decades been replaced by the gregarious principle of language. This paradigm shift tends either to conceal the character of the egocentric principle or to make it seem incredible when from time to time certain aspects make an appearance. A current view of the historiography of the encyclopedists is a case in point. Their emphasis on the origin of science in conflict with religion seems unsatisfactory to some contemporary historians, who prefer to interpret the undeniable innovations of seventeenth-century thought as developments within a basic socio-intellectual consensus. De Santillana's study of the crime of Galileo, for example, denies that it was the collision of religion and

56. *Encyclopédie*, 1: xxvi. The party of "conspirators" to whom d'Alembert refers were the libertines, skeptics, *politiques*, Erastians, Socinians, experimental philosophers, and others who composed the party of progress in the sixteenth and seventeenth centuries. These groupings are discussed in chaps. 2–4. For surveys of early responses to Descartes as a dangerous or irreligious philosopher, see Paul Hazard, *The European Mind*, 88–131, Jean Bordas-Demoulin, *Le Cartésianisme*, chaps. 1, 2, and Cornelio Fabro, *God in Exile*, 91–119, 189–93. Maxime Leroy's *Descartes, le philosophe au masque*, a full-length study of the skeptical, libertine Descartes behind the mask of piety, has been superseded by more systematic investigations of this question: H. Caton, "The Problem of Descartes' Sincerity," *Philosophical Forum* 2 (1971): 355–70; Caton, "Analytic History of Philosophy: The Case of Descartes"; Caton, "Descartes' Anonymous Writings: A Recapitulation."

science that Enlightenment historiography gave it out to be. Pope Urban VIII and his entourage, he advises, were "much less the oppressors of science than the first bewildered casualties of the scientific age," while Galileo represented "the spirit of ecumenic and conciliar Christianity" in the mold of "Ambrose, Augustine, or Bonaventure, reprehending sleepy shepherds and degenerate epigones."[57] The affair was a "tragic misunderstanding" contrived and manipulated by gnomic third parties (the Jesuits, who headed the Inquisition). The conflict, then, was a misunderstanding, not a dramatic clash between entrenched intolerance and ambitious reason. Neither did it illustrate the independence of the new philosophy, since Galileo pressed his claims not merely as a true son of the Church, but in the holy tradition of ecumenic and conciliar Christianity.

This interpretation illustrates how intractable cases, where the evidence is detailed and apparently conclusive, may yet be squeezed into the explanatory models of social consensus. My object here is not to question the value of those models, but to note their limits. Possibly the new philosophy did ground, unbeknownst to its inventors, in "Catholic science" (de Santillana) or "Puritan science" (Merton, Webster), whatever those ominous phrases may mean. But such models are not at their best when explaining how originators of a nongregarious *mentalité* understood themselves and their world. The problem is acute in the present instance, since the Cartesian ego is the unsocial self upon which so much subsequent modern thought was built.[58]

The content of the Cartesian ego is disclosed partly by the way Descartes differentiated himself from his milieu. As we have seen, he created an egocentric frame, the history of his mind, as the vehicle for representing his philosophy. Descartes could not say "I" without committing unsociable acts, such as rejecting the received learning and the authority of preceptors, although they were the emblems of respectability in his time. Authority was rejected because it conflicted with his own "clear and distinct ideas," and he would not endure having his thought coerced, which bespeaks truculence uncharacteristic of a team player. Indeed, the history of this ego was a calculated assault on his socialization. Descartes was determined to think for himself, not merely in some things, or now and then, but on all matters. To assert this "empire of reason" was to deny the legitimacy of authority, particularly the social

57. De Santillana, *The Crime of Galileo*, x, xi, 204.
58. For a survey and criticism of this historiographic tendency, see Caton, "Tory History of Ideas," and "Analytic History of Philosophy: The Case of Descartes."

norms of intellectual life, and brand it arbitrary and despotic. In remarks on morality and the received learning, he indicated that authority arises to enforce a consensus that otherwise would not exist, although an alleged consensus, created by force and threats, is invoked to intimidate dissidents and to undermine their subjective certainties.[59] Descartes delicately depicted himself in just this situation—his purely subjective certainties vs. "the world." From what resources did he draw the strength and temerity for his unsociable disdain for received norms?

He molded his subjective certainty on the certainty of mathematics. Early in the *Discourse* he mentioned that of all the arts and sciences, only mathematics is a true science, prolific in proof and demonstration. The other so-called sciences are medleys of shifting opinions; but mathematical notions are so "natural to the mind" that proof is "simple and easy." Although the evidence of mathematics rests on nothing more exalted than the mathematician's subjective certainty, that certainty is self-sufficient, impervious to special pleading, "unshakable": $2 + 2 = 4$, let the world say what it will. Nevertheless, the subjective certainties of mathematicians achieve an uncoerced consensus of the competent handily surpassing any consensus engineered by authority.

After pointing out these potencies in mathematics, Descartes launched his sharpest image of intellectual isolation—the solitary retreat to his *poêle,* when he constructed his method for reducing physics to mathematics, so that truths about nature could be rendered as theorems of a deduction. By mathematizing physics, Descartes believed he had transformed natural philosophy into natural science, whose notions and proofs also enjoyed the unshakable certainty of mathematics. How must the advent of mathematical physics affect the world of learning? Plainly it must, in time, be wholly transformed. Disputation would yield to proof; authority would crumble before experimental evidence; sundry incompetents and interested potentates who hitherto laid down the correct line would soon be embarrassed by demonstrations, as incorruptible and unanswerable as Columbus's voyage. The dusty, bulky library of Scholastic learning was suddenly irrelevant, or worse, shown to be misguided in principle.

But there was a hitch: show to whom? Descartes often said and more often implied that the *mentalité* of Scholastics was too corrupted by "prejudices," especially deference to authority, to be rehabilitated or even persuaded. Hence he addressed his writings to men and women of "good sense," outside the universities. Yet they inhabited a social milieu where deference to authority was taken for granted, and they too de-

59. Caton, "Analytic History of Philosophy," 280ff., 286ff.

ferred on matters of importance. To alter this outlook, to steel them to follow only the deliverances of reason, the new philosophy required some Baconian "crucial experiment" that would decide the issue once for all.

The Inquisition handed Descartes the issue. As a young man, he followed the yo-yoing of the Holy Office on the Copernican theory at least from 1620, when it was permitted as a mathematical hypothesis. When the axe finally fell on Galileo in 1633, Descartes reacted with cool, implacable resolve. He wrote to Mersenne, that information exchange for the learned of Europe, that he must now suppress his nearly completed treatise *The World*, since if the Copernican theory is false, "the whole foundations of my philosophy are false also, for they most evidently demonstrate this theory." Knowing that the gossip Mersenne would repeat all he said, he sent the Scholastics a stinging message by declaring his intention to "burn all his papers." The Inquisition, Descartes believed, had responded to Galileo's challenge with a classic demonstration of prejudice by expressly demanding that the subjective certainty of individual reason be abandoned for the committee authority of the Holy Congregation. This was the great perversion of intellect that the new philosophy had to meet and defeat.[60]

To bring the issue to a crisis for those who would follow his path, Descartes devised a hyperbolic doubt as a thought-experiment. He supposed that there is some god or demon, omnipotent and infinitely cunning, bent on deceiving him in all that he perceived, however clearly: the existence of the world is an illusion; 2 + 2 does not equal 4; even his own body is a phantasm devised by his deceiver. What certainty can be salvaged from so great an onslaught? That I who think these things do think, and thinking, must exist: I think, therefore I am. Here Descartes found a certainty he called "unshakable" because not even an omnipotent god can overthrow it. Well then, what is the basis and source of that truth? Nothing but the subjective certainty of his own clear and distinct thoughts. The effect of radical doubt, then, is to identify the subjective certainty of thought as the sole region of truth. If so, my thought is the principle or beginning of philosophy in the sense that whatever truth I find is always known as my clear and distinct ideas. Descartes' new foundation of philosophy therefore says in effect: I, René Descartes, born Anno Domini 1596 and nourished on the Catholic faith since infancy, know and affirm my clear thoughts as the sole source of truth within the power of reason. Toward the end of his life he expressed this *mentalité* in wonderfully forthright language: "Since we are born men

60. Caton, *The Origin of Subjectivity*, 66–73, 115–30, 203ff.

before we are made Christians, it is beyond belief that any man should seriously embrace opinions which he thinks contrary to that right reason which constitutes a man, in order to cling to the faith through which he is a Christian."[61] Here is the ego robust and assertive. If faith conflicts with subjective certainties, so much the worse for faith. The strong medicine of hyperbolic doubt, a figure of the conflict between reason and faith, brings consciousness to awareness of its own natural strength and power.

This was the revolution in thought for which Descartes was hailed by so many Enlightenment figures: it was his achievement, his liberation of the mind from despotic and arbitrary power. And one sees that his principle is not remote from the predatory rationalism of the Enlightenment.[62] But we lose sight of the character of "I think" as the beginning of philosophy if we conceive it as *essentially* an assertion of reason's independence from religion. Rather, it is an assertion of the self-sufficiency of the clear and distinct ideas of anyone who wills to embrace his ideas as *his own*. Its critical edge is set against any authority, religious or otherwise. Its positive content is the method of individual self-assertion. D'Alembert presumably had this legitimation of reason in mind when he credited Descartes with having laid "the foundations for a government more just and happy than any seen established."

If the ego finds itself by recovering what Caesar has stolen, Descartes also discovers what he is by "distinguishing" himself from "body," and conversely. The celebrated dualism of thinking and extension, self and world, is an optics of knowledge, a system of conceptual mirrors and inverting lens, that corrects a multitude of natural illusions which prevent the subject from seeing the mechanistic universe as it is. We naturally believe that the earth is at rest; Tycho Brahe even performed an experiment to prove it. The idea that the earth not only rotates on its axis but also around the sun twice contradicts our strongest sense impressions. Or again, the starry sky appears bounded and finite. That roses are red, that marble is shiny and hard, that the night is cold are all certainties to our natural way of thinking. We also believe that we take action thanks to some will or soul in us, and we attribute a similar power to animals.

61. *Œuvres de Descartes,* ed. Charles Adam and Paul Tannery, 11 vols. (Paris: L. Cerf, 1897–1910), 8 (pt. 2): 353–54.
62. I have developed an interpretation of Descartes' writings as advancing militant crypto-atheism. For this interpretation, see my works cited in n. 56, especially "Descartes' Anonymous Writings: A Recapitulation," 303–9, and "Reply to Curley," *Independent Journal of Philosophy,* in press.

But if the world is a machine, these convictions are illusions. Thinking the world mechanistically sets all things in motion: "there is no location of anything in the world which is *firm* and *fixed*, except that we fix it in our thought."[63] And the qualities we perceive in things are not there—"in" them. How could they be? Whoever clutched a geometrical solid, or smelled an acceleration, or heard a ratio? The mechanistic world is pure quantity and absolute geometry, and quantity is perceived only by the mind. The corrective optical system shows that when we say the night is cold, we project onto our conception of body something of "the mind," namely, coldness. The new relation between sense and understanding effected by the optics of dualism locates sense qualities "in" the mind.[64]

Audacious though it is, this conceptual optics, as David Hume remarked, was "the fundamental principle of modern philosophy . . . which asserts [sense qualities] to be nothing but impressions in the mind derived from the operation of external objects, and without any resemblance to the qualities of the objects." But if it is incredible, it is not mysterious. The ego is "attached" to an animal body. This body-machine, Descartes explained elaborately in the *Discourse,* is an automaton, like the intricate wind-up dolls that clockmakers of the day constructed to display their skill. Like the doll, the body "goes by itself," immune to influence of the will and in conformity with the necessity that permeates the universe. But what particularly interested Descartes about this machine was that it receives impacts on its nerve endings, conducts them to a point in the brain, and there converts them into conscious thoughts and ideas, or dreams, as may be. The thinking "thing" is therefore a thinking machine, a mind "attached" to a living body. Because it is attached to the body inside the brain, the mind has immediate and direct knowledge only of its bodily ideas, not of the objects of the world. Descartes' corrective optics explains how those defective and deceptive ideas may be used to acquire knowledge of the machine universe.

These exotic notions at once shrink the subject to a point in space and time and expand it infinitely. There is perhaps no more striking and ridiculous image of human finitude than the mind imprisoned in the damp, dark, silent entrails of the cerebral cortex. And yet, from a scientific and medical point of view, the mind remains today just where Descartes deposited it. This extreme spatiotemporal isolation nevertheless expands the ego infinitely. Though the body-machine is a thing poor

63. Descartes, *Principles of Philosophy,* pt. 2, §13.
64. Caton, *The Origin of Subjectivity,* 74 ff.

and insignificant, it rolls through the world's universal causal net in such a way that its contact with environing bodies communicates the infinite universe to thought. The infinity represented by sense impressions inside the brain goes unnoticed except to mathematical thinking, which learns how to seize its thought and represent to itself the world as a machine. In this way the ego comes to know itself as a thinking machine whose pointlike finitude mediates infinite comprehension.

Moving the World

"I think" is an Archimedean point to move the world, Descartes boasted. The metaphor refers to a hypothetical fulcrum for a lever. But nothing is "firm and fixed, except that we fix it in our thought." Descartes' practical philosophy, whose great motion is the mastery and possession of nature, revolves about the ways and means of unshakably emplacing the ego so that the world may be mastered.

The beginning of ethics, as of science, is to understand clearly what is and what is not "within our power." The thinking subject knows that only his thoughts are in his power, since the body-machine behaves according to its own laws. Descartes did not say, as Hobbes and Spinoza did, that free will is an illusion. He preferred rather to say that he was freest when his will was most determined. To impart to the will the character of necessity consummates ethics, for it roots out and destroys "all the penitence and remorse which usually agitates the conscience of those weak and vacillating minds who allow themselves the inconstancy of practicing as good things which they afterwards judge to be bad." Bad conscience is a bad condition not because it is iniquitous, but because it *enfeebles* the ego, sapping its strength to carry through action. The basic categories of ethics are not good and evil, iniquity and righteousness, but, as in the natural world, power and impotence. Hence Descartes defined virtuous activity in abstraction from good and evil, calling it a "firm and constant resolution . . . never to fail of his own will to undertake and execute all the things which he judges to be best." He is "good" whose strong soul is resolved to will his particular necessity, his fatality as this particular thinking machine whose wishes and desires follow their own character and rhythm. Cartesian ethics, then, is a kind of *mimesis*—an imitation in thought, or a comprehension by thought, of the mechanical necessity that the thinking machine is. Descartes' own necessity impelled him to the maximum enhancement and use of power. He admitted, for example, that it would be wrong for *him*—though not for "weak minds"—to limit in any way his freedom by "vows and promises." As we have seen, he extirpated conscience in himself and patronized it as a weakness.

Similarly, he despised humility, and resolved to rely exclusively on his own strength, taking this so far as to "desire nothing in the future beyond what I could acquire," such as life beyond the grave. In these respects Cartesian virtue resembles the virtue of a Machiavellian captain. Action aims at success, at producing the desired effect, at carrying through one's will. As for morality and social norms, the first rule of action is to observe them when it is convenient to do so. The unsociable self-assertion of the ego thus runs close to outright immorality.

The concluding part of the *Discourse* announces that call to greatness, "the mastery and possession of nature." Once again the autobiographical format provides the clues to the character of the ego. Descartes represented himself as wishing to "lose no opportunity of benefiting the public" by the generosity and *humanité* of a gift that will vastly improve the human condition. Describing the fruits of mathematical physics in brief but unforgettably stirring words, he wrote:

> [The mastery of nature] is not merely desirable for the invention of an infinity of machines that will enable us to enjoy without pain the fruits of the earth and all the good things to be found there, but also principally for the preservation of health, which is without doubt the first good and the foundation of all other goods of this life.

However, he was inhibited from publishing his physics because it would have offended the learned of the day, who might, in his euphemism, "rob him of his leisure." Thus Descartes struck the pose of the embattled public benefactor thwarted by the envy and obscurantism of the learned, who happened to be also the principal guardians of religion and morals. This posture was designed to weld the self-interest and indignation of the public into a powerful force that would overturn those states and institutions that frustrated the public work that Descartes would set in motion. The appropriateness of this posture to their circumstances was realized by the philosophers, who, as we have seen in the case of the *Encyclopedia*, used it to lead the battle for science and *humanité* against the dark powers of superstition and despotism.

Unlike Bacon, Descartes did not invoke any religious tradition or text to legitimate his project, since practical philosophy is expressly based on "natural reason without the light of faith." Indeed, the passage just quoted insinuates a new Garden of Eden restored by man's own efforts. But this end (which Descartes forecast lay centuries in the future, if it were ever realized at all) is not the motive animating the project. The motive is delight in putting one's powers to the test, the glory of breaking new paths and venturing the untried, in short, the set of desires that

Bacon subsumed under the desire for greatness. This, not any sense of charity, is the *humanité* of the philosopher-benefactor. The material benefits of the mastery of nature are, to be sure, not despised, especially when one wants to arouse the interest of all men. But if no material benefits flow from the project, his interest in it would not diminish, for he is charmed, as Bacon put it, by the prospect of "how much more is possible now, if we but knew our strength and chose to assay and exert it." What could be more *interesting*, as an experiment in power and knowledge, than the mastery of nature? This spirit was captured by Nietzsche in one of his glances across the many faces of modernity:

> Even measured by the Greek standard [which prized power], our whole modern existence, insofar as it is not weakness but power and consciousness of power, looks like sheer *hubris* and impiety: things exactly contrary to the ones we reverence today had for the longest time conscience on their side and God for their guardian. Our whole attitude toward nature, our violation of nature with the help of machines and the heedless ingenuity of technicians and engineers, is *hubris;* so is our attitude to God as some putative spider weaving purposes and ethics behind a vast web of causation . . . ; so is our attitude toward ourselves, upon whom we perform experiments which we would never perform on any animal, cheerfully and curiously splitting open the soul, while the body still breathes. What do we care any longer for the "salvation" of the soul? [65]

Methodological Remark

We now have a preliminary description of the party of progress, called the "party of progress" by one of its members, Voltaire. The description was obtained by constructing an event series connecting the encyclopedists with the advent of science as a political force. The event series was obtained initially as a datum embedded in the encyclopedists' history of progress. Independent examination of the writings of Bacon and Descartes confirmed the encyclopedists' construction of events. We ascertained that these men inaugurated programs projecting a progressive politics based on accumulation of knowledge. Their program therefore projected the event series in which the encyclopedists situated themselves as participants and advocates.

Our event series is thinly populated at the moment, consisting only of a few intellectuals. In the next four chapters that population will substantially multiply; and we will see how an unprecedented political pro-

65. Nietzsche, *Genealogy of Morals,* pt. 2, §9.

gram expanded its forces by preempting political traditions. Before entering that more complex narrative and analytic web, it is desirable to stress certain main points.

Novelty and enterprising spirit were distinguishing features of the program; accordingly, they furnish descriptive criteria for recognizing its presence in a given milieu. The three manifestos just examined accord in asserting the novelty of a new politics inaugurated by the subjection of a small part of nature, the cognitive power, by rules of right thinking. This heroic performance defined obstruction of the new force as various sorts of existing literary craftsmanship, pseudo-science, and mental debasement (superstition, prejudice), dominating intellectual institutions at the opening of the seventeenth century. These institutions were, to be sure, in a condition of flux owing to the upsurge of factional competition. Theology had been overtaken by the Reformation, while humanists had opened a strong front against Scholasticism. The existence of these factions meant that there was space for bargaining and coalition, but the party of science was not in any sense the accidental residue of sundry alliances. The humanists were literati who might eulogize Galileo's virtuosity or Bacon's grandeur, or otherwise perform services for the party of science. Yet the scientists were a breed quite distinct from humanists. In place of words there was now the experiment; in place of moral edification there was material improvement; in place of authoritative valorized traditions there was innovation. As for theology, revelation was replaced with inspection of nature, including human nature, by using one's own resources.

Any politics, to succeed, must have a popular constituency. Prior to Bacon, knowledge had never enjoyed a commanding role in politics. Philosophers had fantasized utopias where knowledge and knowers would rule, but neither they nor anyone else had any concrete notions about how to make knowledge the center of actual politics. Bacon thus innovated when he recognized that improvement of the arts and sciences could function as the hinge of a new politics. His legitimating argument, by contrast, was as old as politics: in return for the public trust, the party of progress would benefit mankind by improving their condition. We saw that this sales talk was compromised by another line of thinking which identified as the motivation of the scientists not benevolent intent, but material power and political glory. This duplicity was eliminated by Thomas Hobbes in his detailed integration of Bacon's flamboyant project into the matter-of-factness of everyday politics. Hobbes, we will see, put down Bacon's infatuation with glory as another "idol" distracting the mind from lucid apprehension of the human condition.

chapter 2

The Diffusion of the New Philosophy

IT IS useful to think of the decades between 1630 and 1666 as a critical period in the growth of the new philosophy. The latter date marks the founding of the Académie royale des sciences in Paris under the leadership of Christiaan Huygens, following closely the establishment of the Royal Society of London (1662) and the Accademia del Cimento in Florence (1657). With the founding of these societies under royal protection, the struggle for recognition of the new philosophy had crossed a watershed. Sovereigns could not extend protection to experimentalists without implicitly discarding the accusation that their inquiries were dangerous to religion and public order. Official sanction implied that the temporal powers countenanced, if they did not endorse, the new scientific outlook. This was a substantial victory. Since members of these academies were Copernicans and tended to be mechanists as well, approval of their activities implied relaxation of secular claims to regulate scientific opinion. To be sure, ferocious censorship laws in France and the power of the Inquisition in Italy rendered this implication equivocal, but it became explicit in England when Parliament abolished licensing of books in 1712—not for the sake of experimentalists but as a result of fierce political faction.[1]

1. In 1624, the Parlement of Paris, on advice of the Sorbonne theological faculty, prohibited "to everyone, on pain of death, holding or teaching maxims contrary to ancient and approved authors, or disputing questions other than those approved by the theology faculty" (Charles Jourdain, *Histoire de l'Université de Paris*, 106). Aristotle would no doubt have been amazed that criti-

Science and Its Public

The three academies were initially very promising. Bacon's dream of science sponsored by ambitious authority was about to be realized in 1661 when a high-spirited monarch, Louis XIV, appointed Jean-Baptiste Colbert as successor to Mazarin. While Louis was bred to the outlook of *noblesse oblige* and cultivated the arts and sciences as an ornament of the crown, Colbert was one of the new men who understood the importance of the arts and sciences for enhancing the power of the state. To this end he gave the Académie its own quarters, equipped it with instruments and an observatory, and pensioned its members for full-time research. Leopold de Medici, the initiator and patron of the Accademia, was himself a student of Galileo and a keen experimenter who spared no expense for instruments and specimens. His Accademia consisted of a small group of Galileo's students, led by Borelli, who conducted intensive experimental investigations resulting in the invention of a number of instruments and great refinement of experimental precision.

Charles II was not of this stamp, even though his first cousin, Prince Rupert, was a keen amateur scientist. Referring to Boyle's experiments with the vacuum pump, he derided "philosophers who weighed the air."[2] He endowed the Society with no funds, quarters, or pensions. This neglect was not due solely to Charles's skepticism, for the Royal Society was conceived less as a research institute than as a forum for gentlemen amateurs.[3] Such men funded the publication of the Society's

---

cism of his philosophy should have been a capital offense in a Christian nation; but then, he had never met a Jesuit. In any case, the law was not enforced, but it was used to intimidate, primarily through the good offices of the Sorbonne doctors, as Jourdain's work amply shows. It also shows that the University of Paris faculty tormented themselves at least as much as they harassed those beyond the walls. Things were much the same at Oxford and Cambridge. On French censorship and publishing see J.-P. Belin, *Le commerce des livres prohibés,* and David Pottinger, *The French Book Trade in the Ancien Régime.*

2. Samuel Pepys's *Diary,* February 1, 1663/4, records that Charles "stayed an hour or two laughing at Sir W. Petty, about his boat, and . . . at Gresham College in general . . . for spending time only in weighing of ayre, and doing nothing else since they sat." This complaint seems to have been general. In his *History of the Royal Society,* Sprat goes to some length to establish Charles's good opinion of the virtuosi and claims that he even assisted with experiments (Sprat, *History of the Royal Society,* 133).

3. The founding of the Royal Society is discussed in chapter 4.

Transactions from 1665, the same year that the *Journal des savants* began publication in Paris, subsidized by Colbert from the public purse.

The academies and the circumstances of their founding are perhaps the most stable and conspicuous measure of the impact of the new philosophy. We do well to keep them clearly in view as we attempt to trace the rise and progress of the arts and sciences; for, as Hume noted, they depend on but a few men and effects stemming from such causes are not easy to trace.[4] By 1665 these few had created a receptive public, whose character may be estimated from the audience addressed by the *Journal des savants*. The journal was a review of books meant to report "new events in the republic of letters."[5] Its editor, Denis de Sallo, declared his intention to emphasize "the works of celebrated men" as he focused on the natural sciences and on "new discoveries . . . such as machines and useful inventions."[6] The journal also reviewed works on travel and geography, secular and ecclesiastical history, theological tracts, and law. It adopted a tone of praise rather than censure, although it implicitly censured by its choice of the praiseworthy. The first volume, for example, sketched Bacon's criticism of Scholasticism in the course of reviewing his *Opera omnia* and declared that "this great chancellor is one of those who has contributed most to the advancement of science."[7] The same volume also carried a eulogy to the deceased mathematician Fermat and praised Descartes in the context of a review of the first (posthumous) edition of his *Traité de l'homme*. A book critical of millenarian and apocalypse men was favorably reviewed, while readers were advised that "every day new progress [is made] in the sciences; new experiments are invented; and the discoveries of our century concede nothing . . . to antiquity taken in all its glory."[8]

The *Transactions* and the *Journal des savants* were followed by the *Nouvelles de la république des lettres,* established by Pierre Bayle in Rotterdam (1678), and by the *Acta eruditorum* in Leipzig (1682), initiated by Leibniz. These journals were read by those who had carried or would carry the applications of the new philosophy into every sphere of life. One such application, dubbed "political arithmetick" by Sir William Petty, was so deeply embedded in government that by 1670 it influenced the power of nations. Louis' war minister, Louvois, mastered the logis-

4. David Hume, *Philosophical Works,* 3: 175.
5. *Journal des savants,* 1: 5. The history of the *Journal* and comparable publications is described by Harcourt Brown in *Scientific Organizations,* 185–207.
6. *Journal des savants,* 1: 5.
7. Ibid., 303.
8. Ibid., 288–89; and see 3: 8.

tics of maintaining a disciplined standing army of 300,000 men. The fortifications constructed by his chief engineer, Vauban, showed how mathematical science could counteract artillery by designing fortress walls according to calculations of maximum angles of deflection for cannon shot. Colbert, who understood the problems of scale involved in coordinating a nation of 19 million, taught his subordinates to collect data and to quantify it wherever possible. In the Netherlands and England, the newly discovered calculus of probability was used to draw up the first actuarial tables used to insure life and property.

Political arithmetick, as one sees from Petty's own writings, was a subdivision of a new kind of political thinking called "projecting." The arch-projectors were Bacon and Descartes, and the Ur-form was the *New Atlantis.* Although that work inspired scientific utopianism, projecting was not meant to be utopian in the usual sense of the word, but an altogether practical art of increasing, improving, expanding, and controlling human affairs. The context of practical projecting in the seventeenth and eighteenth centuries was mercantilist political economy, whose exemplary practitioner Colbert was.

The new philosophy had also by 1670 inspired a new literary genre, science fiction, whose first specimens were works that used space travel for didactic purposes. Kepler had originated the genre with his *Somnium* (1612). John Wilkins, who was instrumental in founding the Royal Society, took up the theme in 1638. In his *Voyage to the Moon* (1651), Cyrano de Bergerac staged satiric dialogues about the antipodes, the Copernican system, and religion through an encounter between an earthling and a moonling. Fontenelle made it the theme of *Conversation on the Plurality of Worlds,* and finally Huygens contributed his effort, *Kosmotheoros* (1689). In his introductory remarks, Huygens, who generally avoided controversy, anticipated that his essay would be censured by those whose "credulity submits to human authority," and pointedly named the Jesuit astronomers Kircher and Riccioli.[9] He therefore di-

9. Huygens, *Œuvres complètes,* 21: 694. Huygens may have been settling accounts with Jesuits. His work on the rings of Saturn, which he discovered and reported in *Systema Saturnium* (1659), was attacked by the Jesuits Honori Fabri and Eustachio Divinis, who balked at Huygens's new evidence for the Copernican theory. They abused his evidence even though he explained that his observations were possible thanks to a new telescope of his design (which he described) and to the use of a micrometer, which he invented. Their obstinate defense of ecclesiastical astronomy was no doubt the reason for this sharp rebuke. Athanasius Kircher, another Jesuit scientist, was doubly cursed, for he was also an occultist and Hermetic philosopher who did missionary

rected his remarks to those who approved "rational curiosity" and invoked the examples of Copernicus, Columbus, Galileo, and Kepler. These writings, especially Fontenelle's tome, provided a charming image of the well-ordered infinite universe that had frightened the perceptive Pascal and had cost Bruno his life.

The new philosophy influenced literature less in the themes it generated than through impressions it made on writers. In England, Milton, John Donne, Andrew Marvell, and Dryden initiated that dalliance with philosophy that became a preoccupation of many Augustan writers. In France the literary circles around Gassendi and Port Royale were also digesting the new outlook and interpreting it for the public. In *Le bourgeois gentilhomme* and *Les femmes savantes*, Molière, a disciple of Gassendi, poked fun at the science fashion in the Paris salons. Samuel Butler lampooned the virtuosi of the Royal Society in his *Elephant in the Moon* (1676). Lashing at their indecent heedlessness of common belief, he wrote:

> Resolv'd to give Truth no regard,
> But what was for their turn to vouch
> And either find or make it such:
> That 'twas more noble to create
> Things like Truth, out of strong conceit,
> Than with vexatious pains and doubt
> To find, or think t'have found, her out.
>
> (ll. 450–56)

Butler, who moved in the sophisticated, skeptical company of the duke of Buckingham, was among the first writers to express reservations about the new philosophy. He blamed experimentalists for disregarding the plain truth of the senses and of imagination. The truth they created from "strong conceit" was the counterintuitive mathematical world whose properties were tested by bizarre experiments that tortured nature and offended propriety.[10] Like Jonathan Swift a generation later, Butler was troubled by this clash of truths. There are hints in his

---

work among lapsed Rosicrucians. See Frances Yates, *The Rosicrucian Enlightenment*, 274.

10. Butler's satire alludes to two experiments that brought odium upon the society: blood transfusions and mating animals across species. Human subjects were infused with a mixture of blood from sheep and human beings. Thomas Sprat discussed these experiments, conducted by Christopher Wren, without mentioning their lethal effects. They were soon discontinued.

poem that he was even more alarmed by the prospect that the virtuosi might be on to something: "For if all secret truths were known / Who would not be once more undone? / For truth has always danger in it."

Butler's somber wit expressed a doubt that the Royal Society had hoped to allay in its *History of the Royal Society* (1667). The doubt troubled a number of those friendly to science and indeed scientists such as Boyle. They wondered whether the natural religion of "reasonable Christianity" that alone seemed to survive rational scrutiny was soil deep enough for faith. This common uneasiness was carried to uncommon depths by Blaise Pascal, who discovered the exotic agonies of the soul crucified by the mutual cancellations of faith and reason. In Italy, Pascal's inner conflicts played out on stage. The Medicis had quietly restored science in Florence after the trauma of the Recantation. But in 1667, the Accademia del Cimento was disbanded after Leopold accepted a cardinal's hat—on the understanding, it was rumored, that the institution be quashed.[11] Its members were scattered; one committed suicide to escape torture in Jesuit dungeons.

These remarks sketch the ups and downs of the new philosophy around 1665. Compared with the situation in 1630, it had made immense strides intellectually and politically. The change of fortune over this short period is indeed astonishing. In 1630, the wave of genius critical to the genesis of natural philosophy seemed to have passed. Johannes Kepler died that year in Linz, leaving behind no followers. Bacon died four years earlier, also without issue, while Simon Stevin died in 1620. The only philosopher of European stature was the aging Galileo. Though he had trained brilliant disciples, he and they were dogged by ecclesiastical censure. Stevin's best students continued his work in freer Holland, but they lacked the genius of the master. Kepler had moved from Graz to Prague because his Protestant confession was offensive in Austria; and from Prague to Linz because he could not support himself on his stipend; and in Linz his mother was accused of witchcraft. It was not an auspicious picture.

The dramatic change of fortune in the prestige and public visibility of science over the next decades was due to the second wave of genius that consolidated the breakthroughs of the first. France suddenly blossomed with mathematical talent that in one generation added four new fields to that ancient subject and brought the mathematical treatment of stat-

11. M. Ornstein, *The Role of Scientific Societies in the Seventeenth Century*, 78. One of his students, Isaac Beeckman, instructed Descartes privately in mechanics. Stevin had retired from teaching in Leyden in 1615, two years before Descartes' first visit to Holland.

ics and hydrostatics to new levels of sophistication. In this period, Paris eclipsed Florence and Rome as the center of European culture that attracted leading lights from England, the Netherlands, and Germany. It was during this period too that the consolidation of political power enabled France to surpass Spain as the leading continental power after the Treaty of Westphalia (1648). The Thirty Years' War had wasted large parts of Germany, including its commercial and cultural centers; some regions lost as much as 60 percent of their population. But the Netherlands and England were culturally vigorous despite the destruction and dislocations of wars. In both countries the new philosophy made rapid strides, sometimes in strange garb.

Apart from the Accademia del Cimento, which worked as a group under Borelli's direction, the achievements of mathematicians and natural philosophers between 1630 and 1665 were the fruits of individuals working alone or in occasional collaboration. This indeed tended to be the pattern after the foundation of the academies as well, but the existence of institutional support for science enhanced the activity in many ways. During the decisive decades, however, there was little in the way of organization or infrastructure to support experimentalists. Academic opportunities were limited to mathematics or medicine, and the climate in universities tended to be unfavorable to innovators. Some combined private pursuit of science with professions, especially medicine and civil engineering. Some enjoyed a sinecure or patronage. Others had independent means.[12] This remained the vocational pattern of scientists until the professionalization of science in late eighteenth-century France and Germany and nineteenth-century England.

Nevertheless infrastructures did coalesce in this period, and they were important vehicles for the diffusion of science beyond the small circle of experimentalists and mathematicians. Roughly five types of organiza-

12. Galileo, Stevin, Kepler, and Leibniz enjoyed princely patronage. A number were men of independent means: Torricelli, Fermat, Pascal, Descartes, von Guericke, Tschirnhausen, Römer, van Helmont, Leeuwenhoek, Huygens, Boyle. Others were professionals: Harvey, Swammerdam, and Malpighi were physicians; Roberval, Barrow, Ward, and Newton were university professors; Picard, Cassini, Flamsteed, and Auzout staffed observatories; Mariotte was a priest. Seven of these men were born to families of nobility. Most of the remainder stem from the *officier* class or the gentry. Two (Stevin and Leeuwenhoek) were sons of artisans. None were sons of merchants. Although N. Hans (*New Trends in Education in the Eighteenth Century*) lists no British peers as scientists from 1646 to 1685, there were six: Lord Willoughby, Lord Bruce, Lord Brouncker, the Marquis of Worcester, the Duke of Newcastle, and Prince Rupert.

tion can be distinguished in addition to academies and colleges: discussion groups, systems of correspondence, enclaves in universities and technical schools, salons, and reform-minded religious groups. Although these types endured well into the eighteenth century, they tended to be ephemeral or else became institutionally entrenched. Both the Académie and the Royal Society arose from discussion groups, while the correspondence system was absorbed by the secretaries of these organizations. The support given science by religious groups was indirect and consisted usually of modernizing secondary school curricula.

These organizations were usually inspired or maintained by the most important support that the new philosophy enjoyed, the gentleman patron. Patronage of science began in Italy, where it was an offshoot of patronage of learning and the arts. The social characteristics of patrons varied over time and with place. If we consider the period 1550–1650, several profiles emerge. In Italy of 1550, when science had no clear shape and when the major controversies were between the humanists and Scholastics, patronage came from ranking ecclesiastics as well as the laity; and among the latter, patrons might be nobility or bourgeoisie. Patrons themselves tended to be humanists proud of their learning and taste. This pattern altered as the stress of the Counter-Reformation increased religious factionalism and made ecclesiastics, Protestant and Catholic, defensive about the emerging new philosophy. Gentlemen humanists like Pope Urban VIII were eventually obliged to distinguish between contraband science and Catholic science. The importance of lay patronage naturally increased as ecclesiastical patronage decreased. In the Netherlands, Germany, and Britain, patrons were overwhelmingly lay. The French pattern was similar to the Italian, with the difference that patronage was older and better established in Italy. Gentlemen ecclesiastics like Richelieu were generous with pensions to writers and scholars, but cared little for science. The significance of these patterns is summarized by the observation that not one of the front-rank philosophers or scientists of the seventeenth century enjoyed the patronage of an ecclesiastic.

From around 1600, lay patrons of science tended to be amateur scientists themselves. They were amateurs in the sense that they took to science as much for adornment and diversion as for enlightenment. They were often avid collectors of specimens and instruments, which they liked to display. Their expertise was more likely to be in botany than physics, and their interests often betrayed a penchant for the exotic. They tended to be more interested in languages or machines than in mathematics. Although none seems to have made any signal contribution to knowledge, their support of science was critical to its success. They conferred respectability on science by doing it themselves. They protected scientists by the prior restraining force of their approval, or by using their influence to curb aroused persecutors. Above all they were the cadre who distinguished between science and crackpot ideas. Had they not put their hands to the winnowing process, the labor to free science from mimics and predators might have taken much longer.[13]

Amateur Patrons of Science

One of the earliest and most remarkable patrons was Duke Frederigo Cesi of Rome. He was a skilled experimenter particularly interested in bees and plants; his botanical garden was celebrated for its variety. Sometime around 1600 he organized regular meetings of a small group, but the circle was disbanded by ecclesiastical authorities, who alleged that it practiced black magic—the same allegation brought against Della Porta's group in Naples about the same time. But Frederigo persisted, and in 1609 he organized a larger group of thirty-two experimentalists calling themselves the Accademia dei Lincei. The establishment was what we would recognize as a research institute, complete with library, museum, printing office, laboratories, instrument makers, and botanical garden.

The Accademia was organized as a fraternal order based on dedication to a common larger aim and oaths of personal loyalty. The aim is sufficiently indicated by the membership rule that excluded priests; and by its coat of arms, which showed a lynx tearing the monster Cerberus with its claws, signifying the destruction of superstition by truth.[14] It was Frederigo's intention to clone the Accademia in a chain of like organizations that would eventually ring the world—the pattern subse-

13. The effects of the winnowing are evident in the circumstances of the founding of the Royal Society and the Académie des sciences, discussed below. In the case of the Florentine Accademia, it is direct and unmistakable. The Berlin Academy, founded in 1700 by Leibniz after many years of effort, is an interesting variation that proves the same point. Although Leibniz, the first president, was a distinguished scientist and philosopher, circumstances compelled him to dilute the Academy's membership with clergymen and scholars who envied him and disliked his project. Its rush to sterility proves the importance of the right personnel for the success of these institutions. The Berlin Academy was revived by Frederick the Great, mainly by importing French talent.

14. Ornstein, *The Role of Scientific Societies in the Seventeenth Century,* 75.

quently implemented by Freemasonry. This concept reflected the defensive expansionism of the exponents of science at that time. Events were to prove that the duke's perception of the need of some special solidarity among experimentalists was correct. The Accademia was shaken when the Holy Congregation first condemned the Copernican hypothesis in 1615. Quarrels arose, and some members of the group resigned because others, particularly Galileo, held forbidden views.[15] The association disbanded completely on the death of the duke in 1630. Doubtless it would not have survived the tumult of 1633.

That Frederigo's notions about the organization of science did not prevail throws light on the character of scientists and science at that time. It was a proud boast that since science proved rather than argued, it would terminate quarrels and dissensions. The conclusion alas did not follow from the premise. When experimentalists were not contesting evidence, they accused one another of plagiarism. The Royal Society and the Académie had their share of internal disputes, which in France were so severe that the collaborative effort originally pursued had to be abandoned and the society was reorganized around individual research.[16] The problem seems to have been that the best minds are necessarily solitary, while the rest value their own opinions above solidarity. This behavior stems from the qualities of those who "think for themselves" and who are jealous of their discoveries. Even Newton, after his greatness was assured, was not above falsely accusing Leibniz of plagiarism. These traits of intellectuals indicate why building the infrastructure of science depended so much upon patrons.

The main conduit for the transfer of Italian science to France was Fabri de Peiresc (1580–1637), senator of Aix-en-Provence and member of the Accademia dei Lincei. Peiresc began his journeys in Italy at eighteen, when his main interest was in antiquities and the humanities. But the stimulus of Italian science soon led him to astronomy, botany, and anatomy, and into collecting fossils and crystals. He became a friend of his fellow academician Galileo, staunchly defended Copernican theory during the trying days, and organized astronomical observations that sometimes involved coordinating stations from Aleppo to Lyons. He made the first map of the moon. His interests seem to have had no bounds. A devoted antiquarian, he learned Arabic and Hebrew in order to study ancient coins, inscriptions, and books. He was a patron of science and of the fine arts, upon which he spent liberally, in the Provence cultural tradition. He amassed large collections of fossils, ancient manu-

15. Ibid., 76.
16. Bertrand, *L'Académie des sciences*, 42–43.

scripts, and telescopes. His learning, wealth, and rank, combined with his manifold connections with French and Italian courts, enabled him to establish science in France. For more than two decades, Peiresc *was* French science in the eyes of its small but influential public.

Though his contributions were modest, Peiresc's service to science was immense. In a nation whose taste was molded by the court, he proved that novel science was compatible with good breeding and orthodoxy. He was the great mover and organizer. With his friends the brothers Dupuy, he initiated what became the important tradition of conferences for the discussion of science and *belles lettres*.[17] He carried on an extensive correspondence with like-minded men everywhere in Europe, and thus began the system of international correspondence that was continued by one of his protégés, Father Marin Mersenne.[18] He was intimate with Étienne Pascal and Vietà, who between them fathered the brilliant generation of French mathematicians.

Peiresc's best-known protégé was Pierre Gassendi, who for twelve years assisted him in observations, dissections, and astronomical computations. From about 1635, Gassendi, together with Mersenne, formed the core of a mixed group in Paris who met to discuss science, philosophy, and letters. Until then, science and mathematics had been mainly the diversions of provincial gentlemen, and continued so for some time after.[19] But Gassendi and Mersenne were experimentalists and mathematicians. If they lacked the genius of the provincials Fermat and Pascal, they could appreciate their work and repeat the latest experiments. Gassendi brought to the Paris group the prestige of Peiresc and access to many in Peiresc's vast network of relations, especially Thévenot and Chapelain, who were well connected at court. He was himself a man of many talents. Provost of the cathedral at Digne, and Royal Professor of Mathematics, Gassendi was best known as the reviver of Epicurean philosophy and leader of the literary circle of "libertines"—such things were

17. Harcourt Brown traces in detail the evolution of the Peiresc-Dupuy *conférences* through various versions (the Bureau d'adresse, Mersenne's *conférences*) to the Montmor Academy and finally the Académie des sciences. On collaboration between Peiresc and the brothers Dupuy, see Brown's *Scientific Organizations*, 1–16.

18. Peiresc's scientific writings consist only of a few inconsequential memoirs. He communicated his ideas and observations primarily in correspondence, which was extensive. The *Lettres de Peiresc*, edited by Tamizey de Larroque (1888–98), are in seven volumes.

19. The size and population of France probably account for the diffusion of science in the provinces, where it was vigorous. See Brown, *Scientific Organizations*, 208–30.

possible in Richelieu's France.[20] Mersenne, by contrast, was an eclectic unperturbed by whiplash contradictions. He was one of the few men of his time who believed that both Galileo and the Church were right. To his famous statement that there were 50,000 atheists in Paris, some wit replied that his circle of friends was large.[21] His unfailing good cheer and kindness kept enemies at bay. These qualities, in addition to his learning, soon made him the unofficial envoy between science and the ecclesiastical hierarchy of France. Having formed a friendship with Descartes when both attended La Flèche, he served his secretive friend for twenty years as an aide-de-camp who screened all correspondents and visitors.

It was around these two men that the first important Paris conferences revolved until Mersenne's death in 1648. Among those in Gassendi's libertine group were Cyrano, Molière, La Mothe le Vayer, Gabriel Naudé, and Thomas Hobbes during his French exile. The provincials Fermat and Pascal attended when they were in Paris. Among

20. Richelieu conferred cardinal hats and lesser offices as patronage, irrespective of the religious qualifications or inclinations of his clients. He made an admiral, a diplomat, and a general cardinals. Youths, even infants, became abbés. This was an old practice in France. Sully, the Protestant lord chancellor to Henri IV, had the income of four abbeys. These profane usages, common throughout Europe, were one of the "corrupt" practices that reformers Catholic and Protestant meant to eliminate. Gassendi's revival of Epicurus, whose name was traditionally one with atheism, amply establishes his dexterity. In his *De vita et moribus Epicuri,* he claimed to refute "everything contrary to Christianity," but only after stating Epicurus's positions forcefully and at length. The result was a "Christian Epicureanism" that wavered between incoherence and disingenuousness. In 1669 the Holy Congregation decided that the unstable synthesis was more Epicurean than Christian, and placed his works on Index. This has caused some historians to debate whether Gassendi was merely being politic or whether he was sincere. See Lenoble, *Mersenne, ou la naissance du mécanisme,* 419n.

21. Ibid., 171. Mersenne's association with the thinkers of his time did not leave him unaffected. "You know that he did not believe all his religion," his friend Andre Pineau wrote of him, "also that he was one of those who are glad enough to see church service done, and that he dared not often repeat his Breviary for fear of spoiling his good Latin" (quoted in Brown, *Scientific Organizations,* 36). However, he believed enough of his religion to compromise Copernican astronomy by a modified Jesuit epistemology according to which science knows only "appearances," although it is unchallengeable in this domain. He lacked the lucidity of Pascal, who declared: "If the earth moves, a decree from Rome cannot stop it."

the regulars were Roberval, a mathematician at the Collège de France, Pierre Petit, an engineer, and Claude Hardy, a mathematician.[22]

In 1641 Gassendi published a biography of Peiresc, which was translated into English as *The Mirrour of True Nobility* (1657).[23] Though forgotten today, at the time it enjoyed a success comparable to Sprat's *History of the Royal Society*. Gassendi presented his subject as a "great and rare man, fit to be propounded for an example to after-ages." Though no commander or ruler, Peiresc was nevertheless a model of true nobility because his "unwearied care to advance all ingenious and liberal arts, with a munificence towards all learned men . . . was perfectly Royal, and Princely" (n.p.). This theme was continued by William Rand in his dedication of the English translation to John Evelyn. The English gentry, he said, lacked the education needed to provide political leadership, and thus were themselves led by "mercenary men" who advised according to their own "Interests, Factions, and Trades." The gentry must develop "well-informed, unbiased and generous understandings" if they were to save the nation from its miseries. This political function, though not in accordance with the class orientation of the new philosophy, was endorsed by Sprat's *History,* as we shall see.

Gassendi began his biography with a stereotypical tale of portents and prodigies that reportedly surrounded the hero's birth. These tales, which involve an astrologer and a witch, were nimbly pulverized in Peiresc's name, and dismissed as vulgar superstitions (bk. 1: 9). But since he was writing for polite society, Gassendi bowed to genre requirements and conjured a prodigy of a different kind—Peiresc's precocity. He was "scarcely weaned from the breast" when he began pestering all around him with questions about "what everything was, and how and wherefore it was made." When he began reading, he searched the arguments of authors, and would not endure to be told "that it was above his capacity to understand."

The biography of Peiresc is the story of his inquisitiveness as it might

22. These meetings were well known to English gentlemen who traveled abroad, particularly Sir William Cavendish. For thirty years (1630–60), the Cavendish family was the chief conduit for contacts between French, English, and continental science. William Cavendish introduced Hobbes to Galileo and Gassendi, after Hobbes entered service to that eminent family. For descriptions of these meetings, see Brown, *Scientific Organizations,* 17, 63; for the relation between polite society and science, see Arthur Tilley, *From Montaigne to Molière,* and David Maland, *Culture and Society in Seventeenth Century France,* 114–20.

23. Gassendi's study was entitled *Viri illustris N. C. Fabricii de Peiresc, senatoris*

be told to the fashionable set at the Hôtel de Rambouillet or to the eager readers of Renaudot's very successful *Conférences du Bureau d'adresse* (from 1633), which reported in a gossipy way on conferences he hosted. Nevertheless, Gassendi did indicate something of Peiresc's mind and character. He assigned a rank order to the sciences that lent coherence to his varied investigations. At the head was mathematics, because of its certainty; then astronomy, because of its dignity and majesty; then geography and history, as means of rooting out parochialism by knowledge of "the whole world"; and finally optics, "because it explains many things reputed to be miracles" (bk. 1: 212). The contemporaries he most admired were his friend Galileo and Bacon. He remained a staunch defender of Galileo despite the Inquisition, and attempted, through the sympathetic Cardinal Barberini, to secure his liberty after house arrest was imposed. He regretted that he never met Bacon, with whom he shared a lively desire to improve the mechanical arts (bk. 6: 207, 186). He disapproved of Scholasticism and theology because they were specious and contentious (bk. 6: 177, 207–10). Peiresc's main objective was to begin the painstaking process of piecing together the true history of the earth, in the broadest sense. This was why he studied geology, collected fossils, studied ancient coins and inscriptions, and pursued the comparative history of nations and laws. The geological and fossil record persuaded Peiresc that land masses had drifted and changed place over time, which suggested in turn that all received chronologies were unreliable. His explanations of the formation of geological strata have a Lucretian flavor. His approach to written history was critical and cautious. He used methods of collation and comparative study of documents, coins, and inscriptions, which the Italian humanists had developed, to devise a critical apparatus for winnowing errors and falsehoods from the works of pagan and ecclesiastical historians (bk. 1: 30–37). These were the beginnings of source criticism.

Though Gassendi emphasized Peiresc's rigid performance of religious duties and left no tale of his conversations with popes and cardinals untold, it is not hard to see that Peiresc's researches tended to replace a religious history of the earth with a naturalistic account in harmony with Galilean science. As France's foremost Epicurean, Gassendi was familiar with Lucretius's account of human evolution, which he might well have discussed with Peiresc. But he did not commend Peiresc's researches in terms of discoveries to which they might lead. Instead he commended them for the virtues they inspire and support. They en-

---

Acquisextiensis, vita. The only modern biography is Pierre Humbert's *Un amateur: Peiresc* (1947).

large the mind and raise it above the faction of religion, nation, and age. Like Socrates, Peiresc was a citizen of the world who followed the rule to do good to all and to harm no one. How do these intellectual virtues constitute the true nobility of the gentleman? Apparently Gassendi wished to suggest a reinterpretation of the Roman *honestus*, which informed the meaning of *honnêteté* among the French aristocracy. A gentleman is honest or honorable if he speaks his mind and eschews deceit and intrigue. Gassendi enlarged this sense of rectitude to include Peiresc's marked trait, inquisitiveness, so that the gentleman is honorbound to cultivate a "well-informed, unbiased and generous understanding," not merely of people and politics, but of nature as well. This conception raises the premium on gentility by suggesting that in practice integrity depends on the *honnêteté* of opinions about things in the heavens and beneath the earth. Why is this so? Gassendi suggested an answer in his discussions of Galileo and Scholasticism. The practice of European nations and of the Church depended on beliefs that an honest mind knows to be badly flawed, probably false, and surely sectarian. Gentlemen who despise knowledge will not know how to avoid serving corruption and deceit; therefore, only by exercising the intellectual virtues can he maintain his *honnêteté*. This amounts to iterating in a new context the old Socratic dictum that virtue is knowledge.

The New Gentleman[24]

The limited objective of Gassendi's biography does not allow for adequate discussion of the Peiresc model. Inquisitiveness must eventually harm the interests of the erring and ignorant, but Gassendi was content

24. The theme commenced here is resumed below, pp. 94–100. It is the object of one full-length study by Lewis S. Feuer. In *The Scientific Intellectual: The Psychological and Sociological Origins of Modern Science*, Feuer presents his evidence as a rebuttal to Max Weber's view that the originators of modern science were pietist ascetics. He found that on the contrary scientific intellectuals were self-assertive, guilt-free, hedonic, and libertarian in outlook. These traits describe *libertinage érudit*, discussed below, pp. 167–74. There is substantial concordance between my findings and Feuer's. The main divergence pertains to our different assessment of the sociological origins. Feuer was unable to come to any clear view about the sociological origins of the modern intellectual, but he did not perceive why. The view presented in this study is that polytechnic rationality bears no relation to social class; hence, it has no sociological origin. However, there was an attempt to remodel traditional concepts of gentility to make them fit polytechnic rationality. Feuer did not detect this effort or its result.

to show that Peiresc managed to maintain friendly terms with everyone. Other Frenchmen, however, did address the nonutopian predicament of the aristocracy, who were squeezed between the Counter-Reformation Church and a consolidating monarchy. The pressure eventually erupted in the abortive Fronde conspiracy of 1650, when the cry "République!" was heard in the streets of Paris. The pressure may be detected in the tragedies of Corneille and the reveries of the *dévot*. But we find it earlier in the writings of Rabelais and Montaigne, especially the latter, who was moved by the debasement of aristocratic virtue conspicuous in the bankruptcy of royal and ecclesiastical policy during the Wars of Religion. The court and ecclesiastical hierarchy were after all patrician institutions, yet they threatened to ruin the patriciate and the nation.[25] Montaigne's remedy for decadent belief was purgative skepticism. He used it as a diagnostic that traced the corruption of the leading men to blind attachments to creeds and loyalties. At the same time, skepticism led back to first things, particularly to the dissociated *moi* who insists on judging all things itself. That self, who is consciously interested first and last in itself, was the theme for the reinterpretation of gentility from Descartes to La Rochefoucauld. And it was the core of *libertinage érudit*.[26]

The honesty, even rigorism, common to these interpretations is a hallmark of the individualist political theory that was built on them. The dissociated self knows that it is not moral. It is actuated by neither

25. Arthur Tilley's account of the Catholic Revival describes the decadence of French ecclesiastical institutions circa 1600, in his *From Montaigne to Molière*, chap. 1. See also Robert Mandrou, *Louis XIV et son temps*, 191–223.

26. This development has been described by Krailsheimer in his *Studies in Self-Interest*. He shares with Pascal the view that the *moi* is "morally bankrupt" (66), atheist (41, 70, 142–43, 147), and ambitious for godhood (41, 70). He also emphasizes that the new *moi* is a reinterpretation of the *honnête homme*. But he construes all this as somehow an involuntary response to an unwilled predicament; hence, the *moi* is "*désaxé*." This is hard to square with the chief feature of the *moi*, conscious rational will. For a description of Montaigne's conscious reorientation of values, see David Schaefer, "Montaigne's Political Skepticism," 514–41, and his "Montaigne's Political Reformation," *Journal of Politics* 42 (1981): 766–91. In his *History of Skepticism from Erasmus to Spinoza*, Richard Popkin emphasizes that Pyrrhonism, in Montaigne's writings in particular, was recruited by the Church to combat the inner conviction of certainty assumed by Protestant justification by faith (78ff., 95ff.). While this is true, it was only one of several uses of skepticism in that age; Popkin overlooks its use as an antidote to religious fervor of any kind. For a discussion of Popkin's view and defense of the "Whig history" of skepticism that he rejects, see Caton, "Tory History of Ideas."

justice nor love, but by an *amour propre* that compels self-interestedness as the rule of life. Selfishness is controlled by seemliness (*bienséance*), the art of pleasing others to attain one's ends. Discovery of the amorality of the self put a new face on the concept of the *gentilhomme*. Cardinal de Retz, who intended his *Mémoires* to display himself as an *honnête homme*, was honest enough to write, in italics, that he "*resolved to do evil deliberately, which is without comparison most criminal before God, but it is without doubt most wise before the world.*"[27] We are a long way from Peiresc. Once the self knows that it cannot be morally good, virtue consists in knowing, as Machiavelli put it, how to be bad.

If de Retz and Pascal wrote of the gentleman as man of action, Descartes did the same for the gentleman-philosopher. Despite his recluse existence, he emphasized that he composed his writings for active gentlemen and ladies of "good sense" whose special grace was their freedom from the prejudices that warp the minds of academics.[28] The *Discourse on Method* in particular modeled a new notion of *honnêteté* based on a curious practical reason. The point of the *Discourse* was to show how to "conduct reason" or use it in all the exigencies of life, not merely in science; thus he could, without breaking stride, explain in the closing part of the work how he uses reason to fulfill that desire of every gentleman, *la gloire*. He would do it, he said, by benefiting mankind and smiting its enemies, the clergy who control learning and police discourse. Aware of his wickedness, Descartes contrived a set of "rules" for the conduct of reason that may be read as instructions on how to be bad. They are at the same time the model of the gentleman's honesty, for they yield an elegant solution to a problem of *honnêteté*—the achievement of harmony between conviction and conduct.

The solution is founded on the strength of the isolated *moi*. Descartes acknowledged an incredulity so vast that it tossed him into a state of nature where all received norms and precepts war with one another. Disbelief neutralized the decadent tradition, and Descartes, like Montaigne, relied solely on himself for the guidance of life. In the moment that he takes control of his own thoughts, and puts life in order according to his own wish, the gentleman's love of independence and the firmness of his will successfully assert themselves. Successfully, because

---

27. De Retz, *Mémoires*, 44.
28. That Descartes wrote for the *honnête homme* is understood by students of French culture (e.g. Krailsheimer, *Studies in Self-Interest*, 98, and Maland, *Culture and Society in Seventeenth Century France*, 154). Philosophers tend to believe that he wrote for theologians. Descartes' distinction between these two classes of readers is discussed in my "Descartes' Anonymous Writings: A Recapitulation."

Descartes brought conviction into harmony with conduct by honestly declaring his detached selfishness as rules of life. It is hard to be more forthright than that. But as befits a gentleman, his *amour propre* is presented in a seemly manner that puts the face of innocence on badness.

Descartes distanced his model from Peiresc and from gentlemen humanists generally by repudiating erudition during the skeptical deluge. Erudition makes one dependent on others, the past above all. Instead of Peiresc's wide-ranging researches, Descartes set course on clean, methodical, and uniform investigation of his own present and clear ideas. His demolition of the past was reiterated in the powerful metaphor of the "founding" of science, in which he likened received opinions and sciences to a city built by "many hands" in a haphazard manner over many centuries. Descartes wiped this slate clean. He undertook to found the sciences anew, relying only on himself to generate a single rational plan. The past is dead or decadent.

The first maxim of his "provisional morality" is a rule of seemliness that explains, in a gracious manner, the provisional character of morality as a function of its pure expediency. He resolved "to obey the laws and customs of my country, and to adhere constantly to the religion in which by God's grace I had been nourished since my infancy," and in all other things to follow the most moderate opinion.[29] The free "resolution" to be good was required by the wicked doubt that went before and rooted out all beliefs on which he had been "nourished since infancy." That this good will is a seemly version of politic religion appears true when the status of the resolution is considered: the honest man can conform to external things so long as he makes it clear by other deeds where his conviction lies.[30] The required deeds—in this case, truthtelling—are performed directly in the maxim. Descartes repudiated as immoderate "all promises by which one in some degree limits his lib-

29. Descartes, *Œuvres philosophiques*, 1: 592.
30. Though the possible sources of Descartes' politic religion maxim are numerous, one in particular deserves mention in view of his associations with the Stevin tradition in Holland. In his *Het Burgherlick Leven* (1590), Stevin was anxious to establish the primacy of secular public authority over all objections of private conscience. In the course of his argument he wrote, "Therefore, if your heart says: there is no God (which is dreadful) do not make your mouth utter it, for the sake of your children . . . for the sake of the community, whose welfare is also yours. For what is more foolish than to destroy and prevent wilfully that which one passionately desires?" (*Principal Works*, 5: 555). Nevertheless, he prominently displayed his motto, "Wonder is no wonder," on the frontispiece of his books, and he expressly denied the possibility of miracles (1: 59).

erty." Religious vows or commercial contracts are acceptable as remedies for the "inconstancy of weak minds," but for himself he reserved the right to alter his judgment at any time. Expediency is the rule, and the rule of expediency is reason.

One is struck by the fact that Descartes directed this manly example to women as well as to men. This cannot be discounted as a gallant bow to the *femme savant* fashionable at the time, for his relations with women had a serious cast. He carried on an extensive correspondence with Elizabeth, Princess Palatine, and died in service to the precocious Christine of Sweden. In dedicating his chief work to Elizabeth, he praised her intellectual accomplishments as "an example to posterity." Even when allowances are made for the encomium genre, Descartes' words are remarkable. To this beautiful woman he commended the manly wisdom that "whoever forms a firm and constant will always to use reason to the best of his power, and in all his actions to do what he believes to be best, is truly wise."[31] This "sovereign good" depends upon no divine or objective norm to which the will must conform; instead, the good is good willing—willing firmly to use reason. This "true virtue," as Descartes impishly called it, is hardly distinguishable from audacious Machiavellian *virtù*, which knows how to be bad in knowing how to will its own will.

Such is the quality of the *honnêteté* that Descartes claimed Elizabeth possessed "in the most perfect manner," as she was also said to understand Cartesian philosophy perfectly. He contrasted her teachability with the hardened prejudice of "learned men" and "ancient doctors," who secretly hated knowledge and denied education to women, as he pointedly mentioned. The suggestion was that the representatives of traditional philosophy were feeble and decadent paper tigers, while the princess was strong and bold. The contrast insinuated the wicked thought that once such Cartesians became aware of their strength and beauty, they would withdraw their consciences from the keeping of ancient doctors, in imitation of the master.

Behind Descartes' encomium lies the singular fact that he corresponded with Elizabeth about Machiavelli, whose name he never mentioned to any of his male correspondents. At the end of his second letter on the Florentine, he proposed that they continue in cipher, but Elizabeth declined. What secret thought did he want to convey? A commentary on his notion of good willing as the sovereign good? We cannot say. It does seem, however, that his ardor for the *honnête femme* sprang in part from recognition that the recruitment of women to his project

31. Descartes, *Œuvres philosophiques*, 3: 88.

would double the size of his army. This gambit paid off handsomely. Mistresses of salons were a significant factor in the dissemination of Cartesian philosophy. Women were the main readers of Descartes' books.[32] They, not the men, organized the drawing room lectures where experimental philosophers came to demonstrate the newly discovered truths of science. They were largely responsible for the word-of-mouth transmission of the new ideas in Paris and in the provinces.[33]

Descartes' elegant subversion of female claustration was repeated by others. The long-time secretary of the Académie des sciences, Fontenelle, dedicated his widely read *Conversation on the Plurality of Worlds* to women, with the exhortation that they should prefer the grandeur of nature to the frivolities of novels. When Addison translated this work into English, he added an introductory poem that closed with an admonition:

Assert your claim to sense, and show mankind
That reason is not to themselves confined.

The encouragement of women to assert themselves as rational beings has scarcely been noticed by students of this phase of cultural history. Yet it is a splendid illustration of the thoroughness of the renovation of *honnêteté*, and adds yet more evidence of the uninhibited dynamism and aggressive recruitment efforts of rationalist exponents. By 1670, their combination of skepticism in faith and certainty in science had induced religious indifference among the genteel classes. That insightful observer of this scene, Pascal, said of *honnêteté:* "The 'moi' has two qualities: it is unjust in itself, in that it makes itself the center of everything . . . , and then the 'moi' is the enemy and wants to be the tyrant over all others." The target could not have been more accurately measured from the religious point of view. *Amour propre,* the original sin, had become the core of enlightened gentility. No wonder that Bossuet, the court preacher who spent a lifetime trying to put out the fires of free thinking, finally realized where the secret ember lay:

32. Possibly Descartes' quest for female readership is the reason for his repeatedly classifying his writings in the fictional genre women favored. Thus, the *Discourse* he called a "fable"; the "new world" of his *Le Monde* is styled "une fable du monde." He advised that his major work, *The Principles of Philosophy,* should be read "like a novel"; and his natural philosophy as a whole he styled "le roman de la nature" (Baillet, *Vie de Monsieur Descartes,* 1: xviii). Shortly before his death he composed a ballet for Christine of Sweden.
33. Tilley, *From Montaigne to Molière,* 217ff.; J. S. Spink, *French Free-Thought from Gassendi to Voltaire,* 190–92.

I see . . . preparations for a great onslaught on the Church in the name of Cartesian philosophy. From the womb of that philosophy, from its principles . . . I foresee the birth of more than one heresy. I foresee also that conclusions will be deduced from it, hostile to the dogmas our fathers taught us, [that] will bring down hatred upon the Church.[34]

Colbert's "Projet Vaste de Réforme"

In his will, Cardinal Mazarin, finance minister to the young Louis XIV, thanked his master for many marks of favor and declared that in compensation "I leave you Colbert."[35] The wealthy cardinal knew the value of things. Jean-Baptiste Colbert, born in 1619 to a merchant of Rheims, had made himself indispensable in the ten years he worked as Mazarin's personal assistant. He seemed to know the location of every *sou* in the kingdom and how to bring the king's large share into the royal treasury. Such financial wizardry appealed to a king whose policy of national greatness and royal magnificence required continuous expenditures. When Mazarin died in 1661, Louis accepted the offer and never had reason for regret. Able, ambitious, and indefatigable, Colbert quickly expanded his portfolio to become superintendent of nearly all affairs of state except war and foreign affairs.

Colbert's vast project of reform, as the Abbé de Choisy called it, was a one-legged lurch toward modernity that sprang from the conjunction of Louis' love of glory with his own vision of the means. Like others whose deeds bulk large, Colbert's achievement is subject to continuing reevaluation. He died beloved by his king but hated by many in Paris and the provinces for his *dirigiste* centralizing policies. This old rancor, plus sharp criticism of his commercial policies by early eighteenth-century political economists, kept his reputation low; but he was hailed by Voltaire and the encyclopedists as one of their own. Such oscillations continued until his reputation peaked toward the turn of the century. Jean Clément, the editor of his papers and student of his administration, and Ernest Lavisse, in the monumental *Histoire de France,* restated the encyclopedists' case for Colbert. Lavisse wrote that "among the statesmen who served Louis XIV, one alone, the only one who was great,

34. Bossuet, letter to a disciple of Malebranche, 21 May 1867.
35. The actual sentence in Mazarin's testament is less dramatic: "À Colbert, la maison ou il demeure . . . et prie le roi de se servir de lui, étant fort fidèle" (quoted by Clément, *Histoire de Colbert,* 1: 112).

Colbert, comprehended that this society needed to be reformed from top to bottom. The others seem to have believed in the imperishability of the regime. Louis himself certainly did not doubt it; he saw neither paradox nor peril."[36] Lavisse's portrayal of Colbert as an innovating reformer was endorsed by Pierre Boissonade's study, which hailed his modernizing "socialisme d'état."

Then came the reaction to what Pierre Goubert has recently called "this unconscious falsification of history."[37] In 1939 C. W. Cole published his two-volume study of Colbert's administration and economic policy, in which he claims that Colbert had no ideas and originated no policies. The only novelty of his administration was his own indefatigable energy and relentless work ethic. Nevertheless, this diligent if not overperceptive scholar does from time to time notice something extraordinary, and even writes in an unguarded moment that "if Colbert could have found a hundred men like himself, he would have changed the history of Europe and molded France like a piece of clay."[38] Henri Hauser's studies a decade later endorsed Cole's claim that all Colbert's policies could be found in the mercantilist literature of a hundred years before, and in Richelieu's example especially, with the difference that Richelieu was a true exponent of economic growth while Colbert believed that the volume of trade was constant.[39] The difference between the two was the difference between "a perfect clerk and a statesman." Goubert puts the finishing touches on this now common portrait of Colbert as the arch bureaucrat: "a tireless scribbler, a devourer of documents, avid for details . . . [and borrowing] from more original minds."[40] Yet Goubert, like Cole, marvels at Colbert's financial wizardry and even admits that he engendered "expansion on a scale unprecedented for any French monarch." It seems that Richelieu was not, after all, in Colbert's league.

There are reasons for this ambivalence. Boissonade's state socialism notion conjures certain comparisons that might fruitfully be pursued in a comparative essay, but it forces the facts when used as an interpretive heuristic. On the other side, Hauser and Cole do not recognize that mercantilist balance-of-trade and bullionist doctrines were sound for that period and were compatible with economic expansionism. Beyond these incidentals, there lies the rejection of Whig historiography that

36. Lavisse, *Histoire de France*, 6: 403.
37. Pierre Goubert, *Louis XIV and Twenty Million Frenchmen*, 115.
38. C. W. Cole, *Colbert and a Century of French Mercantilism*, 1: 320.
39. Goubert, *Louis XIV and Twenty Million Frenchmen*, 117.
40. Ibid., 118–19.

guides Cole, Hauser, and Goubert. Critics of Whig history doubt that reason works in the world. They think it especially dormant among statesmen, who of all men are the most absorbed in their time and milieu. Rationalism is itself a time-specific idiosyncracy, which only the naïve take at face value as the motive of a Voltaire or Frederick the Great, much less Colbert. This Tory skepticism of reason, with its underpinning in Hume and Burke, was fresh air that blew away a Whig historiography grown sterile. But it cannot tell the story of modern politics insofar as they have been molded by a succession of rationalist schemes. Consequently it often falls into paradox, and claims, in the present case, that while Colbert had no idea of economic expansion, he was nevertheless the architect of expansion on an unprecedented scale. At such a rupture between effect and cause even Hume would scowl.

Disputes of this kind, if they are not to be futile, must be referred to the facts, for it is from the interpretive effort that they spring. In 1949, James E. King published his *Science and Rationalism in the Government of Louis XIV, 1661–1683*. This book is rarely cited and seems to have had little impact, perhaps because the supposed "unconscious falsification of history" turns out to be admirably supported by the data. King documents in gratifying detail how Louis XIV and Colbert imparted a thoroughly rationalist bent to French administration during the twenty-two years of Colbert's service, very much as Voltaire claimed in his *Histoire du siècle de Louis XIV*. The rationalism was curtailed shortly after Colbert's death, when Louis, dominated by the devout Mme. de Maintenon and his Jesuit confessor, repented his wickedness, revoked the Edict of Nantes, and drove out the Huguenots.[41] He lived on until 1715 without a Colbert to support his mind or a Molière to charm his heart. What the result of another thirty-two years of rationalism might have been is an interesting speculation. In any case, the subsequent three decades overshadowed the initial decades of light, and memory homogenized into one what was in effect two reigns.[42]

41. Princess Elizabeth of Palatine ascribed Louis' weakness in this regard to defective education. She wrote that "the King is a good Christian, but very ignorant in religious matters. Not in his whole life has he read the Bible. He believes everything the priests and falsely pious tell him. So it is no surprise if he is deceived" (quoted by Mandrou, *Louis XIV et son temps*, 209).

42. An example of the homogenization occurs in the historiographical conclusion to Robert Mandrou's *Louis XIV*. Mandrou discusses appraisals of his subject by Voltaire, Michelet, and Lavisse, without noticing that what these authors find praiseworthy in Louis' reign is most pronounced in the first part of his reign, while what they deplore is most pronounced in the second. Although Mandrou emphasizes that the death of Colbert marked a change

Although little is known about Colbert's development, the ten years of service to Mazarin were probably decisive. He was frequently in contact with Nicolas Fouquet, the powerful *surintendant* of taxes, who assembled the Cartesians of Paris into his entourage. When Colbert and Louis drove Fouquet from office, these men gravitated to Colbert.[43] Such contacts establish the transmission of Cartesianism. Yet no stress need be laid on this point, since Colbert's memoranda, letters, and deeds reveal a saturation in Cartesianism that goes well beyond merely learned or heard "doctrine." Colbert was Cartesianism in action.

On approaching Colbert, we notice first the figure of his master. When Louis assumed personal rule on Mazarin's death, he had formed definite ideas about the conduct of government. His observations of the administrations of Richelieu and Mazarin persuaded him that he should be his own chief minister and that high ecclesiastics and patricians should not be admitted to the inner council. He understood and accepted the burden of work that would fall on him, as he indicated in a note to the dauphin (1661): "I have often wondered how it could happen that while love of work is a quality so essential to sovereigns, it is nevertheless one seldom found among them."[44] To the astonishment of the diplomatic corps in Paris, Louis carried out his resolution. Neither the luxury of court nor the labyrinth of his *amours* prevented him supervising the details of government and exercising royal authority. His daily routine he described as follows:

I imposed on myself as a law to work regularly twice a day, and two or three hours each time with various people, not counting the

---

in the regime (295ff.), and is aware that Colbert and Mme. de Maintenon represented very different influences, he does not appreciate, I think, what the transition from *bon sens* to piety means in historical terms.

43. Fouquet's circle included Habert de Montmor; Melchisédec Thévenot, orientalist, mathematician, and member of the Montmor Academy; Samuel Sorbière, Cartesian natural philosopher and secretary of the Montmor Academy; Jean Chapelain, member of the Académie française and former advisor to Richelieu; Pierre Chanut, diplomat and friend of Descartes; Charles Perrault, writer; and Molière (Albert George, "The Genesis of the Académie des Sciences," 386–87).

44. *Œuvres de Louis XIV*, 1: 105; also 1: 6, where he writes that "since my childhood the very name of idle kings . . . has given me pain when mentioned in my presence." There are many other eulogies to work, e.g. "it is by work that one reigns and for work that one reigns." Weberians might wish to note the espousal of this "work ethic" by a Catholic monarch claiming to be the first gentleman of Europe.

hours which I passed privately, nor the time which I could give beyond this to extraordinary affairs if they arose. . . . there was not a moment when it was not permissible to speak to me, provided that the affairs were pressing.[45]

Subordinates presenting written or oral reports could expect them to be examined for accuracy, thoroughness, and clarity. Louis prided his ability to absorb and use detail. It was an important ingredient of ruling "by reason," as he styled it. One might add that, given the level of activity of his servants, it was a condition for remaining their master. And Louis never allowed any doubt to arise about who was master. His continuous and exacting scrutiny of administration foreclosed the possibility that any minister could long persist in a policy that lacked his approval. Even so, he did not rule arbitrarily. Ministers in council were expected to discuss questions freely and vigorously, it being understood that the sense of the council was its decision, even if at times it was contrary to the king's opinion.[46]

This working monarch was nevertheless the first gentleman of Europe, adroit in *bienséance*. He knew how to exact deference while making it seem to come spontaneously from his subjects. He bestowed favors with a charm that created obligations twice as great. He knew how to represent rebukes as forbearance under provocation. His flawless grace was the more remarkable in view of the norms that his conception of the monarch imposed:

All eyes are fixed on him alone; it is to him that all wishes are addressed; he alone receives all respects; he alone is the object of all hopes. . . . Everyone regards his good graces as the only source of all benefits; no one can raise himself but by gradually coming closer to the royal person or estimation; all else is base, all else is powerless, all else is sterile. . . . The shining image of the greatness to which he has risen is carried everywhere on the wings of his reputation. As he is the admiration of his subjects, so he soon arouses the amazement of the neighbouring nations, and if he makes any use of this advantage, there will be nothing, either inside or outside his empire, which he cannot obtain in the course of time.[47]

45. Quoted by King, *Science and Rationalism*, 408–9.
46. Ibid., 87.
47. *Œuvres de Louis XIV*, 1: 121. This passage was written in 1666. On the monarch as god, see Lavisse, *Histoire de France*, 6: 133ff.

While the idea of the monarch as mortal god on earth was not new, the vigor and earnestness of Louis' conception is startling. It cannot have been an easy thing to be such a god, especially when we consider how much he resembles the dynamic ego in the Hobbesean pageant, who ceaselessly strives for power after power to satisfy his boundless appetite for glory. Louis meant to make himself master of Europe and actually succeeded in making France the predominant power. Pursuit of this grandiose goal, with its consequences, gave Europe a foretaste of the expansive egoism that emerged later in Napoleon Bonaparte and others.

Colbert was the right man to translate royal ambition into action. Responsibilities of a magnitude that would have overwhelmed perhaps even Richelieu were for Colbert the relished opportunity for undertaking administrative, commercial, legal, social, political, and cultural programs on a scale that dwarfed the reformism of parliamentary England. Colbert attempted to create, and partially succeeded in creating, a modern administration. The old system of administration duplicated the class and commercial relations of the nation. Patron-client relations, purchased office, and local loyalty were the rule. Members of the *officier* class did not understand themselves as civil servants who were functionaries of national policy; as *noblesse de robe,* they thought of themselves as independent men who served the local interests of the king—insofar as they did not conflict with other local interests. This was the intractable arrangement that Colbert attempted to change. In order to "reduce the whole kingdom to the same law, the same measure, the same weight," as he put it, he realized that he must have an instrument, a civil service, loyal to national policy and trained to administer policy in a methodical manner, based on accurate data and constant reporting to Paris.[48]

48. Colbert, *Œuvres,* 6: 14. Colbert's resolve to reduce the diversity of French national life to a single rational design has struck most students of his administration, including Henri Hauser; and they have accepted his verdict that French society was "confused." But it did not seem irrational to Fouquet, or to the aristocracy, or to the *officiers,* or to the bourgeois of the day, all of whom opposed Colbert's innovations at one time or another. It did not seem incoherent to them because they did not measure things by Colbert's standard of a single rational design, which, incidentally, duplicates Descartes' formula for political reform (see Descartes, *Œuvres philosophiques,* 1: 579ff.). In addition to this suggestive coincidence, Colbert believed that every problem could be solved by application of order and method; and, conversely, that all impediments to action were reducible to soluble problems. This notion is fundamental to Cartesian method. The Cartesian criteria of clarity, exactitude, evidence, and critical spirit appear constantly in his memoranda and instructions. King, who has noticed these similarities, fre-

Though his effort did not entirely succeed, he did create a cadre of provincial and municipal *intendants* who overshadowed other authorities and who were loyal to Paris.[49] It was a skeleton civil service. He also created—and perhaps in the long run this is more important—its esprit de corps and rationale. Administration was to be above local interest, conscious of the interests of the nation and of the requisites for enhancing national power. It was to be rational in aims and method.

Since Colbert's primary responsibility was to raise revenue for a king notably unsympathetic to mere budgetary constraints, this circumstance imparted a certain bias to his policies, particularly the bullionist bias. Revenues could not be raised without ample specie in the nation, widely circulated. According to mercantilist maxims, imports took specie out of the country and exports brought it in. Colbert thus undertook a broad policy of reducing France's dependency on foreign goods and increasing its export capacity by stimulating manufacture and trade. This was often done directly, by launching state-financed manufacturing and trading monopolies or by offering favorable terms to entrepreneurs. Indirect action ran the gamut from campaigns to encourage the nobility to invest and lead commerce, to bringing guilds under control of the crown, to enticing skilled foreign artisans to settle in France. The thoroughness of Colbert's attention to the indirect means of creating conditions favorable to commerce and manufacture was impressive. He built the French Marine, which was nearly nonexistent when he took office. He launched a major program for the improvement of roads and bridges and for the construction of canals. His financial and administrative reforms earned him the hatred of the *officier* class, whose venality and traffic in offices were badly hit. He demanded accurate reporting and accounting from his *intendants*. He labored against entrenched

---

quently draws attention to them (King, *Science and Rationalism*, 100–115). Nussbaum's political history of Europe, 1660–85, construes the whole period as Cartesian (Nussbaum, *The Triumph of Science and Reason*).

As mentioned, recognition of Colbert's Cartesianism runs through the historiographical stream that reaches from Voltaire to Lavisse. Gustave Lanson, in his *Origines et premières manifestations de l'esprit philosophique dans la littérature française de 1675 à 1748*, affirms the Descartes-Colbert link on the authority of Lavisse.

49. Lavisse, *Histoire de France*, 6: 166–67. King rates the change in the quality and functions of the *intendants* as the administrative renovation that was fundamental to all else (King, *Science and Rationalism*, 127ff.). Colbert's concept of a dedicated public service was realized in the course of the eighteenth century; see Paul Ardascheff, *Les intendants de province sous Louis XVI*, chaps. 3–5.

local interests to introduce uniform commercial law and flexible credit. He succeeded in shifting the tax burden from an overwhelming load on the peasantry and artisans to business and the nobles. His dislike of idle hands and idle money disposed him favorably to the Huguenots, and he would have drastically reduced the number of persons in religious orders had it been within his power to do so.[50]

The Technocrat

The vexed question whether Colbert innovated on the mercantilist policies of the French monarchy from Sully to Richelieu is best considered within the framework of action. If we compare Colbert's maxims with those of his predecessors, the similarities are more striking than the differences. But if we consider the magnitude of Colbert's project, the detail in which it was conceived, and his ability to launch and coordinate his program, differences come at once to light. French policy toward its Marine will serve as an example. When Colbert took office, there was firm precedent for improving the Marine, based on the mercantilist maxim that no nation could gain in trade without a substantial merchant fleet and a navy to protect its shipping. Yet in 1661, the French Navy consisted of 18 aged warships and a few galleys. The arsenals and stores were empty, ports had deteriorated, and French sailors had taken service with Dutch and Italian masters. The Merchant Marine, according to a census of 1664, consisted of 2,368 vessels of all sizes, of which only 329 were of 100 tons' burden or over, whereas the Dutch, by Colbert's reckoning, possessed over 16,000 merchant vessels.[51]

Colbert set to work on the Marine immediately upon assuming office. The naval budget was increased rapidly from Mazarin's 200,000 livres per year to several million and then to 10 million. Initially most purchases of materials and stores had to be made abroad. But Colbert recognized that expenditures on such a scale would support large domestic industries. Accordingly, shops for the manufacture of ordinance, sailcloth, masts, tar, rope, and other stores were set up all over France.

---

50. "There are too many priests, monks, and nuns," Colbert remarked. "Not only do they disburden themselves of work that contributes to the common good, they deprive the public of children whom they could engender, and would serve necessary and useful functions . . . there are no monks in Holland and England" (Lavisse, *Histoire de France,* 7: 172). The *dévote* Mme. de Maintenon, who called him *le Nord,* said that "he thinks only of finances and almost never of religion" (Cole, *Colbert and a Century of French Mercantilism,* 1: 300). Cole's inspired gloss on this remark is that "his religion seems to have been more political than personal."

51. Cole, *Colbert and a Century of French Mercantilism,* 1: 451, 468.

To remedy the low estate of French shipbuilding technique, he offered high salaries to entice naval architects and master carpenters from England and the Netherlands, with the understanding that they were to teach their skills as well as exercise them. Meanwhile, missions were sent abroad to study shipyards, and the savants of the Académie des sciences were set to work finding optimal ship designs and other improvements. In Colbert's energetic pursuit of technical knowledge, he even imprisoned a Dutch naval architect who refused to reveal his secrets. Meanwhile ports, arsenals, and bases were renovated or established. Rochefort was built *ab initio* to a bustling shipbuilding town of 9,000 inhabitants turning out thirteen large vessels per year. Brest, which Richelieu had founded, was nearly deserted in 1661. Colbert revived it, along with Toulon and Saint Malo. Dunkirk, long an important port, was soon employing 30,000 laborers. Many other ports were deepened and improved.[52]

Manning the Navy and the Marine presented numerous problems, which Colbert approached with his usual mixture of velvet touch and mailed fist. Rather than depending on impressment, the common method, he established a naval reserve system in which active duty was followed by a period of paid reserve service. Special hospitals were available to sick and wounded sailors, who were exempt from tax. These and other favorable conditions of service were part of an effort to make maritime employment attractive and the Navy an elite corps. The creation of a naval elite was Colbert's tactic for wooing the nobility to the officer corps of a service that attracted neither the king's favor nor the public notice. Other things counted against it—the asceticism and anonymity of long months at sea, learning exact skills, and Colbert's increasingly tight discipline.

Recruits to the officer corps were sent to schools where they learned navigation, hydrology, and artillery. The schools also corrected the feudal attitudes that captains tended to take toward their commands. Captains were disallowed the right to carry cargo, and they could be hanged for deserting French merchant vessels they were assigned to escort. They were required to keep their ships clean and their men

52. Colbert brought the French maritime service to a pitch of technological proficiency that was not excelled until the beginning of the Industrial Revolution. His counterpart in England, Samuel Pepys, repeatedly noted the French technical superiority in his *Naval Minutes*. King's outstanding survey of this activity brings out Colbert's own technological inventiveness (King, *Science and Rationalism*, 252–63). For an illuminating comparative study, see John U. Nef, *Industry and Government in France and England*, especially chap. 3, "Royal Participation in Industrial Enterprise."

healthy. The mailed fist showed in other ways as well. Colbert ordered all Frenchmen in foreign maritime service to return to France and register for French service, on pain of death. His agents scoured France for vagabonds and convicted criminals to feed to the growing galley fleet. One *intendant* wrote apologetically to Colbert of two criminals whose introduction to the oar the executioner had forestalled: "The judges," he wrote, "do not always comply with our wishes."

Although Louis hardly took notice of the Navy until 1680, Colbert's efforts were successful. A census of 1677 showed that it comprised 144 warships exclusive of service vessels, mounting 7,107 cannon.[53] Shipbuilding efficiency had risen to such a pitch that the yard at Marseilles could assemble a vessel in six hours. Naval commanders struck at the pirates of the Barbary Coast. The Navy was integral to Colbert's large colonial undertakings in North America, and it challenged English and Dutch supremacy of the seas. When Duquesne defeated the superior forces of the Dutch admiral de Ruyter in 1676, French naval power proved itself and made Colbert the happiest man in France.

Comparison of the maritime policies of Richelieu and Colbert illuminates the *mentalité* that they brought to bear on the conduct of office. They shared the mercantilist conception that marine, commerce, and national power were intimately related. But they understood it in different ways. Richelieu laid the stress on the end effect—on the exercise of military and diplomatic power in the continuing political struggle with Spain and Austria. For him the linkages with commerce and manufacture were means to the political result. Colbert had a greater appreciation for the means as power in their own right, provided they were understood within a network of systematic linkage. Thus the maritime policy was simultaneously linked with improving domestic manufacture, increasing French technical proficiency, providing employment, goading merchants to new ventures, pressing his outlook on the aristocracy, menacing Dutch and English shipping and encroaching on their trade. For him, the political power that interested Richelieu—and Louis—was a product of the systematic linkage and could not be sustained without it. This conception, and its administrative consequences, were missing in Richelieu, who did not systematically press all the objective ramifications of a policy into new activity across a broad financial, social, and productive front. This "systems approach" distinguished Colbert's rationalism. His memoranda and directives reveal a mind ever alert to the material implications and presuppositions of every policy;

53. Cole, *Colbert and a Century of French Mercantilism,* 1: 457.

his world was a causal net in which every event was connected with every other. The job of the *contrôleur général* of this mechanism was to arrange the forces so that they produced the desired effect. He had to strive to control all the variables, otherwise he could not control the effect. Unfortunately, he was unable to control Louis, who was forever frustrating the system; and when Louis didn't throw sand in the gears, the merchants of Marseilles did. Frenchmen might well have been grateful, considering the Colbertian image of the social order described by his mercantilist disciple, Pottier de la Hestroye (1698):

All subjects must work in the state; everyone must be occupied. The state is properly speaking a machine, whose movements, though different, must be continuously regulated. Subjects cannot interfere with the movements without running risk of destroying the machine. Subjects must act and work in a state to support it and make it flourish.[54]

The gray rigidity of Colbert's social machine fitted his relentless, factual character, which was often the target of ferocious pamphlets and verse. No detail evaded his gaze; he was not above prescribing the number of nails to be used in fastening slate shingles. It was characteristic that he drafted an Ordinance on Forests and Waters as a gloss on his program to make France self-sufficient in ship timber; and in character again that the ordinance was so sound that it required no amendment until 1873.[55] But the practice of systematic rationality often demanded that administrators ignore pleas for custom and manners of the place. Thus he

54. Quoted by Rothking, *Opposition to Louis XIV*, 104–5. The frequent occurrences of the machine analogy in Colbert's works indicate that he thought mechanistically as a matter of course. Addressing the taxation snarl after taking over from Fouquet, for example, he viewed his task as "disentangling a machine that the cleverest men in the kingdom . . . devised so as to make of it a science that they alone know" (quoted by Cole, *Colbert and a Century of French Mercantilism*, 1: 301).

55. The language school that Colbert established illustrates the thoroughness that stemmed from his confidence in the power of methodical procedure to solve all problems. When the Turkey merchants of Marseilles experienced the usual difficulties of those who try to do business through local interpreters, Colbert suggested that French youths be taken to Turkey and taught the language and customs. The merchants opposed this proposal, but Colbert went ahead. He was so successful that merchants were soon clamoring to have their sons admitted to the school.

seemed inhuman to his enemies and to the people of Paris, whose rage was so great that when he died, he was buried secretly to prevent desecration of his tomb.[56]

Here too the contrast with Richelieu is instructive. Richelieu was an aristocrat imbued with the ethos of Renaissance humanism, especially the civic humanism that linked *virtù* with glory and national power. His ecclesiastical, commercial, and diplomatic policy was thoroughly political, focused on the hegemony that depends on statecraft backed by court and cannon. While this humanism was neither very moral nor very pious, it was emphatically oriented on the soul as the thing in the world politically most important and humanly most interesting. Richelieu, like Machiavelli, wrote poetry and practiced the political arts as things that stirred and satisfied the soul. Colbert did not write poetry, and we do not readily picture him attempting it. Though he used the arts of blandishment and manipulation, they were not his cup of tea. He preferred directness without rhetorical flourish, forthrightness to cunning. His substitute for statecraft was technocratic factuality, with its criteria of efficiency, uniformity, productivity, know-how, and control.

While Colbert's conception of his work as polytechnic labor in the social machine resembles the technique of Machiavellian statecraft, they differ in one particular especially: in Colbert's conception, the element of *Fortuna*, or chance, has been eliminated. Technique, Machiavelli admitted, is subject to Fortuna. As a result, his politician must be alert to the main chance and must thrive on the play of cunning. There is an element of the gratuitous in every victory or defeat; and the politician's fortitude in wrestling with the incalculable in men and events is an ingredient of his heroism and glory. This is his humanism. But Machiavelli noticed that it is the nature of art to eliminate chance, and he assigned to

---

56. The poems and epigrams collected by Mongrédien clearly reveal their origin in patrician and *officier* resentment, e.g.:

> De l'avare Colbert j'ai vu la violence
> Renverser de l'État les plus augustes lois,
> Attaquer la noblesse, opprimer l'innocence
> Et forcer sans respect la justice et ses droits.
>
> (Mongrédien, *Colbert*, 213)

Such aggrieved men are the source of his reputation as "un esprit médiocre" and a man "des vues bornées" (ibid., 33, 204). The patrician foreign minister Michel Le Tellier said of him that "il avait tous les dehors d'un honnête homme, l'esprit doux, facile, insinuant; il parlait avec tant de circonspection qu'on le croyait toujours plus habile qu'il n'était; et souvent on attribuait à sagesse ce que ne venait que d'ignorance."

fortitude the capacity to subdue, if not entirely vanquish, Fortuna. Colbert, by consistently applying the logic of technique, banished chance from his conceptual world, however often it might have crossed his efforts. In his world the heroes are experts, and power assumes a new meaning. Effective political power—hegemony—is conceived as an effect of wealth, efficiency, and control. It is the effect not of one art—the political art—but of the systematic coordination of many arts. Colbert's dictum that the power of the state depends on commerce and manufacture is his abbreviated mercantilist formula for his basically Cartesian insight. To treat the social world as a machine is to proceed in some manner as if the beings in it were machines: the world is "extension" or "matter" only. Under the mechanical auspices, humanism is replaced by technocracy.

By linking polytechnic work to rationality and resolute will, Colbert burst the limits of the Cartesian *gentilhomme*, for whom freedom from work is requisite for *générosité*. Despite the modernity of his outlook, Descartes wrote poetry and lived a life of leisure. Colbert was more consistent. That his consistency stemmed from his temperament is not so material, since his letters to his son prove that he reflected on the compatibility of work with the *gentilhomme*. He grasped, as Descartes apparently did not, that in a world of rational power the *gentilhomme* must be effective; and this he cannot be unless he labors to master its complexity and makes himself part of the social machine. To determine what sense of gentility survives in this concept is a difficult question.[57] The symbiotic relationship between Louis and Colbert suggests that something does survive. The aristocratic "pathos of distance" that characterized Europeans who incorporated Colbertian *virtù* suggests it as well. Finally, there is the remarkable fact that Colbert presided over the golden age of French classicism in the arts, sciences, and letters.

---

57. The decisive point seems to be the shift in the meaning of justice from particular and individual right to functional effectiveness in a national system. Using the second criterion, Colbert judged that the patriciate was obliged to become entrepreneurial, even as it seemed right that criminals and vagabonds should be condemned to galley slavery. In a lucid article, R. B. Grassby shows that the patriciate understood what Colbert was about, detested his schemes, and opposed them however they could ("Social Status and Commercial Enterprise under Louis XIV"). Saint-Simon probably summarized aristocratic opinion when he called the Louvois-Colbert government "la tyrannie des roturiers." He forgot that Richelieu, who was no *roturier*, had difficulties not very different from Colbert's. Unlike their English counterparts, the French aristocracy stubbornly insisted on their feudal rights.

The Technique of Aesthetics

As superintendent of buildings, Colbert personally supervised the construction of France's greatest monuments, culminating in Versailles. He reorganized the Académie française (which Richelieu had founded), the Académie royale de peinture et de sculpture, and the Jardin du roi. He founded the Académie royale des sciences (1666) and the Académie royale d'architecture (1671). In the peak years, more than 500 painters and artisans of every skill worked under the direction of the man whose results had to please the taste of Europe's foremost gentleman. In only a decade he collected 670 paintings by Italian, Dutch, and French masters, which were housed in the Louvre for study by France's artists. (When the English National Gallery opened a century later, it could display but 38 paintings). To the Bibliothèque de roi he added 25,000 rare books and manuscripts collected by consuls all over Europe; at the same time he assembled a grand library of his own, which later became the basic collection of the Bibliothèque nationale. Pensions for writers and savants, which rarely exceeded 30,000 livres a year during Richelieu's administration, often exceeded 100,000 livres a year under Colbert. The recipients were not only Frenchmen but also distinguished scholars abroad. He imported artistic and scientific talent from wherever he found it. He organized academies in the provinces. He founded an academy of music. He established industrial museums. He broke precedent by opening the first exhibition of works by living painters. His public works completely changed the face of Paris. And with usual thoroughness, he also changed the smell; he organized crews to remove rubbish and *boue* from the streets.[58]

This prodigious activity was part of his plan to create a technological elite. As superintendent of arts and manufactures, he sought to impart technical proficiency to both. He chose as director of the Académie d'architecture the mathematician-engineer Nicolas-François Blondel, who believed that "beauty is born of dimension and proportion." The curriculum included mathematics, mechanics, and hydrology; its classicist aesthetic was drawn from Vitruvius, antiquity's model artist-engineer. Academy graduates formed a small cohort of architect-engineers who used the principles of applied science to build roads, bridges, canals, harbors, and buildings in classical and baroque style. In Europe of that day, only the technical institute at Bréda offered engi-

58. Maland, *Culture and Society in Seventeenth Century France*, 235ff.; Mandrou, *Louis XIV et son temps*, 159–81.

neering training of equal caliber. When Christopher Wren undertook his building program after the London fire, there were none to assist him possessed of the talents abundant in France. Vauban, the master of fortifications, supervised a corps of engineers for the war minister Louvois. Claude Perrault, an initial member of the Académie des sciences, frequently directed public works for Colbert. But the largest engineering enterprise of Louis' reign was the work of Pierre-Paul Riquet. Riquet, a wealthy tax official, was an accomplished mathematician and sometime participant in Mersenne's conferences. In 1662 he wrote Colbert describing his scheme for the Canal of the Two Seas. The canal was to join the Garonne River to the Aude Valley of Languedoc, where Riquet lived. It would rise and descend 600 feet over Les Pierres de Naurouse, utilizing sixty-five locks to cover a total distance of 175 miles. Riquet proposed to pay half the cost from his own fortune in return for exclusive rights of operation. After careful study of the plan, Colbert was convinced of its feasibility and faithfully backed the project during the fourteen-year period of its construction. It was, after all, his kind of project. It would snatch the Cadiz trade from the Spanish, forestall Dutch shipping in the Mediterranean, and eliminate the long, costly voyage from the Atlantic by a shortcut through French dominion. And all this it would do thanks to the ability of French technology to create the engineering wonder of the age.[59]

The Académie de peinture was placed under Le Brun, who also directed the royal tapestry manufacture at St. Marceou (the Gobelins), with this brief from Colbert: "The desire is that art should have a uniform character, like the state, should produce the effect of formal perfection, like the movement of a [military] corps, that it should be clear and precise, like a decree, and be governed by absolute rules, like the life of every subject in the state." The policy of regimenting art, so apparent here, was begun by Richelieu, who established the Académie française as a state-controlled guild for writers and scholars who were expected to set acceptable standards in taste and learning. Colbert was able to take this process much further, thanks to the Cartesian bent of French classicism.

Cartesian in this context means attention to rules of technique. In his *Rules for the Direction of the Mind*, Descartes had used the rule-governed techniques of manual arts to model the methodology of science; in the *Discourse* he identified art, understood as mathematical technique, with

---

59. Cole, *Colbert and a Century of French Mercantilism*, 1: 380ff.; Pepys, *Naval Minutes*, 390.

method and science.[60] The identification of art (technique) with knowledge had an ancient history, but it was asserted with renewed vigor by Italian Renaissance masters of *bottegas* as artists discovered new rules for producing visual effects. These masters worked out the organizational and instructional methods for mass-producing fine art according to the tastes of patrons. Colbert undertook to hasten the transfer of these methods to France. Cohorts of apprentices were sent to Rome to be drilled in drawing and copying. In Paris, Louis Testelin, the Académie's secretary, labored to refine existing rules for drawing and painting, which he set out as canons binding on apprentices. In his *Table de Préceptes,* he devised a scale for grading "great art" according to composition, drawing, color, and expression.[61] These strictly technical categories—expression, for Testelin, was also a matter of draftsmanship—treated art as technique for producing decorative patterns. Indeed, the Académie's apprentices were trained to teach draftsmanship and design principles to craftsmen in various trades, while their professional work consisted largely of painting to designs drawn by a master.[62] These methods, I emphasize, were not new, nor have they disappeared; they were not stultifying so long as the master was an artist. Colbert's organization of art production was based on the same technical outlook that he applied to manufactures. Though a nonartist, he understood the technical dimension of art. Technique produces art; hence, the product can be controlled by control of technique. This fact was familiar to artists. Colbert used it as a criterion for the selection of personnel to direct his establishments and to supervise artistic endeavors whose scope has not often been equaled since.

The Académie des Sciences

The complications surrounding the establishment of the Académie des sciences comprise a cameo of the state of scientific, philosophical, and religious alliances of the day. It has been mentioned that the conferences of Peiresc had been continued by Mersenne and Gassendi, and, from 1654, by Habert de Montmor as the Montmor Academy. In 1663 it became clear that the Academy was about to dissolve under the pressures of disputes between Cartesians and Gassendists, as well as from

60. See Caton, *The Origin of Subjectivity,* 43–54, for a discussion of this identification.
61. Maland, *Culture and Society in Seventeenth Century France,* 241.
62. Frederick Artz, *The Development of Technical Education in France,* 31.

want of funds to conduct experiments.[63] Several members therefore resolved to take separate initiatives to win support for a Compagnie des sciences et des arts. The ardent Cartesian Samuel Sorbière wrote to Colbert outlining a scheme. The classicist Abbé d'Augingac, who did to Homer what Spinoza did to the Old Testament, told Louis that "God threatens with the fire of his indignation heads of state who neglect to cultivate the arts and sciences."[64] The astronomer Adrian Auzout addressed Louis in the preface of his *Ephémérides des Comète de 1664* with an appeal to honor and utility:

> [to increase your glory] is one of the main objectives of the Society of Sciences and Arts, which desires nothing more than the protection of Your Majesty to work effectively toward the perfection of all sciences and all useful arts. Its project is so great, and it will be so glorious to the state, and so useful to the public, that if it is executed in its whole extent, it is not possible to believe that Your Majesty, who has projects so vast and magnificent, would not approve and favor it.[65]

The project described by Auzout's precarious rhetoric circulated widely in France and abroad. It copied the program of the Royal Society; indeed, contact between the Royal Society and French scientists was at that time intense. Sorbière visited the Royal Society in early 1663, while Melchisédec Thévenot, Jean Chapelain, Montmor, and Auzout were in touch with Oldenburg or other members of the society. Like its English sister, the Compagnie was to advise the king on scientific and technical matters. It would conduct experiments in all fields, with particular attention to increasing longevity through medicine, improving existing machines, and inventing new ones. It would serve as a bureau of standards and review applications for patents. Navigational improvement, flood control, and reclamation of exhausted lands were mentioned as possible areas of contribution. It would correspond with other learned bodies and would publish its findings. Its meetings would be open only to members, who would be amateurs and practitioners alike. Discussions of religion and politics were to be strictly banished.[66]

63. Brown, *Scientific Organizations*, 117–34; J. M. Hirschfield, *Académie Royale des Sciences (1666-1683): Inauguration and Initial Problems*.
64. Quoted by George, "Genesis of the Académie des Sciences," 378.
65. Quoted by Brown, *Scientific Organizations*, 144.
66. Ibid., 144–45; George, "Genesis of the Académie des Sciences," 379–80;

The existence of the Jardin du roi and more especially of the Académie française required that the proposed society be coordinated with these bodies. The Jardin, essentially an extension of the king's medical service, employed physicians, chemists, apothecaries, and botanists. In a society based on jealousy of privileges, the relation of the new organization's functions and personnel to the Jardin had to be clarified. The solution eventually adopted was to include leading personnel from the Jardin in the Académie des sciences while confirming the Jardin's separate functions. The larger and more jealous Académie française presented greater problems. At Colbert's request, Thévenot, Charles Perrault, and Chapelain submitted proposals for coordinating or for merging the two academies. That Colbert sought the advice of these men is significant. Thévenot, Montmor, and Chapelain embodied the Peiresc tradition of the gentleman-amateur. Chapelain had indeed been close to Peiresc and had advised Richelieu, Mazarin, and Colbert on various matters concerning the Académie française. Moreover, he had long maintained contacts with English scientists, especially Cavendish. Thévenot had been closely associated with the Montmor Academy and was secretary of the Accademia del Cimento. Colbert pondered a variety of arrangements before resolving the question. The organizational model of the Académie des sciences was evidently the Accademia del Cimento, not the Royal Society. The Académie restricted its membership to scientists, physicians, mathematicians, and engineers of proven ability; it was organized into specialist sections that met weekly; its quarters were equipped with research facilities. All this followed Italian precedent. But the aims of the Académie, as originally advertised in Auzout's proposal, copied the Royal Society.[67]

The composition of the first appointments to the Académie reveals

---

Hirschfield, *Académie Royale*, 8–14. Perrault notes that the Sorbonne, alarmed about the formation of the Académie, demanded that it not discuss theology (*Mémoires*, 48).

67. The source of the history of the genesis of the Académie is Fontenelle's *Histoire*, supplemented by Du Hamel's *Latin History* and Perrault's *Mémoires*. The papers of Thévenot, which undoubtedly would illuminate the subject, have unfortunately been lost. This material was reworked by Alfred Maury (*L'ancienne Académie des sciences*, 1864), Gaston Darboux (*Institut de France*, 1907), and Ernest Maindron (*L'ancienne Académie des sciences, Les académiciens*, 1895). The account given here is drawn from Brown, *Scientific Organizations*, 149–54; George, "Genesis of the Académie des Sciences," 384ff.; Mandrou, *Louis XIV et son temps*, 182–90; Perrault, *Mémoires*, 43–44; Roger Hahn, *The Anatomy of a Scientific Institution*, 1–18; and Hirschfield, *Académie Royale*, 1–29.

clear patterns of choice.[68] There was a marked preference for scientists and engineers who were already in royal service. However, this class of men was further refined by the exclusion of those who served Colbert's rival, the war minister Louvois. This exclusion carried over in the aims of the Académie, which did not include improvements in military technology. Finally, Cartesians were entirely excluded. This surprising outcome was probably due to the strained religious climate of the day. In 1660, the Jesuits intensified their campaign against the Jansenists and the Cartesian philosophy they had adopted. From that year, Descartes was frequently censured in Jesuit tracts. In 1662, the prestigious theology faculty at the University of Louvain condemned his philosophy in toto. The Jesuit Inquisition followed suit in 1663 by placing his works on Index, pending correction of his explication of the Eucharist. The following year the University of Paris reminded and admonished its faculty that the pagan Aristotle was the basis of all its teaching.[69]

The Jesuits were apparently distressed by the vigor of the Jansenist-Cartesian insurgency. Arnauld and Nicole published their very successful *Logique* in 1661. Cordemoy, Sorbière, Desgabets, and Rohault busily expounded Cartesian physics and recruited followers away from the Aristotelian standard. Port Royal enjoyed the sympathy of fashionable and powerful men and women in Paris society, including the Prince de Condé, La Rochefoucauld, Cardinal de Retz, Mme. de Sévigné, Marquise de Sablé, and Pierre Chanut, counselor of Fouquet and patron of Descartes.

The determination of the Jesuits was exposed by a dramatic event in 1667. Dogged by Jesuit accusations that Descartes' philosophy was heretical, the Cartesians and Jansenists were put on the defensive among the laity, where their influence was strongest. To undercut these harmful cries, Claude Clerselier, equally devoted to Descartes and to Catholi-

68. For discussion of the original membership, see Perrault, *Mémoires*, 43–44; Ornstein, *The Role of Scientific Societies in the Seventeenth Century*, 145ff.; Hirschfield, *Académie Royale*, 30–48.
69. T. McClaughlin, "Censorship and Defenders of the Cartesian Faith in Mid-Seventeenth Century France," 566ff. The harassment continued. In 1671 the archbishop of Paris and rector of the University of Paris demanded of the Parlement of Paris that it forbid teaching any doctrine other than Aristotle. The Parlement declined to do so. In 1675 Louis gave a verbal order forbidding the teaching of Cartesian philosophy, which was to be enforced by regular examination of lecturers. In 1678 the Oratorians were compelled to recognize the validity of Aristotle, after one of their number, Father Malebranche, published his heterodox Cartesian theology. All these events are discussed by McClaughlin.

cism, decided to have Descartes' remains reburied in Paris with proper Catholic obsequies. The minute requirements of sanctity were observed in the removal of his remains from Sweden to France. Clerselier even took the unusual step of producing for the abbé of the church where he was to be buried three testimonials to the piety and orthodoxy of Descartes' life; one was from Queen Christine of Sweden, who attributed her conversion to Descartes. The burial site was chosen with care: it was the beautiful Sainte-Geneviève du Mont, which served the University of Paris. On 25 June a throng assembled to pay their respects and to hear Father Lallement, rector of the University, pronounce the oration. As this consecration of Descartes' innocence was about to be consummated, the service was interrupted by the clamor of the king's officers. The startled assembly were informed that the court of Paris forbade the oration.[70] The assembly was in turmoil and the Cartesians confounded; the Jesuits had contrived to transform, as if by magic, what seemed certain victory into a humiliating defeat. Yet the Jesuits did not gloat. Their sentiments were revealed by the dean of the Sorbonne theology faculty, who commented to his party as they left the cemetery: "the enemy is within our walls; and here our ancient city falls to the ground."[71]

This prediction of defeat in the moment of apparent triumph proved to be correct. Despite continuous censures, despite royal prohibition of the teaching of Cartesian philosophy in 1671 and 1675, despite prohibitions of books, banishments, and the intimidation of the Oratorians, the Jesuit position slowly eroded. In 1690, the *Journal des savants* declared that the struggle against Aristotle and for the new philosophy had triumphed everywhere "except in the schools." In 1720 the University of Paris capitulated and officially allowed Cartesian and other new philosophies to be taught.[72]

The *Mémoires* of Perrault reveal something of Colbert's caution in this superheated theological environment. Although the public record of the initiatives for the founding of the Académie shows that they came from scientists, Perrault records that Colbert had resolved upon an academy in 1662, after confidential discussion with his secret cabinet.[73] As servant to a king whose confessors were Jesuits, he could not oppose their schemes openly, even though they frequently obstructed his plans

70. A. Baillet, *Vie de Descartes*, 2: 440.
71. *Œuvres de Descartes*, ed. Adam and Tannery, 12: 367.
72. McClaughlin, "Censorship and Defenders of the Cartesian Faith," 569.
73. George, "Genesis of the Académie des Sciences," 388. George cites Perrault's *Mémoires*, 9, 34–36, but does not indicate which edition he consulted. I cannot locate this story in the Libraire Renovard edition (1909). George also notes that the secret cabinet was called *le département de la gloire de Louis XIV*.

and crossed his policies. Their control of French education frustrated his desire to introduce mechanical and commercial subjects into secondary schools.[74] Ecclesiastical wealth was exempt from his financial net. He was obliged to acquiesce in Louis' awe of the Jesuits, which eventually led to the persecution and expulsion of his valued Huguenots. The exclusion of Cartesians from the Académie des sciences—a cruel and ironical twist—was doubtless a concession to theological anxiety. The other irony, however, was that the exclusion was nugatory in real terms, for Descartes was indeed "within the walls." He was in Huygens, who declared that "I am one of those who has profited from the wisdom of that great man." And he was in Colbert, who directed the work of the Académie along the lines Descartes laid out in the preface to his last published writing.

In his history of the Académie, Fontenelle called it the *"famille spirituelle* of which Colbert was the father."[75] Colbert largely set its agenda and saw to it that no funds were wanting for research; the Académie's observatory alone cost 750,000 livres. The advancement of industrial arts was one of its principal functions. Auzout and Couplet were sent on tours in France and abroad to collect information on industrial tools, machines, and fabrication processes, and to purchase selected foreign machinery for study and duplication in France. Academicians were sent out to ateliers to teach and learn from master craftsmen.[76] Huygens and Papin experimented on ballistics, the steam engine, and the use of gunpowder as a new power source. Mariotte applied hydraulics and machine design in the construction of the innovative water supply system of Versailles, a labor that produced improvements in the calculation of the strength of beams. Antoine Parent's study of waterwheels was the first use of differential calculus to solve engineering problems. Roberval, Römer, and Blondel collaborated in writing the Académie's joint publication, *Traité de mécanique*. The Académie's continuous review of new machines and inventions documents the high pitch that French technology had reached. The range of devices is impressive: mills, pumps, and steam engines of many kinds; medical equipment, including ingenious artificial limbs; lock and canal designs; calculators; elaborate automatic toys; industrial fabrication techniques.[77]

74. I have omitted discussion of this significant plan for reform. See Boissonade, *Colbert*, 35–36, and Frederick Artz, "Les débuts de l'éducation technique en France," *Revue l'histoire moderne* 12 (1937): 469–519.
75. Fontenelle, *Histoire de l'Académie royale des sciences*, 1: 241.
76. King, *Science and Rationalism*, 294. For the Academy's work on cartography, see Hirschfield, *Académie Royale*, 169–87.
77. M. Gallon, *Machines et inventions approuvées par l'Académie royale des sciences*

Another area of applied science was the Marine, especially in cartography, astronomy, naval architecture, and study of the tides. Colbert was especially eager for the Académie to discover a method of finding longitude at sea. Huygens attempted to solve this problem by inventing an accurate nautical clock based on his path-breaking theoretical studies of the dynamics of oscillating pendulums. Though his design failed to overcome the effects of ship's motion, his effort illustrates the polytechnic finesse of the finest theoretical physicist of his generation.

That Colbert's discerning leadership was largely responsible for the success of the Académie appears from its career after his death. The king's other technocrat, Louvois, assumed control and insisted that the academicians confine themselves to practical applications.[78] Accustomed as he was to working with engineers, he did not understand that applied science, at the Académie's level, could not be separated from theoretical research, and the Académie atrophied until it was reorganized in 1699.

Lavisse summarized his study of Colbert with the famous remark that "if Colbert had one day revealed his whole thought about the society of his time, he would appear as the precursor of revolution." In view of the unusual scope he enjoyed for putting his ideas into action, one wonders whether Colbert's do not reveal more of his thought than is usually conceded. Perfect eyesight is not necessary to see that his vast project of reform was incompatible with the order of privilege and caste that he served. Colbert himself was completely aware of this fact; his tireless efforts to recruit the French patriciate and bourgeoisie to his schemes comprise the clearest proof one needs. But his success in organizing a technological elite, and his attempt to provide for its propagation within the shell of the *ancien régime,* are yet further evidence. The Académie in particular was a functioning assembly of talents whose likes were not to be seen again until Napoleon assembled polytechnics more than a century later. Here, for the first time, in a rich, powerful, ambitious nation, a new type of man found scope and reward for his activity. The contemporary name of this type was "the technocrat." But the neuter character we sense in that term makes it anachronistic as applied to the men of the Académie, who are more aptly described as "polytechnic gentlemen."

---

depuis son établissement jusqu'à présent, 22 vols. (1735). The description of each machine is accompanied by at least two drawings in geometrical perspective, and often as many as eight. The drawings are masterpieces of industrial draughtsmanship. Their consistency suggests that they originated from a single atelier, perhaps the Académie de peinture itself.

78. King, *Science and Rationalism,* 291.

Perhaps the purest representative of this type, besides Colbert, was Christiaan Huygens. Born in the lap of Dutch culture, Huygens received the best education in science and the arts. He proved to be precocious in mathematics and music—he was said to be an accomplished harpsichordist. As a youth he met distinguished men when they called upon his father Constantijn, a diplomat and amateur scientist. Among those who came was René Descartes, who sometimes asked questions to test his talents. When the young Huygens read "that great man's" writings, it seemed to him "that everything in the world became clearer and I was sure that when I found some difficulty, it was my fault that I did not understand this thought."[79] Having begun with Descartes' "roman de physique," Huygens turned it into science, but science that combined lucidity with grace. One is tempted to say that he raised science to a form of art. Newton called him "the most elegant writer [on mathematics] in modern times."[80] Auzout remarked in admiration that "in him nothing is lacking, and nothing is superfluous." That is almost a description of the perfect work of art. And indeed, the signature of French classicism seems to lie on all that he did. There are no laborious struggles through the brambles of Kepler's exhausting calculations or Boyle's trial and error experiments: his path is direct and sure. Blessed with an audience who understood him, as Galileo was not, he wrote calmly and confidently, without polemic. He moved effortlessly among geometry, astronomy, optics, physics, biology, and experimental mechanics, and made fundamental contributions in each of these fields. Huygens knew nature more thoroughly than any man ever had. It was a machine universe, and it was to his liking. He understood the forms of power and did not think them all evil, although Louis' invasion of the Netherlands saddened his heart. He suffered none of Pascal's anxiety; he even sent away unheard a clergyman whom another called to his deathbed.

That was the polytechnic gentleman. It is easy to imagine that had one been on the throne, Colbert would have found a hundred more, and Europe's history would have been different. "We are not in a reign of little things," Colbert once wrote to a sluggish subordinate, "you will see that it is impossible to imagine anything too great."[81] The great thing Colbert imagined was the modern state.

79. Quoted by A. E. Bell, *Christian Huygens*, 20.
80. Ibid., 68.
81. Colbert to de Clerville, 4 October 1669.

chapter 3

Popular Enlightenment: Gutenberg, Conscience, and Leviathan

HISTORIANS of the last century emphasized the invention of printing as a critical factor in the passionate struggles that gripped Europe between 1530 and 1648. This story has been somewhat lost in the preoccupation, during recent decades, with fine-grained economic and social history. Exciting as they are, these new contributions to knowledge do not alter the old estimate of the importance of the invention of printing, which touched off a chain reaction that led to widespread literacy, to the Reformation, and to the first popular enlightenment in human history.

The Reformation broke across Europe just as the consolidation of monarchies from the patchwork of feudal principalities reached a critical phase. The power of magnates had been diminished, particularly in England, France, and Spain, but methods and institutions for governing kingdoms were imperfectly developed; above all, law and institutions to settle a frame of government on the inchoate relations between monarch, clergy, and aristocracy were especially wanting. As we have seen, this problem still was not resolved in France when Louis XIV assumed personal rule.

The Reformation introduced new perturbations into this already precarious political world. Kings discovered that their "political nation" had suddenly expanded to include many artisans and yeomen whose religious opinions made them an active political force propelled along uncertain trajectories. The intrusion of the people into politics, via religion, placed substantial pressures on Europe's nascent states, and few princes could hope to hold their thrones without an ecclesiastical policy that found some defensible ground between papal *fulmen excommunicationis* and the popular cry for reform. A half-dozen kings were crushed by these forces, not counting those assassinated by religious avengers. And England astounded the world by putting a king on trial in the name of "the people of England," on the charge of treason for violating "the fundamental constitution of this kingdom."[1] This unprecedented act, which mortified even the parliamentary soldiers, was not the sanguinary terror of a wanton impulse; it flowed from the impulse of men, in straitened political circumstances, who had originally been determined to affirm the concept of government limited by laws made by representatives of the people. In reality, the regicide merely sealed a new despotism conducted in the name of the people. Such were the adversities of the endeavor to implement republican notions.

That key modern phenomenon, the sovereign state, emerged from these intense struggles of mind and sword; in addition, Colbert enjoyed a partial success in joining the newly discovered technical rationality to its institutions. Had Colbert wished for a theorist to explicate the suppositions and to frame the legitimacy of his state, he would have found him in Thomas Hobbes. Hobbes drew up the plan for a new kind of government, which may be styled a "popular mercantile monarchy." It is a rule of law *imperium* whose sovereign governs in the public interest, by consent of the people. As behooves a court apologist, Hobbes based his state on the *imperium* politics to which the English monarchy had been committed since Henry VIII. But he rationalized the political sense of *imperium* by interpreting it in terms of the "natural rights" of free and equal subjects, whose primary activities are "economic." Since his scheme cannot be disentangled without a clear view of the ecclesiastical politics to which it is opposed, we must examine pertinent features of the Reformation.

The People's Religion

John Gutenberg was a Mainz goldsmith who formed a partnership with a merchant, John Fust, to capitalize Gutenberg's fruitful idea. The market potential doubtless seemed good. Books and other written material could be produced only in single copies, at no greater speed than the movement of a quill. A fair copy of the Bible required about ten months' labor by a copyist, and might sell for as much as 600 crowns.[2] The part-

1. Lawrence Stone, *The Causes of the English Revolution, 1529–1642,* 49.
2. Samuel Smiles, *The Huguenots,* 2.

ners elected to invest eight years' work in producing a complete Latin Bible on their first attempt. The risk paid off, for the first printing brought forth the flawless books that made Gutenberg famous. Fust took a batch to Paris, where they made a great stir and sold in days. But doubts arose about the provenance of perfectly identical copies, which had never before been seen. The wisdom of the day apprehended that they must be the work of the Devil, so Fust was arrested on charges of practicing magic.[3] He secured his release only by revealing the trade secret. This circumstance, in addition to local wars, deprived the company of the commercial rewards of their labors—it was to be a common fate of inventors for the next four centuries—and Gutenberg died a pensioner, honored but poor. Even so, the Gutenberg revolution had begun. In Cologne, Mainz, Treves, Magdeburg, Antwerp, Bruges, and other commercial cities, the book trade grew rapidly between 1475 and 1500. Translations of the Bible into every major European language were the bestsellers, but classical authors, psalters, and theological tracts were also in demand. Once this public was established, publishers in the next century reaped a bonanza. The availability of cheap books made the effort to acquire literacy worthwhile for a much broader public, particularly for artisans and freeholders. By the century's end, innumerable ancient and modern authors had been printed, and probably more than 100 million books were in circulation.[4]

As a European event, printing is indissolubly linked with the Reformation. Popular pietism as protest was familiar long before Gutenberg. When previously the people murmured about despotic bishops, ignorant and licentious priests, and the decay of ecclesiastical institutions, the Church responded by establishing reforming orders. But post-Gutenberg pietism contained an unprecedented element. Simple believers reading the Bible experienced a kind of enlightenment. They found no trace in the New Testament of the hated canon law, which exempted ecclesiastics from criminal prosecution in civil courts. Purgatory, simony, and the pope were missing. They found instead that the Gospel was originally preached to small, humble congregations whose simple practices were a world away from the opulent formality of the Roman liturgy. Their discovery of primitive, historical Christianity was to become the backbone of Protestant theology. To be sure, these discoveries were not without promptings. Among the important pre-Reformation reform movements was the Brethren of the Common Life, founded by

3. Ibid., 6. This episode is thought to be the source of the Faust legend.
4. Ibid., 16, 21n; *New Cambridge Modern History*, 2: 213, 390.

Gerard Groot and Florentius Radewins in Deventer (1378), which encouraged biblical studies and pressed for the circulation of the Bible in the vulgar tongue.[5]

Bible reading among the Gospellers, as they were called in pre-Reformation decades, prompted a fervor that remained a major political and religious force until 1700. Inspiration—or "enthusiasm," as the incredulous called it—was often the result of Bible-reading devotionals unsupervised by priests. Those rustic minds, holding as they believed the very Word of God in their hands, were deeply moved by its resonating imagery. And they discovered cataclysmic new images of Millennium and Apocalypse in the Book of Revelation, which the Church did not preach because they had more than once occasioned heresy. The undesigning elimination of priests through private Bible reading had the effect of democratizing grace, with consequences that Cardinal Wolsey vividly portrayed to Pope Clement VII. If worship in the vulgar tongue were allowed, he declared, "the common people at last might come to believe that there was not so much use of the clergy. For if men were persuaded once they could make their own way to God, and that prayers in the native and ordinary language might pierce heaven as well as Latin, how much would the authority of the Mass fall!"[6] Fall it did. By 1550, the Mass had been declared idolatrous in a number of German principalities.

These dangerous tendencies were noticed well before Luther drew his drastic conclusions from reading his cherished personal copy of the Gutenberg Bible. In 1511, Pope Alexander VI, whose flat-earth geography has been noted, formalized licensing and censorship by prohibiting the publication of any book without permission from an archbishop. The Ninety-five Theses provoked sharper responses. In 1535, the Sorbonne secured a prohibition on the printing of all books whatever. In France, as elsewhere, the Bible was burned, with ceremonial imprecations, as "Luther's book." When that failed to discourage Bible reading, Bible readers were burned as exemplary punishment; when that too

5. Quentin Skinner, *Foundations of Modern Political Thought,* 2: 22–25; John T. McNeill, *The History and Character of Calvinism,* 255.

6. In his *Table-Talk,* Luther testified to the impact of the discovery of the Bible on his own religious sense: "I was twenty years old before I had even seen the Bible. I had no notion that there existed any other gospels or epistles than those in the service. At last I came across a Bible in the library at Erfurt, and I often used to read it to Dr. Staupitz with ever increasing wonder." Staupitz, Luther's mentor, later gave him a copy of the Gutenberg Bible and told him that the Curia believed that "the Bible itself is the cause of all our troubles."

failed, there were massacres of Gospellers.[7] Pope Paul IV carried anti-Bible policy to its logical conclusion when he issued the first Index Expurgatorius (1559), which placed all Bibles printed in modern languages on the list of forbidden books.[8] But it was too late for that root-and-branch policy. Many millions of books were in circulation, and the busy Dutch presses added daily to their number.

Hobbes, a diligent student of fragmented opinion, traced the importunities of conscience and belief in private inspiration to the popular diffusion of the Bible. "After the Bible was translated into English," he complained, "every man, nay every boy and wench, that could read English thought they spoke with God Almighty and understood what He said."[9] The experience of sudden illumination and exaltation—the "tower feeling," Luther called it—lay at the center of Protestantism. The central doctrine of justification by faith was the product of such inspired experience and seems to be integral to it; for to believe, as Luther did, that he had been "altogether born again and had entered paradise itself through open gates," he required an ecstatic emotional upheaval to interpret as a divine sign. The doctrine presupposes other religious experiences, especially belief in one's own corruption, and despair that one can fulfill the Law of Christ. This is the somber dilemma to which justification by faith was revealed to Luther as the solution.[10] Dread of this predicament could not form in the mind of a Catholic who accepted the orthodox teaching that forgiveness was obtained ritually by priestly absolution. Before he discovered his saving solution, Luther had despaired of his own righteousness partly because he was appalled by the spiritual desolation of the Church: if the instrument of salvation was itself debauched and impious, what hope was there for his lost soul? The despairing Luther cursed God for casting him into this wretchedness. Thus, unable to believe that the external signs of a corrupt Church could save him, but needing a way out of this abyss, Luther hit on his solution of a private, internal sign. Given the etiology of his problem, it was an apt solution.

7. Smiles, *The Huguenots,* 49–76. In England, Sir Thomas More contrived an atrocious punishment for John Tyndale, brother of the translator, for possessing a copy of the Bible; see Henry Hallam, *Constitutional History of England,* 1: 82.
8. *New Cambridge Modern History,* 2: 390.
9. *Behemoth,* vol. 6 of *The English Works of Thomas Hobbes,* 190 (hereinafter cited as *EWH*).
10. Skinner, *Foundations of Modern Political Thought,* 2: 7ff.; Julius Köstlin, *Life of Luther,* 39–44.

Protestant soteriology is inseparable from the infamy of rebellion against the Church, for to trust the inner sign of grace is to be heretic, outcast, burnable. Had Luther's way to salvation coursed within the boundaries of orthodoxy, reform would have taken less terrible paths. As it was, Luther constructed an absolute and irreconcilable collision that made Luther and the pope each think the other damned. The infamy of rebellion heightened the Protestant's sense of the overwhelming importance of his inner experiences, which had to withstand the frightful terrors that the Roman clergy knew how to direct against heretics and schismatics. Calvin's predestination soteriology cut the efficacy of these terrors at their roots. The inner illumination, the private "certainty of salvation," was trustworthy because it had been decreed by the Almighty from eternity, even as the Church was predestined from eternity to persecute the Elect.[11] Calvinist militancy and endurance under persecution were to show that this harsh doctrine was a master stroke that hurled the Church to perdition in the same motion that elevated believers from infamy to sainthood. In any case it was essential, once the dangerous leap into faith had been taken, to destroy all vestiges of the legitimacy of the Church. Luther damned it as Antichrist and the Whore of Babylon. These anathemas are not to be set down to the ferocities of a repressed personality. Calvin and Roman ecclesiastics were no less emphatic; all were engaged in the spiritual warfare, or, in the memorable words of an English Puritan, "holy violence."

This would be clearer than it is today if more attention were paid to that pure essence of the Counter-Reformation, the Society of Jesus.

11. Calvin's statement of the criterion of election is worth notice: "The true conviction which believers have . . . of their salvation . . . proceeds in no sense from the flesh nor from reasons human or philosophical, but from the imprint of the Holy Spirit which makes our consciences so assured that they are no longer in doubt." This religious individualism is the obverse of the rational egocentricity of modern philosophy. The Holy Spirit is said to be the cause of the mental disposition of "certainty of salvation." According to the new philosophy, all mental dispositions were said to be caused by "the flesh," i.e. the body-machine at its neurological centrum, the brain. This inference was based on "reasons human or philosophical"—the *only* grounds of belief that the new philosophy admitted as legitimate. Predestination was one of many Protestant doctrines stemming from medieval schismatics. It was first enunciated by the monk Gottschalk in his *Confessio prolixior,* in which he rested his contention on the authority of St. Augustine. Alarmed, prelates convened the Synod of Quierzy (A.D. 853) and designated the theologian Scotus to answer Gottschalk, which he did in his *De divina praedestinatione.* The Catharist and Albigensian heresies were associated with predestination (*Cambridge Medieval History,* 5: 651–55).

Here the militancy of the Calvinists was matched by an elite corps whose first article of faith was entire obedience to the Church Militant. Jesuits alone, of all orders, vowed personal fidelity to the pope. They were trained in a discipline of pious hardness emblematic of the Spanish founder. Bred to rule or ruin, they were master dialecticians and keepers of conscience, adept in the arts of intrigue and confession. They liquidated the Reformation in Spain and stifled learning there; they drove it out of Flanders, Brabant, and eventually proud Italy. They brought Poland back into the Church. They ruled Paraguay outright, and were ambitious for China. They did not hesitate to plot against powerful monarchs, three of whom fell to the daggers of their hit men. Their presence in a nation was so nearly equivalent to subversion that France and Spain were eventually obliged to expel them. They persecuted co-religionists without remorse. They did not scruple to use genocide: in 1569 the Jesuit-run Spanish Inquisition condemned to death 3 million Netherlanders—men, women, and children. Like their Calvinist arch-enemies, they embodied the fascinating tensions of "Christian soldiers"—of force united with charity. The Jesuits were in any event one of the most formidable spiritual forces ever unleashed in Europe. An art of obedience was the basis of the order. Rule 13 of Loyola's *Rules for Thinking with the Church* embraces the last consequence of spiritual authority as the antithesis of Protestant rebellion: "That we may be altogether of the same mind and in conformity with the Church herself, if she shall have defined anything to be black which to our eyes appears to be white, we ought in like manner to pronounce it to be black." The Machiavellian logic of this unflinching consistency charters the higher obscurantism that became the Jesuit hallmark. There is something distinctly modern about it—perhaps the tough, systematic discipline that uses reason and morality as means for concentrating all force at a single point, in this case the love of Jesus, or, more exactly, the Society of Jesus.[12]

The Protestant do-it-yourself salvation kit was not the source of

12. W. C. Cartwright, *The Jesuits: Their Constitution and Teaching*, passim; G. B. Nicolini, *History of the Jesuits*, 151–295; William J. Bouwsma, *Venice and the Defense of Republican Liberty*, 293–338. The staggering qualities and deeds of the Jesuits make them an exceptional challenge for the historian. Jesuit histories of the order, like histories of Freemasonry by Freemasons, remain close to externals and pious expressions. Authors who appreciate their great force in politics and culture usually polemicize against them, as do Cartwright and Nicolini. The polemic is descriptively justified as a means of highlighting the character of the order. Bouwsma writes without a polemic of his own; he acquires one by liberal quotation and summary of hostile opinion.

popular political liberties, as Acton's Whig history declared. Neither the Lutheran nor Calvinist clergy were political thinkers, and in their political tracts they did not advocate republicanism but the "godly commonwealth," whose model was not the pagan Athens and Rome, but Israel. Luther and the Lutheran clergy preached strict obedience to the prince, no matter how iniquitous; as for religious liberty, it consisted mainly in the freedom to be Lutheran. Calvin's polity was a godly autocracy incompatible with political liberties in Geneva, New England, and Scotland. In the Netherlands, the Calvinist clergy opposed the republican, religiously Latitudinarian urban patriciate.[13] In England, they were largely monarchist; and if some laymen like Sir Henry Vane entertained republican notions, their idea of a republic was the rule of saints preparing the world for the Millennium. This was redemption politics, not secular politics.[14] Calvinists made such an unholy mess that by 1680 their policies were everywhere disgraced, and their godly commonwealths returned to the profane hands of politicians, even in Geneva.

13. Pieter Geyl, *History of the Low Countries*, 148–72; H. R. Trevor-Roper, *Religion, the Reformation and Social Change*, 6–37. The view that Calvinism assisted political liberty is not well supported. Calvin and his church tended to distress the free institutions of Geneva. The temper of the *Christian Institutes* underwrites moral regimentation and theological autocracy. See McNeill, *The History and Character of Calvinism*, 176, 186ff., 217, 224–25; below, 222–26.
14. Richard Hooker's *Ecclesiastical Polity* (1594) is a litmus for Puritan politics. Puritans believed that all laws and practices not authorized by Scripture were unlawful. "If they looked to the Mosaic law as the standard of criminal jurisprudence, if they sought precedents from scripture for all matters of temporal policy, much more would they deem the practice of the apostles as unerring and immutable rule for the discipline of the Christian church." This is Henry Hallam's summary of the Puritan outlook that Hooker opposed (*Constitutional History of England*, 1: 203). It was to Hooker, not Cartwright or Whitgift, that Locke appealed in his *Two Treatises of Government*. It is true, certainly, that Puritan zeal backed the Puritan leader Sir John Eliot, who brought in the Petition of Right. But the liberties the Petition of Right espoused were baronial prerogatives or pretensions from the thirteenth century. Puritan support for procedural forms tending to uphold parliamentary prerogative was a marriage of convenience with the political and legal thinking that worked out those forms. The political testament of English Puritanism is the Root and Branch Petition (1640), which called for the abolition of episcopal regiment of the Church and substitution of "government according to God's word," meaning the presbyterian system. One need only consider the Scottish Kirk to recognize the frailty of its connection with political liberty.

Nevertheless, Protestantism did provide an attitudinal substratum that could be used by political heads to the advantage of liberty. This substratum comes to light by contrasting the core of the Counter-Reformation, Jesuit obedience, with Protestant soteriology. Despite all the rigors of Christian directories and moral regimentation, salvation through the inner sign insinuated an abiding individualism. Initially it took the form of rebellious self-assertion against the Church, and continued to manifest itself in the proliferation of sects. By declaring each his own theologian, Calvinism inadvertently undermined its capacity for doctrinal coherence and implicitly attacked the idea of orthodoxy. This was no small consequence, unintended though it was. In its initial phases, each his own theologian was not promising. Clergy and laymen elaborated an immense casuistry to determine whether the Bible commanded that hair should be worn long, whether wedding bands were permissible, whether Christmas should be celebrated, and the like.[15] Nevertheless, this rude biblicism was a training school for many in the habits of literacy, deliberation, and eloquence. If their moral horizon was narrow, this was the price to be paid for making it themselves; partly for this reason, morality among Protestants bore a weight and dignity absent among the broad mass of Catholics. Politics made its appearance in the guise of disputes concerning Church government and the relation of the Church to civil government. Despite the Calvinists' failures in this regard, the debate they opened and the hard knocks they gave and took were the beginning of popular political education, which by itself could never have engaged the attention of multitudes. Finally, Protestantism reshuffled the order of rank of values in a way hostile to aristocracy and favorable to the commons. If the pilgrim makes his progress along puritanical paths, at least he escapes the vices that so often sap the strength of the commons. Frugality and austerity were not cherished for economic reasons, but because they were the godly way of primitive Christianity and a badge of reproach to the aristocratic opulence of the Roman liturgy and sanctuaries. The severe, empty caverns Calvinists built for worship are silent witnesses to a popular revolt against luxury and ostentation in the house of God; they made heaven over for the common man. This is, to be sure, very different from making earth over for the common man. The Deist Mandeville had this difference in mind when he argued, implicitly against rigorism, that private vices confer public economic benefits. Nevertheless, the habits of austerity and personal responsibility, if originally cultivated for pious

15. Daniel Neal, *The History of the Puritans,* 1: 126; 2: 55, 221ff.; 3: 355; 5: 148ff.

motives, can also serve private advantage, provided that advantage and the means of achieving it are understood.[16] But for that, a political critique of ecclesiastical politics was required.

Ghibelline Politics and the Reformation

James Harrington's epigram "An ounce of wisdom is worth a pound of clergy" could stand as the thought that links the two political traditions that framed modern politics. One of these traditions was neoclassical republicanism, which sprang up in Italy, passed through the hands of Guicciardini and Machiavelli, and threaded its way north to France, the Netherlands, and England. Recent studies by Hans Baron and J. G. A. Pocock have charted the continuity of this tradition and demonstrated

16. A trenchant summary of the Puritan economic conscience is Hobbes's observation that "He reads [in Scripture] that covetousness is the root of all evil; but he thinks, and sometimes finds, it is the root of his estate" (*EWH,* 6: 231). The conflict between biblicism and the passions is apparent here; and in regard to economic policy, the Calvinist clergy were equipped with obstructions that they mitigated by platitudes, as Tawney's study of the economic thought of Richard Baxter brings out clearly. Max Weber's conjuration of capitalism from "Protestantism" is alchemical history borrowed from Auguste Comte. I mention one point only. Weber's Calvinism links "unemotional, rationally consistent" predestination with good works as a sign of election, which in that way becomes the "this-worldly asceticism" that powers the drive to accumulation (Weber, *The Protestant Ethic and the Spirit of Capitalism,* 105, 114, 117, 123, 126). But Calvin repeatedly stressed that predestination rules out good works as a sign of election (McNeill, *The History and Character of Calvinism,* 222ff.). This doctrine is not specifically Calvinist or Protestant; it stems from the ninth-century monk Gottschalk and was affirmed by St. Ignatius in his *Spiritual Exercises.* Good works as a sign of grace or salvation was the Dutch "Arminian" doctrine used by the commercial classes of Holland to oppose the morbidity of the *decretum horribile,* as Calvin himself called it (Hallam, *Constitutional History,* 1: 371ff.; below, 232–33, 237–39). Calvinist theologians incorporated touches of the "Arminian heresy" into their theology in response to the criticism that predestination encouraged bigotry (called "holy zeal" by Calvinists and "unemotional" by Weber). That Weber in addition admired the "rationality" of the doctrine (Calvinists themselves thought it a mystery) helps explain some of the derelictions of *The Protestant Ethic.* For a systematic criticism of the Weber thesis, see Kurt Samuelsson, *Religion and Economic Action;* H. M. Robertson, *Aspects of the Rise of Economic Individualism;* and Trevor-Roper, *Religion, the Reformation and Social Change.* The connection between the Protestant ethic thesis and Weber's psychosis is discussed in my *A Method for the Analysis of Neurotic Political Thought.*

its vigor. Thanks to their work, and to recent contributions by constitutional historians, we have an improved grasp of the development of republican political thought from the civic humanism of the Renaissance writers through its stillborn mutations in France, its development in England and the Netherlands, and its mature expression in the republicanism of the American Founders.

By 1700, Europe had settled firmly into the track of monarchy; republicanism had made a lasting impression on the institutions of only two nations. The tendency of Whig historians to identify republicanism with the cause of progress and to cast monarchy as conservative has sometimes made it difficult to keep a steady eye on the modern trends present in monarchical statesmen and advocates. Relics of that presence lie dispersed in the historical memory bank. One knows that monarchs and their chancellors created the modern state as an *imperium* sovereign over law, administration, citizenry, and territory; that they did not lag far behind the commercial cities in pursuit of trade and commerce; that they patronized science and the arts; that France, England, Sweden, Denmark, and numerous German principalities fell more or less into this pattern, while Spain and the Hapsburg empire, where suspicion of science was vigilant, entered orbits of slow eclipse until they eventually resembled the Whig stereotype of reactionary monarchy.

The political thought of modernizing monarchies has not been studied through the panoramic lens recently focused on republican political thought. When this study is completed, it will reveal, I believe, that modern centralizing monarchies were continuations of the medieval political tradition known as "Ghibelline politics," the politics of the German emperors who asserted the sovereignty of temporal (or civil) power against papal claims of *plenitudo potestatis*.[17] The struggle began

17. At the Synod of Worms (1076), the German bishops challenged Pope Gregory's power to excommunicate the emperor. Gregory VIII responded by declaring Henry IV heretic. Henry went to Canossa a penitent in 1078, but at the earliest opportunity (1083) he marched into Italy, subdued Rome, and compelled Clement III to crown him emperor. This was the beginning of centuries of strife. For summaries of medieval Ghibelline political thought, see Henry Hallam, *View of the State of Europe During the Middle Ages*, 2: 259–80; R. W. Carlyle and A. J. Carlyle, *A History of Medieval Political Theory in the West*, 4: 61–306, 5: 152–314; George H. Sabine, *A History of Political Theory*, 198–284; G. R. Elton, "Constitutional Development and Political Thought in Western Europe." An outstanding study of Ghibelline political thought in late Renaissance and early modern Italy is William J. Bouwsma's *Venice and the Defense of Republican Liberty*. W. J. Stankiewicz's *Politics and Religion in Seventeenth-Century France* is of comparable value. W. K. Jordan's

with Henry IV and Frederick Barbarossa and entered a new phase during the reigns of Frederick II and Ludwig IV. From then on, Europe divided into papal and civil factions. I say factions, because the fundamental issue was not the opposition of a Guelf papal league to a Ghibelline imperial league but whether ecclesiastical institutions were to be subordinate to civil power or conversely. The Conciliar Movement, which would subordinate the pope to Church councils, and the Reformation were events in this struggle. Moreover, much of the republican tradition was concordant with Ghibelline politics, since its exponents typically espoused the central Ghibelline thesis, the subordination of church to state. Further, although the German imperial tradition was the chief repository of Ghibelline politics, it was espoused also by

The Development of Religious Toleration in England appears to be the most recent comprehensive coverage of the English case.

There is a historiography that treats Ghibelline politics as Caesarist absolutism opposing a Guelf politics of civic liberty, feudal rights, and local autonomy. In this schema, the Papacy appears as the Guelf mainstay and hence as the defender of liberty (James Westfall Thompson, *Feudal Germany*, 266–91). Episodes in this long struggle, particularly during the reign of Frederick I (Barbarossa), may be read this way. But this approach yields no interpretation of the central issue, the competing legitimacy claims of the pope and emperor. It also romanticizes the Papacy, whose defense of liberty consisted largely in inciting rebellious and despotic barons against the emperors.

Thompson's *A History of Historical Writing* contains a fine summary of Ghibelline historiography during the Reformation and Counter-Reformation. Paolo Sarpi's *History of the Council of Trent* (1614) figures in Thompson's narrative as a landmark antipapal tract (*A History of Historical Writing*, 1: 520–79).

The matter of Ghibelline politics came up at the Vatican Council of 1869–70, when the Church made peace with the arrangement that had been installed in the constitutions of all modern nations. In an authorized publication, Dom Cuthbert Butler has reviewed the history of the old struggle: "The organizing of wars by the Popes for purposes hardly or not at all religious; their leading forth military expeditions to subdue to their authority rebellious cities . . . ; the ruthless use of the spiritual weapons of excommunication and interdict on issues often purely political and secular; the launching of crusades against cities, as Venice in 1309, when no issue of heresy or religion was at stake: it all makes bewildering reading. . . . The great German Emperors of the Franconian and Suabian Houses, who confronted the Popes during two centuries, were terrific men: powerful, able, determined, ruthless, resourceful, often unscrupulous and faithless, sometimes openly licentious" (*The Vatican Council 1869–1870*, 14–15).

French kings (Philip the Fair, Louis IX, Louis XII, Francis I, Henry IV), who integrated it into French monarchy as "Gallicanism," i.e. the right of the king to appoint and regulate the clergy. In literature, Ghibelline thought was typically anticlerical. Dante, Boccaccio, Rabelais, and Montaigne were its exponents. Among historians, Machiavelli led the way with a canvass of Ghibelline politics in his *Florentine Histories*. Guicciardini, Sarpi, de Thou, Raleigh, Camden, and later Voltaire followed that lead. Among theologians, William of Ockham wrote his antipapal polemics from the court of Ludwig IV. Wycliffe, John Hus, Erasmus, and Luther are more or less in that track. In philosophy, the Ghibelline position found support from Marsilius of Padua, the Latin Averroists, Roger Bacon, and Ockham's anti-Scholastic nominalism. This is the tradition of Europe's *politiques*—the men who opposed the double sovereignty of pope and king because of the political disorders and confusion it engendered. When scientific enlightenment became available, Ghibelline thinkers impressed it into the old war on superstition.

A Chronology of Ghibelline Politics

1076–1083	At the Synod of Worms, German bishops challenge Pope Gregory VII's power to excommunicate. Gregory retaliates by deposing Henry IV, who goes to Canossa as penitent in 1078. In 1083, Henry subdues Rome and compels Clement III to crown him emperor.
1121	Würzburg meeting of German princes on the investiture struggle results in Concordat of 1122.
1139	Second Lateran Council ends schism, but Roger II takes Innocent II prisoner.
1154	Victor IV is elected imperial antipope.
1162	Welf IV of Saxony defects from the Hohenstaufen Frederick I (Barbarossa) of Swabia to join the pope and Lombard League against the emperor—thus the origin of the terms *Guelf* (from Welf) and *Ghibelline* (from Weibelungen, a Hohenstaufen stronghold).
1198–1216	Innocent III proclaims the pope Vicar of Christ, superior to temporal authority; claims the right to examine and crown the emperor, or to reject him; uses the interdict to withdraw all church rites from subjects of disobedient sovereigns. Fourth Lateran Council defines heresy and declares transubstantiation an article of faith.
1215	King John seals Magna Carta, but the agreement is annulled by Innocent III in John's favor. Barons revolt.

1217	Magna Carta is reissued, and reissued again in 1225.
1220	Frederick II issues *Confoederatio cum principibus ecclesiasticis.*
1227	Inquisition is established by Gregory IX to subdue the Albigensian heresy.
1230	Frederick is absolved from excommunication.
1239	Frederick appeals to the authority of the Council against Gregory IX; Gregory offers the imperial crown to Louis IX, who refuses it, saying that only a council can depose the emperor. Henry III of England declines to enter a league against the pope on the grounds that he is the pope's vassal.
1245	Frederick is deposed by the Council of Lyons; Hohenstaufen fortunes decline.
1256	Innocent IV issues *Ad extirpanda* against Italian heretics. Dominicans receive permission to persecute sorcery as heresy.
1258	Provisions of Oxford and Westminster establish annual parliaments and expulsion of aliens from office.
1261	Alexander IV frees Henry III from the Provisions of Oxford.
1295–1304	Philip the Fair of France demands that the pope be tried before a council. Boniface VIII asserts the supremacy of the Papacy in the bull *Unam sanctum.*
1310	Thomas of Lancaster and twenty other barons appointed Lords of Ordinaries by Parliament. They govern in place of the king.
1322	John XXII declares heretical the Franciscan poverty doctrine that the Apostles owned no property.
1323	Diet of Nuremberg rejects papal claim of approbation.
1328	Ludwig IV is crowned according to the doctrine of sovereignty expressed in *Defender of Peace.* Pope John XXII is deposed for heresy.
1338	Ludwig annuls all papal verdicts against himself.
1344	German electors reject papal influence in imperial elections.
1353	Statute of Praemumire forbids appeals of English clergy to Rome.
1366	Parliament refuses to pay feudal tribute to pope.
1378	Commencement of the Great Schism.
1414–1418	The Council of Constance, directed by Emperor Sigismund, declares the pope inferior to its authority.

The Council disposes of three antipopes and elects Martin V. Reform measures are aimed at curbing fiscal abuses and weakening the power of the Curia. John Hus is burned in Constance for heresy. Sigismund causes *Gravamina nationis germanicae* (1417) to be issued.

1420–1436   Hussite wars in Bohemia.

1433–1437   Council convened in Basel by Sigismund reasserts the supremacy of the Council, deposes Eugene IV, and elects Felix V.

1438   Pragmatic sanction of Bourges asserts Gallican liberties against the Papacy.

1511   Alexander VI prohibits publication of books unlicensed by an archbishop.

1520   Leo X condemns forty-one propositions in the writings of Martin Luther. Teutonic Knights leave the Church.

1522   Diet of Nuremberg issues *Centum gravamina.*

Ghibelline politics began in earnest when Henry IV clapped the pope and a hundred cardinals into prison and set up the antipopes. But the emperor who molded it into articulate policy was the Hohenstaufen Frederick II, who ruled from his court in Sicily from 1220 to 1245. Frederick did not conform to then-current stereotypes of medieval princes. That his contemporaries found him something out of the common way is indicated by his sobriquets, Stupor Mundi ("Wonder of the World") and Immutator Mundi ("Transformer of the World"). His court alone in Europe could rival the splendor and learning of the courts of Arab princes, and that because it was heavily Arabized. Sicily had for centuries been in Arab hands before it was conquered by Frederick's kinsman Roger II. Rather than driving out the infidels, as Ferdinand did later in Spain, Frederick opened his court to Muslim scholars, natural philosophers, and artisans, and some were entrusted with high political office.[18] Muslim minorities under his jurisdiction were allowed freedom of worship and they were encouraged in agriculture and trade. Frederick himself spoke Arabic, in addition to French and Latin. His tutor in philosophy was a Muslim, and he corresponded with Sultan al-Kāmil about mathematical questions.[19] He was also a keen naturalist. His treatise *De arte venandi* is today regarded as an outstanding empirical study of the anatomy and behavior of birds.[20]

18. T. C. Van Cleve, *The Emperor Frederick II,* 155, 303.
19. Ibid., 304.
20. Ibid., 315. Van Cleve writes in praise of Frederick's qualities: "To the medieval mind, quickened by its intellectual and artistic interests, Frederick II

Frederick enjoyed the admiration of Muslim princes, despite his conquest of Jerusalem, because he did not treat Muslims with loathing. It is characteristic of his cosmopolitanism that when he led the Crusade, he left behind an angry pope who had recently excommunicated him. While his openness to men of other faiths doubtless expressed his enlightened outlook, it was also an instrument of policy against the Papacy. High officials of the Muslim and Jewish faiths were immune to the terrors of papal anathemas. Muslim minorities present among a Christian population opened the door to that subversive doctrine of toleration advocated many centuries earlier by another emperor, Flavius Claudius Julianus ("The Apostate"). Frederick differed from Henry IV and Barbarossa, and resembled Julian in his appreciation of the importance of having court intellectuals to counter the papal canonists and theologians. This was the political reason for promoting Islamic and Greek philosophy. In Sicily a team of scholars was put to work translating manuscripts, chiefly those of Aristotle and Averroës.[21] Both writers were at that time unknown in the Latin culture, which was also innocent of the "natural reason" to which the philosophers appealed. Frederick was particularly fond of Averroës, who had formulated an Aristotelian position on revealed religion. It was that religion is the "milk sister" of philosophy—meaning that religion contains as much of philosophy as the multitude can comprehend. As for the relation between the clergy and civil authority, Averroës affirmed the orthodox Islamic view that the prince is chief of the clergy.[22]

Such doctrines were congenial to an emperor whose reign was one long struggle with the Papacy. For years he conducted the angry propaganda war with Pope Gregory IX that generated much of the polemic that reappeared during the Reformation.[23] His constitutional position

gave a new and powerful impulse, broadening its vision, severing its restrictive bonds, brushing aside the obstacles that held it in restraint for a thousand years" (304).

21. Ibid., 302ff.

22. Averroism was intellectually among the more exciting theories to circulate in medieval Europe. It was closely associated with the doctrine of the Three Impostors, thus with the debunking of religion, with materialism, and with denial of a future judgment. See Georges de Lagarde, *La naissance de l'esprit laïque*, 31–50. Ernst Renan's study, *Averroës et l'Averroisme*, remains valuable.

23. Van Cleve, *The Emperor Frederick II*, 429–45. Papal propaganda depicted Frederick as a second Emperor Julian—an apostate infidel who scoffed at the virgin birth and profaned the clergy. In addition, he was said to have originated the blasphemy of the Three Imposters. Frederick's propaganda to princes maintained that his cause was theirs as well. His appeal to the Ro-

was that the pope had no power to crown or depose kings, and that the pope's authority in matters of faith was subordinate to the College of Cardinals'.[24] William of Ockham and other clerics subsequently developed this doctrine into the conciliar theory that councils of the Church were superior to the pope.[25]

In one more important respect Frederick laid down the pattern that Ghibelline monarchs imitated or attempted to imitate for centuries afterwards. He attempted to consolidate his territories by dispossessing petty barons, by streamlining administration and purging it of corrupt officials, and by promulgating a new legal code. He also realized that the viability of his *imperium* depended upon flourishing commerce and agriculture, which he energetically promoted.[26]

The Ghibelline political testament was written in 1324 by Marsilius of Padua shortly before he entered service to Ludwig IV. He joined the "Munich academy" of antipapists, including William of Ockham, which gathered around the emperor to assist in his war on the Holy See.[27] Marsilius's *Defender of Peace* traced the wars and turmoil of Christendom to the papal claim of sovereignty over all Christians (*plenitudo potestatis*) and declared that the two enemies of truth are ecclesiastical persecutions and the "misreasonings of priests" that lead to threats of damnation.[28] Marsilius declared that coercive power is by definition secular. He cited the New Testament and other historical documents to show that the pope, for three centuries after Christ, was only the bishop of Rome, and enjoyed no special spiritual authority, let alone coercive power. Recognizing that the poverty controversy begun by the Franciscans struck at the roots of ecclesiastical authority, Marsilius ap-

---

mans emphasized their ancient valor and patriotism. Gregory trumped this by a dramatic use of religious relics.

24. Ibid., 435ff. Gregory offered the imperial crown to Louis IX, who declined, saying that only a council could depose a king. Henry III of England, however, characterized himself to Frederick as a "vassal of the Pope."

25. B. Tierney, *Foundations of Conciliar Theory*, 1–20; Sabine, *A History of Political Theory*, 294–310.

26. Van Cleve, *The Emperor Frederick II*, 149–53. Frederick's politics were imitated by Philip the Fair in his struggle with Boniface VIII. See G. A. L. Digard, *Philippe le Bel et le Saint-Siège de 1258 à 1304*.

27. For an account of Ludwig's court and its propaganda machine, see Otto Berthold, *Kaiser, Volk und Avignon*, 45–68. On Ockham's role in the propaganda war, see A. S. McGrade, *The Political Thought of William of Ockham*, 21ff., 31–34; on the propaganda of the French court against the Papacy, see Richard Scholz, *Die Publizistik zur Zeit Philipps des Schönen*, passim.

28. *Defender of Peace*, II. i. 1–3.

propriated it as a weapon that later became the foundation of Protestant criticism: the Church had totally departed from primitive Christianity. The Apostles, lacking royal pretensions, enjoined obedience to Caesar. They eschewed opulence to live a holy life of humble service. They did not quarrel over contentious doctrines, denied the sacraments to none, and acknowledged the right of the civil power to appoint bishops and regulate the Church. Marsilius claimed that papal usurpations of these rights of sovereignty were the chief cause of the disorders of Christian dominions; and he demanded that the clergy, including the pope, return to the humble apostolic example.[29]

Together with John of Jandun, Marsilius directed Ludwig's political and theological war with the Papacy, while Ludwig commanded the military operations. Their depredations of the Papacy in 1328 are particularly notable. In January, Ludwig responded to John XXII's demand for an imperial vicarate and the right to investigate the election of emperors: he made a pilgrimage to Rome—German style, at the head of an army—and crowned himself emperor on the Capital.[30] This "unprecedented arrogance," as the Papacy saw it, initiated five months of political action meant to destroy the legitimacy of the Papacy and to reestablish imperial legitimacy on a strictly political basis. The axis of this politics was the Roman Parliament, which Ludwig treated as competent to provide popular sanction to imperial decisions. On 14 April, he proposed to the Parliament that John XXII was a heretic. This "cleverest of all medieval attacks on the ecclesiastical order," as Sigmund Riezler calls it, was a string taken from the bow of Ockham. Ockham had set a new and startling problem for the canonists to ponder: what does the Church do about a heretic pope? The heretic pope was Ockham's riposte to the excommunicate emperor; and he used this mischievous notion to argue the superiority of councils to the pope. John and Marsilius went a step further to declare that by heresy a pope forfeited his office and obliged the emperor to depose him.[31] The Roman Parliament was further urged to deny popes the right to dwell in Rome without its consent. On May 12, a new barrage was fired. The people of Rome elected pope one Petrus Rainalucci, an obscure monk distinguished only by his poverty and humility. In addition, Ludwig claimed

---

29. Ibid., I.i.3; II.xvi, xviii; III.ii. For a summary of Marsilius's politics that emphasizes their Averroist leanings, see Sabine, *A History of Political Theory,* 271–93.

30. S. Riezler, *Die literarischen Widersächer der Päpste zur Zeit Ludwig des Baiers,* 47–48.

31. Ibid.

his legitimacy from consent of the Roman people, represented by the Roman Parliament, as the *Defender of Peace* had argued.[32] It is scarcely to be wondered that Pope John declared Marsilius to be the "son of corruption and the offspring of damnation."

Marsilius advanced his arguments without the fear and trembling of Luther's version centuries later. He did not agonize about the fate of his soul or invent a new soteriology to support his war on ecclesiastical usurpations. He justified himself by reasoned argument from historical facts and Aristotelian political principles. But this was not the stuff of religion, for it contained no refuge for the people against the thunderbolts of papal anathemas. Frederick II had attempted to sway the people by appeal to Roman traditions of valor and patriotism, but that proved to be less effective than the pope's appeal to the pathos of religious relics.

The Marsilian doctrine of popular sovereignty, as its use in 1328 shows, was meant to open a popular front against the charisma of ecclesiastics. The popular sovereignty doctrine did not achieve its purpose, no doubt because the means for its institutionalization were wanting. Ghibelline doctrine as a whole split into a royal version without roots in the people and a popular version disjoined from politics. The popular version took the form of heresies, as the Church was pleased to call them, in which Ghibelline principles were mingled with prophetic outpourings. The Franciscan poverty movement, with its reprobation of the carnal Church, its denunciation of iniquitous popes, and prophecies of Apocalypse, contributed much toward debunking the Roman charisma. But with John Hus, this popular sentiment reached a turning point from heresy to Reformation. For the first time, protest against the Church took the form of national political revolt, and in the process crystallized the main positions of subsequent Protestantism.[33]

It was Luther's genius that he could see and pluck this ripe fruit. His achievement was to marry Ghibelline politics with an anti-Roman soteriology that eliminated the dependency of the people on the priest-

32. Ibid., 49.
33. Gordon Leff, *Heresy in the Later Middle Ages*, 2: 607, 633; 1: 52. For examples of grievances (*gravamina*) just prior to the Ninety-five Theses, see Gerald Strauss, ed., *Manifestations of Discontent in Germany on the Eve of the Reformation: A Collection of Documents*, 35–51. This volume also contains the *Gravamina nationis germanicae*, formulated at the Council of Constance in 1417, and the Reformatio Sigismundi (ca. 1438) of the Emperor Sigismund. These documents exhibit the continuity between twelfth-century imperial assaults on papal abuses and the doctrine of Hus and Luther.

hood. He was an Augustinian monk trained in the Occamist tradition, which exposed him to Ghibelline doctrine.[34] Shortly before his break with the Church, Luther made a brief retreat to Ockham's Conciliarism; but in the critical year, 1519, he read Hus's radical Ghibelline tract, *On the Church,* of which he later said, "I have taught and held all the teaching of John Hus, but without knowing it." Once Luther resolved to link his soteriology to national politics, he proved to be a master politician with princes as well as with the people. In the year of his excommunication (1520), he published his *Address to the Christian Nobility of Germany* in which he laid down the fundamental theologico-political line he followed throughout his life: salvation by faith alone is the doctrine that will redeem Germany from Roman arrogance, bloodsucking, and oppression. Luther had accurately measured the German nobility, who rallied at once to their mutual cause. The Teutonic Knights of Prussia, led by Albert Hohenzollern, left the Church in 1520, followed a year later by Philip of Hesse, and then many. In 1522 the Diet of Nuremberg issued the *Centum gravamina,* which described Roman indulgences as an insupportable burden, sucking the marrow from Germany and destroying piety by imposture.[35] Tracts and broadsides, which Luther turned out in prodigious quantity, stressed German nationalism and piety in rebellion against Roman iniquity and oppression.[36] Two of Germany's most celebrated knights, Ulrich von Hutten and Frederick von Sickingen, rallied to defend Germany and Luther's doctrine. If their military adventures turned out quixotically, they helped to mold what was to become a permanent alliance between Luther and the German nobility, formally recognized by the Treaty of Torgau (1526).[37]

34. Skinner, *The Foundations of Modern Political Thought,* 2: 49; Bengt Hägglund, *Theologie und Philosophie bei Luther und in der Occamistischen Tradition,* 9, 20, 26.
35. H. C. Lea, *A History of Auricular Confession,* 1: 402. The similar *Gravamina of Worms* (A.D. 1521) is printed in Strauss, *Manifestations of Discontent in Germany,* 52–63. In these few pages are found the Protestant case against the abuses of the Roman Church. For a discussion of reformation doctrine, see E. G. Rupp, "Luther and the German Reformation to 1529."
36. Lea, *A History of Auricular Confession,* 1: 391; Köstlin, *Life of Luther,* 208–12.
37. *On the Liberty of a Christian Man* (1520) declares that a Christian is a "free lord over all things, and subject to nobody." This sort of talk, of which Luther's writings are full, conveyed to the people attitudes that were permissible only among the nobility. In this way Luther helped to create legitimation for popular political liberty in the contest of nationalism. This, of course, is the very same popular sovereignty that Marsilius tried to appropriate to his politics. But Luther, a shrewd judge of men and affairs, realized that popular sovereignty would wreck the chances of reform and conse-

The meeting point for politics, theology, and the people at that moment was money; specifically, indulgences. Indulgences allow the commutation of moral offenses by monetary payment in lieu of penitential acts. The system, as Clement VI put it in the bull Unigenitus (1343), is the means whereby "Christ acquired a treasure for the Church militant."[38] After Sextus VI hit on the idea of selling prayers for souls in Purgatory, the indulgence business became a major source of papal revenue, so large that it was farmed by the Fugger financial empire. To pietists like Luther—and Europe was full of them—who lived in dread of the Lord, indulgences were a scandal to the Church and an offense to anguished conscience. The system also weakened the hold of preachers over their congregations, for whom the terrors of hell seemed less pressing if they could be bought off. Luther's patron, Frederick the Wise, had forbidden indulgences in his territory to stop the outflow of money. He established a religious business of his own by amassing a large collection of relics in twelve galleries for public view; his income from indulgences amounted to 100,000 marks annually.[39] Evidently the whole political economy of penitence could be rationalized to the benefit of the public by dealing the pope out; which is just what Luther and Frederick did.

When Henry VIII repudiated papal claims, he imitated the German princes. The Act in Restraint of Appeals to Rome (1533) and the Act of Supremacy (1534) set forth Ghibelline political doctrine in forceful terms.[40] These acts repudiated the *jus divino* claims of the English bishops and the papacy. Only positive enacted law has binding force, and the legislator cannot be limited in any way.[41] The legislator, however, is the sovereign legislative power, or *imperium*, recognizing "no superior power on earth"; and the legislator is the king in Parliament. The author of these acts, Henry's Chancellor Thomas Cromwell, was well in-

quently preached strict obedience to princes, irrespective of their legitimacy (Köstlin, *Life of Luther*, 141–57, 178, 202, 251, 289).

38. *New Cambridge Modern History*, 2: 75–76; Lea, *A History of Auricular Confession*, 1: 180, 292ff., 581, where Church spokesmen frankly acknowledge that revenue is the object of indulgences.

39. *New Cambridge Modern History*, 2: 75–76.

40. The Marsilian inspiration of this policy is suggested by the fact that its author, Thomas Cromwell, caused the *Defensor pacis* to be translated for use in his struggle with the papists (Elton, *Reform and Renewal*, 171, 195). According to Elton, "Cromwell thoroughly shared the anticlerical feeling that in the reign of Henry VIII dominated so much of English public life: he hated 'the snuffing pride of prelates'" (171).

41. Ibid., 176ff., 182ff.

formed about affairs on the Continent and understood that if Henry's assertion of national sovereignty was to succeed, it would need the support of the commons as well as of the gentry and aristocracy represented in Parliament.[42] The German pattern was to redistribute vast Church lands—in England, about one-third of the realm—to the gentry and aristocracy in order to secure their interest in the new religion and to reform the Roman religion to satisfy the people. Cromwell developed a plan for gradual transition to the reformed religion and began forming alliances with German princes against Spain and France.[43] But Henry, fearing perhaps the power of Spain, decided to retain the Catholic orthodoxy, liturgy, and ecclesiastical regiment, with himself as English pope. Henry had Cromwell beheaded for heresy, and in 1539 the Six Articles decreed Catholic orthodoxy. This half-measure, which seems to have been no more than a temporary expedient ripe for exploitation by papal agents or domestic reformers, was a fateful indecision that haunted the English constitution for the next century. Henry's daughter Mary, a fervent Catholic, took England back into the papal orbit, till Elizabeth took it out again; but like her father, Elizabeth temporized with reform. This set the stage for rebellion against the Stuarts, who lacked the Tudor mettle.

Once the religious wars began on the Continent, the future of England was thought to be closely linked with the success of Protestant armies.[44] Elizabeth's Chancellors Burleigh and Bacon resumed Cromwell's initiatives to create ties with German principalities. Bacon arranged the marriage of James's daughter Elizabeth to the elector Palatine in 1620. The magnificent ceremonies he organized seemed to seal a military alliance with this geopolitically crucial German prin-

42. Ibid., 170–71, 199. Although Elton does not draw attention to the fact, Cromwell's church politics had a long history in England revolving about the king, the pope, and the barons. King John and Innocent III clashed over English internal politics, leading to John's excommunication in 1209, the reduction of England to a papal fiefdom in 1211, and the annulment of the Magna Carta in 1217 and 1225. The Act in Restraint of Appeals to Rome specifically refers to the Statute of Praemunire (1353, 1365), which forbade appeals of English clergy to the Holy See.

43. Ibid., 184–85. See *New Cambridge Modern History*, 2: 238, 241–42, 457–58, for Cromwell's contacts with courts in the Schmalkaldic League. The consistency of Cromwell's policy shows too in his initiation of reforms at Cambridge, where he undertook to replace Scholasticism with an Erasmian humanism. See Elton, *Reform and Renewal*, 40–47.

44. Hallam, *Constitutional History*, 1: 377–89; S. R. Gardiner, *The First Two Stuarts and the Puritan Revolution*, 63ff.

cipality, but James declined Bacon's lead and watched idly as his son-in-law was defeated in Bohemia. Even so, the issue of this marriage came to the English throne when Elizabeth's great-grandson, George I, was invited to establish the Hanoverian dynasty in 1712. Ghibelline influence was also present in England through the Dutch stadholder. William III of Orange, called to the throne in 1689, was descended from the brilliant commander William the Silent, who relinquished his German titles to become the Netherlands' warlord. In general, the political bearing of dynastic marriages and alterations from Henry VIII forward tended away from Spanish and French connections and toward German dynasties. It is therefore not surprising that Ghibelline politics should have left its mark on English politics.

Republican and Ghibelline Politics in England

The Great Rebellion against Charles Stuart culminated sixty years' struggle between king and Parliament to find acceptable settlements of contentious constitutional and ecclesiastical questions. Charles could not endure to have his absolute powers trimmed; Parliament would no longer tolerate them: that was the gist of the conflict. The Parliament that assembled in 1640 was not consciously republican, in the sense that it wished to abandon monarchy; but it was decidedly republican in its determination to have a limited monarchy. This was the message they had sent to the king in the Petition of Right (1620); by the impeachment of the king's ministers; and in the ship-money dispute. When Parliament sat in 1640, the Scottish Assembly, under leadership of the duke of Argyle, had thrown down the gauntlet to the king's supremacy by replacing episcopacy with Presbyterianism. Charles's weakness appeared when the army he called to put down the rebellion proved to be ineffective. Parliament, led by John Pym and John Hampden, took the initiative by impeaching and executing Lord Chancellor Strafford for treason. Later Charles saw his other great minister, Archbishop Laud, impeached and executed. Encroachment followed encroachment, and Charles was compelled to choose his ministers from men approved by Parliament. Finally came the Grand Remonstrance, Charles's abortive attempt to arrest its framers in Parliament, the drawing of swords, and Parliament's making a Great Seal to signify its supremacy.

A distinguished historian of the last century called this plainly revolutionary Parliament "conservative." This was true in several respects. Moderate leaders such as Lord Faulkland and Edward Hyde, later Lord Clarendon, could have been placated had Charles comprehended his unpopularity and come to terms. He did neither. Those who were chiefly concerned about Laud's defense of episcopacy and persecution of Calvinists might have been mollified by reforms proposed in the Grand Remonstrance. The conservatism of the moderates showed when the fighting began, for they joined the king. The conservatism of the religious showed in their insistence on imposing a new orthodoxy once events gave them the upper hand. The parliamentary leaders Pym and Hampden can scarcely be described as conservative. But their deaths in 1643, and the desertion of the moderates to the royalist camp, left Parliament with few skilled politicians to conduct its business and fight its wars.[45] Consequently it stumbled between events, turned first this way by the commonwealth men, now another way by the godly people. There being no settled policy, politico-religious imagination generated innumerable nostrums, including various forms of millenarian communism.

It is idle to nominate spokesmen for a revolution whose course was so erratic. The beliefs and career of Oliver Cromwell are its typical event, if it may be said to have one. Nevertheless, there were three prominent spokesmen for the republicanism that Parliament was unwilling or unable to implement—John Milton, James Harrington, and Henry Parker. Milton was probably the most thoughtful, certainly the most forceful expositor of the parliamentary cause as a politics of the Christian commonwealth. Like Cromwell, he was loyal to the gentry from which he sprang; and like Cromwell, he was one of the few men who were able to sustain a stable vision of a republic dedicated to the perfection of theological virtue. Milton's lofty tone and tough, discerning vindication of Christian liberty against oppression, sacred or secular, dignified the parliamentary cause. Yet, as Macaulay remarked, Milton was not a Puritan. His erudition and love of learning, his baroque literary style, his freedom from doctrinal entanglements and casuistry, his cosmopolitan friendships with learned and scientific men throughout Europe placed him well beyond the limits of the Puritan mind. Richard Baxter, a bellwether Presbyterian clergyman, initially opposed the rebellion, as most Puritans did, and only swung around in support because of the licentiousness he saw in the camps of Cavalier armies. But Milton supported the rebellion from the beginning, for republican and religious reasons. Baxter, like most Puritans and the mass of the English people, was horrified by the execution of Charles I. Though Milton would have advised against the deed, he defended it once the irrevocable act had occurred. Baxter thought Cromwell a usurper, while

45. J. H. Hexter, *The Reign of King Pym*, 66ff.

Milton became his secretary during the Protectorate. Baxter embodied the Puritan suspicion of "heathen learning" and was no enthusiast of the new science. Milton was saturated in the classics and made a pilgrimage to see Galileo. Above all, the consistency of Milton's defense of freedom of conscience was unusual. For many Puritans in England and the American colonies, freedom of conscience meant the obligation to replace episcopal enforced conformity by Presbyterian enforced conformity. Here again the contrast with Baxter is instructive. For all his revulsion at Laud's Arminian doctrine and persecutions, Baxter did not doubt that a Christian monarch was obliged by Heaven to police the orthodoxy of his subjects.[46] Milton's Christian liberty was less Calvinist and more republican. His Adam lost Paradise by a real act of free choice, and his descendants regain it by the same means. Cherishing Christian liberty requires that the faculty of choice be protected, although the Christian commonwealth affirms Christian virtue as the only wise and religious object of the will.

If soteriology linked Milton's republicanism to Christianity, Harrington's republicanism was thoroughly political. He and his companions in the Rota mistook Machiavelli for their Bible, and they aimed at Roman *virtù* based on the freeholder's armed defense of his worldly property. His prescriptions were directed to the gentry, which he wished to enlarge by dissolving the peerage and redistributing their estates. His thoughts on the relations between liberty, property, and political power approach the positions argued by Ireton and Cromwell in the Putney debates. Though he and his companions exercised limited influence—Cromwell thought his politics too "heathen"—Harrington's republicanism later enjoyed a posthumous existence as the "Old Whig" critique of the "New Whig" corruptions of liberty attributed to the Walpole government.

Henry Parker and his colleague Henry Robinson espoused a version of republicanism that deserves recognition as a prototype of the commercial republic. Harrington's armed independent freeholder, ever vigilant of his virtue, is replaced by collaborating commercial and landed interests operating within the constitutional arrangement of parliamentary supremacy. In a voluminous outpouring of tracts, Parker and Robinson drew attention to the importance of commerce and institutional change for a proper understanding of England's altered constitution and position in the comity of European nations. Both men were influential in Parliament throughout the revolutionary period; Parker became secretary to Cromwell and was among those responsible for

46. Richard Schlatter, *Richard Baxter,* 14–15, 22ff.

drafting the Navigation Act (1651), that landmark recognition of England's commercial rivalry with the Dutch.[47]

Harrington, Parker, and Hobbes were representative of the English *politiques*, then known as Erastians. However else they might disagree, they were agreed in the Ghibelline principle that the right to regulate ecclesiastical institutions belongs to the political sovereign. Parker, who declared for religious liberty, was as energetic in his attack on religious sectaries, especially the Puritans, as were Harrington or Hobbes. It was of such men that the broadminded Gilbert Burnet said that they "pretended to little or no religion, and acted only upon the principles of civil liberty."[48] But it was Hobbes who in his own time was singled out by friend and foe alike for having drawn the last consequences of Erastian doctrine.

Hobbes was the witty, argumentative son of an obscure clergyman

47. W. K. Jordan, *Men of Substance: A Study of the Thought of Two English Revolutionaries, Henry Parker and Henry Robinson*, 31–36, 66ff. Jordan recognizes the Erastianism common to Parker and Hobbes, inclusive of their detestation of the clerical spirit (73, 85, 141). He rates the "triumph of religious toleration . . . a victory opposed most violently . . . by the incendiary sects of the age." For a profile of the Erastians influential in framing commercial policy during the Protectorate, see Jordan's *The Development of Religious Toleration in England*, 2: 265–75; Maurice Ashley, *Financial and Commercial Policy under the Cromwellian Protectorate*, 26–37; Charles Wilson, *Profit and Power: A Study of England and the Dutch Wars*, 52–57; Trevor-Roper, *Religion, the Reformation and Social Change*, 358ff. Among the challengers of Erastian influence were the Levellers, who held for abolition of all monopolies and privileges, and complete freedom of trade. This doctrine was to have a future; see below, 484–92.

48. Gilbert Burnet, *History of His Own Times*, 1: 124. Other Erastians according to Burnet were Henry Martin, John Seldon, Algernon Sidney, and Harrington's close associate, Henry Neville. Of Henry Martin, Burnet wrote that "he never entered on matters of religion, but on design to laugh at both of them and all morality; for he was both an impious and a vicious man" (1: 291). Harrington and Neville were accused by Puritans of the Long Parliament of atheism and blasphemy (Jordan, *The Development of Religious Toleration*, 1: 256). Such assessments of politicals were common among clergymen. The Catholic apologist Botero said of them that "they profess to prefer temporal to ecclesiastical peace and the political state to the kingdom of God, to exclude Christ our Lord and his Holy Gospel from the councils of state, and finally to adapt their deliberations not to the law of God but to present occasions. This is the prudence of this world, which Saint Paul calls the enemy of God . . . and the earth is full of this sort of men, and they have thrown Christianity into confusion and ruin" (quoted by Bouwsma, *Venice and the Defense of Republican Liberty*, 300).

from Malmesbury. As a youth he distinguished himself in classical studies and at eighteen became a client of the Cavendish family, whom he
served all his life. The Cavendishes were to science in England nearly
what Peiresc was to French science. Sir Charles, a mathematician, introduced Hobbes to Bacon, Galileo, and the Peiresc network in France.[49]
When the war commenced, Hobbes was "the first of them that fled,"
mainly because he feared reprisals for his vigorous anti-Parliament tract,
The Elements of Law. During his Paris exile, he associated with the
Gassendi circle and tutored the crown prince. When the *Leviathan* appeared in 1651, it seemed to some Cavaliers treasonous, and Hobbes fled
back to England, where Cromwell's publicist, Marchemont Nedham,
was printing large parts of *De cive* to support the government position
on the Engagement controversy.[50] But Hobbes patched up his estrange-
ment from the court, and when General Monck invited Charles II to
England, he had the satisfaction of witnessing the Presbyterian leader
place on the throne a king whom he had taught.

It is not easy to tell whether Hobbes succeeded despite or because of
his notoriety, which he evidently enjoyed.[51] The celebrity of his cynicism matched Machiavelli's reputation for suspecting the worst and
finding it. In any case, Hobbism turned up in many places. The loose
morals and scoffing of Charles II's companions and the young blades
who imitated the court were often attributed to his bad influence. But
equally Hobbism popped up in the sermons of respectable Socinian
bishops of the 1680s. Recent studies of pamphlet literature have shown
that Hobbes's writings were a major factor in turning public opinion
stoutly against "enthusiasm" by 1700.[52] This is not surprising, since he

---

49. Miriam M. Reik, *The Golden Lands of Thomas Hobbes,* 67–68, 81–82.
50. Ibid., 83–84.
51. In his witty autobiographical poem, Hobbes wrote with evident relish that
    the clergy regarded *Leviathan* as "quasi monstrum horrendum informae,
    omni rationis lumines destitutem" (*Opera Latina,* 1: xxxvi). Further, "Interea
    doctrinam ejus academici et ecclesiastici condemnabant fere omnes; lauda-
    bant nobiles et viri docti ex laicis" (1: xvii; also xxvi, xxviii). These and simi-
    lar statements reveal a mind fully conscious of its wicked anticlericism.
52. John Redwood, *Reason, Ridicule and Religion,* 34, 70, 73–78. Burnet's ap-
    praisal of Hobbes's intention and influence (discussed below, 208–9) ex-
    pressed the consensus among Latitudinarians. The consensus was stated in
    the first Boyle Lectures, delivered in 1692 by Richard Bentley, then chaplain
    to Bishop Stillingfleet and subsequently Master of Trinity College, Cam-
    bridge. Bentley's lectures, entitled *Confutation of Atheism,* attacked Hobbes,
    Spinoza, and Descartes as the three fonts of irreligion. Hobbes was espe-
    cially singled out because "not one English infidel in a hundred was other

authored the most penetrating, consistent critique of ecclesiastical politics of his time. Unlike Grotius before him or Locke after, Hobbes did not conciliate or compromise. His jarring bluntness was not calculated to win friends, as he was aware: "I know, by experience, how much greater thanks will be due than paid me, for telling men the truth of what men are."[53]

The truth Hobbes compassed in the course of his study of the Judeo-Christian heritage was the leaden impact on public life of the "ordinary ignorance, stupidity, and superstition of mankind" (*Leviathan,* 289). His writings anatomize these ordinary weaknesses. On his showing, everything hallowed and holy is rank with trifling ignorance, sublimated revenge, despair, and vainglory. The Hobbesian man, more often than not, is a sick animal who deposits his self-loathing in sepulchers adorned with fine words and art. The symptoms of this sickness—the "disease of the state"—are religion and the moral illusion. Like narcotics, they relieve the morbidity of self-loathing by transporting the soul into "fairy kingdoms" where weakness is magically rewarded. But there is a cost— perpetual civil strife and war between nations. Despite this dismal picture, Hobbes was no pessimist; he believed that the symptoms could be arrested by the political arts, even if the disease was incurable. He boasted that he was the first to put morality and politics on a scientific footing. He claimed too much, no doubt. But if we measure his achievement against the classics, as he did in making his claim, we may say that his innovation was fundamental and drastic. His political science laid bare most of the presuppositions of the commercial republic.

It is easier to enumerate those presuppositions than to display their consequences graphically or to exhibit their operation in the new model political thought that Hobbes set in train. Indeed, he is yet today so controversial a thinker that mere descriptions of his doctrine are likely to provoke demurrers meant to protect some vulnerable spot in contemporary political consciousness. Similarly, the story of the triumph of Hobbism in practice is also the story of opposition to it. To thread our way through this thicket, it will be helpful to take our bearings from modern critics.

Ferdinand Tönnies and C. B. Macpherson judged Hobbes with socialist eyes, while Leo Strauss probed with a classical lens, but they

---

than a Hobbist." Bentley claimed that Hobbists were to be found everywhere—in "taverns and coffee-houses, nay, Westminster Hall, and the very Churches" (James Monk, *The Life of Richard Bentley,* 1: 38, 41). As for Hobbism in Westminster and the churches, see Schlatter, *Richard Baxter,* 15.

53. Hobbes, *EWH,* 1: xii.

agreed that Hobbes was the architect of "bourgeois society" or "liberal politics." They also largely agreed on its characterization, which may be displayed in eight cardinal theses:

(1) man is not by nature sociable;

(2) his behavior is "egoistic," or self-interested;

(3) it follows that political association is "artificial," or factitious, and that the state cannot be a "community";

(4) the state cannot effectively or legitimately be concerned with "virtue," "community," or "goods of the soul," because such goods are essentially private;

(5) the state is a tool for promoting the pursuit of private ends insofar as they are mutually compatible;

(6) the common good is rationally defined by the existence conditions for the pursuit of private ends;

(7) these conditions pertain partly to the administration of justice, partly to obtaining the material means of "commodious existence";

(8) economic activity is the legitimate (peaceable) means of obtaining the means of existence.

All of these theses are prominent in Hobbes's writings. Since numerous scholars have scouted them attentively, there is no need to repeat that effort. Our attention is directed instead to the reflections that made these extraordinary presuppositions seem evident. The clue is provided by detractors and admirers alike, who suggest that Hobbes's political prescriptions arose as the negative residue of his thorough repudiation of ecclesiastical politics.

Hobbes's Critique of Ecclesiastical Politics

True to the Ghibelline tradition, Hobbes plainly declared his political interest, which was to defend the sovereignty of the court against ecclesiastical encroachments. He legitimated his doctrine by appeal to the *imperium* policies of Henry VIII and Elizabeth and tossed in a reference to Frederick II for good measure (*Leviathan*, 455–56, 458). Though he rejected Thomas Cromwell's king-in-Parliament concept of sovereignty, he affirmed the doctrine that Cromwell laid down as the basis of *imperium*: there is no law but the positive enactments of the sovereign, whose legislative fiat is encumbered by no limit.

Hobbes's defense of the prince falls into two main works, the *Leviathan* and its monster cousin, *Behemoth*. In the *Leviathan* he took aim at the most recent authorized version of papal claims, authored by Cardinal Bellarmine, who also worked out the papal epistemology that encroached on astronomy—a fact upon which Hobbes did not fail to

comment (450). The Protestant appeal from secular law to sacred conscience also received its most systematic rebuttal in *Leviathan*. In the
Behemoth, which Hobbes wrote during the Restoration and was forbidden to publish, he criticized ecclesiastical politics through a history of
the civil war.

The disputed question he defined as whether the Bible denies the
right of princes to regulate the clergy and the religion of their subjects
(*Leviathan*, 243, 254, 324ff., 342). Like Marsilius, he laid it down that
the argument was about the bare sense of Scripture. The ground rules
for conducting the dispute were that "natural reason" is the "undoubted
word of God"; if supernatural revelation surpasses reason in some
points, yet nowhere is it contrary to reason (242). This premise puts the
knee to reason into the spine of Bible interpretation and compels it to
deliver reasonable oracles. A second doctrine, that God is incomprehensible, closes the escape route opened by the admission of supernatural
revelation; for Hobbes claimed that the mysteries of religion must not
be interpreted, but swallowed whole like a pill.

Superstition

Since superstition was the root of ecclesiastical politics, Hobbes was
obliged to expose its deceptions. The deceptions consisted of errors of
fact easily seen through, but made unassailable by the wall of sanctity
surrounding them. To break the spell, Hobbes adopted an authorial
posture of relentless yet irenic cynicism as he demolished the Kingdom
of God. Rather than mounting a frontal assault, he deployed the expressive modes of irony and mockery to profane it verse by verse; but an
oceanic indifference prevailed at those peak moments of horror when
the weakness of everything religious was panoramically displayed.[54]

His initial premises do not differ in any substantial way from the
Cartesian system—the world is a machine of matter in motion. As
Hobbes put it with Olympian finality: "The world . . . is corporeal,
that is to say, body; and hath the dimensions of magnitude, namely,
length, breadth, and depth: also every part of body, is likewise body,
and hath the like dimensions; and consequently every part of the universe, is body, and that which is not body, is no part of the universe:
and because the universe is all, that which is no part of it, is *nothing;* and
consequently, *nowhere.*"[55] It follows that there are no incorporeal spirits;

54. See especially chapter 12, on religion, in *Leviathan*.
55. *Leviathan*, 440. This celebrated statement scandalized Hobbes's contemporaries. Richard Bentley castigated Hobbes's retention of the word "God" for
the material world as "a mere sham to get his book printed" (Monk, *The Life
of Richard Bentley*, 1: 41).

the very expression is a contradiction. Yet there are spirits—corporeal spirits—particularly the human soul, which consists of minute bodies too rare to be perceived by the senses. The vulgar, ignorant of intangible corporeality, superstitiously imagine these spirits to be immaterial. From this error springs the "disordered imagination" that mistakes "phantasms" or "idols of the brain" for real beings endowed with causal efficacy (*Leviathan,* 418–19, 426, 440). When disordered imagination is mingled with fear, ambition, and fraud, they produce the "kingdom of darkness" where immortal souls are harried in this life, hear voices and see apparitions, and suffer torment beyond the grave. But in truth the human soul is naturally corporeal and mortal and perishes entirely at death.[56]

All this Hobbes had from the "undoubted word of God," his own natural reason. It appears to conflict with that other revelation, Holy Scripture; but since he postulated, with the theologians, that the two orders of truth cannot conflict, he was obliged to show that the Bible teaches nothing contrary to natural reason. Hobbes's reversal of the theological presumption that the Bible is certain while the deliverances

---

56. *Leviathan,* 295. In his essay on Hobbes's eschatological thought, J. G. A. Pocock suggests tentatively that Hobbes's mortalism was inspired by the politically radical sectarians and higher criticism current in England around 1650. However, on more exact comparison of Hobbes's doctrine with the spiritualist materialism of Overton and Winstanley, he concludes that "Hobbes does not share the outlook of these men; it can quite conclusively be shown that his thought does not rest on belief in the primacy of the spirit, but on denial of this belief" (Pocock, *Politics, Language and Time,* 176). This is true but not the whole truth, for Hobbes asserted that "spirit" is the superstitious designation for psychological processes of a wholly material kind, as Pocock sometimes seems to admit. But he resists ascribing to Hobbes a materialistic atheism because he thinks such views "belong properly to the nineteenth century" (177). This does seem to beg the question; there were materialists in antiquity.

Similar objections apply to Eldon Eisenach's attempt to show that Hobbes situated his political doctrine and his interpretation of the Kingdom of God in sacred history as known by faith (*Two Worlds of Liberalism: Religion and Politics in Hobbes, Locke, and Mill,* 55–59). The arguments of books 3 and 4 of the *Leviathan* are to exactly the opposite effect, for they situate sacred history within profane history. The profane framework of sacred history is constituted by specifying reason, rather than the Bible, as the "undoubted word of God"; and by the doctrines of mortalism, the eternity of the human species, and the eternity and materiality of the world. Eisenach simply ignores these assertions, as he ignores Hobbes's demolition of the superstitious basis of ecclesiastical politics. It may be noted that the final position

of reason are doubtful turns his exegesis into a satire of exegesis: the staggering conclusions he drew from well-drilled platoons of citations indicate that anything can be proved from Scripture. In this way he destroyed the independent authority of the Bible and indicated to the sovereign that the Bible can be used to support whatever doctrine one pleases.

Hobbes argued that the immortality of the soul is asserted nowhere in either Testament. The biblical teaching, he maintained, is that the human soul is material, and therefore naturally mortal. Its resurrection is nonetheless assured by a supernatural act of God. Belief in the natural immortality of the soul is a relic of "Greek demonology" that infected the Jews after the conquests (*Leviathan,* 405). Purgatory, which the New Testament does not mention, was "built by the Church" to provide a habitation for souls until Resurrection; but it is an empty prison, since souls are totally destroyed on death. Hobbes's examination of the meaning of "spirit" and "spirits" purports to prove that the biblical authors were materialists. They did not teach that angels and other spirits are like the superstitious pagan entities, i.e. independent spiritual substances; they taught instead that they are phantasms of the brain, or hallucinations, miraculously induced by God (421, 255–65, 418ff.). The same is true of possession by spirits, insofar as the Bible acknowledges such a thing. Hobbes thought it doubtful that the New Testament teaches eternal damnation, which is a "harsh doctrine" (298, 300, 410). He was quite certain, in any case, that no one will go to Heaven or Hell (294, 300). This because Christ will descend to earth to reign in the city of Jerusalem eternally. His views on the reprobate, in whom he had particular interest, were curious. Hell is a place outside Jerusalem (298). The wicked will marry and reproduce, "which is an immortality of the kind, but not of the persons of men" (412). In other words, they are resurrected not for life eternal, but for a second mortal life, which is "condign punishment for [their] contumacy" in the first. This process, which seems so like man's natural, pre-Resurrection condition, will continue "as long as the kind of man by propagation shall endure; which is eternally." The reproducing reprobate must be mortal, else "the earth in a small time would not have been able to afford them place to stand on" (412). A population explosion is unacceptable in Hell, even as punishment, because the reprobate share the earth with the elect, who would be affected and afflicted in their resurrected bodies.

These doctrines erected a counter-universe to the millenarian expec-

that Eisenach ascribes to Hobbes (*Two Worlds,* 67–71) is a particularly crisp summary of the secular politics commonly attributed to him.

tations and visionary politics that grew more pronounced as the fury of the English civil war increased. One of the favored verses of the Millennium Watch was Peter's prophecy of "new heavens, and a new earth, wherein dwelleth righteousness." Preached in hundreds of sermons, it was a battle cry of the New Model Army. This prophecy followed another prediction of the destruction "by fire" of the heavens and earth that are now, for the "perdition of the ungodly." Hobbes cited this wrathful prophecy to contrast with his alternative forecast. His new earth is the same old earth, with the same old unrighteous people going about their business "outside Jerusalem," i.e. everywhere. His assertion of the eternity of the human species and of the earth corrects the astronomy that prophesies cosmic disasters that incite the people to civil disorder. Here we discern the sharpest cutting edge of Hobbesian enlightenment. The messianic doctrine of the Second Coming, which Hobbes construed as the core of Christianity, presupposes that the law of causality is about to be suspended. The counter-assertion of the eternity of the earth affirms the law of causality against religious imagination and reduces the Second Coming to the triviality of Jesus ruling an insignificant town in the Middle East. In this way, reason, "the undoubted word of God," corrects the moralized history of the Jews and subdues the millenarian political intoxication of the English Puritans.[57]

57. Responding to J. G. A. Pocock's claim that Hobbes was a millenarian, Bernard Capp comments: "Hobbes was interested not in the millennium itself but in the millenarian doctrine which he used as a weapon against clerical power and pretensions. . . . By defining salvation as participation in Christ's future kingdom . . . Hobbes was able to reduce the role of the church—any church—to insignificance. He was pursuing ends diametrically opposed to those of the mass of contemporary millenarians: pushing New Jerusalem into the indefinite future, he rejected any attempt by a self-proclaimed Elect to establish a disciplinarian holy commonwealth" ("Godly Rule and English Millenarianism," 393). Pocock's evidence for Hobbes's supposed eschatological theology stems from the doctrine of Christ's future personal reign, which was indeed common to the "mainstream of Protestant thinking," but also to all Christians. However, the Protestant mainstream to which Hobbes, according to Pocock, was most closely associated was the radicalism of the Fifth Monarchists and Levellers, with whom the Anglican Hobbes was notably out of sympathy. These paradoxes lead Pocock to declare that Hobbes's "role in the Protestant tradition becomes visibly enigmatic" (Pocock, *Politics, Language and Time*, 180). This dilemma did not burden contemporary spokesmen for mainstream Protestantism, Anglican or dissenting, who classified him in the atheist mainstream. Mainstream Catholic spokesmen such as Bossuet fully concurred with this view.
    Further evidence of the rationalist character of Hobbes's criticism is that

The Kingdom of God

Ecclesiastical politics requires a priesthood that claims divine sanction for priests' authority over a laity, which they exercise for the glory of God and benefit of men. To Hobbes this was the humbug of priestcraft, "a confederacy of deceivers, that to obtain dominion over men in this world, endeavour by dark and erroneous doctrines, to extinguish in them the light, both of nature, and of the gospel" (*Leviathan,* 397). This great accusation against ecclesiastical politics is repeated unsparingly throughout *Leviathan* and *Behemoth,* with the effect that "clergyman" becomes synonymous with "imposter."

The historian is tempted to register accusations of this magnitude as preposterous abuse. The accused, after all, were honest men according to their lights; they were the consciences of their flocks. Yet this sensible response is not satisfactory. The accusation was not the personal opinion of an apologist captivated by his own hyperbole; it was fundamental to Ghibelline politics. Luther had made the same accusation in clerical form when he indicted the Papacy as Antichrist. The indictment worked itself into a significant historical datum through its assimilation to Protestant attitudes that translated into action. Hobbes's accusation requires evaluation along similar lines. He did not write as one cleric accusing others, but as a court philosopher accusing all clergymen. The difference is not trivial. Ghibelline apologists could not legitimate secular politics without accusing the clergy. As an exponent of *imperium* based on political science, Hobbes had to accuse the clergy of ignorance and fraud. This accusation, too, translated into action. It legitimated the excision of religion from public life and its relegation to private con-

---

his materialist interpretation of spirits and visions, and his psychology of religious emotions, became the core of many subsequent criticisms of religion. The first uptake was by Spinoza; the second by Locke. From these two authors, as well as Hobbes's writings, it spread to Shaftesbury, Bayle, and Fontenelle and to the Deists. Hume reproduced it, adding some nuances, and Gibbon presupposed it in writing on the superstitious ages of antiquity. Vico also assumed Hobbes's account, which came to him via Spinoza. The tradition of French materialism, culminating in d'Holbach's *Contagion sacrée,* is also Hobbist. While the many specialized studies on these numerous authors usually reveal the impact of Hobbes, there seems to be no study of the rationalist critique of superstition that is aware of its Hobbist foundation. Frank Manuel's *The Eighteenth Century Confronts the Gods* focuses on authors of secondary importance, omitting explicitly discussion of Hobbes, Spinoza, and Locke. These three names nevertheless recur frequently in his narrative.

science. It set a stigma upon any counsel clergymen might offer. Above all, it lay at the heart of Hobbes's attempt to demonstrate the fraudulence of the Kingdom of God. In this way it legitimated the secular state that subsequently developed. The documented accusation is therefore no insignificant part of history.

The Kingdom of God, Hobbes said, is no metaphor, but the literal rule of God over the descendants of Abraham, deriving from the initial covenant. The covenant was subsequently renewed by Moses, who established Israel under divine laws. Yet Moses did but comply with "the votes of the people of Israel in a peculiar manner; wherein they chose God for their king by covenant made with him, upon God's promising them the possession of the land of Canaan" (*Leviathan*, 266, 268). The covenant involved a quid pro quo. God promised the Israelites a territory provided that they destroy its idolatrous inhabitants; in return, they were to render God service. However, since God is invisible most of the time, his sovereignty was exercised mediately through the priesthood Moses founded. This arrangement of a sacerdotal kingdom continued through the period of the Judges to Saul, when the people demanded of Saul that he become king in order that Israel might be like other nations. God counseled Saul to accept this demand, "for they have not rejected thee, but they have rejected me, that I should not reign over them" (1 Samuel 8: 7). Thus did the Jews "depose God," as Hobbes's suggestive phrase has it, and terminated his reign.[58] Thereafter the kings, rather than priests, had the whole power of the state, civil and religious, in their hands, for this was the way of the gentile nations.

This constitutional condition continued, interrupted by conquests and captivity, until the coming of Jesus, who declared himself the Messiah promised by the prophets to restore the Kingdom of God, i.e. the sacerdotal rule of priests. Yet Jesus came not to restore the kingdom at that time, but came only as the Redeemer renewing the promise of the prophets; he came, in other words, to announce that the advent of the kingdom had been postponed indefinitely.[59] Jesus gave the Apostles a commission to teach, but gave them no authority to enforce their teaching or warrant to disobey any laws of the civil sovereign and the judges of Israel. Christians remained submissive to Roman authority, even

58. *Leviathan*, 78–79. The classicist and historian Count Volney commended Hobbes's assessment in a thorough study based on better sources than were available to Hobbes. See his *Histoire de Samuel, inventeur sacré des rois*, vol. 7 of *Œuvres de C. F. Volney*.

59. See *Leviathan*, chap. 42, as a whole; on Jesus as seditious, 245, 269.

under persecution, in obedience to Jesus' commission, until Constantine converted to Christianity and delegated the ancient Roman office of Pontifex Maximus to the bishop of Rome. In a short time, the bishops transformed this delegated authority into a sovereign right to order religion and even to inspect the religion and morals of the emperor. This, Hobbes declared, was the origin of ecclesiastical usurpation of civil authority (*Leviathan,* 433–34).

The political substance of a sacerdotal kingdom follows from its fundamental institutions. Since Jehovah's power and invisibility prevented him ruling in his own right, he required a human deputy to exercise the offices of political authority. However, as mere deputy to sovereign Jehovah, the authority of the chief priest depended on his ability to persuade the people, by miracles and other signs, that he conversed with Jehovah and faithfully delivered his oracles. The system might have worked had Jehovah kept the memory of the people fresh by passing many miracles through the priests, and if he had suppressed rival miracles by false prophets (282–83, 288–89). But Jehovah did no such thing, preferring rather to test the faith of his people. Consequently, the fervor of Israel waxed and waned; the people oscillated between idolatrous imitation of the ways of the gentiles, and righteous obedience to Jewish law.[60] Unable to be consistently one thing or the other, "every man did what was right in his own eyes" (314). The people wanted a king, Hobbes suggested, to protect them from the injustices of priests. But once they had a king, they played king and priest off against one another, "so that they always kept in store a pretext, either of justice or religion, to discharge themselves of their obedience, whensoever they hoped to prevail"; on such evidence Hobbes declared that "there was *never* a sovereign power in Israel" (314). The endless sedition, civil wars, and calamitous defeats by gentile invaders recorded in the Old Testament were the woes of a badly ordered polity. The division of sovereignty between powers spiritual and temporal is the legacy of the divine politics of the Mosaic covenant. The problem lies in the divine side of things. The ends and instruments of priestly rule—promises, miracles, apparitions, and colloquies with God—throw a surd into politics that places settled prudence or rational decision at the mercy of ambitious agitators calling themselves prophets; and "by this means destroying all laws, both divine and human, reduce all order, government, and so-

60. Ibid., 312. To underscore the instability of the faith of Israel, Hobbes noted that although Moses was in the mountains but forty days, still on his return he found God's chosen turned to idolatry.

ciety, to the first chaos of violence and civil war." Ecclesiastical politics is preeminently a war of all on all.[61]

It is significant for Hobbes's system that his indictment of God's commonwealth does not assume the impossibility of miracles. The political problem is the inability of Jehovah's deputies to designate a workable procedure for differentiating authentic revelation from competing specious revelations. Since it is impossible to *know* which prophets are false, the faithful accept an authoritative decision, which Hobbes believed should be the political decision of the political sovereign (*Leviathan*, 246, 254). His stricture against the hallucinations of religious chieftains is not that they are false, but that they are inherently *private;* and since exotic psychological states are the very marrow of religion, religion cannot provide stabilizing laws or political prudence.

The differentiation between private opinion and public law is at once the backbone of Hobbes's new political science and a diagnostic of the insufficiency of all previous political thought and practice. The distinction may be conceived as a counterpart to his distinctions between science and fancy. The natural condition of the human mind is a chaos produced by confused mingling of sensation, imagination, and the passions unenlightened by knowledge of the causes of things. Only the methodical application of artificial reason remedies this epistemological war of all on all. The counterparts to this chaos in public affairs are attempts to base politics on despotic will, or on claims to be "better" (aristocracy), or on private visions of the Good, or on private inspiration from Jehovah. Hobbes's concept of public reason as declared law places an objectivity requirement upon the legislator, which is that the sover-

61. Ibid., 285. Hobbes's assimilation of the Mosaic covenant to his concept of the contractual origin of government is a paradigmatic example of reinterpreting the Bible to make it agree with reason. After a detailed comparison of the Puritan notion of the covenant with Hobbes's contractual notion, Winfried Forster concludes that "Hobbes's political theory should be interpreted as a reaction against militant English Puritanism prior to the outbreak of the Civil War" ("Thomas Hobbes und der Puritanismus," 88). During the period of the Glorious Revolution, royalists denounced the notion of an original contract for government "as a republican chimera" (Hallam, *Constitutional History,* 3: 89).

In his *Tractatus theologico-politicus,* the republican Spinoza followed closely Hobbes's interpretation of Israel, including the critique of superstition that disordered the Mosaic constitution; and he concluded, like Hobbes, that the political sovereign by right exercises dominion over ecclesiastical institutions. See especially chaps. 16–18 of the *Tractatus.*

eign is "representative" of the political (and only the political) interests of his subjects. Since I will return to this point subsequently, it suffices to illustrate it with respect to the present question. In Hobbes's state, the sovereign has exclusive right to prescribe and order religion; he is the head of the national church, there being no universal church (254, 285). This right, and the corresponding submission of subjects, extends only to public and visible signs of religion, such as ritual and public confession; it does not extend to the marrow of religion, the subject's private beliefs. The sovereign may therefore require conformity, but he may not set up an inquisition to inspect conscience; for the same reasoning that disqualifies private belief from public function also protects it from illegitimate (unpolitical) incursions (428).

The systematic distinction between public law and private conscience is interwoven with the analysis of priestcraft. In a stunning chapter of *Leviathan*, "Of Religion," Hobbes expounded the sense of his accusation through observations on gentile religion. Gentile politicians, he said, manipulated popular superstition for political ends. By feigning converse with gods and by other deceits, they persuaded the multitude that the laws they wished to introduce enjoyed divine favor or authorship; and they contrived the reading of entrails of birds to suggest that their own decisions about political contingencies of the moment were commanded by the gods (73–74). This politic arrangement worked because the multitude were god-fearing, whereas the politicians looked to advantage; but it worked only when the multitude believed in the piety and honesty of their political prophets (77–78).

The circumstance that prudence, or rational consideration of advantage, must be deceitfully tacked onto religion is evidence that religion, as a condition of confused imagination, can never of its own deliver up laws—it is devoid of prudence. Wherever religion is politically efficacious, then, it is mediated by deceitful manipulation. The evidence that the Roman religion depends on such frauds is the circumstance that its oracles and dogmas tend exclusively to enhance the power of the pope.[62] But Protestant clergymen behave in no other way.[63] One sees then that Hobbes's accusation is not affected by the protest that clergymen sincerely believe their dogmas; the point is that they manipulate belief, even their own, to enhance their power. The common man, Hobbes observed, suspects fraud when clergymen do not practice what they preach (*Leviathan*, 78). But Hobbes traced fraud to the political use of religion.

---

62. *Leviathan*, 79, 376–85, 451ff.; *Behemoth* (*EWH*, 6: 222).
63. *Behemoth* (*EWH*, 6: 212ff., 257, 267, 276–81, 379, 382).

Believing as he did that superstitions "can never be so abolished out of human nature, but that new religions may again be made to spring out of them," Hobbes contrived his solution for the maximum feasible separation of politics and religion. His arrangement of outward compliance and inner freedom is a "civil worship," or a new form of politic religion.[64] The sovereign is head of his national church not because of his intimacies with God, but because he commands the sword that desires what all reasonable men must also desire, civil peace. In his capacity as subject, then, Hobbes's citizen worships as he does on entirely rational grounds that leave him free to believe privately whatever he likes. The logic of this position led Hobbes to recommend that the sovereign tolerate religious dissent, which coincided with Oliver Cromwell's own policy.[65] The dignity of conscience played no role in drawing Hobbes to this conclusion; it followed rather from the circumstance that private opinion cannot and ought not be made a public or political concern.

It is hard to imagine an arrangement that more effectively excludes religion from politics without attempting to extirpate it. Hobbes acknowledged that to succeed, it required that the people be enlightened. He suggested that the pulpit was the appropriate point of contact, and that the pulpit be reformed by reforming those seminaries of sedition, Oxford and Cambridge.[66] The king's clergy should preach that the national religion is the king's peace, and that rival doctrines were the "outworks of the enemy" that ambitious men used to cloak their designs (*Leviathan*, 2). The clergy themselves should be taught Hobbes's interpretation of Scripture, together with the materialism that underpins it.

---

64. *Leviathan*, 425ff.; also 307, 331, 336, 343, where Hobbes emphasizes that public worship pertains only to "outward signs and manners." For a concise statement of Hobbes's politic religion as Erastian doctrine, see Jordan, *The Development of Religious Toleration*, 2: 311.

Since some scholars are unsure of Hobbes's Erastianism, it is pertinent to draw attention to Richard Baxter's reading of *Leviathan:* "I speak of the evil of denying Christ's doctrine to be a law, in that most of the horrid consequences in Hobbes's book arise from that principle, *viz.*, *ergo* Christ doth but teach the Prince to command; . . . *ergo* Scripture is no further a law (saith Hobbes) than sovereigns so make it; nor ministers have any power of governing, or commanding; nor Christ any Kingdom on earth" (letter to Thomas Hill, 8 March 1652).

65. *Leviathan*, 456, where Hobbes declares for toleration of all sects.

66. Ibid., 224–25; *Behemoth* (*EWH*, 7: 212ff.). Hobbes called the universities the Trojan horse of English politics and the "core of rebellion" (*Behemoth*, 236–37).

This might seem a barren education, since it conceded so little to the religious impulse; and in fact, the Great Awakening set off by John Wesley in the 1740s was a revolt against the bloodless rational religion of the Socinian bishops. Yet Hobbes's attempt to place controls on religion was only half of his criticism of disordered imagination and superstitious causality. The other half was his analysis of morality and the controls he devised to limit its intrusions into politics.

Controlling the Moral Illusion

Ferdinand Tönnies noted that Hobbes's examination of ecclesiastical politics implied a rejection of "community" (*Gemeinschaft*). Religion thrives in the fabric of ethos, which a people tend to represent as a moral consensus; when the consensus demand transfers to religion, it becomes a requirement of orthodoxy. Hobbes's withering scrutiny of the Judeo-Christian tradition showed that the purported consensus was only a factional opinion attempting to argue away heterodoxy as schism and unrighteousness. The absence of consensus, the ineluctable heterogeneity, instability, and collision of private opinion is the fact going to show that ethos, or morality, cannot supply the basis of political association. Politics is not based on natural consensus, or ethos, but on effectively applied force. Forced consensus is "artificial," an agreement or compact that, stripped of irrational elements, would stipulate in public law the conditions of the association of citizens to their mutual advantage.

The erroneous outlook of classical authors is distilled in their belief that man is by nature social and political. The consequences of this error were so far-reaching that Hobbes confidently equated its elimination to the achievement of political science. The natural sociability thesis announces a moral interpretation of man. Moral interpretations, however, declare only how man ought to be and castigate departures from the norm as iniquitous. For Hobbes this attitude was adolescent. Political writers who adopt this position begin and end with symptoms and fail to see that their own prescriptions, far from providing any "more than vulgar prudence," merely compound the problem by adding new Oughts to the contentious field of mutually exclusive Oughts. The natural sociability authors—Hobbes had Aristotle primarily in mind—are in the awkward position of being unable to explain why their own moral theory should be unsociable in the very act of negating other moral theories.

To put the unsociability of men in a strong light, Hobbes began his analysis with the true natural condition, the "first chaos and violence of civil war." The drama of a war of all on all produced a resonating icon of the fundamental break with classical political thought, but at the cost of some confusion as to what he meant. The state of nature is not merely the condition of savages, of civilized nations in time of civil war, and so on with other examples he gave. As his analysis of ecclesiastical politics shows, the state of nature is the *typical* condition of man hitherto; and it will remain the typical condition until sovereigns and subjects learn that they are unsociable and draw the appropriate political conclusions.

The moral illusion blinds men to their unsociability. The illusion springs from the belief that the vocabulary of praise and blame refers to moral objects existing independently of private feelings and passions. Moralists unaware of this error fruitlessly attempt to derive from these supposed objects common measures of good and evil. The enlightened mind, however, has understood that "these words of good, evil, and contemptible, are ever used with relation to the person that useth them: there being nothing simply and absolutely so; nor any common rule of good and evil, to be taken from the nature of the objects themselves" (*Leviathan*, 32). If so, moral reasoning or discourse cannot provide a common standard for naming, let alone for judging actions. Janus-faced, moral discourse provides opposite appellations for one and the same action, according as it is liked or disliked. Thus, one man's justice is to another cruelty, one's courage another's recklessness, and so on. The inherent contentiousness and special pleading of moral discourse make it worthless as an analytical tool; it is useful only as a symptomology of the passions.

Hobbes ran these symptoms to the ground in a corporeal motion, peculiar to all animals, which he called "endeavour for power." This impulse impels all animals to conserve their existence and to flee death and injury. In man it diversifies into a range of psychological states and valuations, all of which express, openly or by disguise, feelings of power and impotence. On this showing, shame is "embarrassment of discovering some defect of ability in oneself." Repentance is remorse that one's actions were thwarted. Humility registers perception of infirmity. Laughter is enjoyment of the discomfiture or misfortune of others. Indignation is anger at contumely. Good will is hope of assistance. And "the end of worship is power."[67] These are some of the valuations of a creature conscious of itself as power and impotence, which are the first spring and ultimate reference of all valuation. What men praise in them-

---

67. *Leviathan*, 237, and chap. 10, passim. Hobbes's earliest statement of this psychology, in the *Elements of Law*, remains perhaps the most trenchant he wrote. It is also well expressed in *De homine*.

selves, or disparage, is nothing else than modalities of power and infirmity. Hobbes placed special emphasis on the link between power and honor. All praise and blame, all filiation and fear, are expressions of opinion of power. Each wishes to have the best opinion of himself because the "whole pleasure of the mind" consists in glorifying itself, especially by invidious comparisons with others.[68] Human sociability, then, is a perpetual competition or "race" of egos seeking to enhance their self-esteem by maximizing their powers, real and apparent. This is why they compete for wealth, public honors, and political power and do what they can to check their rivals and make them stumble in the race. The natural trajectory of the appetite for power is to have "all the world, if [it] could, to fear and obey [it]."[69] This not for the sake of security, but because "*every* man looketh that his companion should value him, at the same rate he sets upon himself; and upon all signs of contempt, or undervaluing, naturally endeavours, as far as he dares . . . to extort a greater value from his contemners, by *damage*; and from others, by example" (*Leviathan*, 81). A war of all on all, then, is the natural tendency of man's natural appetite. The tendency is checked when one or a few get the upper hand in the struggle and compel the rest to submit. Political association is the standing proof of man's unsociability. Not love and consensus, but fear, and hope of advantage, is the basis of politics. Only when these facts are comprehended, Hobbes believed, can one define the nature and scope of politics, and design institutions suitable to human nature.

True Political Science

Hobbes wrote against the background of two great traditions—the Greco-Roman and the Hebraic—that had, each in its fashion, stressed justice and virtue. He seems to have been the first thinker to free himself from their charming errors—those "idols" of the theater and of the tribe. As he noted, the labor to disburden the mind of moral prejudice is greater than the corresponding effort in natural science, because it has the heart against it.[70] The political scientist must free himself from the bewitchment of heroes and villains, from cosmic struggles of good and evil, from the glamour of power. He must be immune to the enchant-

---

68. *De cive*, I.i.2. For an analysis of this psychology, see H. Caton, "On the Basis of Hobbes' Political Philosophy," 418–28.

69. *EWH*, 7: 73.

70. See especially "Preface to the Reader," *De cive*. In *Elements of Philosophy*, Hobbes wrote that the "first grounds of all science are not only not beautiful, but poor, arid, and in appearance deformed" (*EWH*, 1: 2).

ment of shining ideals, righteousness, moral regeneration, patriotism, and ethnic solidarity. He must even look down on these things with a certain indulgent contempt, as signs of human weakness and delusion. In every shining ideal he discerns the campaign to crush a competing ideal. He discerns the debris of victims crushed by the bear hug of solidarity. He observes that the wicked whom the righteous persecute out of the world are often no worse than their persecutors. He notices that the weak, and the losers in the struggle for power, are esteemed the only criminals. He discerns the "robust child" in the mightiest monarch. He must have the cold blood and iron nerve to comprehend the appalling chaos of man's natural condition. Then, as the body servant of the sovereign, he begins the creative work of bringing order from the chaos. He does not go about it with Bacon's high-spirited dash, calling help to his standard with promises of intoxicating power: Hobbes was not infatuated with power. He goes about it with a sober, candid toughness meant to inflict no more pain than necessary on the psyche already badly battered by his criticisms.

The problem is to contain the chaos. The overall plan is to establish a hierarchy of values, which legitimates and channels necessary impulses along mutually compatible paths, while repressing impulses destructive of civil life, i.e. civil peace.

The first order of business is to settle the question of justice. Citizens are to understand the exact purpose and conditions of the social contract they are compelled to sign. They are to understand that the whole contrivance of justice and the institutions of the state, regardless of their awesome trappings, are nothing more than rules of expediency and convenient arrangements for securing the safety and welfare of the citizens. They are to understand that their rational self-interest is to keep the compact, but likewise that they must be coerced to sign on, and coerced to law-abidingness, owing to natural impulses that generate the chaos for which the state is a remedy. They are apprised that the contract they sign will certainly be unfair to some; for justice is possible only by arbitrarily adopting a particular set of values from among the many competing values, and crushing the opposition if it cannot be conciliated. Public justice is recommended not because it is perfect, but because it is the alternative to chaos. There is nothing heroic, sublime, righteous, or idealistic about the social contract. It is a deal to be struck by a tough bargainer jealous of his interests but alert to their limits.

The citizen agrees to abandon his private notions of good and evil and accept public law as the norm for his actions. It is normative for him, however, only in his public capacity, as an artificial citizen of the state; the sovereign therefore does not require that he abandon private fancies that the citizen cannot help entertaining. In exchange for this compliance, the sovereign guarantees the life and safety of the citizen. In addition to this vertical relation between citizen and sovereign, the contract constructs a horizonal relation between contracting citizens. Since each citizen agrees to comply with the law for the sake of his own safety, the condition of his submission implies expectation that all other citizens are equally obedient. The safety of all, then, requires the equal submission of all. This circumstance generates the basic premise of the rule-of-law state that citizens are all equal in their claim to the natural rights of life and liberty and in their entitlement to equal application of the law. There can be no enclaves of privileged exemption, as canon law exempts ecclesiastics, and as class once privileged the aristocracy. Hobbesian rule of law thus imparts a democratic bias to politics.

Analysis of the use of political coercion enabled Hobbes to deduce a surprising list of liberties and judicial restraints that came to be engrafted into the polities of Europe. Judicial torture and forced confessions are ruled out because no one can be conceived to will his own damage. Slavery and forced labor are ruled out for the same reasons. There can be no retroactive laws; and wherever the law is silent, citizens may act to their discretion (*Leviathan*, 143). The innocent may not be punished, nor may a judge refuse to hear proof (87, 182, 196). Crimes committed under threats of death are excused, while crimes committed with the tacit approval of the sovereign are extenuated (197, 199). Law must aim at equity and punishment must aim at deterrence (203). One liberty the citizen does not enjoy, however, is the right of participation in government. While Hobbes acknowledged the appetite for politics in "every man" (150), the tendency of his politics was to discourage or redirect it. Here Hobbes parted company with the republican tradition of Machiavelli and Harrington. Their defense of power balanced between the people and the aristocracy, and their seductive depictions of manly, dashing citizens keen on public affairs, were for him signs of infatuation with the glamour of power.[71] He rejected republicanism not out of a contrary infatuation with monarchy, but because he believed the republican "balance" was a standing invitation to faction and civil tumult. In republican government, public-spiritedness enjoys respectability and prestige—and provides the ambitious a convenient cover to advance their private interests at the expense of public order. Ancient republics

71. *Leviathan*, 214. Spinoza, though a republican, agreed with Hobbes on this point, and shared in particular Hobbes's low opinion of the republicanism of the English parliament. See below, 208–9, for Bishop Burnet's appraisal of Hobbes's intention and influence.

had established a solid record of incessant foreign wars and colonialization, culminating in the Pax Romana, which extinguished the free cities of the Mediterranean. A political science aiming at peace should therefore seek to confine participation and public spirit to a small compass.

If Hobbes deprived citizens of participation, he did equip them with a remarkable array of liberties that extended the latitude of private action much farther than any republic theretofore had allowed. Of these, one especially highlights the scientific character of Leviathan: the status of capital crimes. According to the social contract, the citizen enters society to preserve his life; but when capital sentence is pronounced, the condemned man's natural right to life is, from the sovereign's point of view, abrogated. But since safety is the purpose of the contract, Hobbes declared, the situation reverts to the state of nature: the condemned man and the sovereign are on equal footing, and each may justly destroy the other (91–92, 196–97). Neither the character of the crime, nor actual guilt or innocence, have any bearing on the question. Should the accused succeed in overthrowing the sovereign to save himself, he cannot be said to have committed injustice, however iniquitous he might have been. The same reasoning holds for deserters or for those who refuse military service; their acts are dishonorable, but not unjust, since the natural right to life excuses. Even so, the sovereign may justly have them hanged.

This amazing impartiality proves Hobbes's freedom from bias even toward established justice, let alone patriotism and codes of honor. The impartiality was not a private attitude, but followed from the logic of his system. Political association is a contractual relation for mutual advantage. When an absolute conflict of right occurs, the contract is dissolved and the parties return to their precontractual status (214). By refusing to paper over this conflict with excuses, Hobbes emphasized that the world order is not moral, but a competitive striving of wills. People will not learn to live in peace by trying to improve their virtue; they must instead learn "how to be bad"—how to channelize their nonmoral, necessary power-strivings so that they are as far as possible mutually compatible. The best channel for badness, Hobbes thought, is work and accumulation of wealth (163–65, 226–27). Dr. Johnson expressed it in an epigram: "Men are rarely so innocently employed, as when they are making money."

Leviathan: A Popular Mercantile Monarchy

It has often been noted that Hobbes's writings contain substantial elements of Whig or Liberal political doctrine, under whose auspices the commercial republic developed in England and America. The notion of natural equality and natural rights, the model of the human being as a competitive individual, the legalist approach to politics, the repudiation of natural or moral limits on the accumulation of national wealth—in these ways and more Hobbes prepared the ground for subsequent developments. Yet they occurred within the framework of republican government, and Hobbes was no republican. This perplexity of situating Hobbes under current political rubrics was unintentionally expressed by Tönnies when he declared that Hobbes was equally the father of liberalism and socialism. A related approach, worked out in detail by C. B. Macpherson, interprets *Leviathan* as the description of the newly born "market society" that succeeded the feudal order. Hobbes is said to be a theorist who tells the "rising" bourgeois how to put their house in order. Since Macpherson's approach is representative of a current line of thinking, a few comments on it may be useful.

To exhibit Hobbes as a conscious theorist of the "market society," in which value is determined by impersonal market price, Macpherson must systematically replace Hobbes's apparent object, political society, with an economic object; for him the political sovereign becomes the despotism of the market, and political equality is equal subjection, not to civil law, but to the market.[72] Macpherson is undaunted by Hobbes's ignorance of the phrase "market society" and his preoccupation with religious disorders; *Behemoth* seems to him a description of England "as a fairly complete market society."[73] As for Hobbes's recognition of the market and its mechanism, he finds it in chapter 10 of *Leviathan*. Although this chapter opens with a definition of political power and appraises power relations throughout in terms of the individual psychology of harm and benefit, Macpherson construes "power" to mean the impersonality of market exchange.[74] Although Hobbes traced the natural condition of unsociability and war to the necessary collision of selfish wills unintimidated by superior power, Macpherson takes it to be an expression of the artificial "market morality."[75] Although Hobbes is alleged to be a "more or less conscious" analyst of a unique historical development, Macpherson admits that Hobbes's universalist treatment of political society rendered the market society he described indistinguishable from Greece or Rome.[76] Macpherson notes the anomaly that this alleged theorist of bourgeois society failed to identify the bour-

72. C. B. Macpherson, *The Political Theory of Possessive Individualism*, 89, 106, 272.
73. Ibid., 66.
74. Ibid., 39–40, 45, 55.
75. Ibid., 40–41, 65.
76. Ibid., 38, 46, 67, 88.

geoisie or their class function; indeed, his theory abstracts from class altogether.[77] Macpherson does not conclude from this remarkable fact that Hobbes meant his science to be class-neutral; instead he reproaches Hobbes for not recognizing class bias that Macpherson's superior wisdom knows must be there. Other anomalies obtrude. Hobbes drew attention to the fact that trade and commerce in England were clogged by government regulation, protectionism, monopolies, and privileges. These practices are correctly characterized as "mercantilist economics," which is clearly distinct from the "market society" construct as drawn from Marx's descriptions of England two centuries after the publication of *Leviathan.*[78]

Macpherson's interpretation serves a moral purpose which he often insinuates and sometimes formulates: "If the real basis of Hobbes's political obligation is . . . the rational perception of men in possessive market society that they are all irretrievably subject to the determination of the market, then the somewhat inhuman flavor of Hobbes's political obligation is at once explained and justified."[79] Hobbes the realist troubles utopian dreams, secular and religious. To turn the flank of this danger, and even to parlay Hobbes's realism into a help to idealism, his analysis of political society as such is construed to be an analysis of a contingent historical society.

If we discard anachronistic periodizations, and discard as well the mirror epistemology, with its conviction that political writers, however they may contradict one another, nevertheless "reflect society," we may arrive at a better estimate of Hobbes's thoughts on economics. "Capitalistic" elements are certainly present, not however as "reflections" but as a political program that wants execution. We have noticed the striking modernity of Colbert's royal mercantilist policies, which he carried out in the teeth of opposition from the French bourgeoisie, *officiers,* and aristocracy. Similarly, Hobbes accepted the mercantilist policies of the Tudor and Stuart dynasties. For him, as for mercantilist writers generally, the primary phenomenon was not commerce, but the political arrangements that tend best to enhance commerce to the benefit of national power. The idea of an economics independent of political aims and requisites did not occur in this period; hence, the concept of a "market society" was alien to it. By putting the accent on politics, where it belongs, we find that Hobbes, far from contriving a state to the advantage of a particular class, laid the groundwork for a social order in

77. Ibid., 93, 99–100.
78. Ibid., 53, 62.
79. Ibid., 106.

which inherited class would be replaced by stratification of socially mobile individuals. For in defining politics as a system for mutual advantage operating under law, he shifted the legitimacy of the state from the aristocracy and clergy to the people. The sense of the shift as it concerned the clergy should now be clear. They stood accused of fomenting civil strife and of duping the people. Their instruments of rule had been exposed to public view and their doctrine was in ruins. Their one remaining legitimate function was to preach what the king commanded them to preach. Hobbes's politics was nearly as severe with the aristocracy. The thesis of natural equality, together with its implications, undermined the aristocratic claim to privileges on the basis of birth. The equality doctrine is not an assertion of equal worth; instead, it establishes a new rank order of values that gives first priority to what is common and necessary. All have a right to life, and, moreover, a life that is not miserable; hence, the leading purpose of the social contract is life secure and commodious for all. His new rank order of values discarded the divine right theory and substituted the assertion that the sovereign rules by consent of the people—the thesis for which Hobbes's books were burned at Oxford in 1683. The sovereign is the "representative" of the people and rules in their name, according to the principle that their safety is the supreme law. Wars of glory and ambition, the vice of kings, are not compatible with this principle; the king is better advised to pursue a policy of peace and prosperity, to be obtained by "labor and thrift."

Hobbes acknowledged the necessity for institutionalized inequality, but he declined to ground aristocratic privilege on expediency or merit. It was enjoyed as a "free gift," by grace of the sovereign, which he compared to chance (*Leviathan*, 115). This downgrading of aristocratic legitimacy was followed by a denial of Aristotle's view that some men are by nature more worthy to command (100). In numerous passages he spoke sharply against arrogance and contumely, and obliged the sovereign to restrain it (94–101, 224ff.). Although the equality thesis contains no assertion of equal worth, it does contain a demand for recognition of worth: "And even if [all] are not equal," he wrote, "still they think they are." Those who trample down the self-esteem of others invite contention and strife. It is a rule, therefore, that the "honour of great persons, is to be valued for the beneficence and the aids they give to men of inferior rank, or not at all" (226).

Having denied the aristocratic conceit, lately battered by Cromwell, that some men are more worthy to command, Hobbes sallied out against the two great privileges of the aristocracy, legal immunities and great wealth. As mentioned, he demanded the equal application of law, especially as concerns grievances of commons against the offenses of the great. This was not a passing criticism or a random slap at abuses; it was a systemic demand without which Leviathan could not be a rule-of-law state. As for poverty and wealth, he reminded the sovereign that "poverty afflicts the mind of men more than anything," and warned that hungry men are not obedient subjects.[80] He rebuked those "that by asperity of nature, will strive to retain those things which to himself are superfluous, and to another necessary; . . . for seeing every man, not only by right, but also by necessity of nature, is supposed to endeavour all he can, to obtain that which is necessary for his conservation; he that shall oppose himself against it, for things superfluous, is guilty of the war that thereupon is to follow" (*Leviathan,* 99–100). Accordingly, he suggested equal taxation on the aristocracy at a time when they liked to claim exemption from taxation; and he proposed that it be a tax on items of consumption, to encourage those who "laboureth much, and sparing the fruits of [their] labour consumeth little," and to penalize those who "living idley, getteth little, and spendeth all they get" (226).

These counsels are not pastoral homilies dangling in a policy void. The *Leviathan* advances a thoroughgoing mercantilist economic policy. Hobbes accepted that the organs of a centralized monarchy could and should be used to create a national economy, and the substance of his recommendations tends toward that end. Thus, he advocated a uniform commercial code; emphasized the importance of the circulation of money to the stimulation of commerce; disapproved feudal obstructions to geographic and social mobility of the work force, which is the sense of his famous remark that labor is a commodity exchangeable for price (57, 161). He also criticized monopolies and defended market price as a measure of value. Toward corporations, which he styled "bodies politic for ordering of trade," he was favorably disposed. He pointed out that the most convenient system of governance of corporations is "an assembly of all the members," in which each may contribute to deliberations and decisions (151). He seems to have toyed with the thought that business enterprise might provide an outlet for the political appetite otherwise frustrated by his monarchical system.

*   *   *   *   *

Hobbes was a court philosopher at a time when monarchies were dynamic, innovative forces. Even so, it may seem remarkable that proposals so radical got a hearing from the court and aristocracy. Surprise vanishes, however, on remembering that those were times "that never were before." The king had been executed for treason, the House of

80. *De cive,* XII.8; XIII.3.

Lords abolished, and estates confiscated. The confusing new order of things had to be reckoned with, and in such a climate even Hobbes might gain a hearing. His writings prior to the outbreak of the civil war show that he anticipated the main flow of events with astounding accuracy. His study of the struggles between the commons and aristocracy in antiquity doubtless sharpened his insight into the cycles of political change.[81] But unprecedented new elements, rich in possibility, were at work in the world; and of these, the most important was the advent of science, which equipped the mind with the power of methodical thought. This was the linchpin that enabled thinkers to terminate their hidden concessions to superstition and confidently step forward with a programmatic politics.

In the course of his study of the human chaos, Hobbes, like Bacon and Descartes, discovered the infinite: the striving for power after power which drives the cosmos and which in man "ceaseth only in death." His shift of political legitimacy to the people was in part a consequence of this discovery. *All* men alike strive for power, regardless of rank or degree of blessedness. In this decisive respect, nature equalizes. In political terms, the discovery meant that the people have to be reckoned an active, volatile chaos rather than as the passive matter favored by Aristotle's aristocratic metaphysics. Stable government is possible only if their power drives are harnessed and channeled.

Hobbes seems to have believed that modern conditions imperceptibly shifted power toward the people. Bible reading had "caused each man to judge for himself." From writers on ancient republics he learned that when the people begin thinking for themselves, they hit on the idea of increasing their power, especially by challenging inequalities of wealth and rank.[82] If the invention of printing, like the invention of writing, were an irreversible discovery, then the communist agitation of the Levellers and Fifth Monarchy men had to be accounted a permanent presence with an enlarged audience (modern nations were far more

81. For a statement of the cycles notion of political change, reminiscent of Machiavelli, see *Behemoth* (*EWH*, 6: 252, 418). This statement should be compared with Hobbes's emphasis on man's perpetual discontent and love of novelty, summarized in the attribution to man of a perpetual striving for power after power. Hobbes meant to break the cycle by providing a true political science that would undeceive the people. The same point is made also in the preface to *De cive*.

82. Hobbes's study of the commons began with his study of Thucydides. In the preface to his translation of the *Peloponnesian War*, he commented at length on the ruin of the patriciate by the plebes, a phenomenon studied by Machiavelli in the *Florentine Histories*.

populous than ancient republics) accessible at any time, anywhere the printed word could be read.[83] With the old restraints on the people weakened or broken, and their numbers greatly increased, Hobbes foresaw that their political force must substantially increase. And foreseeing, he attempted to forestall the demagogues and tribunes with a monarchy based on the people.[84]

The unrivaled audacity of his conception is not adequately described without observing that its practicability depends upon discovering a solution to what seems an intractable problem. Hobbes documented the weakness of the people as few writers have. They are running sores of superstition, easy to dupe, warmly attached to tribal ignorance. Yet his politics required that they be enlightened about themselves; and that enlightenment cross their self-image in the severest manner. What remedy was available? Hobbes conceived it as a coordinated attack on two fronts. Reform from the top would eliminate the nurture of superstition: reform preaching by reforming Oxford and Cambridge, and reform Oxford and Cambridge by crushing superstitious philosophy with the hammer of the new science. The other front is a formulation of enlightened doctrine in terms that the people will *want* to believe: teach them their self-interest. Hobbes was too arrogant and detached to rewrite his doctrine for the people; he occupied the closing years of his life by translating Homer. But not long after, a colonial philosopher, and printer by trade, who had studied Newton, pondered Locke, and conversed with Mandeville at a café in Atheist Alley, invented Hobbism for the people. He called it *Poor Richard's Almanack;* and it was a raging commercial success.

83. The printing press altered English politics in Hobbes's lifetime. In 1641, 741 political and religious publications appeared; in the next year, the number swelled threefold to 2,134. Between 1640 and 1660, over 30,000 tracts, broadsheets, pamphlets, and books were published (Perez Zagorin, *The Court and the Country,* 204–5). John Pym was the first parliamentary leader to use the press as a political weapon, but the application had been pioneered a century previously by Martin Luther.

84. In the passage on sedition and revolutions cited in note 81 above, Hobbes says they depend on a combination of ambitious men raising vain hopes in the ignorant multitude, i.e. on empty promises. But if the common people were instructed in the true grounds of justice, the cycle of revolutions could be broken.

chapter 4

Enlightenment and Religion
in England, 1620–1700

Prospectus

When the Dutch Stadholder William of Orange accepted the British throne from the Convention Parliament in 1689, he and they concluded the Settlement that laid the keel of British politics for the next century and a half.[1] To commons, the new dynasty marked the liberation of England from Stuart tyranny and the specter of popery. To the political men who made the revolution, William's bloodless conquest was the outcome of more than a decade of negotiations and plots to supplant the Stuarts by a Dutch king skilled in the politics of constitutional monarchy.[2] These men—Buckingham, Shaftesbury, Halifax, Russel, Somers, Mordaunt, Locke—were *politiques* in every sense of the word. They understood the use of power. Unlike the parliamentary leaders of 1640, they pursued clearly defined political aims undistracted by notions of a godly commonwealth. They understood that either king or Parliament must be supreme, and they found the formula for parliamentary supremacy in the new coronation oath and in the Bill of Rights. Theirs was not a politics of righteousness, but of religious toleration and national expansion.[3] And they were fortunate in their monarch. Holland

1. David Ogg, *England in the Reigns of James II and William III*, 510–47.
2. Stephen B. Baxter, *William III*, 243–57, 269ff.
3. Comparison of the Petition of Right (1629) with the Bill of Rights written by the Convention Parliament of 1689 illustrates the growth of political sophisti-

had been the refuge of leading Whig political figures for more than a decade; William's abilities as the head of an advanced commercial nation were well known to them. His ministers at once set about modernizing the English administration and military forces; and he established an anti-French foreign policy that was to endure, with brief interruptions, for more than two centuries.[4] The Settlement of 1689 marked England's decisive turn toward the commercial republic.

The Glorious Revolution laid down a frame of government whose basic precepts were tempered by knowledge drawn from the new political science. Also important to the success of the Revolution was a new theology that may be called establishment theism, thanks to the support it enjoyed in the high Church and even in the universities. Establishment theism was the gospel of "reasonable Christianity," which taught hardly anything above reason and nothing contrary to it. It held that inspiration and miracles ceased when the Apostles ended their ministry. God rules the universe remotely, an honorary mechanician overseeing his vast clockwork. Morally speaking, the Deity behaves himself. He is not jealous, inspires no terrors of double predestination, and does not meddle in human affairs. This theology was developed during the Restoration largely by low Church clergymen who drew on a substantial corpus of English and continental liberal theology. Its effect was to disengage religion from competition with natural reason, particularly in science and politics. In the English context, it was anti-Puritan, as its counterpart in Holland was anti-Calvinist. Practical morality was emphasized, while visitations from the Holy Spirit to communicants were held to be infrequent and certainly not necessary to salvation. Reasonable Christianity jettisoned the biblicism of Calvinists because it sought rules for life in a book utterly uncontemporaneous with the present. Establishment theism increased the latitude of reason by weakening the hold of tradition; this was its appeal to the *politiques* who made the Revo-

---

cation among parliamentarians. The Convention's deliberations show a Parliament aware that in a constitutional monarchy, Parliament must be supreme. The Bill of Rights reveals comprehension of the institutional arrangements and procedural requisites necessary for maintaining king and Parliament in balance. The texts of these documents are printed in *The Constitutional Documents of the Puritan Revolution,* ed. S. R. Gardiner; and see Henry Hallam's evaluation of them in *The Constitutional History of England,* 3: 90–91.

4. Hallam characterizes the constitutional change as a transition from monarchy to aristocracy and calls the new principles of the Whigs "liberal" (*Constitutional History,* 3: 89). See J. H. Plumb, *The Growth of Political Stability in England,* 5–14.

lution. To be sure, there was nothing new in it. It had been the theological preference of *politiques* in Holland, France, Switzerland, and indeed England for more than a century.[5] Still, the Restoration combination of parliamentary politics, rational religion, and science became the public face of enlightenment throughout Europe, owing perhaps to the prestige of Parliament, Locke, and Newton. The synthesis was preached by Voltaire and Montesquieu. It was the creed of the American Founding Fathers. It was advocated by Lessing and Kant in Germany and by Becarria in Italy. Its hold was firm until evolutionary theory destroyed the credibility of Providence.

Historical classifications, if they are to be useful, must be broad enough to compose a significant group but not so broad as to include incompatible elements. Few classifications actually meet this ideal. "Establishment theism," as I use the term, includes John Wilkins and the young men he influenced, the Cambridge Platonists, and laymen like Newton, Locke, and Shaftesbury. All shared a distaste for biblicist Puritanism and a confidence that religion could be ethically improved by bathing it in the waters of the new science. But the Cambridge Platonists were more conservative than the Wilkins group; the former did not welcome the new regime and soon found themselves reproaching its "materialism." Locke and Newton, by contrast, held lucrative, prestigious appointments under the new regime; Newton was Master of the Mint while Locke was the dominant figure on the Board of Trade. This difference between the enlightened low Church bishops and the two enlightened laymen may be referred to their respective pay-packet interests. Clergymen have an interest in the belief that the good order of the nation depends on the moral uprightness of citizens; otherwise they could not justify their keep. But the new philosophy, as we have seen, puts paid to this ancient notion. Priestly morality, far from being useful to the state, is a standing threat to peace. The new philosophy preached calculated self-interest as the means to methodical acquisition, which was to substitute for morality. The most enlightened clergyman must hesitate here, and we find, not surprisingly, that the arch exponent of acquisitive egoism, Thomas Hobbes, was the bête noire of the Platonists and the Wilkins group.[6] The clerical exponents of establishment theism

5. H. R. Trevor-Roper, *Religion, the Reformation and Social Change*, 24–25, 203–36; J. W. Thompson, *A History of Historical Writing*, 1: 543ff., 554–69; and see above, 123, 136, 141–42.
6. John Redwood, *Reason, Ridicule and Religion*, 34ff., 51–52, 50, 73–78; Margaret Jacob, *The Newtonians and the English Revolution*, 52ff., 56–57, 197ff.; and see below, 195, 208–11.

were anxious not to take enlightenment too far. But once that tram is boarded, it is hard to get off before the end of the line. Establishment theism was no sooner established than the hideous head of the atheistical Hobbes rose again in the shape of Deists—most of them renegade clergymen and self-styled disciples of John Locke.

In the present chapter this cat-and-mouse game will be explored from the perspective of the new philosophy. We have seen that the only God consistent with it must be something like the God of Descartes, Hobbes, and Spinoza, who is pledged to endorse the findings of reason (the "undoubted word of God"). Clergymen who embraced this rationalism were driven into dilemmas and inconsistencies. Henry More's belated backtracking from Cartesian metaphysics once he recognized its inherent irreligion was an orbit often traced. There was a certain necessity in this half-enlightenment. Clergymen were faced with the alternative of continuing in the tracks of Luther and Calvin or coming to terms with the new philosophy. The clerical instinct was to sacralize it, as the Patriarchs had sacralized the Greco-Roman heritage; and, characteristic of this impulse, they reached back to the mainstay of Christian theology, Plato. The Patriarchs were able to jerry-build a steeple on Platonic metaphysics because Platonic philosophy, like all ancient philosophy, was not science. There was plenty of latitude for opinion—"right opinion" (orthodoxy) Plato called it. But the new philosophy was science; and this fact set limits on how much one could fiddle to make it subserve orthodoxy. The new philosophy, in short, was Plato-proof and clergy-proof. Plato-proof, because Ideas are a play of fancy in a mechanistic universe. Clergy-proof, because science is no respecter of persons, parties, or sects, however sacred. Since they were clergymen before they were philosophers, the Cambridge Platonists did not understand that the new philosophy represented a new force impervious to the tried and trusted methods of verbal manipulation. So it transpired that, despite the mountains of theology that were heaped upon the mechanistic universe, not one scientific law or principle was ever altered owing to changes in theological fashions. On the other hand, every theology or religious attitude that attached itself to science cohabited with a dangerous bedfellow who sooner or later forced a divorce. The dilemma that cropped up in establishment theism was that it must either be consistent, and become cryptoatheist, or pious, and commit itself to inconsistency. The dilemma was resolved by the discovery of a third position, pious atheism. This was the religion of Newton and Locke.

Aubrey's Record of *Libertinage Érudit*

It has been mentioned that views similar to those contained in establishment theism had circulated among *politiques* throughout Europe for more than a century. They took many forms, skeptical and dogmatic, and bore many names, but the inspiration of Erasmus or Montaigne was usually traceable in them. A low estimate of Scholastic theology and a positive valuation of worldly practicality were common elements that made this new way of thinking appealing to the laity. But laymen did not digest it independently of other influences, especially the impact of political events and of the new philosophy, with which it was often associated. To appreciate what the new theology meant to the laity, one must consider it in this context.

Gentlemen and patricians were the transmission belt between the new philosophy and active life. The generation of gentlemen who came of age during the English Revolution was the first to be exposed to it. For many it provided a refuge from the wordy clatter of wartime *Kulturkampf.* John Aubrey was one of these men. He went up to Oxford in 1642, a youth troubled by the nation's travail. His lawyer grandfather made the family fortune in service to the court, and this background disposed him to the royalist side. But as he matured, and as the king's cause faltered, he came under the influence of James Harrington. For a time he attended the Rota meetings, where republican politics were intensively discussed. But Aubrey's friendships were wide. At the age of nine he met in the family home a philosopher whom he described as "a proper man, briske, and in very good habit . . . who was pleased to take notice of me" (*Brief Lives,* xxvi). This man was Thomas Hobbes. Friendship followed, and at the same time Aubrey was attending Rota meetings, he corresponded with Hobbes in France, giving him all the local news. He was in addition among the thirty or so men who attended John Wilkins's science group meetings at Wadham College, Oxford. He became a founding fellow of the Royal Society largely on the strength of his connections with Wilkins and other prominent members. He was less a scientist than a scholar and collector, particularly of choice anecdotes. This talent he put to work in *Brief Lives,* where he sketched 426 biographies of contemporaries or near contemporaries.

The work is incomplete. Many of the biographies are drafts only. There is also an air of randomness about them. Some fasten on a single character trait or narrate one long anecdote; some of the anecdotal material reads like a Chaucerian tale. Even so, the typical biography conveys a strong sense of factuality. Aubrey avoided praise and blame and made no attempt to explain the behavior or character of his subjects.

The absence of edifying narrative, the mode in biography at that time, must be considered together with the unusual candor of the work. Thanks to this combination, Aubrey often allowed iniquity to pass unreproached. It is not easy to know which aspects of the work are due to art, and which to chance, but Aubrey did think that he had been unusually candid. Other biographers, he wrote, "treading too neer on the heeles of truth . . . dare not speake plaine," whereas he wrote to "laydowne to you the . . . naked and plaine trueth" (*Brief Lives*, cix). The stylistic realism and candor of the work are characteristic of the *honnêtes hommes* who made the new philosophy. They were men Aubrey admired and attempted to imitate. Indeed, they are the heroes of *Brief Lives;* and in reading his biographies of those associated with the new philosophy, we find that Aubrey unobtrusively mapped cryptoatheism and *libertinage érudit* in England. At the time he wrote, libertinage—not always learned—was fashionable among the coffeehouse set.[7] The court of Charles II set the tone, and men of rank, notably the duke of Buckingham and the earls of Rochester and Shaftesbury, encouraged mockery as a means of putting fanatics on the defensive. Since moral intimidation is a potent weapon, it is natural that the Ghibelline politicals should make common cause with the exponents of liberty. The tradition of their association was old, running from Boccaccio to Machiavelli; from Rabelais to Montaigne and the French libertines, including Gabriel Naudé, Gassendi, and Molière; and in Geneva, the dismayed Calvin discovered that his political opposition used libertinage to batter his moral rigorism.[8]

Brief Lives belonged to this ambient. While some of its characters were scoffers, its thrust was against the mystification of morality. The blows were struck by direct and honest means: Aubrey merely told some truths about the immorality of his heroes. In this way he pulled the rug from under Puritan and Royal Society hagiography concerned to present some of these men as models of conventional piety. One such man was Francis Bacon, who even today is surrounded by halos. The canonization began in the 1630s, when the Puritan gentry endowed him with the virtues of the right-thinking squire, while the Royal Society

7. G. T. Buckley's *Atheism in the English Renaissance* (1932) has not been followed by more contemporary studies.
8. On the libertines of Geneva and their leader, Ami Perrin, see John T. McNeill, *The History and Character of Calvinism*, 168–77. On the libertine tradition, see Don Allen, *Doubt's Boundless Sea;* René Pintard, *Le libertinage érudit;* François Perrens, *Les libertins en France au XVIIe siècle;* and Jacques Denis, *Sceptiques ou libertins.*

continued the canonization on a somewhat different plane. Aubrey demolished the halo with one laconic sentence: "He was a παιδεραστές. His Ganimeds and Favorites tooke Bribes; but his Lordship alwayes gave Judgement *secundum aequum et bonum*" (*Brief Lives*, 11). It is not hard to imagine what drolleries this sentence must have occasioned among the smart set. It was comic enough that the austere Puritans lionized a man who spent a fortune annually to support his opulent living; but that this man should in addition be a pederast! It goes to show of what stuff saints are made.

Aubrey took his readers into Bacon's circle of intimates to show that the corruption was general. Sir Walter Raleigh, recently acclaimed by an eminent historian to be a great Puritan, was a womanizer and pederast. He was also a proud man whose opinions put him in need of denying that he was an atheist.[9] Except for this observation, Aubrey was silent about the religion of Bacon and Raleigh. But he threw light indirectly with a comment on Thomas Harriot, the gifted mathematician who made important contributions to algebra and astronomy: "He made a Philosophical Theologie, wherein he cast-off the Old Testament, and then the New-one would (consequently) have no Foundation. He was a Deist. His Doctrine he taught to Sir Walter Raleigh, Henry Earle of Northumberland; and some others. The Divines of those times look't on his manner of death as a Judgement upon him for nullifying the Scripture" (*Brief Lives*, 123). The divines knew their enemy, for Harriot's "theology" was a formula for cryptoatheism. Harriot was possibly familiar with Bacon's views on cryptoatheism. Bacon had said that the atheist denies God "in his heart" from "fear of law and opinion: as one says, it is a hard matter to deny God in a public assembly, but in familiar conference it is easy enough. For if this restraint were removed, there is no heresy which strives with more zeal to spread and sow and multiply itself than atheism" (*Works*, 7: 251). One means of spreading atheism without denying God openly is to put up a theology that tends to the ruin of religion. This is what Aubrey intimated of Harriot. He scoffed at the association of Harriot's death with divine wrath by explaining that the man died of a pimple on the nose—the comedy of his tragic end underscores the capriciousness of nature,

9. John Aubrey, *Brief Lives*, 254, 259. Aubrey said of Raleigh that "he was such a person (every way), that . . . a prince would rather be afrayd of than ashamed of. He had that awfulness and ascendancy in his Aspect over other mortals" (257). It is not surprising that a man of this stripe should have proposed, on the death of Elizabeth, setting up a Commonwealth "to keape the government in their owne hands" (257).

which often slaps some indignity on Aubrey's heroes. One who understood nature's caprice was Bacon's physician, William Harvey, who thought man a "great, mischievous Baboon." This sentiment was apparently the reason for his staunch monarchist politics and for his disapproval of political meddling. Nature embarrassed Harvey by endowing him with a "cholerique" disposition that made him "apt to draw-out his dagger on every slight occasion" (*Brief Lives*, 131). He took opium during his declining years and committed suicide when he recognized his terminal illness.

Aubrey detected several lines of transmission of Elizabethan free-thinking to the parliamentary interregnum, the most important being Lord Falkland's circle at Great Tew, an estate a few miles from Oxford. The authentic Elizabethan presence there was Ben Jonson, who had dined with the queen, tippled with Shakespeare, and slept with Raleigh. But the younger men of Bacon's circle, Harvey and Hobbes, themselves fast friends, were also regulars at Great Tew. Politics, religion, and morals were the main topics of discussion. When Hobbes set down an affection for republicanism among gentlemen as one of the causes of the civil war, he would have had Falkland in mind. Together with Edward Hyde, later lord chancellor to Charles I and Charles II, he was among the patricians who in 1640–41 pressed parliamentary claims against the royal prerogative. Falkland's republicanism was not inspired by a religious vision. He was a *politique* who took his models from secular writers—had it been otherwise, Hobbes would scarcely have been a welcome guest. The religious outlook of the men of Great Tew harmonized with the circle's political orientation. The resident theologian was William Chillingworth, whose *Religion of the Protestants* (1637) undercut the biblicism of Puritan theology and paved the way for the Latitudinarianism developed a decade later at Oxford by the Wilkins group. Falkland himself, Aubrey claimed, was the first Socinian in England (*Brief Lives*, 56). Sir William Davenant, another member of the group, looked forward to the day when religious sectarianism would exhaust itself and subside into a Quakeresque indifference to confession.

In Aubrey's *Who's Who* of anti-Puritan politicals, a network emerges that ties together men of very different political persuasions. Henry Briggs, the mathematician and astronomer, fought a private war against the lingering belief in astrology among mathematicians. The republican radicals Henry Martin and Thomas Chaloner fought running battles with the Puritans in Parliament. The republican James Harrington argued politics with Charles I, whom he deeply loved and whose death caused Harrington's health to fail. Sir Charles Danvers, Sir Kenelm Digby, Edmund Gunter, Sir Robert Moray, John Pell, Sir William

Petty, Sir Philip Sydney, Edmund Waller, Walter Warner—all figure among Aubrey's politicals. But the name most frequently mentioned in the *Brief Lives* is Thomas Hobbes. The biographies of Bacon and Hobbes are much the longest in the book, and Aubrey took care to link them by twice telling the story that Bacon preferred Hobbes to his other secretaries because he alone understood what was dictated. Aubrey also underscored the link by stressing Hobbes's friendship with Harvey and Jonson. In these ways, Aubrey suggested that Hobbes was the true heir of Bacon's philosophy. And Hobbes was named the conqueror of superstition; for he, "being but *one,* and a private person, pulled downe all their Churches, dispelled the mists of ignorance, and layde-opene their Priest-craft." [10]

The theme of irreligion is suitably complemented in the *Brief Lives* by numerous anecdotes about magic, astrology, premonitions, inspirations, divinations, and ghosts. Their juxtaposition in the work evokes the image of a great struggle in the minds of Englishmen. Aubrey was not merely an observer. Despite his rationalist sympathies, he could not abandon his fondness for astrology. In an autobiographical passage written late in life, about the time *Brief Lives* was completed, he characterized the change of opinion he had observed:

When I was a child . . . the fashion was for old women and mayds to tell stories nighttimes, of Sprights and walking of Ghosts, &c. This was derived down from mother to daughter, from the Monkish Ballance which upheld Holy Church, for the Divines say, Deny Spirits, you are an Atheist. When the Warres came, and with them Liberty of Conscience and Liberty of inquisition, the phantoms vanished. Now children fear no such things, having heard not of them; and are not checked with such feares. (*Brief Lives,* xxv)

This statement, a classic description of the progress of enlightenment, was based on more than casual observations. As a student of the antiquities of his beloved Wiltshire, Aubrey was steeped in west country lore. He had studied its people, monuments, and ways back to the Ro-

10. Ibid., 165, quoting Edmund Waller, who was afraid to praise Hobbes openly. Shaftesbury, in his "Essay on Raillery," said that "Hobbes defined theology, with his ordinary precision, as *regnum tenebrarum,* the kingdom of darkness. Hobbes made every effort to make us see that there is nothing that naturally inclines us to a religious life." In his translation of Shaftesbury's *Essays,* Diderot remarked on this passage that "Hobbes was a good citizen, a good parent, a good friend, and did not believe in God."

man conquest. His intimacy with country opinion came to the fore vividly in another similar comment, this time on John Wilkins's group:

> Till about the yeare 1649, when Experimental Philosophy was first cultivated by a Club at Oxford, 'twas held a strange presumption for a Man to attempt an Innovation in Learnings; and not to be good Manners, to be more knowing than his Neighbours and Forefathers; even to attempt an improvement in Husbandry (though it succeeded with profit) was look'd upon with an ill Eie. Their Neighbours did scorne to follow it, though not to doe it, was to their own Detriment. 'Twas held a Sin to make a Scrutinie into the Waies of Nature; Whereas it is certainly a profound part of Religion to glorify God in his Workes: and to take no notice at all of what is dayly offered before our Eyes is grosse Stupidity. (*Brief Lives*, xxvii)

This is the country spirit pure and undiluted. The agriculture improver Arthur Young found it barely shaken when he made his famous tours of England's farmlands a century later. Certainly it lay heavily on the revolutionary Parliament, through the dominance of the gentry. When the Visitors from Parliament brought down the hammer on Oxford and Cambridge in 1649–50, they insisted on the old curriculum, not the new science.[11] The Barebones Parliament of 1653 considered "suppressing Universities and all Schools of Learning, as heathenish and unnecessary."[12] Although this Luddism was beaten back, it does illustrate that the radical wing of the Revolution, though it sometimes invoked Bacon's name, was animated by the worst country prejudices.

Aubrey's characterization of settled attitudes toward inquiry stresses a thought that comes out repeatedly in *Brief Lives*. Knowledge and its pursuit were at that time socially disruptive. To be sociable in Wiltshire, one deferred to the village myths, to the established order, to venerable opinion. What made beliefs true was not their objective content, but their importance in channeling the endless process of social negotiation and grooming. Village consensus was the truth. But in science, none of

11. Barbara Shapiro, *John Wilkins*, 93.
12. Ibid., 97. Wilkins's appointment to Wadham was due to Cromwell, and thus reflected the more tolerant spirit of the Independents. At no time in the seventeenth century were scientists more than a tiny fraction of the total number of tutors in the universities, and science studies were not encouraged. For a review, see Phyllis Allen, "Scientific Studies in the English Universities of the Seventeenth Century," 219–53.

these social values carries any weight. "Nothing in words" was the motto of the Royal Society, regardless of the social importance of received beliefs. Only the things themselves count. Whereas the village mentality will not separate truth from the standing of those who purport to speak it, science is cosmopolitan in its disregard of the human provenance of truth. Cosmopolitanism is scandalous to the village consensus. Aubrey's portraits of the men who nurtured science established the connection between the cosmopolitanism of science and the socially disruptive honesty that it underpins and perhaps requires. "'Twas held a Sin to make a Scrutinie into the Waies of Nature," he wrote, and to attempt improvements "was look'd upon with an ill Eie." Thus, Harvey's discovery of the circulation of the blood departed so far from established opinion that his practice fell off dramatically and his medical colleagues ridiculed him as a crackpot.[13] That in a nutshell was the predicament of the men of science. They reaped an awesome discovery to which ancient philosophy had been the overture. It was possible for the brains of individuals to grasp in a methodical and systematic way the truth of things, independently of time, place, and circumstance. But this fact, which today we take for granted, was at odds with the village conception of knowledge as social negotiation and grooming. How were they to defend themselves in these circumstances? They made honesty their virtue and set out to cut the roots of the village mentality through war on superstition and moral intimidation.

Guardians of the village mentality in Restoration England were quick to point out the connection between freethinking and moral reprobation: whoever prefers his own conceits to the settled wisdom of the village is contumacious toward the collective conscience, and therefore will not be "guided" by it in his actions either.[14] But this coin has another side; those who find themselves in odium may hunt around for cosmopolitan justifications. That this was the common notion among the coffeehouse set we need not doubt: the irreligion of the new philosophy was a handy stick to lay to village righteousness. Here Bacon's Titanism is again relevant to our story. It was previously noted that in his *Wisdom of the Ancients*, Bacon emphasized the immorality of Daedalus, Prometheus, and other mythic symbols of the new philosophy. They were headstrong individuals who unscrupulously executed the grand designs they conjured from imagination. Bacon's unnatural

13. Aubrey, *Brief Lives*, 131. Harvey also offended the men whom Charles Webster calls Puritan "world reformers," owing to the incompatibility of his "physick" with Paracelsus's; see Webster, *The Great Instauration*, 323, 275.
14. Redwood, *Reason, Ridicule and Religion*, 23–30.

vice placed him beyond the pale of respectability; what he loved was detestable to every right-thinking person. In Plato's *Symposium* Bacon discovered the wisdom of ancient pederasts. Some controlled their passion, and took revenge on the village by implanting a corrosive skepticism that removed the sting from moral reprobation. Others, dissatisfied with this half-measure, would storm Mount Olympus, displace the old village gods, and remake the village in their image. This manly insurrection was Bacon's option. The audacity of his design, the charm of his vehemence, and the thoroughness of his attacks on the old gods probably owe something to the infamy of his passion.

Bacon was not the man to place this contest in perspective. He needed a Hobbes to show that it is not a question of a few iniquitous renegades opposed to the moral consensus of the village. Hobbes showed that the consensus is phony because no one is virtuous. Honest acknowledgment of human depravity, and recognition that the village consensus is merely an expedient for living together, paved the way for cosmopolitanism.

Puritan Science

In the years prior to the outbreak of civil war, Bacon's philosophy advanced in favor among the English gentry who were conducting the protracted struggle with Charles I. As the constitutional crisis deepened and the need for justification and direction grew, the parliamentary party transformed him into a national saint and his philosophy into a watchword of the millennial era that many believed the war heralded.

Although Bacon is not the only man to achieve posthumous glory at the expense of misunderstanding, in this case the paradoxes are stunning. The same gentry who saluted him in 1640 had demanded his impeachment on twenty-eight counts of bribery and corruption only two decades earlier.[15] The gentry complained bitterly of the extravagance of the court, yet Bacon was among the worse offenders. His writings make no secret of his admiration for Machiavelli and Henry VII, whom he styled "the most rapacious" English king;[16] he was a power politician and monarchist to the hilt. Nevertheless, he became a patron saint of the godly commonwealth. His secular philosophy was hallowed as the

15. Two decades later, these same gentry composed a Parliament fervently attached to the Anglican Church. Presbyterians were lumped together with fanatics who attacked property, and the gentry warmly approved the severe Clarendon Code to keep the Presbyterians down. See Hallam, *Constitutional History*, 2: 305.

16. Quoted ibid., 1: 294.

paradigm of philosophical piety. How could two things so antithetical—royal Titanism and country Puritanism—have attained this affinity?

Bacon framed his domestic policies in the tradition of Thomas Cromwell. He recognized that Calvinism appealed to the gentry in the measure that the Anglican Church had not corrected abuses obnoxious to most Protestants. Parishes were staffed with ignorant or dissolute clergy, or none at all. Parish administration was neglected, with poor relief falling on local shoulders unsupported by the court. Inequities of taxation were exacerbated by royal extravagance. Law had not been updated despite two centuries of substantial social change. In matters of liturgy and ritual, so important to Protestant pietists, the Anglican Church was unyielding despite decades of pleas and agitation. Bacon put forward policies meant to redress many of these grievances. It has been suggested that, had James accepted them, the civil war might have been averted.[17]

It had been a maxim of English politics since Thomas Cromwell that church reform implied a foreign policy oriented on Protestant alliance; and conversely, that Henrican Anglicanism implied bilateral alliances with Catholic or Protestant powers as opportunity might suggest. Events proved that Cromwell had correctly diagnosed the drift of things. Henrican middle ground was progressively less viable. If England were to cast off the papal supremacy, it must ally with Protestant powers against formidable Spain and France; to make Protestantism strong at home, it must redress the Protestant grievances. Bacon attempted to set this policy once more in motion. For a time, James I seemed to have crossed the watershed. He adopted predestination, which at that time was a badge of the Protestant cause. He agreed to Bacon's arrangement of marriage between the Protestant hero Frederick of Palatine and James's daughter Elizabeth. This marriage was immensely popular in England because it seemed to seal the Protestant alliance. The Palatinate was in the geographic center of the Thirty Years'

17. *Dictionary of National Biography,* s.v. "Bacon." Hallam describes as "healing counsels" the policies of Burleigh and Bacon toward Puritan dissent and contrasts them with the policies of Neile and Laud, who are "low-born and little-minded men" (*Constitutional History,* 1: 366).

Charles probably could have avoided the Revolution as late as 1641 had he shut the queen up in a closet and brought parliamentary leaders into the Privy Council. But Pym and Hampden, sitting in the Privy Council, would have constituted implicit recognition of the supremacy of Parliament, and Charles would not have it. See Perez Zagorin, *The Court and the Country,* 216; Trevor-Roper, *Religion, the Reformation and Social Change,* 84–85; J. H. Hexter, *The Reign of King Pym,* 48–62.

War; with Elizabeth on the throne, James could not but throw eager English forces into the fray; and with that, church reform must soon follow.

As it happened, James lifted not a finger to save Frederick from defeat, nor to reform the Church. When Charles I came to the throne, he reasserted Henrican ideas of carrying royal prerogative high. He rejected Calvinist theology and appointed Archbishop Laud to root it out of the Church. These two actions were connected. "Predestination is the root of Puritanism," Dr. Samuel Brooke wrote to Laud, "and Puritanism is the root of all rebellion and disobedient intractableness and all schism and sauciness in the Country, nay, in the Church itself."[18] Charles I acted consistently with this policy when he rejected the Protestant alliance and began those overtures to France that culminated in his son's secret treaty with Louis XIV to convert to Catholicism and bring England back into the papal fold.[19] Charles I's untimely reassertion of Henrican absolutism thus joined together what previously had been two separate causes, Church reform and limits on the royal prerogative.[20] Discontented clergy and discontented parliamentarians joined forces, primarily through the gentry, who experienced both discontents.

In those circumstances, Francis Bacon began to look like a champion of the good old causes, even as Queen Bess was fondly remembered for her open-arms policy toward refugees from Catholic persecutions, while her persecutions of English Puritans were conveniently forgotten. Furthermore, Bacon had polished his rhetoric to make it consistent with the policies he advocated. His tireless exhortations to reform the

18. Quoted by G. R. Cragg, *From Puritanism to the Age of Reason*, 15.
19. Hallam, *Constitutional History*, 2: 401, 369ff.
20. Puritan clergy, as distinguished from laymen, kept clear of the struggle between the Crown and Parliament until persecution finally drove them to seek refuge from episcopal ire. Parliament, in their eyes, was swollen with *politiques*—worldly nobility and gentry whose ambition was more conspicuous than their piety. Richard Baxter complained that "gentlemen think us such fools in Politics that they will disdain to be told what to do." On the other end of the social spectrum, they also despised and feared the "rabble," whom they thought naturally sensual and licentious. They looked to the Crown as the rock of the Church because they agreed with the Anglican principle of clerical monopoly. The alliance between the Puritan clergy and Parliament was forced and short-lived, ending when the Independents got the upper hand on the Presbyterians. See Brian Manning, "The Godly People," 95, 103; Richard Schlatter, ed., *Richard Baxter and Puritan Politics*, 4, 9, 15, 17, 22, 38, 93; Hexter, *The Reign of King Pym*, 63.

sciences were read in Wiltshire and the north country as referring to the only kind of learning they knew, religious learning. Among the religions of that age, grand designs for reform were often represented in terms of the defeat of Antichrist and the advent of the Millennium.[21] Bacon played with these notions by quoting occasionally Daniel 12: 4, which at the time was a way of signaling one's belief in the glories to come. But he had his own eccentric anticipations of the coming age, signified by the three inventions that had changed the face of Europe. The compass had unleashed powers that planted European flags throughout the world, while crushing a superstition in the process. In gunpowder he read the promise of a new empire; linked with sail and printing, who could say how far it might extend? This was Bacon's notion of Millennium: a new empire, commanded by Machiavellian Titans and backed by a technological science that made nature itself obey. Such was the utopian bliss lost by Adam's fall, now to be restored.[22]

Out in the back country these pyrotechnic notions could make no impression. Country gentlemen would haul *The New Organon* down from a shelf that held Foxe's *Book of Martyrs;* John Everard's *Some Gospel Treasures Opened;* the devout, ecstatic gibberish of the ever-popular *Theologica Germanica;* Raleigh's *History of the World;* Joseph Mede's *Clavis Apocalyptica* (*Key to Apocalypse*), a major inspiration text to Puritans preparing politically to meet their Maker; Cartwright's *Book of*

21. English millenarianism is later than, and partly derives from, German pietists and mystics reaching back to Jacob Boehme. German chiliasm is reviewed in the *New Cambridge Modern History,* 4: 169–97.
22. Charles Webster's *The Great Instauration* is a valuable compendium of opinion about Bacon among the learned clergy in the 1630s and '40s. They predictably considered Bacon a religious thinker, often with absurd results. John Stoughton, for example, compared Bacon with John Dury and St. John Chrysostom, while William Twisse believed that Bacon's citation of a few Bible verses in *Valerius Terminus* was enough to establish a religious foundation for his philosophy, even though in that work Bacon warned that anyone who believes in such foundations "dangerously deludes himself" (Webster, *The Great Instauration,* 19ff.). As for assimilation of the conquest of nature to millennialist ideas, Webster's study contains the best documentation to date. Its usefulness, however, is somewhat impaired by Webster's view that Bacon's philosophy was an "expression of the dominant viewpoint in the Jacobean scientific movement" (345), by which he means "Puritan science." Bacon was not conscious of such a "movement," unless it consisted of William Gilbert and William Harvey; and he consistently represented himself as a trailblazer rather than an imitator. Webster's study does not identify a body of Jacobean scientific writings of which Bacon's philosophy could with any plausibility be said to be an "expression."

Discipline; and sundry tracts by Erasmus and Calvin, sprinkled with books on the number of the Beast, astrology, Hermetic wisdom, Paracelsian natural wonders, and horticulture.[23] Some catalyst was needed to bundle these disparate worlds into a usable farrago. The catalyst arrived at a providential moment, bearing the name of Jan Amos Comenius.

Comenius was a clergyman of the Bohemia Brethren, a sect whose doctrine mixed Calvin with Luther. To Protestants, particularly to English Calvinists, Bohemia was sacred to the faith. It was in Bohemia that Calvinist princes, defending their liberties, began the Thirty Years' War. Elizabeth's husband was defeated there when her father refused to come to his aid. The land was devastated by Catholic armies; one-sixth of the population were destroyed or forced to flee. By these sufferings Bohemian Protestants acquired the martyr's badge, as the Huguenots had previously.[24] Comenius, the spiritual leader of this community, enjoyed enormous prestige as well as the patronage of the rich and powerful, particularly the Dutch finance minister and moving spirit in the Swedish court, Louis de Geer. In 1659 Comenius was offered the presidency of Harvard College. Cardinal Richelieu even invited him to the French court, but Comenius smelled the Machiavellianism behind the flattery.[25]

Comenius's prestige seems to have derived from his doctrine, for his personality was unexceptional and his deeds few. He preached a doctrine called Pansophia, dedicated to the unification of Protestants. It was an all-embracing doctrine laid down on the pillars of Universals: Universal Knowledge, Universal Language, Universal Schools, Universal Books. Universality was demanded by the scope of Comenius's

---

23. Puritan reading is surveyed by William Haller in *The Rise of Puritanism,* 405–50. Haller, Webster, and other authorities agree that *Clavis Apocalyptica,* a high-flying millenarian tract full of prophecies, was the epitome of Puritan pietism. This view is not supported by Daniel Neal, writing in the 1720s (see his *History of the Puritans,* vol. 5). He stated that millenarianism was a heresy among them, attributed to the Anabaptists. Puritans were above all concerned with Church regiment, which meant the divine right of the presbytery; strict observance of the Sabbath, and strict conformity to catechisms and directories; elaborate casuistry about the abolition of Christmas, the use of the Apocrypha in service, the exchange of wedding rings. John Bunyan, not Comenius or Milton, expressed their searching piety. The gentry Puritans of Parliament were of a somewhat different stripe; see Trevor-Roper, *Religion, the Reformation and Social Change,* 237–391.

24. G. H. Turnbull, *Hartlib, Dury and Comenius,* 351–56, 380, 462.

25. Ibid., 368, 460–61.

projected reform. It was to be world reformation in anticipation of the advent of Millennium.

In Pansophia there was something for everyone. It absorbed currents of high and low culture and united them into a Protestant philosophy missing theretofore. But Comenius recognized a precursor in Bacon, although his clerical eye spotted the defect in Bacon's philosophy that prevented it serving religion. Bacon insisted that philosophy and religion be kept strictly separate, lest both be spoiled. Comenius knew better, and what Bacon put asunder, he once again joined together. In this way he sacralized Baconian philosophy.[26]

A Protestant philosophy to guide them through the briers of Antichrist was what the English gentry urgently needed. After they discovered Comenius's writings in the 1630s, he was all the rage. His Puritan patron, the parliamentary leader Lord Brooke, praised him as "that mighty man [who] doth happily and rationally endeavour to reduce *all* into one." By reducing all distinctions into one mighty unity, Comenius enabled Puritans to look backward to Jerusalem, and at the same time look forward to a Baconian Millennium. They could admire Paracelsian medicine, and at the same time approve Harvey's new physiology, which contradicted it. They could have experimental philosophy as well as ghosts, witches, and astrology. They could adorn their cause with the emblems of science, and at the same time believe that the law of

26. For details of Pansophia, see Purver, *The Royal Society*, 206–34, where Comenius's mingling of philosophy and religion is stressed. On the Puritan conception of the relation between reason and faith, Haller writes that "the key to Calvinistic reasoning was that the Bible gave a rule to be followed in church and state as in all other affairs of life . . . the theory was that truth in scripture when brought to bear upon conscience by the force of reason would lead men to early agreement unless those chose wilfully and maliciously to resist the light. The fact was . . . that scripture, which had more poetry in its pages than law, worked upon the men of uncritical minds, lively imaginations, differing temperaments and conflicting interests not as a unifying but as a divisive force" (*Rise of Puritanism*, 14). Webster reproduces the purport of this assessment when he says that novelties in philosophy and science were acceptable to Puritans only if they conformed to "their basic religious premises" (*The Great Instauration*, 15; see also 498, 504–5, 520). It is more pertinent to note, however, that science and philosophy altogether lacked spiritual importance for Puritans because the whole saving message was believed to be in the Bible. This point is forcefully made by John Morgan, "Puritanism and Science: A Reinterpretation."

On Comenius's life and career, see the essay in Trevor-Roper, *Religion, the Reformation and Social Change*, 237–93.

causality was about to be suspended by the Second Coming. They could approve the new science of mechanics, since Comenius had proved that the Millennium would be powered by perpetual motion machines, which would run on metaphysical gas.[27]

Comenius was induced by parliamentary leaders—John Pym, Bishop Williams, Oliver St. John, Sir Cheney Culpeper—to visit England in 1642, in the hope that he would become the spiritual director of reform.[28] He was present during the summer of euphoria, when all things seemed possible. But in November the Irish rebellion broke out, and for the next eighteen years the world reformers were enmeshed in local distractions. Comenius left England, never to return.

Two disciples, John Dury and Samuel Hartlib, remained to work for the faith. Refugees from Bohemia, they had settled in England around 1628 and had established their reputations for piety and good works by ministering to their refugee countrymen. Hartlib's modest legacy from his merchant father enabled him to operate a hostel for Bohemian clergymen. But this charity soon reduced his private means, and he himself became dependent. Collections were taken for him among the gentry, and friends occasionally petitioned Parliament to pension this "man of very publique spirit, a zealous promoter of all parts of good learning, of Christian unity and the power of godliness in many forraine states."[29] Parliament retained him as a brain truster at large, with no definite commission and on a pension too small to meet his personal needs. Nevertheless, for twenty years Hartlib was the provocateur to godly works, the central data station of Millennium Watch, the learning exchange for "correspondencies" among Puritan Baconians. He began his labors in the right way by publishing a short utopian tract, *Macaria* (1641), which set out programmatically what was to be done. The substance of the work was derived from Thomas More's *Utopia* and Bacon's *New Atlantis*. In Macaria, worldly vices give way to "piety, learning, morality and other exercises of industry." There is no luxury nor great imbalance of fortune. Land is privately owned, but a condition of ownership is tillage and improvement. Each parish has its own medical service, staffed by Baconian clergymen-scientists, and technology is

27. By 1660, Comenius's faithful disciple Samuel Hartlib admitted that he had given up the master's *Perpetuum Mobile* "after 15 years hopes" (Turnbull, *Hartlib,* 381).

28. On Comenius's relations with parliamentary leaders, see Turnbull, *Hartlib,* 342–70.

29. Ibid., 28. Hartlib said of his poverty that he had obeyed the New Testament injunction to give all to the poor.

freely cultivated and used. In all, *Macaria* is more conservative than either of its models. More's sharp criticisms of the abuse of wealth are missing, and the work carries none of the complex suggestiveness of *New Atlantis*. There is not a single grand idea in the work that Frank Manuel, the leading scholar of utopian literature, styles "one of the most insipid of an unbearably dull literary genre."[30] Such is the fate of big ideas in little minds.

Hartlib's main function on behalf of sacralized science was to be the "conduit pipe for things communicable," as Dury fondly called him. The Bohemian Brethren stressed communication, believing as they did that if all men of true learning united against false knowledge by apprising one another of their findings, the battle was virtually won. The knowledge that came through his exchange station concerned horticulture and herbal medicine chiefly, since they were the main interests of the gentry. He was closely associated with the agricultural improvers Gabriel Plattes and Walter Blith, and his name was for generations linked with theirs as the men who made the idea of methodical agricultural improvement acceptable among the gentry. Their notion of improvement might be styled "critical lore." They were concerned with methods of field drainage, efficiency of plows, techniques of tillage, grafting, harvesting—the kind of thing that Arthur Young and his gentry following called "scientific farming" more than a century later. Neither had any notion that agricultural science must be based on experimental studies such as Stephen Hales's description of the respiration of plants.

Hartlib, and others he was able to prompt, kept a stream of proposals flowing to Parliament concerning educational reform and the organization of science under an agency of universal learning, called the Office of Publicke Addresse in Spiritual and Temporall Matters. The Office was modeled on Theophraste Renaudot's Bureau d'adresse, a successful privately owned welfare agency in Paris.[31] But Hartlib's fertile imagination took him well beyond the suggestions of Renaudot's precedent. The Office was to have two main sections, one dealing with the address of "communications concerning spiritual matters," the other with the address of "accommodations for bodily matters." Knowledge fell under

30. Frank Manuel, *Freedom from History*, 107.
31. At the time Hartlib sought a patent from Parliament for the Office, there were six other applicants for patents to similar agencies (Turnbull, *Hartlib*, 80–88, 123–24). Hartlib knew of the Bureau d'adresse through his friend Arnold Boate, who described its operations, including the sharp practices that made it yield a lucrative trade in charity (124).

matters spiritual, and the bureau was to advance knowledge by functioning as an information and learning exchange. Exchangers of knowledge were described as those who "hath a feat in any Science which is extraordinary. Either a new discovery of a Truth, or an Experiment in Physick, Mathematicks, or Mechanicks; or a method of delivering Sciences or Languages, not ordinarily known, and very profitable; or some intricate Question and difficulty which he would have resolved by the most experienced in any or all Arts."[32] Hartlib's religio-magical conception of science is apparent from these remarks. He had no conception of method in science, whereby a plan of research led ineluctably to the accumulation of knowledge by scientists working independently or in association. Instead, science was for him something exotic, mysterious, scarcely comprehensible: it consisted of "extraordinary feats" or solutions to "intricate questions." Given this subjective notion, the *only* mode of cooperation was communication of results. Like many with no head for things technical, machines seemed to him little miracles, as his favored term for them—"ingenuities"—implies. If he possessed any systematic knowledge, he kept it to himself; his one publication on horticulture consists entirely of "correspondencies," "addresses," or in plain language, reports of the experiments of others.[33] His learning appears to have consisted mainly of anecdotes about natural wonders and the occult.[34]

As for public addresses concerning bodily accommodations, Hartlib's bureau cut a wide path. It was to be an employment agency for the poor, and it would furnish a listing service for those in need of, or willing to provide, medical and other services to the poor. It would provide information about commerce, including a travel service for commercial men and strangers. It was to be a matrimonial agency, but also a newspaper giving all foreign and domestic news. There was even to be a parcel-checking service to complete the domestication of London.

Such was the program of Puritan science that some historians have lately hailed as a bold step toward modernity. Despite the bewildering variety of these humanitarian schemes, there is system in them. Hartlib merely drew up a list of things that he would like to do for others and called them "accommodations," evidently to foreshadow a resumption of the charitable hotel and hostel business that in the 1630s had ruined his private fortune. These plans struck the improvers at Westminster as

32. Quoted by R. F. Jones, *Ancients and Moderns,* 149.
33. Ibid., 153.
34. Lynn Thorndike, *History of Magic and Experimental Science,* 7: 272–332; Keith Thomas, *The Decline of Magic,* passim.

worthwhile. In 1649, shortly after the publication of his design for the Office of Address, Parliament named Hartlib State Agent for Universal Learning and increased his pension to £300 per year. But that was not enough to support his schemes, which came to nought. Such was the fate of Comenianism. Already in 1646 Dury wrote to Hartlib that Comenius had only "raised expectations" and "shamed" his lieutenants, who were left holding the bag of "so many promises and so little performance." Hartlib, however, lived on hopes. A few kind words or casual promises were enough to make him hope that the Office of Address must soon become the divine instrument for world reform, that his income would be secure, that Parliament would take an interest in his secret weapon, which could sink ships with a single shot. And he was a man of faith. He believed that he would find the mechanic to build Comenius's perpetual motion machine, so vital to the success of Macaria. He believed that the Millennium would arrive in 1655, because Comenius had promised it. Ill and impoverished toward the end of his life, his dreams of reform foundered when Charles II returned to England. Despondently he wrote that England had "proved a great nothing" as the site of Macaria; "the name and the thing are as good as vanished." Yet even in this somber moment hope did not desert him, for he believed that the Lord might install Macaria on Bermuda.

The flawless ineptitude of Puritan Baconians is doubtless why previous historians passed them by as a lost cause of no particular importance. The revival of interest in Puritanism sparked by Max Weber has produced a mass of evidence to confirm that "Puritan science" was indeed a blind alley. Nevertheless, we may read from the new data several significant lessons about the brief career of evangelical science.

Hartlib's personal ineffectiveness and bad luck do not alter the fact that he pioneered a new role for an old social type: he discovered social welfare entrepreneurship as a new type of chaplaincy. He always stressed the public character of his activities. He consistently identified Parliament as the appropriate institution to support his activities. And he believed that the public purse owed him an income in return for his services. When he was offered a benefice to supply his needs, he declined because, he said, he was not suited to the clergy.[35] He realized that he had a valuable product to sell. The young patrician Robert Boyle supported enthusiastically his "glorious design" for the Office of Address. To young William Petty, Hartlib was "that painful and great instrument" of the Office.[36] These endorsements do not signify acceptance of

---

35. Turnbull, *Hartlib,* 27.
36. Purver, *The Royal Society,* 201.

Hartlib's religious conception of science, since both men took Bacon's point about the necessity of banishing religious notions from science. What they signify is Hartlib's hold on their consciences. In neither case was the conscience Puritan. Even as young men they disapproved Puritan enthusiasm. But if they were secular in the head, they were religious in the heart. Hartlib's reorientation of Christian charity toward regeneration and "reformation of the whole world" seemed to them a sensible and generous outlook. It does not matter so much that the mature Boyle's reformism was directed overseas, to the conversion of the heathen, while the commoner Petty acquired a knighthood and lands for his services in Ireland. The point remains that Hartlib sensed the humanitarian shape conscience would take among nondoctrinal, scientific laymen. His edifying, vague prose displays the pastoral flare for yoking the mind to sentiment. His skill in inventing titles for himself ("the sollicitor of humane learning for the reformation of schooles," and the like) suggests a realistic appreciation of the economic and political importance of investing his new role with suitable dignities.

If Hartlib's efforts were fruitless and sublimely sentimental, it is because he was ahead of his time. Boyle and Petty were atypical of his natural constituency. Most parliamentarians had no concrete idea of science at all. The Puritan clergy, like the clergy of most sects, looked upon science as a suspicious rival spiritual force beyond their ken and control. It was not clear to them how a philosophy that displaced the earth from the center of the universe into a cosmic backwater could be made to serve religion.[37]

37. I draw attention here to the amusing historiographic scandal created by the attempt to attribute to Puritans and Puritan religious beliefs the English civil war, the rise of science, and the origins of capitalism in England. The joke is on the "discipline" of intellectual history, which is so wanting in methods and principles that leading historians cannot agree among themselves whether modern science, which was originated by professing Catholics, owes an essential debt to Puritan theology or religiosity. This "historical" thesis of Puritan origins stems from a neurotic philosopher, Auguste Comte (see chap. 1, n. 14), and was reiterated by a neurotic sociologist, Max Weber, and by another sociologist, Robert Merton. It is part of the scandal that the disputation is conducted without much regard for the origin of the thesis and none whatever for the theoretical presuppositions involved in asserting either thesis or antithesis. As I undertake to show in this work by examination of the thought of the founders of modern science, the Puritan origin thesis is at odds with the essential structure of scientific rationality. That is why the evaporation of Puritan piety had no effect upon the scientific enterprise. Exponents of the thesis are twisted into unhealable confusion by the reductions they undertake to perform: science springs from religion; but

In this they were correct, and their more up-to-date brethren who believed in Puritan science were mistaken. "Puritan science" ranks with the persecution of Galileo as a paradigmatic error. "Belief" in evangelical science indeed involves the same error as the Inquisition committed, but now from the point of view of advocacy rather than opposition. Neither Puritans nor Jesuits could imagine nonsectarian knowledge or truths inconsistent with the communal good (faith). The Inquisition innocently reasoned that since Copernican astronomy prejudiced faith, it must be "absurd and false philosophically." Similarly, the notion of Puritan science expresses a sectarian conception of science that opens the door to exotic possibilities—Catholic botany, Jewish physics, socialist genetics. Had this mentality prevailed it would have been the ruin of science. Charles Webster's study of Puritan Baconians highlights this fact. They opposed Harvey and his influence on the College of Physicians because Harvey's physiology was incompatible with Paracelsian medicine, and "a negative attitude to Paracelsus was taken as a sign of reactionary social and intellectual attitudes. From the point of view of the Puritan Revolution, the intellectual priorities of the college resulted in an insensitivity to the severe social problems of the time and a lack of interest in proposals to establish more adequate medical services for the community."[38] This is country prejudice vigorous and unashamed; the tribal idol that insists on "virtuous knowledge."

---

religion is in turn referred to social interaction and consensus, which is supposed to be the primitive explainer. However, the precise content of this explainer is never specified. It is easy to see why: sociality is common to all human groups, whereas science is a late evolutionary arrival cultivated by less than 0.0001 percent of human beings, however large the audience for scientific ideology might be. The attempt to attribute a specific activity to so vague and comprehensive a cause cannot but fail, since the supposed cause proves to "explain" every specific human activity. In the present work, the cause of science is assumed to be the polytechnic brain. For episodes of the scandal, see A. R. Hall, "Merton Revisited, or Science and Society in the Seventeenth Century," 1–16; A. R. Hall, "The Scientific and the Puritan Revolution"; H. R. Trevor-Roper, review of Christopher Hill's *Intellectual Origins of the English Revolution,* in *History and Theory;* numerous essays in Charles Webster's edited volume, *The Intellectual Revolution of the Seventeenth Century;* and, similarly, essays in Donald Pennington and Keith Thomas, eds., *Puritans and Revolutionaries: Essays in Seventeenth-Century History Presented to Christopher Hill.* The thesis of the social origin of science serves psychological, professional, and social functions for scholars anxious to level science to ideology. As Bacon said, "Infirmarum virtutum apud vulgus laus est."

38. Webster, *The Great Instauration,* 323.

The recent studies of Puritan Baconianism have restored the social background of entrenched prejudice against which thinkers and scientists struggled. This work supplies materials for a fresh appreciation of the tenacious confusions that stood in the path of science and so also of the ferocious critique directed against it. Bacon and Hobbes did what they could to root out the error of virtuous knowledge. Bacon bluntly declared that knowledge is power. In *Wisdom of the Ancients,* he underscored his point by exhibiting knowledge dissociated from virtue and cavorting with ambition, revenge, rapacity, and other antisocial behaviors and attitudes. In this way he showed that the number of moral requisites for knowledge is zero. The personal qualities of the scientist are no more relevant to science than the personal qualities of an architect are relevant to architecture. Science is religion-proof and ideology-proof.

The Baconian link between knowledge and practice is instrumentality. Knowledge can be used to relieve the human estate only because it is power. The religious mind of Comenius and the Puritans was bound to misunderstand this relationship. The morally neutral notion of relieving man's estate became for them an eschatological expectation, or a humanitarian work of charity bent on moral improvement. This misconception was not confined to the Comenians. Science usually made its way among modern publics under the banner of some comparable sacralization. It is important to stress that Bacon did not commit this error. Artillery and empire are not humanitarian weapons. Hobbes for his part struck at the roots of the Platonic-Christian tradition by maintaining that "the Good" is nothing else, in its natural state, than a chaos of contending wills.

These repudiations of tribal idols are closely linked with the *honnête homme.* The idols declare that in order to know truth, the man of knowledge must be virtuous. But the honest Descartes believed that the search for truth needs the assistance of transcendental iniquity. "I think" ties the search for truth to the impiety of preferring one's own clear and distinct ideas to communal norms and faiths, however sacred or "necessary."

The dissociation of knowledge from moral virtue is at the heart of the anticlericism and irreligion of "true philosophy." It is equally at the heart of its antisectarian, cosmopolitan political outlook. Plato's moralization of truth had as its political correlate the supervision of morals and opinion by a council of elders. Political thinkers of the seventeenth century recognized this for what it was: a carryover of prepolitical, tribal mentality into the cosmopolitan milieu of the city. The historical expression of this conflict was of course not Plato's writings, but the struggle of Europe's *politiques* with religious sectarianism. The *politiques* understood that city life is not compatible with the supervision of morals and opinion. The diversity of social ranks, the division of labor, the range of public and private roles ensure and require diversity of character and opinion. This diversity they championed by espousing toleration and by insisting on the subordination of religion to civil authority. Since science was independent of sects and morals, it provided powerful support to the cosmopolitan outlook. This linkage between science and politics is a basic theme of Sprat's *History of the Royal Society.*

The Political Program of the Royal Society

Charles II had scarcely warmed the throne when returning royalist scientists presented him with a plan for the Royal Society. In less than two years they achieved what Hartlib and his Puritan associates could not accomplish in two decades. The reasons for their success are apparent. The returning scientists who took the lead were Sir Robert Moray and Lord Brouncker, the Society's first president. Moray, who has been called "the architect of the Society's incorporation," was a member of the Privy Council and enjoyed Charles's confidence thanks to his many military and diplomatic services to the house of Stuart.[39] He and Brouncker were competent mathematicians conversant with the most advanced continental science and scientists. They distinguished science from its imitators and shadows, from antiquarianism to natural magic. Aware that science is cosmopolitan, they jettisoned the idea of tying the Royal Society to confessional orthodoxy or political allegiance. They joined forces with John Wilkins's science group, then meeting in Gresham College, London, and formed a planning committee which met under Moray's leadership until the Society's first charter was issued in 1662.[40]

39. D. C. Martin, "Sir Robert Moray, F.R.S," 250. Anthony Wood characterizes Moray as "a renowned chemist, a great patron of the Rosicrucians, and an excellent mathematician" and asserts that "though presbyterianly inclined, he had the king's ear as much as any other person, and was indefatigable in his undertakings" (*Athenae Oxon.*, ed. Bliss, 1: 725). In politics, he preferred that the royal prerogative be carried low rather than high. Clarendon called him a "cunning and dexterous man"; Gilbert Burnet praised his gentility and kindness. Charles II was so fond of Moray that he gave him quarters in Whitehall and buried him at his own expense in Westminster Cathedral. As for Moray's religion, Charles said that he was "head of his own church." See Martin, "Sir Robert Moray, F.R.S," 245–46; Alexander Robertson, *The Life of Sir Robert Moray*, 170–91.

40. On 28 November 1660, the Wilkins group proposed to establish a "society for promoting experimental philosophy." The proposal was communicated

Early in its deliberations, the planning committee resolved to open membership to nonscientists. This was not an obviously sound decision, as Moray knew. Between 1660 and 1665, Moray was in touch with Christiaan Huygens, who kept him informed of the deliberations in France concerning the founding of the Académie.[41] The painful failures of the Montmor Academy contained many cautions against a large membership, a fact that figured in Colbert's decision to model the Académie after the Florentine Accademia, with membership restricted to a small number of working scientists. Moray favored this model, but opted for a large association because financial considerations left no alternative.[42] When Charles returned to England, the exchequer was empty, and the prospects for improvement in the immediate future were bleak. The Society certainly could not hope for funding on the

---

to Moray, who was able to report the king's approval on 5 December (Purver, *The Royal Society,* 109–10). The rapid approval suggests that Moray had discussed the prospectus of a scientific society well in advance of the Gresham resolution. Purver repeats the current belief that Wilkins was the architect of the Society (109). The record does not bear it out. Moray chaired all meetings until Brouncker was elected president in 1662; he and Sir Paul Neile were the liaison with Charles; Moray alone was the liaison with the principals in France who were organizing the Académie; and Moray was the Society's chief fund raiser (Henry Lyons, *The Royal Society, 1660–1940,* 21, 26–27, 33, 36f., 44, 55–56). John Evelyn, whom Moray brought into the group in January 1661, said that Moray, together with Brouncker and Boyle, "were the persons to whom the world stands obliged for the promoting of that generous and real knowledge which gave the ferment that has ever since obtained" (*Diary,* 3: 481). Gilbert Burnet called him "the first former of the royal society, and its first president; and while he lived he was the life and soul of that body" (Burnet, *History of His Own Times,* 1: 109). Moray's leadership is also acknowledged by Sprat in *The History of the Royal Society,* 58–59, 135–36. On Brouncker and his role in the Society, see J. F. Scott and Harold Hartley, "William, Viscount Brouncker, F.R.S.," in Harold Hartley, ed., *The Royal Society, Its Originators and Founders,* 147–58.

41. Lyons, *The Royal Society, 1660–1940,* 36; Robertson, *Life of Sir Robert Moray,* 156.
42. Ibid. In a letter to Huygens (14 May 1663), Moray described the act of incorporation of the Society as "necessaire à la rendre capable selon les lois des pays à recevoir donations et standi in indicio etc., de sorte que nous nous appliquons aux autres moyens necessoires à la prosecution du dessein que nous nous sommes proposés." On 3 February 1664, Moray moved in council "that everyone of the council might think of ways to raise a revenue for carrying on the design and work of the Society." The council decided, on Moray's motion, that they attempt to acquire Chelsea College. Legal title was acquired, but the Society never got any revenue or use from that crumbling institution. See Robertson, *Life of Sir Robert Moray,* 156–57.

lavish scale that the Académie enjoyed from its inception. Moray's strategy was to raise money for the Society's activities from dues and subscriptions. The pattern of enlarging membership clearly reflects this intention. The founding group of 11 in 1661 soon became 56, which for a time was declared the maximum number. But this restriction was soon removed. By 1663, there were 131 fellows, a figure that remained typical of the Society's size.[43] The membership included some of the wealthiest men of the nation, who were promptly solicited for dues and subscriptions. But these efforts did not immediately succeed. By 1663 fellows were £158 in arrears with dues; by 1676 the figure had reached £2,000. Until 1700, the annual income of the Society rarely exceeded £300, a sum so beggarly that the modest salaries of its secretary and curator could not always be met.[44] In these financial circumstances, a program of research in applied or theoretical science could scarcely be mounted. Funding the Royal Society at a level equivalent to the Paris Académie would have cost about £15,000 per year.

The decision to publish *The History of the Royal Society,* advertising its aims and purposes, seems to have been part of the fund-raising effort. A publication committee consisting of Moray, Brouncker, Wilkins, Robert Boyle, and John Evelyn was set up in 1663 to supervise the writing by Thomas Sprat, a Wilkins protégé.[45] Sprat was not a scientist but a young clergyman and publicist who wrote in the cause of science, after the fashion of Joseph Glanvill. The breezy style of the work is doubtless his own, but it may be safely assumed that Moray and Wilkins, especially, either dictated or approved all matters in the work that might be subject to controversy.

Sprat was out to do a selling job with his amiable picture of the Society's success, prestige, and respectability. The most powerful men of the land were portrayed as having formed a united front with renowned scientists to advance knowledge. The actual situation was rather different. When the *History* appeared, the Society was still largely a paper organization; its council, to be sure, had been active, but the first meeting with its full membership was not held until that year. And as we have seen, the Society's membership was badly in arrears with dues—a pertinent but compromising fact that Sprat chose not to mention. Undoubtedly the council hoped that the *History* might serve as a suitable vehicle for conveying its intentions to its own uncooperative members, whose combined wealth and power might easily finance all the research its scientific members could pursue. To cajole support, the *History* set forth a

43. Martin, "Sir Robert Moray, F.R.S.," 249ff.
44. Lyons, *The Royal Society, 1660–1940,* 79.
45. Purver, *The Royal Society,* 11–12.

program whose political bearing the gentlemen members of the Society could readily understand; and it argued that scientific contributions from the Society were indispensable to the program's success.

The program was comprised of two main points. One was envisaged by the Society's charter, which defined its "business and design" to be "to improve the knowledge of naturall things, and all useful Arts, Manufactures, Mechanick practices, Engines and Inventions by Experiments."[46] The *History* labored to establish that applied science, of great potential profitability, was a going concern. This matter had to be treated with a certain caution, however. The marquis of Worcester had spent a fortune estimated at £60,000 in search of commercial applications of science and had precious little to show for it. Confidence men had already tried to cash in on the applied science El Dorado by selling shares in perpetual motion machines, methods of finding longitude at sea, and updated versions of the alchemical swindle.[47] The *History*'s strong emphasis on Society fellows' bona fide achievements in applied science doubtless addressed a justified skepticism toward pie-in-the-sky Baconianism. The *History* accordingly located applied science as integral to a politics of national economic and political expansion, which at that time was topical. The program was nonpartisan in the sense that it might be carried out by a monarchy or a republic, as the then-current examples of the Netherlands and France would show. But by 1670, this program came to be associated in Charles's mind with his troublesome Whig factions and the Nonconformists.[48]

The second point of the program concerned that nerve of Restoration politics, religion. The *History* invoked the authority of science for "rational religion" against "enthusiasm," "fanaticism," and "superstition." Although the Society pretended not to meddle in politics or religion, it is not obvious that this critique was politically neutral in the Restoration context. Events up to that time may be described as a wrestling match between Charles's determination to achieve conformity and the Nonconformists' determination to resist. Between 1662 and 1665, Parliament approved four very restrictive acts against Nonconformists (the Clarendon Code), which Archbishop Sheldon enforced with severities that exceeded the persecutions that decades before had cost Archbishop Laud his head.[49] The Nonconformists, led by Baxter, Calamy, Jacomb, and the like, affirmed the rights of the depressed Puritan con-

46. Sprat, *History of the Royal Society*, 46.
47. Marjorie Nicholson, *Pepys' Diary and the New Science*, 122–30. See Defoe's comments on fraudulent projectors in his *Essay upon projects*, 8 ff.
48. Plum, *Restoration Puritanism*, 45, 51.
49. Ibid., 35, 40.

science while protesting their loyalty to the throne. Charles's Lord Chancellor Clarendon retorted that political loyalty implied submission to the king's Church.

Rational religion represented a third and ultimately triumphant force in this struggle. Rationalism provided no support for the Nonconformists' plea for toleration on the grounds of liberty of conscience. That liberty was the shadow of the Calvinist belief in election, which rational religion effectively demolished. High churchmen might therefore look upon it as an ally. In fact they did not, for the good reason that rationalism did not prop up the Anglican rationale for persecution, passive obedience, and divine right. The whole tendency of rational religion, or Latitudinarian theology, was to supersede high Church *and* Nonconformist theology with a doctrine largely independent of tradition or the Bible—reasonable Christianity, Locke called it.

The alliance of Whig politics with Latitudinarian theology was officially recognized when William III named John Tillotson, the son-in-law of John Wilkins, archbishop of Canterbury. But the alliance was probably formed around 1660, when the duke of Buckingham, a notorious libertine of no confirmed religious beliefs, became the patron of Wilkins and Thomas Sprat. Buckingham was an original fellow of the Society; his collaborator, the Whig Shaftesbury, was elected fellow in 1663.[50] The *History* discreetly avoided direct comment on the controversial Clarendon Code. But it made a show of its own nonsectarianism as a model for the nation, and implications for ecclesiastical policy were obvious. It was not gratuitous, then, that the *History* appeared in the same year that the Clarendon Ministry fell to the Cabal Ministry, an alliance of Whigs and Catholics led by Buckingham, Shaftesbury, and Arlington. Buckingham at once used his influence to promote his clients. In 1668, Wilkins, whom Archbishop Sheldon had kept in limbo, was consecrated bishop of Chester with great ceremony, while Sprat, who was Buckingham's chaplain, was appointed to the canonry of Westminster.[51] In the same year, Sir Paul Neile, a Shaftesbury associate, sponsored the membership of John Locke and saw to it that he went directly onto the Society's governing council.[52]

A year later, the purport of this backstairs politicking was made public in a sensational sermon at Oxford. Notables had gathered to cele-

50. Lotte Mulligan, "Civil War Politics," 342.
51. On Buckingham's influence in these appointments, see *Dictionary of National Biography*, 20: 340. On the hostility between Wilkins and Sheldon, see Shapiro, *John Wilkins*, 167 ff.
52. Purver, *The Royal Society*, 73, 82. Locke had entered Shaftesbury's service in 1667.

brate the opening of the Sheldonian Theater. The university orator, Dr. Robert South, took the occasion to eulogize the donor of the Theater and his high Church theology. South also identified and castigated the enemies of the Church. They were, he maintained, the Royal Society, which tended to undermine religion and the universities.[53]

South's allegations were substantially correct from the Oxford perspective. Prior to 1700, three Whig chieftains—the earl of Pembroke, the earl of Halifax, and Lord Somers—held the presidency of the Society, while no Tory leader did. One of the main broadsides in the war of words leading up to the Glorious Revolution was the *Essay concerning Human Understanding*, which Locke dedicated to Pembroke as president of the Society. Despite his caution and secrecy, Locke was known as the brain truster to Shaftesbury, Halifax, Mordaunt, and Somers. No man could aspire to more solid Whig credentials.

That the *History* may be reckoned an early, perhaps the first, Whig manifesto is apparent from its integration of the political program with theology. The theory was meant to remove religious quarrels from the political agenda so that the nation could get on with the business of economic expansion. In the political arena, Buckingham and Shaftesbury deployed a parallel argument against Clarendon and the high Church bishops. Irrespective of conscience and other religious questions, they argued that persecutions were economically harmful.[54] Besides the costs of enforcement, persecutions drove artisans and merchants from the nation in tens of thousands, to the detriment of commerce.[55] This experience was neither new nor specifically English. It had been observed in France, Flanders, Holland, and Germany since the wars of the Reformation began. The link between toleration and prosperity was clearly articulated at that time by Colbert in France and John de Witt in Holland. In England, the politicians who advocated policies to enhance this link came to be called "Whigs." The cardinal Whig maxim—that the liberty of the subject and the prosperity of the nation stand together—was completely distinct from Nonconformist defenses of toleration on grounds of conscience. Nonconformists suffered considerable loss of life, and property losses estimated at £1,400,000, for the sake of conscience—proof enough that for them, the salvation of the soul rated higher than worldly prosperity. Whig politicians placed the opposite value on this state of affairs: what counted was not souls saved,

53. Evelyn, *Diary*, 3: 485, entry for 9 July 1669. For a review of ecclesiastical opposition to the Royal Society, see Nicholson, *Pepys' Diary*, 100–175.
54. Plum, *Restoration Puritanism*, 41–42, 52, 56.
55. Ibid., 43 ff.

but property lost and commerce burdened. Whig defenses of liberty of conscience were supplementary to the defense of property. Thus, whereas Baxter and Calamy defended conscience in terms supportive of the Calvinist sect, Locke's defense of conscience tended to reform it in the direction of "reasonable Christianity," which was detested by Puritans and high churchmen alike.[56]

That the linkage between liberty and property, or prosperity, owns a pedigree independent of Calvinist theology is apparent from the *History*'s vehement attack on zealots as the enemy of public order, the enemy of science and sober thinking, the enemy of true religion. Sprat pointedly described the origin of the Royal Society as a refuge from the fury of Puritan righteousness. It began in 1649 with the men who assembled in Wilkins's lodgings at Wadham College:

Their first purpose was no more, than only the satisfaction of breathing freer air, and of conversing in quiet with one another, without being engaged in the passions, and madness of that dismal age . . . that by this means there was a race of young men provided, against the next age, whose minds receiving from them their first impressions of sober and generous knowledge, were invincibly armed against all the enchantments of enthusiasm.[57]

56. The Whig leanings of the Royal Society have been recently investigated by J. R. Jacob in a series of articles that draw attention to Pett. Jacob does not explore the similar attitudes held by parliamentary Whigs such as Shaftesbury. It is important to note that the politics of prosperity and national expansion were espoused by both Whigs and Tories in the period 1670–90. In drawing attention to this fact, Jacob seeks to detect an Anglican tilt in the Royalist case, and a Puritan tilt in the Royal Society case. He arrives at this reading by disregarding the anti-Puritan polemic of Sprat's *History* (Jacob, "Restoration Ideologies and the Royal Society," 30–33).

57. Sprat, *History of the Royal Society*, 53–54. The *History*'s sharp repudiation of Puritanism, and its denial of any "connection" between Puritanism and science, are embarrassing to those who are keen to prove some "connection." Thus, Charles Webster attempts to explain away the *History*'s testimony by suggesting that the Society's fellows were attempting to cover up or disavow their Puritan past (Webster, *The Great Instauration*, xxxff.). This is merely a surmise. Webster's remark assumes that most fellows had a scarlet past to hide or exculpate; actually, the fellows were overwhelmingly royalist (Mulligan, "Civil War Politics," 334ff.). Webster's surmise applies at most to a few fellows, preeminently John Wilkins. But Wilkins was no more a Puritan than other *politique* commonwealth men like Harrington or Shaftesbury (Shapiro, "Latitudinarianism and Science in Seventeenth-Century England," 293ff.).

The full significance of the *History's* repudiation of religious passion is not appreciated without exchanging these epithets for the characterizations used by the Puritans. They preferred to say not that they were mad, but zealous; and the zeal stemmed from conscience stirred by divine inspiration. To repudiate zealotry, then, was to abandon that bedrock of Puritanism, conscience as a self-sufficient theologian and moralist. The Wadham group's common pursuit of science was defined by its replacement of conscience by another code, the genteel virtues of sobriety, moderation, and generosity. Sprat was indeed concerned to establish in the *History* the mutual consistency of gentility and experimental science. Prince Rupert's assiduous experimentation was not enough to eliminate doubts in this regard, provoked according to Sprat by the experimentalist's minute investigations and mechanical practice. Experimentalists were gentlemen, Sprat maintained; but they were gentlemen of a new stripe. Their sobriety did not stem from a traditional conception of seemliness and due measure, but from turning their thoughts from words to the order of nature. Their generosity was not animated by the ancient *noblesse oblige*, but comprised a cosmopolitanism recognizing no difference in "country, interests, or profession of religion" (*History,* 63, 56–57). The experiences of the Interregnum proved that generosity among the English gentry was compatible with bitter and narrow sectarianism. The experimental philosopher, as Sprat portrayed him, was incapable of bigotry because he had overcome the naïvetés of conscience. The Society accordingly "profess not to lay the foundations of an English, Scotch, Irish, Popish, or Protestant philosophy, but a philosophy of mankind" (63).

Cosmopolitanism placed the experimentalist into a chronology altogether nonbiblical—a "rational age" whose "universal disposition . . . is bent on rational religion" (370, 374). Sprat represented the rational age as the most recent consequence of the historiography of progress outlined by Bacon. The light of reason first dawned among the Greeks, albeit imperfectly, for they were captivated by the thrill of rhetorical display. The Romans passed this legacy to the Church doctors, who used it to refute the pagans after miracles ceased. Having defeated the heathens, the subtle doctors turned their weapons on each other, darkened their minds with captious reasoning, and ushered in an age of barbarism and war (11–22). The restoration of learning in the Renaissance led to that decisive discovery in the mind's itinerary toward reason, experimental philosophy. Experiment was the breakthrough to "things" that eliminated the mind's dependency on "words." Language is inadequate as a medium of knowledge because the signifying relation between words and things is defective. Words are the medium of subjective rhapsodies. In an obvious reference to seditious preaching, Sprat declared that "eloquence ought to be banished out of all civil societies, as a thing fatal to peace and good manners" (III, II2–13, 427). The *History* did not disguise the consequences of its repudiation of "words." Ancient authors might be respected as venerable relics, but the experimentalist emancipated himself from the "slavery to dead men's minds" (29, 37–38, 42, 46). Late in the *History*, Sprat itemized seven objections to erudition, which set at nought, as Dr. South complained, the value of the curriculum of the universities (331, 340).

From the perspective of the secular chronology of the rational age, miracles were the product of "dark and ignorant ages." Religious beliefs generally had to be trimmed to the average mentality of an age:

> The medicines for religious distempers must be changeable according to the Diseases. . . . in a gross and sensual age, the deepest mysteries of our religion may be proper, to purify the stupidity of men's spirits: but there must be an application of quite different and more sensible prescriptions, in a subtle, refined or enthusiastical time. (376–77)

This smacks of Hobbism. Hobbes had maintained that the mysteries of religion are symptoms of human stupidity. The more palatable line taken here is that religious mysteries are medicines for ferocious superstitions. Sprat neglected to defend the efficacy of the biblical medicines; and no wonder. In a previous statement, he had maintained that the mysteries were taught by miracles during the age of the Apostles; when miracles ceased, monks fell to theorizing about them, which led to darkened minds and civil turbulence. Sprat thus provided little evidence to support his marginal disagreement with Hobbes. The dictum that miracles ceased sometime in the first century terminated sacred history well in the past and freed nature for rational investigation. Hobbes had repudiated that central miracle, inspired conscience, as a disguise used to introduce political novelties; so did Sprat (360, 363). The experimentalist accepted miracles because they were part of the public religion. Having repudiated speculative inquiries as unsound, he had no way to investigate them; and even if he had had a method of investigation, he would not have used it because he would not mingle faith with reason. Sprat's experimental philosopher, in other words, followed Hobbes's advice to "swallow" articles of public faith "whole like a pill."[58]

58. The Hobbism of the *History* is not surprising in view of Wilkins's own reputation as a trimmer and his tendency to accept Hobbes's view of the political status of religion (Shapiro, *John Wilkins*, 150, 157).

Such rationality in matters of religion has the advantage of allowing the experimentalist's "incredulous temper" a wide berth. But what is to prevent the latitude carrying off Anglican religion together with Puritanism? Sprat approached this topic with circumspection prompted by the possibility that experimentalists might "bring the strictness of holy life out of fashion: and that so they will silently, and piece-meals, demolish religion, which they dare not openly encounter" (356). Here the *History*'s readers confronted the Restoration atheism anxiety. Glanvill, More, and Cudworth, to mention only Latitudinarian clergymen, perceived an irreligious tendency in experimental philosophy and detected a conspiracy to demolish religion "by piece-meals." And Sprat admitted that Christianity was menaced by cryptoatheist subversion; for religion teetered on the brink of the "fatal condition" that preceded the destruction of religion in the ancient world, when men paid lip service to it while "in private [they] regarded it not at all" (376). Private irreligion was especially prevalent among "many modern naturalists," which fits the pattern, discerned by Bacon, that enlightened ages tend to be the most skeptical.

We need not mention all the parries and thrusts Sprat used to counter the destructive effects of the medicine meant to cure religious distempers.[59] Suffice it that the Anglican Church was "safe amidst the consequence of a rational age" because it held a trump card: "the true and certain interest of our Church is to derive its doctrine from the plain and unquestioned parts of the Word of God, and to keep itself in due submission to the Civil Magistrate" (370). The operative part of this statement is the due submission clause. One and the same magistrate, Charles II, approved both the Anglican Church and the Royal Society; consequently, the Anglican faith was safe in the Age of Reason by royal fiat. Sprat drew up a Hobbesian contract between the experimentalist and the bishop, enforceable by the sovereign, which specified their agreement. Atheism would not be tolerated. However, the epithet "atheist" was to be applied only to "bold and insolent defiers of Heaven in their words and actions" (377). The experimentalist, in other words, was safe from dangerous accusations, provided that he paid lip service to the little bit of public credulity required by the sovereign. No Anglican inquisition would inquire into cryptoatheism and its propagation. However, those tempted to propagate irreligion should know that there were imperative reasons for them to desist.

59. The precepts of rational religion are elaborated on pp. 347–68 of the *History*. In a curious argument against materialism, Sprat instances the impalpability and insensibility of subtle fluids as material "spirits" so wonderful that they must have a creator (349).

Sprat took the line common among Latitudinarians, that the cryptoatheists were drawn to irreligion by the "late extravagant excesses of enthusiasm." But they had so successfully spread irreligion that Christianity was threatened with ruin. The result would not be to free politics from the influence of superstition, but a new calamity: "a revolution that cannot be thought on without horror. The subversion of all Europe would attend it" (378). Sprat did not further explain, but the context suggests that triumphant irreligion would provoke a fanatical countermovement. Puritanism, of course, was just such a movement, animated against the many guises of "Antichrist." In Restoration England, Puritan epigones continued evangelical work by founding societies—not scientific societies, but the Society for the Reformation of Manners, the Society for the Promotion of Christian Knowledge, and the Society for the Propagation of the Gospel in Foreign Parts.[60] This anguished moralism was the danger.

According to a currently influential interpretation of seventeenth-century intellectual history, the "Restoration mind" could not seriously entertain the possibility of irreligion. The *History* shows, however, that it was considered in cold blood as a serious political option. The argument just reviewed was probably the strongest that could have been thrown against the current of political atheism inspired mainly by Hobbes and Descartes. It did not invoke the traditional plea that religion is the bulwark of morality. This appeal would have had no force with the political atheists, whose anticlerical polemic asserted the opposite: religion is the bulwark of priestly intrigues and destructive political passions. Sprat was therefore compelled to argue that irreligion taken too far would provide a backlash that would stir once again the very passions the atheist hoped to defeat: untethered atheism is politically self-defeating. Sprat's Hobbist contract with the atheists did not require them to abandon their views but to alter their public face. The atheist should adopt a pious tone, if not from fear of God, then from fear of the God-fearing. He might, if he pleased, hold with Hobbes that man's natural condition is a state of war, provided that he presented these views reverently, as Locke did. He might espouse the godless machine universe, provided that he invoked a few emblems of natural religion, as Newton did. Let him, in other words, defer to local prejudice; let him adopt *pious atheism,* and abandon Hobbes's mocking epigrams and Descartes' destructive irony. But pious atheism was a two-way street. If experimentalists were required to adopt a pious attitude, clergymen were required to give sound reasons when they discussed political matters with political men. The *History* is piously atheistic in this

60. Plum, *Restoration Puritanism,* 90.

sense. Apart from a few canards, like the contention that Jesus' miracles qualified him as an experimental philosopher, the argument does not at any point depend on premises that could not be granted by atheists.

The fundamental political change signified here in the phrase "pious atheism" is usually expressed by the observation that during the Restoration, political deliberation in national councils shifted from religious to secular presuppositions characteristic of the modern state. While the grounds for this shift can be seen in various writings by individuals, the *History* is of special value as the work of a group, for a prestige association, who declared that the shift to secular values was conscious and deliberate. It should be emphasized that the *History*'s secularism—or, as we call it, pious atheism—does not refer to supposed private attitudes but to an argumentative strategy objectively present in the work. The private attitudes of Sprat and the publication committee are immaterial to the interpretation advanced here.

The operation of pious atheism as the fundamental premise of the *History* is apparent in Sprat's description of the doctrine that ought to be preached to the people:

> Men must now be told, that as religion is a heavenly thing, so it is not utterly averse for making use of the rules of human prudence. They must be informed, that the true holiness is a severity over ourselves, and not others. They must be instructed, that it is not the best service that can be done to Christianity to place its chief precepts so much out of the way, as to make them unfit for men of business. They must remember, that the chief of the Apostles became all things to all men, that he might gain some. (377)

Prudence takes precedence over mysteries; millenarian obsessions give way to the practical concerns of business. There is nothing here to offend a Hobbist, and the remainder of the *History* is devoted to an exposition of this turn to worldliness. England, we are informed, was about to embark on a program of commercial, manufacturing, and political expansion that would make the nation great as an empire. Science, under the auspices of the Society, would be the hub of a wheel linking commerce and manufacture in a grand expansion calculated to create unheard-of opportunities for the English "genius" for "governing and command" (420). In this remarkable manifesto, the roles of churchmen, scientists, merchants, and mechanics are defined; and in the system of expanding economy, a secular remedy for religious distempers is found. It is work; more precisely, work as efficient, productive enterprise directed toward fruitful ends, as exemplified by the Society itself:

Nor is it the least commendation the Royal Society deserves, that designing a union of men's hands and reasons, it has proceeded so far in uniting their affections. For there we behold an unusual sight to the English nation, that men of disagreeing parties, and ways of life, have forgotten to hate, and have met in the unanimous advancement of the same works. There the soldier, the tradesman, the merchant, the scholar, the gentleman, the courtier, the divine, the Presbyterian, the Papist, the Independent, and those of Orthodox judgment, have laid aside their names of distinction, and calmly conspired in a mutual agreement of labors and desires. (427)

Sprat held up the cosmopolitan toleration and mutual endeavor of the Society as a political model for the nation. Work is the practical correlate of the intellectual cosmopolitanism of science. Work unites men of all confessions by subordinating sectarianism to common interest, thereby establishing a basis for the arts of peace (396, 422, 426ff.). Work is neither the curse of Adam nor an exercise in the remission of sin. It is the effective means to increase the advantage, strength, and power of the nation. The *History* implied that the nation had very little option but to adopt this program. In 1666 a Dutch naval force boldly sailed up the Thames to destroy the English fleet anchored at Chatham; and the grand ambitions of Louis XIV were no secret. Pointing anxiously to these commercial and territorial rivals, Sprat advised:

It is true concernment of England to secure itself from the dominion of strangers, both ecclesiastical and temporal; to advance its industry in peaceful arts; to increase its people; to improve its own manufactures; to introduce the foreign, of which our soil is capable; to make use of the two kingdoms that are joined with it under the same monarch, for those productions that grow not at home; to obtain union of mind, both in civil and spiritual matters; and to preserve the ancient form of government. (421)

By enhancing their advantage, and experiencing the wealth and power they afford, men acquire a taste, even a passion for work (422). Methodical work within a national system of growth remedies religious distempers by filling morbid imaginations with concrete objectives that the hands of men can do something about. Thus, the age of rational work moves ineluctably forward toward improvements on all fronts—toward increase, toward empire, toward "capitalism."

The *History* proposed this program not merely as the antithesis of what came to be called "the Protestant ethic" but as a remedy for its distempers. Its diagnosis is scarcely unique. The greatest practitioner of the commercial republic in the seventeenth century, John de Witt, based his policies as grand pensionary of Holland on the same diagnosis. Of his opponents, the Calvinist clergy, he wrote that "they do in all these countries think fit to teach and preach up all that can have a tendency to their own credit, profit, and ease, yea, though it be to the ruin of the whole country; . . . when the doctrine, counsel, and admonition of these men is not received by any of their auditors, . . . they do then very unmercifully prosecute them *odio theologico*."[61] There is nothing especially ethical about the secular remedy for the distempers of the Calvinist salvation ethic. The motive for work is tangible advantage and power, not spiritual reward. No reliance is placed on charity or benevolence; for to assume benevolence is to believe that something can be had for nothing.[62] But this is only to say that the matrix of work is the rational world system of determinant causality, which provides the basis for all calculation of productive increase.

The firm insistence on the law of causality in matters economic upsets more than the Protestant ethic; it also upsets traditional notions of generosity. As mentioned, the *History* was anxious to reconcile gentility with the practice of experimental philosophy. The prejudice of traditional gentility spoke in the witty reproaches to experimental philosophers that circulated in Restoration England. Dr. South complained that experimentalists "admire nothing but fleas, lice, and themselves"; Charles II laughed at Boyle's "weighing the air" and ridiculed William Petty's catamaran. The experimentalist, with his contempt of letters, his minute and mechanic investigations, his bizarre ideas (blood transfusion, crossing of species), seemed some new barbarian. Sprat cited these common reactions as the greatest obstacle to the acceptance of the new philosophy (421–22). He met the objection frontally with a demand that the traditional education of gentlemen in polite arts and erudition be replaced by training of the head and hand in mechanical philosophy (409, 413). He demanded a new kind of gentility—the polytechnic gentleman—exemplified on the Continent at that time by Colbert, Huygens, and de Witt.

61. [Pieter de la Court], *The True Interest and Political Maxims of the Republic of Holland and Westfriesland*, 59.

62. Speaking of the random discovery of inventions by tradesmen and engineers, Sprat said: "For in all ages by some casual accidents those things have been revealed which either men did not think of or else fought for in vain. But of this the benevolence is irregular and most uncertain: this indeed can scarce be styled a work of man. The heart deserves as much praise of invention, for lighting on the herb that cures it; as the man who blindly stumbles on any profitable work without foresight, or consideration" (*History*, 394). These words echo Descartes in *The Discourse on Method*.

Under the auspices of Whig politics, England did embark on the program of commercial and manufacturing expansion announced in the *History*. But the Society's role in it was not what the Council of 1667 had hoped it would be. It was unable to persuade its own members to fund a research program. Had the fellows been in earnest about research, they would have provided funds for quarters; but in the event, the Society could not purchase accommodation until 1712, a half-century after its charter was issued. Nor did the polytechnic gentleman find influential sponsors. In France polytechnic academies for engineers and military officers were founded early in the eighteenth century. The English establishment proved to be so indifferent to the idea that England did not acquire its first engineering schools until late in the nineteenth century, and then only under the duress of foreign competition.

The idea was not wholly without effect, however. At Cambridge, where the influence of the Latitudinarians was greatest, and where Newton held the Lucasian chair of mathematics, Richard Bentley, the Latitudinarian master of Trinity College, pushed through a reform of the curriculum that made mathematics and physics required subjects for all students.[63] While laboratory demonstrations were part of the physics course, the curriculum was taught as a dignified and contemplative subject, more in the spirit of astronomy than of mechanics. That approach was evidently congenial to Latitudinarian theology, since astronomy is more apt than mechanics to direct the minds of undergraduates to the Creator. There was indeed a symbiosis between Newton and the academic Latitudinarian clergymen. He encouraged them to use his world system to underpin their rational theology, while they repaid the debt by legitimating and endorsing his physics from lectern and pulpit.[64]

This alliance against the high churchmen was clearly to Newton's advantage. His political career began in 1689, when Cambridge colleagues elected him to represent the university in the Convention Parliament. A year later he was introduced to Locke, then a potent advisor. The impoverished Newton was soon in touch with the lord treasurer, Halifax, and in 1694 he was appointed Master of the Mint. The sanctification of his natural philosophy by the Latitudinarians made him the most celebrated and widely admired man of his age. Newton responded

63. John Gascoigne, "'The Holy Alliance,'" 281ff.
64. Manuel, *Freedom from History*, 156, 160, 164. Newton's disciples included Samuel Clarke, William Whiston, Edmund Halley, Gregory Cotes, Richard Bentley, and Fatio de Duillier. Newton ejected Fatio from his circle when he became involved with religious millenarians in London. For a "social origins" view of Newton's self-perpetuation, see Margaret Jacob, *The Newtonians and the English Revolution*.

to canonization with cool, pious cupidity. He concocted a noble ancestry from his gentry stock, got about London in a sedan chair, and had himself painted in the costume of the Knights of the British Empire. Scientific rivals were made sensible of his jealousy: the gentle Royal Astronomer Flamsteed he crushed without compunction or cause, and he used foul means to destroy Leibniz's reputation, meanwhile imposing his own inferior version of the calculus on British mathematics.[65] When he became president of the Royal Society in 1703, he set about rescuing it from decay. Finances were set in order, administration was improved, quarters were purchased, and scientists acquired more representation on the council. But he did nothing to restore the Society's original emphasis on applied science; instead he used the Society as a platform for projecting the image of science as a lofty religious metaphysics.[66] By 1754 the Royal Society had veered so far from applied science that the Society of Arts could be established without fearing to tread on the older society's territory.

The genteel objection to the new philosophy doubtless played some part in discouraging the Royal Society from pursuing its original aims. The "airy speculations" of the experimentalists, with their projects for airships and a universal language, seemed to Sir William Temple an ominous sign of an unhinged imagination destructive of proportion and sobriety. His essay *Of Ancient and Modern Learning* (1690) commenced the English version of the Battle of the Books with a defense of the ancients against the overweening claims of the moderns. Temple was by no means merely nostalgic. As English ambassador to Holland, he supported alliance with a people whose enterprise he admired; his *Observations on the United Provinces* was a modern defense of a modern nation. But modern taste offended him. The idea of progress seemed brash arrogance that attacked the roots of refinement, a respectful attitude toward the legacy of the fathers over millennia. He would not concede that moderns had surpassed the ancients in the arts or in moral subjects, and he was unconvinced that the progress of the sciences was not offset by their barbarous character.[67] Richard Bentley and William Wooten replied on behalf of the moderns; they were answered by Temple's secretary, Jonathan Swift, in two satires. In his subsequent fable, *Gulliver's Travels*, Swift penned the most bitter attack on the Royal

65. Manuel, *Freedom from History*, 175ff.
66. According to Manuel, Newton wove a "sacred and aristocratic aura around science through the development of ceremonials" for the Society (ibid., 157, 169).
67. H. E. Woodbridge, *Sir William Temple*, 316ff.

Society to emerge from the literature of Augustan England. Although Swift's response to the new philosophy was unusually cross, it did, like Pascal's response, identify a tendency by representing it in the extreme. But genteel reserve toward the Royal Society's aims cannot be the whole story. That reserve carried even more weight in France, which nevertheless became the pacesetter for technical education in Europe. The reception of the new philosophy was burdened in England by disagreements among its advocates.

There occurred something like a factional fight within the Whig-Latitudinarian camp concerning how far secularization should go. The controversy concerned the Trinity, revelation, miracles, and the basis of morality. John Locke conveniently located himself at the hub of the controversy as the exponent of a more secular Whiggism against the episcopal Whiggism of the Latitudinarians and the genteel Whiggism of Locke's former pupil, the third earl of Shaftesbury. Locke's critique of innate ideas attacked the Platonic component of Latitudinarian theology necessary for the sacralization of Newton's mechanistic system. Bishop Stillingfleet's criticism of Locke's reasonable Christianity meant to salvage the divinity of Christ from Locke's alleged depredations. Most telling of all, however, was the young Shaftesbury's repudiation of his master's moral doctrines as "barbarous."

Locke, Whiggery, and Deism

Our proposal to consider Locke as the founder of Whig political philosophy runs against a certain drift in contemporary scholarship. John Dunn's study dares perhaps the most explicit statement of recent demurrers at the canonical picture of Locke as a rationalist progressive. Dunn maintains that Locke passed from an early "conservative" position to the later "liberal" phase, in which all his main works were written; but throughout both phases, "Locke's ideas remain . . . profoundly and exotically incoherent."[68] Dunn suggests as well that the "liberal" Locke was rather more conservative than scholars such as Fox Bourne have believed, for his principles merely reiterated "the most indubitable and parochial political orthodoxy" of the day. Dunn's incoherent Locke was part of the evidence prompting J. G. A. Pocock to declare that Locke was not the central figure he was once thought to be, and to wonder where he "fits in" the stream of British political consciousness.[69] Other

68. John Dunn, *The Political Thought of John Locke*, 29; also 4 ff.
69. J. G. A. Pocock, *The Machiavellian Moment*, 424. Pocock's diminution of the place of Locke and Hobbes in the political thought of Great Britain and the

historians have expressed similar reservations about the Whig picture of Locke.

There was indeed something conservative about Locke—his manner. His languid, long-winded prose never crackles with the sauciness of the rebel or the vehemence of faction. He never boasted of the novelty of his ideas; he even deprecated them. He did not seek attention through authorship; on the contrary, he went to great lengths to keep his authorship of major tracts secret years after their anonymous publication. His entire manner bespoke caution and sobriety. Lord Acton suggestively characterized such conservatism as Whig moderation, which he contrasted with the radicalism of the Long Parliament: "The very essence of the new party was compromise. They saw that it is an error to ride a principle to death, to push things to an extreme, to have an eye for one thing only, to prefer abstractions to realities, to disregard practical conditions. They were a little disappointing, a little too fond of the halfway house. Their philosophy, or rather their philosopher, John Locke, is always reasonable and sensible, but diluted and pedestrian and poor."[70] It is but a short step from here to Dunn's conclusion that the *matter* of Locke's thought is incoherent. To take Locke's measure, we should hold firmly to these impressions while searching out the fugitive Mr. Hyde in the closet of Dr. Locke.

There is one index of Locke's opinions that remained consistent throughout his life: he did not get on well with that citadel of high church conservatism, Oxford. As a student he disliked its scholastic curriculum. He left Oxford at the first opportunity to embark on a diplomatic and political career in Shaftesbury's household. His fellowship in Christ College was canceled in 1684 for his part in Shaftesbury's po-

---

United States is part of a strategy to exhibit the "civic humanist" paradigm in contrast to the "liberal" paradigm, which assigns these two thinkers so large a formative role. His challenge to an orthodoxy has had a tonic effect on slumbering dogmatists, and he has lent the civic humanist tradition a vividness and historiographic fullness that it never previously had. But at the end of the day it cannot explain why the liberal tradition prevailed in Europe and North America. The reason, on the present view, is that liberalism locked arms with the cognitive structure of science, which made it a formidable rational and rhetorical instrument even in the hands of more superficial thinkers and publicists. For a particularly clear statement on this historiographic quest, see Pocock, "Cambridge Paradigms and Scotch Philosophers," 235–52. For Pocock's statement on the place of Locke in the Anglo-American political tradition, see "The Myth of John Locke and the Obsession with Liberalism."

70. Lord Acton, *Lectures on Modern History*, 217.

litical machinations. Two decades later, university officials contemplated a ban on his *Essay concerning Human Understanding*, to whose influence they attributed the decay of logical exercises in the university. The idea was dropped, however, for fear that its effect would be the opposite of that intended. And in the survivals of Oxford gossip, Locke appears as a corrupter of morals, a Hobbist, and an "arrant atheist."[71] At Oxford, then, Locke did not seem a pedestrian endorser of parochial orthodoxies but a dangerous innovator in the mold of Hobbes and Spinoza.

A second index to the man and his thought is his political activity. The politics of that time was marked by persecutions, plots, intrigue, treason, show trials, and political executions. In 1672, the king committed treason by providing, in the secret clauses of the Treaty of Dover, for the conversion of England to Catholicism in return for large payments from Louis XIV meant to make Charles independent of parliamentary supply. Shaftesbury was deep in intrigue to thwart this popish intention, and Locke faithfully served his master throughout. The timid Locke was watched by court spies but managed to evade them for weeks at a time. He probably helped Shaftesbury manufacture the Popish plot.[72] After the Rye House plot he burned his papers and fled to Holland. In Amsterdam he associated with Whig refugees and intriguers; on moving to Utrecht, he was again in the web of conspiracy, particularly through Viscount Mordaunt, whom he probably counseled on the Monmouth rebellion. In 1686, the magistrates of Utrecht ordered him from the city when James II sought his extradition along with other suspected enemies of James's regime.[73] As conspirators sometimes do, Locke earnestly denied all involvement in conspiratorial politics, as

71. In a letter to Dr. Charlett, president of Trinity College, John Hutton wrote: "I think that both Locke and my Lord Shaftesbury were as arrant atheists as Spinoza, and more corrupt than any sect of heathen philosophers" (4 February 1706). Thomas Cherry is the source of a report that, on his deathbed, Shaftesbury refused confession and talked of the Socinian notions that he had "imbibed from Mr. Locke and his tenth chapter of 'Human Understanding'" (H. R. Fox Bourne, *Life of John Locke*, 1: 469). The Tory historian Thomas Hearne wrote that Locke was a man of "very bad principles . . . [who] hath been cried up and magnified by a set of men of Republican principles, but Orthodox and truly honest men have detected his errors and fallacies and endeavoured what they could to obstruct his infection" (quoted by J. W. Gough, *John Locke's Political Philosophy*, 134).
72. Locke's involvement in Whig intrigues is detailed by Maurice Cranston in *John Locke*, 246–79.
73. Ibid., 227, 250, 253, 262, 285.

he denied having read the Socinian tracts that he copiously annotated in his notebooks, as he feigned unfamiliarity with Hobbes's writings, and as he concealed his authorship of timely political tracts.[74] But Maurice Cranston's splendid biography shows that Locke established a solid track record as a revolutionary conspirator—a record that presumably would be even more telling had Locke not burned incriminating papers on fleeing England. Reviewing this evidence together with his own findings, Peter Laslett declared that Locke "went much further towards revolution and treason than his earlier biographers knew, anxious as they were to present him as a man of unspotted personal and political virtue."[75] This was the state of opinion until Richard Ashcraft made a fresh review of the evidence in light of the Laslett and Cranston findings. He found that even in debunking the myth of Locke's political innocence, they understated the evidence on a number of points which, taken together, establish unequivocally that Locke was a pivotal figure in Whig conspiracies from 1680 to the Revolution.[76] To the politics of such a one the label "conservative" cannot be meaningfully attached.

Locke's role during and after the Revolution was significant. He was not present for the Convention Parliament, but one of his associates, Lord Somers, chaired the committee that drafted the Bill of Rights.[77] When he returned to England in the company of the queen, William promptly offered him an ambassadorial post, which poor health compelled him to decline. In 1690 he published anonymously the *Two Treatises of Government*, which were read as a defense of the new regime. This work is unparalleled by any other Whig tract of the period, for in it Locke became the first political thinker to build the legitimacy of revolution into a comprehensive theory of government. Locke was no

74. Ibid., 249–50, 392.
75. Peter Laslett, ed., *John Locke: Two Treatises of Government,* 31. Laslett also remarks the "secular drift in England" that became a "rapid transformation after 1688" (40). In 1722 Defoe could write that "no age, since the founding and forming of the Christian Church, was ever, in open avowed atheism, blasphemies, and heresies, equal to the age we now live in."
76. Richard Ashcraft, "The *Two Treatises* and the Exclusion Crisis," 45ff. and notes. Ashcraft's specific findings, contra Cranston, are: Locke *was* involved in the Monmouth rebellion; he *was* among the hundred exiles that James II sought to have extradited from Holland to stand trial (Locke took Dutch citizenship to secure his safety); he *was* closely associated with several of the "most notorious revolutionaries in the Whig movement," Robert West, Thomas Dare, and John Wildness; he fled England *prior* to official disclosure of the Rye House plot; he *did* associate with Thomas Dare in Utrecht and indeed lodged with him.
77. On this association, see Cranston, *John Locke,* 325.

sooner in England than he began to exercise influence as advisor to the Junto Whigs, Somers, Halifax, and Mordaunt. He returned to the Board of Trade, which he tended to dominate, and later became an initial subscriber to the Bank of England. Together with Halifax and Newton, he designed the important currency reform of 1694–96. He wrote extensive critical notes on proposed parliamentary legislation that promoted Whig principles, not least of all by providing models of legislative draftsmanship.[78] The quandary about where Locke fits in the English political tradition is thus no puzzle at all. He stood where the Whig tradition said all along he stood—"at the very seat of political power," to borrow Laslett's phrase. No English thinker before or since exercised such direct and immediate influence on public affairs at a turning point in constitutional history and in national development.[79]

Locke collaborated with Whig grandees on the basis of certain shared attitudes: dislike of the Stuart tendency to ally with Rome against Parliament; a desire to diminish the power of bishops in English political life; a sense that the nation had settled its political will on Parliament; belief that enterprise was more important to the national weal than piety. In his tracts for the times, he repeated the favored Whig phrases of the day, as Dunn notes. But the sense of those phrases was altered by the philosophical grounding he gave his theory of government. This fact is clear even from Locke's spectacular silence: he made no use whatever of the basic Whig mode of political thought, exegesis of the ancient constitution.[80] The silence was not due to Locke's personal lack of interest in constitutional history. It was due to the fact Locke had a rational political science whose relevant evidential experience was not limited to the political history of the English nation, however important that might be.[81] This is why Locke's theories of right, sovereignty, the

---

78. Fox Bourne, *Life of John Locke,* 2: 312–26, 336, 375ff.
79. Laslett writes that Locke's political influence in 1690–91 was "truly extraordinary" and that "during the years after the revolution there was a sense in which liberal or Whig philosophy did in fact inform the government and affect politicians in the person of Locke the Whig philosopher" (Laslett, ed., *John Locke: Two Treatises of Government,* 39–40). Cranston writes that Locke was the man behind the scenes "advising and prompting" the men who walked the stage (*John Locke,* 324).
80. This point is canvassed by J. Richards, L. Mulligan, and J. Graham in "'Property' and 'People': Political Usages of Locke and Some Contemporaries." The authors say that the *Treatises,* "although more radical than the preferred Whig case, echoed too much of the language and principles of other Whigs easily to be repudiated by them" (30).
81. Ibid., 35–51. Locke's silence about the ancient constitution might have been dictated by the need to avoid identification with Hobbes, who was well

people, property, and the rest survived the parochialism of the day to exercise influence for a century. The philosophical grounding he gave the Revolution was, and was perceived by his political allies to be, suggestive of innovations they did not approve.[82] This complex position may be expressed by saying that Locke was a conservative member of the Whig left, although he represented his position as centrist.

Once we have Locke back where he belongs on the political scene, it is easier to solve that other puzzle: where does Hobbes fit in the Whig Settlement? Hobbes has been an ambiguous figure in the Whig canon. His anticlerical materialism was repellent to many, while his theory of indivisible sovereignty was incompatible with the Whig theory of balanced power. Yet his concept of natural right, his orientation of politics on power and replacement of justice by expediency, his theory of political representation, his defense of liberty and encouragement of commercial enterprise, his excision of religion from the political agenda, all place him in the Whig camp. Moreover, Hobbes was a living force in the political debate of this period, for his doctrine was *the* stumbling block to the Latitudinarian sacralization of the mechanical world system. The Latitudinarian and very Whig Bishop Gilbert Burnet was explicit about it. In a passage on the Latitudinarians, he summarized the views of Tillotson, Stillingfleet, Patrick, Wilkins, Cudworth, and More, who "studied to establish men in the great principles of religion against atheism, that was then beginning to gain ground, chiefly by reason of the hypocrisy of some, and the fantastical conceits of the more sincere enthusiasts." Without further explanation he went to the root of the matter with this comment on Hobbes:

> Hobbes, who had long followed the court, and passed there for a mathematical man, though he really knew little that way, being disgusted by the court, came into England in Cromwell's time, and published a very wicked book, with a very strange title, *The Leviathan*. His main principles were, that all men acted under an absolute necessity, in which he seemed protected by the then re-

---

known for his assault in the name of rationality on common law and, by implication, on all inherited institutions. This is suggested by the details of Locke's association with James Tyrrell, a Whig devoted to historical political theory. See J. W. Gough, "James Tyrrell, Whig Historian and Friend of John Locke," 580, 594. On Locke's awareness of Hobbes's views on law, see n. 85 below.

82. Martyn P. Thompson, "The Reception of Locke's *Two Treatises of Government* 1690–1705," 189.

ceived doctrine of absolute decrees. He seemed to think the universe was God, and that souls were material, thought being only subtle and imperceptible motion. He thought interest and fear were the chief principles of society: and he put all morality in the following that which was our own private will or advantage. He thought religion had no other foundation than the laws of the land. And he put all the law in the will of the prince, or of the people: for he writ his book at first in favour of absolute monarchy, but turned it afterwards to gratify the republican party. These were his true principles, though he had disguised them, for deceiving unwary readers. And this set of notions came to spread much. The novelty and boldness of them set many on reading them. The impiety of them was acceptable to men of corrupt minds, which were but too much prepared to receive them by the extravagancies of the late times. So this set of men at Cambridge studied to assert and examine the principles of religion and morality on clear grounds and in a philosophical method. In this More led the way to many that came after him.[83]

The young John Locke at Oxford was among the many to whom Hobbes's notions spread. His first effort in political theory, *Essays on the Law of Nature* (1660), shows that he had assimilated the doctrine of man's naturally chaotic condition; he was also a firm monarchist opposed to religious toleration on the Hobbesian ground that the chaos of private religious opinion jeopardized peace.[84] However, Hobbes was able "to gratify the republican party" without abandoning his theory of sovereignty because, from his earliest tract, he maintained that the theory was equally applicable to republics and monarchies. As for toleration, Hobbes said that it was much the same as having no religion at all—a view that Shaftesbury expressed in his spirited attack on Holland. Those who label Hobbes a "conservative" thinker cannot but be mystified by Locke's transition from the monarchism of 1660 to the "republican" politics midwifed in the association with Shaftesbury. Why would the leading advocate of parliamentary supremacy and religious toleration seek the assistance, at a critical political moment (1667), of an untested client whose views were profoundly opposed to his own? And how *could* that young brain truster renovate his thinking so rapidly that in scarcely twelve months he was producing tracts for his patron? Not only Locke but also Shaftesbury must, on this supposition, be "pro-

83. Burnet, *History of His Own Times*, 1: 340–41.
84. Cranston, *John Locke*, 57–63.

foundly and exotically incoherent."[85] However, if Hobbes's radicalism is the thread connecting the young Locke with Locke the client of Shaftesbury, this political reorientation expresses no more than a prudential judgment that parliamentary supremacy is, in the circumstances, preferable to high royal prerogative. In any case, Locke's Whig politics were based on Hobbesian principles. The state of nature doctrine, the contractual character of political justice, the natural rights interpretation of civic liberty, the theory of political representation, the substitution of acquisitive individualism for the pursuit of virtue or righteousness as the aim of the commonwealth, and the reduction of Christian faith to a single article—all this Hobbism Locke repackaged in his own peculiar way.[86]

His soft packaging of hard doctrines did not deceive contemporaries who looked beyond the manner to the matter. The high churchmen of Cambridge, ever watchful of new dangers emanating from their old enemy, quickly spotted him in Locke's writings on religion. In a polemic endorsed by the Cambridge vice-chancellor and dedicated to both universities, John Edwards reproached Locke for continuing Hobbes's assault on university learning and perpetuating Hobbes's specious interpretation of Christianity:

> Nor is [Locke] pleased with our old Christianity, but hath offered a new scheme to the world, the same . . . with what Mr. Hobbes

85. According to Locke's intimate friend Lady Masham, the friendship between Shaftesbury and Locke was based on the benefit each derived from their conversations. Just what was said in these conversations is not known, but John Aubrey recommended to Locke, in 1672, Hobbes's *Dialogue between a Philosopher and a Student of the Common Laws of England,* saying that "I have a conceit that if your Lord saw it he would like it" (K. H. D. Haley, *The First Earl of Shaftesbury,* 217–19).

86. The appropriation of Hobbes's doctrines by Locke has been reviewed by Richard Cox, *Locke on War and Peace,* xix–xx, 22–23, and Roger D. Masters, "Hobbes and Locke," 116–40. Both build on Leo Strauss's meticulous exegesis meant to show the continuity between Hobbes and Locke; see *Natural Right and History,* 165–251. In a decree against "certain pernicious books and damnable doctrines," Oxford University condemned a number of propositions that Locke took from Hobbes, viz. all civil authority is derived originally from the people; there is a contract between the prince and the people; self-preservation is the fundamental law of nature; in the state of nature, there is no difference between good and evil; the foundation of society is natural right; on entering society everyone retains the right to self-defense. This text is printed in *Somer's Tracts,* 8: 420–24.

propounded as the perfect and complete mode of faith viz: To believe in Christ is to believe nothing else than to believe that Jesus is
the Christ: and no other faith, besides this article, is required to
eternal life (*De Cive*, cap. 18). . . . This is the doctrine which is revived and furbished up in the pretended *Reasonableness of Christianity:* and you see whence it is borrowed.[87]

Not only did Locke borrow this simplification from Hobbes; he put
it to exactly the same use as a tool for undercutting sectarianism. All
Christians share that article of faith; and if it is sufficient to salvation,
then the attempt to impose a catechism and liturgy, shored up by learning, is misguided. Locke did, however, depart from Hobbes on the matter of toleration and established church. Locke maintained that the
competence of civil authority extends only to "outward" matters—the
procurement and preservation of life, liberty, health, property, and ease.
Compulsion can and must be used to secure government, but in respect
to religion this is impossible; for "true and saving religion consists in
the inward [uncoerced] persuasion of the mind, without which nothing
can be acceptable to God."[88] Locke tirelessly repeated this Protestant
appeal to the sanctity of conscience to draw readers to the *political* principle of toleration. The argument would have been unnecessary if the
Protestant religious experience somehow suggested the principle. In
fact it did not. Protestants enforced doctrinal conformity on tender, sacred consciences with the zeal of bishops. Locke, by contrast, endorsed
Hobbes's observation that the Protestant conscience is chaotic; but he
said this in sugared tones of sweet reasonableness that made it seem
plausible that "saving religion consists in the inward persuasion of
the mind."

If one looks at what this formula actually asserts, abstracting from the
aura of piety Locke threw around it, it is clear why he so upset the
churchmen: his definition of religion is broad enough to include sincere
atheists. Hobbes's defense of the sovereign's prerogative to enforce conformity is not inconsistent with Locke's defense of the "rights" of conscience; as we have seen, Hobbes also limited the prerogative to the requirement of *outward* conformity, while interdicting inquisition of
conscience on the ground that the end of government does not require
it. In a reference to this formula, Locke surmised that "none but an
atheist" would advance it; yet he came around to very much the same

87. Quoted by Cranston, *John Locke*, 107.
88. Locke, *Works*, 7: 11. See Strauss's discerning examination of Locke on reason
    and religion in *Natural Right*, 207–14.

view; for he maintained, as Hobbes had, that laws respecting the regulation of religion are binding, and there is *no* "right of conscience" to disregard them (*Letters on Toleration*, 85). The differences between Hobbes and Locke on this crucial question therefore come to little more than different judgments about the feasibility of a particular policy in changed political circumstances.

Hobbes's discovery of the chaos of man's natural condition led by one route to his critique of religion and by another to his critique of morality. In his *Two Treatises of Government* and the *Essay*, Locke devoted careful scrutiny to the latter questions, and reiterated the affirmative position he had reached by 1660.[89] He accordingly followed Hobbes in assimilating moral principles to the public reason of political science, founded on nothing else than the advantages and expediencies of government.[90] This cardinal aspect of Hobbes's doctrine was also detected in Locke's works by that discerning moralist, the third earl of Shaftesbury. Deference to his former teacher prevented Shaftesbury including Locke in his repeated criticisms of Hobbes, but in private correspondence he made his opinion known:

> In general truly it has happened that all those they call free writers now-a-days have espoused those principles which Mr. Hobbes set a-foot in this last age. Mr. Locke, as much as I admire him on account of other writings . . . and as well as I knew him . . . did, however, go in the self-same track, and is followed by the Tindals, and all the other ingenious free authors of our time. It was Mr. Locke that struck the home blow: for Mr. Hobbes's character and base slavish principles in government took off the poison of his philosophy. 'Twas Mr. Locke that struck at all fundamentals, threw all order and virtue out of the world and made the very idea of these . . . unnatural and without foundation in our minds."[91]

The "home blow" was struck, Shaftesbury believed, in Locke's political writings and the *Essay*, where all "ideas" are said to depend solely on

89. Cox, *Locke on War and Peace*, 68–84.
90. In typically ambiguous prose, Locke wrote that "true politics I look on as a part of moral philosophy, which is nothing but the art of conducting men right in a society, and supporting a community amongst its neighbours" (quoted by Cranston, *John Locke*, 428).
91. Quoted by Jason Aronson, "Shaftesbury on Locke," 1103. For further discussion of the young Shaftesbury's deep reservations about Locke and his teaching, see John A. Dussinger, "'The Lovely System of Lord Shaftesbury': An Answer to Locke in the Aftermath of 1688?"

experience, so that morality, justice, virtue, and beauty are deprived of all natural foundation and are "nothing in themselves." This interpretation of Locke was common among his Tory and university critics, who thought he taught "very bad principles" that corrupt morality. Shaftesbury himself was so appalled that he called Hobbes and Locke "barbarians."

Shaftesbury's response to Locke's allegedly depraved principles contains an important lesson about the way in which enlightenment spread in Whig England. Despite his reservations, he was able to appreciate Locke's service to their common causes of liberty, religious peace, and commercial expansion. He was willing to accept an intellectual alliance with Locke's doctrine up to a point. But like other Whig gentlemen, Shaftesbury feared Locke's basic principles; and he was among the first of a long line of moralists to seek a new basis for morality consistent with Whig politics. Although Whigs such as Somers and Halifax lacked Shaftesbury's acute perception of the radicalism of Locke's principles, they shared his view that classical moral philosophy was an irreplaceable source of moral thought and suasion; in practical terms, this attitude translated into general approval of the curricula of the universities, improved by some modernizing here and there. With the bishops and politically active aristocracy in agreement on this question, the polemics of Hobbes and the gentle persuasion of Locke directed at reform were bound to fail. But above all, Shaftesbury's judgment is a bellwether of the radicalism of modern political philosophy. Despite all his muffling and muting of Hobbes's principles, despite his patient and conciliatory prose, despite frequent repetition of pious formulas, Locke's philosophy was too radical for enlightened Whig gentlemen. The circumstance that laymen and politicians came to measure its radicalism so late in the day suggests that in earlier decades they had not understood the implications of the philosophic critique of ancient learning and superstition. To be sure, in 1670 Lord Clarendon urgently sounded the alarm against Hobbes in roughly the terms Shaftesbury used, but gentlemen might dismiss it as an expression of bitterness about his displacement from office. Many no doubt also took a similar attitude toward the numerous cries from bishops and university clergymen. Yet even after compensating for their exaggerations, a solid core of accurate criticism remains.

The most pertinent clergymen were the Latitudinarians. Bishop Burnet, we saw, singled out Henry More as the champion of religion against Hobbes's atheism. It was previously mentioned that More's introduction to modern philosophy was through the system of Descartes, which gradually changed its aspect from pious modernity to dangerous godlessness. In his *Antidote to Atheism,* More claimed that Descartes followed the "lower road of Democritism, amidst the thick dust of atoms" while he himself had taken leave of Descartes for "the high and airey hills of Platonism" (*A Collection of Several Philosophical Writings,* xii). All that remained of the Cartesian system for More were "some select theorems. For that part of it which insinuates that the world was either created or consisted of mechanical reasons, I not only refuse to admit, but explode" (xxvii). The doctrine of innate ideas was More's weapon against all mechanical atheism, Cartesian or Hobbesian. His innate ideas had to be Platonic, not the Cartesian variety, for Descartes' innate ideas merely lead back to materialism by the indirect route of *l'homme machine* who entertains ideas (35ff.).[92] Platonic innate ideas support notions of God, spirit, soul, purpose. These notions, combined with the doctrine of "signatures" of divine purpose on all creatures, enabled More to generate a religious outlook on nature whose effect was to replace mechanical explanations of natural phenomena with teleological and spiritual explanations. We are not surprised to find More filling his reenchanted world with all those phantoms that the mechanists had overthrown. No village gossip of witches, sprites, apparitions, premonitions, or prodigies was too gross for his credulity. More's scarcely believable crudities were not repeated by his Cambridge colleague, Ralph Cudworth, whose *True Intellectual System of the World* expounded the godless world system intelligently and sought to undo it by conjuring teleology and moral principles into the mechanical universe. Yet for this large undertaking he too used the speculative tool of innate ideas.

This background helps identify the polemical target of Locke's *Essay concerning Human Understanding.* By opening the book with a claim that the mind is a *tabula rasa,* he fired a broadside against the Cambridge Platonists, who denied that the mind is "abrassa tabula, a tablebook wherein nothing is writ."[93] In a typically understated comment on the "rubbish" he set out to remove, Locke noted that innate ideas "derive from no better original than the superstitions of a nurse, or the authority of an old woman," which by many repetitions acquire the "dignity of a principle in religion and morality" (*Essay,* I.ii.22).[94] That ideas

92. On the materiality of Cartesian ideas, see Caton, *The Origin of Subjectivity,* 76, 94–95.

93. More, *A Collection,* 17.

94. See also I.iii.81, where Locke denies the innateness of the idea of God by referring to the Chinese mandarins, whom the Jesuits reported to be atheists.

such as divine signatures needed clearing away signifies more than the endurance of spiritual metaphysics. The rubbish emanated from the leaders of modernizing enlightenment in the Anglican Church. It was expressly contrived to counteract the perceived godless tendency of modern mechanistic philosophy—the very philosophy they hoped to harness to pious enlightenment. More and Cudworth burned their fingers on a philosophy whose secularism they did not fully understand. Theirs was a no-win situation: it was incoherent to appropriate Descartes, and later Newton, for enlightenment purposes, while attempting to hedge in reason with superstitions.

It was in this atmosphere of the first sharp reaction to rationalism by the leading ecclesiastical exponents of rationalism that Locke rose to his timely defense of the genuine article. The *Essay* defends rationalism in characteristic Lockean fashion: he trimmed and softened the jagged edges of the modern theory of mind to make it more palatable. His main innovation in this regard was to set the task of philosophy as sifting the origin of ideas from "experience." In its chaotic natural condition, "experience" throws up kobolds and numbers, witches and fevers, in random fashion. Locke would bring order to the chaos by patiently enumerating classes of ideas and deriving them from their "original" in the senses. The jagged edge suppressed by this empiricism is the hard core of modern philosophy: the ordered mechanistic world. At no point is the reader required to face it squarely; instead, Locke allowed it to emerge subliminally to those who realize that the "primary qualities" he detected in experience happen, by happy chance, to be the *quantities* with which the new physics operates. This tedious backstairs route to the mechanistic universe is apparently recommended by the fact that "*morality* and *mechanism* . . . are not very easy to be reconciled" (*Essay*, I.ii.14).

The enlightenment of Locke and Newton eventually bore unwanted fruit in the scandals of rationalist heresy among their clerical disciples. The strict discipline and surveillance that Newton exercised over the men he chose to propagate his version of pious science was largely successful: only two—William Whiston and Samuel Clarke—were prosecuted for heresy.[95] Locke, who did not control his men through patronage, as Newton did, was not so fortunate. In 1696 John Toland touched off the Deism controversy with his *Christianity Not Mysterious*, in which he argued from the precepts of Locke's *Essays* and *The Reasonableness of*

---

95. The tendency of Newtonian metaphysics to disintegrate into heresy is reviewed by Larry Stewart, "Samuel Clarke, Newtonianism, and the Factions of Post-Revolutionary England."

Christianity that rationally tenable religion could contain nothing above or below reason. Toland maintained that the mysteries of Christianity are corruptions of the original Christian message, which intended nothing more than simple, rationally valid moral teaching. The corruptions were introduced by priests who imitated the gentile practice of concocting religious mysteries in order to control the consciences of believers.[96] In this attack on the deceits of priestcraft, there are overtones of an obscure clergyman's resentment of the hypocrisy of masters, whom he intended to punish by revealing their secrets.[97] This rebellion may also be detected in Anthony Collins's *Discourse of Free-Thinking* (1713). Collins, another Lockean, pointedly remarked that Archbishop Tillotson's Latitudinarian theology was scarcely distinguishable from the Deist repudiation of all theological anthropomorphism; and in reply to the practical objection that freethinking would promote atheism, Collins constructed a dilemma for the bishops: if freethinking is suppressed, atheism will decline but superstition and enthusiasm will increase; but superstition is socially more mischievous than atheism; consequently, atheism ought to be endured as the lesser evil.

The controversies over Deism, the Trinity, the antiquity of the earth, and the like were each and all traced by contemporaries to the hardcore rationalism ensconced within the pious facades erected by Locke and Newton. Newton had no compunction about punishing William Whiston for incautiously expressing Newton's own anti-Trinitarian views because, like Locke, he was anxious to preserve the Anglican

96. Toland, *Christianity Not Mysterious* (1696), chaps. 3, 4. Bishops Berkeley and Butler, who led a counteroffensive against establishment theism, located its source in Hobbes, Locke, and Spinoza. Samuel Johnson declared that the "deplorable progress of infidelity and apostasy in this age of mighty pretense and reasoning" stemmed from "the well-meaning but too conceited Mr. Locke" (Roland Stromberg, *Religious Liberalism in Eighteenth-Century England,* 108; also 93, 103).

97. One such retaliation was John Craig's *Theologiae Christiania principia mathematica* (1699), dedicated to his patron Bishop Burnet of Salisbury. Craig combined Newton and Spinoza to construct a probability calculus for computing the evidential value of Scripture. Proposition XVIII, Problem XI ("To define the space of time in which the probability of the written history of Christ will vanish"), concluded that the evidential value of the Bible would disappear 1,454 years thence. Craig invoked Luke 18: 8 to support his assertion that when Christ returns at that time, there will be no believers remaining. This is a remarkable expression of confidence in the progress of unbelief. Well might Robert Boyle say that "the difference between an atheist and a deist is almost negligible."

Church as essential to the Whig Settlement under which both men prospered.[98] Their delicate balancing of enlightenment and public faith eventually jelled into a stable, moderate enlightenment force that did not overtly attack the basic articles. Public faith, after all, was necessary, and Locke gave the reason. Enlightened minds, he pointed out, presuppose leisure as well as ability: "and you may as soon hope to have all the Day-Labourers and Tradesmen, the Spinsters and Dairy Maids perfect Mathematicians, as to have them perfect in *Ethicks* in this way. Hearing plain Commands, is the sure and only course to bring them to Obedience and Practice. The greatest part cannot know, and therefore must believe" (*Works,* 1: 410). Reason for the gentlemen who govern, faith for the multitude—this is the formula for politic religion espoused by Machiavelli and Sarpi, by the *politiques* of the French court, by the Erastians in Holland and England, and expounded in classic fashion by Hobbes and Spinoza. Locke, ever oblique, noted in the *Essays* that the mandarins had perfected this system in China; the mandarins were atheists, but they kept to the forms of traditional religion. Lest the point of this traveler's tale be lost, he spelled it out in his usual stuttering prose:

> And perhaps, if we should with attention mind the lives and discourses of people not so far off, we should have too much reason to fear, that many, in more civilized countries, have no very strong and clear impressions of a Deity upon their minds, and that the complaints of atheism made from the pulpit are not without reason. And though only some profligate wretches own it too barefacedly now; yet perhaps we should hear more than we do of it from others, did not the fear of the magistrate's sword, or their neighbour's censure, tie up people's tongues; which, were the apprehensions of punishment taken away, would as openly proclaim their atheism as their lives do. (*Essay,* I.iii.8)

Locke's epistemology clarified the status of politick religion. To deny innate ideas is to imply that all people are born atheists, and that religious beliefs consist entirely of conventional opinions. These conventions owe their force to something like an established church backed by the magistrate's sword. Locke's version of the religious settlement kept the established church intact, because its offices were necessary for instructing the commons in their duties. At the same time, by restricting the coercive warrant to outward conformity and by characterizing reli-

98. Manuel, *Freedom from History,* 165.

gion as conventional belief, the effect was to remove the stigma from unbelief.

That effect was visible in the Lockean bishops Hoadly, Hare, and Warburton, who defended the established Church on grounds of "civil polity" while urging that it must impose no requirement of doctrinal conformity at all. How could it? Learned controversies concerning two core doctrines of traditional belief, the Trinity and the Resurrection, had shown that the texts supposed to support them were so flawed, inconsistent, and equivocal that a scholarly consensus about their meaning was out of the question. Thus Bishop Hare declared that study of the Bible is the surest way to become a heretic (echoing in this Catholic bishops of 200 years before), while Conyers Middleton's scholarly studies led him to conclude that Christianity is more useful than true.[99]

The diffusion of this enlightenment is manifest in broad lines in what Herbert Butterfield calls a "colossal secularization of thought in every possible realm of ideas" at the turn of the century. Those large aims of the Christian commonwealth, the salvation of the soul and the glory of God, found few advocates in public life, and political deliberation became nearly as free from religious belief as science had become. The secularization process is ill described by those who, misunderstanding the Erastian position, infer from the utterance of pious formulas that the Augustan mind was deeply religious despite its secular outlook. The Augustan Age, like every other, was of many minds; it included those who rejected miracles as well as those like Bishops Berkeley and Butler who began a counterattack on the secular temper dominant in political circles. Deep religious convictions were by no means dead among the people or the clergy. But the people did not manage affairs or imbue the age with their attitudes: Reformation preaching had been driven from the public arena. As for the secular minds, their private religious convictions are of no consequence to the historian because they are inaccessible. What matters is that men of standing and influence, such as Halifax, analyzed religion in terms stemming from the odious Hobbes. Thus Halifax could say that men would be reconciled in their religious views if they were reconciled in their interests, and that religious sects were "little more than so many spiritual monopolies."[100] In his "Advice to a Daughter," he advised that true religion had nothing to do with

99. Stromberg, *Religious Liberalism in Eighteenth-Century England,* 96, 76–77.
100. *The Complete Works of George Savile, First Marquess of Halifax,* 221. Halifax was a Hobbist also in his first maxim of politics, "that in every constitution there is some power which neither will nor ought to be bounded" (ibid.). In limited governments, this power is the law.

conceit, zeal, persecuting anger, brutish and melancholy temper, or barbarous opinions. "Religion is exalted Reason . . . it dwelleth in the upper region of the Mind, where there are fewest clouds or mists to darken or offend it . . . it is morality improv'd and rais'd to its height . . . it doth not want the hopes and the terrors which are made use of to support it" (5). Halifax's rational religion was not a renovation of traditional religion, but the alternative we call pious atheism.

chapter 5

John de Witt and the Dutch Commercial Republic

Dutch Politics

The Low Countries were a microcosm of the conflicts that bulked so large in the glory and misery of seventeenth-century Europe. Born of bloody war with Spain, the Dutch Republic survived the dangerous chaos of dynastic politics by agile diplomacy and military prowess. Though it was a small territory of scarcely two million, its commanders, statesmen, and people frustrated Spanish designs on its independence, thwarted the awesome power of Louis' armies, and managed to evade, when they could not neutralize, the preponderant naval force of England.

The tenacity and resourcefulness of the Dutch won the grudging admiration of their enemies. But their domination of trade stirred the wonder of many observers, who could not conceal their envy. The Dutch indeed seemed to have passed a miracle. It was a common observation among English writers that although the Dutch had no natural resources, they sold timber, iron ore, naval stores, and flax to all Europe; that although their agriculture was negligible, their warehouses were full of corn and grain; that although they had no mines, they exported bullion and controlled international finance.[1] The Dutch were

1. The tone was set for English writers by Thomas Mun, who observed in 1620 that "it seems a wonder to the world that such a small country, not fully so big as two of our best shires, having little natural wealth, victuals, timber, or other

the original rags-to-riches success story. Lacking all natural wealth, lacking indeed even good harbors, they nevertheless made themselves the wealthiest maritime nation of Europe. They had discovered the secret of acquisition. Statesmen and political economists of other nations studied their methods in hope of imitating them.

Observers traced the Dutch success to a variety of factors. Thomas Mun claimed that profits from herring fishing—in English waters, he noted irritably—had bankrolled the spectacular growth of the Dutch economy. William Petty and Sir William Temple believed that the nation's want of natural resources compelled its people to be frugal and enterprising. Colbert was impressed by Dutch technical and entrepreneurial skill. Dudley North emphasized financial stability and the 4 percent interest rate. Still others traced the Dutch success to their republican political system.

The Protestant work ethic was not among the factors of the Dutch success formula mentioned by contemporary observers. Although writers routinely stressed the importance of frugality to accumulation, Calvinist austerity was not cited as an incentive. The economic literature of the period stressed other incentives instead: bare necessity, hope of advantage, sumptuary laws, duties on imported luxuries, and similar measures.

If early students of the Dutch success did not hit on the Protestant ethic as the motive for primitive accumulation, doubtless that was because of their familiarity with the origins and history of the Dutch nation. The centers of trade in the sixteenth century were Flanders—especially Antwerp and Bruges—and the Hanseatic cities. When the Reformation swept the Low Countries, Philip II determined to root heresy out of the Spanish monarchy's richest possession. In 1573, the Inquisition placed every Protestant man, woman, and child under decree

---

necessary amunitions either for war or peace, should notwithstanding possess them all in such extraordinary abundance, that besides their own wants (which are very great) they can and do likewise serve and sell to other princes, ships, ordnance, cordage, corn, powder, shot, and what not, which by their industrious trading they gather from all the quarters of the world" (*England's Treasure by Forraign Trade*, 183). Josiah Child's widely read *A discourse about trade* (1693) began by holding up the Dutch example for emulation: "The prodigious increase of the Netherlands in their domestick and foreign trade, riches, and multitude of shipping, is the envy of the present, and may be the wonder of all future generations. And yet the means whereby they have thus advanced themselves are sufficiently obvious, and in a great measure imitable by most other nations."

of death, and the duke of Alba was dispatched to execute this pious work. The ruin of Antwerp's trade drove many thousands northward to the independent states still resisting the Spanish yoke. The effects of Spanish policy were reflected in the population growth of Holland. Between 1514 and 1622, its population increased from 275,000 to 672,000, a rise of 145 percent. Most of this increase occurred after 1580, when persecution was at its height in the south. In the subsequent half-century, this dramatic growth rate slowed to about 35 percent, but Holland continued to receive refugees from strife-torn Europe.[2]

The northward emigration of merchants, financiers, and tradesmen transferred Antwerp's trade to Amsterdam in scarcely two decades. Many Catholics were among those who fled; indeed, they became the majority denomination in Amsterdam. The mingling of peoples and religions in the Netherlands impressed a certain cosmopolitan tolerance on its civil and commercial life. What struck observers about the relation between commerce and religion in the Dutch Republic was not its Calvinists or its many-colored Protestantism but its religious liberty. In contrast to Spanish policy, Dutch liberty opened the nation's courts and counting houses to Christian and Jew alike. As one English commentator put it, "God may be more safely offended [in the United Provinces] than the States General."[3]

2. Pieter Geyl, *The Netherlands in the Seventeenth Century,* pt. 1, 18–38; Ralph Davis, *The Rise of the Atlantic Economies,* 176–84. In the period between 1585 and 1622, the population of Amsterdam increased 250 percent, from 30,000 to 105,000. William Temple interpreted the relation between population growth and economic growth in the following way: "I conceive the true original and ground of trade to be a great multitude of people crowded into small compass of land, whereby all things necessary to life become dear, and all men, who have possessions are induced to parsimony; but those who have none are forced to industry and labour, or else to want. Bodies that are vigorous, fall to labor; such as are not, supply that defect by some sort of inventions or ingenuity. These customs arise first from necessity, but increase by imitation, and grow in time to be habitual in a country" (*Observations on the United Provinces of the Netherlands,* 211). There is no suggestion here of a connection between prosperity and Protestantism.

3. J. L. Price, *Culture and Society in the Dutch Republic during the Seventeenth Century,* 170ff.; Geyl, *The Netherlands,* 63–70. After describing the political means used to control the clergy, the anonymous author of *The Dutch Drawn to Life* (1664) wrote: "Amsterdam is a university of all religions, which grow here confusedly . . . without either order or prunings. If you be unsettled in your religion, you may here try all, and take at last what you like best. If you like none, you have a pattern to follow of two that would be a church to themselves. It's the fair of all the sects, where all the pedlars of religion have

This is not to suggest that the Calvinist faith had no bearing on commercial enterprise. Its impact was substantial in Holland but mostly negative. The Calvinist clergy, who drew their following mainly from tradesmen and the gentry, were the chief support of the Orangist faction. The Dutch Republic owed its existence to the military leadership of the founder of the Orange dynasty, William the Silent, who led Calvinist armies that blocked the Spanish advance. The basis of this coalition was mutual advantage. The clergy espoused holy war against the Spanish Antichrist, whom they hoped to expel from the southern provinces. The house of Orange, for its part, could best promote its dynastic ambitions through war. Orange princes, or stadholders, were not sovereign in the Dutch constitution. They were brought in as warlords, elected by the states of the Netherlands, when the war with Spain commenced. (They converted from the Catholic faith to accept this ambiguous position in the Dutch nation.) Never satisfied with their subordination to civil government, they aspired to royal power. Victory over Spain would have enabled them to overawe the civil government; and, failing victory, protracted conflict provided opportunities for enhancing their prestige at the expense of the government.[4]

This war-and-religion faction was opposed by the party of peace and prosperity, led by the commercial patriciate who dominated government. Dutch political institutions reflected the urban power of the merchant princes. The political unit was the city, headed by a mayor and council. Cities elected a state government (the Regents) from among representatives of the councils; and the states in turn allied in a confederation that composed the Republic. The formal equality of cities and states gave way in practice to domination by the principal city in each state and domination of the states by the leading state. Holland enjoyed this leadership thanks to the position of Amsterdam as the most populous and prosperous city.

When the northern provinces rebelled against Spain, the civilian gov-

---

leave to vend their toyes, their ribbands, and phanatique rattles. Their republic is more to them than heaven, and God may be more safely offended there than the States General" (49). William Temple, whose *Observations* became a text in the Whig tradition, derived Dutch toleration in religion not from veneration of sacred private conscience but from the "force of commerce," which mingled and mixed people in a cosmopolitan setting (207). In his diatribe against the Dutch on account of their supremacy in trade (the Delenda est Carthago speech), Shaftesbury equated Dutch toleration with no religion at all.

4. Geyl, *The Netherlands*, 54–55, 61.

ernment adopted the Ghibelline policy of subordinating the clergy to civil power. At that time (1578), the reformed clergy were content to accept subordination in return for recognition as the national church. But Calvinism was a militant religion that placed high value on salvation, whereas the civil authority valued its own sovereignty as well as trade. The tensions inherent in this difference were expressed in domestic conflicts over war policy. Clerical support for war against Spain would commit the Netherlands to wars of territorial acquisition, but merchants wanted maritime markets, not territory, and therefore favored a potent naval force. Besides, it was not to the advantage of Dutch commercial interests to liberate Ghent, Bruges, and Antwerp, which could soon become rivals in trade.

The conflict between the Regents and the Calvinist clergy grew into an explicit, institutionalized opposition in the course of the Arminian controversy. In 1605, Arminius, a theologian at the University of Leiden, denied that written creeds were binding on conscience and impugned predestination as offensive to the divine majesty. Orthodox clergymen spotted heresy in this repudiation of Calvin's core doctrine; Arminius was forthwith anathematized as a secret papist. As the disturbance raced beyond seminary walls and excited the people, it became apparent to Oldenbarnevelt, the head of government, where the conflict must lead. If Arminius and his small following were not protected and tolerated within the reformed Church, the impassioned clergy would encroach on the prerogatives of government until they usurped its jurisdiction.[5] The Regents declared therefore that predestination was not part of the creed of the reformed Church, and reformed clergymen were forbidden to preach this "high mystery" to their congregations. This ruling in effect reconstituted the national church as "libertinist" or Latitudinarian. The aggrieved clergy set out to usurp the civil power to regulate religion. They agitated for a synod to lay down a confession binding on reformed clergy. They played on popular feeling by equating Arminianism with lukewarmness in the national cause. Had the Regents not negotiated a truce with Spain? Were they not tolerant of Catholics in the Netherlands but unsympathetic to the plight of Huguenots in France? Such men, the clergy exhorted the people, must be secret heretics and traitors. This sectarian syllogism battered the authority of the Regents. The aging Oldenbarnevelt recruited the young Hugo Grotius to the government's cause. But this new effort was offset when the stadholder Maurice of Nassau, who had held aloof from the fray, supported the clergy. He divided the councils of the Regents by encouraging

5. Ibid., 46–47.

Oldenbarnevelt's political enemies, until at length the stadholder was able to arrest the great statesman. A show trial found him guilty of crimes against religion and the nation, and on the morning of 12 May 1619, he was hanged.

With Oldenbarnevelt's cause disgraced and his party cowed, orthodox clergymen ruled the roost. The Synod of Dort imposed predestination as an article of faith in the reformed Church and Arminian clergymen were purged. Incited by these victories, rigid churchmen grew bolder in their demands that the Regents suppress the public worship of non-Calvinist sects and silence heterodox opinion. These experiences reminded the Regents of the bigotry that Oldenbarnevelt had attempted to contain, and their resolve gradually returned. For two decades Orangists and Regents struggled for supremacy. New heroes entered the fight for orthodoxy and for the civil government. From his exile in Antwerp, Hugo Grotius defended the principles of Oldenbarnevelt. Gilbert Voetius, the leading Calvinist theologian, discovered a new source of godlessness more sinister than the teachings of Arminius: the crypto-atheism of René Descartes, whose method of doubt, Voetius urged in numerous pamphlets, was meant to undermine all faith. Although nothing seems to have aroused his passion more than the progress of Cartesianism in Dutch universities, Voetius was a tireless opponent of every immorality, which included Sunday recreations and usury.[6]

This sour temper temporarily spent its force through Voetius's exertions. His best effort achieved no more than the silencing of a few disciples for a time, and a temporary prohibition on discussion of Cartesian philosophy at Utrecht, where he was rector. But to those less morbid than the theologians, a game of tennis on Sunday seemed harmless. Usury is integral to commerce, and blood continued to circulate in the veins of vertebrates notwithstanding theological disapproval. The Regents showed their weariness with theological intransigence when they named the Cartesian Abraham Heidanus to the chair of theology in Leiden.

Voetius lived to see his worst forecasts about the influence of Cartesian philosophy come true. Even as his crusade was at its apex, three young Dutchmen pondered Cartesianism and parlayed it into bold strides toward secularism in science, politics, and philosophy: these were Christiaan Huygens, John de Witt, and Benedict Spinoza.

De Witt came from a Dortrecht family prominent in the Regents' faction. He attended the Latin School of Dortrecht, famous across Eu-

6. For a résumé of the Regents-Orangists conflict, see Pieter Geyl, *History of the Low Countries: Episodes and Problems*, 148–72.

rope for the quality of its schooling. It was there that young de Witt encountered Cartesian philosophy. The school's founder and master was Isaac Beeckman, with whom Descartes had discussed problems in mechanics when both were young men. The mathematics instruction at the Latin School was thorough, and de Witt was precocious in this subject. At the age of twenty-three he drafted his *Elementa curvarum linearum* (*The Elements of Curved Lines*), which was conceived as the successor of Descartes' *Geometry* in that it recast Cartesian analysis into the form subsequently known as analytic geometry. It attracted the high praise of Huygens and Newton and won him a place among the ranks of distinguished mathematicians.[7] De Witt subsequently put this ability to use in devising new quantitative methods for fiscal problems, but he prepared himself for a political career by enrolling in law at the University of Leiden. On completing his studies he traveled widely in France with his brother Cornelius and sojourned in England at the time Charles was taken prisoner by Cromwell.

When the de Witts returned home, the nation was in the throes of another constitutional crisis. The ambitious young Stadholder William II had combined with the clergy to discredit the men who had negotiated the Treaty of Westphalia (1648), which had ended eighty years of war with Spain. Jacob de Witt, John's father, was among six men whom William had arrested. Just as it seemed that the scenario of Oldenbarnevelt's disgrace and execution was about to be reenacted, William suddenly died. Jacob de Witt was released from prison and restored to honor. The moment was opportune for the Regents' party to seize the initiative in its struggle against the Orangist faction. John de Witt, learned in constitutional law but lacking experience, chose that moment to enter politics. He began his career as pensionary of Dortrecht, which made him the chief civil servant in the municipal government. He took the lead in formulating a law to exclude the infant heir of William II from the office of admiral general, traditionally held by the house of Orange. So skilled was his handling of these and other matters that when Adrian Pauw vacated the office of grand pensionary of Holland in 1653, de Witt was elected to the nation's most powerful office.[8] Never

7. The *Elementa* was published with Descartes' *Géométrie* in a 1659–61 edition undertaken by Frans van Schooten. The English mathematician John Wallis said of de Witt that had he not elected for politics, he would have been unequaled among the geometers of his time. See Germain-Antonin Lefèvre Pontalis, *John de Witt*, 1: 84, 298–99, 2: 301; Herbert H. Rowen, *John de Witt*, 412–16.

8. It was characteristic of the Dutch constitution that its highest officeholders had little formal power. The title grand pensionary designated the senior public servant, who acted as secretary to the Regents and enjoyed no formal

had it been so powerful. The Orangists were unable to prevent de Witt from excluding the infant William from military command until he reached his majority. De Witt thus became the first Dutch statesman to control the military forces as well as civil government and foreign affairs. For two decades he gave the Netherlands government in the spirit of the commercial republic, relatively uncompromised by concessions to the opposition. His program of peace and prosperity worked. Skillful diplomacy kept the Netherlands at peace with continental powers. The three wars with England were initiated by the English as challenges to Dutch trading supremacy. They did not achieve their end. The war of 1665–67 indeed brought the destruction of the English fleet anchored at Chatham, just below London, by a bold surprise attack that de Witt conceived and directed. With trade flourishing despite increased competition from France and England, de Witt attempted to put public finance on a sound basis by reducing the debt and revising the tax formula.

The Interest of Holland

De Witt predicated his domination of domestic politics upon the Perpetual Edict (1654). The edict excluded the Orangist party from power by excluding the infant Prince William's guardian, Frederick William, from exercising the stadholder office in William's name.[9] It also gave the custody and education of the prince to the States General. This bold initiative succeeded only because de Witt was able to present it as one of Cromwell's conditions for a peace treaty. Even so, de Witt inscribed the edict upon the banner of his party under the party slogan, "True Liberty."[10]

The party had no infrastructure and was not visible in a government dominated by the elected members of the States General. Its presence was felt through influence and through publicist activities supportive of

---

powers of state (Rowen, *John de Witt*, 141). In fact, though, grand pensionaries exercised considerable power, and de Witt's exceptional talents quickly made him master of his masters. Constantine Huygens, one of Descartes' few intimates, said of de Witt that not even Descartes had discovered anything comparable to de Witt's method of government, which was to possess power and dare to use it (416). Given his qualities as a statesman, and the legal infirmity of his office, de Witt's motto, *Ago quod ago* ("I do what I do"), was particularly apt.

9. Lefèvre Pontalis, *John de Witt*, 1: 99–103.
10. Rowen, *John de Witt*, 148, 381.

de Witt's position. He did not project himself as the chief of these people, preferring instead to persist in his identity as grand pensionary. He treated the activists as representatives of a sector of public opinion who required from time to time his protection against attempts by the Orangist clergy or local authorities to threaten their liberties. The activists were reformers in university posts (popularly styled "Cartesians"), sundry publicists and operatives, and the occasional philosopher or theologian, chief of whom was Benedict Spinoza.[11] While de Witt kept a close watch on these activities, particularly in the universities, the degree of his collaboration in them is uncertain. But he was intimately involved in the anonymous publication of a book that was perceived to be the political testament of his government, *The Interest of Holland* (1662).[12]

Pieter de la Court composed this work on de Witt's prompting and with his party's collaboration. The book opens with a self-characterization tailored to de Witt as much as de la Court: "I am a true Hollander who always calls a spade a spade and hates all indirect paths." The establishment of this identity was not a perfunctory self-assertion but was integral to the legitimation of the Regents' domination. The Regents, we have observed, were subject to allegations of lukewarm patriotism. Oldenbarnevelt and Jacob de Witt were said to be traitors because they opposed wars of territorial aggrandizement. These accusations were credible among the tradesmen and shopkeepers who composed the Orangist constituency. De la Court therefore addressed to this audience some general political maxims which he claimed were not well understood by the public (*The True Interest,* 6).

All men without exception, he declared, are motivated by care for their

11. Ibid., 148–53; J. Freudenthal, *Spinoza: Leben und Lehre,* 150–55.
12. The manuscript of *The Interest* shows numerous corrections in de Witt's handwriting. The second edition, which appeared a year later, included two chapters by de Witt. The book was subject to immediate controversy in Holland (Rowen, *John de Witt,* 394–98) and made an impression abroad. Louis' minister for foreign affairs, de Lionne, wrote Ambassador d'Estrades: "If you can find a volume entitled *The Interest of Holland* in which they say all the secrets of trade are contained, you can oblige me by sending a copy, and M. Colbert still more by sending him another" (Lefèvre Pontalis, *John de Witt,* 1: 300). In 1669 a revised and enlarged edition appeared in Dutch under the title *Aanwysing de heilsame politike gronden en maximen van de republike Holland.* This edition was the basis of the first French translation, *Mémoires de Jean de Witt, grand pensionnaire de Holland* (1702). The first English translation (1707) was made from the French translation. It bore the title *The True Interest and Political Maxims of the Republic of Holland and West-*

own private interest; they care for the public interest only insofar as it touches their own. Theories of government that deny this truth either endorse the utopianism of moral perfectability, as Plato and Aristotle did, or advocate despotic rule of the better, or the pious, over a base and wicked commons (13–15). On either alternative, the origin and aim of good government is misconstrued. Government is required by the weakness and selfishness of men, which cannot be checked without the right of public authority to compel obedience. That the public good must be imposed by force defines its character as "the joint welfare of governors and governed" consisting in the "prosperity of all the inhabitants" (xxviii, 2). The best government, then, is designed to enhance the private economic interests of the whole population. This is a possible object of government because the "harmony and union" of private interests unite Dutchmen in a political economy of mutual dependence and mutual advantage (36). Politics and economy are effectively linked by republican government because this form of government unites the interests of the governing class with the interests of the citizens. De la Court stated this relationship in a maxim that became the backbone of republican thought from Locke to Alexander Hamilton:

The public is not regarded but for the sake of private interest [in any government]; and consequently that is the best government where the chief rulers may obtain their own welfare by that of the people. It follows then to be the duty of the governors of republics to seek for great cities, and to make them as populous and strong as possible, so that all rulers and magistrates, and likewise all others that serve the public either in the country or city, may thereby gain the more power, honor and benefit, and more safely possess it, whether in peace or war. And this is the reason why we see that all republics thrive and flourish far more in arts, manufactures, traffic, populousness and strength, than the dominions and cities of monarchs; for where there is liberty, there will be riches and people. (6–7)

The claim that republics are not only more prosperous and free but also more powerful than monarchies was acknowledged to be an assertion contrary to the "general and ancient prejudices of all ignorant persons." The claim was a rejoinder to the Orangist claim that a warlord

Friesland. Written by John de Witt and other great men in Holland. In 1743 John Campbell made an English translation from the Dutch, and it is cited here.

was necessary for the defense of the nation against foreign enemies. De la Court did not minimize the need for a strong defense. More than half the book is given to a discussion of foreign affairs as geopolitics and power relations between states. The argument is that civilians conduct these Machiavellian exercises more reliably in the public interest than do monarchs.

The maxim that power follows liberty and prosperity was defended by an extended comparison of Spanish policy in Flanders with Dutch policy. The depredations of Flanders illustrated de la Court's contention that monarchs weaken and divide their people in order to live securely at their expense. If the Spanish imposed taxes that depressed trade, it was in order to weaken opposition to the regime (51–52, 91). These skilled mercantile and manufacturing classes immigrated to Amsterdam rather than to France and England because the tax and import laws of those countries discouraged settlement and because Amsterdam had no inquisitorial apparatus to inspect conscience. Its open policy toward persons of all faiths was based not on a religious belief in the inviolability of conscience but on the cosmopolitan openness of a maritime trading nation to strangers (65–68).Considerations of this kind might explain why the prosperity of Spain declined while the prosperity of Holland increased; but unless money is the sinews of war—a view rejected in the book— they do not explain how Holland successfully resisted Spanish might. Did the Dutch owe nothing to the militant fervor fostered by the clergy? Was nothing to be conceded to the military genius of William the Silent and Maurice of Nassau? How did the ruling class of the mercantile republic tap the resources of self-interest to man its armies and navies, so essential to the nation's survival?

De la Court would not concede that the stadholder or the clergy conferred any benefit on the Dutch nation.[13] He berated them for burdening the nation with unnecessary wars and needless expense. The house of Orange, he claimed, advanced its secret ambition for royal authority under pretenses of national defense. This would not be objectionable, according to de la Court's maxim, if Orange interest coincided with the national interest. That it did not was proven by the fact that the stadholder fought the wrong wars—land rather than maritime wars. The maritime forces were diverted from their proper functions—the protection of shipping, and clearing sea-lanes of pirates and English freebooters—to engage in short-lived but costly colonial wars of territorial

---

13. This was not the view of de Witt, whose model of a Dutch politician was William II, because he made an inchoate Dutch political system work (Rowen, *John de Witt*, 140).

acquisition. De le Court estimated that the cost of wresting Brazil and Angola from the Portuguese had been 118 million guilders. Even if they had not been immediately lost to the Spanish, they would have been of no material benefit, for these acquisitions were not based on the kind of realistic commercial considerations that turned the Dutch conquest of Java into a lucrative trade in spices. The indictment of Orange continued with charges of maladministration of the Army and Navy. The fault was chronic and could not be remedied because Orange princes, like all princes, had to find offices for their courtiers, whose primary object was not to promote competent, efficient discharge of public business but to abuse and mulct the people.

The Dutch reformed clergy were alleged to be scheming men who abused credulity. As pensioners of the state, they were insulated from the ebb and flow of prosperity that affected others. Consequently, "they . . . teach and preach up all that can have a tendency to their own credit, profit, and ease, yea, though it be to the ruin of the whole country; . . . when the doctrine, counsel, and admonition of these men is not received by any of their auditors, . . . [they] do then very unmercifully prosecute them *Odio theologico*" (59).[14] In a vigorous statement of Ghibelline doctrine, de la Court urged that the public interest requires that ecclesiastical institutions be subordinated to the civil power. It is in the public interest that there should be a national church, supported by the public purse; but to lay down a requirement of religious conformity that penalizes or even persecutes those not of the national religion stultifies trade and business. Yet this way was sought by the Calvinists, whose violent intolerance matched the inquisitorial brutality of the Jesuits.

By following the implications of these accusations of the prince-clergy axis in Dutch politics, the reader becomes sensible of the claim the author makes on behalf of the Regents' legitimacy. These men did not seek to disguise their motives or to mystify politics by grandiose rhetoric. They wanted to conduct public affairs because it served their interest. Every ruling group sought its own interest, but only the merchant princes could and even had to admit this. They could admit it because mercantile prosperity could not benefit a few without benefiting all. They had to admit it in order to distinguish their solid claims from the specious claims of the stadholder and the clergy. Wars of conquest and wars of religion did not serve the national interest because they were beneficial only to courtiers and clergymen. Hence, the Orangists had to disguise their interests. But the merchant princes could not disguise the

14. *The Interest* was vehemently anticlerical; see especially 320ff.

fact that they sought their own advantage; the nature of their profession made them in this respect honest men. It was therefore to their advantage to pull away disguises and draw the fangs of their rivals by frankly declaring that all politics is based on interest and by arguing that only mercantile prosperity is truly consistent with the national interest. This was Adam Smith a century before *The Wealth of Nations,* with the difference that whereas for Smith the invisible hand in the economy achieved its effects despite the intentions of individuals, for de la Court the system had to be cultivated and maintained by policy and statesmanship, lest it collapse under the weight of sectarian strife. It was right that the Regents should rule because they were proficient in the art of political economy.

By establishing that the Regents represented the national interest, de la Court justified their claim to be good citizens and patriots. It did not follow that those they ruled would remain steadfast in the national defense. What benefit in the system of interests might impel Dutchmen to undergo the hardships and sufferings of war? De la Court did not expressly answer this question, but the one implicit in his position was liberty. He could point out that the French and English navies were manned by press-gangs. Dutchmen would not tolerate such intrusions on personal liberties by the government. Love of their liberties would animate them to patriotic devotion and to defense of their country, if fight they must.

The System of Interests

It has been remarked that Colbert's administration was distinguished not so much by the novelty of his maxims of government as by the systematic linkage he established—and attempted to establish—between adjoining sectors of national life. In the current state of research, it is not possible to say to what extend Colbert modeled his administration on the de Witt administration. The French diplomatic service, outstanding for its intelligence-gathering, had been reporting on de Witt for a decade prior to Colbert's receipt of his first portfolio, and de Witt's qualities were well known to Louis' privy council. Ambassadors Chanut and d'Estrades were impressed by de Witt's charm, by his incorruptibility, his simplicity of habits, his self-control, lucidity, firmness of mind, and by his "perfect knowledge of affairs, as they all pass through his hands."[15] Colbert, well briefed on de Witt, made no secret of his jealous admiration. However, it would be misleading to press insis-

15. Lefèvre Pontalis, *John de Witt,* 1: 126.

tently the possible influence, since Colbert's administration bears all the marks of an original, regardless of models he might have studied. The point of a comparison should be rather to stress the close resemblance of their administration. Both were indefatigable workers operating with a machinelike regularity and thoroughness—de Witt's state papers run to forty volumes. Both were polytechnists. De Witt designed the chain shot for cannon that tore sail and masts from enemy ships. He put his mathematical knowledge to many uses in government, where he was expert in finance, taxation, and accounting. He designed the first modern system of pensions, which he worked out by applying the recently discovered theory of probability to mortality tables that he had caused to be drawn up.[16] The famous 4 percent interest rate on the funded public debt was a direct consequence of this scheme, which saved the government 1.5 million florins per annum on interest paid under the old scheme. His skill as a diplomat enabled him to keep the United Provinces free from land war until 1672, when Louis IV invaded with his huge army. Louis' ambition for universal monarchy, apparent to everyone, de Witt used to his advantage. "France," he argued, "cannot increase her power without becoming dangerous to all the rest of Europe, and after the conquest of the United Provinces there will be nothing to prevent her universal domination."[17] Above all, he grasped the systematic linkage of politics, economics, and foreign policy that lay at the base of the Dutch

16. One of de Witt's memoranda on the pension scheme described it in the following way: "As has been made clear to us by reasons which are perfectly well known to us, it is much preferable to negotiate stock on annuities which are certain to be redeemed in the course of nature, rather than on perpetual annuities or redeemable stock. On the other hand, it is more advantageous for private individuals who employ the surplus of their saving in augmenting their capital, to invest their money in life annuities rather than in annuities or interest at 4 percent, for although these same annuities are now being bought at 7½ percent, the profit upon them is comparatively much greater than upon an annuity of 4 percent. I have, therefore, to submit very respectfully to their Noble and High Mightinesses the unanswerable proofs of my assertions, and feel bound at the same time to defer to their wish of having this demonstration in writing." De Witt could claim "unanswerable proofs" of this complex scheme because he had brought it under mathematical discipline. Here, again, is Cartesianism in action. It may be noted that de Witt's scheme mandated that each age cohort should fund itself, rather than one generation funding the previous. The first method provides, over time, a large capital stock, while the second generates, over time, an insupportable tax burden. De Witt developed probability theory and the actuarial system. Condorcet credited him as the pioneer of "social mathematics."

17. Lefèvre Pontalis, *John de Witt*, 2: 153.

republic. Our concern here is with this system as de la Court sketched it in *The True Interest of Holland*.

Summarizing English opinion about the Dutch economic miracle, Joyce Appleby wrote that "what the Dutch success suggested more strongly than anything else was the productive possibilities of well-organized human efforts," which proved "the possibility of human ingenuity triumphing over the limits nature seemed to have set to productivity."[18] In view of our emphasis on the promise of economic growth through the application of scientific technology, we must now stress that *actual* rapid economic growth in Holland without such aids was doubtless a more important stimulus to the emergence of a politics of growth than was the Baconian project. The Dutch performance and Bacon's project were of course complementary. This is nowhere made clearer than by de Witt himself, who was that man of the seventeenth century in whom Dutch performance and Baconian-Cartesian ideas were authentically united in thought and practice.

The Interest of Holland declared that productivity is the basis of the Dutch nation. Its land "yields almost nothing out of its own bowels." The place would not be fit for habitation but for the "wit," "inventiveness," and "constant work" that the people apply to their inhospitable natural circumstances (*The True Interest*, 25, 28, 30, 38). Their own ingenuity and application, then, are the most important resources the Dutch possess: they must think in order to exist. Owing to this priority of wit to nature, of town to land, the Dutch system took shape as a set of interlocking demographic/productivity relations. The "four pillars of prosperity" were manufacture, shipping, fishing, and trade, which supported an estimated 650,000, 250,000, 450,000, and 650,000 people, respectively (36). The two basic, symbiotic industries were manufacturing and trade, and of these manufacturing took precedence. The large re-export trade depended on manufacturing, which attracted trade in the first instance and which capitalized raw materials taken in trade on manufactured goods (113).

The manufacture-trade linkage mandated an agenda of political priorities. One previously emphasized was cosmopolitanism, which in institutional terms means that strangers and immigrants had to have full access to the instruments of commerce and property and could not be burdened with arbitrary taxes that nationals might be reluctant to pay. Another mandate shaped financial policy—taxes calculated to enhance manufacturing, for example, by low import duties on raw materials.

18. Joyce O. Appleby, *Economic Thought and Ideology in Seventeenth Century England*, 77–78.

Manufacture might also be encouraged indirectly by tax incentives that "excite the commonality to ingenuity, diligence and frugality" (109, 91). There was no magic vector capable of satisfying these and other desiderata simultaneously. To encourage savings by taxing consumption must disfavor manufacturing. Free trade, or reduced duty agreements with trading partners, provided better markets for Dutch goods but deprived local manufacturers of protection. Policy thus invariably involved trade-offs. To affirm the complementarity of Dutch interests did not deny, but presupposed, competition between them. Short-term shifts of advantage and disadvantage between various economic sectors had to be manipulated to strike a balance. The premise of policy was that these interests, despite their competitiveness, were mutually supportive.

Histories of economic thought accustomed to contrast free trade with state manipulation are confounded by de la Court's tract, where a marked preference for free trade is combined with a developed sense of the role of policy in promoting economic growth. This combination was common in the mercantilist literature of the period. Its occurrence is usually associated with confidence in growth. De la Court endorsed a thoroughgoing free trade policy by opposing monopolies and guilds as artificial refuges from the discipline of the market, by chiding the States General for their timidity in occasionally imposing limits on the export of bullion, and by advocating open immigration. As we have seen, Colbert, like many statesmen, was cautious about the export of bullion although he knew that it "drove trade." He reasoned that, owing to France's weak trading position, exported bullion might not return in favorable quantity or within an acceptable time. That the States General restrained the export of bullion from time to time, even in their strong trading position, shows that apprehension about immediate losses could easily override considerations of long-term gains among men whose business was business. By opposing stoppages on bullion export, de la Court aligned himself with a growth outlook on the Dutch economy. Similarly, he opposed the East India monopoly and guilds, both of which were entrenched in Dutch commercial life. Optimism shows again in his attitude toward immigration, which he maintained stimulated manufacture by increasing demand, on the part of the more prosperous, and by lowering productive costs, in the case of the poor. As for the poor who, failing to accumulate, threatened the public purse with pauperism, the remedy lay in opportunities afforded by the colonies (142).

The Interest of Holland was designed for reading in a context that it does not, and need not, fully describe. Comparing it as a manifesto of the de Witt party with de Witt's actual conduct of government, we observe that the manifesto compromised rather less than the politician did. It lashed out at the house of Orange and the clergy, whereas de Witt could not afford to be so forthright. It was remarkably explicit about the Machiavellian character of international affairs; de Witt was more tactful, though he shared that view. *The Interest* blithely affirmed a harmony of interests that in practice was often exhaustingly difficult to attain. In these and other ways, the manifesto diverged from actuality, as political persuasion so often does. That divergence disqualifies *The Interest* as a history of de Witt's deeds, which it did not in any case purport to be. But the divergence does not affect its value as an expression of the thought that shaped his deeds. It was unusually bold thought, both in content and expression. De la Court often compressed into a few taut paragraphs notions that Locke three decades later would need fifty long-winded pages to express.

Pieter de la Court was not the only publicist in the de Witt circle who called a spade a spade. Benedict Spinoza was another. Spinoza's association with the de Witt circle began in 1663, four years after the reformed clergy had initiated a campaign to discredit the de Witt government.[19] In 1659, the States of Holland had allowed strict laws of Sabbath observance to lapse. The indignant clergy responded with a series of demands on the government, including the withdrawal of toleration of Roman Catholics and of minor Protestant sects. When these importunities were rebuffed, the clergy slandered the Amsterdam Regents as freethinkers and atheists. Ledewijk Meyer and others responded with strong defenses of the Erastian principles that had been incorporated into the

19. J. Freudenthal, *Spinoza: Leben und Lehre*, 150–55. Members of this circle were another Jan de Witt, Pieter de la Court, Lambert van Velthuysen, and Ledewijk Meyer. While Spinoza's admiration for de Witt is well documented, the degree of de Witt's reciprocation is disputed; this literature is summarized by Rowen, *John de Witt*, 411 n. 24. Rowen accepts the view that the alleged association is legendary, largely, it would appear, on the ground that in his view de Witt was not philosophically inclined. In the absence of evidence of de Witt's association with Spinoza, the dispute remains speculative. But Rowen's attempt to distance de Witt from philosophy, particularly Cartesian philosophy, is unconvincing. De Witt was educated by men who knew Descartes. His mathematical tract was a commentary on the *Geometry*. He owned Descartes' complete writings. His methodical manner was in the Cartesian mold, as Rowen admits. His motto, "Ago quod ago," is "Cogito ergo sum" revised for the man of action. Rowen makes much of de Witt's statement that he was the disciple of no man but himself (Rowen, *John de Witt*, 414). He does not note that emancipation from discipleship was just the "revolution in philosophy" that so excited his public. De Witt, like Colbert, was Cartesianism in action.

constitution of Holland in 1591. The episode was known as the "affaire de Witt."

Spinoza composed his *Tractatus theologico-politicus* as part of the counterattack that defended subordination of the clergy to civil authority. His reputation until then was based on an essay concerning the principles of Cartesian philosophy, which established him as the foremost Cartesian in Holland; and from the moment that the *Tractatus* appeared in 1665, Voetius's alarm about Descartes' crypto-atheism seemed to be fully confirmed. No writing of that century, the *Leviathan* possibly excepted, provoked more violent and continuous attacks than the *Tractatus*.[20] It was condemned as the devil's own corruption, as blasphemy, as a tool calculated to subvert all morals and civil order, let alone religion.

This literary sensation soon became a political cause. The Synod of South Holland resolved to demand that the government "suppress and forbid all heretical books, especially the wicked and blasphemous book, the theological-political tractatus."[21] The resolution was evidently meant to test the mettle of the de Witt government. Would de Witt defy public indignation to defend a man known to be of his party, and a miserable Jew at that? De Witt stood his ground: the Regents declined to use the civil power to suppress opinions odious to the clergy.

Despite the sensation created by the *Tractatus*, its innovations on the repertoire of Ghibelline arguments are few. Spinoza was not the first to assert that the Bible contains no rational teachings, or to deny Moses' authorship of the Pentateuch, or to take a text-critical approach based on the premise that the Bible is the work of human hands. But he was the first author to treat the Bible with disdain, as unworthy of the attention of a rational man: one turns to it not for instruction, which it cannot give, but to dispel the veneration of prejudiced minds who invoke

20. On the embarrassed efforts of the Dutch Cartesians to dissociate themselves from Spinoza, see Freudenthal, 236–42. Limborch, one of the endangered Cartesians, said of the *Tractatus* that it "ridicules the prophets and the Apostles; he thinks no miracles ever occurred. God is bound by fatality. But he describes God so as to seem to deny his existence altogether. . . . Such men attack not this or that credo, but the soul of religion itself" (Freudenthal, *Spinoza*, 220).

21. Ibid., 231. Although opposition to the *Tractatus* was especially vehement, it should be noted that most of the works by de Witt publicists, including *The Interest*, were subject to appeals from the clergy to municipal authorities to suppress their printing or sale (*Tractatus theologico-politicus*, preface, chaps. 6, 12).

biblical sanctions to suppress freedom of thought.[22] The insolence of this posture impressed even Hobbes, who had ventured in this direction, and who said of the *Tractatus* that he "had not dared to write so boldly." Spinoza's method of text criticism was meant to show that the Bible is a historical document, composed over a period of centuries, embodying the superstitions and mores of a defunct nation. From his rational perspective, the religious xenophobia of the Hebrews seemed barbarous and their beliefs childish. The implications against the reformed clergy were clear: their xenophobia and Sabbatarianism, their biblical mentality generally, was an anachronism uncontemporaneous with modern states steered by rational men.

Between 1670 and 1672, increasing pressure from domestic and foreign affairs seriously damaged the authority of de Witt's government. The young head of the Orange house, destined two decades later to take the English throne, had come of age. Astute, and mature beyond his years, he began a well-organized assault on de Witt by promising rewards to political rivals who would desert his camp. In Paris, the war that de Witt had so long attempted to avoid by negotiation and treaty was in preparation. In the summer of 1672, Louis launched his war for domination of the Continent by attacking the United Provinces with an overwhelming force whose impact discredited de Witt's government. But even this did not satisfy the Orangists or the clergy. Some weeks after a failed assassination attempt, John de Witt, master of European diplomacy and author of Holland's new prosperity, was violently torn to pieces by an enraged mob set upon him by his enemies.[23]

Holland survived Louis' assault by the last-resort device of opening the dikes. But it was a Holland subdued by the prince and substantially influenced by the clergy. De Witt's barbaric end and the execution of the English regicides had humbled the republican spirit. This was the Holland known to the exiled English Whigs of the 1680s. Had caution

22. This point has been brought out with particular force by Leo Strauss's study of the *Tractatus* in his *Persecution and the Art of Writing*.
23. The ghastly destruction of de Witt and his brother Cornelius was a sensational event comparable to regicide. His epitaph in an old church in the Hague memorialized his virtues as follows: "Here lie the remains of a man of universal genius, the profoundest statesman and the most adroit diplomatist of his age, in war as well as in peace; the prop of the republic of which even his enemies regarded him as the surest oracle. He was laborious, indefatigable, vigilant, sober, and modest; always serious, but easy, affable, and agreeable. As disinterested as a man could be, proposing to himself no other object but the good of his country and the establishment of her liberties."

not been native to John Locke, he might have learned it during his Dutch exile. Among his friends were the Cartesian Limborch and the historian LeClerc. If Locke discussed philosophy and politics with these men, their conversations must have turned more than once to Spinoza and the de Witt government. He would have learned that Spinoza's uncompromising posture renewed the clergy's suspicions of Cartesianism; they brought pressures to bear on reformists such as Limborch. Heidanus had been obliged to resign his chair at Leiden in the aftermath of de Witt's fall, and Spinoza escaped de Witt's fate only because of a premature natural death. LeClerc would have emphasized that lessons were to be learned from the fact that Holland's two great republican statesmen, Oldenbarnevelt and de Witt, had perished by political execution. The times were out of phase, the old and the new sat juxtaposed in sharp antagonism. Advance, then, with caution. Pay court to the prejudices you intend to demolish. Call a spade an implement. Condescend to treat trifling opinions with respect. Rebut them with a thousand petty objections, among which the main point is buried. Preserve the appearance of piety, if you would cast political institutions and practices into a secular, rational mold.

The Dutch Constitution

Dutch supremacy was eclipsed after the War of the Spanish Succession by the political and fiscal costs of war and by other nations' growing aptitude for trade. The influence Holland exercised for a century was disproportionate to its size and staying power, given jealous, potent neighbors. In this sense its ascendancy was a lucky chance that even exceptional political skill could not perpetuate.

The Dutch Republic was an exotic adaptation of old institutions to new requirements and practices. Most of its liberties—and the taste for liberty—were ancient. So were its political institutions. They had been developed in the Middle Ages by an urban mercantile patriciate who looked to the emperor for protection and who never contemplated democratic government. When Netherlanders rebelled against their royal masters, they did so in defense of "ancient liberties"—the old system of privileges and immunities. For the first time in their political experience, the patriciate bore the entire burden of government, including provision for defense. As we have seen, the Regents were not successful in leading the nation in war; this power they shared with the stadholder and the clergy. This division of power, and the factional struggle between Regents and clergy, was of a piece with the formal exclusion of the people from government. The Regents' inability to renovate institutions so that the people could participate in government was the defect that Spinoza detected in the regime; and he was probably correct in regarding the de Witt government as occupying a critical juncture in the development of the Dutch constitution. If the Perpetual Edict were to succeed, it had to be followed by a renovation of institutions that would bring the Orange constituency into the government.

What de Witt might have thought of Spinoza's schemes is not known. There is no evidence that he contemplated some enfranchisement of the people. The people were a force in Dutch politics, despite their exclusion from office; government might not require their approval, but no government could long survive their aroused disapproval. De Witt was entirely aware of the force of public opinion and hoped to win it over by conducting his administration in a popular manner. He lived modestly on his salary of 3,000 florins, although he had married into the wealthy Bicker family. He avoided any suggestion of favoritism, luxury, or corruption. He often went about official business on foot, accompanied only by a secretary and a servant "carrying in a velvet bag the most important papers in Europe," as the astonished French Ambassador d'Estrades reported. To these simple habits he added a reputation for unimpeachable rectitude: in contrast to the universal practice in Europe, his favor could not be bought, and neither would he buy favor.[24] In these ways he set examples for republican service. But to this popular manner he joined autocracy in practice. His effective day-to-day constituency consisted of the oligarchs in Amsterdam and Dortrecht. Although he was an effective speaker, he disliked even the small assembly of the States General. His was the distaste of the supreme technician for the social grooming and fence-mending of mere politics.[25]

The narrow political base of the Republic was the unresolved problem of politics of interest in Holland. The public interest was to be served by optimizing the liberty and prosperity of the Regents and the people. The determination of this optimum was largely a technical matter for the political economist. To the extent that interest could be reduced to "unanswerable proofs," in de Witt's proud phrase, expertise might replace the social grooming and dominance struggles characteristic of popular political deliberation. But the elimination of mere politics by knowledge reaches its limit when the expert's formulas are im-

---

24. Lefévre Pontalis, *John de Witt,* 1: 178, 500–506.
25. Rowen's chapter "The Craft of Politics" describes graphically de Witt's manner of conducting office. The fluidity of Dutch politics has been contrasted with the less porous Venetian regime by Peter Burke, *Venice and Amsterdam: A Study of Seventeenth-Century Elites,* 32, 42, 47, 74.

plemented by the inexpert interested public. How may assent to enlightened policy be secured? Or, turning the problem around, how may
republics secure enlightened government? This old question had never
received an adequate answer, although the advent of progressive rationalism made it urgent. The solution that emerged was the system of
representative government—that, plus the insight gathered by David
Hume from study of ancient republics: political stability is not compatible with the small compass of city-states; they must have a large
territory.

In addition to this domestic difficulty, de Witt's politics of interest
confronted serious problems in foreign affairs. By the time he took
office, the *politiques* in England and France were convinced of a close
relation between commercial ascendancy and national power. A typical
expression of this conviction occurs in Benjamin Worsley's assertion
that "it is by trade and the due ordering of government, and by no other
means, that wealth and shipping can either be increased or upheld, and
consequently by no other, that the power of any nation can be sustained
by land, or by sea. . . . it is by a knowledge of trade and commerce . . .
that one nation . . . knows perfectly how to straighten and pinch another, and to compel a compliance from them" (*The Advocate*, 12).
Worsley was among the men of the Rump Parliment who goaded
Cromwell into a war on the Dutch, after a massive buildup of the fleet,
to break their hold on the Baltic trade. Charles II's two Dutch wars had
the same object, and Colbert was keen to reduce the Netherlands to a
client state of France. Peace was in Holland's interest because war jeopardized its trading advantage; but for that very reason its trading rivals
might hope to gain from war. Interest politics thus seems to undercut
itself by setting in motion a perpetual international struggle for commercial supremacy, since one nation purchases its advantage at the cost
of another. Here the situation differs from domestic politics. Increased
national prosperity can alleviate the domestic struggle between rich and
poor by increasing the ease and convenience of the poor. But this
mechanism does not operate internationally, since even a strong trading
nation, if weak relative to a rival, may lose its liberty. Consequently, if
the strength of nations is grounded in economic power, states seem obliged to engage in endless competition and war for trade advantage. Or
to express the same thought more explicitly in the perspective of the
Bacon-Descartes program: although the subjection of nature by the arts
and sciences opens the *prospect* of infinite acquisition, all *actual* acquisition occurs in a condition of relative scarcity of trade, bullion, or resources. The competition for these things will be sharpest precisely
among men who know that they are the sinews of national power.

Political thinkers of the seventeenth and eighteenth centuries did not set the compass of progress for utopia partly because they fully appreciated this fact and its consequences. International politics remained, in their thinking, a "state of nature." Hobbes had accordingly recommended a large population and maximization of national wealth; Locke, writing *Considerations on Money* with hindsight on the Colbert and de Witt governments, declared that "riches do *not* consist in having more gold and silver, but in having *more in proportion than the rest of the world, or than our neighbours,* whereby we are enabled to procure to ourselves a greater plenty of the conveniences of life, than comes within the reach of neighboring kingdoms and states, who, sharing the gold and silver of the world in a less proportion, *want the means of plenty and power,* and so are poorer" (*Works,* 4: 13).

Locke shared the view of Shaftesbury that England should, as a matter of national policy, "break the trade" of the Dutch.[26] As it happened, the accession of William III to the English throne made England the senior partner in an alliance with Holland against France, which also aspired to Dutch trade.

Despite the permanent competition for trade projected by the politics of interest, its spokesmen argued that commercial nations are peaceful ("la douce commerce," Montesquieu called it). There are two reasons for this. Hobbes, de la Court, Locke and the republican writers of the eighteenth century agreed that wars of ambition or righteousness are not in the national interest. Such wars serve the vanity of monarchs or flatter the aroused passion of a nation; they do not promote the solid interests of the people. The commercial republic, then, is peaceful without being pacifistic: it fights only wars necessary to maintaining its national power, and even then, as de la Court said, it is not ashamed to *buy* peace as an alternative to war. Commercial republics are also peaceful in the sense that the nature of trade sets limits to the degree of control that is in a nation's interest. Trade is inherently reciprocal; it cannot be conducted with trading "partners" that are totally impoverished. Trading nations have an interest therefore in the solvency of their partners and in the markets they may provide. Their rational interest is not in the ruin of their rivals but in maintaining a marginal advantage over them. This conception of interest politics on the international scale is expressed by the maxims of the two great "balances," the balance of trade and the balance of power as reference points for national policy.

26. Richard Cox, *Locke on War and Peace,* 175–80.

chapter 6

The Whig Commercial
Republic

IN THE half-century that elapsed between the Glorious Revolution and
Sir Robert Walpole's resignation from office, the "Revolution Principles" of Whiggism transformed England into a commercial republic
dominated by a loose alliance of gentry, peers, and "monied men." Although its institutions were makeshift and its rhetoric followed expediency as much as principle, the overall performance is unmistakable.

Parliamentary supremacy was irrevocably settled when the Hanoverian dynasty was brought to England in 1714. Ministerial government
had ruled England for two decades, although the legitimacy of this political form was still moot. Similarly with political parties: formal party
organization did not exist, and many publicists, Whig and Tory, decried
factional spirit. Nevertheless, party allegiance was a major factor of parliamentary politics. Ministerial and parliamentary business were supported by a civil service that attained a certain professionalism, particularly in the Treasury and the Navy. Legislation, which was increasing
dramatically in volume now that Parliament sat every year, was drafted
largely by lawyers who might be members of Parliament or civil servants.

The English liberty so admired on the Continent expanded unobtrusively, thanks largely to benign neglect of repression. The licensing
of books ended in 1696, and the last political censorship in 1712. Watered-
down laws on religious conformity were weakly enforced except in the
universities. Habeas corpus was secure. Everyone was free to buy and
sell, and government annuities attracted investment from many thousands of the "middling sort." A court ruling of 1699 extended the law of

property to the protection of securities and bills of exchange against theft. Prejudice against foreigners relaxed. In 1753 a Naturalization Act allowing citizenship to Jews was passed. But it proved to be premature, for the public outcry forced its repeal in the next session.

The tone of public life changed with the disappearance of political violence. There was no Jeffries to hang dissenters, nor did angry Parliaments send impeached ministers to the Tower for execution. In the entire period there was but one political execution, arising from the Jacobite attempt on the life of William III; and even this order carried narrowly in Parliament. Although his actions accused him of treason, Bolingbroke obtained pardon to return from the court of the Pretender in France to lead the Tory opposition against Walpole. Violence was replaced by fierce political satire, partisan vehemence on the hustings, and duels between gentlemen. Masculine passions were dissipated in the coffee houses, in Exchange Alley, in the theater, at gaming tables, or in the numerous foreign wars. In all, public life was lively, stable if not always sensible, a little voluptuous, and literate. For these qualities it came to be called the Augustan Age; and numerous diaries registered the feeling that it was a good time to be alive.

Whigs laid the foundations of England's commercial supremacy by combining far-reaching innovations in public finance with a foreign policy meant to keep French political and mercantile ambitions within bounds. In the first decade of their dominance, Whigs gave England a sound currency, reformed funding of the national debt, and set up what proved to be the catalyst of investment, the Bank of England.

These were the things that put flesh and blood to Liberty and Prosperity, slogans whose prestige was so great that even Tories were compelled to endorse them. As a political program their success was impressive. Between 1700 and 1750, England acquired effective control of the East India trade and took the lead in the Levant and Baltic trade. The volume of its reexport trade increased fourfold. Numerous industries showed marked gains in output; in little more than two decades, linen production in Scotland doubled, to 7.7 million yards stamped in 1750. The capital assets of the Bank of England rose from £100,000 to £18 million and drew the center of international finance from the great Amsterdam Exchange Bank to London. And the national debt rose from £12.8 million to £75.5 million.

Monetary Theory and Practice

"The ancients speak only of virtue; the moderns speak only of money." Thus spake J.-J. Rousseau. But he exaggerated. Rousseau himself warmly defended virtue, and political debate in Augustan England revolved around the antithesis between virtue and money. But these were words. Concerning the world of affairs Rousseau was about right; monetary and fiscal policy were the levers that raised England from a trading nation to a great commercial power.

The springboard of this transition vindicated Shaftesbury's insistence on Protestant succession. With William on the throne, the religious division that distracted the reign of Charles II and ruined James suddenly tumbled down the agenda. Holland was no longer a rival but an ally whose expertise in trade, finance, and administration could be transplanted to England, providing that it was suitably disguised. This was what the Whig junto did. The four years between 1694 and 1698 were a period of dazzling financial change: the Board of Trade and the Bank of England were chartered; the East India Company became a major creditor to the government; the coinage was reminted; and the earl of Halifax, as treasurer, consolidated the public debt. These mechanisms, so critical for the subsequent development of trade and credit, were copies of Dutch models, as many publicists noted. Among them was that merchant of malice, Jonathan Swift, who wrote:

> The present Bishop of Salisbury [Gilbert Burnet] is said to have found out that expedient (which he learned in Holland) of raising money upon the security of taxes that were only sufficient to pay a large interest. I am satisfied that the pernicious counsel of borrowing money upon public funds was taken indigested from the like practices among the Dutch, without allowing for any difference in government, religion, law, custom, extent of country or manners and disposition of the people.[1]

Swift ventilates here a fragment of the Country attitude, to be considered later, that encumbered England's course to becoming a monetized economy. I mention this example to indicate that the reforms and mechanisms of the commercial republic carried no small political liability. The public did not quite understand these mechanisms. Publicists often depicted them as mysterious forces manipulated by shadowy "stock jobbers" and "money'd men" of foreign origin and sinister intent. These publicists voiced the sentiments of the squires, who dominated Parliament. Often they were suspicious of the qualities of city life—money, trade, brains, and cosmopolitanism. They formed the "Country party" in Parliament, opposed to the "Court party," and their

1. Jonathan Swift, *The History of the four last years of the Queen*, in *Works*, 12: 87.

influence accounts in part for the makeshift quality of public finance in this period. But the publicists also spoke for strong Tory sentiment that could be found in London's mob. The Tory mobs that rioted during the Sacheverell trial threatened to storm the Bank of England, which they believed to be full of gold and Whiggery.

The impact of Country opinion is discernible in the circumstances of the founding of the Bank of England. Schemes for a national bank had been rejected by Parliament several times during the seventeenth century, even though the experience of trading cities indicated the necessity of that institution. But with public finance distressed by England's wars, the proposal of the Scots financier William Paterson to found the Bank of England squeezed past Parliament. To mollify old prejudices against national banks, Paterson presented his proposal obliquely. His scheme was to form a consortium to lend the government £1.2 million at 8 percent, the security being a new tax on ship's tonnage. The Bank itself was presented as a concession to the consortium, which was to be issued a charter of incorporation allowing it to conduct a range of banking operations, exclusive of trading.[2] The initial grant of charter was for but ten years, renewable on Parliament's approval. This meager proposal encountered heavy opposition in Lords, especially from bishops, who complained of privileges being granted to monied interests. Nevertheless, Parliament approved the scheme as the Tonnage Act, to indicate that the life of the bank was tied to a specific tax.

These were crumbs, but Paterson's consortium evidently had not expected more. The high 8 percent interest they demanded is a measure of their estimate of the risk involved. And they were not wrong. The government could not pay the first installment of interest from the tax monies voted and had to borrow to meet its obligation. By March 1695, the government, requiring funds to pay William's troops, borrowed £100,000 per month from the Bank, which it in turn obtained from the Exchange Bank of Amsterdam.[3] But the consortium had foreseen these risks; they showed their muscle by subscribing the entire £1.2 million in only twelve days after the issue of the Bank's charter and promptly transferred the first installment of the loan to the Treasury.

The Bank and the Exchequer moved at once to open up the credit

2. Herman van der Wee, "Monetary, Credit and Banking System," in *The Cambridge Economic History of Europe*, 5: 385.
3. David Ogg, *England in the Reigns of James II and William III*, 422; E. L. Hargreaves, *The National Debt*, 9–10. Under the terms of its incorporation, the capital of the Bank was to come from the interest on its loan! This truly was a shoestring beginning.

system in England and to consolidate government finance. The Bank circulated £1.7 million in paper money, backed by an equivalent amount of discounted government bills and tallies. Halifax began issuing his famous Exchequer bills, which were negotiable at the Bank. He also raised large loans by annuities schemes. In 1696, he brought down to Commons what may pass as England's first budget. Until then government debts had been regarded as independent debts to be redeemed by repaying the loan from specific taxes. Halifax declared that these loans totaled about £10 million. He proposed to approach them as an aggregate. They were to be consolidated under a new fund, called the sinking fund, which was to receive monies to repay the principal on government loans. The sinking fund in effect created a budget line for what was soon called the national debt. It gave fiscal expression to government indebtedness by providing a mechanism for paying it off. To the investor the sinking fund represented an increase in the security of his loan; for it meant that the return of his principal was not tied to a particular tax vulnerable to shifts in parliamentary opinion, but to the whole of the national revenue.[4]

These credit mechanisms were improvised during a period of danger to the ruling Whig junto. Financial resources were strained by war debts. A sharp price inflation sprang from the effects of extensive new credit coupled with the sorry condition of the English coinage. Merchants had formed an unnatural alliance with country squires resentful of the foreign dynasty. The alliance acquired a flag in the Jacobite assassination attempt on William and in the French-backed invasion force that gathered at Calais but did not sail.

In this unsettled atmosphere, there occurred one of the most important monetary debates in English history—the debate on the recoinage. The shilling had been debased over decades by "clipping," that is, by slicing silver off the edges of the coins. This little theft, which became a big theft through repetition, was meant to be stopped by the introduction of milled edges in Charles II's reign, but the result was that the milled shilling was driven out of circulation by the bad coin. By the time the recoinage debate began in 1694, Treasury Secretary William Lowndes estimated that the bullion value of the English coinage was at least 25 percent less than its face value, representing a loss of about £1.8 million.

The Privy Council asked Lowndes to review the coinage matter and submit a recommendation. His thorough report, *Essay for the Amend-*

4. Van der Wee, "Monetary, Credit and Banking System," 413; P. G. M. Dickson, *The Financial Revolution in England,* 46, 50.

ment of the Silver Coin, marshaled the evidence and arguments for what had then become the opposing views. The hard-money men proposed that money should be recoined according to the old standard, eighty-six grains of silver to the shilling. The cost of bringing the coinage back to the standard was to be borne by taxation. The opposing point of view was that the standard should be lowered by minting not eighty-six but sixty-nine grains of silver to the shilling, about par with the average debasement through clipping. This scheme, it was argued, would avoid the rigors of a return to hard money by bringing the mint standard in line with the average value of clipped coins.

Lowndes's *Essay* recommended the soft-money option, which tended also to be the preference of the merchant-Tory alliance. The Privy Council, then dominated by Somers, Pembroke, and Halifax, decided to seek reports from eight leading scientists, philosophers, and merchants, among whom were Locke and Newton. Locke had already established himself as a spokesman for hard money in a publication on the subject the year previous. He was at the height of his influence with Somers and Pembroke, who consulted him closely on all important matters.[5] Locke's initial publication drew fire from a wide range of authors, including successful merchants and some of the best economists of the day. His response to Lowndes took the soft-money arguments to pieces chapter and verse. Newton in his report concurred with Locke, and on this basis Pembroke rushed the recoinage legislation through Parliament early in 1696. The consequence was to install hard money as the basis of British monetary policy for the next two centuries.

Locke's Theory of Money, Credit, and Trade

It is scarcely surprising that in an era of soft money and demand-side economics, the high praises of Locke by McCulloch and Macaulay turned to blame and even scorn. William Shaw set the tone when in 1896 he wrote that Locke's "interference" in the recoinage debate "affords one of the most conspicuous instances of the weakness of even piercing intellects before a purely practical and technical question."[6] Locke, he maintained, confused capital and money, did not understand that money was a medium of exchange, and argued "in the abstract without reference to, or acknowledgement of, the commonest facts

5. Peter Laslett, "John Locke, the Great Recoinage, and the Origins of the Board of Trade: 1695–1698," 380–81, 388–89.
6. William Shaw, ed., *Select Tracts and Documents Illustrative of English Monetary History, 1626–1730,* 103.

which are daily transacting under our eyes."[7] Three decades later C. R. Fay more generously drew attention to the far-reaching historical importance of Locke's argument, which "every head of the Bank of England . . . would have endorsed."[8] But he maintained that Locke's reasoning was obtuse, and that he "was like those general historians who shrink from the subtleties of economic thought because it appears to be leading them to conclusions they believe to be politically impossible." These criticisms have more recently been parlayed by Joyce Appleby into the ideology accusation. The soft-money men, she claims, understood from experience that the serviceability of currency was not dependent on its silver value, but depended merely on the fiat of the political sovereign who decreed that clipped coin was legal tender. Locke drew a veil of pretended natural laws over this insight into the factitious character of money. His views prevailed against the facts because of the connection he drew between "economic and political freedom, an association predicated upon the dogma of natural, universal, inexorable laws working outside the purview and power of human legislators."[9]

Appleby's indictment of Locke as the doctrinaire architect of liberal economics has the advantage of placing him in the Whig camp, where he belongs. He did indeed insist on inexorable laws that define objective economic structure. The discovery of these laws, or general maxims, about the behavior of the market were to his mind central to the formation of policy; for to strain against them was to court calamity. They were also, like the discoveries of natural scientists, a great deliverance from error and quackery. The axis of his essays on money and interest is the fundamental scientific axiom, the law of causality, which in economic terms means that you cannot get something for nothing. The advocates of soft money, Locke believed, were trying to get something for nothing. They did not call it devaluation, a term then unknown. They called it "raising the value of money" and denied that this was the old practice of debasing coin, done up as an *increase* in its value! Locke scorned these reasonings. "This business of money and coinage," he wrote at the conclusion of a rebuttal, "is by some men, and amongst them some very ingenious persons, thought to be a great mystery, and very hard to understand. Not that truly in itself it is so, but because interested people, that treat of it, wrap up the secret they make advan-

7. Ibid., 105.
8. C. R. Fay, "Locke versus Lowndes," 149.
9. Joyce O. Appleby, "Locke, Liberalism, and the Natural Law of Money," 56. See also the chapter "An Ideological Triumph" in her *Economic Thought and Ideology in Seventeenth-Century England*.

tage of in a mystical, obscure, and unintelligible way of talking." But if the facts were declared in their "plain, true, honest sense, [they] would prove very easy and intelligible."[10] The issue in the recoinage debate was simple. As the Royal Astronomer Flamsteed said, the real point was whether five was six or only five. Or as Lord Macaulay put it, Lowndes's *Essay* had become the "text book of a party composed partly of dull men who really believed what he told them, and partly of shrewd men who were perfectly willing to be authorized by law to pay a hundred pounds with eighty."

Locke's conviction that clear and distinct ideas about these matters were available led him to attempt, in these essays, to educate the public in basic economic concepts. The relevant public consisted of the country "squires," as he called them, who dominated Parliament. He entertained no very high opinion of their economic competence. But they occupied a decisive position in the new constitution that Locke himself had defended; and it was now important to bring what he considered to be economic enlightenment to them. In these essays, where religion was of no relevance, Locke was free to speak openly about a national economic policy. England might acquire wealth by conquest or by trade. To opt for the first was to imitate Rome and Spain. The second fork led down the path taken by Holland, whose example Locke repeatedly held up for emulation. He frankly described the conflicting and complementary interests of the landed men, merchants, financiers, and people. He outlined monetary and fiscal policies for reconciling these interests, without disguising where pinches would be felt. He declared, for example, that land must bear the chief burden of taxation, and that it was in the interest of landed men to do so. In sum, Locke wrote as the new intellectual, the *honnête homme* whose unmoralizing, toughminded honesty grounded in his certain knowledge of the world.[11] Since he drew his power from knowledge, interest compelled him to drive deceit from the pulpit of moral posturing and subterfuge from its dark closets.

Locke's description of the function of money linked three ideas current at the time. Money was said to be a medium of exchange (currency); it was said to be "treasure"; and it was said to "drive trade." These maxims express experience with chronic money shortages that hampered trade; often there simply was not enough coin to circulate through the manifold markets of the kingdom. One of the arguments

10. John Locke, "Considerations of the Lowering of Interest and Raising the Value of Money," in *Works*, 5: 104.
11. Laslett, "John Locke, The Great Recoinage," 395.

for "raising," i.e. lowering, the value of money was that by coining less silver in the shilling, the nation's money supply would be stretched, whereas recoining at the old standard would contract the money supply. Locke opposed this attractive solution because he did not believe that the money supply could be stretched. He undertook to show that silver specie is the fundamental medium of exchange upon which all others depend. Specie performs this function, and drives trade, only because it is "treasure," or possesses "intrinsic value." Finally, he argued that silver alone had to be the currency if the national currency was to be a stable money of account. These three points led to his conclusion that money is the indispensable pillar of national wealth, presupposed by the credit superstructure. In advancing this argument, Locke acknowledged that he sailed against the winds of current opinion. He emphasized that paper credit, in its many forms from I.O.U. to bill of exchange to debenture stock, had confused public opinion about the nature of money.[12] That clipped coins were commonly received in payment at face value seemed to many the clinching argument against hard money. One of Locke's critics did him the favor of carrying this reasoning to the end of the line by declaring that "if money were leather, it would pass." Locke's argument was meant to rebut schemes for any currency other than silver.

His argument for the unique suitability of silver as currency has been subject to misunderstanding in his time and our own. His dictum that the "general consent" of mankind has placed an "imaginary value" on silver and gold has been derided as speculation. But the evidence he cited to support this statement bears him out—the dictum merely summarized universal practice. Silver has been in fact the medium of exchange and money of account of all trading nations ancient and modern. Occasional experiments with copper coinages, as in Ireland, Sweden, and portions of Germany, were quickly visited by economic punishments. Silver is unique because it happens to be the one material answering all the requirements of currency. It is durable, portable, easily recognized and not easily counterfeited, and divisible with precision into uniform units. These purely physical properties are required in order that a currency may perform the function of stable "counters."[13] The physical properties of money must, as it were, mimic the stability of numbers. Many materials that have these properties lack one further property that is unique to silver and gold, which is their "intrinsic value" as "treasure." The expression "intrinsic value" is not especially well adapted to

12. Locke, *Works*, 5: 19, 22–23, 149.
13. Ibid., 22–23, 29–30, 35.

Locke's analysis. But it was then the accepted terminology for denoting the silver content of coin, distinguished from the "extrinsic," or face value, of coin. For Locke, the intrinsic value of specie meant specifically its *commodity value as bullion*. This point requires emphasis because it lies at the base of his monetary analysis and also because his critics, then as today, take him to be saying that the intrinsic value of silver was fixed from eternity by some Platonic money god. But Locke, who wrote always with a view to fact, maintained that not only silver, but money generally, "is in the same condition with other commodities."[14] This statement could be verified simply by entering any exchange bank and inquiring about the price of bullion or the exchange rates on various currencies.

While gold and silver are in the same condition with copper, paper, or leather as commodities, they differ in that mankind has placed an "imaginary value" on them as precious metals; silver is far more valuable than an equal amount of copper. This value is not fixed, but fluctuates with market demand—it has no more "standing, settled value" than any other commodity.[15] To underscore this point, Locke traced the gradual price inflation of the sixteenth and seventeenth centuries to the great influx of these metals from the Americas, which cheapened their price in Europe. But if the price of precious metals fluctuates, it is still far more stable than the prices of other commodities, especially foods, which fluctuate seasonally and annually. The relative stability of the price of gold and silver is the reason that people "consent" to measure the value of all other commodities relative to them. Gold is, however, less suitable as specie than silver; for gold is too dear and scarce to function as a national currency usable as a uniform money of account throughout the kingdom.

14. "Money has a value, as it is capable, by exchange, to procure us the necessaries or conveniences of life, and in this it has the nature of a commodity. . . . Money therefore, in buying and selling, being perfectly in the same condition with other commodities, and subject to all the same laws of value. . . . To money, considered in its proper use as a commodity passing in exchange from one to another . . ." (Locke, *Works,* 5: 34, 36, 42, 45). William Shaw and Joyce Appleby, among many other writers, deny that Locke asserted what he did assert in these citations; see especially Appleby, *Economic Thought and Ideology,* 222–23. When Locke's position is acknowledged, little remains of Appleby's case that Locke fabricated counterfactual evidence to support his "ideological" defense of property.
15. Locke, *Works,* 5: 46ff. The second item of Locke's twenty-one-point economic primer declares that "there is no such intrinsic, natural, settled value in anything, as to make any assigned quantity of it *constantly* worth any assigned quantity of another" (42; italics added).

In summary, then, the unique suitability of silver as money is that it may be readily coined into uniform units of known weight and fineness, from which commodity value may be readily calculated; hence, it is suitable as a standard measure of all other commodities. The function of currency is comparable to the function of uniform weights and measures. By reducing things to comparable magnitudes, it generates a calculable system, called the market. Credit instruments, including paper currency, can function only if backed by silver currency, for paper credit is a "promise of money." The medium of exchange must itself be valuable because otherwise someone exchanging a bushel of wheat for leather money, for example, gets nothing valuable in return. The basis of all exchange is barter.[16] The mint stamp on the silver adds nothing to the commodity value of the silver. Even so, coinage is valuable, even indispensable, because it enables exchange to be carried out by reference to a settled standard of value that immeasurably facilitates exchange. Money is a prime condition for the creation of the market and its values.

The basic elements of the market are price, supply, and demand. They stand in a fixed relation: price is the ratio of supply to demand ("the quantity of goods to their vent").[17] This proposition was in low credit in Locke's time. The House of Commons, to look no further, was the scene of innumerable rebellions against this concept. Indeed, Locke may have been the only man of his age who accepted, with full appreciation of the implication, the proposition that the market objectively determines the values of commodities. This startling notion is implicit in a good deal of the free-trade literature of the period, but few authors seem to have recognized its drastic implications. The market expresses the human drive to acquire in circumstances of relative scarcity and uncertainty. The acquisitive drive is not optional; those who do not acquire depend upon the charity of those who do.[18] There is no free lunch. Exchange of commodities is the peaceful mechanism devised by people to acquire the produce of the labors of others in exchange for their own.[19] Individual buyers and sellers bring their subjective evalua-

16. Locke, *Works*, 5: 24ff. John Law accepted this analysis in his *Money and trade consider'd* (1705); reprinted in *Somers' Tracts*, 13: 779.
17. Locke, *Works*, 5: 36, 40, 42–51. In one of several criticisms directed expressly against Locke, John Law remarked of this statement that "the vent of goods cannot be greater than the quantity, but the demand may be greater" (*Money and trade consider'd*, 777). This is the correct expression for what Locke certainly meant to say.
18. Locke, *Second Treatise of Government*, chap. 5, pars. 27–28, 32, 34–35, 40, 43.
19. Ibid., pars. 48–50. In these passages Locke maintains that the "acquisitive desire naturally extends only to commodities for immediate use, in the ab-

tions to the market hopeful of a good result. These evaluations are necessarily partial and self-interested; taken as a whole, they are chaotic. The market provides a testing ground for resolving conflicting subjective judgments of value into an objective measure: market price. Price represents a *consensus of exchange;* it expresses the coherent, directed pressure generated by demand against a supply. There are of course many markets, like wheels within wheels. Some extend no farther than the parish. Locke's focus was on the English national economy as a part of the European market. In his criticisms of proposals to fix the rate of interest at 4 percent, Locke described in detail the general conceptions just mentioned.

Among the gentry, complaints about interest were as common as complaints about taxes and the weather. Since interest and taxation, like the rain, fell more heavily on landed men than any other group, their complaints were not contrived miseries. The gentry therefore provided a steady clientele for schemes to shift the burden of taxation to merchants and the costs of borrowing to the monied men. Like most nations, England had long regulated the official interest rate; in Locke's time, it was 6 percent. Proposals were abroad that it should be reduced to 4 percent. High interest, it was argued, lowered the value of land, because interest rates must be charged against profits. Low interest would therefore raise the value of land, to the advantage of the burdened gentry. Publicists argued that since in Holland money was lent at 4 percent, higher interest in England put the nation at a trade disadvantage while at the same time mortgaging the gentry to Dutch money.

To all this Locke replied that the rent on money follows market price. The rate of interest is a function of risk plus supply relative to demand. The legal rate of interest is but a "fence to hedge in cuckoos": neither lenders nor borrowers pay it any regard. The 4 percent rate in Holland, which astonished so many, was no mystery at all. He correctly observed that there was no legal rate, so that a contract for 25 percent was enforceable in the courts. The popular belief that the government effectively legislated a 4 percent rate Locke traced to John de Witt's conversion of the rate on the funded debt from 5 percent to 4 percent. This transaction did not occur, Locke observed, by legislative fiat. In reducing the interest, de Witt allowed any creditor dissatisfied with the new rate to withdraw his principal. That few did withdraw proved de Witt

---

sence of money. It was the invention of money as a medium of exchange that released the desire for boundless accumulation." This assertion is based on the assumption that the customs of the American Indians exemplify the condition of man in the "state of nature."

right in thinking that the market price for annuities in Holland was 4 percent.[20] Although better returns could be obtained in Holland and abroad, investment at that rate was still attractive to investors seeking low-risk returns. By parity of argument, the high rates paid by the English gentry expressed scarcity of money and high risk. To establish the objectivity of this market, or "natural," value, Locke traced the consequences of reducing the rate to 4 percent. If the measure were successfully enforced, capital needed to improve lands and finance would dry up and the Exchequer would be required to deliver large amounts of principal to investors.[21] Monied men would be losers, but so would other lenders, such as orphans and widows; and the nation would be the great loser.

However, the assumption that the law could be enforced was contrary to experience. In the real world, such a law would create a lending black market very profitable to creditors. Many innocent but ignorant persons would invest their money with scriveners and goldsmiths at less than the legal rate, as usual, but these would lend at the market rate plus an increment to compensate the risk of illegal trade. Trade would thus not be thwarted, merely hindered. The common view that interest rates could be controlled by legislation was therefore mistaken. So was its moralizing corollary, that financiers engaged in a conspiracy to cheat the public.[22] The real reasons for high interest in England were scarcity of money and the relatively high risk of lending on English lands. Lending was risky because so many landowners managed their estates poorly. Rents fell owing to negligent farming; debts for imported luxuries piled up; mortgages were sought not to improve yields or to extend tillage, but to pay wages to improvidence. Here indeed was the crux of the matter. Produce of the land was the anchor of the English economy, but the gentry were poor businessmen:

> If the virtue and provident way of living of our ancestors (content with our native conveniences of life, without the costly itch after the materials of pride and luxury from abroad) were brought in fashion and countenance again amongst us; this alone would do

20. Locke, *Works*, 5: 67–68.
21. Ibid., 9–10, 12–16.
22. Ibid., 71. Locke noted two exceptions to his general rule against official interest rates. There should be a nominal official interest rate to provide a rule for courts that settle matters pertaining to debts and contract. Further, he conceded that a fixed rate of interest might in some cases be an appropriate weapon to break the hold of financial cartels, should they develop (63–64).

more to keep and increase our wealth, and enrich our land, than all
our paper helps, about interest, money, bullion, &c. which, however eagerly we may catch at, will not, I fear, without better husbandry, keep us from sinking. . . . spending less than our own
commodities will pay for [abroad], is the sure and only way for the
nation to grow rich; and when that begins once seriously to be
considered . . . we may hope to have our rents rise, and the public
stock thrive again. Till then, we in vain, I fear, endeavour with
noise, and weapons of law, to drive the wolf from our own to another's doors: the breed ought to be extirpated out of the island;
for want, brought in by ill management, and nursed up by expensive vanity, will make the nation poor, and spare nobody.[23]

Locke tried to persuade his readers that attempts to remedy their economic distress by laws and regulations, besides mistaking effect for
cause, merely postponed the needed recognition that, compared with
the Dutch, the English husbandman was backward and self-indulgent.
The Dutch with far less fertile soil obtained better yields. In a lapidary
response to a complaint that high interest depressed shipbuilding,
Locke wrote:

The Dutch buy our rape-seed, make it into oil, bring it back to us,
and sell it with advantage. This may be as well said to be from high
interest here, and low there. But the truth is, the industry and frugality of that people make them content to work cheaper, and sell at
less profit than their neighbours, and so get the trade from them.[24]

To curse high interest is to curse the rain. English husbandmen and
merchants, like it or not, were in competition with the Dutch because
they were linked in the system of money and commerce.

The expression of this competition was the balance of trade. It was a
truism of commercial and financial practice that money follows trade,
meaning that the flow of coin and bullion coursed through the same
routes as merchandise. This truism, we saw, was the cornerstone of
Colbert's colonial and international trade policy. A nation must be
drained of the silver needed for domestic traffic and taxes if it does not

---

23. Ibid., 72–73; also 19–20, 53–54, 58–59.
24. Ibid., 80. Locke's pointed criticisms of the shoddy managerial practices of
    the gentry deserve emphasis, especially since they have not been noted in
    the secondary literature. They show how far he was from being an uncritical
    apologist for the landed interest.

export more to its neighbors than it imports. Locke, too, underscored this truism, as he also made it the cornerstone of his analysis of interest and coinage. High interest was due to shortage of money, which in turn was due to trade deficits. To establish this point, Locke was obliged to correct crude misconceptions. He explained at length that prohibitions on the export of specie did not work, since it was merely melted down and exported as bullion. Nor did payment for imported goods with bills of exchange stop one farthing going abroad, since that credit instrument, like all others, was a promise of money. But Locke's most telling argument was the contrast between Spain and Holland. Spain acquired an abundance of silver and gold by conquest, but could not keep it against the pressure of an unfavorable balance of trade. But Holland, having no mines and no conquered territories, acquired the Spanish treasure.[25]

In one of the most trenchant paragraphs of these essays, Locke spelled out a usually neglected connection between money supply, domestic produce, and international trade. Any nation, regardless of where it may be, must incur an unfavorable balance of trade and experience decline in its domestic produce if its prices do not maintain a rough parity with prices in other nations enjoying a favorable balance of trade. This parity is *high prices*. The reason is that a nation with a favorable balance of trade will have plenty of money; and abundance of money means price inflation. Such a trading nation will export relatively expensive commodities. The dearness is parity with like nations, and therefore does not drain away specie. But export to money-poor economies carries away their fund of money needed for domestic traffic and investment and further depresses trade.[26] This unusual observation, which was prompted by trading patterns in Spain, drew attention to the demand for luxuries or expensive staples even in money-poor countries.[27] The lesson was clear. The alternative to England's becoming richer and experiencing a long-term price inflation was not price stability, but depression.

The hard-money line Locke took in the recoinage debate expressed

25. "It is death in Spain to export money: and yet they, who furnish all the world with gold and silver, have least of it among themselves. Trade fetches it away from that lazy and indigent people, notwithstanding all their artificial and forced contrivances to keep it there. It follows trade against the rigour of their laws; and their want of foreign commodities makes it openly to be carried away at noon-day" (Locke, *Works*, 5: 72). This statement is exemplary of the thoroughgoing empiricism of these economic writings.

26. Ibid., 51.

27. Ibid., 48–50. This maxim holds interesting implications for England's colonial expansion, which Locke unfortunately did not spell out.

his perception of the independence of the market, including the money market, from political prescription. He did not defend the view that government should "do nothing" or "let it be." This for Locke was not an option, since taxation and regulation of trade alone constitute substantial market parameters. He held rather that government policy should as far as possible harmonize with the known laws of the market and with sound fiscal policy. He opposed attempts by wishful thinking to evade facts with prescriptive "solutions" that worsened the problem. The proposal to "raise the value of money" was an attempt to evade a number of unsettling facts and the hardship they must impose. The fact was that the mass of clipped coins had debased England's legal tender and had robbed England of an amount equal to about one-sixth of the annual gross national product. The hard-money line accepted the loss as irretrievable; it could be made good only by temporary austerity and improvements in the balance of trade. Recoinage at the old standard had the disadvantage of making money scarcer and pinching trade. But that consequence could not be evaded. The soft-money advocates believed that it could be evaded. They reasoned that since clipped coin passed at face value as legal tender, this state of affairs could be perpetuated by recoining the shilling at a lower silver content. Locke pointed out that the common people and revenue officers accepted devalued coins because they had no alternative. But merchants and others who drew up contracts for payment specified the specie of payment and adjusted their prices accordingly.[28] Above all, face value of the shilling meant nothing on the international exchange, where bullion value determined the exchange rate of money.[29] Locke scorned the argument that the exchange rate fluctuated with changing demands for different currencies: this effect was strictly marginal, a plus or minus 2 percent effect. To mistake this marginal effect for the main highway, where exchange value equaled bullion value, was more evidence of wishful thinking.

Lowndes's report contained a detailed analysis of the probable effects

28. Ibid., 168. Locke threw down a droll challenge to the soft-money men: "Silver, i.e. the quantity of pure silver, makes the real value of money. If it does not, coin copper with the same stamp and denomination, and see whether it will be of the same value. I suspect your stamp will make it of no more worth than the copper money of Ireland is, which is its weight in copper, and no more" (88).

29. "Bullion is silver, whose workmanship has no value. And thus foreign coin hath no value here for its stamp, and our coin is bullion in foreign dominions" (ibid., 148). The subsequent pages present a lucid exposition of the foreign exchange market.

of recoinage at the old and the new standards, on melting down. He believed that a relationship obtained between face value, silver content, and the illegal practice of melting coin into bullion. He stated that it is "a truth so apparent, that it may well be compared to an axiom, even in mathematical reasoning; to wit, that whensoever the intrinsic value of silver in the coin hath been, or shall be, less than the price of silver in bullion, the coin hath, and will be melted down." Locke politely conceded Lowndes this "apparent truth," but pointed out that the circumstances to which it purports to give the rule can never arise, since the value of silver in coin is precisely the same as its value in bullion.[30] He dismissed as irrelevant the argument about melting down and the export of specie. The cause of both had nothing to do with the relationship between face value and intrinsic value of coin, but with balance of trade. This point has been missed by a number of recent commentators on this debate. Lowndes predicted that recoinage at the old rate would result in melting down, whereas recoinage at the new rate would lessen it or stop it altogether. Locke's prediction has unfortunately been ignored by his critics. He said that melting down would continue, *irrespective of coinage*, so long as the export of specie was prohibited and the balance of trade remained unfavorable.[31] Events confirmed both men, but Locke had the right reason. Lowndes's argument distracted attention from the fact that the very prohibition on the export of specie, which alone induced melting down, confessed trade deficits. To believe that adjusting denominational values of currency had any bearing on the balance of trade was yet another confirmation that soft money and spongy thinking were helpmates.

Locke wrote at a time when the multiplication of credit generated confusion about the nature of money. Considerations of convenience and security aside, the shortage of silver in Europe made paper credit necessary to conduct trade. Clever men of the day looked upon Locke's hard-money position as obtuse about this circumstance: money drives trade, but credit drives it even more. One such man was the redoubtable John Law, who proposed a paper currency. In his scheme, currency was released from the straitjacket of gold and silver and secured by land.[32] Law won the ear of the duke of Argyle and other Scottish magnates, but the Scottish Parliament rejected his proposals. He was more successful in France. The regent, the duke of Orléans, obtained letters pa-

30. Ibid., 156.
31. Ibid., 159–61, 171–73. On the chaos of Lowndes's argument, see 171–72, 182, 188, 190–91, 193.
32. Law, *Money and trade consider'd*, 809–12.

tent for the establishment of the Banque Générale to test the scheme of issuing paper currency. In its initial phase, the scheme was sound. Law's currency was a silver certificate for repayment on demand in coin of a stated weight and fineness. This was the decisive proviso that made the currency an instant success. French coinage was in chaos owing to frequent alterations of silver ratios in the coinage. Law's currency ended the uncertainty about the value of money and gave his clients a stable money of account. As a result, his currency was preferred to silver, and French industry expanded dramatically.

In a very short time, Law acquired control of French fiscal policy. He introduced reforms to facilitate taxation, trade, and agriculture. The Banque Générale became a golden bowl offering loans at low interest and high returns on investments. In only four years (1716 to 1720), Law raised himself from his private station as a man grown wealthy at gaming tables (he had a gift for mathematics) to a figure so powerful that he dared boast to Lord Stair, the British ambassador, that he could elevate France on the ruins of England and Holland; he could, he claimed, break English trade and destroy the Bank of England and the East India Company at will. These boasts foundered on a fatal weakness in his system: the issue of paper money in amounts far beyond his silver reserves. When rumors to this effect circulated, investors demanded redemption of their paper money and began a run on the Banque Générale. Harsh and arbitrary measures were useless to stem the debacle. Within six months the Banque was in ruins and Law fled France for his life.

The glory and misery of John Law underscore the strengths and limitations of Locke's monetary theory. As we would expect, Law was among Locke's many critics.[33] The hard-money line seemed to him ob-

33. Although every mention of Locke in Law's *Money and trade consider'd* is critical, the tract shows him to have been a close student of Locke's writings who absorbed far more than he rejected. For example, Law agreed with Locke against Lowndes that the mint stamp added nothing to the value of bullion; that the movement of goods in international markets followed laws that lie outside the power of the sovereign to alter; that hard money was the condition of a stable money of account (779, 782ff., 788–89, 791, 793–94). His most significant departure from Locke was his denial that silver was uniquely suited to be the money of account. Law maintained that the value of silver was much less stable than Locke had maintained, although his evidence for this contention amounts to no more than Locke's own observation of the long-term gradual depreciation of silver subsequent to massive importations from the New World. Law thought it an advantage of land-secured currency that, having little value abroad, it would remain in the country and relieve the depression of trade caused by want of specie. But how a currency

tuse because he realized the measure of truth in the dictum that if money were leather, it would pass. Locke rejoined that it will pass only so long as it is not known to be merely leather. His hard-money line was meant to thwart speculative flashes and to discourage the standing temptation of governments to fund revenue shortfalls by debasing the coin or by raiding annuity funds. In this strategy there was not a farthing of originality. Hard money was the backbone of the Amsterdam Exchange Bank and every other great banking institution of Europe. Without hard money, there could be no stable money of account; and without a money of account, market values were incalculable and chaotic.[34] With a stable money of account, banking costs were greatly reduced, transactions were hastened, credit could be measured, and market values were calculable.

The ignorance exemplified by the gentry and the ambition of speculators like Law epitomize what historically have been the two great hazards of sound fiscal and monetary policy. Ignorance and ambition have combined repeatedly to achieve by force of law or outright confiscation what could not be achieved by ordinary economic means. The rise and prosperity of Europe's great banks coincided with governments that refused to override the market by *force majeur,* while the decline of great banks, such as the Fugger financial empire, occurred when the kingdoms with which they were associated ceased to honor the discipline of the market. When Spanish monarchs defaulted on their debts, Fugger demanded economies of government and reforms of fiscal policy. They were not forthcoming, so Spain and Fugger sank together. This example illustrates the unique role of banks in the market. An institution whose commodity is credit sells a very peculiar product: banks lend money to people who do not have it, in order that they may get it. The creditor thus speculates on the future gains of his clients; and he must show a net gain in these inherently uncertain transactions. Banks man-

---

worthless in London or Amsterdam could maintain its value in Aberdeen, Law did not explain. Land-secured currency is full of unworkables, and the Scottish Parliament wisely rejected it. The scheme was revived in recent times by the Social Credit Party in Canada and New Zealand.

34. Throughout his essays Locke stressed the essential role of a stable money of account for the conduct of trade. One of his most telling arguments against debasement was that it was the thin edge of a wedge to ever-renewed debasements until coin became worthless at home and abroad (ibid., 87–88, 151). Here again Locke simply reproduced the wisdom of the great banking houses of Europe. See Herman van der Wee, "Monetary, Credit and Banking Systems," 295ff.

age to win this gamble by reducing uncertainty as far as possible. One means of reducing uncertainty is an exacting scrutiny of values offered in security for loans. This procedure establishes the "credit" of a company or government. It also functions as a disciplinarian and drill sergeant against fraud, mismanagement, and aberrations of market price. Merchants of course carry out an analogous vetting procedure with respect to one another. But bankers are professionals in this business, since they alone trade in credit. It is a curious but unparadoxical fact that the profession whose commodity is the most speculative should operate with estimates of value that are consistently lower, more "conservative," than market value: conservatism minimizes liability in an inherently risky business.

The conservatism of Locke's monetary theory is the conservatism of bankers. As one of the initial subscribers to the Bank of England, he wrote with a vested interest. Other investors, financially much more heavily committed than he, disagreed with his views. In attempting to persuade his contemporaries to act in their own interest, his chief problem was to make it known. To this end he penned a lucid résumé of the wisdom of the great banks. He won the battle in the recoinage question. But this was not enough to assure England's prosperity. The apple cart could be tipped over by Parliament's acting in ignorance, anger, or haste. The danger of haste and frustration was present in the enormous demands of England's continental war—over £120 million between 1689 and 1710. The danger of anger came sharply to the fore when the South Sea Company went bankrupt in the same year that the Banque Générale failed. The sting of investors' loss of some £35 million pounds brought out parliamentary knives against the whole system of finance. The man who salvaged that grim situation was Robert Walpole, under whose two-decade dominance England's finances were placed on the track that carried the nation into the Industrial Revolution.

The Whig Supremacy

It is usually gratuitous to say of any statesman that he typified the politics of his age, but in the case of Sir Robert Walpole, this may be so. Walpole stemmed from a prosperous gentry family of Norfolk. The pater familias, the elder Robert Walpole, was an improving Whig farmer who copied Dutch agricultural methods and who tightly controlled the account books to ensure that profits were wisely invested. The Walpole estates were models of Dutch husbandry.

The enterprising gentry from whom Walpole sprang were an important part of his constituency, and in his political triumph they no doubt saw their own. The taste of the gentry for upward mobility became explicit in the struggle over the Peerage Bill of 1719. Walpole led the struggle and engineered its defeat under the slogan "What, shall I consent to the shutting the door upon my family ever coming into the House of Lords!"[35] This frank avowal of ambition occurred when a government led by Whig peers attempted to thwart Walpole's drive to batter his way into a high government position. They failed. A year later the crises created by the collapse of South Sea stock forced Sunderland to call Walpole to become lord treasurer and set the nation's finances in order. Walpole thus became the first commoner to thrust himself into high office by a combination of ability, stamina, and command of a parliamentary following. His two-decade dominance of government was itself an exercise of the "Revolution Principles" that had shifted the axis of English politics from the Crown, peerage, and bishops to the Crown, commons, and peers. From his resignation to the end of the century, all but two prime ministers were commoners. Walpole's success signified that "the people" had found the will and the means to push their way into the privileged places in English society. This was the free England that Voltaire admired in the *Philosophical Letters;* it was the constitutional and enterprising England that Montesquieu praised in *The Spirit of the Laws.*[36]

Walpole's ability was recognized soon after he entered Parliament at age twenty-four. He was invited to the Kit-Cat Club, where the Whig magnates and their publicists assembled to talk shop, divert themselves, and blaspheme in the fashionable bawdy style. The club's weekly dinners brought Walpole into association with the Junto Whigs—Somers, Halifax, and Thomas Wharton—and with the Whig election masters—Wharton, the dukes of Richmond and Somerset, the earls of Carbery, Essex, Cornwallis, and Dorchester. The young Stanhope, subsequently to become Walpole's rival, was there, as were two of the most prolific publicists in the Whig cause, Addison and Steele. Much later Walpole said of this group that though "generally mentioned as a set of wits, in reality they were the patriots that saved Britain."

The political legacy that Walpole derived from the first-generation Whigs bears the stamp of Thomas Wharton, who more than anyone

35. The speech is quoted in its entirety by William Coxe, *Memoirs of the Life and Administration of Sir Robert Walpole,* 1: 206–17. In the absence of an edition of the works of Walpole, Coxe's *Memoirs* remains the best single source of Walpole's expressed opinions.
36. Voltaire's contacts with Whigs during his English sojourn are discussed by John Carswell, *The Old Cause,* 162–66. Montesquieu's contacts were primarily with the Bolingbroke circle.

else epitomized Whig parliamentary politics. Wharton's father had been among the Puritan squires who believed in godly politics. Thomas shed religious trappings from his politics and from his pleasure-loving private life. On entering Parliament in 1672, he looked to Shaftesbury and learned from him the craft of election management and the manipulation of crowds.[37] These skills he used to organize the Whig electoral victories of 1695 and 1708. Like Shaftesbury, he understood the value of docile intellectuals and publicists. Joseph Addison was his most distinguished protégé, but he was also instrumental in launching the career of Daniel Defoe. He rejected the services of the young Jonathan Swift, who subsequently found employment with Tory masters and took revenge on Wharton by reviling him as the fountain of Whig indecency and corruption.

Wharton was representative of the wealthy, powerful, self-interested men who made the Glorious Revolution. He took the lead at the Convention Parliament as party whip, collaborated with Somers in drafting the Bill of Rights, and became one of the five magnates who comprised the junto Privy Council of William III. He boasted in Parliament that "I own to driving King James out, and I would do it again." Such forthrightness earned him the sobriquet "Honest Tom," for he insisted through thick and thin on fidelity to the Revolutionary Settlement. To him Whiggism meant the rejection of the divine right of kings and bishops. It meant that Parliament could alter succession to safeguard Protestantism, not because Protestant faith was favorable to liberty, but because Catholicism entailed the Stuart dynasty and its penchant for absolutism and divine right. Wharton favored the balanced constitution that limited the powers of royal prerogative and correspondingly enhanced the powers of Parliament. He favored religious toleration, but not because he was a dissenter: he had no scruples about becoming a communicant of the Church of England in order to further his career. He favored toleration on the political ground that dissenting sects were a check on the power of bishops.

Wharton's honesty expressed political toughness. Those Whigs who went over to the Country Tories merely to gain political advantage earned his warm hostility. One such renegade was Edward Harley, subsequently the earl of Oxford, with whose family the Whartons had been allied politically for generations. Harley, with Bolingbroke, another renegade Whig, defeated the Whigs in the election of 1698 by exploiting Country discontent about the cost of William's wars. To Wharton, such political maneuvering placed a man on the slippery slope to betrayal

37. Ibid., 40.

of the Revolution. The war with France (a consequence of the Revolution) and patriotic duty demanded that the costs of William's wars be accepted.[38] He was particularly determined that anyone involved in Jacobite plots should be given a one-way ticket to the Tower. It was due to his efforts that in 1695 Parliament issued the Act of Attainder that took the life of the Jacobite conspirator Sir John Fenwick.

If Walpole cut the cloth of his politics from Wharton's template, perhaps it was because their aptitudes and tastes were similar. His first government appointment was to the Admiralty Council in the coalition government of Marlborough and Godolphin. He soon showed himself to be an able man by mastering the intricate problems of supply and finance for a navy at war.[39] Three years later (1708), he became secretary of war in a shift of political alliances that enabled him to displace his rival, Bolingbroke, who had come under suspicion in the aftermath of the pretender's abortive invasion attempt the year before. The patriotic feeling that this event provoked proved to be only a ripple, if one large enough to win the elections of that year. Popular feeling against the war was strong. Soldiers could not be recruited, and in 1709 two regiments mutinied. In November of that year, Dr. Henry Sacheverell, preaching before the mayor of London at St. Paul's, brought popular feeling to a head in a thundering attack on the Whigs and a fiery defense of the High Court principles of divine right and passive obedience. The government, or rather its head, Lord Godolphin, whom Sacheverell had personally insulted with his wide-ranging invective, felt that the challenge could not go unanswered. He wanted an impeachment despite the advice of other members of the Privy Council that a show trial would only create a Tory martyr. But Godolphin was adamant, and articles of impeachment were drawn in Parliament for a trial that produced what Edmund Burke called the ablest and most authentic expression of Whig principles since 1688.

Sacheverell's sermon was a catechism of the current high Church line that the Whigs had "put the Church in danger" by their combination of Deism, dissenting sects, irreligion, and seditious republicanism. His sermon was viewed as an attack on the Toleration Act, which so rankled high churchmen; on William III, whom they loathed; and on the Revolution Settlement. The Whigs sent in a prosecution team, which included John Locke's nephew Sir Peter King, Nicholas Lechmere, and Robert Walpole acting as leading prosecutor. The speeches of Lechmere, Walpole, and James Stanhope reproduced Locke's defense of Revolution

38. Ibid., 80, 88, 116.
39. Coxe, *Memoirs of the Life and Administration of Sir Robert Walpole*, 1: 34–38.

Principles: when the sovereign breaks the original contract between himself and the people, when he subverts the constitution and endangers the
liberties of subjects, it is the right of the people to rise against him. The
explicit defense of the right to armed revolution against a despotic sovereign was specifically Lockean, not the defense of the Revolution made
by the Convention Parliament, which had dodged this crucial question
by the legal fiction that James had "vacated" the throne by his flight.
The articles of impeachment discarded this fiction in the opening sentence, which declared that William "did with an armed force undertake
a glorious enterprise, for delivering this kingdom from popery and
arbitrary power; and divers subjects of this realm . . . joined with and
assisted his late Majesty in . . . the late happy revolution." Thus did
Parliament finally acknowledge the plain facts that the empirical philosopher had presupposed two decades previously in his legitimation of
contractual government by consent. In his speech, Walpole emphasized
that the right to resistance was entailed by limited and constitutional
government. "The doctrine of unlimited, unconditional, passive obedience," he said, echoing Locke, "was first invented to support arbitrary
and despotic power, and was never promoted or countenanced by any
government that had not designs of making use of it." He excoriated
high churchmen for their persecuting zeal. Their seditious preaching,
he declared, had no other object than to prepare for the return of the
Stuart pretender. These accusations he followed up in a pamphlet that
described the political consequences of the trial. The French government, encouraged to hope for the pretender's chances, had withdrawn
from peace negotiations; England's credit was shaken and its allies
doubted its resolve.[40]

40. The Lockean character of the Sacheverell prosecution requires emphasis.
    Paraphrases of Locke abound in prosecution speeches; for example, Nicholas
    Lechmere urged: "The nature of our constitution is that of a limited monar-
    chy, wherein the supreme power was—by mutual consent and not by acci-
    dent—limited and lodged in more hands than one; and the uniform preser-
    vation of such a constitution for so many ages, without any fundamental
    change, demonstrates to your lordships the continuance of the same con-
    tract. The consequences of such a form of government are obvious; that the
    laws are the rule to both, the common measure of the power of the crown
    and the obedience of the subject; and if the executive part endeavours the
    subversion and total destruction of the government the Original Contract is
    thereby broke, and the right of allegiance ceases, and that part of the gov-
    ernment thus fundamentally injured hath a right to save or recover that con-
    stitution in which it had an original interest. Nay, the nature of such an
    Original Contract of government proves, that there is not only a power in

The Whig House of Lords impeached Sacheverell by a vote of 69 to 51, but imposed a penalty of three years' silence—a verdict that many deemed equivalent to acquittal. The light penalty was doubtless a concession to the fiercely pro-Sacheverell London mobs, who had menaced Whig parliamentarians throughout the three-and-a-half-week trial and who lit the London skies in one night of wild rioting. In the elections of that year, the Whigs lost ground and pious Queen Anne turned against a Ministry that had never been to her taste. Harley was called to form a Tory government in which Bolingbroke had the satisfaction of taking Walpole's portfolio as secretary of war. The new government brought down legislation meant to satisfy popular feeling and high Church rancor. It was a feeling against foreigners, especially Germans. The General Naturalization Act of 1709 had allowed 10,000 German refugees displaced by war to enter the country. The presence of these numerous poor strained further a system already pressed by bad harvests and high prices. The act was annulled. The Schism Act was brought in to suppress dissenting academies and to reestablish the education monopoly of the Church. Bolingbroke, meanwhile, diligently prepared his masterstroke against the Whigs by opening secret negotiations for James's re-

---

the people, who have inherited its freedom to assert their own title to it, but they are bound in duty to transmit the same constitution to their posterity also" (quoted by Geoffrey Holmes, *The Trial of Doctor Sacheverell*, 22–23; also 57ff., 74–75, 121, 285). We should note as well the strong presence of Junto Whiggism in the prosecution. Lechmere and Walpole were closely allied with Wharton; Sir Joseph Jekyll was Somers's brother-in-law; and Dr. Peter King was Locke's nephew. Evidence of the Lockean character of the prosecution is provided by two recent studies, J. P. Kenyon's *Revolution Principles*, 128–45, and Holmes's *Trial of Doctor Sacheverell*, 135–48. Kenyon, who opens his book with a denial that Locke exercised any considerable influence on the Revolution or its principles, does not remark on the Lockean character of the prosecution; but Caroline Robbins, in her *Eighteenth-Century Commonwealthman*, 78–86, has seen it clearly. Holmes's study reprints the articles of impeachment (279–82) and presents a valuable study of the rearguard battles of high churchmen attempting to defend divine right and passive obedience after 1688. Here again we see the presence of Locke in the doctrine of Bishop Hoadly. A. C. Ewald's *Sir Robert Walpole*, 35–44, and Coxe's *Memoirs of the Life and Administration of Sir Robert Walpole*, 1: 41ff., may also be consulted with profit. The tendency to read Locke out of the Court Whig position may be inspired by agreement with Burke's assessment of 1688 in his *An Appeal from the Old Whigs*. Burke claimed that "in truth and substance" 1688 was "a revolution not made but prevented . . . we made no revolution, no, nor any alteration at all."

turn. Although a cosmopolitan himself, Bolingbroke meant to exploit the English hatred of foreigners. It had been difficult for many to endure a Dutch king; now, with Anne ill, they faced the devolution of the Crown upon Hanover. Many of the gentry, he believed, would prefer a Stuart—provided that he was Anglican. But there was the snare. James would not renounce Catholicism, even though his confessor urged that Rome would gain more from it in the long run. Bolingbroke took what precautions he could to secure his position in this dangerous game. He turned Whigs out of all offices, taking particular care to remove them from military commands. By deft manipulation of the dying queen, he managed to oust Harley. But, apprehensive that the queen would die before his coup was ripe, he began negotiating with Whig leaders for a coalition government. This was duplicity on a grand scale, but the Whigs were not deceived. They prepared for war and bluntly warned Bolingbroke that there were only two places for him—James's exile court or the scaffold. When Anne died the following day, Bolingbroke heeded the warning and fled to the St. Germains court.

Illness had kept Walpole out of action during those intense days, but when he returned to Parliament in the next session, he took the lead in demanding the impeachment of Harley and Bolingbroke. In this way he used events to turn the flank of the Tories by setting Hanoverians against Jacobites. By and by this strategy effectively destroyed the Tories as a party; for a Hanoverian Tory was one who accepted the Revolution Settlement; and whoever accepted that was a Whig despite himself. With George I on the throne, the Tories had twice in twenty-five years endorsed the keystone of Whig politics, the right of Parliament to regulate succession. To withdraw that endorsement was treason against the reigning monarch. Walpole recognized this fracture in the foundation of Tory politics, as he also realized that, skillfully managed, it placed the initiative permanently in Whig hands. Walpole's skills in parliamentary management were unexcelled. He kept the Whig-Tory distinction alive, insisting always that a Tory was a Jacobite enemy of the new constitutional settlement. Thus he overcame the liability of a foreign-born monarch by shifting political loyalty from the Crown to the nation: Whigs were patriots, Tories were Jacobites, papists, and persecutors.

The hammerlike logic of this aggressive Whiggism forced the Tories to evade their identity. This they did by declaring that the Whig-Tory distinction was meaningless except as a red herring to tar honorable men with the brush of treachery. None were louder in espousing this line than Henry St. John, Viscount Bolingbroke. This ill-starred man was one of those magnificent calamities that fortune tosses across the path of statesmen destined for greatness. By his brilliance and organizational prowess, Bolingbroke managed to dominate the opposition to Walpole, even though permanently debarred from office. His journal, *The Craftsman*, might rail against the corruption of Parliament by patronage; yet it was well known that Bolingbroke, of all Tory ministers, had used patronage to the last degree. He might invoke integrity, cry up the Church, and reproach the irreligion of Whig leaders; but Bolingbroke was a notorious libertine who indulged his expansive amorous appetite and who privately mocked religion and the clergy. He might attempt to coopt patriotism and flatter the crown prince, but everyone knew that he was the turncoat whose impeachment Walpole led and whose pardon Walpole allowed. Had Walpole himself written the script, he could not have invented an opponent more surely condemned to futility by the mismatch between exhortation and manner of life. The Tory leader William Shippen could, without undue sarcasm, commend the honesty of Walpole's forthright defense of Whig principles. But in Bolingbroke, grand ambition dominated so entirely that little remained to be honest about. So it was that this splendidly corrupt man led the opposition attack on the corruption of Walpole's government. That the Tories should have taken cues from such a leader signifies the confused political will characteristic of stagnant opposition parties.

Walpole's Politics of Interest

The central problem of interest politics, mentioned in chapter 5 in connection with the de Witt government, is to find the politico-economic vector that promotes special interests and reconciles them, when need be, to temporary disadvantage inflicted by the requirements of competing interests. This vector is graphed on the axis of liberty and prosperity—the two public goods that interest politicians may invoke to rally support for policies really or apparently injurious to some special interests. The interest politician must discern the real relations of interests to one another and frame policies that will promote them. For this he requires expertise in finance and economics. In addition, he must know how to combine persuasion with the power of office to carry his policies through. Walpole fit his age so well because Englishmen largely acquiesced in the politics of which he was master.

The most potent interest was the one dominating Commons—the small and medium-sized landed interest. Walpole rose to power thanks to his capacity to persuade, mollify, charm, stall, divert, manipulate, and outlast the parliamentary gentry. Lord Chesterfield, one of his detractors, said of him that "he was the best parliament-man, and the ablest manager of Parliament, that I believe ever lived. An artful rather than an eloquent speaker, he saw as by intuition, the disposition of the house, and pressed or receded accordingly." He steadfastly declined the peerage repeatedly offered lest he forfeit control over this key institution of the Revolution Settlement. This decision proved to be fundamental to the evolution of the English constitution. Walpole began the tradition of prime minister as chief of a parliamentary majority. Prior to Walpole, a defeat in Commons, or even electoral defeat, did not mandate even a change in the Ministry, let alone a change of government; as the constitution was understood at that time, ministers were appointments of the Crown. But Walpole justified his policies by appeal to parliamentary majority. He underscored this legitimating principle by retreating on issues that threatened his majority. He created precedent by resigning from office when he believed that he could no longer sustain a majority. This consistent adherence to an innovative principle made the popular element of the constitution supreme in government.

The main fiscal interests of the gentry who dominated Parliament were low taxes on land and the increase of its value. Walpole's fiscal policy successfully aimed at both results. From 1722 to 1726, and from 1733 to 1739, he was able to lower the tax on land to two shillings on the pound. In 1731–32, it dropped to one shilling. During this period, the value of land increased from twenty years of rent to about twenty-six. Since war always drove the land tax to four shillings or more, and usually disrupted trade, he pursued a peace policy in the Dutch style, which meant being less concerned to avenge minor insults to the British flag than to ship exports to foreign ports. At the same time he upgraded the nation's fleet to make it the preponderant naval force in the world and a silent deterrent to mercantile wars. His peace policy was successful in part thanks to his counterpart in France, Cardinal Fluery, who wished to rebuild the French economy in the wake of the depredations inflicted by Louis XIV's incessant wars. This combination of diplomacy with war capacity helped increase total exports from £6,911,000 in 1720 to £9,993,000 in 1738, with an increase of trade balance from £800,000 to £2,720,000 per annum.[41] The importance of his peace policy to English commerce was amply demonstrated by the consequences of the Spanish war of 1739–42. Walpole was pushed into this war by South Seas trading interests collaborating with the opposition in Parliament. The legal South Seas trade, which was conducted under the Asiento Convention with Spain, was worth scarcely £30,000 per annum. The contraband trade, on the other hand, was lucrative, although it irritated the Span-

41. Norris A. Brisco, *The Economic Policy of Robert Walpole*, 204.

ish, who from time to time took merchant vessels as prizes. Walpole was willing to accept this loss quietly in return for peace and the trade. But an emotional press campaign to avenge injuries forced Walpole into a conflict that cost England £1 million in trade every year of the war. This ill-advised war, from which England gained nothing, prompted Walpole's retirement.

In the king's address to Parliament in 1721, Walpole signaled his intention to take a systematic approach to the promotion of trade and commerce. "We should be extremely wanting to ourselves," he had the king declare, "if we neglected to improve the favorable opportunity given us of extending our commerce, upon which the riches and grandeur of this nation chiefly depend. It is very obvious that nothing would more conduce to the obtaining of the public good, than to make the exportation of our own manufactures, and the importation of the commodities used in the manufacturing of them, as practicable and as easy as may be." Although this policy was not controversial, previous ministries had not been particularly effective in identifying means to these ends. Indeed, the whole customs system was in a state of decay. The official rate books of the value of duty leviable on each taxable article had not been revised since 1660. Multiple duties were imposed on single items. Heavy customs were charged against commodities needed in domestic manufacture for export. High duties made extensive smuggling lucrative. Walpole renovated this archaic system. In 1722, he eliminated duties on 106 articles of export and 38 articles of import. Export duties were lifted on all agricultural produce and many manufactured goods that had a ready market overseas. Import duties were removed from many articles required in manufacture. A new book of rates was issued, and multiple duties were eliminated. One of the main features of the duty-free import scheme was borrowed from Dutch practice. Selected commodities—chief among them tea, cocoa, coffee, and wines—were landed duty-free and stored in bonded warehouses. Reexported commodities went out untaxed; commodities sold to the domestic market bore an excise tax that substituted for import duties. In this way smuggling was undercut, revenue increased by £120,000 per annum, and the reexport trade expanded. To enhance further the marketability of British goods, he introduced legislation requiring manufactured goods destined for export to meet standards of quality and measurement. Action was taken to enhance colonial trade as well. He set aside protectionist provisions of the Navigation Act, which required goods produced in the colonies to be carried in English bottoms to English ports only. Planters were allowed to ship rice, sugar, and other commodities directly to Europe, provided British ships were used. The result of these and similar measures was a fourfold increase of colonial exports during the Walpole administration. The value of British exports increased about one-third during the same period, while the value of imports increased by only one-fifth.[42] Although some historians have disparaged the importance of these policies, their effect on England's prosperity was palpable. The favorable balance of trade brought an abundance of money into the nation. The land tax was reduced, £6.5 million of the national debt was retired, and the interest on gilt-edged government securities dropped to 4 percent—all according to Locke's forecast concerning the relation between balance of trade and prosperity. We learn from one recent historian that these policies were the beginning of protectionism in England. While it is true that Walpole erected high tariffs to protect selected industries, particularly textiles, the basic thrust of his policies was aptly characterized by Robert Morley in 1889 as the "first full, general and distinct approach . . . made by an English statesman towards those enlightened views of trade which were fifty-five years later given in systematic shape to the world by the genius of Adam Smith."[43]

Such policies often went into effect in the teeth of heated opposition. The hue and cry about the excise tax may serve as an example. The excise scheme implemented in 1723 had been successful in raising revenue, expediting trade, and reducing abuses. Walpole proposed to extend the tax to include tobacco and wine, for tobacco was a major reexport item while the smuggling trade in both was brisk. In his speech introducing this legislation, Walpole proposed that the projected £200,000 revenue from the tax should be used to eliminate the land tax. To the mercantile constituency he threw out the bait of making London a free port "and by consequence, the market of the world."

This legislation came under violent attack even before it reached the floor of Commons. *The Craftsman* abandoned all restraint in denouncing the new tax as a covert assault on the prosperity and liberties of Englishmen. The excise on tobacco, it was said, would be followed by taxes on food, clothing, and other necessities, thus driving the common man to beggary. As for liberty, the authority of tax officers to search premises for untaxed stores was inflated into a dastardly "plan of arbitrary power." Thus, from revenue officers *The Craftsman* conjured a secret police whose right to search would be used to inspect minutely all private dealings, thereby paving the way to the enslavement of the nation.

---

42. Ibid., 129–35.
43. Robert Morley, *Walpole*, 167. Cf. Ralph Davis, "The Rise of Protection in England," 313.

This polemic was driven by the emotional charge Englishmen attached to the word *excise*. In the village memory, an excise tax was associated with unpopular taxes of earlier reigns. This was why Walpole avoided the term, calling his excise "inland duties." Opposition leaders supposed that by waving the flag of excise, they could inflame the nation. And they did. Petitions were circulated and demonstrations organized. Boroughs instructed their members of Parliament to vote the scheme down. Walpole himself was assaulted by a mob outside Westminster. But he was not a man easily intimidated, and he stood his ground inside the chamber. The tide could not be stemmed, however; and when his majority shrank to seventeen, he threw in the sponge.[44]

The excise on tobacco was one of several measures that were defeated by an aroused public. Many years after the event, Adam Smith reproached politicians for avoiding this sound fiscal device, and the elder Pitt admitted in Parliament that his opposition to it had been misguided. These cases illustrate a standing problem of interest politics. The program of growth endorsed by the founders of Whig politics greatly increased the complexity of public affairs. Increased complexity required a commensurate increase in the skills needed to manage the complexity. Whig politics accordingly placed a premium on the coincidence of technical rationality, including political knowledge, with political power. Moreover, increased complexity increased the risk of damage from mistakes of analysis or management. Yet interest politics legitimates the competition of political factions for power, irrespective of the competence of those factions to govern. These power struggles are played out before a public whose capacity to judge competence is limited and whose ability to judge the character of public men is shaped by propaganda. Interest politics thus appears to be distressed by the absence of mechanisms that assure the coincidence of knowledge and political power presupposed by the program. The crash of South Sea stock cogently illustrates this problem, as well as the solution that emerged in those years of England's apprenticeship in interest politics.

The South Sea Company was chartered by Harley's Tory government in a bid to offset what many parliamentarians believed to be the overweening power of the Bank of England and the East India Company. Many Whigs, although not Walpole, approved this new company to engage the trade of Latin America and to fund some portion of the national debt. In the event, the company pursued finance more than trade, and in 1719 it secretly put to the Whig Ministry a grandiose scheme to take over funding of the entire national debt. The company at that time

44. See Ewald, *Sir Robert Walpole*, 229 ff., 454.

already held £11.75 million of the public debt. It proposed to assume the £6.5 million held by the Bank of England and the East India Company, plus £16.5 million in redeemable stock and £15 million in unredeemable annuities. This vast scheme for a national financial monopoly was inspired by John Law's financial wizardry, which at that time dazzled the world and drew investment funds from England. Once the proposal became public, it understandably attracted the determined opposition of the Bank of England. The Bank's spokesman in Parliament, Walpole, managed to persuade Commons to seek a bid from the Bank, which promptly offered £4 million for the privilege of assuming the debt, as against the £2 million bid of the South Sea Company. The South Sea Company's directors responded with an offer of £7.6 million for the debt concession, and agreed to take 5 percent interest until 1727, thereafter 4 percent. This offer was extremely generous. The government owed holders of long-term annuities (70 to 85 years) 7 percent on their capital. The short-term annuities, paying 9 percent, expired in twenty years. Servicing the annuities alone cost the government £778,235 per annum. By converting the debt, Chancellor of the Exchequer Aislabie calculated that the entire debt could be retired in twenty-five years.[45]

This easy road to financial disencumbrance bore the marks of razzle-dazzle; and indeed its crucial weakness was evident at the Bank of England and was pointed out by Walpole in debate on the measure. The scheme could not work unless holders of unredeemable annuities were induced to exchange annuities yielding 7 percent to 9 percent for South Sea stock paying 5 percent. There was nothing in the South Sea proposal indicating the mechanisms by which this conversion would be made. However, the conditions that the South Sea Company's directors sought and won assumed that annuities holders could be induced to exchange South Sea Company stock by the prospect of capital gains; and that prospect they expected to make tangible in the form of a rapid rise in South Sea Company stock. The company thus in effect bought the national debt on margin, and meant to raise the remainder of capital by pushing secured debentures (the annuities) into money market futures, which they counted on falling relative to South Sea Company stock! An incredible scheme indeed.

An essential feature of the scheme was that the conversion rate of annuities to South Sea Company stock not be set aside at a fixed ratio, as sound finance would require, but be allowed to follow market value. The effect of this provision of the charter was to empower the South Sea Company to manufacture stock. For example, if the whole of the

45. P. G. M. Dickson, *The Financial Revolution*, 93ff.; J. H. Plumb, *Sir Robert Walpole*, 1: 298–99.

£31 million of subscribable debts could be exchanged for, say, £15.5 million of South Sea Company stock valued at £200 per share, the company was entitled to sell another £15.5 million in stock at the highest price; if the £31 million could be changed for only £7.75 million in stock valued at £400, the company could sell £23.25 million in stock. This was the escalator to paper values that provoked objections from the Bank of England. Yet without this provision, the South Sea Company proposal lacked all plausibility. The company's financial commitments on taking over the debt required not only a rise in the value of South Sea Company stock, but a rapid rise. When it began issuing stock in February 1720, it already had a liquidity problem, which was overcome by borrowing £1 million in Exchequer bills to pay arrears on the debt, some £200,000 of which was owed the South Sea Company! Without the capital gains promise of a rising market, annuitants would not convert to South Sea Company stock, and the company could not raise the capital needed to meet its obligations, totaling £1.7 million annually for debt servicing. Since half of this service charge was for annuities, the rapid conversion of annuities to stock was essential. Thus were paper expectations backed by paper promises.[46]

Such a scheme could win credence only in a buoyant investment climate. John Law's fabulous overnight success in France created one. French investors expected a bonanza from Law's Mississippi trading company, whose stock tripled in value in a few months. English investors caught this fever, and gladly believed that the South Sea trade would land El Dorado in London. The fact that neither company had realized profits from the colonial trade did not trouble investors hooked on speculative fever and gullible about every Exchange Alley rumor. The investment fever was not confined to South Sea Company stock. Hundreds of companies, springing up like mushrooms, projected slight and even frivolous enterprises and raised enormous subscriptions. In a single heady week in June, subscriptions of capital to new companies soared to £224 million. A Dutch observer of this craze wrote that it was "as if all the lunatics had escaped the madhouse at once. I don't know what to make of it all." So it was that South Sea Company stock made its amazing rise from £300 in April to £1,000 by June 17. The nominal value of company stock soared from £6.75 million to £50 million in June, topping out at £75 million in August, just before the plummet back to earth. The fall was jarring. By September 1, stock had dropped to £775; by October 1 it had plunged to £290; and on December 15 it bottomed out at £155, which had been its value in February before the climb began.

Investors shrewd enough to sell early reaped fortunes from the bubble.

46. Dickson, *The Financial Revolution*, 100ff.

But the typical story was a tale of woe. A stockbroker might lose £100,000, a duke £50,000; but thousands of dependent annuitants were wiped out. A distressed and enraged nation cried out for remedies, and the Parliament that assembled in October was determined to bring culprits to justice. This scarcely went to the root of the matter, since the principal fraud was the company's charter, which had been drafted into legislation, debated, and approved by Parliament. The experts had so miserably failed that the entire financial structure was in jeopardy.

The failures were of varying degrees and kinds. The Treasury expert who drafted the legislation was Secretary William Lowndes, whose advice to the Privy Council on recoinage has been canvassed in this chapter. The directors of the company were men of reputation, experience, and substantial business interests. Most were as shocked by events as the public, and not a few suffered financial losses. Nevertheless, they had committed serious management errors. They relinquished control of the company to a "Cabinet Council" led by Sir John Blunt, who worked closely with Exchequer Aislabie. They did not oversee the council's operations; and after the horse had bolted the barn they endorsed a fatuous attempt to stop the fall of stock—a promise of 50 percent interest on a new issue. Leaders in the government had accepted large "gifts" of stock in return for services rendered the company. Thus even the Bank of England, which had pinpointed the defects in the South Sea Company charter, failed to comprehend the magnitude of the danger; or comprehending, failed to sound the alarm clearly enough.[47]

Walpole belongs to this last group. In parliamentary debate he had pointed out the fatal flaw of the charter, which allowed the conversion rate of annuities to South Sea Company stock to float. The bullish rise of the company's stock should consequently have alerted him to the bear in the wings. While no letter or comment of his on the rise of stock survives, J. H. Plumb has argued from circumstantial evidence that Walpole did not foresee the crash; or if he did, his timing was out. He summered in Norfolk, where he spent large sums buying land in a market that was rising in response to South Sea Company stock. And he sent orders for purchases of South Sea Company stock as late as August, although he had received communications from two well-placed businessmen expressing grave doubts about the bubble.[48] The nation's financial intelligence dozed through the summer even though the collapse of Law's empire in June might well have put it on red alert.

47. For a description of the careers and financial worth of some principal South Sea Company directors, see ibid., 112ff.
48. Plumb, *Sir Robert Walpole*, 1: 304ff.

The crash dramatically transformed Walpole's political fortunes. The Ministry that had denied him high office was now under fierce attack, which it could survive only if Walpole gave his support in Parliament. Circumstances thus tossed an unusual choice in his path. He might stand aside and watch the destruction of his rivals; or he could take up their defense, and bear the onus of shielding men who had outraged the public. Yet a third option was to take the offensive in the cry for the scalps of Sunderland and Stanhope. In what terms Walpole weighed these alternatives is not known. The course of action he followed proved to be the most difficult in the short term; and yet, by prevailing, Walpole turned it to his own and the nation's interest. Instead of joining the chorus of accusers, or conveniently retiring to a sickbed, he hastened to London to formulate a plan to restore national confidence. The plan was to "engraft" Bank of England solvency into the tottering South Sea Company. This scheme foreshadowed the strategy that he was to follow for the next twelve months. As the Bank's principal parliamentary advocate, no one knew better than he the hostility that must meet such a proposal: as the bitter rival of the South Sea Company, the Bank of England's directors would not gladly extend a helping hand, especially when doing so placed the Bank at risk in a stew not of its own making. But he persuaded the directors to swallow this bitter pill. In a complementary maneuver, Walpole accepted the onerous task of defending the Whig Ministry. In session after rugged session, he faced down a public that vilified him as the "Skreen-Master General" protecting villains in high places, which was true. And this he was said to have done to conceal his own complicity in the swindle, which was false. Walpole went even further in offering himself up as a potential victim of an enraged public by insisting, successfully, that all contracts for purchase of South Sea Company stock must be honored, although contractors were partially compensated by distribution of assets of the confiscated estates of the South Sea Company's directors.

A politician who knowingly pursues a course that must make him, as it did, the most unpopular man in England two years before elections was probably animated by a farsighted perception of the coincidence of the public interest with his own. Evidence about Walpole's thinking at this time comes mainly from his parliamentary speeches, which are tailored to occasion. But his reasoning seems to have run along the following lines. Throwing the South Sea Company's directors to their accusers would have pleased his Bank of England constituency, but it would have deprived the nation of a large fund of commercial talent and capital not easily replaced. It was therefore in the nation's interest to minimize the discredit of the monied men and to salvage what could be salvaged of their reputations and fortunes. Similar reasoning applied to the Whig Ministry. Walpole might have ascended to the highest office by leaving his rivals to defend themselves as they could. But the impeachment of Sunderland, Stanhope, and Aislabie would have seriously damaged the Whig cause, jeopardized the Revolution Settlement, and perhaps precipitated a revolution. The king himself, after all, was governor of the company and a substantial investor in its stock. It was therefore necessary to defend them, however distasteful that might be. A similar logic prevailed respecting the public outcry for cancellation of contracts for the purchase of South Sea Company stock. Investors who had contracted at peak price were loud in their demands for relief, once it had fallen by 500 percent. Having entered the lion's den to defend the directors and the Ministry, Walpole must have been tempted to compromise on this demand. But instead he upheld the sanctity of contracts, although investors were compensated in some measure by proportional awards from confiscations of director's estates, in the amount of about £2 million.[49]

The positions Walpole took thus showed a consistent effort to salvage the public credit; and in doing so he consummated the highest act of statesmanship possible on the political principles by which he stood. Fixed purpose and iron nerve were needed to pursue this course in the face of personal abuse in Commons and the obloquy of the press. Would-be government writers and poets perceived in this conduct a heroic steadfastness. But its true political significance runs in a rather different direction. The quality that distinguished Walpole's conduct during the South Sea Company crises was the quality that distinguished his career—professionalism. He discerned what the circumstances required and set out to do it. To place this matter in the correct perspective, a comparison of Walpole's professionalism with the conduct of the first wave of philosopher-scientists is pertinent. The defiance of common opinion characteristic of the founders of science was suitable material for a heroic epic in the Galilean manner. But however colorful their heroic deed, and however important its function in registering on the public mind the case against imposed orthodoxy, still from an objective point of view it was all ruffles and flourishes. The inner character of science that enabled scientists to engage superstition in a heroic contest

49. This reconstruction of Walpole's strategy is advanced by Plumb, ibid., 329–58. Plumb's version differs from Coxe's mainly in denying that Walpole foresaw the crash of the South Sea stock. See Coxe, *Memoirs of the Life and Administration of Sir Robert Walpole*, 231–75.

was the same character that enabled them to persevere in serene or merely indifferent research environments, namely, objective knowledge of natural process. This was the basis for the professionalization of science. Similarly, the discovery of basic political facts and principles prepared the professionalization of politics. The statesmen who initiated political professionalization were de Witt and Colbert, whose technical political innovations have been discussed. Walpole must be placed beside them as the statesman who introduced professionalism into English politics. He discovered how the legislative power, lodged in a representative assembly, could be made to work. He did not, to be sure, invent the ingredients of the system. But prior to Walpole, those ingredients—the committee system, patronage, elections, and so on—were not enough to settle Parliament into a steady course of legislative business. This Walpole achieved in part by replacing the dependence of government on great men with steady, unheroic performance.

The most conspicuous index of this change was his alteration of the constitutional standing of the king's ministers. The king was of course the great man of English politics, and quarrels over dynasty and prerogative had been the most significant destabilizing force in English politics since the Petition of Right. The Revolutionary Settlement had laid down the principle that the legislative power, binding on the kings, lay in Parliament. But no one had discovered how to institutionalize this principle. This was Walpole's discovery: the king's ministers were transformed into parliamentary ministers who commanded a majority. The practicability of this solution depended upon the capacity of ministers to retain the confidence of Commons and of the king simultaneously. Possibly Walpole succeeded only because the Hanoverians were more interested in their German dominions than in English politics. This was the element of luck in success. But his refusal of a peerage and insistence on basing his administration's legitimacy on parliamentary majorities was the effect of policy. The dynamics of this politics was that while he commanded a majority, he enjoyed the confidence of George I, mainly because he held down the Jacobites and secured the income of the royal household. George II, although initially disposed to dismiss Walpole as chief minister, soon confirmed him in office because he came to appreciate the importance of business and political competence in chief ministers. George II spoke of Walpole as a "magician" able to make "gold from nothing." This was as much as to say that he did not understand Treasury matters, and would therefore leave them in the hands of his minister. Recognition of the competence requirement amounted to a tacit transfer of power. The absence of business competence in the

Hanoverians should not be set down merely as a flaw of that dynasty. In the last fifteen years of his reign, Louis XIV could not effectively direct his ministers; Louis XV never could. William III was probably the last English monarch competent to direct his ministers. This devolution of power from monarch to ministers occurred because the great-man ethos of monarchy was incompatible with the polytechnic skills required in an age of new technical complexity.

chapter 7

Faction, Party, and the Rhetoric of Opposition

The Problem of Faction: Aristotle, Machiavelli, Hobbes

Systematic recognition of the contentiousness of politics may be said to have begun with Aristotle's criticisms of Plato's attempt to banish faction from his utopia. To promote amity and suppress discord, Plato modeled the institutions of his guardian class on the family practice of holding property in common. But family solidarity, Socrates noticed, depends on selfish parental regard of offspring as one's own; he therefore argued that the extension of family sharing to an entire class requires the community of wives, so that, none knowing who fathered whom, all adults will consider themselves parents to all children, while children are to regard one another as brothers and sisters. Even this drastic measure is insufficient, for Socrates observed yet a further source of discord in the male bias of conventional political institutions, for which the remedy is to rear males and females identically and to have them share all tasks, including warfare.

Aristotle objected that in his pursuit of concord Plato had indeed reduced his ideal city to a large family, but at the cost of eliminating the political component from government. If so great a unity could be achieved, the political tasks of government (as distinguished from administration) would be superfluous and society would be stateless. Aristotle held that this result is not desirable. Human nature cannot achieve its full development in the household, however large, for it requires the association of heterogeneous groups engaged in the diverse pursuits characteristic of civic life. Only in this more complex mode of association is there leisure to pursue the arts and sciences necessary to sustain the complexity of urban life. But diversity entails inequality of fortune and circumstance; and this inequality sustains the perpetual contention over who should rule.[1]

Aristotle supposed that the statesman should reconcile the factiousness implicit in diversity, and should do so in a way that promotes the dignity and dominance of virtue. The chronic antagonism between the commons and aristocracy over property and office was for him the substance of faction. When the commons prevail, they institute democratic government and menace the aristocracy. When the patricians have the upper hand, they become oligarchs. The supremacy of one faction creates a climate favorable to the rise of a champion of the other; and when he liberates his party, he often converts government into a tyranny. The best remedy for faction, Aristotle advised, is "mixed government," which gives each faction a moderate satisfaction of its desire for wealth and power while checking the tendency of both factions toward extremes. The extremes are checked partly by institutional arrangements, but also by virtue, especially moderation. Aristotle's statesman is concerned to prevent the polity degenerating into one of the vicious forms of government, where factional arbitrariness and partiality expel justice, prudence, and moderation from public affairs.[2]

Aristotle's negative view of faction was not challenged until Machiavelli claimed that Roman practice did not conform to his theory. Although Rome was antiquity's foremost example of a durable mixed government, Roman politics were less conspicuous for moderation than for the turbulent strife between the commons and the patriciate. Rome indeed achieved greatness not despite but because of faction; for the commons' love of freedom combined with patrician ambition to propel Rome to ever new and more glorious endeavors. Machiavelli's enumeration of the causes of this success largely endorsed the assessment of ancient historians. The piety and energy of its commons, the astuteness and good faith of its patriciate, the rule of law in domestic affairs were the keys to its success. But Machiavelli noted that these characteristics did not distinguish Rome from other Latin republics. What made it unique was the steady progress of its expansion from a rustic agricultural village to a potent warrior city and eventual empire. A foreign pol-

1. Aristotle, *Politics*, 1261a 15–40, 1277a 5–20, 1296b 17–34; *Œconomica*, 1343a 10–15.
2. *Politics*, bk. 4, especially 1296a 22–62.

icy of predatory military expansion enabled Rome to resolve the problem of faction by directing its energies outward. Since conquest gave ample scope to ambition, the patriciate had less need to oppress the commons. Conquest benefited commons as well by bringing the booty of many nations into the city, where it was used to celebrate the grandeur of civic virtue in magnificent public works.[3]

These observations led Machiavelli to reassess classical concepts of virtue. For Aristotle, virtue was the habit of acting according to a mean between extremes of passion, a view consistent with his emphasis on moderation as the golden rule for public and private life. Machiavelli was however persuaded that the vehemence of passion and the vicissitudes of life reduce the political effectiveness of moderation to nothing. The Roman commons were honest and law-abiding only when in awe of the gods, fearful of harm, or hopeful of reward. And Rome's leadership did not conform to Aristotle's notion of the statesman as an impartial arbiter devoted to the common good. This concept, Machiavelli thought, did not square with the divisiveness of politics in Rome or elsewhere. A statesman who stood above faction also stood outside politics and therefore could have no effect. Real statesmen were invariably interested men called to office by ambition. Roman statesmen in particular were singularly lacking in moral goodness. Instead, their virtue was adroitness in a kind of statecraft that has come to be identified with Machiavelli's name. The Machiavellian statesman combines a nimble intelligence unfettered by scruples with a capacity to mimic emotions at will. It may be called the art of getting away with murder, since it enables the politician to do the unthinkable and yet sell it to the public as moral superiority to his opponents. Machiavelli signaled the importance of this Protean capacity to assume all forms by giving it the honorific name *virtù*. *Virtù* is required by a world in constant flux, ever on the brink of chaos. Since law and morals do not discipline action into stable forms, political stability depends upon the directive force of statecraft to discover safe or salutary channels into which the force of aroused passions may be diverted.[4]

If this is a solution to the problem of faction, it is not one encouraging to the prospects of political stability. That Machiavelli himself was not content with it may be guessed from his situating *virtù* in a moralistic scheme of political change—the cycle of regeneration and decay that Polybius discerned in his study of Roman history. In adopting the Polybian cycle, Machiavelli committed himself to the vocabulary of

3. Machiavelli, *Discourses on the First Ten Books of Titus Livy*, 1: 1–4; 2: 3.
4. Harvey C. Mansfield, Jr., *Machiavelli's New Modes and Orders*, 139–77.

"corruption" and "renewal" to characterize the foci of political revolutions; and the corruption metaphor pulled Machiavelli's thought back into Aristotle's moral orbit.[5]

The metaphor originates in the analogy of virtuous and vicious regimes to health and disease. Tyranny is a sick or corrupt monarchy. The analogy is intransitive, for one may not say that monarchy is a healthy tyranny. It is intransitive because in Aristotle's cosmos, virtuous regimes are "forms," that is, fixed and settled norms from which governments depart by contracting diseases (vices), which, if unchecked by a return to the norm, result in revolutions or even the dissolution of the body politic.[6] Polybius's cycle reworked Aristotle's static regime types into a schematization of political change suggested in part by Aristotle's own analysis of revolutions. In adopting the cycle schema, Machiavelli implicitly conceived change as a movement away from a norm, followed by a corrective back-to-basics movement, which renews the norm. Thus, Machiavelli's Romans were loaded with passions that tended to drive the polity toward despotism or anarchy; the degenerative motions were rectified by leaders who brought Rome back to its original norms, the ancient laws and customs (*ritorno ai principii*). The notion of return to norms is not very different from the Aristotelian statesman's preoccupation with constitutionalism and virtue or indeed from prophets calling Israel back to righteousness, despite Machiavelli's boast of having cut his ties with moralizing political science. The resemblance is especially marked when one notices that his descriptions of faction often sound like heroic struggles to maintain civic order against the disintegrating corruption of passions inflamed. In the *Florentine Histories* especially, faction is displayed as the bane of politics, the woeful father of innumerable calamities public and private.[7] Those who fixed their attention on this aspect of Machiavelli, especially his English disciples, read him as a political moralist who portrayed republican politics as a great drama of Virtue vs. Corruption.

Machiavelli's new modes and orders in fact contain no general solution to the problem of faction; they even presuppose the perpetuity of the old strife between commons and patricians. This one sees in his ren-

5. J. G. A. Pocock, *The Machiavellian Moment*, 243, 317, 484.
6. Aristotle, *Politics*, bk. 5.
7. In book 3 of the *Florentine Histories* Machievelli painted a vivid picture of faction by liberally quoting, or inventing, inflammatory orations. The speeches suggest that in Florence rioting had become popular theater, as it did subsequently in the Netherlands and colonial Boston. The speech of the Plebeian is particularly notable as containing much of the repertoire of democratic prejudices.

dition of that cornerstone of his politics, anticlericism. Christianity was for Machiavelli something of an enigma. Although Christian morals seemed prima facie apt to legitimate only an ascetic life, the clergy had nonetheless made themselves a force cutting across national and class lines. This paradox was achieved, Machiavelli suggested, thanks to the despotic organization of the clergy under the pope, who conducted affairs according to the maxims of the world rather than according to the precepts of Christ. Machiavelli embedded the paradox in his depiction of Christian antinomianism: the clergy preached poverty, humility, and charity, but lived in arrogant splendor supported by the rewards of avarice perpetuated upon a laity they had reduced to penitential compliance. The puzzle was that the clergy had somehow immobilized the passions that ordinarily guaranteed opposition to oppression. He expressed this puzzle in the formulas stating that Christianity had "disarmed the world" or had "made men weak," meaning that somehow Christianity had produced a pusillanimous and servile attitude in the natural political leadership.[8]

This line was a variation of Ghibelline criticism of ecclesiastical politics, which would break priestly hegemony by subordinating ecclesiastical office to secular control. The "unthinkable" deed was to be le-

---

8. Machiavelli's main statement on the emasculation of moderns by religion occurs in *Discourses*, 2: 2; other references are scattered throughout his writings, e.g. in chapter 15 of *The Prince*. The notion that Christianity had weakened the political potency of modern men is inevident on its face, especially when it means, as for Machiavelli it so often did, that the modern military institutions were weaker than the ancient. The assertion is more understandable if for "moderns" we read "modern Italians." Machiavelli's dread may then be referred to the humiliation of Italian armies by Charles VIII in 1494. This defeat gave rise to the *Italia* movement of national renewal, whose spokesmen shared Machiavelli's scapegoating of religion. Paolo Giovio made this point by writing enthusiastically of Turkish military institutions. Alberti blasted religion and urged his countrymen to "la iustitia di Torquato, qual per osservare la militare disciplina non perdonò al figlivolo." Guicciardini, an authority among Harringtonians, was prompted to write *Storia Italia* by the shock of the event, which clearly marks his description of it: the Italians displayed "nè virtu nè animo nè consiglio, non cupidità d'onore non potenza non fede"; and the battle ended "con summo vituperio e derisione della milizia italiana e con gravissimo pericolo e ignorminica di tutti." The *pro pátria* writings of the humanists undertook to exorcise the humiliation of Italian manhood; hence the romantic strain in their writings. A similar connection between manliness, anti-Christianity, and romanticism is found in Nietzsche's writings and their culminating heroic idea, the *Übermensch*. For discussion, see Hiram Caton, "Toward a Diagnosis of Progress," 1–14.

gitimated by the argument that the divine right claimed by the Church had no basis in apostolic doctrine. Machiavelli produced a variation of that argument with his accusation that the example of iniquitous priests had corrupted the morals of the people. But he never developed an anticlerical politics based on institutional analysis: he did not examine the most stable institution in Italian politics, the Curia, and his ruminations on the paradoxical inversion of Christian precepts in practice were unilluminated by attention to the circumstance that a religion that began as a revitalization movement was subsequently coopted by the feudal aristocracy.[9] Analysis along such lines might have restrained his tendency to depict politics as pure flux of riot, war, and perfidy and might have suggested some lessons about political stability.

But Machiavelli loved dramatic ideas and the glamour of power. He represented the presiding political problem of his times as the misfortune of an age stalled in the corruption segment of a Polybian cycle; the remedy he prescribed against the malignancy of *Fortuna* was a back-to-basics renewal, which in Italy's case meant a revival of the Roman republic. But his prospectus of the character and institutions of the projected revival consists mainly of rules of thumb teased from incidents in Livy's history. The incidents centered upon battles, riots, and conspiracies, while the lesson Machiavelli drew from them usually brought him around to the one theme of which he was indisputably master: statecraft. He had little to say about the operation of political institutions and their relation to social and economic institutions. This is why his *Florentine Histories* and *Discourses* convey the impression that politics consist of harangues, intrigues, tumults, wars. Characteristically, his one sustained interest in institutions was in the Roman citizen militia, which he attempted to revive in Florence. He urged that Florence's dependency on mercenaries weakened the city's capacity to resist despots. His militia was meant to purge this "corruption" by instilling citizens with patriotic ardor, which he viewed as the first step toward the revival of militant republicanism. Not surprisingly, he downplayed the importance of artillery in modern warfare, maintaining that it did not invalidate Roman infantry tactics. Virtue subdues even technology.

9. This is the theme of Bernard Mandeville's *An Enquiry into the Origin of Honour and the Usefulness of Christianity in War*, especially book 3, which answered Machiavelli's belief that virtue is threatened by Christian humility: the real problem was romantic feelings of honor that reshaped Roman *virtus* into its Gothic form. This tract, like the *Fable of the Bees*, was directed against Harringtonians. The description of the desired qualities of a statesman, given in the *Fable*, seems to be tailored to Robert Walpole.

Machiavelli's chosen themes, as well as his omissions, tend to identify politics with the moments of its peak emotions in dramatic confrontation. They are, certainly, a part of politics; and his ability to convey a sense of emotions typical of politics has perhaps never been equaled. But euphoria and depression are not the whole stuff of government, whose business requires organizational structure and rational policy. No one, I believe, has ever suggested that Machiavelli was a romantic, and I should not like to be the first to propose it. But J. G. A. Pocock's study of his legacy demonstrates that an important tradition, which we are about to discuss, read him as a moralist and idealist of liberty; while in France his Romanism helped inspire the romantic element of the French Revolution.[10]

Hobbes made a fresh beginning on the problem of faction by breaking cleanly with notions of virtue and its corruption. These notions construe faction as a struggle between good and evil, or else diagnose faction as a symptom of virtue's decay. In either case, the remedy for faction requires the recovery of lost goodness or righteousness. Hobbes observed that the application of remedies of that kind only perpetuates factions, since they cannot cope with the fact that moral valuations are inherently contentious. A grip on the problem of faction requires that virtue be recognized as part of the problem. The problem is that moral judgments, upon which people chiefly rely for orienting themselves and others, are illusions conjuring imaginary moral orders.[11] The correspondence between these norms and actual government is not high: every government is condemned by some morality and magnified by another. This chaos of opinion is the truth about the "moral faculty"—it is a rhapsody of unstable, factious emotions. To place government under the direction of morality is to set the fox to watch the chickens. In contrast to the chaos of opinion, behavior follows the principle of maximizing advantage, or, correspondingly, of minimizing damage. But self-interested action generates all-sided competition for marginal advantage—the war

10. Pocock, *The Machiavellian Moment*, 385ff. A document bearing on the reception of Machiavelli as a republican moralist is Henry Neville's translation of his *Works* in 1675, to which is appended "A letter to Zenobius Buondelmontius in Vindication of Himself and His Writings." This letter, which purports to be by Machiavelli, was probably Neville's invention. It was meant to pacify the English perception of Machiavelli as the sycophant who encouraged princes to play the tyrant. Neville claimed that the advice was given with ironical intent, namely, to provoke indignation against despots. This interpretation was adopted by Spinoza, Rousseau, and other republican writers.

11. See above, 144–52.

of all on all. Moral opinions are weapons in this war, functioning to attract help to oneself while creating troubles for rivals. The remedy is not more virtue but rather its elimination as a criterion for judging politics. What is wanted is not a return to a goodness lost, but a step away from nature toward artificial means of controlling the chaos. In a word, the remedy is not a recovery of manliness and heroic emotions, but brains applied to organizational problems.

Government is the artificial means of controlling the chaos of political competition. Its effectiveness depends upon achieving those ends that it can achieve, and no others. As we saw, Hobbesian government rests on three great principles: the common good, equality, and the rule of law backed by force. The common good is objectively determined as those advantages that all seek to secure to themselves, regardless of what they say they seek. These advantages are life, liberty, and the means to life, property. The common good, defined by "natural rights," establishes the ends of government in a rank order of values. Equality is decisive to that order. All are equally compelled by natural necessity to strive for life, liberty, and the means to life. If people were under no other necessity, government would amount to no more than the administration of things. But they also seek to have more than others and to dominate. Here is the root of faction. We see that it is also the root of government: if people did not seek to dominate, government would be unnecessary and indeed impossible. In the event, however, dominance is a certainty, since the clash of contending wills eventuates in some individual or faction forcing the remainder into submission. Such hegemony is unstable if it menaces the lives and liberties of those excluded from government, for they must rebel. Stability may be achieved if the power of government is used to promote the common good; and submission is sweetened by leaving citizens private liberties. But some will use liberties to attempt to oppress others, even if the sovereign refrains from doing so. Consequently, the use of liberty must be regulated by law as declared norms binding on all.

This is the kernel of the solution to the problem of faction emanating from Hobbes and Locke. It was unprecedented, for it undercut what in Western political history had been a fundamental source of faction, inherited social class. While inequalities of fortune and status are inevitable consequences of competition among people unequal in age, talent, and luck, the sovereign may not write privileges or disabilities of birth into law.[12] The implementation of this program implies the replacement of class inequalities by inequalities of status, to which no le-

12. See above, 157–58.

gally sanctioned disadvantage accrues; for legal endorsement of disability would show that government harbors a systematic bias against a segment of the population, and hence encourages faction.

Governments ordered in accordance with these principles may use them to deal with factions that inevitably arise. Factions are "great," in Burke's sense, if they challenge the constitution, or "small" if they do not. Small factions, which may have a large following, seek marginal advantages over other groups. Since they do not challenge the constitution, they legitimate their endeavors by appeal to its principles. In so doing, they become self-limiting, since the principles to which they appeal circumscribe private interest within the bounds of the rights of others. Great factions, on the other hand, openly or covertly challenge the fundamental order established by government. Such challenges entail rejection of some element of the common good. Great factions therefore menace the common good to promote factional advantage, and this fact can be mobilized as a weapon against them. At the same time, the deployment of this weapon tends to compel government to adhere to its own nonfactional principles.

Hobbes and Locke attacked the two most prestigious ideological factions in the Western political traditions—ecclesiastical regiment and the classical republican tradition. As we have seen, the accusation against the religious faction was that ecclesiastical politics operated in a kingdom of darkness whose moralism conjured a network of specious causes of human action. Its effect was not only to compound calamities by denying such reliefs as might be obtained from knowledge of the human predicament; its faith was hostile to attempts to bring light into the cave. There was no relief short of a campaign to discredit it in matters concerning public policy. By 1700 the enlightenment party enjoyed the advantage. When David Hume surveyed the battlefield in 1742, he issued this situation report:

> There has been a sudden and sensible change in the opinions of men within these last fifty years, by the progress of learning and of liberty. Most people, in this island, have divested themselves of all superstitious reverence to names and authority: The clergy have much lost their credit: Their pretensions and doctrines have been ridiculed; and even religion can scarcely support itself in the world. The mere name of *king* commands little respect; and to talk of a king as God's vice-regent on earth, or to give him any of those magnificent titles, which formerly dazzled mankind, would but excite laughter in every one. Though the crown, by means of its large revenue, may maintain its authority in times of tranquillity, upon

private interest and influence; yet, as the least shock or convulsion must break all these interests to pieces, the royal power, being no longer supported by the settled principles and opinions of men, will immediately dissolve. Had men been in the same disposition at the time of the *revolution* [of 1688], as they are at present, monarchy would have run a great risque of being entirely lost in this island.[13]

Throne and altar were no longer legitimated by settled opinion. If they nevertheless endured, it was due to their conformance with private interest and influence. Although Hume overstated the fragility of the British monarchy, he exaggerated in the right direction. Hobbes's basing monarchy on its expediency for the common good; Locke's legitimation of revolution to the same end; followed by Walpole's transfer of the law-making power to the first minister in Parliament—all subordinated the Crown to Parliament.

The linkage between throne and altar was uniform throughout Europe, regardless of whether the national church was Roman or evangelical. The Church, like the Army, received the sons of the landed classes. As clergymen, these sons taught the people their duties; as soldiers, they enforced the king's will. Dissenting sects were viewed as subversive of this order because they withdrew tithes, personnel, and loyalty from the regime. Thus, the high churchmen linked dissent with republicanism, sedition, and atheism.[14] The sentiment animating these charges was that the Church supported monarchy by providing an institution of privilege and preferment for sons of privileged classes who could not inherit the family estate. The Church was exactly what Tory doctrine always said it was—a bulwark of the landed interest. To legitimate toleration implied a veiled attack on the privileges of landed men, the backbone of social class throughout Europe. Locke's legitimation of toleration, and his insistence, in economic writings, that land and trade were complementary interests, must be understood in this context. His apologia for trade—and finance—was not a defense of a "rising class"; it was the leading edge of the *dismemberment of class, as the condition for*

13. David Hume, *Philosophical Works*, 3: 125.
14. Geoffrey Holmes, *The Trial of Doctor Sacheverell*, 26–32, 35–41; J. P. Kenyon, *Revolution Principles*, 83–101. Sacheverell's sermon *The Perils of False Brethren* (1709) and Bishop Atterbury's *English Advice to the Freeholders of England* (1714) were high points of the "Church in danger" scare. The danger was that the Whigs intended to reduce the Church to the Dutch model by eliminating hierarchy, possessing Church lands, and prescribing doctrine. It would be interesting to know whether these allegations had a basis, perhaps in the shop talk of the Whig inner circle. No one seems to have investigated this question.

the program of political equality. In the American colonies, where Locke-
ans had a freer hand, this is exactly what they did, consciously and
deliberately.

The second great faction Hobbes attacked was that amorphous group
of writers and politicians who perpetuated the errors of classical republicanism. Republicanism for him was the factious politics of leading
men who stir the people against government by representing themselves
as champions of the oppressed. But the faction no sooner captures
power than its adherents fall to quarreling about how power may be
shared; and this occurs because all are rivals for public eminence.[15] With
government thus weakened by power struggles, and the public distracted by turmoil, the leading men seek to remedy public discontent by
an expedient that also enhances the opportunities for glory: they embark on wars of conquest. To sustain public support for war, republican
politicians must hold out the rewards of booty while confecting a moral
order to justify the sacrifice of native and foreign blood to the glory of
the republic, i.e. its leading men. Every step of this politics, Hobbes
thought, is specious and multiplies fantasms, such as "corruption" and
"virtue." In one of his few references to the Polybian cycle, Hobbes rejected the corruption-and-virtue interpretation, substituting instead a
scheme where sharp operators persuade a gullible public to overthrow
the government, followed by a new government as oppressive as the
old, which is then in turn overthrown, and so on. This cycle of revolution occurs, he said,

all for the want of rules of justice for the common people to take
notice of; which if the people had known in the beginning of every
one of these seditions, the ambitious persons could never have had
the hope to disturb their government after it had once been settled.
For ambition can do little without hands, and few hands it would
have if the common people were as diligently instructed in the true
principles of their duty, as they are terrified and amazed by their
preachers.[16]

These words are from *Behemoth* (1672), which the aged philosopher
would have launched against the renewed exertions of English republicans, except that Charles forbade its publication. Hobbes had forecast,
with uncanny precision, where the mishmash of republicanism and biblicism would lead from the events of 1642. He repeated that forecast in
Behemoth; but this time political thought had matured sufficiently to

15. Hobbes, *Leviathan*, 140–41, 219.
16. Hobbes, *Works*, 6: 252; also 212–13, 343, 362, 418.

effect a change of regime from a troubled mixed monarchy to a stable commercial republic.

The First Modern Electoral Party

The political controversy of the 1670s and 1680s amply documents the currents that came to fruition in the Revolution. Whig and Tory were established as factional names in this period, especially during the Exclusion Crisis of 1679–81, when the Shaftesbury Whigs made an attempt on the government. Whigs combined under the slogans "No popery, no slavery" and "Liberty and Property." The prospect of a Catholic king was the issue that might momentarily unite incompatible elements into a single front. Few Protestants of any class warmed to the idea of a Catholic king, and it aroused the vehement resistance of many. Charles's revocation of corporation charters as a means of imposing control on Parliament by controlling selection seemed the beginning of absolute despotism; persecutions under the Clarendon Code were not forgotten; and it was feared that the Catholic James would confiscate lands to restore to the Church after it had been consecrated Catholic. Such were the apprehensions that gave flesh to the slogan "Liberty and Property."[17]

The Whigs of that time sorted roughly into two types—the Harringtonians, led by Henry Neville, and the mercantilists, led by Shaftesbury. In his Exclusionist tract *Plato Redivivus,* Neville revived the master's notions about equal distribution of land and projected the image of the virtuous freeholder (£2,000 per annum, no more, no less) rotating in office and living in armed liberty. The prospect of Catholic James confiscating estates breathed life into Harrington's battered conceit that power followed land (it had led him to predict in 1656 that neither peers nor monarch could ever again be raised in England). Even before this prediction was falsified, Harringtonian agrarianism was pulled to bits by the royalist writer Matthew Wren, who showed that the power-follows-land maxim could not account for the obvious relationships between land and trade.[18] Political economy was not a strong suit of Harringtonians, who contributed little to the political economy debate of the 1670s and 1680s.

Shaftesbury Whigs, by contrast, placed political economy in the forefront. The position taken by Shaftesbury writers during the Exclusion

17. Richard Ashcraft, "The *Two Treatises* and the Exclusion Crisis," 54.
18. The Dutch Republic, Wren urged, is a standing refutation of Harrington's system: "Spain or England are either of them by nature endowed with all advantages for taking the whole traffique of the world into their hands, and

Crisis was substantially the program of the Cabal Ministry that persuaded Charles to cashier Clarendon in 1667. Clarendon's Toryism was the common wisdom on monarchists throughout Europe, whether Catholic or Protestant: the stability of the throne depends upon a united clergy to discipline the people and loyal landed classes to put down invaders and rebels. But this policy entailed persecution to curb religious dissenters; and these persecutions in turn destroyed productive labor and small capital. The alternative policy, vigorous in de Witt's Holland, was that national power is better enhanced by trade and prosperity than by religious conformity; and that accordingly religious toleration and political liberty, which unleash the energies of the people, should form the axis of politics. Shaftesbury meant to implement Dutch politics in England; but the more Charles saw of it, the less he liked it, and by 1673 Shaftesbury was turned out of the Privy Council. From that moment, Shaftesbury was persuaded that a new struggle over the English regime was unavoidable. Its public face would be a dynastic struggle precipitated by the religious question; but its inner core would be a struggle for the commercial republic.[19]

Shaftesbury was the arch exponent of the commercial republic. Maurice Cranston declares that he was among the first English statesmen to be "the complete progressive capitalist in politics."[20] What did this pioneering "capitalist" do when turned out of office? Shaftes-

---

are inferior to the Dutch who enjoy it, in nothing but industry. What the importance of this is or might be, the Dutch will best help us to understand, who by that alone without any considerable land, have been able to baffle Spain, and contest with England" (*Monarchy asserted, or the State of Monarchicall and Popular Government*, 30). Wren also derided the rigidity of Harrington's "agrarian," e.g. the supposition that land may be equally divided and that those divisions may be held constant over time; and the requirement of universal military service and of universal political participation, etc. (146–52). Harrington acknowledged that commercial states did not conform to his axiom about the balance of power and property; but this was because commercial states were "corrupt" regimes about to dissolve.

19. This has been the prevailing opinion among such historians as John Morley and H. R. Fox Bourne (*The Life of John Locke*, especially vol. 2, chap. 13). Richard Ashcraft's "The *Two Treatises* and the Exclusion Crisis" is a good contemporary statement of this contention. The difficulty with the teleology of my "inner core" concept is that the political intention of the Shaftesbury party seems to become more obscure as knowledge of minutiae increases. See n. 21 below.

20. Maurice Cranston, *John Locke*, 107. See also his "The Politics of John Locke," *History Today* 2 (1952): 621; and Ashcraft, "The *Two Treatises* and the Exclusion Crisis," 42–43, 51, 77–82.

bury built up a party, backed by a party apparatus. And a formidable party machine it was. It could call out a London crowd of 150,000; it could produce petitions with 60,000 signatures; it commanded a private army, the "Boys from Wapping"; it was geared for electioneering throughout the kingdom; its agents canvassed opinion and harangued in coffeehouses, pubs, markets, and other public places; propaganda broadsides from its presses kept the party line constantly before the public. Its Clandestine Activities Department could move persons and goods undetected from place to place, or carry orders or intelligence great distances in a twinkling; it could move arms, contrive riots, rig specious plots, and attempt a real coup d'état of its own.[21] Shaftesbury was the inventor and chieftain of the first mass party machine. A machine was what the de Witt government needed to support its popular

21. Despite the hillock of books on this critical period and its leading men, there is still no authoritative study of Shaftesbury's party. One must accordingly refer to numerous larger and smaller fragments. Cranston's *John Locke,* Laslett's introduction to *John Locke: Two Treatises of Government,* and Richard Ashcraft's "The *Two Treatises* and the Exclusion Crisis" are accessible sources containing much information essential to the eventual construction of an adequate narrative. J. R. Jones's *The First Whigs: The Politics of the Exclusion Crisis, 1678–1683* promises the wanted story but falls short, particularly on the conspiratorial side of politics. Another study in the same vein is Francis S. Ronalds's *The Attempted Whig Revolution of 1678–1681,* although it contains a valuable bibliography of primary works and early history. Lois G. Schwoerer's *The Declaration of Rights, 1689* recognizes the continuity between the Exclusionists and the men of 1688, including their conspiratorial politics, but her account is very brief. Iris Morley's *A Thousand Lives: An Account of the English Revolutionary Movement, 1660–1685* is more biographical than analytical. J. R. Tanner's *English Constitutional Conflicts of the Seventeenth Century, 1603–1689* devotes but four pages to Shaftesbury's politics, although he notes that Shaftesbury was "the first pesty organizer and wire puller, the modern demagogue, and the modern parliamentary debater." Other pertinent studies are William L. Sachse, *Lord Somers: A Political Portrait;* J. R. Western, *Monarchy and Revolution: The English State in the 1680s;* Henry Horwitz, *Parliament, Policy and Politics in the Reign of William III,* and the same author's *Revolution Politics: The Career of Daniel Finch, 2nd Earl of Nottingham;* John Kenyon, *The Popish Plot;* K. H. D. Haley, *The First Earl of Shaftesbury.* Examination of these studies suggests that the historiographic mission is perplexed by a wish not to expose the great scandals of Shaftesbury's politics. Thus John Dunn and J. G. A. Pocock downplay Locke's role in the events of this period and John Kenyon could write of the Whig claim, at the Sacheverell trial, that there had been armed resistance to James, that "there is very little evidence for it, and what there is comes mostly from James II" (Kenyon, *Revolution Principles,* 5). It is to be hoped that someone will make a study of this curious historiographic knot.

politics, but did not have; and for want of it, de Witt was destroyed by a furious mob about the time Shaftesbury was turned out of office. Shaftesbury realized that a popular politics could not be conducted without a broad political base and a party apparatus manned by men representative of its constituency. The constituency consisted of types gentlemen might call "the rabble"—tradesmen, shopkeepers, laborers, plus some freeholders and petty gentry. To this largely unenfranchised but political public the Whig machine directed its propaganda about toleration, liberty, government by consent; and spoke of Parliament as representative of the people and as the chief law-making body, although it was neither.[22]

Court publicists taking their cues from Privy Council were not slow to smell the sedition in Whig propaganda. The court publicist Roger L'Estrange recognized the weak point in the Whig front and set his axe into it. The single issue meant to unite the front was the Exclusion Bill. It could not succeed without strong support from the gentry dominating Parliament. But parliamentary commonwealth sentiment was dominated by Harringtonian ideas; and the commonwealth Harrington envisaged was not a commercial republic but a virtuous agrarian republic where equality extended only to the landed class. L'Estrange recognized this fault line in the Whig front. Gentry who knew their interest must support the Crown, not Shaftesbury's commonwealth, which would "reduce all degrees to a parity; for as titles and honors are incident to kingship, so also are equality of place and birth, to democracy."[23] In a sparkling analysis of the conditions of English monarchy, L'Estrange pointed out that the arbitrary power of the king, castigated by Harringtonians, was of the same nature as the arbitrary power exercised by the landed men over their tenants, servants, and laborers. Abolish arbitrary power in the king, and the arbitrary power of the landed classes must follow.[24] The example of the Dutch republic, which Whig propaganda dangled before the gentry, L'Estrange dismissed. The Dutch republic, having no land, was dominated by trade; its institutions could not be transplanted to England, whose "laws, genius, and interest" were very different.[25] England, in a word, was a class society dominated by gentlemen, whereas the Dutch were organized by the spirit of "traffic, navigation, handicrafts, and sordid thrift."

Harringtonians like Neville and Algernon Sidney, captivated by visions of agrarian virtue, might be vague where L'Estrange was lucid.

22. Ashcraft, "The *Two Treatises* and the Exclusion Crisis," 62ff.
23. Quoted ibid., 75.
24. Ibid., 72–73.
25. Ibid., 74.

But most in Parliament would not join Shaftesbury's "rabble" to oppose the king. The Exclusion Bill was defeated. The party apparatus, smashed by Crown constables, was reassembled in Holland by refugees. Sidney, the Garibaldi of his day, died in the Tower a martyr to liberty.

Shaftesbury had counted on changing the regime by momentarily uniting disparate elements on a single issue where popular emotion co-incided with political intention. His calculation of the vector of forces needed for this purpose was correct; but his timing was out. A few years later gentry who had forsworn commonwealth politics found their re-solve weakening as the obstinate James prepared to take England back into the papal fold. When the Whig machine produced William the De-liverer on English soil, backed by 15,000 troops, the gentry deserted James with an uneasy conscience. The Dutch warlord, supported by the Shaftesbury Whigs, steered the nation toward the commercial republic.

The *force majeure* that accomplished the Revolution was intellectual as well as military. Many of the gentry who sat in the Convention Par-liament could not tell exactly what was in the "contract" between king and people that they were supposed to endorse. Others who could read the fine print did not like what they saw, or liked some clauses but not others. In the reign of Anne, these differences about the Settlement came to light. At the extreme of discontent were the nonjuring bishops and Jacobite gentry. They were able to make common cause with Har-ringtonians, who were in high dudgeon against the novelties of the commercial republic. These two strains of opinion and sentiment—Tory and "Old Whig"—blended to generate the rhetoric of opposition to the Court Whig oligarchy.

Opposition Rhetoric, 1700–1750

Opposition publicists were known variously as commonwealth-men, Old Whigs, the Country party, constitutionalists, and Tories. They may be said to have originated in the 1690s in a circle encompassing Robert Molesworth, the third earl of Shaftesbury, John Trenchard, Charles Davenant, John Toland, Anthony Collins, James Tyrrell, Thomas Gor-don, and Andrew Fletcher. These men enthusiastically endorsed the Revolution, although only Molesworth had any involvement, and that but minor. William dispatched him to Denmark as an envoy, but ap-pointed him to no post because of his uncontrollable temper. He was created an Irish peer by George I. Between 1716 and his death in 1724 he was a highly visible Old Whig in Parliament who spoke warmly against the South Seas directors. He was a friend and admirer of Lord Somers and John Locke, but otherwise he was not well disposed to the Junto

Whigs.[26] James Tyrrell was among the Whig publicists of the Exclusion Crisis, and for years was close to Locke. Toland and Collins initiated the Deist controversy, claiming to take their doctrine from Locke's *Essay*.

These men shared with Locke certain programmatic agreements: preference for a balanced constitution and rule of law; mistrust of clergymen and dislike of religious persecution; a sense that export trade and plantations were important determinants of Britain's influence and power. But none proved to be a disciple of Locke or an exponent of his politics; and some were, probably unawares, key figures in opposition to it. Only the third earl of Shaftesbury seems to have detected the disharmony between Locke's notion of human sociability and their own. They drew their inspiration from classical authors, mediated through Machiavelli and Harrington, without appreciating the historical distinctiveness of the classical republic and the commercial republic. Lord Somers put his finger on the problem when he noted, in his discussion of faction, that among the nation's republicans "some are for aristocracy, others for democracy, and they are not agreed among themselves whether Holland, Venice, Switzerland, or Harrington's *Oceana* shall be the model."[27] *Oceana*, we may say, did not understand Holland.

The failure of the Old Whigs to comprehend events had two consequences. Their opposition to the commercial republic impeded the thorough articulation of its principles into institutions. That did not occur until the American Founders renovated the Lockean heritage. The second consequence was that opposition rhetoric burdened English political thought with a prestigious nostalgia for the ancient constitution, the patriot king, and other arcadias. This potent tradition might have been dissipated by the American and French revolutions. But a writer of unusual expressive gifts remodeled the old rhetoric into a new criticism of the commercial republic that elevated tradition above reason. That writer was the self-styled Old Whig Edmund Burke.

Opposition rhetoric revolved about a short list of iniquitous practices threatening the moral fiber of the nation, viz. standing armies, placemen, long parliaments, stockjobbers, corruption, and influence. Behind most of these complaints there was a history of parliamentary engagement with the Crown. Exclusionist Whigs had contested Charles on the first three points. When Charles increased his guard to offset the menace of Shaftesbury's private army, this was denounced as a standing army that might be used to throttle the liberties of Englishmen. When the Whigs

---

26. Caroline Robbins, *The Eighteenth Century Commonwealthman*, 94–100.
27. John Lord Somers, *Anguis in herba, or the fatal consequences of a treaty with France*, 20.

came to power, they wrote a standing army clause into the Bill of Rights. Point 4 declared "that the raising or keeping a standing army within the kingdom (in time of peace) unless it be with consent of Parliament is against the law." This provision of the Settlement might have pleased the Harringtonians, but it was rather less than their idea of replacing professional armies with the citizen militia. The provision gave a very wide mandate. Standing armies were permitted with parliamentary consent; and they were permissible overseas, or at home during war, regardless of Parliament.

If actions are indicative of intention, the Shaftesbury Whigs never believed a word of the Harringtonian complaint about standing armies and only took up the cry to harass Charles, for the Junto had no sooner assembled in William's Privy Council than it began a rapid buildup of the Army from James's 16,000 to 35,000 at the height of William's wars. Between 1700 and 1750, no government reduced the Army below 17,000, which was barely sufficient to keep Ireland quiet and assert the nation's presence on the Continent. It is a rare militia that can hold its own against a professional army. The notion that Britain might exercise imperial powers with such a force was robust persiflage.[28]

The career of the antiplacemen grievance was similar. Had the Junto believed the antiplaceman rhetoric of the Shaftesbury opposition, it would have put through the place bill so often blocked by the Crown in the past. It did no such thing. Numerous place bills were introduced in Commons between 1690 and 1710, but those that were reported out were killed in Lords. Country spokesmen ritually lashed placemen as constitutional corruption; and no politician was more maligned for his placemen than Walpole. The government response to this complaint was that placemen, far from unhinging the constitution, were necessary to make it work; for placemen represented the Crown's legislative interest in Parliament. In his survey of party struggles, David Hume agreed: without placemen as balance, Parliament's control of supply would lead to a gradual usurpation of the crown's powers.[29] Subsequent events confirmed this analysis. The administration that succeeded Walpole did not pass a place bill; indeed, no government ever did. Placemen were phased

28. A work by the Country publicist James Ralph gives, in rich detail, opposition parliamentary speeches on the standing army. The speeches repeat the standard themes: that the support of the Crown is the affection of the people; that armed force betrays mistrust and fear of the people; that fearful sovereigns become despots; that standing armies degenerate into Pretorian guards (*Of the Use and Abuse of Parliaments,* 1: 215, 223, 268, 399, 484 ff.).

29. Hume, *Philosophical Works,* 3: 120–21.

out between 1784 and 1832 as an indirect consequence of administrative modernization.[30] When they did disappear, parties as remote as the duke of Wellington and the *Edinburgh Review* worried about what would replace "the essential basis for co-operation between King and Commons," as a recent student of this subject has called it.[31]

These examples show that the Country criticism was at variance with the facts discernible to informed opinion of that period. Stubborn opposition to standing armies and the rest are best described not as a criticism but as an aversion to the commercial republic. Yet the aversion proved to be more durable than the gentry who first gave it utterance. Indeed, many subsequent "criticisms" of the commercial republic reproduced some of the Country attitudes.[32]

Andrew Fletcher

The moral core of the virtuous republic was the independent freeholder as active participant in government, ready to defend liberty with arms. The root of this idea, as J. G. A. Pocock has shown so well, was Machiavelli's notion that the citizen's independence requires his moral capacity to bear arms. The leading expositor of the citizen militia among the commonwealth-men was the Scot Andrew Fletcher, whose political career was typical of men who formed the Country opposition after 1689. An outspoken critic of Danby's policies, he joined the duke of Monmouth's attempt on the government. He escaped arrest and returned to the society of political exiles in Holland. He was among those who accompanied William's invasion. However, this "enemy to all monarchical governments" and "admirer of both ancient and modern republics" was soon disaffected from the Junto and came to bear William great hatred.[33] Fletcher was typical in despising the names Whig and

30. Betty Kemp, *King and Commons*, 52–65; see also Archibald Foord, *His Majesty's Opposition*, 175–85.
31. Kemp, *King and Commons*, 64.
32. The connection between Country criticisms of the commercial republic and subsequent criticisms has been underlined by Pocock. He styles the Old Whigs "the first intellectuals of the left," denouncing their own party for "betrayal of secular principles" (*The Machiavellian Moment*, 477). He points out that in the development that moves through the *Wealth of Nations*, the classical concept of corruption "merges with the modern concept of alienation, and the humanist roots of early Marxism become visible" (502). The link between the first and subsequent intellectuals of the Left is disaffection based on class rancor.
33. "Characters of the Author," by Lockhart, reprinted in Fletcher's *Discourse of*

Tory, and in being "a strict and nice observer of all points of honour." It was not despite but because of these attitudes that Fletcher "liked, commended, and conversed with high-flying Tories, more than any other set of men, acknowledging them to be the best countrymen, and of most honor, integrity, and ingenuity."[34]

In his *Discourse of Government with Relation to Militias*, Fletcher described the character of the militia and how it was to enhance the virtuous republic. He thought it "the chief part of the constitution of any free government," since it is the gymnasium for training in virtue.[35] Militia service teaches gentlemen to value arms as "the only true badges of liberty; and ought never, but in times of utmost necessity, to be put into the hand of mercenaries or slaves" (50).

Fletcher advocated universal military service for a period of two years. Properly the Spartan training would mandate that uniforms be plain and coarse and that the diet be bread and water. Swearing, gambling, and consorting with women would be severely punished; masturbation, sodomy, and homosexuality were to be punishable by death (58). In this "school of virtue" inculcating equality and discipline the youth would learn

> to stand in need of few things; to be content with that small allowance which nature requires; to suffer, as well as to act; to be modest, as well as brave; to be as much ashamed of doing anything insolent or injurious, as of turning their back upon an enemy. They would learn to forgive injuries done to themselves, but to embrace with joy the occasion of dying to revenge those done to their country. (64)

These sentiments about manly endeavor were inspired by the books of classical authors, which Fletcher read in the original languages. He admitted that no such behavior could be found in the camps of real armies, with the possible exception of Cromwell's. Fletcher did not conclude from this fact that Plutarch had perhaps dressed up his stories; instead, he believed that among moderns, virtue was distressed by all-sided corruption. The current education, he observed, "debauched" the minds of youth "from all duty and business to which they are born; and in the place of moral and civil knowledge and virtue, addict themselves

---

Government with Relation to Militias; there is no pagination for Lockhart's "Characters." Lockhart, it may be noted, was a Jacobite.

34. Ibid.

35. Fletcher, *Discourse of Government with Relation to Militias*, 49.

to mathematical, natural and metaphysical speculations" (379). Here was Cato's old accusation against schoolmasters and philosophers; an accusation that Rousseau voiced again at mid-century. Indeed, Rousseau shared Fletcher's anxiety that civilization itself was incompatible with virtue:

> Experience has taught us that no human prudence can preserve the manners of men living in great cities from extraordinary corruption; and that when great power, riches and numbers of men are brought together, they not only introduce a universal depravation of manners, but destroy all good government, and bring ruin and desolation upon a people. (371)

This is the Rustic's Perplexity. The liberty of Europe, Fletcher believed, was based on the "ancient constitution" established by Gothic tribes. In that arrangement, the king distributed lands to his warrior chieftains, the barons, who possessed them with their vassals. When the king required arms, he could have them only from the barons. This arrangement secured liberty "because the vassals depended more immediately on the barons than on the king, which effectively secured the freedom of those governments" (8). This free government, as Fletcher understood freedom, endured for a millennium, until the consolidation of monarchy was touched off by "the restoration of learning, the invention of printing, of the needle and of gunpowder" (11). Although Fletcher allowed these inventions to be excellent in themselves, they excited "man's natural propension to pleasure," which led in turn to enslavement by absolute monarchy. The progress of the arts, sciences, and commerce, then, generate a Polybian cycle dooming freedom and virtue—vigorous in the feudal system—to decay. This was disconcerting to Fletcher, who hoped to alleviate the poverty of Scotland by agricultural improvement; for the more improvement advanced, the more certainly virtue-blight must follow. Fletcher was troubled by another paradox as well. A consequence of the Polybian corruption is the decay of military valor, followed by exposure to foreign conquest. Yet France, that Sodom of depraved manners and absolutism, not only showed no sign of collapsing under the burden of vice, but bid fair to impose empire. This design was repeatedly thwarted by the Dutch, who were more advanced in the corrupting arts than any nation in Europe. The Netherlands defense force was composed of a reserve militia plus a professional army of about 20,000, supported by the most advanced technologies of the day. With a population only a third of England's, the Dutch fielded armies of 80,000 to 100,000, twice the size of the largest army ever raised in the virtuous nation. The Dutch also employed foreign mercenaries to good effect, although Machiavelli had dismissed them as useless. The Dutch were in addition the most free, prosperous, and money-grubbing people in the world. A totally corrupt people, then. Fletcher groped fitfully to understand why vice should be the cause of prosperity to foreigners but the nemesis of Britons.[36]

The institutional progress of enlightened political science is more readily appreciated by attending to the confusions it encountered and overcame. Fletcher's works enjoyed high standing among the English gentry because they confirmed a self-image of honor supported by a fictitious history drawn up from a gallimaufry of classical, medieval, and modern elements. Since it lacked a solid basis, it was unstable, and might lead anywhere. It took Fletcher into the company of Jacobites, although he had helped drive James from the throne. But it took the choleric Robert Molesworth in a different direction; he embraced the conquering virtuous republic, spreading its evangel of liberty:

> No man can be a sincere lover of liberty that is not for increasing and communicating that blessing to all people; and therefore the giving or restoring it not only to our brethren of Scotland and Ireland, but even to France itself, were it in our powers, is one of the principal articles of Whiggism.[37]

Charles Davenant

An exquisite expression of the Country *mentalité* as moral dilemma is in Charles Davenant's essays on the new commercial order. Davenant was

36. The Country writers formed no consistent or distinct opinion of Dutch institutions, although to be sure they had an ample supply of attitudes. During the de Witt era a number of authors emphasized the potency of the Dutch land force, e.g. the anonymous tract *The Dutch Drawn to Life* (1664), 48ff. In his *Observations on the United Provinces of the Netherlands* (1673) William Temple praised the power of the Dutch Army. The Country hatred of William and the "Dutch captivity" probably reflected the same wounded manliness that smoldered in the rhetoric of the Italia movement. The Dutch had *invaded* England and disarmed England's unresisting forces. It was a humiliation for the "true Briton." That, combined with the downgrading of the gentry in the Whig dispensation, would help explain the morbid obsession with virtue. For further discussion, see the afterword in this volume. On the marked anti-Dutch temper of Tory election propaganda, see James O. Richards, *Party Propaganda Under Queen Anne,* 39–40, 125.

37. Robert Molesworth, *The Principles of a Real Whig* (1711), 6–7 (1775 edition is

of an old family whose political connections might have lodged him with either Whigs or Tories. He held a number of government posts, mainly in Treasury, under the Junto and Godolphin governments, but never sat in Parliament. Davenant accepted trade as integral to English national existence. He accepted as well that liberty and prosperity are consistent; and he was unembarrassed to say that England's loss of liberty would ruin her prosperity.[38] An ardent monarchist, he identified public spirit with patriotic loyalty. These opinions might have been a formula for contentment in Whig England. But Davenant also espoused the opposite of these views and expressed them in somber tones. We must hear him:

> Trade, without doubt, is in its nature a pernicious thing; it brings in that wealth which introduces luxury; it gives a rise to fraud and avarice and extinguishes virtue and simplicity of manners; it depraves a people, and makes way for that corruption which never fails to end in slavery, foreign or domestic. Lycurgus, in the most perfect model of government that was ever framed, did banish it from his commonwealth. But, the posture and condition of other countries considered, 'tis become with us a necessary evil. We shall be continually exposed to insults and invasions without such a naval force, as is not to be had naturally but where there is an extended traffic. However, if trade cannot be made subservient to the nation's safety, it ought to be no more encouraged here than it was in Sparta; and it can never tend to make us safe, unless it be so managed as to make us increase in shipping.[39]

The ineluctable rotation of the Polybian cycle exacted from Davenant a documentation of its melancholy dilemmas. Trade promotes liberty and prosperity; but the law-givers of antiquity recognized that trade also introduces the vices that ruin liberty and prosperity. Anxiety about virtue's distress bullied Davenant into asserting, in an essay devoted to advocating methods of improving England's trade balance, that trade is "in its nature" pernicious. But it is a necessary evil; for England requires a navy to guard against French invasion; and it cannot raise a navy of the

---

cited). This tract was among the important statements of Whig republicanism in the post-Junto period. The political evangelism of Thomas Jefferson found its voice here.

38. Charles Davenant, *An Essay Upon the Probable Methods of Making a People Gainers in the Balance of Trade*, 135.

39. Ibid., 102.

requisite size without a large mercantile fleet; therefore, a condition upon English trade is that it must move in English bottoms. By such lateral thinking Davenant justified the Navigation Act.

Davenant's moral economy is dominated by obsession with the cyclic movement of virtue from *libertá* to *licensiositá*. Everywhere he saw virtue in decay. He was certain that the virtue of the nation reposed in the landed men; ardent for king and liberty, they exercised their wholesome influence in Parliament. Yet iniquity sent its harlots even into this sanctuary to corrupt the flower of the nation. The corruptor was none other than the hinge of the constitution, the king; and he compassed this evil by inviting landed men into his service in return for pay and preferments: he created placemen with money.[40]

Tableaux of crumbling virtue also dominated his views on foreign affairs. He believed that France was a new Persia aspiring to "universal monarchy" menacing Spartan England. The moral imperatives operating in England mandated that subservience entailed poverty and military weakness; but in France, enslaving absolutism produced wealth and might in disconcerting proportions. This cruel paradox suggested that England for its safety should ally with Holland against France. But alas, there was no safety here either, for Holland would infect Spartan England with its commercial vices:

> The busy men of the town . . . have a different interest from that of their country. They neither mind peace nor war, but as their bank, new or old East India stock, may be affected; the interest of Europe weighs nothing with them, in comparison with the interest upon their tallies; they think a high discompt upon Exchequer Bills, Bank Notes, Matt or Lottery Tickets, would be a worse consequence than the King of Spain's will. . . . They say, if we have peace, their stocks will rise in value; if a war comes, they can again bring money to thirty or forty per cent interest; so they shall find their profit either way.[41]

Here was patriotism and military valor ruined by the Dutch vice. Davenant did not pause to consider how, if this were true, Holland managed

---

40. Davenant, *Essays Upon the Ballance of Power, the Right of Making War, Peace, and Alliances, Universal Monarchy*, 2.

41. Ibid., 4–5. Davenant styled paper credit "imaginary wealth" and "chimerical treasure." J. G. A. Pocock ascribes to Davenant an epistemology of finance capital, based on the imaginary character of credit and mobile property and distinguished from the solidity of real property (*The Machiavellian Moment*, 439–41, 451–60).

to raise from its citizens large armies to oppose French force. He turned his mind instead to ponder that subject of dread to the Country writers—the new modeling of England on the Dutch pattern. What was one to think of the patriots who made the Revolution and cast England into the Dutch mold? For a brief moment, the cycle paused in the arc of generation: prosperity increased and England was confirmed as a world power. But "distempers" soon darkened the stage. The patriots were corrupted; they gave and received bribes, engrossed the places of profit, and corrupted the boroughs.[42] Finally untethered from virtue, the Junto Whigs "used their utmost endeavors to discountenance all revealed religion."[43] Amazed by this discovery, Davenant exclaimed, "What a strange mixture of men we have seen lately on the stage! Irreligious fanatics and arbitrary republicans!"

Davenant disburdened himself of these paradoxes a year later in a philippic that may count as the opening shot of what was to be four decades of violent pamphleteering. *The True Picture of a Modern Whig* exhibits the new men as nimble knaves who gloried in acting only for their private interest. The work was composed as a dialogue between an honest but naïve Old Whig and a New Whig, Tom Double. This is how Double explains himself:

> WHIGLOVE: It would serve as a good instruction if you would please to let me know how you did rise in the world. I am a gentleman born to some fortune and have good relations, yet I can do nothing, and rather grow worse than better in my estate, notwithstanding that all along I have been as hearty a Whig as the best of you.
>
> DOUBLE: That's true, but you have always been a Whig out of principle, and we have no regard for such people at all; they are volunteers that will serve us for nothing; we value none but those who are Whigs out of interest, and who like Captain Bessus in the play, are ready to do anything, good, bad, or indifferent, that may promote our designs. I'll lay you a guinea you think I was always a Whig.
>
> WHIGLOVE: Truly, sir, I ever took you for an original staunch Whig, and for one who despised the Church, and misliked kingly government from your very cradle.
>
> DOUBLE: Alas, you are utterly mistaken, and if you can make any profit from example, I will give you a short narrative of my whole life. I was first bound to a shoemaker in London, and

---

42. Davenant, *Essays Upon the Ballance of Power,* 33, 35, 45.
43. Ibid., 38.

being an impudent young rogue, I got into a gang of loyal apprentices that addressed to King Charles II, and I was one of those who were treated with Hyde Park venison at the Wonder Tavern. My Grandmother, who sold barley-broth and furmity by Fleetditch, died and left me three hundred pound, with which I set up for a gentleman and a spark; and I was so remarkable a Tory, that I got a place in customs of about a hundred pounds a year. But in King James' time, the Commissioners of the Customs detected me in a notorious fraud, and turned me out, upon which I became a malecontent. . . . I became a furious Whig. . . . I went to all the discontented clubs in town, where we drank confusion to the government, and talked treason dagger out of sheath.[44]

Double was a parvenu who migrated to Shaftesbury's party out of personal pique. Honest gentlemen who opposed arbitrary government and the standing army, who favored triennial Parliaments and impeachment of corrupt ministers, made the error of allying with such riffraff. They grabbed power after the Revolution, and then fleeced honest gentlemen, pillaged the Treasury, and betrayed all Revolution Principles. Davenant left no doubt that the corruption of the Whig party began with the Junto; or rather, with Shaftesbury's recruitment of the rabble to politics.[45]

The anxiety about virtue's decay expressed, in the vocabulary of an available political tradition, the apprehension of a ruling class whose dominance had been challenged. The revival of Sparta and Rome, the celebration of the ancient constitution, the opposition to professional armies and placemen—these reveries were an attempt to repossess in words the virtue that the Harringtonians thought they ought to possess. *Oceana* was born a fanciful anachronism that might warm the breast without very much enlightening practice. But until the Junto swept aside the Country version of Revolution Principles, the gentry could not know how marginal they were in the new order. The financial revolution of the 1690s administered the shock of recognition. In a decade the nation was transformed. England became Great Britain, with a permanent need for imperial arms and a large corps of government officers, tilting power toward the court. These changes were financed by a large national debt that committed the nation to commercial expansion

---

44. Davenant, *The True Picture of a Modern Whig*, 15–16.
45. Ibid., 33ff. The Junto also came under criticism in *Essays Upon the Ballance of Power,* for extravagance, misconduct of foreign policy, and setting up the institutions of public credit. See *Essays,* 50–51, 77, 81, 86ff., 92ff.

by mortgaging the future. Many of the gentry mortgaged their estates either to pay for luxuries or to improve their yields. On coming to London, they found the city abustle with new men acquiring wealth and wielding power in government, business, and finance. Dominant classes usually resent intruders; and the gentry, accustomed to think that positions of power and influence belonged to them by imprescriptable right, were mortified. Comparing their own imagined virtues with the character of the new men, they drew the all-too-human conclusion that the parvenus were worthless rogues while they themselves were pillars of integrity. This seems to have been the root experience calling up anxiety about virtue. It was certainly the experience that produced the gut reaction to which opposition rhetoric addressed its strongest appeal. The dialogue between Whiglove and Double identifies the gut reaction as self-righteous resentment that honest patriots should lose their status and patrimony to the likes of Double.

This attitude was the signature and spirit of opposition rhetoric. It was rebutted by government writers claiming that opposition grievances were malicious exaggerations. They attacked the opposition image of the stockjobber as a monster of avarice and deceit. Stockbrokers, they said, practiced an honorable profession incident to a market in stock and securities. Projectors, who were only a little higher in the nine circles of commercial iniquity described by Country writers, were stoutly defended for their vision, risk-taking entrepreneurship, and resourcefulness. Merchants were praised for their moderation, honesty, intelligence, and piety. And they turned their guns on the squires who launched the grievances. The *London Journal* quoted Locke's criticisms of Country indolence and extravagance and suggested that they should look to their own house before casting stones at others. Joseph Addison brought forward his enduring image of the rural statesman in fox-hunting garb, feared equally by his spaniels and servants, spouting prejudices in crude language. But to follow this side of "the paper war" is not our object.

John Trenchard

To sample resentment against the new men, we may examine John Trenchard's *Some Considerations upon the State of Our Publick Debts* (1723). Trenchard had co-authored "Cato's Letters" in the *London Journal* during the South Sea fraud, which he mightily castigated. Cato combined spleen with wit ("All men, as I humbly conceive, have an equal right to cheat the public"), engaging informality, and classicism. That combination won acclaim and wide circulation for the "Letters."

Some Considerations urged fiscal reform to cleanse the nation of corruption's blight. Parliament should establish a commission to audit all expenditures from the Exchequer and Civil List. Strict auditing would achieve more than economy in government. By eliminating hundreds of useless places, it would break the spine of the court oligarchy. Trenchard also proposed to eliminate placemen by making it treasonous for parliamentarians to receive "any pension, sum of money or other gratuity from the crown" (34). These proposals are supported by no factual analysis. A moment's thought shows that it cannot be criminal for a member of Parliament to engage with the Crown in an action that is not criminal for the latter. What would the law say if gratuities were conferred by royal command? Similarly, parliamentary audit of the Civil List would usurp the Crown's right to superintend its own monies. Thus both proposals were short on legal intelligence. Country propaganda tended toward rhetoric because fact, logic, and institutional analysis were low on its scale of values. At its best it was a literary language rich in metaphor, sounding phrases, and ardor. It was always moralistic. *Some Considerations* is typically moral: graft and peculation must be eliminated. Trenchard knew that they *could* be eliminated because ancient historians testified to their absence in ancient virtuous republics prior to the onset of corruption.

It was an ardent moralist, then, who contrasted gentlemen and the parvenus in the following ways:

What can be more invidious than for a nation, staggering under the weight and oppression of its debts, eaten up with usury, and exhausted with payments, to have the additional mortification of seeing private and worthless men riot in their calamities, and grow rich, whilst they grow poor; to see the two every day glittering with new and pompous equipages, whilst they are mortgaging and selling their estates; to see blazing meteors suddenly exhaled out of their jakes, and their mud (as in Egypt) warmed into monsters? (10)

* * * * *

In the prosperous condition of their affairs such a servile crew [of courtiers], like the scum of fermented liquors, will rise uppermost, and appear always in sight, haunting their courts, flattering their persons, indulging their vices, and promoting their expenses; whilst wise and good men, conscious of their own virtue, and abilities, will expect to be sought after, tho' are seldom enquired for, till the remedy is too late, and 'tis out of their power to help the prince, and save their country. (27)

* * * * *

Men who are contented in their own obscurity, when they see worthlessness rewarded and bought up at a high price, will put in their claim too; and think themselves upon a level in merit with those that have none, and so ruin themselves and country in spite, if they are not gratified. (29)

* * * * *

I wish [courtiers] would not spend all their time in [Exchange] Alley, or in carousing with one another over champagne and burgundy, but would now and then descend to drink a cup of ale in the company of poor dispised and mortgaged country gentlemen, where it may be of use to them to hear other language. It's true their ears will be offended with the unusual and ungrateful [tales] of extortion and bribery, of juggling bargains made between former ministers and stockjobbers; money then borrowed by the same persons in one capacity and lent in another; desperate debts bought up by confederacy for trifling sums, and then made good; public money got into private hands, and then lent to the public again for great premiums, and at great interest, and afterward squandered away to make room for new projects. (7)

The discussion of Colbert's administration notes that his commercial politics attracted the hatred of landed men unwilling or unable to adjust *noblesse* to new national requirements. Their refusal to assume a new kind of leadership, as polytechnic gentlemen, was a partial cause of the strife that followed the overthrow of monarchy. In Trenchard's acrimonious, unsubstantiated accusations—proud men do not stoop to proof—there is a like stubbornness that he admitted might seem to betray spite, envy, and disaffection.[46] It is instructive to note that the initial phase of "capitalism" generated a class antagonism and that publicists writing as spokesmen for the rightful governing class were not only envious of the new men, but cast themselves in the posture of exploited victims of what came to be called "finance capital." Although these facts are well documented,[47] they have not received an interpretation that

46. *Some Considerations*, 8, where Trenchard wrote: "How unreasonable so ever these suggestions and discourses are, (which perhaps may be said to proceed from emulation, envy, and often from disaffection) yet 'tis certain they come from those who have, and always will have, a great share in our legislature, in spite of all that can be done to prevent it." Trenchard clearly did not foresee the changes that the commercial republic would work.

47. The class feeling of "rural statesmen" was criticized and lampooned by numerous authors of the day, e.g. Addison, Defoe, and Mandeville. Representative of this genre is the anonymous *A brief history of trade in England. By a*

brings out their entire significance. The needed interpretation would not be historical but psychological.[48] In the present context it may be emphasized that the Country lament was moral aggression against men perceived to be rivals in power, and winners (exploiters) to boot. Although the aggression was packaged as action for the public good against men who acted only from private interest, factual assessments of the public good were not brought forward to support these claims. As we have seen, such policy recommendations as they did make were wind eggs, which as policy would have put the nation at risk. Similarly, Country issues were usually jeremiads. Jonathan Swift led the successful campaign against Wood's halfpenny, which denied Ireland a needed recoinage; the sensation of Jenkins's ears pushed England into war with Spain; the legend of £35 million embezzled by evil ministers fortified indignation for decades despite its repeated rebuttal. Long after these events, Horace Walpole reflected upon them in a quiet moment:

> Last night at Strawberry Hill, I took up, to divert my thoughts, a volume of letters to Swift from Bolingbroke, Bathurst, and Gay and what was there but lamentations on the ruin of England, in that era of prosperity and peace, from wretches who thought their own want of power a proof that their country was undone! Oh, my father! Twenty years of peace, and credit, and happiness, and liberty, were punishments to rascals who weighted everything in the scales of self.[49]

Walpole's Party Politics

Modern parties are composed of people who, aggregated by enduring interests, seek to promote them by dominating government. Since in-

---

merchant (1702), whose author stated that contempt of tradesmen and merchants betrays failure to appreciate that their activities create the luxuries gentlemen adore (106–7). And then, putting in the knife, he dismissed the pretensions of birth by remarking that nine out of ten of England's gentry stem from artisans and tradesmen (109). For observations on the envy of the "declining gentry," see J. H. Plumb, *Sir Robert Walpole*, 1: 20; Isaac Kramnick, *Bolingbroke and His Circle*, 56–62; H. T. Dickinson, *Bolingbroke*, 208ff.; J. M. Robertson, *Bolingbroke and Walpole*, 126–33; P. G. M. Dickson, *The Financial Revolution*, 29, 33–35.
48. See the afterword in this volume.
49. Quoted by H. T. Dickinson, *Bolingbroke*, 210.

terests are tangible activities of acquisition or advance, party allegiance cuts across the lines of religion, class, and locality. To that extent the orientation of parties is cosmopolitan.

Country Whig political thought expressed a class conception of politics in which landed men ranked as moral patrons of the polity. In their world, mere interest was plebeian. What counted was the goodness embodied in the judgment and action of virtuous men. The exercise of virtue was held to be the purpose of government. The notion that politics might or should be regulated by party was repugnant, since it implied the dominance of gross interestedness to the detriment of the elevated view of the social order from atop the Great Chain of Being, which assigned a ranked value to each class and individual.

The clash between these conflicting concepts of government was the point at issue in the long duel between Robert Walpole and Bolingbroke. The contest commenced in 1726 when Bolingbroke and William Pulteney established *The Craftsman* as a journal of opinion to oppose the Walpole government. *The Craftsman* defined itself as a public-spirited, nonparty censor of political morality. Each issue was a sermon on corruption and maladministration. It eschewed the informational content common among journals of the day, i.e. news of commerce, the colonies, scientific and technical discoveries, and current events. The programmatic manifesto of 1731 accurately described what the journal had been and would continue to be: an organ pledged to patriotic opposition to party spirit, to the defense of liberty against the menace of corruption; to the defense of prosperity against the extravagance of government; and to the defense of the Church.[50] The journal's success formula was to rehearse tirelessly the Country opinions previously reviewed. Thus readers were regaled with the idea that "money is the root of all evil."[51] Money was the means whereby the plebeian invaders exercised their dominance. Bribery corrupted the gentry; sinecures maintained the influence of the court over Parliament. This conception defined *The*

50. *The Craftsman*, 1731, "To the People of England," vi–xxi. Bolingbroke put forth the same program, unchanged, in *The Idea of a Patriot King* (1735).

51. *The Craftsman*, 1726, nos. 5, 12; 1727, no. 172. The crudity of *The Craftsman's* ideas and invective is best appreciated by comparison with the political prints of the day. They were gross, the iconographic repertory being substantially oriented toward scatological references. The prints have been systematically studied by Herbert M. Atherton, *Political Prints in the Age of Hogarth*. Other useful sources on journalism during the Walpole era are Bertrand A. Goldgar's *Walpole and the Wits: The Relation of Politics to Literature, 1722–1742* and W. A. Speck's essay "Political Propaganda in Augustan England." This research is essential to any assessment of the contents of the Augustan mind.

Craftsman's view of the party. Party was equated with private interest, in opposition to the patriotic public spirit assumed to be the natural inheritance of the gentry. Party was therefore an index of virtue's decay.

The Craftsman's interpretation of Britain's recent party history followed from such ideas. The Whig and Tory appellations, it maintained, were a smokescreen used by "Robinarchs," i.e. Walpole's men, to conceal corruption behind specious principle. Whig and Tory had been relevant only during the Exclusion controversy and again in 1688, when the constitutional principle of liberty had been at issue. "Whig" had not designated an aggregate of interests organized for the conduct of government, but a patriotic assertion of constitutional and moral principle at a critical political moment. This principle was the Old Whig or Country legacy, which *The Craftsman,* in company with most of Walpole's opponents, identified as the authentic political heritage of Britain.[52]

This identification was at stake in the debate over the ancient constitution conducted by *The Craftsman* with Walpole's magazine, the *London Journal*. Ancient-constitution thinking, we have seen, located political norms in the primitive political practice of the Britons—their Witenagemot or Parliament. All subsequent political history was construed as a genealogy from the original heritage. The story read as a history of oscillations away from liberty into despotism and corruption, and recoveries from these declines. Ancient-constitution theory, in other words, was the Polybian cycle or Machiavellian renewal. Bolingbroke's political thought was completely in tow to this conception. In *Letters on History* and *Remarks on the History of England,* he identified the reign of Queen Elizabeth as the modern embodiment of virtuous liberty, and the Whig Junto as the great corruptor of political virtue.

The *London Journal*[53] took on *The Craftsman* with great zest. It dis-

52. Bolingbroke, *Works,* 3: 4, 43ff., 126, 132ff. Bolingbroke was anxious to have an interpretation of parties that eliminated Tories, since that appellation was his albatross. He maintained that Whig and Tory became obsolete upon the Settlement, since it determined the legitimacy question to which "Whig" and "Tory" pertained. But the Junto Whigs kept these terms alive to cloak their ambition. The real division, Bolingbroke held, was between Court and Country. This analysis conveniently forgot the Jacobites. It also overlooked the fact that London municipal politics would not classify into these categories, nor, for that matter, into Whig and Tory.

53. Walpole bought the *London Journal* in 1721 and turned it from a Country to a Court publication. This did not require any change of personnel, for journalists had become professionals and could write for either side. Daniel Defoe, the preeminent journalist of the day, excelled also in this flexibility. See David Stevens, *Party Politics and English Journalism,* 37, 40, 46–55, 60, 100.

missed the appeal to patriotism as the rant of disaffection. In one of its mischievous sallies, it quipped that "methinks the child of liberty should not always be crying."[54] *The Craftsman* was cruelly vulnerable on the patriotism issue owing to Bolingbroke's conviction for Jacobite treason. His claim to be the authentic spokesman of the principles of the Revolution Settlement was accordingly not difficult to discredit. It might be that Walpole secured Bolingbroke's pardon and readmission to England just for this reason. Without a Bolingbroke on the scene, the political struggle over the legacy of 1688 was between the virtuous republic notions of the Country Whigs and the commercial republic notions of the Court Whigs. It would be much easier to disburden himself of Country doctrine if he could brand it as Tory; and there was no doubt that Bolingbroke had been a great Tory. His readmission to England, permanently debarred from office, created for Walpole the ideal solution of an opposition led by a man identified with a party whose legitimacy had been repudiated.[55] Well might the Country Whigs complain of being branded Tories: but the admission of Bolingbroke to their company enabled the Walpole propaganda machine to make the label stick.

The *London Journal* forthrightly defended the concept of party. "'Tis so far from being a reproach, 'tis an honor to us; and shows, that we have a sense of liberty and public virtue."[56] The *Journal* traded heavily

54. Quoted by Isaac Kramnick, *Bolingbroke and His Circle*, 133. On complaining as a strategy for promoting political disaffection, see Hiram Caton, "Whingeing," *Quadrant* 26 (January 1982): 45–49. Bolingbroke's endless winter of discontent prompted J. M. Robertson to observe: "We feel that he exemplifies the force of waste and frustration in things; that no more than his corivals, and much less than Walpole, did he see life steadily or whole; that his inner light was ever darkened by the smoke of his egotism; that between his flaws and his evil circumstance his work was largely fitted to be cast as rubbish into the void" (*Walpole and Bolingbroke*, 79; also 134–35).

55. The story of the mechanics of Bolingbroke's pardon has not in my opinion been correctly told. According to William Coxe, the decision was not Walpole's but the king's, or rather Lady Kendall's, who is supposed to have taken an £11,000 gift from Bolingbroke in return for influencing the king (*Memoires of the Life and Administration of Sir Robert Walpole*, 1: 365ff.). This is improbable. The readmission of Bolingbroke to Hanoverian England was a decision of the first magnitude, and George left political decisions to Walpole. When he took the bill of pardon into Parliament, Walpole received a tremendous thumping from anti-Jacobites and from colleagues who thought his judgment quite unbalanced. But if Walpole recognized the consequences I have described, this momentary cost was more than offset by the long-term gain. For J. H. Plumb's account of this affair, see his *Sir Robert Walpole*, 2: 69.

56. *London Journal*, 1734, no. 786. A bibliography of government tracts on party is contained in Archibald Foord, *His Majesty's Opposition*, 153.

on the one sense of party respectability acknowledged by most Englishmen. Writing on this matter in 1742, David Hume said that

> There are few men of knowledge or learning, at least, few philosophers, since Mr. Locke wrote, who would not be ashamed to be thought of [the Tory] party; and in almost all companies that name of Old Whig is mentioned as an uncontestable appellation of honor and dignity.[57]

The problem was the construction to be placed upon the consensus for constitutional liberty: was its basis to be interest or virtue? Walpole's strategy was to discredit virtue by branding it a Tory. This is especially clear from the debate between the two journals over the ancient constitution. *The Craftsman* and the Old Whigs held that liberty was maintained by virtue, and that virtue was something primeval and enduring. The Court position, by contrast, was Lockean, for it held that liberty was the function of constitutional arrangements that replaced virtue by calculable interests.[58] Consequently the *Journal* took the view that the liberties of Englishmen dated from the Revolutionary Settlement. All notions that liberty was of ancient vintage were disparaged as "heroic tales." It declared the "first principles" of English government to be "absolute slavery. The primitive purity of our constitution was that the people had no share in government, but were the villains, vassals, or bondsmen of the lords: a sort of cattle to be bought and sold."[59] It followed that Machiavellian renewals were nonsense: "A renewal of what? A renewal of a nonentity. We never before had a constitution as was settled at the Revolution. . . . new England, or the present state of things caused by the Revolution, as far exceeds the old, as light does darkness, as liberty does slavery; or as happiness does misery."[60] Liberty

---

57. Hume, *Philosophical Works*, 3: 143.
58. This point has been emphasized by Isaac Kramnick: "The basic positions of Walpole's political thought, as articulated by his publicists, were derived from the writings of John Locke. An important position was thus achieved for Locke's ideas when they were given the official stamp of the government and the Whig Establishment. Cited in Walpole's press, Locke's ideas became part of the general political debate for large numbers at the level of the coffee house" (*Bolingbroke and His Circle*, 117).
59. *London Journal*, 1 September 1733, no. 740.
60. *Daily Gazetteer*, 23 August 1735, no. 48. For a discussion of this debate, see Kramnick, *Bolingbroke and His Circle*, 127–36; also Duncan Forbes, *Hume's Philosophical Politics*, 233–62. Hume, of course, rejected the ancient constitution theory, and wrote his *History of England* partly to discredit it. See Pocock, *The Machiavellian Moment*, 493–94.

meant the rule of law in contradistinction to the appetites and unreasonable passions such as were so apparent in *The Craftsman*'s attempt to sow disaffection.[61]

Walpole himself defended the party principle in a notable speech on yet another place bill in 1740. By that time the term "opposition" had firmed into the concept "The Opposition." Two years later, the spatial reference of this concept to the opposing benches in Parliament came into use.[62] The moment was opportune for a statement on party. Walpole maintained that party was incident to liberty. For in all matters that "do not admit of demonstration, there must be a variety of opinions"; and when men are at liberty to judge, a host of opinions give wings to the variety of interests. In political society the fact of government polarizes opinion into government and opposition factions because the exercise of government power inevitably benefits some more than others. The root of party, then, is the fact of government.[63]

Country thinkers could not accept this view. Their notion was that if "evil counsellors" were dismissed and replaced by "men of ability," all faction and dissension would cease.[64] Walpole dismissed this opinion as bombast. In language reminiscent of Hobbes on endeavor for power, and Locke on the "uneasiness" that goads men ceaselessly to augment their power, Walpole maintained that discontent would raise a party against the wisest government:

61. Rule of law in a decidedly Lockean vein was frequently the subject of *Journal* harangues. Thus: "The rights of the people (for the sake of securing which all government was instituted) consists in framing their own constitution, and choosing their own governors. When the constitution is broke through, or dissolved, by wrong use of power in the hands of the chief magistrate, then the power that was originally derived from the people reverts to them" (1 September 1733, no. 740; see also nos. 552, 557, 744, 745). The virtue of the Country party was denounced as bombast and pretense. Thus: "These men, under the marks of piety and rigid virtue, are only satisfying their natural appetites, or gratifying their unreasonable passions" (30 May 1730, no. 565). Pocock accurately summarizes the Court position in the following terms: "In place of virtue it stressed the ego's pursuit of satisfaction and self-esteem. . . . Since it did not regard virtue as political paradigmatic, it did not regard government as founded upon principles of virtue which needed to be regularly reasserted; it readily accepted that men were factious and interested beings and, instead of regarding these characteristics as fatal if unchecked to [*sic*] virtue and government, proposed to have them policed by a strong central executive" (*The Machiavellian Moment*, 487).

62. Foord, *His Majesty's Opposition*, 153–57.

63. This speech is printed in *Parliamentary History*, vol. 2, cols. 363–66. I am quoting from J. A. W. Gunn's edited volume on party, *Factions No More*.

64. The "evil counsellors" theory is summarized by Foord, *His Majesty's Opposi-*

All men feel some wants, pressures, or misfortunes; and very few are willing to impute them to their own folly, or to any mistake in their conduct. To such men, the administration is in politics, what the devil is in religion; it is the author of all their misdeeds, and the cause of all their sufferings.[65]

One sees that Walpole fashioned his rhetoric to fit his conception: moralizing idealism is brought back to earth by measured portions of cynical realism. In a passage that smacks of Hobbes's tart phrases, Walpole declared:

In all countries it is honorable to have a share in the government of one's country: in rich countries, it is profitable as well as honorable; and as there are but a very few in any country that can have a share of the government, and still fewer that can have such a share as they think they deserve, there must be many candidates for every title of honor, or post of profit, that is to be disposed of. Of these candidates, one only can be chosen, and all the rest will, of course, think they have had injustice done them; for few men are so modest as to think such a disappointment owing to their own want of merit, or to the superior merit of their rival; and from thence they will begin to entertain a secret animosity.[66]

Monarchists seek their advantage by appealing to the monarchical component of the constitution, while republicans seek theirs by appeal to the popular element. It is in the nature of the constitution that the government party seeks to balance between these two elements; for the interest of the government party is the continuance of the regime, which would be destroyed were the balance destroyed. The government party must indeed seek this balance to govern at all; for it governs by commanding a majority in Parliament; and it can command majority assent to the wisdom and justice of its policy only by satisfying the *interests* of the majority. From the fact of government, then, Walpole fashioned a handle on the problem of insatiable desire that Hobbes could solve only through the fiat of an absolute sovereign. Although few are ever satisfied with what they have, the Ins can recognize that they are advantaged

---

tion, 37–42, 103–6, 151ff. The theory heightens the lash of faction by accusing persons rather than contesting policy.

65. Quoted by Gunn, *Factions No More*, 128.

66. Hume analyzed parties along similar lines in his essay "Of the Original Contract," in *Works*, 3: 443–59.

relative to the Outs, and that it is in their advantage to collaborate, as a party, to keep the Outs out.[67] A common interest is thus created in political society in a way analogous to the state of nature: just as society, though imperfect, is better than the natural condition, so collaboration in party is preferable to having nothing at all.

The analysis holds regardless of which party of principle might obtain the government. Republicans cannot be wholly republican, nor monarchists wholly royal, without destroying the government from which they benefit. If, moved by enthusiasm or ambition, either party attempted to make the government wholly republican or wholly monarchical, it would be resisted by the Outs; for under the Settlement, Englishmen have the *right*, and the wherewithal of liberty and property, to resist arbitrary and despotic power. Reducing this to the compass of Walpole's speech, the guarantee of balance is the permanence of opposition inherent in the constitution. The constitution is a self-adjusting mechanism precisely because of the perpetuity of party.[68]

This is not to say that the mechanism is indestructible. Forceful combinations of panic, ambition, ignorance, or false accusations might throw sand in the gears. In explaining the dynamics of the constitution to Parliament with a view to defeating a place bill which he contended would unbalance the constitution, Walpole implied that the constitution would be unworkable if there were not, somewhere in it, a conjunction between political science and the power of interest. He also implied that the conjunction happened at that time to exist in the government, yet he emphasized that the claim to political knowledge must

67. Walpole's achievement as a spokesman for party was to legitimate a kind of reasoning that had previously had the quality of intrigue. Thus, Sir John Perceval, in a letter to George Berkeley (31 August 1714), wrote: "There can justly be no reason to keep up our divisions when the King is once happily seated on the throne, but . . . parties are exceeding high, and the disdain to see the opposite side enjoy most favour, together with the practices of some leading Tories who have no preferment and now despair of any or think to lose those they have, will certainly occasion the continuance of our parties for some time" (quoted by Foord, *His Majesty's Opposition*, 41). Similarly, the duke of Newcastle wrote to Stanhope (October 1719): "The great point I think we ought to aim at is, that there should be but two parties, that for and against the Government" (ibid., 65).

68. Walpole managed to make his concept of party prevail to the extent that by 1747 the Tory publicist James Hampton embraced it in his *A Parallel Between the Roman and British Constitution*, discussed by Foord, *His Majesty's Opposition*, 268. In the reign of George III, the party principle was confounded by George's attempt to replace party by the rule of virtue.

appear contentious because "questions of a political nature are less capable of demonstration than any other." Walpole went on to explain why this is so: vanity, especially the vanity of seeming wise, makes men obtuse toward political knowledge. The maintenance of the constitution under the Settlement thus required a coalition between knowledge and interest in order to give knowledge political effect. But this is to say that knowledgeable men must become "interested," i.e. party men. Walpole implied that he was such a man. It was superfluous for him to emphasize that he was the chieftain of the party that made political enlightenment fundamental to its program. One of the founders of that party, John Locke, had been the foremost enlightener of his age; and the Walpole press cultivated that legacy.

chapter 8

"This Progress of the Arts and Sciences . . ."

IN 1756, a symptomatic if minute outrage occurred at Cambridge University when the dissertation of William Bell was awarded the Townshend Prize for the best essay on population and trade.

Charles Townshend had established the prize to encourage public awareness of the importance of trade, especially the important role that population mobility played in trade expansion. Townshend had been a leader in the drive to allow continental immigrants into England and to grant citizenship to Jews. The Naturalization Bill had passed in 1753, but reaction by clergymen, the gentry, and artisans obtained its repeal in the next Parliament. These conflicts registered the tremors of cosmopolitan commercialism colliding with village xenophobia. Townshend, whose family had been politically allied with the Walpoles for three generations, was among those who helped to fashion laws that gradually reformed English institutions into the mold of the enlightened commercial republic.[1]

The most consistent institutional opposition to this progress came from the universities. I previously emphasized the hostility of the universities to the small islands of science that for a time were established. By the late 1660s, all trace of the Wilkins group had vanished at Oxford. Something more might have been hoped for at Newton's old college, Trinity at Cambridge. The Maths Tripos was introduced, and students

---

1. Townshend's son, Lord Shelbourne, was a patron of the Lunar Society and a principal advocate of electoral reform.

long-suffering enough to endure the curmudgeon Master Richard Bentley might learn that the New Testament text had had to be constructed from manuscripts flawed by 2,000 variants and lacunae. But these small mercies were offset by impediments. Bentley lacked vision and leadership. Most of his four-decade tenure was occupied with legal proceedings brought by his Fellows, who wished to remove him for his abundant malfeasance. Newton's legacy at Cambridge evaporated in such pedantic squabbles.[2] But it reappeared at Oxford, where Newton's protégé Dr. John Keil, and Keil's successor, J. T. Desaguliers, for many years taught a course in theoretical and applied physics. The published version of Desaguliers' lectures, *A Course of Experimental Philosophy* (1734), was the major engineering text until it was superseded by the writings of John Smeaton.[3]

Walpole understandably had no wish to stir the pedagogues. He confined his efforts to creating a Whig majority of bishops in Lords and to controlling church patronage through his appointee, Archbishop Gibson, who was content with modest reforms. But in the event, clerical social grooming prevailed against these pressures. Science drifted to the

2. The absence of science at Oxford and Cambridge has been amply documented by the many annalists of the universities. See particularly D. A. Winstanly, *Unreformed Cambridge*, Christopher Wordsworth, *Scholae Academicae: Some Account of Studies at the English Universities in the Eighteenth Century*, and Robert T. Gunther, *Early Science in Cambridge*. For more recent studies, see Robert G. Frank, Jr., "Science, Medicine and the Universities of Early Modern England: Background and Sources, Part II," 239–69; and A. E. Musson and Eric Robinson, *Science and Technology in the Industrial Revolution*, 10–59.

3. Keil, who was Savilian professor at Oxford, was a close associate of Newton. He defended Newton's priority claim for discovery of the calculus, and he put the Newtonian position in the controversy over the history of the earth. In the preface of his book, Desaguliers described the apostolic succession linking himself to Newton through Keil; he also asserted that Locke was the first to teach the Newtonian physics. This curiosity is not so eccentric as first appears. Desaguliers purported to give the inside story on the Descartes-Newton-Locke combine. Descartes presented a cosmology, but it was only a scientific fable. Newton refuted this fable, but offered no cosmology of his own. The correct cosmology is based on Cartesian principles ("nature knows no bounds," and matter is infinitely divisible) articulated as an atomistic cosmology operating under Newtonian laws (Desaguliers, *A Course*, 2–27). Readers are informed that Newton always aimed at applied science (as had Descartes), which can come only from experimental science (67–69). It would seem that Locke taught Newtonian physics implicitly in the *Essay*. Desaguliers, a Huguenot, was an ardent Freemason.

Scottish universities, while the classics survived at Oxford and Cambridge to lead the fight against Darwin.

In that context, the Townshend Prize was a small effort to encourage freer spirits. The prize committee showed what it thought of the intrusion by selecting for distinction a dissertation that repudiated commercial values in the name of the Spartan ideal. "The only way to become free, virtuous, and happy," Bell advised, "is to renounce commerce and the arts, and to stick only at tillage and husbandry. I advise you therefore to leave your smokey cities, your trades and manufactures, and to build huts in the country." Englishmen were admonished to "burn all your ships," to renounce luxuries and "imaginary wants."[4] This policy would rapidly increase population because the healthier agrarian life would enhance fertility. When the numbers became too great, they might be reduced again by the reintroduction of commerce. This persiflage was the Cambridge response to Townshend, and a message to others who might be tempted to prod the universities out of their aggressive medievalism.

Bell's polemic against cosmopolitanism and urbanization was timely. In 1751, the first volumes of Diderot's *Encyclopédie* rolled from the press bearing a library of information on the arts and sciences, with advice on their increase. Three years later, Lord Folkestone and William Shipley founded the Society for the Encouragement of the Arts, Manufactures, and Commerce, known as the Society of Arts. In the colonies, Ben Franklin established the American Philosophical Society in 1769. These were straws in the wind that in the 1780s was to bring the most fundamental and portentous of all Baconian projects, systematic linkage between science and industry on a commercial basis. This was the development to be sketched in the present chapter.

The development may be pictured as traveling along two axes. One was the deeds and projects of the men who brought it to pass; the other was the environment of policy formation, foresight, and legitimation within which action occurred. A few individuals, notably C. L. Berthollet and Ben Franklin, were effective along both axes; but mostly

4. William Bell, *A Dissertation on 'What Causes Principally Contribute to Render a Nation Populous, and What Effect Has the Population of a Nation on Its Trade,'* 2. Bell's dissertation was answered by William Temple in *A Vindication of Commerce and the Arts, Proving that they are the source of the greatness, power, riches and populousness of a state* (1758). Temple was furious about the award of the Townshend Prize to Bell, but even more furious that Bell's opinions should enjoy currency at Cambridge. "What politicians are they like to turn out," he asked, "when the first university of Europe can give the stamp of approbation to such crude and superficial performance?" (*A Vindication,* xiv).

there was a division of labor. The case for the expansion of the arts and sciences was put by many writers. David Hume's reflections were outstanding for their range and succinctness, as well as for a decisive incompleteness made good by Diderot and the encyclopedists. At about the same time, Rousseau penned a memorable attack upon the progress of the arts and sciences. These evaluations and policy proposals were taken up by men who led modernizing revolutions in America and France.

Hume's Argument for the Arts and Sciences

When Hume arrived in Paris as secretary of the British Embassy, he was lionized as his nation's leading philosopher and as a citizen of the world. The philosophes did not mistake their man. Few could match Hume's grasp of the essentials of European politics and culture as they stood circa 1750. Upon his return from Paris, he found that London had fallen further into the torpor that overtook it in the late 1740s. He removed to Edinburgh and supervised the building of his house in St. David Street, an odd choice. Throughout his mature years Hume took an active, sometimes leading role in Scottish societies founded to promote industrial applications of science. Some of the men with whom he met in these associations, particularly the Philosophical Society of Edinburgh, promoted the linkage between science and industrial technology.[5] The autumn years he lived as the amiable, unpretentious philosopher who helped inspire the Scottish Enlightenment. Having lived without benefit of clergy, he died in the same way, cheerful and without dread, to the dismay of Samuel Johnson.

In recent decades a rumor that Hume was a Tory has spread through the historical literature. Since the rumor is symptomatic of some uncertainty about Whigs and Tories, we must address it briefly. The source of the rumor is the reaction of some Whigs to his *History of England*, where Hume discarded the myth of the ancient constitution and, with it, the Country Whig dogma that Stuart kings governed despotically. This led to his being stigmatized as an "atheistical Jacobite."[6] The usual Country muddle was at work here. As we have seen, the ascription of English liberties to the ancient constitution was the Country Whig position, whereas Court Whigs denied that the ancient constitution

5. Hume organized the Select Society, which grew from an initial fifteen members to more than three hundred. He was a member of the Poker Club (devoted to political discussion) and exercised considerable influence upon similar societies in Glasgow and Aberdeen without being a member. See Ernest Mossner, *The Life of David Hume*, 272–73, 281–84.

6. Ibid., 309–10. Hume took no part in Jacobite or any other politics.

guaranteed any liberties, all of which they ascribed to the Settlement and Revolution Principles. Hume's study endorsed the Court Whig position by refusing to reprobate the Stuarts; and he explicitly asserted that the Revolution Settlement was "the firmest foundation of English liberty."[7] When he learned of his supposed Toryism, he declared that "with regard to politics and the character of princes and great men, I think I am very moderate. My views of *things* are more conformable to Whig principles; my representations of *persons* to Tory prejudices."[8] Hume wrote agreeably to Tory prejudice by denying that the Stuarts were tyrants. He wrote contrary to Tory and Country Whig prejudice in declining to condemn Walpole as a monster of corruption and constitutional mayhem. He declared that the only "great error" of Walpole's administration was his failure to reduce the national debt farther than he did.[9]

Hume was an Enlightenment thinker and cosmopolitan Whig. He promoted the Enlightenment program but entered a *caveat emptor* after reflecting upon its progress. He was more circumspect than Locke, and much more cautious than the philosophes, about the power of rationally contrived institutions to shape or constrain irrational passions. This is the key to his political moderation, to his unzealous monarchism, to his apprehension that republican politics might become the vehicle of a new fanaticism. It may also account for Hume's novel conceptualization of the politics of progress. Thinkers from Bacon to Locke emphasized that progress depended upon opportune moments when

7. Hume, *Philosophical Works*, 3: 138. See the endorsement of the Court Whig position in his essay "Of the Protestant Succession," where he attributes the growth of English liberty and the prosperity of the arts, sciences, and commerce to the change of dynasty, whose significance lay not in the elimination of wicked Stuarts but in the new policies brought in by the Junto Whigs. Hume, *Philosophical Works*, 3: 470–79, especially 475–76. In *Hume's Philosophical Politics*, Duncan Forbes observes that Hume rejected the linchpin of Country politics, "that Machiavellian moralism, or political pathology concerned with the degree of corruption and lack of public spirit in the state" (224–25), and accepted the converse Lockean premise that institutions are critical to politics (227). Hume was regarded as the heir of Hobbes and Mandeville (Mossner, *Life of David Hume*, 139–223).
8. Hume believed that "gradual improvements" are far preferable to "violent innovations." This preference is reflected in his belief that opinion, not science, is the final arbiter in politics (Hume, *Philosophical Works*, 3: 157, 452, 460).
9. Ibid., 45. Hume's brief, even-handed "Character of Sir Robert Walpole" was withdrawn after being published in two editions of his essays. The brevity of the essay, and its subsequent withdrawal, imply that only those judgments made of Walpole in other essays represent Hume's considered opinion.

men seized the occasion to remodel institutions according to rational design. A new beginning in the sciences was one model of a radical break with the past; another was the representation of political society as sharply distinguished from "the state of nature." The emphasis on rupture and reform implied that progress was to be conceived, in the manner of the *Encyclopedia*, as the progress of the mind (*l'esprit*) exercising its influence like some demiurge operating on resistant matter. Hume was dissatisfied with this model. He was more impressed by the prospect that the achievements of a Galileo or a Hobbes stood little chance of cultural uptake unless there was some nonrational force impelling irrational passion toward rationality despite itself. One may say that Hume took the politics out of progress by conceiving it as a gradual process of advancing civilization, of which the development of rational politics is itself a part.[10] Hume did not give this process a name, although he discussed its mental vehicle—habit—at length. I will call it "domesticating the passions."

Testimony to the existence of this process was what Hume took to be conclusive evidence that modern Europeans were "milder"—less ferocious and erratic—than ancient men. Thanks to the gradual domestication of the passions under the influence of continuous civilization, political maxims valid in antiquity were invalid for moderns, and conversely. The chief instance of this change was the alteration that the relation between political power and commerce had undergone since antiquity. In modern states, political power and liberty were not only compatible with commerce and consumerism ("luxury"), they depended on them; but in antiquity, the growth of commerce and luxury were usually fatal to power and to liberty.[11] Ancient moralists stigmatized luxury as vice ruinous to liberty. And so it was in the setting of ancient republics, where manners were coarse, brutality was commonplace, and the arts still rudimentary. To express Hume's thought in contemporary

10. The gradualist, social-process concept of progress was understood and applied by the encylopedists as well. In the article *Représentants,* Diderot wrote: "The necessity of circumstances forces political ideas and institutions to change; morals are softened; iniquity perishes of itself; tyrants of the people perceive by and by that their follies are contrary to their own interests; commerce and manufacture become necessary for the state, and demand tranquillity; wars are less necessary; frequent dearth and famine make one sensible of the need for good agriculture." However, unlike Hume, the encyclopedists had a sense of the importance of "violent innovations."

11. See "Of Commerce," "Of the Rise and Progress of the Arts and Sciences," and "Of Refinement in the Arts," all in volume 3 of Hume's *Philosophical Works.*

idiom: ancient states were "developing nations" whose political coherence—such as it was—depended on austerities that are unnecessary and undesirable in advanced nations. The main points of his description of ancient politics are these:[12]

12. This summary is drawn from "Of the Populousness of Ancient Nations." Hume's analysis focused on the Greek cities. Montesquieu drew similar conclusions from his less detailed analysis of the Roman polity in his *Considerations on the Causes of the Greatness of the Romans and Their Decline,* chaps. 1, 2, 6. Montesquieu stated that "since Rome was a city without commerce, and almost without arts, pillage was the only means individuals had of enriching themselves . . . Rome was therefore in an endless and constantly violent war" (chap. 1). This opinion prompted his criticism of heroic virtue (see Thomas L. Pangle, *Montesquieu's Philosophy of Liberalism,* 68, 76, 80–90). The *Encyclopedia* published a slashing attack on classical political models in the article "Œconomie politique" (by Boulanger). During the height of the French Revolution, the classicist Count Volney wrote that "the more I study antiquity and its vaunted governments, the more I realize that the Mamuluks of Egypt and the Bey of Algiers do not differ essentially from Sparta and Rome; and that to trace their character, we need but supply the names, Huns and Vandals. Perpetual wars, disembowelment of prisoners, massacres of women and children, treachery, factions, domestic tyranny, oppression of strangers: there is the picture of Greece and Italy during the five hundred years recorded by Thucydides, Polybius, and Titus Livy" (*Œuvres de C. F. Volney,* 7: 127).

This assessment of the difference between ancient and modern polities was challenged by only one significant political writing prior to 1835—*The Federalist Papers,* discussed below in chapter 11. The findings of modern scholarship suggest that the distinction is not well founded. The public, family, and economic life of the Roman commons during the century on either side of the Augustan Age was remarkably like that of the Dutch in the seventeenth century or the English commons from the Restoration till 1720. They were literate, gregarious, loving of entertainments, religious, and freely mixed politics with religion. Stigmas and legal prohibitions on combining occupations of gain with various levels of social rank were comparable to, but more lax than, prerevolutionary France. The Roman political regime was based on *aequa libertas* and *aequum jus* as rights of citizens upheld in law. Mortality rates associated with domestic strife and war never reached the levels of the wars of the Reformation. Admittedly, there is no modern counterpart to gladiatorial games. Hume's distinction is more persuasive when applied to Greek cities, whose small size, strong sense of rivalry in internal and external politics, and cult of the masculine (inclusive of pederasty and degradation of women) kept politics in a turbulent condition. See Claude Nicolet, *The World of the Citizen in Republican Rome;* P. A. Brunt, *Italian Manpower 225 B.C.–A.D. 14;* E. S. Gruen, *The Last Generation of the Roman*

1. Ancient peoples were slave masters brutalized by that institution. Slaves were not allowed to reproduce because the economy could not sustain the population growth; consequently, slave populations had to be replenished by war.

2. Ancient cities were composed of a small number (5,000–20,000) of free citizens holding women, aliens, and slaves in subjection. The citizens were on a relative parity of wealth and equality. This prevented the formation of a dominant nobility; yet the citizens were too numerous to govern through an assembly. Rotation of office and representation could not be given effect because kinship and factional loyalties overwhelmed institutional form. Consequently, ancient cities were disturbed by frequent revolutions, banishments, and sanguinary revenge.

3. The tendencies that kept domestic politics in turmoil also thrust cities into frequent wars for booty and honor. The butchery of civilian populations was not an unusual outcome of these wars.

4. Depopulation through warfare and slavery lessened the pressure to improve the productive arts. The dominance of citizens over women, artisans, and slaves signified the low esteem for productive labor and the high prestige of political emulation.

Hume's remarks suggest that the productive and political processes of barbarous nations were uncoordinated. Political institutions were not only not geared to enhance productivity, they tended to depress it by wars of booty and by low-yield slave labor. Yet in the midst of this brutish irrationality there was, he believed, a civilizing tendency: the arts, manual and liberal. The arts are not optional to the human species, since they are requisite for survival. Promotion of the arts, however limited or sporadic, must occur everywhere. Indeed, desire for the benefits of the productive arts furnishes a steady motive for their improvement. Consequently, even among savages there is a mechanism tending toward the domestication of their wild passions.

Cultivation of the arts tends in this direction by disciplining the mind and invigorating it with the pleasure of achievement and the delight of new thoughts; by rewarding diligence; by at length instructing the people in the arts of politics and legislation. But the decisive gain is their tendency to soften cruel or austere passions into urbane sociability and humanity:

Republic; M. Rostovtzeff, *Social and Economic History of the Hellenistic World;* Paul A. Rahe, "The Primacy of Politics in Ancient Greece."

The more those refined arts advance, the more sociable men become; nor is it possible, that, when enriched with science, and possessed of a fund of conversation, [men] should be contented to remain in solitude, or live with their fellow-citizens in that distant manner, which is peculiar to ignorant and barbarous nations. They flock to the cities; love to receive and communicate knowledge; to show their wit or their breeding; their taste in conversation or living, in clothes or furniture. Curiosity allures the wise; vanity the foolish; and pleasure both . . . so that, beside the improvement which they receive from knowledge and the liberal arts, it is impossible but they must feel an increase of humanity, from the very habit of conversing together. . . . Thus industry, knowledge, and humanity are linked together by an indissoluble chain, and are found . . . to be peculiar to the more polished, and . . . the more luxurious ages.[13]

This is enlightenment optimism in a cheerful mood. Advanced civilization doesn't require austerity of manners or severe government. By a sort of attitude contagion men are prompted by an agency beyond their will or knowledge to accomplish collectively what perhaps none wills:

We cannot reasonably expect, that a piece of woollen cloth will be brought to perfection in a nation, which is ignorant of astronomy, or where ethics are neglected. The spirit of the age affects all the arts; and the minds of men, being once roused from their lethargy, and put into a fermentation, turn themselves on all sides, and carry improvement into every art and science. Profound ignorance is totally banished, and men enjoy the privilege of rational creatures, to think as well as to act, to cultivate the pleasures of the mind as well as those of the body.[14]

13. Hume, *Philosophical Works*, 3: 301–2. This argument was put very emphatically by Temple, *A Vindication*, 102ff.
14. Temple, *A Vindication*, 102ff. Montesquieu argued in the same fashion: "The spirit of commerce produces in men a certain sentiment of exact justice, opposed on the one hand to brigandage, and on the other hand to those moral virtues which make it so that one doesn't always discuss one's own interests with rigidity, and that one can neglect them for the interests of others. . . . one can say that the laws of commerce perfect morals for exactly the same reason that these very laws destroy morality. Commerce corrupts pure morals; this was the subject of the complaints of Plato; it polishes and softens barbaric morals, as we see every day" (*Spirit of the Laws*, bk. 20, par. 1). See Pangle,

If this sounds too good to be true, we recall that Hume published these essays against the background of two decades of Country invective against the commercial republic. It was a piece of droll effrontery to invest the spirit of the age with a character that excluded the Bolingbroke circle from it; and to discard all classical models as barbarous and unsuited to modern times.[15] But there was more to Hume's utopian prognosis than *jeu d'esprit*. Deployment of the arts was demanded initially by necessity. But the improvement of tillage created so great a surplus that half the population could produce enough to supply all. This was the beginning of capitalization. In earlier ages peasants and mechanics derived little benefit from their productivity. But owing partly to increased productivity, and partly because masters became less violent and rapacious, farmers and artisans could improve their fortune by diligent application.[16] This, Hume believed, was a happy development. In the end, "every thing in the world is purchased by labor; and our passions are the only causes of labor."[17] If the labor of the primary producers is encouraged by allowing laborers to enjoy the fruits of their industry, the wealth of the whole nation will increase. But if, as happened in Poland, every advantage won is swallowed up by the avarice of nobles, the whole nation will be depressed by the indifference of workmen. Wise policy, then, will follow this "natural bent of the mind" and allow the regards of increased productivity to take their natural course: a gradual price and wage inflation, a diminution of inequalities, and upward mobility.[18] In the end, progress does depend importantly, if not exclusively, on the defeat of ignorance and its replacement by rational policy.[19]

Montesquieu's Philosophy of Liberalism, chap. 8, for a discussion of Montesquieu's conception of the role of commerce in the French constitution.

15. The editors of Hume's writing, T. H. Green and T. H. Grose, observed that Hume's political essays "frequently read like a running criticism upon the arguments of the *Craftsman*" (Hume, *Philosophical Works,* 3: 44).

16. Ibid., 293, 296.

17. Ibid., 293.

18. Ibid., 293–97, 136–39. Eugene Rotwein has stressed the importance of Hume's grasp of the "appetite for activity" as a more potent motive for gain than the traditional notion of avarice (Hume, *Writings on Economics,* introduction). The other side of this coin is Hume's perception that laborers were not so besotted that they were compelled to work only by necessity, which was the common view (e.g. Temple, *A Vindication,* 27ff., 56ff.).

19. On the relationship between the course of the world, its comprehension, and action, Hume wrote: "general principles, if just and sound, must always prevail in the general course of things, though they may fail in particular cases; and it is the chief business of philosophers to regard the general course

Rousseau's Jeremiad

Cambridge's award of the Townshend Prize to an essay that slapped its benefactor in the face is not astonishing. Strange, though, that the Dijon Academy awarded the prize for the best essay on its question (Has the restoration of the sciences and arts tended to purify morals?) to Rousseau. The Dijon Academy, a provincial spin-off from the Académie des sciences, was located in a commercial and manufacturing town keen on economic development. Rousseau's essay took the negative in an open question; but it did so in the exaggerated manner of Bell's advice to burn all the ships. Bell probably wrote fashionable Swiftian satire; Rousseau composed the *Discourse* inspired by a rapture in which he "saw another world and became another man."[20] The experience converted him to his new vocation as a political moralist, and literary success confirmed him in it. But having attained celebrity, he repudiated its benefits, perhaps in order to make himself a cult figure to the alienated and to the merely malcontent.

The posture Rousseau adopted in the *Discourse on the Arts and Sciences* remained a prominent feature of his varied works and inspired many imitations. He put himself forward as the spokesman of the com-

---

of things. I may add, that it is also the chief business of politicians; especially in the domestic government of the state, where the public good, which is, or ought to be their object, depends on the concurrence of a multitude of causes" (*Philosophical Works*, 3: 288).

20. It was certainly so composed—*if* we believe the *Confessions*. But according to a story that circulated in Paris, Rousseau took the negative in his Dijon Prize essay at the suggestion of Diderot. Rousseau is said to have mentioned to Diderot his intention to write on the prize theme; and when Diderot asked him which side he would take, Rousseau announced that he would take the affirmative. Diderot responded puckishly, "Eh bien! vous serez un enfonceur de portes ouvertes." Struck by this conceit, Rousseau adopted Diderot's suggestion. It was only later, when he came under attack by critics, that Rousseau began to treat his *jeu d'esprit* as the truth. (This anecdote is related by Count Volney, *Œuvres*, 4: 412–13.) George R. Havens in "Diderot and the Composition of Rousseau's First Discourse" has challenged the story on the grounds that the *First Discourse* can be seen as an outgrowth of Rousseau's prior writing, especially the *Épître à M. de l'Étrang* (1749). Havens's evidence doesn't establish that the *First Discourse* "grew out of" the *Épître* without the midwifery of Diderot's suggestion. Diderot might well have understood Rousseau's propensity better than Rousseau himself did. This would account for Rousseau's astonished discovery that he *believed* the negative case.

mon man against the pernicious influence of a few whom the philosophes praised as the benefactors of mankind—the founders of modern philosophy and science. Living at the heart of the European Enlightenment, Rousseau attacked it. Rousseau's insight—the ecstatic illumination that converted him to political moralism—was the idea that science is wicked because it corrupts the morals of the common man. He did not pretend to have discovered this distressing conflict. Leaning on Socrates and Cato, he maintained that the phenomenon was endemic to civilized life, whose history shows "how luxury, licentiousness, and slavery have in all periods been punishment for the arrogant attempts we have made to emerge from the happy ignorance in which eternal wisdom has placed us."[21] Eternal wisdom created people free, ignorant, and happy; but by plucking forbidden fruit from the tree of knowledge, they fell from their original happy ignorance into licentiousness and slavery.

Rousseau's mingling of classical and biblical sentiments enabled him to reinstate a pious moralism. He maintained that since the sciences corrupt, they must originate from wicked or sinful passions. Thus he asserted that geometry originated from avarice, astronomy from superstition, and physics from vain curiosity.[22] The sciences corroded virtue partly as idle diversions from the serious business of being virtuous, partly through their licentious intellectual content. Under the first heading, Rousseau was especially upset that science introduced a nonmoral criterion for judging men by talent and achievement rather than by the rightness of their sentiments and fidelity to the group.[23] On the second point, science attacked virtue by demystifying the universe. Evidently distressed about the scoffing current among the smart set in Paris, Rousseau deplored the dangerous opinions of Hobbes and Spinoza and penned a petition for deliverance: "Almighty God, thou who holds all spirits in thy hands, deliver us from the enlightenment and fatal arts of our forefathers, and give back to us ignorance, innocence, and poverty, the only goods that can give us happiness and are precious in thy sight."[24] These sentiments were more than oratorical decoration. In subsequent defenses of his paradoxes, he reaffirmed that the sciences caused impiety, heresy, and obscene error, while those who cultivated

21. Rousseau, *The First and Second Discourses*, 46.
22. Ibid., 48.
23. Ibid., 58ff.
24. Ibid., 62. The nostalgia for salvation in Rousseau's thought has been described by Paule-Monique Vennes in *La ville, la fête, la démocratie: Rousseau et les illusions de la communauté*.

them he castigated as prideful, avaricious, jealous, flatterers and lick-spittles, liars and back-stabbers.[25] While all this might have been true, it missed the point being made by the philosophes. Religion had been the cause of more heresies than science could ever hope to be. Nevertheless, Rousseau's exaggerated oratory and need to feel moral did enable him to bring out the predatory character of modern rationalism. In full flight against the astronomers, he wrote that

The philosopher, who imagines that he penetrates the secrets of God, dares to associate his pretended wisdom with eternal wis-dom: he praises and blames, he corrects, he prescribes the laws of nature, and limits to the Divinity . . . [but] the laborer who sees the rain and sun daily fertilize his field, admires with praise and gratitude the hand from which he receives these graces, without mixing in anything of his own judgment. He does not attempt to justify his ignorance or vices by his incredulity. He does not cen-sure the works of God, nor attack his Master in order to puff him-self up.[26]

Here astronomy is compared with peasant piety and found wanting on moral grounds. The astronomer is represented as a heartless destroyer of simple reverence, a quality assumed to be integral to simple and spon-taneous goodness. Science is thus deprived of the benevolent effects that among the philosophes were the cardinal dogma supporting the war on superstition. But in reversing Enlightenment values, Rousseau remained silent about the violence of religious contention.

The virtue Rousseau defended was neither passive nor humane; it was the martial *virtus* of ancient republics mingled with sentimental nostalgia popular in all ages. He described atrocities committed by decadent intellectuals, who replaced virile austerity with softness and luxury, who ridiculed religion, and who undermined patriotism by pro-moting commerce and cosmopolitanism. The reader's curiosity to learn how sturdy virtue was so easily traduced by feckless intellectuals is never satisfied. Warrior courage is praised to the skies, without mention of its sanguinary brutality. Nowhere in the *Discourse* or its two defenses is there any suggestion that virtue might be subject to critical analysis. The very idea of objectivity toward virtue seems to have been repugnant to him. When pressed on this point by a critic, he simply withdrew from argument:

25. Rousseau, *Œuvres complètes,* 3: 36.
26. Ibid., 41.

I know in advance with what grand words one will attack me. Enlightenment, knowledge, law, morals, reason, seemliness, respect, delight, comfort, manners, education, etc.; to all this I respond with only two other words, which sound even stronger in my ears. Virtue, virtue! I cry ceaselessly; virtue, virtue! To those who know not their meaning, I have nothing to say.[27]

Here as elsewhere we run against the sentimental moralism that led Rousseau to call for the suppression of wicked science.[28]

Canvassing perceptions of Rousseau's writings by his contemporaries, we find that few could separate comment on his thought from comment on his personality. From the motto of his first publication ("Here I am the barbarian, because no one understands me") to the posthumous *Rousseau, Judge of Jean-Jacques,* Rousseau portrayed himself as the moralist and folk genius misunderstood and persecuted by the mighty. In Paris he was as much despised by the philosophes as he was the darling of youths and rich women, in both cases because of his manner, not his opinions. Those detectors of political cant, Horace Walpole and Voltaire, set him down unhesitatingly as a mountebank.[29] Hume's opinion progressed from an initially warm affection for "that nice little

27. Ibid., 33. With Abbé de Mably, Rousseau was foremost in a generation of writers who made a sentimental revolution by projecting the romanticized values of antiquity into his present. This was the nostalgic vice that Hobbes had attacked in the political writers of his generation. See R. Spaemann, *Rousseau, Bürger ohne Vaterland;* Elizabeth Rawson, *The Spartan Tradition in European Thought;* Harold T. Parker, *The Cult of Antiquity and the French Revolutionaries;* and below, pp. 395–406.

28. Rousseau said that "a thinking man is a depraved animal" because he believed the rational powers released men from communal attachments: "It is reason that engenders self-love, and reflection that strengthens it; it is reason that makes man shrink into himself—it is philosophy that destroys his connections with other men." See his *Fragments politiques, Écrits sur l'abbé de Saint-Pierre,* and *Consideration sur le gouvernement de Pologne, système économique.* In the preface of *Narcisse,* Rousseau designated the *First Discourse* as the work that "discovered his principles." He denied that he had recommended burning libraries or closing academies. He declared his view to be that "the same causes that have corrupted are sometimes able to prevent a greater corruption. The arts and sciences, having made vices blossom, are necessary to prevent them turning into crimes." This lesser-evil argument for the sciences is found in Lactantius, Augustine, and other religious writers. It is not the position of the *First Discourse,* which poses civic virtue as the antithesis of *l'esprit scientifique.*

29. Mossner, *Life of David Hume,* 523.

man" to a disparaging "little better than a Christian" to "atrocious villain" after Rousseau made insane[30] accusations against him.[31] But it is better not to be drawn into discussion of Rousseau's personality. The point to be remarked is that despite the dismissal of his work by discerning contemporaries, it entered the canon of political thought as the product of a "great mind." In this century, Émile Durkheim paid him homage by appropriating the general will to sociology. Leo Strauss was more circumspect. Drawing attention to Rousseau's defense of the primacy of passion to reason, Strauss judged that the protest of the *Discourse* and subsequent writings signified a "crisis" in modern political philosophy.[32] I suggest that the crisis was a personality disorder, and that Rousseau's effect was as a writer whose great eloquence influenced

30. Rousseau suffered from a physical disorder believed to be uremic poisoning. There is a mass of psychiatric opinion on his mental disorder. Paranoia is diagnosed from 1766, but prior to that he suffered hallucinations and what appears to be circular manic depression with delusional episodes. Rousseau was quite explicit about these events. He described his reaction to the Dijon Prize topic in the following way: "Tout à coup l'esprit ébloui de mille lumières . . . ; je sens ma tête prise par un étourdissement semblable à l'ivresse. Une violente palpitation m'oppresse, soulève ma poitrine; ne pouvant plus respirer en marchant, je me laisse tomber sous un des arbres de l'avenue et j'y passe une demi-heure dans une telle agitation qu'en me relevant j'aperçus tout le devant de ma veste mouillée de mes larmes sans avoir senti que j'en répandais" (*Œuvres complètes*, 1: 1135). See Suzanne Elosu, *La maladie de Jean-Jacques Rousseau,* and Wilhelm Lange-Eichbaum, *Genie, Irrsinn und Ruhm,* 415–18.

31. Hume seems never to have taken Rousseau seriously as a thinker, but regarded him as a man of feeling, a litterateur, a lover of extravagant notions and paradoxes, a "Roman orator" (Mossner, *Life of David Hume,* 508, 523). The onset of paranoia in 1766, which spoiled the relation between them, prompted not only Rousseau's letters denouncing Hume's plots against himself, but also this statement (to Mme. de Verdelin): "I should find it difficult to retain belief in Providence if I knew that Mr. Hume would not be unmasked before his death" (ibid., 532).

32. Leo Strauss, *Natural Right and History,* 252. The crisis is of the following description. Rousseau claimed that the state of nature doctrine was merely an intellectual artifact. A concept of human nature able to support a political doctrine of natural rights must needs make an evolutionary-historical trace of human development. This onset initiated the historicist phase of modern natural right, which Strauss believed culminates in the nihilist or relativist doctrine that all justice claims are baseless. However, it will be apparent that Rousseau did not originate the idea that human nature was to be understood in a historical-developmental framework: it was a leading idea of the age. As for the nihilist doctrine, it is no threat to the Hobbesian natural

attitudes and implanted confused ideas.[33] His espousal of the virtuous republic was more up-to-date than the Country jeremiad because he purported to speak on behalf of "the people." This broad term has no fixed designation in Rousseau's writings; its very flexibility made his writings serviceable to various mutually incompatible forms of political opposition or idealism. To explicate "the people" as a confused idea demands a description of the sundry manic icons Rousseau generated.

   1. *The virtuous people*. Whereas Country rhetoric espoused the virtuous republic from the point of view of the gentry, who were implicitly identified with the Roman patriciate, Rousseau tacitly identified "the people" with the Roman commons. This difference was scarcely consequential in America, where slave-holding agrarian democrats could embrace Rousseau and Harrington. But interpolated into monarchist France, the Rousseauean virtuous republic could be supposed to sanction a populist, antiaristocratic politics. After 1755, virtuous republic ideas received an additional force from the writings of the Physiocrats, who wished to make Frenchmen virtuous patriots and farmers. The physiocratic doctrine that land was the sole source of wealth downgraded commercial, manufacturing, and financial enterprise as derivative from land. The Physiocrats also engaged in an anticommercial rhetoric similar to the Country jeremiad.[34] Although Rousseau was not skilled in political economy, his criticisms of corrupt civilization were sufficiently close to physiocratic doctrine that a leading exponent, Mirabeau, could come forward as one of Rousseau's patrons. This association is important for the light it throws on the diverse and mutually incompatible interpretations that were placed upon Rousseau's criti-

---

   right doctrine at all since it is *presupposed* in the initial condition of war of all on all.

33. The affectations of Rousseau's oratorical prose style were noted by many of his contemporaries. "He has many cries and gestures in his style," wrote one observer, "and his epileptic eloquence is irresistible to women and youths. An ambidextrous orator, he writes without conscience, or rather, he allows his conscience to wander adrift to the taste of all sensations and affections." Mme. du Deffand said of him: "His mind is false. His eloquence is fatiguing, and it has the effect on the mind that dissonant music has on the ears. He is a conjurer: he offers you virtue, you follow it, and you find that it was vice that he has preached to you." These and other observations on Rousseau are in Marcel Hervier's *Les écrivains français jugés par leurs contemporains*, 2: 198, 195, 141–202.

34. Georges Weulersse, *Le mouvement physiocratique en France de 1756 à 1770*, 1: 78ff.; Elizabeth Fox-Genovese, *The Origins of Physiocracy*, 27ff.

cisms. Like the Physiocrats, Rousseau put himself forward as reformer of a corrupt world; and again like the Physiocrats, the reforms he proposed, insofar as they had a definite character, were a step backwards to a more primitive stage of political and economic understanding than was available in the advanced culture of which he and they were critical.

The same denunciations of corrupting wealth that might titillate decaying aristocrats could also appeal to the urban artisans who organized as the *sans-culottes* during the Revolution. Rousseau sometimes identified the people with those who had been defrauded of their liberty and property by an avaricious few, particularly at the beginning of civil society. In addition, his notion that the people exercise their law-giving power through the "general will" revived the politics of moral consensus so carefully dismembered by Hobbes and Locke. The injection of the general will into revolutionary politics in 1793 led to sanguinary persecutions of "counterrevolutionaries," i.e. those obdurate nonparticipants in the general will. With the advent of the Committee of Public Safety, the general will of the people came to reside in ten men. Rousseau of course had sited the general will in the participatory assembly of a small agrarian republic; but since such political societies did not exist in modern Europe, his ideas were applied in contexts wholly uncontemporaneous with them. But this is more evidence of their anachronistic character.

2. *The noble savage.* The people as virtuous citizens was Rousseau's manic alternative to depressive, corrupt civilization. But even the free citizen was not free enough; he was indeed a prisoner of laws, family, and a network of obligation. To escape corruption required a flight from civil society back to the state of nature. It would take us too far afield to describe Rousseau's notions about how natural freedom might be recovered in civil society. Suffice it that the corrupt urbanite sheds his chains by retreating to Walden Pond to commune with nature's harmonies, and perhaps to scribble epiphanies for urbanites whom he now pities more than he despises. Or he may devise permissive education schemes meant to allow free nature's spontaneous expression. In either case, the noble savage icon expressed the poet's alienation from political society, which placed high value on organizational performance, regularity and discipline, mechanical know-how, precise thinking, and scientific knowledge. Rousseau understood enough of "the moderns" to realize that the idea of a return to nature was diametrically opposed to their intentions. Possibly for this very reason he projected his private fantasies into the realm of public business under the pretext that they could or should be made part of the public agenda. But the fact that a private individual did this is no more the sign of a "crisis" in modern

political thought than the endurance of superstition signifies a "crisis" of enlightenment thought. Rousseau's jeremiad was only one instance of the entropic or chaotic tendencies that permanently attend artificial political society. Indeed, the "return to nature" slogan, confusedly represented as a political alternative of some kind, e.g. education reform, does not contradict but illustrates Hobbes's thesis that political society is burdened constantly by tendencies toward its dissolution by the chaos of private opinion. If force is the ultimate resort against this tendency, it is by no means the only one. The arts and sciences may be represented as the greatest benefactors of mankind, and their practice as the perfection of man's natural powers rather than their alienation.

The Society of Arts: Transition to Economic Growth

In *A Brief History of Trade in England,* Daniel Defoe declared that "there is not a government in the world that hath so much reason to encourage and regard sciences, arts, and trades as the English government have." When he wrote these words (1702), their original sponsor, the Royal Society, took only a perfunctory interest in promoting useful arts through science; and no government heeded the call.

The founding of the Society of Arts marked a sudden termination of this neglect. From a small founding group the Society expanded rapidly to a membership of about 2,500, including a large number of magnates and peers in addition to the bulk of the membership, which was a cross-section of English society. The Society was an instant social success. In its aims and composition, it was typical of the "œconomical societies" that sprang up throughout Europe in this period. There had been a great deal of talk about the utility of inventions and their potential for economic gain. But in the 1700–1750 period, the English establishment channeled its energies into commerce and finance. Once commercial enterprise was consolidated, attention might be given to manufactures. The immediate success of the Society of Arts is a benchmark of public recognition that manufacturing stood on a par with commerce as an economic sector.

It was manufacturing with a difference. Drum-beating for industrial arts remained edifying rhetoric until there was evidence that a program of invention and manufacturing innovation paid off. By 1750 it was apparent that the benefits were already at hand. Textile manufacturing was quietly being transformed by the introduction of new dyes, bleaches, and machines. Waterwheels had undergone great improvement, and steam engines ("the miner's friend") were used in more than a dozen locations to pump water from mines. Innovations in fermentation techniques enabled English brewers to bottle ale for the India trade. Gas had been separated from coal, and patents for its use had been issued. Sugar had been extracted from beet juice. New industrial chemicals were steadily reaching the market. Industrial processes were constantly refined by use of new devices for measurement. The sense of these changes was captured by an observer who remarked that in Birmingham of 1757 "almost every master-manufacturer hath a new invention of his own, and is daily improving on those of others." New inventions, but even more, daily improving, framed the new perspective on manufactures: *continuous* manufacturing innovation had taken hold.[35] This point bears emphasis. The endeavors of œconomical societies did not initiate but presupposed the process of invention and improvement that gave currency to the phrase "the progress of society." The process itself—the thoughtful search for inventions and improvements—was initiated by the two academies during the first decades of their existence, as we have seen.

The Society of Arts was founded to promote productive improvements in agriculture, mechanics, manufacturing, chemicals, and fine arts. The means to this objective was a system of premiums, bounties, and medals to inventors and innovators. Each year the Society announced cash prizes for inventions in numerous classes, sometimes as many as four hundred; one class might be improvements in threshing machines, another in paper manufacture. Bounties were awarded for most acreage of reforestation, for the most imports or exports of specified commodities, and the like. First prizes varied from £5 to £100, occasionally more.[36]

Bounties had long been used by governments to reward or subsidize selected commercial ventures. The prizes idea was suggested by the practices of country fairs, where competitions in many kinds of domestic and agricultural produce were held. The Society's shrewd exploitation of this type of popular competition no doubt partly accounts for the large public following it attracted. Indeed, the Society's approach to the public bears the signature of public relations genius. The system of premiums was so contrived as to attract the largest number of participants. Prizes were established for virtually every kind of productive ac-

35. Peter Mathias, *The First Industrial Nation*, 134–44; David Landes, *The Unbound Prometheus*, 65–86; Richard Hills, *Power in the Industrial Revolution*, passim.
36. For a complete list of classes and prizes, see *Register of Premiums and Bounties Given by the Society from 1754 to 1776 inclusive.*

tivity, including especially those engaging women and girls. The number of prizes in small amounts was multiplied not so much to increase incentive as to spread the sense of participation and achievement. The organizers were well aware that a £10 prize awarded to a cottage spinner was a windfall; and that a £1 prize awarded to a youth was an unforgettable event. The Society kept itself in the public eye by holding exhibitions, by newspaper advertising, and by organizing contests at county fairs.

The effect of the Society's premiums system was remarkable. It became a popular fashion, like a lottery; thousands and tens of thousands of ordinary men and women set their minds to "improving." [37] The old prejudice in favor of accustomed ways was painlessly replaced by a new prejudice in favor of change—change initiated at the workface by workers. [38] And the inducement was the new conception of innovation as a source of wealth or even as a form of it. The importance of this new popular participation in what was soon to become the industrialization of Europe may be gauged by comparing it with the annuities system invented in Holland. Annuities were a stroke of financial and political genius. Annuity funds attracted the savings of small investors, an estimated 30,000 in de Witt's Holland. These funds simultaneously provided secure if small incomes, encouraged saving habits, and assembled capital to finance public debts. They also created a material interest in the stability of government for the tens of thousands of small investors. If the annuities system was the first popular institution of finance capital, the Society of Arts premiums system was the first popular participation in routinized innovation inherent in industrialization. The Society's premiums in effect created an artificial market for amateur inventions. It was a cheap means of buying a large amount of labor-intensive inventiveness, without the trouble or cost of organizing that labor.

Impressions of the impact of the Society's activities are confirmed by an examination of its accounts. For the period 1756–66, its income from member subscriptions was £33,300, a large sum; during the same period Royal Society members subscribed only £5,600 to that older prestige institution. The Society's outlays were reported as in table 8.1:[39] The

37. Derek Hudson and Kenneth Luckhurst, *The Royal Society of Arts*, 126–48; Robert Dossie, *Memoirs of Agriculture and Other Œconomical Arts*, 1: 32.
38. The Society declared that "one great and general effect of the rewards . . . has been the removing . . . old vulgar prejudices against all new inventions" (*Register of Premiums and Bounties*, 38).
39. Dossie, *Memoirs of Agriculture*, 1: 27. I have excluded the years 1754–55, when income was low, so that a more accurate notion of average annual expenditure may be obtained. Total outlay for awards from 1754 to 1776 was

preponderance of the fine arts in the share of premiums is notable, and there is a reason for it. One of the objectives of the premiums system was to improve England's balance of trade by improving its export and import position.[40] A substantial portion of the nation's imports were luxury goods, brought mainly from France. Fine arts classes of premiums were meant to help engraft luxury industries on a small native stock, emphasis being placed on textiles, carpets, porcelain, and cameos. Another notable item was the premium reserved for competitors in the colonies. Society officers were keenly aware of the economic importance of colonial produce. (The Society's colonial agent was Ben Franklin, a friend of the Society's moving spirit, William Shipley.) During the 1756–66 period, the Society distributed an average £1,400 per year in premiums and bounties. In addition, it spent £3,500 on a special project for the inland transportation of fish.[41]

How do these expenditures compare with other contemporary forms of investment in industrial innovation? The two points of comparison are private investment and premiums voted by Parliament to inventors or discoverers of medical cures. Parliamentary premiums were worth £2,000 to £5,000; but they were few and irregular and for that reason were probably not a stimulus to discovery. Figures for private investment in research and development at that time are not available; the anecdotal evidence, in addition to what is known about the research and development practices of some high technology manufacturers, suggests an annual national investment of perhaps £15,000.[42] This national minimum is still very modest; Colbert's outlays for research and development were on the order of £60,000 annually. The Society's outlays are therefore by comparison miniscule. However, this figure is not a measure of expenditures for innovation that the Society's premiums stimulated. For reasons to be mentioned presently, I believe that this figure would be substantially less than my notional figure for manufacturers' research and development.

£24,616, which averages to £1,070 annually. This average slowly decreased as commercial opportunities for inventors increased.

40. Ibid., 33, 89ff.

41. For an account of this undertaking, see Walter M. Stern, "Fish Supplies for London in the 1760s: An Experiment in Overland Transport," *Journal of the Royal Society of Arts* 118 (1970): 355–71.

42. This figure is impressionistic; moreover, it is derived from few impressions. There seems to be no study of developmental costs of technology. Figures mentioned in the primary literature almost always pertain to a particular inventor or developer's expenses for a specific period, not the total cost.

Table 8.1

Premiums and Bounties		Running Costs	
Fine Arts	£ 6,964	Exhibitions	£ 371
Agriculture	2,202	Advertisements	854
Manufactures	1,885	Printing and stationery	1,098
Mechanics	2,358	Salaries and allowances	3,847
Chemistry	941		
Colonies (all categories)	2,273		
	16,623		6,170

The Society's classes of premiums were not limited to encouragement of manufacturing innovations, but were deliberately spread broadly to encourage "improvements" of every kind.[43] Readers who have visited museums of science and technology may recall that exhibits dating from this period indicate a surge of innovative ingenuity applied to domestic appliances. Some improved energy efficiency; others improved quality; some improved safety; others reduced costs; some generated new products. This was what the Society of Arts was about. It operated on the assumption that in the nation's laborers and farmers, male and female, there was an untapped potential for improvements that could be made simply by use of the mind and a few tradesman's tools. The Society's role in what became a national fashion for gadgets was to assess the "state of the art" of these many arts and to advertise premiums for innovations both useful and feasible for the amateur. There is no doubt about the Society's success in this effort. Its advertisements of prizes and publication of the inventions of prizewinners are a running commentary on the state of the arts. One index of this success is that the Society correctly identified junctures where innovative breakthroughs were technically feasible and commercially significant. Of these, the most important was the mechanization of spinning.

In a Society publication, the industrial chemist Robert Dossie dwelled on the commercial and mechanical challenges of spinning machines. The problem, he suggested, was to design a machine enabling a single operator to spin more than one thread at once. This problem was not posed by raw, mindless "need." It was in the first instance an engineering fascination: it seemed that there should be a simple solution, yet the solution strategy was elusive. Second, it was a problem whose solution

43. Dossie, *Memoirs of Agriculture*, 1: 32ff.

could be readily translated into economic gains. A machine enabling an operator to spin two threads doubled productivity; three tripled it, and so on. After describing a successful two-thread machine that took a £50 society premium, Dossie wrote: "The advantage of spinning with so great dispatch tends to the emolument of the public, not only by occasioning more work to be done by the same number of hands, and extending the manufactures dependent on spinning, by lowering the price of the commodities produced by them, but by inciting numbers to apply themselves to spinning, in consequence of their being able to earn more money by their labour."[44] The awkward prose notwithstanding, Dossie conveyed the formula for economic growth by means of mechanical innovation: Invention → Increased Productivity → Lower Price → Enlarged Market → Increased Employment + Increased Wages. This formula shows that Dossie understood the difference between commercial economics and the new perspective of growth economics. Commercial prosperity is based on commodity exchange. Exchange may, and often did, stimulate production; and knowledge of market demand can channel production. This indeed was the situation in the English textile industry when Dossie wrote. Merchants organized the cottage operators because merchants knew the market best. But the prosperity obtainable by commercial entrepreneurship is limited to volumes and efficiencies that can be achieved on the basis of a given productive technology. Commerce does not of itself enhance production. Consequently, commerce can only marginally enhance national wealth.

Substantive increase of wealth depends upon increasing the ratio of output per unit of labor time, or, generally, increasing the total volume of produce relative to population size. Such increases may be obtained in two ways: by the system of incentives that Hume stressed, or by "labor-saving devices." Dossie and the Society of Arts projected a transformation of the national economy by harnessing it to the engines of incentive and labor-saving devices. Concerning spinning machines, specifically, Dossie assumed that increased profit would accrue to operators because at that time spinning and weaving were cottage industries. He did not foresee that the successful spinning machine would demand the reorganization of cottage labor into the factory system. As far as the textile industry was concerned, the scenario that actually developed resulted in productivity increases based on mechanical innovation and factory discipline designed around machines.[45] Grim as this development

44. Ibid., 96.
45. Musson and Robinson, *Science and Technology in the Industrial Revolution*, 473–509; S. D. Chapman, *The Early Factory Masters*.

sometimes was, it did not invalidate the new manufacturing economics, which achieved lift-off, around 1800, to high-volume machine production whose output increases created the unprecedented wealth of the nineteenth century.[46]

Although the Society did not foresee the factory system, Dossie's remarks on the Society's efforts to stimulate improvements in spinning foreshadow consolidation of production. The Society offered a premium for a machine that would spin six threads simultaneously. Lewis Paul came forward with a machine that seemed to be the answer. It could take its power from wind or water; and it would spin "in the most perfect manner any number of threads without other assistance of the hand than to supply the carded cotton, take away the finished roll of thread, and rectify any accidental disorders of the operation."[47] But there were bugs in Paul's machine; its complexity and fragility made it subject to frequent breakdowns. Dossie reported that a consortium of investors poured about £60,000 into Paul's machine before it was finally abandoned.[48] Capital outlays of this magnitude for machines that never reach production clearly take the economics of some innovation beyond the means of amateur inventors. To mention one example of capitalization in high technology industry, the Carron Ironworks of Scotland, a pioneer of industrial research and development, was set up in 1759 with a capital of £12,000, which in two decades had increased to £130,000. This example was typical of high technology manufacturing investment in the late eighteenth century, when increasing initial investments for plant, machinery, and stocks demanded bigness in order to attain economy of scale. These developments did not eliminate the amateur inventor, who became a heroic figure in the next century. But his inventions could not usually be marketed without large capital backing. By 1770 it had become clear that the mainstream of industrial innovation flowed

46. Landes, *The Unbound Prometheus*, 78–85; Walter G. Hoffman, *British Industry, 1700–1950*, 130ff., table 54. The same trend has persisted in the present century. R. M. Solow estimates that from 1909 to 1949, only about 10–13 percent of the growth of productivity was due to capitalization, the remainder having resulted from technological innovation ("Technical Change and the Aggregate Production Function," *Review of Economics and Statistics* 39 [1957]: 312–20).

47. Dossie, *Memoirs of Agriculture*, 1: 98.

48. Lewis Paul's spinning rollers were subsequently adapted by a series of inventors, particularly Richard Arkwright, and in this way entered the mainstream of the Industrial Revolution. The development of the Paul machine is described by Richard Hills, *Power in the Industrial Revolution*, 32–72.

from a linkage of scientific research conducted in universities with engineering research carried out within industrial firms. What contribution, then, did the Society of Arts make to industrialization? In the authorized history of the Society, Hudson and Luckhurst assert that some claims can be made with confidence. Considerable reforestation was achieved. Agriculture received a powerful impetus through the introduction of new crops and the improvement of implements. Draftsmanship and mechanical design skills, critical to a machine age, were fostered. And the stimulation of mechanical and chemical inventions, they say, "contributed largely to the progress of the Industrial Revolution."[49] This list probably wants some additions and subtractions. Domestic production of luxury commodities, particularly porcelain and woven goods, was stimulated. So, probably, was investor confidence. The Society's campaigns alerted workmen and entrepreneurs alike to gains to be made by innovation, which came to be regarded as a source of wealth thanks partly to the Society's modest but steady reward of invention. But it is doubtful that the Society's efforts contributed substantially to the industrial innovation at the core of the Industrial Revolution.[50] A £100 premium for a spinning machine would be marginal incentive to an inventor who hoped to sell his machine for ten or a hundred times that amount; or who dreamed of becoming a manufacturer himself, as many inventors did. In brief, the Society's artificial market for inventions was as nothing compared to the real market. Apart from some scientists who from a philanthropic impulse put their inventions in the public domain, most inventors were secretive and obsessive about their work. The inventions critical to industrialization typically required decades of concentrated work, and capital expenditure well in excess of an artisan's resources. The Society's small rewards and honors could have little effect here. Besides, for many inventors, wealth and glory were not the principal motivation. Inventors were men obsessed with their work, and they often persisted in it despite the hardships that the pursuit of technical success inflicted. The Society's pump-priming was a congenial penumbra surrounding this core of self-generating activity. It helped to turn public opinion favorably toward inventors, whom the Bolingbroke circle despised as fraudulent "projectors"; and it subdued residual moral atavisms of the kind retailed by Rousseau. These effects are seen most clearly in the success of

49. Hudson and Luckhurst, *The Royal Society of Arts*, 16.
50. See the Society's own modest estimate of its effects in this area in the *Register of Premiums and Bounties*, 38.

the Society's program among the gentry, particularly the "mercantile gentry," who took to agricultural improvement with gusto.

There was another effect, less conspicuous, perhaps, but no less important. The Society's patronage of popular inventors proclaimed a new self-image for the common man or woman. The popular propaganda of the commercial republic, which culminates, we will see, with Ben Franklin, projected a self-image that valued labor and promised rewards for steady work. But the image of everyman as inventor conveyed a new and startling idea that came to fruition in the nineteenth century: the common man as a hero, and a hero who triumphs over disease, misery, and poverty thanks to his practical intelligence. This new Prometheus in overalls was the popular self-image impelling philosophies of "self-help" and Horatio Alger fantasies. To be sure, the image is more latent than articulate in Society of Arts propaganda. But it is present; and it deserves attention because it is an unprecedented development of the equality principle set in train by modern political science. Religions and moralities had previously provided the urban commoner with many self-images of defeat, subjection, and compliance. Here for the first time was an image of labor dignified to heroic dimensions by the power of technical thinking.

It is pertinent to remark that the genesis and organization of the Society of Arts projected this image. The moving spirit was William Shipley, an art teacher of no particular social or professional distinction. He was one of Ben Franklin's English acquaintances, and shared with him the attitudes of benevolence or philanthropy then current among the scientifically oriented intelligentsia. Lacking influence himself, Shipley took his idea to Stephen Hales, a leading scientist and inventor who enjoyed influence at court. Hales liked Shipley's plan, and won Lords Folkestone and Romney to the scheme; together with Shipley and several of Hales's colleagues from the Royal Society, they founded the Society of Arts in 1754. Œconomical societies were commonly run on democratic principles; members were admitted irrespective of social status, and Society business was conducted by rules of parliamentary order. This was true of the Society of Arts. Although it quickly became a prestige club housed in its own luxurious neoclassical building, it was celebrated or notorious for its in-house-democratic tincture.[51] It did not espouse political causes, of course. But the fact that the obscure Shipley was acceptable as secretary of a club that included peers was a straw in the wind that was to blow many a new man to fame and fortune.

51. D. G. C. Allen, "The Society of Arts and Government, 1754–1800."

Technology Arrives

In his *Elements of Technology* (1829), a publication arising from his Rumford lectures at Harvard College, Jacob Bigelow wrote that

> There has probably never been an age in which the practical applications of science have employed so large a portion of talent and enterprise of the community, as in the present; nor one in which their cultivation has yielded such abundant rewards.

At about the same time, Heinrich Leng declared in the introduction to his *Lehrbuch der Gewerbskunde* (1834):

> Natural history, physics, chemistry, mathematics and mechanics are indispensable adjuncts to technology, for the sciences confer [knowledge] answering to its practical requirements. It is only by learning how to apply the sciences to technical crafts that the marvelous progress made in recent times in nearly all branches of the trades was possible.[52]

These two statements typify manuals on technology that began to appear around 1800. *Technology* was the term newly coined to mark the difference between traditional artisan practices and the new practices generated by the application of science to fabrication processes of every kind. To the authors of this successor of traditional arts manuals, technology meant fabrication in which scientific methods or principles played an important part.[53]

Technology in this sense was the invention of Archimedes, who was the first to apply mechanics to a range of civil engineering problems. The Archimedean tradition was revived by the Renaissance mechanists; Simon Stevin elevated it to a new plateau with his discoveries of several laws of statics and by his virtuosity as an engineer. From that niveau it was a straight march to Bernard Belidor's *Les sciences des ingénieurs*

---

52. Jacob Bigelow, *Elements of Technology*, 3; Heinrich Leng, *Lehrbuch der Gewerbskunde*, 1. See also Karl von Langsdorf's *Erläuterung höchwischtiger Lehren der Technologie* (1807), preface. This volume was a "classic" of the manual genre.

53. For a study of the changed uses of "technique," see Wilfried Seibicke, *Technik: Versuch einer Geschichte der Wortfamilie in Deutschland vom 16. Jahrhundert bis etwa 1830.*

(1729), which shaped the latest advances in mechanics into a civil and mechanical engineering textbook.[54]

Although this older technology was included under the new definitions, the new term was needed to signify the dramatic changes that had occurred between 1780 and 1800. Mechanical engineering was limited by the absence of a science of materials; for without knowledge of the properties of materials, exact calculations were impossible. This deficiency was remedied by rapid progress in chemistry and metallurgy. The second development demanding a new word was the institutionalization of technological innovation, chiefly in manufacturing industries. These two things—the transformation of chemistry into science, and the development of an infrastructure for technological innovation—mark the advent of the Bacon-Descartes program as practical reality.

Adam Smith's Legacy

This grand event has long since been assimilated under the economic category of industrialization. In this scenario, technology appears incidentally, masked as the sudden increase of national income and per capita output. Paul Mantoux expressed a broad consensus when he stated the relationship between technology and the market in the following way:

> Two fundamental facts, closely interwoven, transforming one another, infinitely varied in their consequences and always the same in principle, govern this whole evolution: the exchange of commodities and the division of labor. . . . From this point of view the use of machinery itself, important as are its consequences, is only a secondary phenomenon. Before it became one of the most powerful causes influencing modern societies, it began *by being a resultant, and as it were the expression of these two phenomena,* at one of the decisive moments of their evolution.[55]

While it is certainly true that modern technology arose in the industrial setting, that fact is not merely economic; to be precise, it is not a fact that can be elucidated by commercial economics. We broach here a theme that will require our attention in subsequent chapters. Our

---

54. Musson and Robinson, *Science and Technology in the Industrial Revolution*, 39, 45.

55. Paul Mantoux, *The Industrial Revolution in the Eighteenth Century*, 259; italics added.

present objective is to situate the originator of classical economics, Adam Smith, vis-à-vis the Industrial Revolution, which commenced shortly after the publication of *The Wealth of Nations* (1776).

Smith's tract culminated two centuries of economic writing in a restatement of the physiocratic "system of natural liberty," or free trade. This double perspective is indicated in the title. Although nations are the units of analysis, Smith rejected the privileged status conferred upon particular nations by mercantilist *political* economy. He rejected the use of tariffs, monopolies, export bounties, and other "artificial" means to promote national wealth. The "liberal and generous system" of free trade emphasizes the cosmopolitan character of commerce and denies the coherence of a merely national economy. The wealth of a nation increases or diminishes according to the performance of its productive population within the transpolitical economic system.[56]

Economies are characterized by the division of labor, which enhances productivity, and exchange, which supplies the diverse wants of specialized production. These two activities generate the dynamo of the system, the market. To the market all commodities flow; in it all wants seek satisfaction; there price is ultimately determined. Its force is so great that it catalyzes ever-new division of labor and even influences the birth rate, as the demand for labor ebbs and flows. Smith credited the force of the market, operating through medieval commercial towns, with dissolving the feudal order and installing the mercantile system. The market exercises this power because people in their natural liberty seek to improve themselves, and the market provides opportunity for improvement through profit in exchange. Smith opposed manipulation of trade because he believed that he had discovered fixed relationships between production, price, and profit that might be temporarily deflected but could not be altered by policies. State seed-money for new manufactures was otiose because it ignored supply-and-demand laws. When there is a demand for certain commodities, someone will supply them.

56. Smith's argument for the internationalism of commerce is presented in his attack on mercantilism, particularly the balance of trade doctrine (*Wealth of Nations*, IV, iii, 2) and in his discussion of physiocratic free trade (IV, ix); Campbell and Skinner edition cited herein unless otherwise indicated. Smith's mercantilist critic, Friedrich List, wrote that Smith "speaks of the various systems of political economy in a separate part of his work solely for the purpose of demonstrating their non-efficiency, and to prove that 'political' or *national* economy must be replaced by 'cosmopolitan' or world-wide economy. Although here and there he speaks of wars, this only occurs incidentally. The idea of a perpetual peace forms the foundation of all his arguments" (List, *The National System of Political Economy*, 97–98).

Similarly, the effect of state policies devised to improve agricultural efficiency was feeble compared to the efficacy of market competition: farmers who would not produce grain at competitive prices had to alter their crops or yield to those who would improve.[57]

Although Smith's description of commercial economics was a splendid achievement, his system was not adequate to a completely new phenomenon, exponential growth powered by technology, that broke across Great Britain in the decades immediately after the publication of his study. For reasons not readily understood, his commercial orientation was not subsequently rectified by successors. The consequence is a curious persistence of commercial economic thinking in an era dominated by industry. A few references will serve to indicate the existence of the problem.

1. In a bicentennial volume of essays on Smith, the lead paper by C. P. Kindleberger discusses the question whether "Adam Smith was fully aware of the industrial revolution taking place around him. . . ."[58] Thus, in 1976 it was still moot among economic historians whether Smith knew about the central economic event of modern times. Kindleberger holds that Smith had not discerned the growth of technologies that would lead to the commercial breakthroughs of the 1780s; but he does

57. Smith's systematic treatment of the market occurs in *Wealth of Nations*, I, vii–ix. His view that the modern political order was the outcome of the gradual transfer of wealth from feudal lords to merchants is stated in *Wealth of Nations*, III, iv. His economic reading of political history closely follows Hume's domestication-of-the-passions orientation, e.g.: "Commerce and manufactures gradually introduced order and good government, and with them the liberty and security of the individual . . . who had before lived almost in a continual state of war."

How this happened is not clear. The main point that he made in this regard, that kings granted commercial towns liberties in return for support against usurping barons, is a political explanation. Moreover, the Reformation is passed over in silence. It comes up late in the book, in an aside on schooling (*Wealth of Nations*, V, i, 3, 3). Curiously, we find a decidedly Hobbesian account of the struggle between political and ecclesiastical government. Although he noted that science was involved in this struggle ("science is the great antidote to the poison of enthusiasm and superstition"), Smith denied any influence on events by Erastian politics: "The gradual improvements of arts, manufactures, and commerce, the same causes which destroyed the power of the great barons, destroyed in the same manner, throughout the greater part of Europe, the whole temporal power of the clergy" (2: 325, Cannan ed.).

58. C. P. Kindleberger, "The Historical Background: Adam Smith and the Industrial Revolution," 1.

not inquire whether Smith's economics adequately described industrial markets. Neither of the two bicentennial essay volumes discusses the economic effects of technology. Nor is there an essay on economists who have identified this flaw in Smith's system, e.g. Say and List.

2. An economist alert to technology, W. W. Rostow, has chastised his colleagues for neglecting it. "The trouble," he writes, "started with Adam Smith's assertion that 'the division of labor is limited by the extent of the market.'" This proposition is patently false, "and Smith's successors, living in times when technological change was inescapable, massive, and the central fact in the world economy, have generally followed his lead: they made technological change a function of expanding demand . . . ; they viewed it as a diffuse, incremental process that could be assumed rather than examined; and they did not explore the interactions among science, invention, and innovation and their place in a general theory of production and prices."[59]

3. Rostow is among the economists who in the past three decades have attempted to rectify the distortion created by the legacy of classical economics. They have pointed out that the process of technological change "is the *terra incognita* of modern economics." They estimate that technological innovation may account for as much as 70 percent of economic growth, which exceeds by far estimates of the growth stimulus provided by investment.[60]

The problem is that for two centuries *The Wealth of Nations* has been understood implicitly as a tract on industrial economy, whereas in the agrarian-commercial economy it actually describes, the distinguishing features of capitalism are missing. Those features may be set out by discussing why Smith's system fails to describe them.

The Wealth of Nations is a study of the "progress of opulence" on the grand scale of Montesquieu's study of political institutions. Its scope is global and its temporal horizon encompasses man's development from his primitive conditions as a savage hunter. Smith's object was to explain

---

59. W. W. Rostow, *Why the Poor Get Richer and the Rich Slow Down*, 159.
60. The received view that economic growth is due to capital investment is disputed by E. F. Denison in *The Sources of Economic Growth in the United States;* Denison holds that technological innovation is the mainspring. The same argument was put by E. E. Hagen, *On the Theory of Social Change: How Economic Growth Begins;* S. A. Hetzler, *Technological Growth and Social Change;* W. E. G. Salter, *Productivity and Technical Change;* Simon Kuznets, *Six Lectures on Economic Growth;* Jacob Schmookler, *Invention and Economic Growth;* and John Jewkes et al., *The Sources of Invention.* For a review of the literature, see A. E. Musson, "Editor's Introduction," *Science, Technology and Economic Growth in the Eighteenth Century.*

as far as possible the "progress of society" by referring social change to economic change. His concept of progress is situated in the thought matrix created by David Hume, the physiocratic economist Quesnay, and the encyclopedists.[61] But he was the first to set out a systematic model of economic growth, and it is with this model that we are concerned.

The index of growth is accumulation of circulating and fixed capital, which occurs by reinvestment of savings or profits. The dynamics of growth follows from relationships between components of the economic system. The critical component of the production of wealth, at all stages of development, is agriculture.[62] Agricultural surplus was the gain that enabled a cohort of the population to enter trades, and for another to specialize in exchange. The relations obtaining between agriculture, manufacture, and trade determine growth. Growth is a slow, demand-led momentum that induces productivity increases. It works like this. Price competition rewards productivity efficiencies that reduce productive costs. Efficiencies are achieved by the division of labor. Since price competition is exerted uniformly through markets, constant productivity increases characterize advancing economies. The strength of the demand that rewards efficiency depends on the extent of the market and its continued expansion. When markets are sufficiently large and growing, the demand for labor increases wages and spreads opulence among laborers. Their wages seek goods and further expand the domestic market.[63]

Wage increases would menace growth if, by cutting into profits, they reduced the rate of investment. This does not happen immediately because productive efficiencies attained by the division of labor increase output together with wages.[64] However, as productive efficiencies advance, they induce a circumstance that tends to diminish the rate of accumulation and investment. New efficiencies entail increased investment per worker in plant or equipment. Such investments stimulate

61. Dugald Stewart's *Account of the Life and Writings of Adam Smith* presents an extended account of these influences. See also Hiram Caton, "The Preindustrial Economics of Adam Smith."
62. The systematic statement is in *Wealth of Nations*, III, i. In I, xi, 3, Smith wrote, "The land constitutes by far the greatest, the most important, and the most durable part of the wealth of every extensive country." See also II, v.
63. Ibid., I, viii.
64. Ibid., I, ix. In I, xi, 3: "It is the natural effect of improvement, however, to diminish gradually the real price of almost all manufactures" (1: 269, Cannan ed.).

growth so long as new efficiencies are attained. But they have limits, and when they are reached in a particular productive enterprise, high wages and price competition begin to squeeze profits.[65] The squeeze had actually occurred, Smith thought, in English manufactures. The remedy was that artisans moved to the country and converted the productive efficiency from manufactures to agriculture.[66] He implied that this respite could not last long. England's prosperity had lasted since the reign of Elizabeth, "a period as long as the course of human prosperity usually endures."[67] Once the profit squeeze sets in, the rate of investment falls, although a constantly increasing rate is required to sustain growth in productive facilities with high per-worker capital costs. As a result, markets contract; wages, profits, and productivity decline; and the great mass of people, previously happy, are miserable.[68]

Stagnation and decline are as much a part of Smith's economics as

65. "The increase of stocks, which raises wages, tends to lower profit. When the stocks of many rich merchants are turned into the same trade, their mutual competition naturally tends to lower profit" (ibid., I, ix; Cannan ed., 1: 98). This passage must be compared with I, vi, where Smith maintained that the rate of profit on investment must increase with the amount invested: "The profits must always bear some proportion to the capital" (1: 58, Cannan ed.). If this were so, profits in developed economies would be enormous (proportionate to capital), whereas large profits are characteristic, Smith believed, of retrograde economies.

66. Ibid., I, x, 2 (Cannan ed., 1: 143).

67. Ibid., III, iv (Cannan ed., 1: 443).

68. Ibid., II, iii (Cannan ed., 1: 364–65). The growth model sketched here largely coincides with the models of W. A. Eltis, "Adam Smith's Theory of Economic Growth," and of Adolph Lowe, "Adam Smith's Model of Equilibrium Growth," both in *Essays on Adam Smith*, ed. A. S. Skinner and Thomas Wilson. I differ from Eltis in that I suppose agriculture to be the primary source of accumulation and in discounting the rate of accumulation as having a significant effect. We concur, however, that Smith's growth economy is so structured that it must level off into a steady state (as happened in China) or enter a decline phase (as in India). We also agree that the profit squeeze is decisive in this scenario (Eltis, "Adam Smith's Theory of Economic Growth," 428, 440). Ricardo made the declining rate of profit into a basic thesis, believing that it followed from Smith's doctrine: "Adam Smith . . . uniformly ascribes the fall of profits to the accumulation of capital, and to the competition which will result from it" (Ricardo, *Works*, 1: 289). Ricardo believed that this effect was due to rising wages. However, a decline scenario can also be read out of Smith's premises by considering a *wage* squeeze that must eventually result in an advancing economy. See R. L. Heilbroner's sketch in "The Paradox of Progress: Decline and Decay

growth. Although he frequently referred to them, he never set out a systematic statement on the causes and conditions of the onsets of decline in advanced commercial economies. For this reason it is not clear just how far Smith was conscious of the implications adduced here. Possibly he expected European economies to enter a decline phase in the near future, while North America would continue for some time in its boom. This reading is consistent with two cardinal theses of *The Wealth of Nations*. One is the primacy of agriculture to commerce and manufactures. There is no more solid evidence of Smith's preindustrial perspective than his unequivocal assertion that agriculture leads growth because the rate of profit in that sector is far greater than in trade or manufactures.[69] Furthermore, agriculture is less vulnerable to disturbance by war and natural disasters, and its recovery from calamity is faster. While it is natural for agriculture to lead accumulation, Smith admitted that in fact it had not led the growth of European economies since about 1400. He regretted this fact as "contrary to the order of nature and to reason."[70] He spelled out the particulars in his vigorous critique of mercantilist economics, whose policy was to foster accumulation by artificially stimulating trade and manufacture. His free trade doctrine was intended to return an unbalanced economy to its natural course, in which trade and manufacture do not grow faster than the demands of an agricultural economy. And if Europe were too far gone to be rescued, as Smith believed, still there was hope for North America, where mercantilist-inspired prohibitions on manufactures and restrictions on trade had the unintended effect of keeping the economy agricultural and sound.

These conceptions are intimately related to Smith's second cardinal thesis, that productive efficiency is achieved by division of labor, which

---

in *The Wealth of Nations,"* in Skinner and Wilson, eds., *Essays on Adam Smith*, 524–39.

69. *Wealth of Nations*, II, v: "No equal quantity of productive labor employed in manufactures can ever occasion so great a reproduction. In them nature does nothing; man does all; and the reproduction must always be in proportion to the strength of the agents that occasion it. The capital employed in agriculture, therefore, not only puts into motion a greater quantity of productive labor than any equal capital employed in manufactures, but in proportion too to the quantity of productive labor which it employs, it adds a much greater value to the annual produce of the land and labor of the country, to the real wealth and revenue of its inhabitants. Of all the ways in which a capital can be employed, *it is by far the most advantageous to the society*" (1: 385, Cannan ed.).

70. Ibid., I, x, 2 (Cannan ed., 1: 143).

is limited by the extent of the market. This thesis is a dagger in the heart of mercantilism; for if it is true, growth attained by restraining or forcing trade and manufactures is paid for by penalizing agriculture, which is by far the source of the greatest revenue.[71] Rather than promoting growth, mercantilist policies hobble what, left to itself, would have been a greater and more solidly based growth. In the natural order, agriculture and population grow in tandem, pulling trade and manufacture after at a rate corresponding to market demand. But the fact that they had swollen to unnatural proportions, thanks to mercantilist meddling, meant that Europe's economies were unbalanced and highly vulnerable to decline or stagnation.

These ideas are as far as can be from an industrial economy. There is no inkling of the exponential growth of productive efficiency, output, and markets that was about to eventuate. That growth was not achieved by the division of labor, but by its consolidation in machines.[72] The machines were not produced in response to market demand. When Boulton and Watt opened their Soho plant, the demand for steam engines was miniscule. Demand boomed in response to their supply of a new product. A completely free market was not what inventor-manufacturers desired. They wished to restrain trade by patents protecting their inventions. Factory owners, too, had doubts about free markets in labor when they imposed the thirteen-hour day.

In addition to this evidence that Smith was describing an agricultural-commercial economy, there is the fact that his description of the behavior of price was not accurate for the industrial economy. We have seen that in his model, demand-led markets linked supply, wages, and price in a feedback system. Industrial technology upset his price equilibrium by (1) generating demand from supply, thereby rendering demand the dependent variable; and (2) generating long-term price declines in markets where demand exceeded supply. The first grand commercial success of the Industrial Revolution illustrates both points. Woolens had been the leader in textiles for centuries, with silk and cotton distant runners. If demand determined supply, this market force would have fetched looms to increase the efficiency of woolen manufacture. Demand, however, is not very good at inventing machines. Inventors found that the long, springy fibers of wool were resistant to mechanical spinning and weaving, while the short, soft fibers of cotton lent themselves well to machines. They were successful after fifty years of trials. The result was

71. See nn. 62 and 69 above.
72. The division of labor in relation to industrial production is discussed in chapter 12 of this volume.

a sharp decline in the price and the *creation of a demand* for cotton on a completely novel order of magnitude. In the decade 1770–1779, British imports of raw cotton were 4.8 million pounds; in 1800–1809, they rocketed to 60 million pounds. The corresponding sales bonanza might be described as "latent demand" by anyone minded to save Smith's commercial economics by ad hoc hypotheses. But that such constructions would be the artifact of crippled theory is shown by the performance of wool in the same period. Market economics must predict that the rise in cottons would result in a proportional decline of woolens. This did not happen. British woolen weavers increased their wool intake 11 percent over this period, to 107.4 million pounds in 1800–1809.[73]

Cottons did not take a "share" of the woolen market because the entire market was rapidly expanding. The expansion was due to falling price. No. 100 cotton yarn, which in 1786 sold at 38s. a pound, began a decline that by 1804 brought the price to 7s.10p. per pound. Commercial economics predicts that falling price will be arrested when demand exceeds supply. Yet manufacturers were unable to keep pace with demand during this period, except for two brief periods of market glut.[74] These events were not anomalies of the war period; they described the market profile typical of nineteenth-century growth economy. Rising wages, declining price, steady profits, and momentous increases of productivity and output—that was the market performance of capitalism. It cannot be squared with Smith's system.

The reason is that division of labor, Smith's mechanism of productive efficiency, is only an organizational arrangement making no contact with the essential breakthrough of the machine age—the replacement of animal energy by mechanical energy in fabrication processes. This was why rising wages and declining prices were compatible with increased rate of capitalization. The capitalism of which Smith was an advocate was not industrial but agrarian capitalism.[75] And it was Jeffersonian America, not Manchester, that furnished a political rationale for small producers, as we shall see.

73. Peter Mathias, *The First Industrial Nation*, 487.
74. Paul Mantoux, *The Industrial Revolution in the Eighteenth Century*, 259.
75. That Smith's thinking on productivity remained foreign to the Industrial Revolution is demonstrated in his reason for asserting that agriculture is far more productive of wealth than are manufactures or trade. It is that the agriculturalist's produce incorporates nature's work (energy), whereas the artisan "does all," i.e. is the sole source of the energy required to raise his produce; hence, the farmer is three to five times more productive in equal times than the artisan thanks to his capitalization of nature (*Wealth of Nations*, II, v; Cannan ed., 1: 385). Of course, industrial machinery capitalizes natural pow-

The Science-Arts Linkage

There are no more fitting emblems of the advent of technology than the École polytechnique and the steam engine, the former representing demiurge software, the latter its engineered products. With the founding of the École polytechnique in 1794, the tradition of technical education in France reached maturity in an institute staffed by leading scientists teaching a general engineering curriculum to a corps of students selected by competitive examination. The polytechnic system became the model of engineering institutes everywhere. The steam engine initially took shape in the laboratories of the Académie des sciences, where Huygens and Papin began a series of experiments. It migrated with Thomas Savery to England, where he and Thomas Newcomen built the first commercial engine in 1712. James Watt resumed experimentation in loose collaboration with the metallurgist and ironmaster John Wilkinson, and in symbiosis with Dr. Joseph Black, the discoverer of the latent heat principle. The firm of Boulton, Watt & Co. brought the engine into production.

The École polytechnique and Boulton, Watt & Co. represent the two types of technological infrastructure that were the major vehicles for the transition to high-energy civilization accomplished during the course of the nineteenth century. My object is to convey an impression of how the intellectual and organizational ambient of these institutions mediated the science-arts linkage.

L'École Polytechnique

The École polytechnique was founded in one of those auspicious moments when a brilliant older generation of scientists passed the torch to equally gifted successors. Representative of the older generation were the physicists Laplace, Lagrange, and Coulomb; the chemists Lavoisier, Haüy, Cuvier, Chaptal, and Berthollet; the mathematicians Condorcet, Carnot, Fourier, and Monge. Among the younger men were Gay-Lussac, Poisson, Malus, Cauchy, Ampère, Arago, and Biot, all Polytechnique graduates. The achievements of these men do not readily compress into a synopsis. When the Institut de France officially reported the progress of science in France for the period 1789–1808, sixty-eight pages were needed to list the achievements. Suffice it, then, that

----

ers as well, as Smith might have gathered from study of a pulley or a water-driven mill. The capitalization of natural powers was *the* Bacon-Descartes insight. See Caton, "The Preindustrial Economics of Adam Smith."

between 1780 and 1820, this cadre completed the transformation of chemistry from a trial-and-error search into science. Quantitative and qualitative analysis, volumetric analysis, thermochemistry, the chemistry of gases were all introduced, and industrial applications were exploited. The nomenclature of chemistry, shifting and chaotic until then, was reformed into the modern style. Crystallography was initiated. Optics received a new impetus from Malus's mathematical description of polarized light. Electricity and electromagnetism were subjected to mathematical analysis. The French genius in science had always blazed brightest in the more abstract fields; and in physics the French were peerless. From d'Alembert's landmark *Traité de la dynamique* (1743) to Lagrange's *Mécanique analytique* (1788), the principles of mechanics received their modern form and laid the foundation for clusters of technologies, from naval architecture to construction to the mechanics of engines.

The older generation were trained chiefly in medical faculties and military colleges, where chemistry and physics, respectively, were taught prior to the Revolution. Their career tracks were largely bound to such teaching institutions, which involved them in medical, engineering, or industrial practice, usually in one of the royal manufactories. A few with independent means maintained their own laboratories and ranged over whatever problems might attract their interest. Still others obtained pensions as royal professors or as members of the Académie des sciences or the Jardin du roi. These posts were sufficiently numerous (probably over a hundred), and the qualifications for them sufficiently exacting, that the pre-revolutionary situation of science may be described as professionalized, but for a small cadre only. The founding of the École polytechnique altered this situation by professionalizing science and engineering on a far larger scale.[76] The Polytechnique enrolled on average

76. F. B. Artz, *The Development of Technical Education in France, 1500–1850*, 159. Studies of the social contexts of science and technology now furnish a satisfactory picture of their infrastructure. R. E. Schofield's *The Lunar Society of Birmingham: A Social History of Provincial Science and Industry in Eighteenth-Century England* is an authoritative study of the most productive and effective of the informal groups of scientists and engineering entrepreneurs. Minute descriptions of personal and molecular interactions are given by Archibald Clow and N. L. Clow in *The Chemical Revolution*. Musson and Robinson's *Science and Technology in the Industrial Revolution* is essential. Morris Berman's *Social Change and Scientific Organization: The Royal Institution, 1799–1844* describes the personnel and functions of Britain's earliest polytechnic institute. Louis Figuier's four-volume study, *Les merveilles de la science* (1867–69), contains much valuable information that has disappeared from more recent studies.

300 select students for three years of intensive work in mathematics, physics, and chemistry. Successful completion of a degree was the ticket to a career in science, in military or industrial technology, teaching, or administration. Career prospects in science were considerably expanded with the reorganization of the academies as the Institut de France, which salaried sixty full-time scientific research posts. Engineering was upgraded by the conversion of the École des ponts et chaussées and the École des mines into postgraduate schools for Polytechnique graduates and by the founding of schools of naval, hydrographic, and civil engineering. The reorganization of 1794 created in France a scientific-technical civil service whose senior members often moved between scientific, industrial, military, administrative, and political appointments, or might be active in several fields at once.

Official establishment of the École polytechnique was not enough to assure its success in a period when government was dominated by the cares of revolution and war: the government that established it also removed the heads of the great Lavoisier and Condorcet in the same year. Its success was due to a combination of favorable circumstances, the most important perhaps being that three outstanding scientists were also gifted organizers and public servants. The presiding spirit among scientists was Claude Louis Berthollet; their most senior public servant was Jean Antoine Chaptal, minister of interior from 1801 to 1804; while Pierre Laplace, called "the second Newton" by his contemporaries, excelled Newton in his ability to use institutions to the maximum advantage of science. Berthollet and Chaptal received their chemical training in medical faculties, and both were adept at industrial applications of their chemical researches.

In 1781, at the age of twenty-five, Chaptal was nominated to teach chemistry at the celebrated Montpellier medical faculty where he had taken his degree. He divided his time between teaching and operating a chemical plant, chiefly for the textile industry. His scientific and business interests prompted him to search for new applications of chemistry, which he did first in dyeing, then subsequently in a wide range of industrial preparations. In 1790 he published his three-volume *Éléments de chimie;* in 1794 he began his career in state service as inspector-general for gunpowder. Thereafter he shuttled between the Institut de France, the École polytechnique, and his chemical business. As minister of interior he used his broad powers to promote industrial technology, particularly in the public manufactories, which were under his direct control. École polytechnique graduates who were not drafted into military service Chaptal set to work as chemical and mechanical engineers in factories that previously had been innocent of technological pretensions. An energetic and enterprising minister, Chaptal often designed and sometimes directly supervised industrial research programs in the factories under his control. He was also a strong advocate of the expansion of technical education for craftsmen, which he advanced by his superintendence of the Conservatoire des arts et métiers.[77]

A second factor important to the success of the École polytechnique was the protector that it and French science found in Napoleon Bonaparte. As a former artillery officer trained in mathematics and physics, Napoleon appreciated the importance of engineering to modern warfare. The École did not disappoint his expectations; from its establishment to 1806, about a third of its 1,664 graduates entered service in artillery and military engineering.[78] But Napoleon's view of science encompassed more than its military applications. He fully approved the program advertised by the encyclopedists, to replace traditional crafts by technology; and he appointed Chaptal minister of interior with a mandate to this effect.[79] He also established numerous prizes and honors for industrial innovation and scientific achievement. At one time his government offered a prize of one million livres (about £40,000) for a machine to spin flax.

Napoleon was among the few nineteenth-century chiefs of state who felt a personal affinity for science and technology. In addition to patronizing science and scientists, he mingled with them, particularly as a member of the First Class (natural sciences) of the Institut de France. Election to the First Class was a mark of the highest scientific distinction. Scientists who wished to retain his favor elected him no doubt because he fancied that he might have become another Galileo had destiny not called him to politics.[80] This was one of Napoleon's many expressions of admiration for science. He esteemed scientists for their effective rationality and freedom from ordinary prejudices; he entertained no high opinion of literary men, who he thought were "good for nothing under any government." In declining to authorize a school for literature and history in the Collège de France, Napoleon wrote that

mathematics, physical and natural science, medicine, and jurisprudence are sciences because they are built on facts, observations,

77. Maurice Crosland, The Society of Arcueil, 113–16.
78. Artz (The Development of Technical Education in France, 159) gives the following breakdown of destinations of 1,664 students graduated between 1794 and 1806: artillery, 312; military engineering, 194; naval engineering, 38; mines, 29; bridges and roads, 194; cartography, 24; merchant marine, 45; teaching, 29; administration, 14. The remainder, about 800, entered manufacturing and commerce.
79. Crosland, The Society of Arcueil, 49.
80. Ibid., 16.

comparisons; because discoveries that they make successively accumulate from century to century and come to increase daily the domain of science . . . [yet] we have not surpassed the Greeks either in tragedy, comedy or in epic poetry.[81]

The policy rationale stated in this communication of 1807 is about the same as guided the reforms of 1794. Until then, the Académie française had been senior to the Académie des sciences. The reorganization of the academies as the Institut de France reversed this standing. The natural sciences became the senior First Class; the moral and political sciences were the Second Class; while literature was relegated to lowest position as Third Class.[82] The reorganization plan, put forward by Condorcet, implemented the reform program devised by Diderot and d'Alembert, which they published in the *Encyclopédie*.[83] It may be noted that upon the restoration of the monarchy, the seniority of literature was reestablished, and the École polytechnique was designated an engineering school for the sons of the nobility, who it was hoped would form a new technocratic elite.[84]

The prestige of science and technology during the 1789–1815 period was due partly to the support they gave to the antiaristocratic bias of French politics. What counted in science was performance, not birth. The École polytechnique gave a palpable demonstration of this fact by drawing 46 percent of its students from artisan and peasant classes.[85] Scientific institutions could therefore be interpreted publicly as consistent with equality, since they were a proven means to upward mobility. They also lent themselves to Napoleon's version of equality, institutionalized during the Empire, which was a new aristocracy of merit composed of men of demonstrated achievement, irrespective of social origin.

A survey of the organizational ambient of the science-arts linkage would not be complete without mentioning the face that organized scientists presented to their various publics. The image of science during this period was influenced by the fashion for heroism. If equations could not be dramatized, everyone could perceive the powers of "wondrous science" in the balloon flights of the Montgolfiers or in fairs and

81. Quoted ibid., 52.
82. Ibid., 148–49.
83. Ibid., 149. *Encyclopédie*, "Discours Préliminaire," xxiii.
84. Crosland, *The Society of Arcueil*, 149, 202.
85. Ibid., 202. In 1805, students were required to contribute 800 francs per year for food and lodgings; in 1816, Louis XVIII raised this charge to 1,000 francs, although some scholarships were available for students without means.

expositions that attracted many thousands to view the latest achievements of scientific technology. The men of science, however, did not
adopt a heroic or aggressive posture. The style of professional science
was set by the presiding spirit, Berthollet. His steady judgment, calm
demeanor, and reliability inspired confidence in his colleagues and politicians alike. He was open in his dealings. He practiced the rule that
truth takes precedence over persons, even when it meant that the distinguished Berthollet must bow to the better knowledge of his young assistant, Gay-Lussac. The same rule, he realized, must also prevail in
dealings between scientists and government. Berthollet put himself at
risk with the Committee of Public Safety when he reported that a quantity of brandy supposed to contain poison, implicated in a plot against
the Committee, was in fact free from contamination.[86] He upheld the
cosmopolitan character of science by treating scientists of belligerent
nations as men exempt from the enmities of war and patriotism. He
placed his discoveries, including the commercially valuable chlorine
bleaching process, in the public domain. Most of these standards had
been implicit in French science since the founding of the Académie.
Nevertheless, their firm reassertion at the moment when applied science
became a force in public affairs helped codify the standard of professional conduct for the young men passing through the École polytechnique. These standards established scientist-engineers as a corps of
impartial men who might make mistakes but who did not cheat.

A sign of the success of the professionalization of science in France
was that leading scientists like Berthollet served every government,
from the Bourbon monarchy through the Revolution and the Empire
and back again to the Bourbons. These were the men who trained a
generation of young men who took with them to Germany, Austria,
and Switzerland the scientific adroitness that in a single generation carried German science to preeminence. One such man was Joseph Louis
Gay-Lussac, whose career epitomized professional science in France as it
embodied the traditions of the École polytechnique. Upon completing
his course of study, Gay-Lussac entered the École des ponts et chaussées
for advanced study. At the age of twenty-three, he made his first discovery of an empirical law, the thermal expansion of gases. Shortly thereafter, he ascended 7,000 meters in the Montgolfiers' balloon to make
scientific measurements. In 1806 he commenced his long career of industrial chemistry by joining the Bureau consultatif des arts et manufactures. He was subsequently involved in plate glass manufacturing at
Saint-Gobain, in the manufacture of scientific instruments and chemical

86. Ibid., 99–100.

apparatus, gunpowder, cannon, candles, and industrial chemicals, in addition to the devising of assaying methods for the mint and tests for alcohol content of wines and spirits. The Gay-Lussac tower was a device for recovering oxides of nitrogen in the manufacture of sulfuric acid, which combined the commercial advantage of recycling chemicals with eliminating an industrial pollutant. His method of volumetric analysis was a quick and inexpensive test of the purity of compounds. In 1831 he was elected to the Chamber of Deputies, where he joined several other distinguished scientists in providing the legislature advice derived from his experience as an academician, scientist, industrial chemist, and entrepreneur. Such was the career pattern of the distinguished men of the École polytechnique; and it does not surprise that the founder of industrial chemistry in Germany, Justus von Liebig, was Gay-Lussac's pupil and imitator.

The Steam Engine: Knowledge Is Power

The critical events for the take-off to exponential growth were innovations in spinning and weaving machines that resulted in productivity increases on the order of five- to tenfold. These machines were initially made of wood, and were powered by water. Their cost was astonishingly low. A forty-spindle jenny cost about £6 in 1792; a slubbing billy with thirty spindles cost £10.10s.[87] Hundreds of small entrepreneurs, including craftsmen, were therefore able to set up small shops. High yields on these low capital costs enabled small proprietors to prosper alongside larger entrepreneurs.

The golden egg of textiles would have been a temporary bonanza had it not ramified through manufacturing industries. It did ramify through mining, chemicals, metallurgy, construction, and transportation, because these traditionally high-technology industries had undergone technological improvements that made possible two new technologies essential to industrialization. One was the capacity to fabricate iron to exact dimensions and fine calibrations. Precision work had already been achieved in brass and other soft metals by instrument makers, but to work hard metals into large though exact dimensions required a new technology, machine tools, that sprouted from the workshops of ironmasters.[88] The other new technology was engines, especially the steam engine. This artifact became the symbol of the initial phase of indus-

87. Landes, *The Unbound Prometheus*, 65.
88. Robert S. Woodbury, *Studies in the History of Machine Tools;* Musson and Robinson, *Science and Technology in the Industrial Revolution*, 473–510.

trialization because it summarized what men who made the Industrial Revolution believed they were about. It was a high technology machine whose commercial success exercised strong flow-through effects on half-a-dozen high technology industries. Its applications multiplied from its original function as a pump to traction; it was rapidly applied to ocean and land transport. It delivered power in unheard-of concentrations. One horsepower is equal to the labor of 12 men, operating through equal times. A 50-horsepower engine delivered the equivalent of the labor of 600 men in 8 hours, or of 1,800 in a 24-hour day. By 1825, the fixed engines alone of Great Britain delivered work equivalent to the labor of 5,400,000 men. By 1900, steam engines throughout the world delivered work equivalent to that of 5,000,000,000 men.[89] These figures display in an arresting fashion the exponential growth of power which was the basic material cause of those changes designated by the term "Industrial Revolution."

The steam engine was also the symbol of the transformation of production because it was a stunning example of the rational cause upon which the process depended, scientific technology. The spinning and weaving machines that cast up the first exponential productivity increase were not scientific artifacts, even though their development drew upon engineering studies of machinery. It is conceivable that these artifacts might develop in an advanced culture, such as the Chinese, in which formal science of natural laws did not exist. But the steam engine could not even be conceived except on the basis of a cluster of seventeenth-century scientific discoveries.

The steam engine depends upon knowledge of the odd fact, unknown in any culture until its discovery by Pascal and Torricelli, that the earth is enveloped by an atmosphere that exerts a uniform pressure at sea level of 15 pounds per square inch. This fact is fundamental to the physics of fluids and vacuums, which Pascal reduced to empirical laws in a series of brilliant experiments; and which he applied in his investigations of the action of piston and cylinder, the basic mechanism of pumps. Independently of Pascal, Otto von Guericke of Magdeburg conducted experiments on the vacuum in the 1650s. He astonished the world by demonstrating that teams of horses could not pull apart two hemispheres of brass enclosing a vacuum. Another series of experiments showed how the newly discovered force of atmospheric pressure could be harnessed. By a pulley arrangement, von Guericke attached a piston and cylinder to weights amounting to 2,686 pounds. A lad then evacuated the cylinder by means of a pump. As the cylinder emptied, air pressure exerted on the outer surface of the piston pressed it into the cylin-

89. Andrew Carnegie, *James Watt*, 191–94.

der, raising the great load. Well might the people of Magdeburg marvel at such feats. The very existence of atmospheric pressure cannot be detected by uninstructed senses; its properties can be discerned only by experiments conducted on the basis of mechanical principles.

Realizing the potential of atmospheric pressure in relation to pumps, Huygens and other men of the Académie des sciences set about harnessing it in a vacuum engine. The problem was to achieve regular action of the piston by devising a means of alternately filling and emptying the cylinder chamber. Huygen's assistant, Denis Papin, hit on the steam solution in 1691. The ascending stroke of the piston could be effected by filling the cylinder with steam; the evacuation of the steam would create a vacuum and thus produce the descending stroke. Thus was the concept of the atmospheric steam engine born from apparently useless scientific investigations involving weighing air.[90] According to Adam Smith's economics, the cause of this development was bourgeois society acting through market competition to "divide labor." Inspection of the relevant series of events reveals no trace of this agency. It does reveal a completely different agency: polytechnic intelligence.

Boulton, Watt & Co.

Papin's idea of the atmospheric engine was one thing; midwifing it into a workable machine was quite another. It was in this midwifery that Englishmen displayed the superior mechanical talent that gave them leadership in engineering until about 1850. Thomas Newcomen, collaborating with Thomas Savery, fabricated the first commercial engines for colliers, beginning in 1712.[91] The Newcomen engine was a single-

90. D. F. J. Arago, *Historical Eloge of James Watt*, 40–54.
91. Recent studies of the origin of the Newcomen engine have left this matter in some obscurity. L. T. C. Rolt and J. S. Allen have partially clarified it by showing that Newcomen and his collaborator John Cawley arrived at their ideas for the Newcomen engine independently of Thomas Savery. Newcomen entered a business partnership with Savery only because Savery's patent was written broadly enough to cover Newcomen's innovations (Rolt and Allen, *The Steam Engine of Thomas Newcomen*, 36–41). Where then did the ironmaster Newcomen get the idea for his engine? Rolt and Allen do not say. There is, however, an extensive history of the development of the steam engine in Louis Figuier's *Les merveilles de la science*. The transfer of steam technology to England traces a path running between the Académie des sciences and the Royal Society, involving as principals Papin, Boyle, Hooke, Huygens, Leibniz, and Savery. Newcomen was the beneficiary of this work through two channels. His interest was first aroused by the Savery engine that was installed at a mine in his native Dartmouth. His knowledge of

action, reciprocating engine, very inefficient and bulky. But these engines worked, some of them for more than seventy-five years.

Newcomen's engine inspired further studies by Belidor, Desaguliers, and John Smeaton. Smeaton was England's foremost engineer at mid-eighteenth century. His application of mathematical methods of mechanical design to waterwheels greatly improved their efficiency and power. Turning his know-how to the Newcomen engine, he doubled its efficiency.[92] But he did not redesign the steam engine to make it the power plant of manufacture. That was the achievement of the Scottish instrument maker and experimentalist, James Watt.

The polytechnic achievements of Watt are subject to a misunderstanding that Sir Humphry Davy, his friend and a leading chemist, characterized in the following way:

> Those who consider James Watt only as a great practical mechanic form a very erroneous idea of his character; he was equally distinguished as a natural philosopher and a chemist, and his inventions demonstrate his profound knowledge of those sciences, and that peculiar characteristic of genius, the union of them for practical application. . . . Mr. Watt's improvements on the steam engine were not produced by accidental circumstances or by a single ingenious thought; they were founded on delicate and refined experiments, connected with the discoveries of Dr. Black.[93]

Watt collaborated with Dr. Joseph Black, Dr. John Roebuck, and James Keir to investigate alkali manufacture; and he brought Berthollet's chlorine bleaching process to England.[94] He was a principal, with Priestley, Cavendish, and Lavoisier, in the round-robin of discoveries that finally led to the decomposition of water into oxygen and hydrogen.[95] Watt's mechanical genius was distinctive; his polytechnic talents were the very substance of that first generation who pioneered industrial science and at the same time possessed entrepreneurial skill. John Marshall in the woolen industry, James Nasmyth in engineering, John Roebuck and David Mushet in metallurgy, James Keir, Joseph Black, and Josiah Wedg-

---

steam was indeed not drawn from Savery, but from his correspondence with Robert Hooke at the Royal Society, who explained Papin's experiments (*Les merveilles de la science,* 1: 3-73, especially p. 68).

92. Charles Singer et al., *A History of Technology,* 4: 179–80.
93. Quoted by Carnegie, *James Watt,* 221.
94. Musson and Robinson, *Science and Technology in the Industrial Revolution,* 352–71.
95. Arago, *Historical Eloge of James Watt,* 97–115.

wood in chemistry—these and others of like talents discovered how to make science productive.

Watt's circumstances and career were typical of the breed. His father's modest means just sufficed to enable him to complete an apprenticeship with a London instrument maker. His precocious talents enabled him to complete in one year training that normally required three. On return- ing to Edinburgh in 1762, he was taken by Black, professor of chemistry at the university, into his circle of friends, which included Roebuck, founder of the Carron Iron Works, and Keir, a chemical manufacturer.[96] Watt quickly became a collaborator in their efforts, and initiated his experiments with steam that in the next five years led to his main inventions.

Watt's attention was first drawn to steam in 1758 by John Robison, then a student of Professor Black, subsequently the successor to Black's chair. Robison suggested that the steam engine might be applied to "the driving of wheel carriages." Watt made some trials of this idea by con- structing models of a two-cylinder engine. The trials taught him that he understood little of steam or engines. "Everything became science in [Watt's] hands," Robison said years later. Watt acquired the science he lacked partly by learning French so that he might read Belidor and others on the steam engine.[97]

The function of steam in the Newcomen engine was to create a vac- uum. This was accomplished by flushing cold water into the steam-filled cylinder. It became apparent to Watt that alternately heating and cooling the cylinder taxed the engine with great inefficiency. He ultimately rec- onciled this problem by devising a separate vessel, a condenser, to draw off the steam from the cylinder and quench it, meanwhile keeping the cylinder at about 100°C by surrounding it with a jacket filled with steam. But before having this flash of insight, Watt had to know the properties of water and steam. By measuring volumes of steam and water, and their behavior at given temperatures, he discovered that water at 100°C and steam at the same temperature differ, in a proportion of 1 to 5.3, in the amount of heat they possess. To illustrate, a kilogram of water at 100°C added to a kilo at zero will heat the cold water to 50°C. But a kilogram of steam at 100°C will heat 5.3 kilograms of water at zero to 50°C.[98] The puzzled Watt took this peculiar finding to Dr. Black,

96. On the development of industrial chemistry in Great Britain, see Clow and Clow, *The Chemical Revolution*.

97. Eric Robinson and A. E. Musson, eds., *James Watt and the Steam Revolution, A Documentary History*, 27.

98. For Watt's own account of these experiments, see ibid., 39–40, 46–47, 50–51.

hoping for an explanation. He was not disappointed. Only three years previous, in 1761, Black had himself discovered this difference between the thermometric heat and the composition heat of water as it passes from the solid to the liquid state; he had called it the "latent heat" principle.

At the mention of latent heat, we are obliged to pause and note one of the little piles of debris that mark the progress of scholarship. When D. F. J. Arago, physicist and secretary of the Académie des sciences, published his *Historical Eloge of James Watt* in 1839, it was evident that the latent heat principle had been as important to Watt's invention of the separate condenser as the discovery of atmospheric pressure had been to Papin's invention of the atmospheric engine.[99] It was also plain to Watt, who declared that "the latent heat of steam was a piece of knowledge essential to my enquiries . . . leading to the separate condenser."[100] Although various scholars have lately declared this to be a "legend,"[101] the evidence presumed to dissociate Watt's invention from his scientific investigations turns out to be persiflage. In the course of testifying on Watt's behalf in a patent suit, John Robison recounted that "Mr. Watt had learned from Dr. Black somewhat of his late discovery of the latent heat of Fluids and of Steams" and had proceeded to incorporate this knowledge in his investigations. In a marginal gloss to this remark, Watt wrote: "Dr. Robison is mistaken in this. I had not attended Dr. Black's experiment or theory on latent heat until I was led to it in the course of experiments upon the Engines when the fact proved a stumbling block which the Dr. assisted me to get over."[102] In other words, while Robison believed that Watt's prior knowledge of latent heat was the basis of his experiments, Watt says that he independently discovered the phenomenon that he later learned that Black had previously discovered and explained. Watt's correction of Robison's testimony does not dissociate his research from the latent heat principle, but instead affirms that association.

The discovery of latent heat gave Watt's investigations a quantitative and conceptual basis enabling him to refine the intuitive sense that Newcomen's cylinder performed opposite functions. By measuring heat lost by condensing steam in the cylinder, he was able to define the prob-

99. Arago, *Historical Eloge of James Watt*, 15–20, 61–68.
100. Watt to Andrew Ure, quoted by Samuel Smiles, *Lives of the Engineers: Boulton and Watt*, 71n. See also Watt's remarks on latent heat in Robinson and Musson, *James Watt and the Steam Revolution*, 40.
101. Charles C. Gillispie, "The Natural History of Industry," 123.
102. Robinson and Musson, *James Watt and the Steam Revolution*, 27.

lem as a search for a contrivance to keep the cylinder hot throughout the cycle. Watt not only invented the separate condenser as an effective response to the problem precisely defined; he was also able at the same stroke to redesign the cylinder as a "steam vessel" that replaced atmospheric pressure as the motive force on the piston by steam.[103]

At this stage Watt's engine was still only a bright idea; capital for development and entrepreneurship was needed to translate it into a commercial product. Roebuck was keenly interested both because of his enthusiasm for the new machine and because of its commercial advantage to a firm engaged in mining and iron manufacture. Watt agreed that Roebuck should have two-thirds interest in his patent in return for bearing the unknown development costs. But liquidity problems in 1774 made Roebuck seek a means of divesting this commitment. The man who stepped in was Matthew Boulton, an engaging combination of enthusiast, amateur scientist, and astute entrepreneur. He was the moving spirit of the Birmingham circle of scientists and entrepreneurs calling itself the Lunar Society.

Boulton sustained a multitude of scientific pursuits, as well as two fortunate marriages that netted some £30,000, from which he was able to establish his Soho manufactory. He met Watt in 1768, and entered partnership with him in 1775 after Roebuck had divested his interest in Watt's engine. That year they sold four engines; the next year, five. In 1783, the first year they marketed rotative engines, they sold ten engines. The rotative engine sparked a doubling of sales by 1785, which rose to another doubling ten years later. By 1800, Boulton, Watt & Co. had sold a total of 451 engines, producing 11,251 horsepower, whose estimated value was just under £1 million.[104] In the next quarter-century, these figures approximately doubled again.

When Watt's patents expired in 1800, new manufacturers entered the field with prices 10 to 15 percent lower than the Boulton and Watt charges, and soon engrossed about 80 percent of the market. By 1825, Britain had an estimated 150,000 horsepower in fixed engines, representing a capital value of about £10 million.[105] To form a rough notion of the growth of fixed capital value this figure represents, we need but consider that a century earlier the total value of all fixed capital in Britain would scarcely have exceeded £2 million.

The same figures viewed from the perspective of a later date impress

103. Arago, *Historical Eloge of James Watt,* 63–67; Robinson and Musson, *James Watt and the Steam Revolution,* 46–47, 50–53.
104. Jennifer Tann, ed., *The Selected Papers of Boulton and Watt,* 1: 6–7, 19.
105. Ibid., 19.

us by their smallness. Like so many firms that contributed to industrialization, Boulton, Watt & Co. began with very modest capital. For two decades the firm manufactured only smaller parts for their engines and subcontracted the larger parts to ironmasters, particularly the firm of John Wilkinson, who in collaboration with Smeaton had developed techniques for precision boring of cylinders. Income was based not on the cash sale of engines, but on semiannual royalties, calculated on the basis of horsepower rating—a measure Watt devised partly for that purpose. The firm did not finally break free of liquidity problems until about 1790, some two decades after the separate condenser was patented. Meanwhile there were other business complications. During the 1780s, patent infringements kept them in court; even their valued ironmaster Wilkinson did some illicit trade in Watt engines. Organizing production was a constant headache. Since manufacturing precision had not attained the grade required for interchangeable parts, every engine was in effect built from parts manufactured at various foundries. Not until the engine was assembled at its site was it possible to know whether compatibility of parts had been achieved. Moreover, the manufacture of parts had to be synchronized to ensure their completion and transportation by an established date, while minimizing the time lag between the completed manufacture and the erection of the engine. This process was further complicated by the circumstance that Boulton, Watt & Co. supplied engines at fifteen different power ratings, requiring that many different cylinders and nearly as many boilers. Further, metallurgical technology could not at that time produce an alloy adequate to engine stress, so the supply of noninterchangeable spare parts was a problem. Nevertheless, by persistence, close supervision, and exacting calculations of all aspects of the business, Boulton and Watt could pay their senior engineer £600 per annum, plus commission, while at the same time steadily reducing the cost per horsepower unit of their engine.

It is not usually possible to isolate the motives that animate people engaged over a long period in a complex enterprise. Still, the papers of Boulton and Watt do plainly show that the smell of profits was scarcely their only incentive and certainly not their only reward. Work was achievement, and achievement was its own reward. There were several dimensions to this "work ethic." Watt was anxious lest others would pirate his inventions; and anxious too that baseless charges of his pirating the inventions of others would sully his name with the posterity that he knew must remember him. Boulton was similarly animated by a concern with honor. His firm was no mere manufactory; it made "the most *powerful* machine in the world."[106] The world had always paid respect to

106. Ibid., 72.

great power. In the past, great power was exercised primarily through institutions, and therefore might be challenged by other institutional power. But here, for the first time, was great power exerted through machines.

The origin, character, and destiny of this power became an object of debate almost from the moment of its emergence. The debate lies heavily under the invisible hand of Adam Smith. Four critical misinterpretations of the Industrial Revolution he either expressly formulated or suggested. Two have been mentioned: his idea that the transformation of feudal Europe was due to the progress of trade, which introduced the bourgeois epoch, and the notion that the development of productive technologies was due to market demand. We now consider two additional points: the idea that the "profit motive" is the motivation for invention as well as business, and the belief that industrial innovation and invention were primarily the doing of "common workmen" actuated by a desire to lessen their burdens. Although Smith's brief comments on these matters suggest a gentleman's ignorance of the science, engineering, and industrial technology of his day,[107] and might therefore have been quietly forgotten, they were broadcast by numerous influential writers. One of them was Samuel Smiles, the celebrant of engineers, who wrote that

> One of the most remarkable things about Engineering in England is, that its principal achievements have been accomplished, not by natural philosophers nor by mathematicians, but by men of humble station, for the most part self-educated. The educated classes of the last century regarded with contempt mechanical men and mechanical subjects.

This statement illustrates how spokesmen for the common man perpetuated the class distinctions they resented. The contrast between

107. In a seminal essay on this subject, R. Koebner states that "not a single line" in Smith's writings provides evidence that he foresaw the manufacturing innovations that we call the Industrial Revolution. He points out that Smith was in this respect well behind contemporaries such as Josiah Tucker and the encyclopedists, who had grasped what was in the making. This backwardness is all the odder in that Smith knew James Watt and was familiar with the entrepreneurial and financial circumstances of important high-technology firms, such as the Carron Iron Works. See Koebner, "Adam Smith and the Industrial Revolution," *Economic History Review* 11 (1959): 381–91; also Caton, "The Preindustrial Economics of Adam Smith," 834–35, 848–49. Smith's one thematic discussion of manufacturing technology (*Wealth of Nations*, I, i) exhibits a very rudimentary understanding.

natural philosophers and self-taught mechanics implies that scientists issued from university high culture while mechanics were prevented by their inferior social station from attaining the intellectual status of scientist. The facts are about the reverse of this. England's great scientists of this period—Davy, Dalton, Faraday—were low-caste and self-taught. The mechanics whose engineering talent industrialized England were unusually gifted and steeped in the sciences relevant to their interests, as Smiles's own studies amply show.

This opinion continues today in the historiography of science and the Industrial Revolution, where it takes the form of a denial that the science-technology linkage was forged in the last quarter of the eighteenth century.[108] The denial depends strongly on a definition of science as "basic science" characterized by a substantial body of empirical theory, as distinguished from an empirical prospecting for facts or for successful fabrication processes. However, basic science so defined scarcely existed outside the precincts of the Institut de France and the École polytechnique. Sir Humphry Davy probably could not solve quadratic equations; but he was recognized by the mathematically accomplished Gay-Lussac as an equal. Davy left a deep mark on the industrial science of Manchester as Gay-Lussac did on the industrial centers around Paris. The dismissal of industrial science as mere empiricism forgets that every science except physics did a long empirical apprenticeship before arriving at basic theory. The intuitive mechanical genius of Watt invented the steam engine using crucial scientific facts. The theoretical explanation of how the steam engine worked was not available until thermodynamics reached maturity around 1850. There is indeed an important difference between these two modes of understanding. But it is not a difference between science and nonscience.

His division-of-labor principle was in particular alien to industrial manufacture, as Andrew Ure pointed out; see below, 533–37.

108. The debate is reviewed and assessed in *Science, Technology and Economic Growth in the Eighteenth Century*, ed. A. E. Musson, and in Arthur P. Molella and Nathan Reingold's "Theorists and Ingenious Mechanics: Joseph Henry Defines Science." See also the literature cited in note 60 above. That the science-manufacture linkage was forged between 1780 and 1800 seems to me conclusively documented by Musson and Robinson, *Science and Technology in the Industrial Revolution*, and by Schofield, *The Lunar Society of Birmingham*. Maurice Crosland's *The Society of Arcueil* and *Gay-Lussac* document the French case.

chapter 9

Enlarging the Political Public

MODERN democracies consist of large populations politically organized in democratic institutions. Human populations become large by natural reproductive power in the absence of countervailing restraints, traditionally infant mortality, epidemics, and famine. Between 1700 and 1900, these restraints were either eliminated or greatly diminished, with the result that Europe's population doubled in the nineteenth century despite considerable emigration. The population of the United States doubled every twenty-five years during the nineteenth century, exactly according to the prediction of Benjamin Franklin.

The organization of these many millions in democratic institutions required political technologies whose fabrication and application are the subject of the next two chapters. Presently our interest is in the rapid expansion of the political public that occurred from about 1770 to the termination of the Napoleonic wars. In Great Britain, expansion occurred as the campaign for parliamentary reform, particularly the elimination of rotten boroughs, the extension of the franchise, and the removal of civic disabilities from non-Anglicans. In France, dramatic national events abruptly made citizens of 25 million who had been passive subjects. The execution of the king and of 40,000 counterrevolutionaries, the suppression of the Church, and two decades of war throughout Europe made every Frenchman aware of his political identity and spread the democratic gospel to every European nation. In America, the tradition of local government made the political public, from the beginning, nearly inclusive of adult white males; but the War of Independence and the subsequent founding of the nation gave this public new vehicles of political expression.

Our objective here is to examine a few of the rhetorics that were used to bring millions within the ambient of democratic institutions then aborning. In attending to certain writings of Ben Franklin, we look to their long-range influence on the American ethos of the self-made man. Our examination of Samuel Adams's revolutionary agitation and the fetes of the French Revolution direct attention to high-impact rhetoric and symbolic performance meant to achieve immediate results, although in both instances there was the long-range effect that a new political sensibility was formed.

Ben Franklin: Hobbism for the People

Toward the end of his richly varied career, Ben Franklin composed a pamphlet meant to promote immigration to the new nation. British publicists had for some time disparaged America's harsh conditions and barbarous culture, partly to dissuade skilled workmen from deserting Britain's industry. (Their persuasion proved to be ineffective against the lure of independence, so laws prohibiting emigration were passed; they too were ineffective.) Franklin's pamphlet, *Information for Those Who Would Remove to America* (1787), was meant to counter this propaganda by describing the charms of the new nation's simple life. In it he wrote that

> whoever has travelled thro' the various Parts of Europe, and observed how small the Proportion of People in Affluence or easy Circumstances there, compar'd with those in Poverty and Misery; the few rich and haughty landlords, the multitude of poor, abject, and rack'd Tenants, and the half-paid and half-starv'd ragged Labourers; and view here the happy Mediocrity, that so generally prevails throughout these States, where the Cultivator works for himself, and supports his Family in decent Plenty, will, methinks, see abundant Reason to bless Divine Providence for the evident and great Difference in our Favour, and be convinc'd, that no Nation that is known to us enjoys a greater Share of human Felicity.

America's "happy mediocrity," or equality of conditions, was a Franklin theme from his *Silence Dogood Letters* through *Poor Richard's Almanack* to his *Autobiography*, a period spanning seventy-five years. He succeeded so well in blending his moralism with the provincial ethos that Poor Richard's sayings became folk wisdom, while the *Autobiography* went through many printings and was held up to two generations as a model of how to combine good morals with worldly success.[1]

The symbiosis between Franklin and the American ethos cannot be ascribed to his socialization in Puritan Boston or Quaker Philadelphia; indeed, the young Franklin was guilty of antisocial behavior. At age sixteen he was a "thorough Deist" whose precocious *Silence Dogood Letters* parodied the Puritan ethos and landed him before Boston's magistrates for chastisement as a factious spirit. He fled Boston for more tolerant Philadelphia; but, finding it also "bigotted and besotted," he made his way to cosmopolitan London. The mediocrity young Franklin found everywhere in the colonies did not then register on him as especially "happy." Later in life, his defense of America against European detractors did not deny the superiority of European high culture to American rusticity.[2] The irony of the phrase "happy mediocrity" helps signify that the symbiosis he achieved with his compatriots was an artificial bond that he fashioned as a means of mutual accommodation between his exceptional genius and democratic equality. He achieved this accommodation by redirecting the existing popular ethos into channels tending to favor the private liberty of all, which was the refuge of exceptional men from the envy of multitudes. But laws not confirmed by manners, Franklin thought, were without force. In vain did the exceptional man claim protection of the law if he did not adopt the manners of the common man. He made himself particularly vulnerable if he set up any goal or standard superior to the common good as commonly understood.

Franklin's symbiosis between the exceptional man and the democratic public I call "Hobbism for the people" on two accounts. He invented a popular style that used moral attitudinizing as a lever to replace moral norms by maxims of utility and enlightened self-interest. In this way he gave popular force to the Hobbesian program to remove morality from the public agenda.[3] Secondly, by relinquishing any claim on behalf of

1. From Franklin's death until 1850, seventy-three editions or printings of his works were issued, mainly by American publishers. In addition to these multi-volume issues, which usually contained the *Autobiography*, this work was printed separately in the United States fourteen times until 1850. After this date, there was a sharp drop in the frequency of Franklin printings. See the *Library of Congress Catalog*, vol. 51.

2. For surveys of Franklin's statements on American culture, for and against, see Melvin H. Buxbaum, *Benjamin Franklin and the Zealous Presbyterians*, 36–37, 44–45; Paul W. Conner, *Poor Richard's Politics*, 96–110.

3. Franklin countenanced no morality that was not useful. Not all scholars have appreciated how deeply this opinion was founded. In the *Autobiography*, he described his philosophizing as having led to the view that "there could be no

his superior values and merit, and rebaptizing the exercise of his talents as "benevolence" toward his fellows, Franklin gave effect to Hobbes's hard but consistent strictures against arrogance, as a condition for achieving the equality his politics mandated.

It is not inconsequential that the moralizing Franklin usually wrote using the mask of a fictional persona: Mrs. Silence Dogood was succeeded by Busy Body, the censor of morals, by Father Abraham, and by Poor Richard Saunders, the time-is-money efficiency expert. Franklin's fictional spokespersons embraced the pervasive ethos of his popular audience, whether Franklin shared that ethos or not. It is easy to pick out differences between Franklin and his personae. Mrs. Dogood represents herself as a Christian woman, albeit one who reprobates the clergy, while the author styled himself a Deist. Poor Richard pens admonitions against idleness and recommends piling up wealth, while his creator abandoned the printing trade to make leisure for idle scientific experiments. The exceptional Franklin did not necessarily practice what his spokespersons preached.[4]

The parodist's humor is apparent in the names Franklin gave to his personae. Widow Silence Dogood is a nonstop wag whose inept name parodies the pious hopes expressed by the Puritan custom of bestowing names of the virtues on offspring. "Dogood" parodies Cotton Mather's tract, *Essays to do Good.* Silence Dogood's scolds were launched in the struggle to thwart a renewed effort by Boston clergymen to impose church discipline on the secular community, a repetition of the endless attempts of Puritans to achieve moral goodness through legislation.

---

such thing as evil in the world; that vice and virtue did not in reality exist, and were nothing more than vain distinctions" (*Works,* 1: 80). This bedrock Hobbism occurs in his account of the development of his opinions about religion and morals. Franklin said that although he was socialized into "the principles of Calvinism," he was "scarcely . . . fifteen years of age" when he "began to doubt revelation itself" (ibid., 79). These doubts led him to read "sermons preached at Boyle's lectures," i.e. the answers to the then-current atheism that were argued mostly by Newton's minions under the sponsorship of the Boyle endowment. Franklin identifies these lectures as Deist. Their statements of the atheist positions they were intended to refute appeared to Franklin "much more forceful than the refutation itself. In a word, I became a perfect Deist." This can only mean that Franklin's "perfect Deism" was atheism; or to be precise, perfect Hobbism, since Hobbes was *the* atheist that Clark and others were concerned to refute. Franklin never repudiated this initial atheism; he merely put it aside on practical grounds as "not very useful" to espouse.

4. An extensive and discerning analysis of Franklin's literary personae may be found in Buxbaum, *Benjamin Franklin,* 7–46.

The sixteen-year-old Franklin entered this controversy equipped by his reading of Locke's *Essay on Human Understanding*, Shaftesbury's *Characteristics*, and the writings of Anthony Collins.[5] Franklin ingeniously adapted this sophisticated rationalism to the unlettered Silence. She accepts her spiritual mentors' do-good morality only to turn it against them. Whereas they understand doing good as the exercise of ecclesiastical discipline, because it signifies the reform of conscience, Silence understands doing good as good behavior, especially charity and decency. Silence inserts the Deist blade between the ribs of Cotton Mather's tribe when she contrasts Christian charity with the aggressive moralism of the preachers. She puts Hobbes's old accusation that their pious zeal was a mask for their desire to lord it over others. She appeals to the democratic resentments of the "good people" of Boston in her attacks upon the snobbishness of Harvard College, the training ground for clergymen. She discerns in Harvard arrogance a confirmation of the allegation that clergymen promoted ecclesiastical discipline solely as a means for acquiring power over the people. It was a confirmation because only the sons of the moneyed and powerful could afford to attend Harvard, where they were encouraged to believe that their piety and rarefied minds made them better than others, although—and here Franklin twists the knife—everyone knew that Harvard students loved their ale and went gaming and whoring when they could.[6]

Hobbes had declared that "the contest of opinion is the fiercest" because it is borne by the pride of seeming to be wise. Thanks to their sense of election, saintly Puritans were liable to manifest this pride as moral rigorism and by bullying the lax and reluctant through public law. Young Franklin's reading helped him realize that this anger endangered private liberty. But he also realized that the democratic ethos provided leverage against its own excesses. The "tyranny of opinion," as it was later called, always stakes a claim to superior goodness and wisdom; since this claim is inconsistent with democratic equality, a threatened minority can hope to turn the flank of a threatening majority by appealing to their egalitarian prejudices. But this appeal will be ineffective if it is not spoken in the democratic idiom. It would not have done for

5. *Works*, 1: 21.
6. For an account of the Boston controversy, see Buxbaum, *Benjamin Franklin*, 47–75. This episode is mentioned only allusively in the *Autobiography*, as if to let sleeping dogs lie. This estimate would seem to be confirmed by a letter Franklin wrote to Mather's son, at the time he was composing the *Autobiography*, in which he credits *Essays to do Good* with having inspired his endeavors. On the present interpretation, this was in a way true: Mather inspired Franklin's attempt to overcome Puritan zealousness.

young Franklin to appeal to the "good people" of Boston to repudiate the unsound wisdom of the Puritan faction and embrace the superior wisdom of the Boston politicals. Instead, he presented the conflict as a cabal of preachers and the affluent to lord it over the "good people." Willingness to arouse popular envy of success to screen private liberty from the importunities of clergymen showed that the young Franklin was a natural for democratic politics.

His early contest with the exponents of the Protestant ethic in Boston proved to be the beginning of a long struggle against Presbyterian leadership in colonial politics and educational institutions. His popular writings on morals and "the art of virtue" were similarly a struggle against the Puritan obtuseness that saw "epidemical corruption" and worked itself into zealous fervor against swearing, Sunday sports, witches, prostitution, and ordinary prudent regard for one's affairs. Puritanical contempt of worldly prudence is conveyed in a typical passage from a Cotton Mather tract:

How full of devices are we for our own security and advantage! and how expert in devising many little things to be done for ourselves! We apply our thoughts with mighty assiduity to the old question, 'what shall we eat and drink, and wherewithal shall we be clothed?' . . . We carry on the business of our personal callings, with numberless thoughts how to perform them well; and to effect our temporal affairs we 'find out witty inventions.' But O rational, immortal, heaven-born soul, are they wondrous faculties capable of no greater improvements, no better employments?[7]

Franklin's popular morality may be fairly described as a device for procuring security and advantage. People do not ordinarily know how to secure their advantage. They consult the wrong sages and are duped by their passions. If the admonitions of Busy Body and Poor Richard strike us as banal, even primitive, their reception by the colonial public as wise advice tells us something about the accuracy of Franklin's estimate of his countrymen. Primitive or not, Poor Richard's advice on "the way to wealth" conveys elementary truths about the management of time, labor, money, and oneself. It was the original "philosophy of self-help" (or, as the elevated Emerson called it, "self-reliance") that chartered the independence of millions of farmers and working men. "If you were a servant," Poor Richard advised, "would you not be ashamed that a

7. Quoted by Conner, *Poor Richard's Politics,* 198.

good master should catch you idle? Are you then your own master? Be ashamed to catch yourself idle."[8]

Poor Richard's epigrams aimed to inspire in the colonials a zest for their rare good fortune at being free, while admonishing them that they would remain free only if they mastered themselves. Poor Richard relentlessly stressed industry, frugality, and punctuality, not because work functioned in the divine plan for salvation but because debt was the common path to dependence and misery. Luxuries, like idleness, were to be avoided for this reason. Franklin's witty ingenuity contrived numerous illustrations of the power of small savings and compound interest. While residing in Paris he advised Parisians that they could save 96 million livres annually on candle purchases if they would but rise with the sun rather than in late morning, as was their habit. The root of all domestic economy was self-management and elementary prudence about the ways of the world. "In the affairs of this world," Poor Richard wrote, "men are saved, not by faith, but by the want of it; but a man's own care is profitable; for if you would have a faithful servant, and one that you like, serve yourself."[9] The "want of faith" recommended here is not an indiscriminate suspicion but an "art of virtue," consisting of a good-humored cynical canniness about oneself and one's fellows.

Franklin's most enduring representation of the art of virtue as the way to worldly success is his *Autobiography*. The book is offered as a narrative of how "I have raised myself to a state of opulence and to some degree of celebrity" after having been born in "the bosom of poverty and obscurity."[10] In these words Franklin sketched the plot line of the story of the self-made man. This figure achieved heroic dimensions in the nineteenth century and embedded itself in the American ethos as a motivating and legitimating icon. It was tangible to Tocqueville when he visited America in the 1820s. Americans extol equality, he observed, but no man wants to *remain* equal; all want to rise, to excel, to succeed. Franklin's story reconciled the inequality implied by the success of a fortunate few with the political requirement of equality. This he did by mingling the tale of his rise with the rise of the nation. Franklin's poverty and obscurity corresponded to the wilderness, "the state of nature" Americans possessed; natural talents that through diligent application he turned to advantage corresponded to the wealth the wilderness yielded when cultivated. The celebrity that satisfied his ambition was achieved partly through the na-

8. *Works*, 3: 456.
9. Ibid., 3: 457.
10. Ibid., 1: 1.

tional struggle for independence, which could be a source of pride to all citizens. Above all, Franklin told his story so as to inspire the lowly and obscure. The art of success is not esoteric, but clear and simple, well within the capacities of millions. By showing success to be a popular art, Franklin inspired gratitude for his benevolence and commendation of his democratic solidarity, instead of envy. Reciprocity between the self-made man and the aspiring millions must be repeatable *ad libitum* to become effective ethos. It can be so repeated because the opportunities for rising and for benevolence are inexhaustible.

The upwardly mobile Franklin was constantly on the move. The years of apprenticeship took him from Boston to Philadelphia to London, back to Philadelphia, then back to England and France. Trials of his own strength and observation of others during this period taught him the difference between those who would and those who can. Those who would but don't, fall; their downward motion sometimes makes room for the upward bound. Downward mobility might be occasioned by anything. Franklin's youthful friend James Ralph persisted in his desire to become a poet although he was warned that he had no talent for that ill-rewarded office. The Philadelphia printer Keimer managed his business badly. Most of Franklin's youthful friends were subject to the distractions of women, gaming, and drink, while Franklin dissipated his small gains by supporting his penurious friends. Young Franklin thus learned that seemingly trivial indulgences or negligence can make all the difference to men on the margins. Working as a compositor in London, he discovered that it was not an economy to spare money by refusing to pay union dues, for the union members then sabotaged his work. He observed that the drinking habits of London workmen kept them in debt while doing nothing to promote their health.

Setting up in business himself, he found that diligence and competence were not enough to attract trade; he needed the influence of friends, as it was also advantageous to create an image of himself as a hard-working, honest, reliable tradesman. Franklin thus made himself partly by judicious alliances with others moving upward through the Old Boy network. These alliances were much more permeable in the colonies than on the Continent because they lacked the footing in great families. Alliances in the colonies had more the character of artificial associations freely made by their members. Franklin constantly projected such associations, ranging from his small, private Chamber of Commerce to the establishment of lending libraries, fire companies, colleges, and the militia. These public service activities, as well as Franklin's political involvements, made business sense. By becoming postmaster, he was in a strong position to ensure the distribution of his publications.

Philanthropic undertakings enhanced his public standing, besides generating news to print. Lending libraries and colleges promoted literacy, upon which printers depend. Benevolence, like honesty, was good business. The net gain of a lifetime of philanthropy was the $500,000 Franklin left his heirs.

Franklin's striking demonstration of the compatibility, and even mutual support, of "doing good" and enhancing private advantage stole the march on Cotton Mather's perception of tension between goods of the soul and cares for the body. The tension is eliminated by tacitly identifying spiritual goods with the public good, so that benevolence becomes the virtue most esteemed by the public. It also eliminates the disharmony, stressed by Bolingbroke as an objection to the parvenus, between public spirit and private advantage.

Franklin's demonstration of the practicability of enlightened self-interest did not depend on his anomalous parlaying of the printing trade into a political career. The point is rather that any tradesman or merchant operates in the envelope of public opinion; and in the absence of inherited privilege, he sells his product best by selling himself also. Good opinion is good business. The linkage of business success to public standing is a natural effect of local markets undistorted by inherited privilege or monopolies. Franklin's insight parlayed this fact into a democratic-commercial ethos. Individuals rise and succeed; but they cannot enjoy their eminence untroubled unless their success in some measure promotes the rise of all. Or, to put it in different terms, the spectacular rise of a few can be sanctioned by a democratic society if upward mobility, or "improvement," is an opportunity widely available. This coincidence of private and public advantage inspired the American Dream. The self-made man who by his own efforts rises from nothing becomes a manic icon because it is in some measure within the reach of the great majority; it is within reach because the entire society is upwardly mobile. Once this imagery is embedded in ethos, a class society can be established only by a great upheaval.

Sam Adams and the Evangel of Liberty

If Ben Franklin instructed his countrymen in the pursuit of happiness, persuasion of a very different kind was needed to generate the political will to a war of independence.

The Declaration of Independence is a great document of that will. The Declaration signers represented themselves as reasonable men, sensible of the blessings of government, moved to rebellion only after patiently suffering a "long train of abuses and usurpations, pursuing invariably the same object, [and evincing] a design to reduce them under absolute despotism." From "decent respect for the opinions of mankind," which denies that government long established may be changed for "light and transient causes," the Declaration briefly states the nation's political principles and purports to document, in a list of twenty-eight abuses, the aspiration of George III to tyrannize over the colonists.

The political principles of the Declaration were rendered as a trim statement of basic Whig doctrine after 1689. All men equally are endowed by their creator with natural rights to life, liberty, and the pursuit of happiness. The object of government is to secure these rights, by consent of the governed. A right to resist established government is a corollary of these principles, since no man can consent to a government destructive of his natural rights. Such assertions were political commonplaces; George III himself did not deny them. In rebelling against British dominion, the patriots invoked and applied principles derived from the fatherland. Indeed, a common view of the matter in Britain was put by John Grenville, who introduced the Stamp Act, when he advised Parliament that "the seditious spirit of the colonies owes its birth to factions in this House."[11]

11. Grenville's speech is printed in *The American Revolution through British Eyes,* ed. Martin Kallich and Andrew MacLeish, 12–13. The American enthusiasm for rebellion does indeed seem to have been inspired partly by English factional politics and by the colorful resistance of the Corsicans to Genoese rule. See Pauline Maier, *From Resistance to Revolution: Colonial Radicals and the Development of American Opposition to Britain, 1765–1776,* 161ff., 198–227; and Isaac Kramnick, "Republican Revisionism Revisited." The British internal contest, as well as British reaction to colonial disturbances, was tracked by two journals of the day, *Gentleman's Magazine* and the *Annual Register.* This aspect of revolutionary politics, which will not be pursued here, is important for the light it throws on a significant element of modern politics, namely, how a subordinate faction, in its drive for power, may attack the very legitimacy of a national regime in the name of an enemy's cause. See Max Beloff, introduction to *The Debate on the American Revolution,* ed. Max Beloff.

While Grenville's judgment highlighted the linkage between parliamentary faction and colonial unruliness, it erred in attributing leadership exclusively to Grenville's English rivals. The colonials were exceptionally jealous of their privileges and routinely obstructed British colonial administration. It was this insubordination—or, equally, the failure of colonial administration—that animated the attempt to impose control after the conclusion of the Seven Years' War. These events are succinctly reviewed by Jack P. Greene, "The Seven Years' War and the American Revolution: The Causal Relationship Reconsidered."

This fact was not acknowledged in the Declaration; it was even denied by implication in a paragraph devoted to affirming that appeals to "our British brethren" had fallen on deaf ears. The Conciliation Proposition passed in Parliament by Lord North's government in a final effort to avert war is unmentioned in the Declaration's catalogue of the government's alleged obstinate refusal to compromise or negotiate. The Declaration's insistence upon British tyranny as the cause of the rupture creates another misleading impression. Between July 1774 and late 1775, Lord North's efforts to conciliate the colonists had been met by harsh rebuffs, calculated offenses, and, in Massachusetts, armed attacks on British forces.[12] Continuing insults led the North Ministry at last to declare the colonials in rebellion. These facts went unmentioned in the Declaration because they were difficult to square with the representation of colonials as victims of oppression. Yet in 1774, the alleged oppression was exercised by a naval force composed of one warship, a few frigates, and a dozen smaller vessels; the land force holding North America numbered no more than 2,000 troops. The government was unprepared for war, reacted sluggishly when it finally came, and was in no wise able to impose despotic government on the colonies, even had it wished.[13] The specter of tyranny evolved by the Declaration's strategic silences thus appears to have been a propaganda bogey.

The twenty-eight count indictment of British tyranny confirms by their weakness the specious character of the allegations. Most of the grievances were scarcely more than inflated complaints. For example, the Declaration charges that the Crown had "called together legislative bodies at places unusual . . . for the sole purpose of fatiguing them into compliance with his measures." Apart from the oddity of a tyrant tolerating defiant assemblies, this reference is to Governor Hutchinson's removal of the Massachusetts Bay assembly from Boston to Cambridge— solely to reduce the high-pressure lobbying of Sam Adams's minions. Again, the Declaration objects to "quartering large bodies of troops among us," although the colonials had demanded *more* troops to secure the frontier against Indians. Several grievances drag up the persiflage of two centuries of parliamentary malcontent: the objection to standing armies puts in an appearance, together with the payment of Crown officers from the civil list, the multiplication of officers, and so on. The

---

12. Even after British forces were attacked at Lexington, Lord Dartmouth, the minister responsible for the colonies, still hoped for reconciliation. See Bernard Donoughue, *British Politics and the American Revolution,* 244ff.; and J. Steven Watson, *The Reign of George III,* 199–212.
13. Donoughue, *British Politics,* 204, 209–10, 274.

Declaration also objects to proroguing legislative assemblies, although that was a certain Crown right. The Crown similarly had the right to revoke charters, although the Declaration discerns in its exercise the lawlessness of "absolute tyranny." The Declaration complains that the Crown had protected its troops "by mock trial," from punishments, "for any murders which they should commit on the inhabitants of these states." This is a reference to the "Boston Massacre," Sam Adams's exaggerated phrase for the shooting of five rioters. An officer and several troopers were tried and acquitted by a jury of Boston citizens. The trial was styled "mock" because it was held six months after the event, when the passions of the moment had passed. The reasonable men addressed by the Declaration were asked to believe that tyrannical governments allow their soldiers to stand trial for crimes they are allegedly encouraged to commit.[14]

Examination of the remaining twenty accusations would come to similar results. The charges were gross exaggerations, flat reversals of fact, and conversions of normal Crown entitlements into usurpations, all culminating in a charge of tyranny against a very mild, free government. But in the colonies, first the Stamp Act (1765) and then every revenue act aroused the patriots to loud declamations against tyranny, echoing in this the parliamentary forces of disaffection, or, as may be, of constitutional reform.[15] Moreover, the jeremiads against tyranny were

14. Hiller B. Zobel, *The Boston Massacre*, 180–205.
15. Taxation in the colonies was less than 3 percent of the gross revenue in the years prior to the Revolution. The Stamp Act was meant to raise £60,000 per annum. Annual revenues in the years 1771–74 were about £47,000 per annum. See Peter D. McClelland, "The Cost to America of British Imperial Policy"; Oliver M. Dickerson, *The Navigation Acts and the American Revolution*, 185–86, 198–201; Julian Gwyn, "British Government Spending and the North American Colonies, 1740–1775," 74–84. Despite these small sums, there was a significant fiscal question at stake, as Grenville realized. For the Stamp Act was a direct tax, and direct taxes theretofore had been raised through colonial legislatures. Colonials had never objected to import duties or other indirect taxes levied by the Crown; but the Stamp Act could be and was interpreted as an invasion of a right conferred by usage. This was the matter referred in the otherwise confusing slogan "No Taxation without Representation." The colonists' case was undoubtedly solid, if not conclusive. But they did not put it as a distinct case in common law. Instead it was inflated into much larger questions of the nature and legitimacy of parliamentary authority over the colonies. Publicists writing in defense of the Crown accepted the unmanageably large front, so the road to an insoluble legitimacy dispute was opened. The argumentation on this question is a touchstone of constitutional thinking at that time. Major statements were:

uttered without any embarrassment about the institution of slavery. Jefferson's draft of the Declaration had sharply attacked the slave trade, but wiser heads in the Convention, perceiving that its inclusion would create disharmony among the patriots, excised the argument against slavery from their denunciation of "absolute tyranny."[16]

Soame Jemyns, M.P., *The Objections to the Taxation of Our American Colonies* (1765); Daniel Dulany, *Considerations on the Propriety of Imposing Taxes on British Colonies, for Purposes of Raising Revenue, by Act of Parliament* (1765); Benjamin Franklin's testimony before Parliament (1767), printed in Kallich and MacLeish, eds., *The American Revolution;* and Samuel Johnson, *Taxation No Tyranny: An Answer to the Resolutions of the American Congress* (1775).

16. Jefferson's paragraph on the slave trade ran as follows: "The King waged cruel war against human nature itself, violating its most sacred rights and liberty in the persons of a distant people, who never offended him, captivating and carrying them into slavery in another hemisphere, or to incur miserable death in their transport thither. This practical warfare, the opprobrium of *infidel* powers, is the warfare of the *Christian* king of Great Britain. Determined to keep open a market where MEN should be bought and sold, he has prostituted his negative for suppressing every legislative attempt to prohibit or to restrain this execrable commerce; and that this assemblage of horrors might want no fact of distinguished die, he is now exciting those very people to rise in arms among us, and to purchase that liberty of which *he* has deprived them, by murdering the people upon whom *he* also obtruded them; thus paying off former crimes committed against the *liberties* of one people, with crimes which he urges them to commit against the *lives* of another." One looks twice at this passage to verify that Jefferson was actually blaming the king for *foisting* ("obtruding") slavery on the colonists! No note was taken of the reason why Privy Council did not prohibit slave trading: it was a political concession to southern planters. This paragraph attempted to parry British criticisms of the colonists' righteous denunciations of British tyranny even as they held 800,000 human beings in bondage. The speciousness of Jefferson's response is transparent. While slavery was acknowledged to be inconsistent with the principles he declares, the colonists, who bore nearly all the responsibility, were exonerated while the Privy Council, which bore very little responsibility, was loaded with the whole moral guilt. The paradox of slaveholders espousing liberty and equality is a piquant example of misfits between interest and apologetics. Had the principles of the Declaration been tailored to interest, the black man would have been excluded from the scope of natural rights. But to make one exception is to abandon the case, and the claimed liberties of the colonists would be carried away with it. Logic therefore compelled the planters to subscribe to a principle contrary to their interests. In the course of time, the entire polity was obliged to conform to this principle, contrary to wish and interest.

As a final comment, we note that Jefferson's charge that the British had

These observations expose that standing embarrassment of American historians, the absence of a threat to the principles of liberty, which seems somehow to lower the dignity of the Revolution. Gordon Wood expresses the embarrassment in his seminal historiographic essay "Rhetoric and Reality in the American Revolution":

The Americans were not an oppressed people: they had no crushing imperial shackles to throw off. In fact, the Americans knew they were probably freer and less burdened . . . than any part of mankind. . . . Never in history . . . had there been so much rebellion with so little real cause. . . . The American response was out of all proportion to the stimuli."[17]

The embarrassment seizes political principle as well as historical explanation. The Lockean doctrine of the Declaration justifies the grave act of rebellion only in the extremity of despotism, whereas in reality the Revolution was a free act. What then was the object of the act, and what set it in motion? The object, evidently, was "independence," i.e. sovereignty. But this object is always animated by the same cause, a political will. Thomas Paine, whose *Common Sense* inflamed Americans in January 1776, displayed this will in his remark that it was after all "ridiculous for an island to possess a continent."[18]

---

encouraged slaves to "murder" their masters referred to a threat by General Gage to recruit blacks to the ranks of British forces. That this threat was never executed is yet another proof of Privy Council moderation, stemming from its conservatism.

Jefferson's draft of the Declaration is reprinted by Carl Becker in his *The Declaration of Independence*, 174–84.

17. Gordon Wood, "Rhetoric and Reality in the American Revolution," 106.

18. The development of this political will may be detected in Greene's summary in "The Seven Years' War." The Declaration of Independence is, as a whole, a manifestation of it. But it is worth noting that the Declaration expressly repudiated the sovereignty of Parliament as "a jurisdiction foreign to our constitutions." This was a response to the Declaratory Act of 1766, which asserted the absolute sovereignty of Parliament over all colonies; see Paul Langford, "Old Whigs, Old Tories, and the American Revolution."

The will to independence was often coupled with the vision of empire. In April 1774, Sam Adams wrote to Arthur Lee: "It requires but a small portion of the gift of discernment for any one to foresee, that providence will erect a mighty empire in America" (*The Writings of Samuel Adams*, 3: 102). The architect of empire, however, was Ben Franklin. See Gerald Stourzh, *Benjamin Franklin and American Foreign Policy*, 54–82, and below, pp. 470–75.

Paine's thought had been signaled by colonial agents in proposals to move the capital of the British empire to America when its population should outnumber that of the British Isles. It was available also in the opinion often repeated that the colonies were full of refractory Whigs. This political will generated most of the disputation, yet neither party could place it on the agenda. That was partly because the political will became a conscious national will only through the disputation process; and partly because neither party possessed the conceptual means to accept the free will to sovereignty as legitimate. The consequence for British policy was incorrigible incomprehension: sincere attempts at conciliation were followed by attempts to reduce to obedience by force. The consequence for Americans was to install in the national political ethos a hypocrisy of monumental proportions.[19] Patriots claiming to base their position on reasoned principle and fact had to find a way of replacing the fact of mild British government by the myth of British tyranny. The replacement was accomplished by an overwrought rhetoric, which may be evaluated from the Hobbesian perspective as the shape injustice took in this particular establishment of sovereignty. This point will bear elaboration.

Political will is essentially despotic because political association can be created only by a magisterial act of sovereignty that settles an order on the chaos of contending private wills. This remains true even when citizens say or believe that they consent to government, because consent too is extracted by force, which becomes a permanent fixture as courts and constabulary. There is not a drop of righteousness in this description of sovereignty, since it is based on rejection of the moral illusion that political order derives from an act of justice: in fact, it derives from a contention of wills between which there can be no justice until order is settled by force. The American founding became enmeshed in monumental hypocrisy because it posited the Hobbes-Locke principles, but then put upon itself the mask of morality.

The process of moralizing Hobbes-Locke principles is conspicuous in the thought and action of Samuel Adams. His career, which extended

---

19. The hypocrisy and cant of the colonials is the theme of Peter Oliver's devastating tract *The Origin and Progress of the American Rebellion: A Tory Point of View*. A number of writers, among them Adam Smith and Josiah Tucker, were quite willing to see the colonies granted independence peacefully, but nevertheless held the patriots' accusations and political agitation in contempt. See Josiah Tucker, *Four Tracts* (1774), tract 3; and David Stevens, "Adam Smith and the Colonial Disturbances," in *Essays on Adam Smith*, ed. A. S. Skinner and Thomas Wilson, 202–17.

from 1745 to 1796, spanned the formative years of the republic. His ceaseless activity as publicist, organizer, and politician won Boston its sobriquet, the Cradle of Liberty. His reputation was at its height in 1775–76, for he, above all, had engineered the break with Britain. This destiny had been foreshadowed decades previously when he wrote his Harvard master's thesis arguing that it was "lawful to resist the Supreme Magistrate, if the Commonwealth cannot be otherwise preserved." By 1768 he was calling his compatriots to arms against Britain. It was he who made a word father to a thought by coining a defiant phrase that resounded through the colonies—"Independent we are, and independent we will be." His political career up to 1775 had been a relentless, well-planned assault on the legitimacy of the British government. It was no secret that Adams was the dynamo of the independence movement. He was so thoroughly identified with it that colonial Tories called the Revolution "Adams's conspiracy," while Lord North called the rebels "Sam Adams's crew." Jefferson, who was well situated to know, called him "truly the *Man of the Revolution.*" And a British Army officer wrote of him in 1775: "Would you believe it, that this immense continent from New England to Georgia is moved and directed by one man; a man of ordinary birth and desperate fortune, who by his abilities and talent for factious intrigue, had made himself of some consequence, whose political existence depends upon the continuance of the present dispute, and who must sink into insignificancy and beggary the moment it ceases!"[20]

Adams's moralization of Lockean political science may be conceived as having occurred on two levels. On the conceptual level, it occurred by his amalgamating Locke's teaching with the republicanism of Harrington and the Old Whigs. Locke provided the doctrine of natural right, including the right to resist despotic government. The Harringtonians furnished him an accusatory, heroic rhetoric and the notion of virtue as the basis of a free society. Both notions are absent from Locke because, as we have seen, they are excluded by the rational self-interest that lies at the basis of his political science. Adams's merger of these heterogeneous doctrines armed him with a political rhetoric of great flexibility, which easily moved from deliberative assemblies to newspapers and street harangues. Its effect was to treat Locke's rational political will as if it were righteous; but, conversely, the rhapsodic Harringtonian virtue rhetoric acquired a measure of rational principle by

20. Quoted by John C. Miller, *Sam Adams: Pioneer in Propaganda*, 343–44. For Adams's control of the propaganda machinery in the colonies, see Philip Davidson, *Propaganda and the American Revolution, 1763–1783*, 48–62.

association with Locke's doctrine.[21] This description applies to much of the Whig rhetoric of the period.

Adams's moralization of political science also occurred on what deserves to be distinguished as a psychological plane. Here our attention is directed to his amalgamation of Old Whig virtue, whose chief sources were classical writers, with remnants of Puritan moral fervor anchored in biblical imagery. Of his many arresting expressions of this fusion, we may cite his notion of Boston as a "Christian Sparta," where "Old Puritans" and "Romans" would establish a regime of virtuous simplicity and austerity. The association of Calvinist rigorism with the rigorism of classical virtue could be easily made once the doctrinal element of Calvinism was discarded. Calvinist prohibitions upon drinking, gaming, reveling, the theater, and frivolous entertainment were congenial with the jeremiads of John Trenchard or Andrew Fletcher condemning luxury and vice as instruments of the undoing of that sturdy, manly virtue upon which freedom was thought to depend. It will be recalled that the Old Whig writers were particularly emphatic about targeting commerce and finance as the newly arisen corruptions spreading luxury and selfishness. Adams was no less persuaded than Trenchard and Fletcher that commerce endangers virtue and liberty. Indeed, the love of luxury among the British and the colonial Tories was for him a reliable sign of their decadence and certain decline into despotism.[22] In his Christian Sparta there was no toleration for private wealth, nor entertainments other than those political. As governor of Massachusetts, he attempted to suppress the theater and to curb the growth of religious denominations other than the Congregational Church. Like Trenchard and Bolingbroke, he was dismayed by the parvenus, who swarmed into Boston during the postrevolutionary prosperity. Here is another negative correlation between the "Protestant ethic" and commerce; and one

21. Adams's political thought was thoroughly constitutionalist. The documents of 1688 were the bedrock of his argumentation—the Bill of Rights, Locke's *Two Treatises,* Blackstone's interpretation of the British constitution recur frequently. The Harringtonians he most resembled were Algernon Sydney and Robert Molesworth, whose choleric tempers Adams shared. His blend of natural right and legal reasoning with moralism was the authentic American political idiom of that period. For particularly clear examples of the Locke-Harrington mix, see *The Writings of Samuel Adams,* 1: 134–52, 250ff., 316–18.

22. The widespread view that Britain had become decadent is probably attributable to seventy-five years of Country Whig jeremiads. See Donoughue, *British Politics,* 43; Bernard Bailyn, *The Ideological Origins of the American Revolution,* 136–37; and Maier, *From Resistance to Revolution,* 198–227.

symmetrical with the views of the Boston expatriate Ben Franklin. Whereas Franklin endorsed frugality as a means to wealth and security and believed moralistic austerity to be a danger to liberty, Adams linked austerity and liberty into a political religion hostile to commercial acquisition.

The Old Whigs conducted their critique of commerce as a part of an apology for land. It has been noted that while land was depicted as the virtuous agrarian, its cash value in Augustan England was a defense of the gentry as a social class against inroads on their power. The urbanite Adams could not deploy the anticommerce critique in that manner. His father, a prosperous brewer, might have combined with the commercial elite who dominated the politics of that port town. But Sam Adams, Sr., associated instead with the popular Whig faction opposed to the "oligarchy" composed of the colonial administration, most of the clergy, and the dominant merchants. This coalition corresponded more or less to the Court Whigs in England. Opposition to them in Massachusetts could not duplicate the Country party because there was no gentry. Tradesmen, small merchants, and backcountry farmers formed the natural constituency of the opposition that arose in the 1740s over the government's suppression of the Land Bank—a popular scheme of paper credit based on John Law's ideas. Adams senior was a principal investor in the Bank; its suppression cemented his alliance with the popular faction.[23] Thus it transpired that a brewer and financier headed a popular faction denouncing corrupt manners and oligarchy.

The hard edge of this paradox was removed for Adams junior, whose business ineptitude caused his inherited fortune to decay. But that circumstance did not affect the matter in question. The basis of faction in Boston was not a conflict between despotism and liberty, but the ambition of the subordinate interest to impede or even supplant the dominant interest. (This same factional pattern of tradesmen and small merchants opposed to the "oligarchy" was duplicated in New York and Pennsylvania.) There being no moral difference between the two factions, opposition rhetoric, if it was to depict its cause as a struggle of principle rather than interest, had to fabricate a moral illusion. The overriding illusion that came out of this struggle was the bogey of British tyranny. This allegation was so plainly unfactual that it did not become effective nationally in that form; in the critical months after 1774, Boston patriots succeeded in persuading moderate colonial leaders that there was a "well laid conspiracy" to impose despotism on the colonies.[24]

23. Miller, *Sam Adams*, 8–13, 25.
24. Bernard Bailyn stresses the prominence of the conspiracy theory in the pam-

To create the illusion of British tyranny, Adams needed to deploy an array of images best adapted to evoke emotion potent enough to drive his politics. This was why he invoked the Old Whig virtue-in-distress imagery and spun out a rhetoric of crisis and of the cataclysmic redeeming event. It was why his accusations were so violent and extreme. For example, he unfailingly represented taxation acts as plots "for taking away all our money . . . [and] our lands will go next or be subject to rack rents from haughty and relentless landlords who will ride at ease, while we are trodden in the dirt." In commercial England he could allow nothing short of "total Depravation of principles and manners" that had "irrevocably undone" its sense of honor as well as its political will. Speaking in the Continental Congress against conciliation, he revealed something of his thinking about propaganda when he warned that conciliation promoted the "total Stagnation of the Power of Resentment, the utter loss of every manly Sentiment of Liberty and Virtue." The impulse for the jugular evident in these phrases, the propensity to stark contrasts of good and evil, reveal the mind of a fanatic.[25]

If incendiary language were enough to make a revolution, governments could scarcely afford to tolerate a free press. Adams made his rhetoric politically effective by his skill in assessing the mood of his constituency and integrating words with events. "We cannot make events," he once said of his activity, "our business is wisely to improve them."[26]

---

phlet literature. He does not point out what his evidence clearly indicates, that the events and Privy Council acts taken to be evidence of a conspiracy against American liberty were overwhelmingly Boston events and government measures against the unruliness of Boston. The interpretation of these events was also primarily made by Boston politicians—Sam and John Adams, James Otis, John Hancock. See the chapter "The Logic of Rebellion" in Bailyn, *Ideological Origins of the American Revolution.* Southern delegates to the Continental Congress were acutely aware of the Boston patriots' attempt to project their radical republicanism as a national cause. Of Sam Adams in particular it was said that he "wished to see Massachusetts at the head of America, Boston at the head of Massachusetts, and himself dictator of Boston" (Miller, *Sam Adams,* 316). To the extent that Massachusetts politicians were suspected of wishing to push the colonies into independence to launch their own ambitions, they in turn needed to stress that the Coercion Acts of 1774 were not measures merely to restore order in Massachusetts, but betrayed a well-laid conspiracy against liberty.

25. Most of the revolutionary orators were chiaroscurists. See Philip Davidson's documentation in his *Propaganda and the American Revolution, 1763–1783,* as well as Bailyn, *Ideological Origins of the American Revolution.*
26. Quoted by Miller, *Sam Adams,* 342. It was one of Adams's strengths as a

He commanded numerous improvement techniques. One of these was riots. Staged spontaneous riots were perhaps his chief means of playing on the emotions of the citizenry and of recruiting them to his cause. Understanding the feelings of solidarity that well up in a group who participate in a strong emotion, Adams ritualized riots and made them integral to Boston politics. Rioters usually assembled at the Liberty Tree on Boston Common. The new outrage was announced and brief harangues were delivered. The crowd discussed what its actions should be. Sometimes they drew up angry petitions; sometimes they marched on an offending Tory's home or business and menacingly demanded satisfaction; sometimes they went on rampages of vandalism, sacking Tory homes or businesses.[27]

The use of riots as a political technique depended on the capacity to control them. Control was exercised through a seasoned riot squad, the Loyal Nine, a covert operations group chosen from the local Sons of Liberty, who were themselves selected from among the more steadfast members of the Whig party. Adams's force masked their manipulation of riots by alternating between "black" and "white" varieties. Black riots were staged spontaneous protests used to threaten the administration, intimidate Tories, and excite the public. The Whig leadership seldom made an appearance at these riots. White riots were peaceful celebrations or festivities organized to mark some political event or to commemorate a political victory of the past. These occasions initiated the broader public into the thrills, techniques, and rituals of black riots by subtly inculcating and sanctioning violence. Leaders delivered intemperate orations; threatening gestures, such as effigy burning, were staged; torchlight parades aroused that lawless hankering that the Shaftesbury Whigs had exploited during the Exclusion Crisis. The frequency of popular gatherings of this kind made black riots seem to be only popular assemblies and authentic expressions of warranted indignation. When it was convenient to do so, the Adams men prompted such assemblers to treat their decisions as binding on public authorities and to regard constituted authority as usurpations of the "rights" of such "town meetings." In this way, *de jure* authority was subverted and made to seem illegitimate; and, conversely, the *de facto* power of Whig political gimmicks was made to appear to be legitimate power repressed by the government.[28]

---

popular politician that he could estimate very accurately how far his constituency was willing to go at any given time; and that when he occasionally misjudged the situation, he quickly backtracked. See ibid., 126, 160.

27. Ibid., 53, 61–62, 65, 112, 208.

28. Dirk Hoerder, *Crowd Action in Revolutionary Massachusetts, 1765–1780*, 78–84,

Subversion of legitimate authority was the basic strategy of Adams's practice as well as his rhetoric. As tax collector of Boston, he built party patronage by excusing favored persons from taxes. When an audit showed the revenues to be £7,000 short (in a town of 15,000), Adams set up a smoke screen of legal delays and apologetics that thwarted Tory cries for his scalp. A court eventually required him to make good only £200 of the loss. As a member of the legislature, he used his influence to cause a gallery to be installed in the House; he then packed the galleries with Whig partisans whom he used to intimidate Tory members. The colonial constabulary force he paralleled with an enforcement unit of his own, known as "Adams's Mohawks." The most important action of the Mohawks was the Boston Tea Party of December 1773; they destroyed a cargo of tea being imported under provisions of the Tea Duty Act, which the Whigs opposed as illegal. This sensational raid was a watershed event on the path to revolution, because the open defiance obliged Privy Council to consider whether its long indulgence of usurpations and lawlessness was not leading to destruction of its authority. Unfortunately for the British, the Council's authority had already been seriously weakened by the clandestine muscle of the Mohawks, by which Adams assured that every Whig sympathizer voted, regardless of legal qualification, while Tory voters were intimidated. Mohawks enforced the Nonimportation Agreement on unwilling merchants. They harassed Crown officers and obstructed the performance of their duties, particularly the commissioners of customs. Off-duty British soldiers were beaten in alleys; on duty, they were taunted and insulted. This baiting eventually provoked the shootings that Adams sanctimoniously canonized as the Boston Massacre.[29]

These are but a few of Adams's numerous subversions of law that prompted Tories to ironize him as "the patriot dictator" and to call his coterie "lawless banditti." In Governor Thomas Hutchinson the Tories had an able and steady leader who accurately reported to Privy Council on Massachusetts politics. Had he been given adequate support, he might have rallied Boston sentiment against Adams's political thuggery. The Boston Tea Party for a moment stiffened the North government to appropriate action. Privy Council resolved to punish Adams and five

---

185–89, 207–15; Peter Shaw, *American Patriots and the Rituals of Revolution,* 177–232.

29. Miller, *Sam Adams,* 70, 105, 110, 128, 135, 141, 160, 173, 208, 273. When Adams went to the Continental Congress in Philadelphia, he took his tactics with him. Joseph Galloway, speaker of the Pennsylvania Assembly and a moderate who espoused a conciliation agreement with Britain, was threatened by mobs stirred by Adams, and was sent a death threat (ibid., 323).

others for treasonous actions as officers of the House of Representatives in support of the Mohawk raid. But this resolve soon weakened. Instead of punishing a leadership for publicly visible sedition, the feckless North government brought down the Coercion Acts to strengthen Crown officers in Massachusetts and to punish not the few offenders, but Boston, by closing the port and moving customs to Salem.[30] These acts merely encouraged solidarity with Mohawk illegalities and left Adams free to exploit those feelings. He lost no opportunity to do so. For decades he had endeavored to turn the Committees of Correspondence, an intercolony network of the Sons of Liberty, into an effective organization for the dissemination of propaganda and extension of Mohawk intimidation. The North government's response to the Tea Party enabled Adams to activate this system; by mid-1774, he had organized 300 Committees of Correspondence in Massachusetts alone, while in Pennsylvania and Virginia, similar committees hatched Adams's "egg of sedition." The Jacobin Clubs of France probably copied this model.

Samuel Adams ought to be numbered, after Lord Shaftesbury, as the second modern master of the politics of agitation and subversion. His incendiary rhetoric and clever exploitation of events carried colonials into a war unwished by John Dickinson of Pennsylvania and other great figures of prerevolutionary colonial politics. Adams "co-opted" these men, as he co-opted James Otis and John Hancock in Massachusetts. But unlike Shaftesbury, Adams's political understanding was limited to the rhetoric of Old Whig complaints, which he manipulated to good effect. His animus against standing armies made him an advocate of a militia force to oppose the British; but state militias proved to be worse than ineffective against professional troops, and the American war effort required professionalization as well. He was predictably among the anti-Federalists who opposed the Constitution from fear that it would raise despotic government, although he could not discern the despotism in his own conception of Christian Sparta. His moralization of the liberty of self-interest was thrust aside by postrevolutionary Boston, eager to seize commercial opportunities.[31] Yet it remained a

---

30. For an account of Privy Council deliberations, see Donoughue, *British Politics,* 35, 38, 53ff., 65ff., 73–126.
31. Diarist William Bentley, a Boston clergyman, wrote a lucid characterization of Adams in which he said: "No man contributed more towards our revolution, and no man left behind him less, distinctly to mark his resolutions, his peculiar genius, and his communications. He was feared by his enemies, but too secret to be loved by his friends. . . . he was not known till he acted and how far he was to act was unknown. . . . he preserved the severity of Cato in

heritage of the American ethos, renewed, expanded, and transformed for generations of political moralists.

Spectacles of the French Revolution

The American Revolution was made by a nation of 3 million, thinly spread along 2,000 miles of seaboard. The largest cities, Philadelphia and New York, held fewer than 50,000 inhabitants; Boston's 15,000 were enough to make it a large town. France was a nation of 25 million whose capital contained over a half-million persons; and this large population was enclosed in an area less than half that of the colonies.

These differences of scale may partially account for the different emotional intensity of the two revolutions. Small towns may be seized by paroxysms of enthusiasm or fear, but cannot sustain them over time. A nation of 25 million, by contrast, can and did sustain almost twenty-five years of agitation, riot, persecution, terror, civil and foreign wars. There were other reasons why the two revolutions followed courses so different. The colonies fought a war of independence against a remote power, whereas in France revolution everywhere and at once set class against class, citizen against citizen, the new against the old. The colonials had no need to build democratic institutions from the debris of absolute monarchy. They merely detached mature parliamentary institutions from British sovereignty and remodeled them into the federal system. The American struggle could be and was conducted through intact structures. But in France the old regime had to be dismantled and rebuilt *ab initio*. This could be done only by steady, directed application of force, yet stability evaporated with the collapse of the *ancien régime* and did not reappear until Napoleon imposed his rule a decade later.

Sharp collisions in France generated feelings of rapture, righteousness, paranoia, and hatred that entrenched themselves as patriotism and republican zeal. The passions were also current in America, where they were called "the Spirit of '76." But the revolutionary élan did not take hold in America so fiercely as in France. Indeed, by the 1790s, American democrats, alarmed by the rise of Hamiltonian "monocrats," strove to revive the Spirit of '76 by founding Jacobin Clubs that would reimport

---

his manners, and the dogmatism of a priest in his religious observances, for theology was not his study. Our New England Fathers were his theme and he had their deportment, habits, and customs. Often as I have conversed with him, I saw always this part of his character zeal. He was a puritan in his manners always. In Theory he was nothing, he was all in himself. He could see far into men, but not into opinions."

the fervor that the new nation had exported to France two decades earlier.[32]

In the absence of democratic political institutions, popular action in France flowed into the only channels readily available—riots and demonstrations that gave citizens a sense of solidarity and of inclusion in the political public. The press, particularly the radical press espousing popular sovereignty, ascribed great significance to these tumults. This it did partly by devoting much more space to street actions than to the actions of the National Assembly or other formal bodies.[33] Highlighting street actions was a means of expressing opposition to the distinction made between active and passive citizens by the Constitution of 1789, which enfranchised only about 3 million citizens, the remainder being excluded as deficient in the civic virtue then believed to be necessary for participation in republican politics.[34] Riots and other informal political action demonstrated the *de facto* activity of *de jure* passive citizens. The press was also anxious to establish the civic virtue of the supposedly uncivic passive citizenry, and to this end reported glowingly on their honesty, wisdom, and moderation.[35]

Although such concrete political objectives partly accounted for the celebration of riots and demonstrations by the radical press, another element, pervasive in the Revolution's first phase, tended to romanticize all revolutionary politics. This element was the classicism of the revolutionary leadership; for all factions, from constitutionalists to radicals, con-

---

32. Eugene P. Link, *Democratic-Republican Societies, 1790–1800*, 44–70.

33. Jack Richard Censer, *Prelude to Power: The Parisian Radical Press, 1789–1791*, 81ff., 132ff., 167. Censer's quantitative study covers six newspapers of the many hundreds that published during this period.

34. Eric Thompson, *Popular Sovereignty and the French Constituent Assembly, 1789–91*, 48ff.

35. On 23 October 1790, for example, the *Révolutions de Paris* reported: "I have seen an Englishman stupefied these days with astonishment meeting clusters of citizens, poorly dressed, but rich in luminous and profound ideas. I have seen the more subtle efforts of the aristocracy upset by the instinct of the assembled people which is coarse but just and penetrating. From the moment that the people opened their eyes at the first glimmer of liberty, nothing has deceived them; the names, the titles, all the social considerations, which formerly held them in a stupid respect, have ceased to impose on them. . . . This people is not at all a ferocious beast, which as soon as it felt itself unleashed, threw itself on its enemies; it is rather a people which, after a long denial of justice, first manifested an only too just impatience and today reasons all its actions" (quoted by Censer, *Prelude to Power*, 47).

ceived their objective as the founding of a virtuous republic on Greek or Roman models.[36]

The classicism of the Revolution, which dominated until the Thermidor reaction of 1794, is an anomaly for historians operating according to Adam Smith's historiography, which interprets these events as the destruction of feudal monarchy by a rising bourgeoisie. On this view, zeal for the virtuous republic is an aberration inconsistent with the inherent tendency of events. Reasoning in this way, one readily arrives at Karl Marx's epigram that revolutionary classicism was "the reenactment of tragedy as farce"; and one agrees with H. A. Taine that revolutionary politics was "a sort of opera played in the streets." These judgments suggestively direct attention to the theatrical quality of the revolutionary political style but dismiss the style as window dressing of no importance to the substance of events.

This view is burdened by many paradoxes. Had the French Revolution been led by the *haute bourgeoisie*—the great men of commerce, finance, and manufacturing—espousing Lockean political doctrine and economic expansion, we would without hesitation conclude that it was indeed a bourgeois revolution. But the *haute bourgeoisie* did not combine as a class at any time during the Revolution, and men representative of that group did not acquire influence until Napoleon suppressed factions. The faction whose economic doctrine was the best candidate for "bourgeois" was the Girondists; but their position was indistin-

36. The first historian to draw attention to the formative influence of the classics upon the French Revolution was Constantin François Chasseboeuf, Comte de Volney, in his *Leçons d'histoire*, delivered at the École normale in 1794. Volney was a classical scholar and a deputy in the National Assembly from 1789. In the *Leçons* he urged that the tendency of European politics to cling to classical and biblical models was pernicious. He said that the liberty of Sparta was the freedom of "3,000 nobles to oppress 100,000 serfs," and that their virtue was nothing but a warrant for murder and brigandage. In a passage resembling Hobbes's statement on the Polybian cycle, he wrote: "The actors change on the scene, but the passions do not, and history presents only repetitions of this cycle of calamities and errors . . . while at the same time all history proclaims that these errors and calamities are caused by general and primitive human *ignorance*, which does not know its true interests, nor the means to arrive at the end desired by the passions . . ." (*Œuvres de C. F. Volney*, 7: 133). Also like Hobbes, Volney was struck by certain similarities between Homeric Greeks and the New World savages (4: 442–581). Volney's views on the classicism of the French Revolution were revived toward the end of the nineteenth century by Rioux de Maillou and his pupil André Aulard.

guishable from the mercantilism of the encyclopedists. The short-lived Americanists espoused Physiocratic doctrine, which as we will see was deeply rooted in classical ideals and was emphatically agrarian in orientation.[37] Among other factions economic doctrine meant little more than the politics of class conflict, another notion inherited from antiquity but rejected by modern political science.[38] From that perspective, the classicism of the French Revolution is of a piece with the chronic uproar of revolutionary politics and its theatrical quality.

The classicism of the French Revolution derived from the classicism of French secondary education. The generation that made the Revolution learned their politics from Cicero, Livy, Sallust, Plutarch, Virgil, Horace, and Seneca.[39] That there should have been a classical revival at the very moment when Europe was gearing up for the Industrial Revolution will not startle readers sensitive to frequent occurrences of noncontemporaneity of events in history. The revival betokened the awakening of an appetite for politics, which classical writers encourage and refine.

Hobbes had said that the rebellion against Charles I was due in no small measure to the influence of classical authors. This was certainly a prime factor making for the French Revolution. The dry institutional analysis of Locke and Hume is scarcely traceable anywhere but in the constitution-making aspect of the Revolution. Eloquence held sway. Revolutionaries were enraptured by stories of Manlius Torquatus, who had his own son executed for engaging the enemy contrary to orders; of the Horatii brothers doing battle for the fatherland; of Quinctius Cincinnatus, the mighty statesman living in bucolic simplicity. Classical writers evoked manic images of disciplined legions massed on the field of battle; of Scipio Africanus gloriously annihilating corrupt, commercial Carthage. The tumults of Roman politics they made appear as occasions fit for civic exertion. They praised the wisdom of the Roman

37. See below, chap. 10.
38. Victor Advielle, *Histoire de Gracchus Babeuf,* 1: 66ff.
39. Harold T. Parker, *The Cult of Antiquity and the French Revolutionaries,* 8–36. Expressly denying that the classicism of the French Revolution derived from modern philosophy, Volney traced it to "the system of education which has prevailed in Europe for a century and a half: these are the vaunted classical books—these poets, orators, historians—which, thoughtlessly placed in the hands of youths, have imbued their principles and moral sentiments. It is the models of men and actions found in these books that have inflamed the natural desire to imitate, which have habituated them to passionately desire virtues and beauties real or imagined, but which . . . have served only to implant the blind sentiment called *enthusiasm*" (*Œuvres,* 7: 124).

people, and extolled their respect for law, so forceful among them that obscure citizens enjoyed immunity from arbitrary punishment. They told of the surpassing virtue of Rome's many chieftains, who sometimes aspired to tyranny and compelled their kinsmen to put them to death in order to save liberty. They told of the gradual spread of corruption in Rome, of its slow but deadly civil effects, culminating in despotism.

Such was the stock of exhilarating tragic anecdotes that inflamed the imaginations of revolutionaries and supplied them with a common idiom. They caused the bust of Brutus, the scourge of Caesar, to be prominently displayed in the chamber of the National Assembly. Oratorical expostulations invoking Brutus's name were fashionable, e.g.: "Je jure sur la tête de Brutus." Factional rivalries in the Assembly were expressed as struggles between advocates of Athenian freedom (Desmoulins) and advocates of Spartan moral rigorism (Saint Just, Robespierre). The dechristianization movement initiated by the Assembly in autumn, 1793, meant to replace Christian iconography by pagan symbols applied to the cult of the Supreme Being. Atheism and Epicureanism were officially execrated because classical authors said that they were corrupted virtue—a notion endorsed by Rousseau's epigram that "nations are born Stoic and die Epicurean." The Committee of Public Instruction drew up a comprehensive plan for spartanizing the nation. The plan called for a gymnasium (*théâtre*). Citizens were to be taught a variety of skills meant to enhance the civic capacity, particularly dance and music, poetry, oratory, and art. Newspapers of the day, many of them managed by Assembly politicians, were profuse in their citation of classical authorities, whereas modern political writers tended to be cited to the extent that they endorsed the virtuous republic.[40]

In the provinces the antiquity cult was expressed by the renaming of streets after classical heroes or cities. Birth registers showed a rash of Brutuses, Gracchuses, Lucretias, and Antigones coming into the world. Prominent politicians sometimes entered into the spirit by changing their names to Greek or Roman names. The red Phrygian *bonnet* became a symbol of the Revolution. At Nevers enthusiasm ran so high that citizens celebrated a festival to Brutus in their cathedral.

If the republican idiom sprang directly from the curriculum of Bourbon schools, it was also under official direction that republican iconography was revived in French art. From 1745, superintendents of the King's Buildings began to encourage the "grand style" of neoclassicism as part of a sustained effort to reassert the didactic function of art. This was nothing new. It had been policy since Richelieu founded the Aca-

40. Parker, *Cult of Antiquity*, 131–48.

démie française that art and letters were to serve the throne. The turn
from the prevalent rococo style to neoclassicism was meant to revive the
aristocratic spirit and magnify the nation in historical painting.[41] This
policy happened to coincide with the classical revival stemming from
the archaeologist Johann Winckelmann and the painter whom Winckelmann's work inspired, Raphael Mengs. Little prompting from Paris was
needed to fire the Rome campus of the Royal Academy of Painting and
Sculpture with enthusiasm for Winckelmann's excavations at Herculaneum and Pompeii.[42]

One of the young artists to win the Prix de Rome in 1774 was Jacques-
Louis David. Shortly before his departure, he told his teacher that "antiquity will not seduce me; it lacks warmth, and does not move." Perhaps he had heard of Winckelmann's formulation of the classical style as
"noble simplicity and serene grandeur" and felt that an art so quiescent
could not excite him. In any case, he was mistaken about what lay
ahead. When he viewed Winckelmann's excavations at Herculaneum and
Pompeii, he was enraptured. He said that his "eyes had been opened"
and that he had become "another MAN."[43] David joined dozens of artists compiling sketchbooks of exact drawings of sculpture, decorative
motifs, and buildings. He began painting in neoclassical style and
quickly made himself a master of its technique and tragic passion. By
1781 he was the lion of the salons and the favorite of the king. From 1784
he began to celebrate civic virtue in his *Oath of the Horatii*, *The Death of
Socrates*, *Coriolanus*, and *The Lictors Bringing Back to Brutus the Bodies of
His Sons*. The response to these paintings in Rome and Paris was sensational. One observer wrote from Rome of the exhibition of the *Horatii*
that "Everyday it was like a procession: princes and princesses . . . , cardinals and prelates, monsignori and priests, bourgeoisie and workers, all came to see it."[44] At Paris these paintings created a stir far beyond
the aristocratic revival intended by royal initiatives. Coupled with André
Chénier's tragedy, *Charles IX*, which depicted the tyrannical depredations of the St. Bartholomew's Day Massacre, and new performances of
Voltaire's *Brutus*, David's art incited the passion for the virtuous republic with which he was himself filled. When the first acts of defiance
to absolutism occurred, the Revolution possessed in David an artistic
hand willing and able to arrange great multitudes into living tragic tab-

41. David L. Dowd, *Pageant-Master of the Republic: Jacques-Louis David and the
    French Revolution*, 3–4.
42. Ibid.
43. Quoted ibid., 12.
44. Ibid., 17.

leaux, the revolutionary pageants (*fêtes révolutionnaires*). He became artistic director of pageants in 1790 and retained this position, despite his Jacobin fervor, for the next thirteen years.

At least one major pageant was staged annually from 1790 to 1801. The first was the Federation pageant, followed by a festival commemorating martyrs of the Châteauvieux street fighting. Successive years celebrated Law, National Unity, Reason, the Supreme Being, Victory, the Foundation of the Republic, the Gods of Rome, Peace, and Bastille Day. The funerals of Mirabeau and Marat (1791 and 1793) were grand occasions, as were the transfers of the remains of Voltaire and Rousseau to the Pantheon. Attendance at the festivals was estimated by contemporaries to reach 400,000.[45]

Pageants were usually held at the Champ de Mars, a large review ground on the fringe of Paris, where the Eiffel Tower now stands; or else on the Champs Élysées, bounded at either end by the Place de la Révolution and the Arc de Triomphe. They were sequenced as a procession followed by rites of consecration. Processions included military units appropriate to the occasion, choirs and bands, youth groups, public officials, and heroes of the hour. These groups were variously costumed. Some might wear togas, others were garlanded with flowers. They carried symbols and emblems of the republic. Among these were medallions of honored men, particularly Ben Franklin, Marat, Voltaire, Rousseau, and Brutus. The pyramid and sphinx, signifying wisdom, were also popular. The statue of liberty and the liberty tree were still other common icons.[46]

The procession marched to the sound of tambourines and drums. Its course included pauses at designated stations, where flags of military units were blessed and revolutionary hymns were sung. Onlookers sent the procession off with delirious shouts of the words of Ben Franklin that became the revolutionary slogan, "Ça ira! Ça ira!"[47] On arriving at

---

45. Marie-Louise Biver, *Fêtes révolutionnaires à Paris*, 41, 43, 72.

46. Numerous eyewitness descriptions of fetes are quoted by Biver, ibid. See also Albert Mathiez, *Les origines des cultes révolutionnaires, 1789–1792*, 29–34, 51–52, 60. James A. Leith's *The Idea of Art as Propaganda in France, 1750–1799* surveys the conception and use of art for political edification.

47. *Ça ira* is equivalent to "She'll keep rollin'" in colloquial English. Franklin used this phrase in response to queries about the progress of the American Revolution. The French took to it with gusto not only because it was a vintage Poor Richardism (*Poor Richard* was popular in France), but because America's rise meant Britain's decline. France had lost its North American territories in the war with Britain terminated by the peace of 1763. Frenchmen, smarting from this defeat, found it easy to support the rebels. *Ça ira!*

the Champ de Mars the procession entered an immense arena presenting grandiose proportions. The oval space was bounded by an embankment where spectators sat. At the closed end of the oval were a dais for dignitaries and a large arch of triumph; the procession entered at the open end. The centerpiece was a set especially constructed for the occasion. At the Federation pageant, it was the Altar of the Nation, a huge structure resembling a terraced pyramid. On each face of the square base, wide steps led to the second square tier of lesser circumference. A conical mound was erected on the second tier, at whose peak was the altar. Marching units in serried ranks, perhaps 10,000 in number, arranged themselves before the altar. The rites consecrated the Law, the Constitution, the Nation. Long lines of maidens marched up the steps to lay flowers on the altar. The king made his obeisance and priests blessed the altar and other talismans. Hymns were sung and a hundred thousand voices joined in shouting choral responsives. Trumpet blasts and the roar of cannon brought the rites to a suitably assertive conclusion. Pageants often included grave or frolicsome dances and much display of artful emblems. They also included symbolic destruction of objects of hatred. After Louis XVI's execution, the emblems of monarchy were ceremonially burned. At the Voltaire pageant, the monster of superstition was crushed by the wheels of a neoclassical chariot.[48]

Such was the political theater that Taine likened to opera. It cannot be brushed aside as an aberration, for it documents the classicism of the Revolution's initial phase.[49] Pageants were the first step toward the transformation of civic virtue into a civic cult. The dechristianization movement followed as a logical second stage. Christianity, which Rousseau had said was not and never could be a civil religion, was to be replaced by a cult of the Supreme Being and the new religion Théophilanthropes, which deified political man. All this, Albert Mathiez aptly notes, was nothing else than "an attempt to implement the last chapter of [Rousseau's] *Social Contract*."[50] He also notes that the rage for tragic

---

became a prominent revolutionary slogan; it was made into several rousing songs. See Julien Tiersot, *Les fêtes et les chants de la révolution française*, 19–27.

48. Ibid., 31–32. This work describes numerous fetes.

49. Like the neoclassical revival in art, fetes on a large scale were begun during the *ancien régime*. That they could be so easily adapted to revolutionary purposes is yet another testimony to the continuity of the classicism of the two regimes. See Alain-Charles Gruber, *Les grandes fêtes et leurs décors a l'époque de Louis XVI*.

50. Mathiez, *Les origines des cultes révolutionnaires*, 19–20. For a study of Rousseau's views on civil religion, see Roger D. Masters, *The Political Philosophy of Rousseau*, 87–88, 408–9.

theater during this period was closely connected with cultism. The same men who signified the rejuvenation of the nation by mass rebaptisms of infants with classical names also believed that dramas about tyrants and patriotic apotheosis inculcated civic virtue.[51]

There can be no religion without superstition. The overt superstition of Théophilanthropes was the belief that the God of Newton's universe—which Laplace had shown was no longer necessary even as a hypothesis—took the part of Frenchmen as they fought wars against despotism and superstition. Its deeper superstition, however, was the notion of man's deification. Only confused ideas are possible here. Rousseau generated this confused idea in his attempt to sacralize Hobbes-Locke political science. A central feature of that doctrine, we have stressed, is insight into the problem of justice as a mirage created by moral illusion. Righteous wills, religious or secular, are among the bully tactics human beings use to get the advantage over other human beings. The contentious concept of justice is replaced in political science by the notion of a contract or agreement of particular amoral wills interested in their natural rights; and this agreement must be imposed by force of political sovereignty.

Rousseau's sensibility recoiled from this blow to "sociability" and priestcraft. He revived the righteous will as the "general will," posited as the basis of legislation. But the general will cannot be clearly described nor unambiguously identified in its political operation. It is a kind of superorganism, like God, that embraces each individual and yet is not reducible to the sum of individual wills. Nevertheless, Rousseau knew what he "meant." The general will is a confused ideational rendering of *feelings* of solidarity apt to arise when people are in the grip of shared emotions. In these moments, the mood of the group is perceived as a "general will," i.e. as *mood contagion*. Rousseau was keen to revive civil religion because he had learned from classical authors that festive occasions evoke those emotional experiences he called the general will. One sees how far Rousseau traveled from Hobbes's political rationalism. For Hobbes, the sovereign political will was a cold-blooded calculation of political cost-benefit. For Rousseau, the general will was activated by the rhapsodies of manic crowds. The mummery of civil religion was needed to dignify and sacralize this revival of tribal euphoria, signified as *fraternité*.[52]

51. Mathiez, *Les origines des cultes révolutionnaires*, 50–64.
52. Robespierre was a warm advocate of pageants, which he recommended as follows: "L'homme est le plus grand objet qui soit dans la nature, le plus magnifique de tous les spectacles c'est celui d'un grand peuple assemblé. On ne parle jamais sans enthousiasme des fêtes nationales de la Grèce; cependant elles n'avaient guère pour objet que des jeux où brillaient la force des corps,

The Rousseauean background helps explain why the doctrine of popular sovereignty was felt by revolutionaries to imply pageants and cults, patriotic fanaticism, and crowd action: political theater was the vehicle for the manifestation of popular sovereignty, i.e. the general will, expressly said by the Declaration of the Rights of Man to be the foundation of law. But since neither the Third Estate nor any other part of the population is endowed with a general will, French revolutionary politics degenerated into a war of factions all claiming to be sovereign.

Rousseau's histrionic politics can be readily traced in the deeds and rhetoric of revolutionaries. It accounts for the great store set on the power of gesture, on the magic of words, on the overriding importance of right attitudes ("virtue," "patriotism," "revolutionary fanaticism"). As an illustration, we consider an account of the events immediately following the fall of the Bastille, as described in Prudhomme's influential newspaper, *Révolutions de Paris*:

Meanwhile, the victors get ready to march, they leave amidst an enormous crowd, the applause, the outbursts of joy, the insults, the oaths hurled at the treacherous prisoners of war; everything is confused; cries of vengeance and of pleasure issue from every heart; the conquerors, glorious and covered in honour, carry their arms and the spoils of the conquered, the flags of victory, the militia mingling with the soldiers of the fatherland, the victory laurels from every side—all this created a frightening and sublime spectacle. On arriving at the square, the people, anxious to avenge themselves, allowed neither De Launay [the Bastille commander] nor the other officers to reach the place of trial; they seized them from the hands of their conquerors, and trampled them underfoot one after the other. De Launay was struck a thousand blows, his head was cut off and hoisted on the end of a pike with blood streaming down all sides. . . . This glorious day must amaze our

---

l'adresse, ou tout au plus le talent des poètes et des orateurs: mais la Grèce était là; on voyait un spectacle plus grand que les jeux; c'étaient les spectateurs eux-mêmes, c'était le peuple vainqueur de l'Aise, que les vertus républicaines avaient *élévé quelquefois au-dessus de l'humanité*; on voyait les grands hommes qui avaient sauvé et illustré la patrie; les pères montraient à leurs fils Miltiade, Aristide, Épaminondas, Timoléon, dont le seule présence était une leçon vivante de magnanimité, de justice et de patriotisme. Combien il serait facile au peuple français de donner à ses assemblées un objet plus étendu et un plus grand caractère! Un système de fêtes nationales bien entendu serait à la fois le plus *doux lien de fraternité et le plus puissant moyen de régénération*" (*Œuvres de Robespierre*, 329–30).

enemies, and finally usher in for us the triumph of justice and liberty. In the evening, there were celebrations.[53]

This report is not an objective account of events. The taking of the Bastille is attributed to the valor and skill of citizens spontaneously acting together. There is something miraculous about undisciplined citizens armed only with pikes overrunning a fortress defended by professional troops using cannon and musket. This miracle did not occur; the Bastille was taken by men of the National Guard, then loyal to Lafayette. The account says nothing of the fact that the emblem of despotism, when pried open, was found to contain just seven prisoners, all persons of rank. Factual reporting is not the writer's purpose. Instead, we are presented the tableau of a crowd scene, a *mise en scène* of revolutionary fervor. The writer calls it a "spectacle," and suggests the tragic genre by characterizing its emotions as sublime horror. These emotions are plainly experienced as euphoric, as an ecstatic "spectacle."

That gruesome and terrible events can have a tonic effect on the human psyche has perplexed moralists since Aristotle attempted to interpret Greek tragedy. Aristotle, and after him the Aristotelian critics of French classical theater, did not make the most obvious observation about tragedy—that in it the taste for cruelty disports itself. The tragic genre cultivates emotions that express themselves more crudely in war fever and in the appreciation of public executions at all times. War against neighboring cities and horrendous executions of faction by faction were staples of the classical virtuous republic. Moralists notwithstanding, they loved it. Indeed, ancient moralists glorified war and the slaughter of virtuous heroes by other virtuous heroes. In France the taste for cruelty waxed as the zeal of its leaders for the virtuous republic grew. The erection of the guillotine in the Place de la Révolution simultaneously with wars on two fronts was not the deed of the barbarous scum of the earth led by deluded intellectuals, as Edmund Burke pretended in his *Reflections on the Revolution in France*. The people who gathered to cheer as heads dropped from Dr. Guillotine's infallible machine were the same good patriots who fought gallantly in wars and who wanted their daughters to marry as virgins. The civism of the French Revolution brought forth the greatest outburst of moral fervor since the Reformation. Frenchmen catechized themselves with hundreds of manuals designed to teach the virtue. Thus Poitevin's *Catéchisme républicain* taught French youths:

53. Quoted by John T. Gilchrist and W. J. Murray, eds., *The Press in the French Revolution: A Selection of Documents, 1789–1794*, 55.

QUESTION: What is baptism?
ANSWER: It is the regeneration of France, commencing on July 14, 1789, and soon supported by all the French nation.
QUESTION: What is confirmation?
ANSWER: It is the call and formation of the National convention which corrected the numerous faults of the first two Assemblies, having totally abolished royalty by substituting republican government.
QUESTION: What is communion?
ANSWER: It is the association offered to all reasonable people by the French Republic for forming on this earth a great family of brothers, who no longer know nor flatter idols or tyrants.
QUESTION: What is penitence?
ANSWER: It is today the erring life of traitors to their country; it is the exile of all those monsters who, despising life in the light of liberty and participation in advantages which their iniquity only retards, will soon be driven to the four corners of the earth; and taking horror of nature itself, their only refuge will be the bowels of the earth, which they will soon stain with their crimes.[54]

Such was the moralizing republicanism that for millions of Frenchmen presented itself as their first education in democracy. To sustain it, the revolutionary leadership would have been obliged to follow Marat's exhortation to cut off 100,000 heads—a small price to pay, he thought, for the future of mankind.[55] But these excesses cost the Jacobins the carefully nurtured friendship of Washington's administration and lost them support among many Catholic laymen who balked at worshiping philosophical chimeras. Thus the Jacobins did their turn on the scaffold. But the Jacobins created a radical tradition whose fanatical faith in *fraternité* sprang from the emotional experiences crowds may have of themselves. Memory of these intoxicating experiences was the liquor that charged the word *revolution* with an enormous positive emotional valence, of a power comparable to the emotions tapped by religion. In this way a new political superstition arose, and in time became *the* modern superstition serviced by a priesthood and believed by millions.

54. R. Poitevin, *Catéchisme républicain*, 4.
55. Louis R. Gottschalk, *Jean Paul Marat*, 121. As further documentation of Rousseau's influence upon revolutionary leaders, we note that Marat was among his most ardent admirers; and that his theory of the dictatorship of the people was taken, Gottschalk notes, directly from the *Social Contract*.

chapter 10

The Formation and Reformation of Government (Europe)

Overview, 1770–1830

In the preface of *Democracy in America,* Alexis de Tocqueville cast his eye across an epoch of bewildering complexity, littered by the wreckage of some brave new worlds yet resplendent with the shining towers of others. He discerned in events a clear and indubitable line of advance: the march of democracy. It was a democracy such as had never before been seen; its resources and liabilities had yet to be charted; but he was certain that democracy was the destiny of European civilization. Since America had pressed farthest on the frontiers of the new dispensation, an examination of its ethos and institutions was high on the agenda of the historical political science Tocqueville hoped to establish.

The historical perspective was meant to have a moderating influence on political thinking, which, lately blinkered by abstract ideas, was paying court to Benthamite or Saint Simonian reform programs generated from systems. From systems Tocqueville did not expect enlightenment. Theories recommended by nothing but logic and fact often proved to be barren in practice because they paid no regard to cultural and institutional inertia. Disciplined historical inquiry, Tocqueville believed, would reveal the roots of national politics. Descriptions of their character and transformation by events through time would enable the political scientist better to project their possible future forms.

The common sense of Tocqueville's historical method avoided the arbitrariness of systems, yet it encountered difficulties of its own. If the system builders could not agree on principles, neither could historians. Tocqueville's belief that institutions follow ethos, particularly the ethos of social class, led him to trace modern democracy to an origin in the eleventh century and to project subsequent social and political change as a long predestined march to the present. But his contemporary Auguste Comte projected a quite different time-scale whose dynamic principle was not the evolution of a specific political form, such as democracy, but the progress of the mind (*l'esprit*) from a primitive credulity to the positive sciences. Tocqueville was not interested in scientific rationality, which he thought was at best a secondary influence in the arena of events dominated by opinion and institutions. For Comte, however, opinion and institutions were dependent upon the level of enlightenment attained in a given society. Yet another developmental scheme would emerge from Marx's rewrite of the economists' notion that commerce was the dynamic factor in social change.

Although these thinkers knew that recent events had in some measure been experiments of applied political theory, none was particularly concerned to assess theory in the light of outcomes. The most sustained effort, by Marx, was so heavily committed to polemics that laborious efforts are required to extract the sense from the *Kulturkampf*. Let us accordingly draw up a score sheet independently.

• The Hume-Montesquieu idea that modern men are less violent and more sociable than ancient men cannot be said to have been confirmed by the great convulsion that began in 1775 and continued until the Treaty of Vienna thirty-five years later. Eight million dead and a wide path of physical destruction did not argue that ferocity had been subdued by the domestication that was supposed to have been the long-term effect of the progress of commerce and the arts. The postulate of the fixity of human nature seemed warranted until a more satisfactory anthropology emerged. Nevertheless, the concept of the plasticity of human nature prevailed because to explain rapid and extensive social change seemed to require it. Homo was pictured as a creature of his sensations and of his habitat. The coevolution of man and habitat signified the progressive animal. Nineteenth-century liberalism deployed this conception to batter down prejudices of class and race, as it was also the fundament of the Liberal faith in the "moral progress of mankind." To be sure, the self-interested creature of Hobbesian anthropology remained the dominant image in politics and economics. But it was not consistent with the new image of the progressive man of plastic nature; and the inconsistency took revenge as radical reformism, impatient with gradualist Liberal measures, cut to the cloth of the self-interested accumulator. The imprint of this unresolved tension was found everywhere.

• Napoleon's decade-long economic war against Britain seemed to yield an airtight demonstration of the futility of trade regulation: not even the might of the conqueror could divert trade from paths it wanted to follow. Free trade, then, was wisdom.

• The war also demonstrated the resilience of credit institutions erected in the eighteenth century. In 1750, Bolingbroke shuddered at the national debt of £80 million, but in 1814, the national debt stood at £600 million. Nevertheless, the private and political liberties of Britons had never been more vigorously exercised.

• The long debate over political parties now seemed decided. We previously observed that Robert Walpole made a defense of party consistent with Lockean principles. Faction, he claimed, is a consequence of government. Modern factions express interests in property, liberty, and equality—interests that must prosper under Lockean constitutions. Free government should encourage factions to organize as parties, to enhance the orderly conduct of government. This argument did not long survive Walpole's government. Acting on Bolingbroke's antiparty political notions, George III confounded British politics by attempting to dissociate ministers from party allegiance. This backward step was remedied when war conditions compelled the king to seek stability in the government of Pitt. Similarly, the American Founders were antiparty men who tended to look with disfavor upon the patronage system that party seemed to imply. Yet by the fifth year in the life of the new republic, two great parties vied for power; and both used patronage to cement the allegiance of adherents. The emergence of party and of "corruption" among men opposed to them furnished evidence that both were necessary to representative government.

• Purifying fanaticism had twice arisen to purge the corrupt world. Americans, believing in America's primitive regenerative forces, challenged supposed British decadence. The French, longing for regeneration, destroyed the monarchy and its feudal system. Even so, evangelical politics proved to be unable to construct a new order. The American Constitution was contrived to produce maximum benefits from the private interests that men were assumed to be promoting, whereas stability returned to France only after the virtue mania was terminated. The Treaty of Vienna, which established peace in Europe for a century, was effective because the victorious allies did not punish France for national iniquities, but sought instead a balance of power that respected national interests.

• The equality doctrine of Hobbes and Locke survived emotional overflows that threatened to arm it with vindictive righteousness. It more than survived. Equality was now embedded in ethos as "individualism." Linked with the fever for "improvement" and acquisition, it propelled Europe toward the wealth required to sustain a long trend of upward mobility.

• Classical writers had said that liberty could be maintained only in small, nonmercantile republics. Modern writers asserted the opposite, claiming that a large population, spread over an extensive territory and possessing many kinds of property, formed the requisites of liberty. No ancient republic except Rome had remotely approached the size and diversity of European states. That these could be established at all, and that they enjoyed vigorous growth, were hopeful signs that the touchstone of free government had been found.

• Two centuries had elapsed since Bacon and Descartes ventured extravagant prognostications about the success of science, if men would but cultivate it. In the interval, science, while recruiting only a fraction of the numbers recruited to the clergy, had nevertheless established itself as perhaps the most potent "spiritual" force in human history. The base of knowledge enlarged daily. Linked with technology, its dominion over the material world expanded to subdue space and time. The plainest man perceived the effects; perceived too that they redounded to his benefit, besides providing new entertainments, new careers, new heroes, and new wailing walls for romantics. The common man believed in science; he exalted progress, the new god whose heaven was earth.

The human powers released by modern natural and political science had helped frame the institutions of mercantile monarchies in the seventeenth century. By 1770, they had become a major force generating a requirement of constant reform of government. The heir to earlier politics of progress took the name of Liberalism. The nineteenth century was its triumphal epoch. No antecedent political movement rivaled the fullness of its program, the appeal of its rhetoric, the amplitude of its argument, or the generosity of its intentions. It gave Europe humane government and confidence in the future.

Physiocratic Reform in France

The liberal doctrine of free trade originated in France, and in the same mind that invented "enlightened despotism" as a political ideal. We have the authority of Adam Smith for this identification, for he praised François Quesnay's doctrine as the "liberal and generous" system of physiocracy. The curious name *physiocracy* was the coinage of another Quesnay admirer, the agricultural reformer the Comte de Mirabeau. It was meant to indicate the scientific orientation of Quesnay's teaching.

This grand scheme for the reform of law, administration, and the economy arose partly as a negative against the policies of Colbert and of Law. Contra the Colbertians, who were well represented in the *Encyclopedia*, Quesnay argued that national prosperity depended primarily upon agriculture.

The central dogma of his system was that land is the sole source of wealth or economic growth, while commerce, manufacture, and government are "sterile." As for Law, the Physiocrats were suspicious of credit systems. Quesnay was critical specifically of the attempt to foster circulation of goods by expanding money supply through issues of paper currency. Abundance of money drew agriculturalists into towns, whereas the one thing needful was encouragement of agricultural productivity. Quesnay was certain how this was to be achieved. The complex system of licensing for export and for internal sale, the inland duties, the privileges and monopolies, the price controls—all these were to be swept away. They were to be replaced by nothing, or rather, by a system of free trade in agricultural produce as well as all other goods, which he called *laissez-faire*. Moreover, the cumbersome and arbitrary tax system was also to be replaced by a single tax on cultivated land.

These dogmas sound like the dictates of a simplifier determined to cut knots that he knows not how to untie. Critics of physiocracy, particularly among the philosophes sympathetic with its reformism, harped on this evident shortcoming. Yet in situations perceived to be intractable, grand simplifications can have great appeal; probably for this reason physiocracy became a flag of reform in France from 1760 to the Revolution. Cultivators stymied by bureaucratic regulation and damned to the purgatory of chaotic taxation rallied to Physiocratic formulas as the sign of a will to reform.

Quesnay enhanced the hypnotizing simplicity of his system by composing in a style imitative of mathematical deduction, shunning prolixity and adornment of language, his only eloquence the intransigent march of dictates and prescriptions. The *General Maxims*, which were published with his celebrated *Economic Table* (1758), exemplify the style:

Maxim i

The sovereign authority ought to be unique and superior to all individuals of society and to all unjust enterprises of interested groups; for the object of dominion and obedience is the security and licit interest of all. The system of balanced power in government is a baneful opinion which disguises the strife among the great and the oppression of the small. The division of society into different orders of citizens, some exercising sovereign authority over others, destroys the general interest of the nation and introduces dissension of particular interests between different classes of citizens: this division weakens the public order of an agrarian state, which ought to collect all interests in a capital object—the prosperity of agriculture, which is the source of all the riches of the state and of all citizens.

ii

The nation ought to be instructed in the general laws of the natural order, which constitute the most perfect government. The study of jurisprudence is not sufficient for composing men in a state; it is necessary for civil servants to study the natural order most advantageous to composing men in society. It is necessary that the practical and evident knowledge acquired by experience and reflection should be united in a general science of government in order that the sovereign authority, always enlightened by evidence, institutes the best laws and requires their exact observance for the security of all and to promote the greatest possible prosperity to society.

xiii

That each ought to be free to cultivate his land with such crops as his interest, his faculties, and the nature of the terrain suggest, for achieving the greatest yield. . . .

xv

That fields cultivated in grain ought to be consolidated, as far as possible, in large plots exploited by rich farmers. . . .

xxv

There ought to be complete freedom of trade; FOR THE SUPERVISION OF INTERIOR AND EXTERIOR COMMERCE WHICH IS MOST SECURE, EXACT, AND PROFITABLE TO THE NATION AND THE STATE, CONSISTS IN THE COMPLETE FREEDOM OF COMPETITION.

xxix

To meet the extraordinary needs of the state, one ought to depend only on the prosperity of the nation and not on credit; FOR FINANCIAL FORTUNES ARE CLANDESTINE WEALTH THAT KNOW NEITHER KING NOR COUNTRY.[1]

---

1. François Quesnay, *Œuvres économiques et philosophiques de F. Quesnay*, 329–37.

Although these are but six of thirty maxims, one discerns intimations of a far-reaching reform from above. The sovereign—Quesnay never mentioned "king"—is invested with irresistible authority, unchecked by constitutional balance or a multitude of group interests. The sovereign will is meant to secure the legitimate private interests and welfare of all citizens. It suppresses particular interests that encroach upon the common good, among them the system of class privilege. Quesnay's natural law doctrine, an adaptation of Hobbes, mandates equality of rights before the sovereign.[2] He replaced distinction by social class with an economic classification that situates citizens relative to their contribution to the net annual produce of the nation. In this scheme, the "producing class" are the agricultural laborers; the propertied class are the landowners who provide capital for agricultural production. All others— merchants, manufacturers, the professions—are classified as "sterile" because they take, but do not add, to the net agricultural produce, from which all wealth is deemed to derive. The immediate object of reform

2. Quesnay's adaptation of Hobbes's natural-right teaching marks one of those interesting and critical points in the evolution of a concept from initial clarity to subsequent obscurity. In his short tract, *Le droit naturel*, Quesnay commenced with a criticism of the Hobbesian right of each to everything. This he criticized as "abstract," and substituted his improved version, which was the right of each to those things necessary to "obtenir la jouissance." He did not consider whether that right might not be exactly as extensive as the right to everything; nor did he explain how the enlightened despot was to determine what is necessary to enjoyment. The physician Quesnay entertained vague hopes of physiological answers to these questions. He postulated that all society operates according to certain natural, i.e. physical, laws. Civil or positive law should institute an order of society corresponding to these physical laws; it is the task of enlightened legislation to discover those physical laws and implement civil laws accordingly. In this way Quesnay lost the critical distinction between the state of nature and civil society, whose organization is not natural but artificial. The "organicism" of Quesnay's agricultural society, plus his idea that political organization followed unknown natural laws, was the beginning of the end of the Hobbes-Locke conception in France; it paved the way for the absorption of politics into economics, understood as the study of the natural laws, or "physiology," of society. This is the germinal idea that Adam Smith took over from the Physiocrats. The research program did not produce a natural science because it articulated as natural a subject matter that was artificial. Eventually the natural and artificial were confused in the materialist conception of history, which was forced to do service as a "science." These vicissitudes were visible in the writings of the Physiocrats, e.g. in Mercier de La Rivière's *L'ordre naturel et essentiel* (1767).

was to increase net produce by increasing agricultural yields. To this end trade was to be freed from legal restrictions on price and market destination, and capital was to be funneled into large-scale agriculture.

Abstract though they are, these dicta cut a deep path into the discordant realities of French agriculture. About 85 percent of the nation lived on the land; 50 percent of the cultivated land was owned by peasants, most of whom worked small strips of two to three acres. Physiocracy projected the regeneration of the mass of Frenchmen by lifting them from poverty. From his personal experience as an improving farmer, Quesnay knew (or believed that he knew) how urban, patrician, and court interests depressed agriculture. Trade in agricultural produce, especially in grains, had for centuries been regulated to ensure supply to urban areas at prices affordable by the people. Townsmen looked upon surrounding lands as their larder; they were anxious to secure their food supply by subjecting local production to their requirements. Regulation of price and prohibitions on export or circulation of produce excluded farmers from the benefits of market price. Since incentives to agricultural entrepreneurship were limited, most farmers were content with subsistence farming. This stagnation kept town and country on the chafing leash of recurrent food shortage. Regional *parlements* and Crown officers responded by tightening controls to squeeze more wheat from the land, whereas wise policy, the Physiocrats argued, would set its course on improving productivity. This was Quesnay's main insight into the confusion of the French economy.[3] His peremptory dismissal of commerce, manufacture, and finance as sterile may have been one of those deliberate blunders that cunning men sometimes commit to highlight a great problem.

3. Brilliant analyses of free trade as the remedy for France's grain shortages were composed by A. R. J. Turgot. Of his many statements of this position, the most succinct is his memorandum to Bertin in 1761. Price regulation, he argued, discourages production. In times of dearth, producers are obliged to sell cheaply; in times of abundance, the market price is low and again they sell cheaply. Producers therefore have no incentive to increase supply; hence the nation revolves perpetually in the cycle of abundance and dearth. The solution to the supply problem is not regulation but *circulation* of grains in open markets, combined with a system of storage facilities to preserve the abundance of one year against the poor harvest of the next. This system would achieve an even supply at all times, eliminate panic, misery, and violent price fluctuations (*Œuvres de Turgot*, 2: 122–28). The argument overlooks two critical factors: the capital cost of storage facilities and shipping costs. The difficulty and cost of circulating grain in France was the reason why the scheme could not work. See below, 419–21.

Agriculture lay under heavy political and fiscal disadvantages as well. Only the great landowners were able to take the lead in entrepreneurship, yet these men passed their days mainly at court or in the cities. Leadership fell largely to parish priests. But the inferior clergy supplied a cadre scarcely less ignorant than the peasants, for it too was a neglected and starved group. The peasant population was required to supply the nation's soldiery. Labor for construction and repair of roads was obtained from peasants by the *corvée,* a system of temporary impressed labor. The power of privilege also showed in the tax system. Great landowners were exempt by France's feudal law. The bulk of the state's annual revenues was squeezed from 21 million farmers. This was the circumstance that impelled Quesnay to declare that the revenue of the state derives from agriculture, not trade in luxury goods. The Physiocratic program was meant to bring the nation's economic and fiscal priorities in line with these facts. Until agriculture was put in order, all schemes for enhancing national wealth through commerce and manufacture were, he believed, froth and tinsel.

Quesnay came to economics late in life, after decades as royal physician had familiarized him with ministerial thinking and after his own experiences as an improving farmer showed him firsthand the problems of the countryside. His first publication was an article on grains for the *Encyclopédie.* The attraction of his personality, added to the urgency of the problems he addressed, soon won him a following. One of the first and most zealous of his disciples was Mirabeau, a reforming aristocrat and the author of *L'ami des hommes* (1756) and *Philosophie rurale* (1759). The Quesnay-Mirabeau axis provides a window on the contradictory influences bearing down on France at that time. Whereas Quesnay realized that the feudal order was intractable, Mirabeau wished to restore its former vigor. Rehabilitation of agriculture and Arcadian ideals were central to his program of luring the aristocracy back to the land. They had been corrupted by the frivolities of court life and by involvement in commercial or financial affairs. In his picture of revived aristocracy, ostentatious wealth and towering pride had no role. His model was the improving English squire who lived modestly among his equals and servants, and who took satisfaction in working the soil. Mirabeau's patriciate bears a close resemblance to Harrington's agrarian "natural aristocracy."

In the immediate context, his reform program was more realistic than Quesnay's. The nobility at that time numbered perhaps 250,000. Most lived in petty splendor on small estates; many were indistinguishable in fortune from successful farmers. Few could afford the gay life in Paris or other urban centers, although Mirabeau was aware of the importance of their example and, for that reason, wished to draw them back to the land.

Thus, while retaining and abandoning privilege represent two irreconcilable alternatives, they were not a barrier to practical collaboration.[4]

While Mirabeau wooed the aristocracy, Quesnay kept his eye on court travails. When the Seven Years' War commenced in 1756, neither the Treasury nor the Marine was capable of supporting it.

The British fleet quickly ruined France's maritime trade, which accounted for about 25 percent of the annual national gross. The defeat of the Army at Rosbach in late 1757 was followed by the Crevelt defeat six months later. Public credit, precarious prior to the war, fell under the strain. Finance Minister Bernis believed that bankruptcy was imminent and suspended payment to creditors. In October he advised the king that "the state is in danger."[5] Attempts to raise revenues by a *don gratuit* on all towns and villages met resistance. The Parlement of Besançon prohibited its collection; the Parlement of Paris defied the finance minister with an appeal to the right of the nation. Other *parlements* followed these examples. Late in 1759, Bertin, the third finance minister in eighteen months, advised that he was "reduced to contemplating violent means" to collect taxes.[6] Shortages of grain caused anxiety in the cities that experienced a rash of bread riots. Religious antagonism, which had been running strong for a decade, intensified to the point that the king was obliged to expel the Jesuits. By 1763, the national debt had increased to 1,400,000,000 livres; major creditors were compelled to extend new credit to avert state bankruptcy that would ruin them. In the midst of this chronic political, administrative, and financial crisis, Voltaire penned his famous phrase on the "revolution which will inevitably occur, but which I will not have the pleasure to witness."

In these straitened circumstances, physiocracy came to power: on 25 May 1763, a decree of council proclaimed freedom of trade in grains in France, although not for export trade.[7] The Physiocrats had by that date

---

4. The contrary impulses in physiocracy that arose from the Quesnay-Mirabeau collaboration are, to say the least, exotic. One sign of the difficulty is that interpreters are uncertain whether physiocracy is capitalist or socialist; it is not unusual for them to declare it capitalist on one page and socialist on another. On Mirabeau's system, see Lucien Brocard, *Les doctrines économiques et sociales du Marquis de Mirabeau,* and Elizabeth Fox-Genovese, *The Origins of Physiocracy,* especially 153–60.

5. Georges Weulersse, *Le mouvement physiocratique en France,* 1: 61–62.

6. Ibid., 68.

7. The decree was far-reaching and overturned the restrictive practices that had been hallowed for so long in France. It declared that "We permit to all our subjects, of whatever quality and condition they may be, even nobles and the privileged, to do as seems good to them, in the interior of the realm, respect-

become an allied group that might be loosely called a party. Two journals, the *Journal de l'agriculture* and the *Éphémérides de citoyen,* broadcast Physiocratic doctrine. Men of influence were persuaded to support the program. Le Trosne, king's counsel in the court of Orléans, Mercier de la Rivière, honorary counselor to the Parlement of Paris, and Turgot, then intendant at Limoges, subsequently controller general, were among the early adherents. Support also came from the *parlements* of Languedoc, Brittany, Aix, Toulouse, and Grenoble. Relations with the philosophes were ambiguous. Diderot published articles by Quesnay and other Physiocratic authors in the *Encyclopédie,* but Voltaire was consistently critical, while the *côterie holbachique* kept their distance when they were not directly critical.

The ascendancy lasted only as long as good harvests. In 1769 there was widespread popular agitation against free trade in grains, while the *parlements* of Rouen and Paris prohibited it. The following year brought more resistance from *parlements,* traditionally advocates of trade restrictions, as well as more riots against shortages of corn. Turgot acknowledged in communication to intendants that France had been in "famine" for a decade, while Abbé Galiani blasted free trade as "an enthusiasm, a fashion, a literary caprice . . . and finally one of those epidemic aberrations that sometimes attack the French nation, causing cruel ravages until the calm of reason returns."[8] In December 1770, Controller General Terray closed the brief era of free trade by restoring all the old restrictions. The sole benefit of reversion to the old policy was that loud complaints from *parlements,* intendants, and the poor against free trade ceased. It did nothing to rectify inadequate grain supply to France's rapidly growing population. Bread riots continued and became a training school for popular actions in the Revolution. Food shortages in Paris and Lyon proved to be potent sources of unrest and agitation during the Revolution.[9]

---

ing commerce in grains—to buy or sell or store . . . without restraints or formalities." The decree is printed in full in *Œuvres de Turgot,* 2: 129. Permission to export grain was granted the following year.

8. Weulersse, *Le mouvement physiocratique,* 1: 212. The main economic writer for the *Encyclopédie,* François Forbonnais, regarded physiocracy as mystagogy.

9. The incidence of poverty was 10 percent to 20 percent in many areas. The poor were not a separate section of the population but were socially integrated rural and urban groups whose fortunes varied with harvests, natural disasters, and diseases. One component of their condition was ignorance. They refused to accept rice as a substitute for grain, even during extreme shortage, because they believed that it spread disease. They resisted new tech-

The significance of physiocracy for prerevolutionary reform lies partly in the emergence of an articulate school of political economy, and partly in the school's capacity to prescribe measures to cope with a major problem. The traditional identification of free trade with industrial capitalism requires us to emphasize that this first school of political economy to attract extensive public attention made its appearance as a panacea inscribed on the flag of an agrarian reform movement. It was cool or hostile—depending on the spokesman—to everything "bourgeois": finance, commerce, manufacture, artisans, towns.[10] The country prejudices espoused by Mirabeau comprise physiocracy's claim to be a progressive reform movement. Quesnay's lopsided idea of a single tax on the single productive industry places the doctrine well below the economic sophistication attained by de Witt, Colbert, or Locke. Nevertheless, his emphasis on the power of market forces to increase produc-

----

niques for improving yields. Mortality rates were high. In some regions only about 35 percent of the population attained their twenty-first birthday. Infanticide was common. See Olwen Hufton, *The Poor in Eighteenth-Century France, 1750–1796.*

10. As an example of the violent abuse of commercialism, we might cite Mirabeau's exclamation: "O voracious nation! the tyranny and fraudulence of the cities is the excrement of the country!" He was equally violent in his attitudes toward finance: "Unhappy is every society where finance seduces and dominates government or economic administration and makes a state within the state. Thrice cursed are those societies where one knows the words: *high finance!*" We are not surprised to learn that Mirabeau was an admirer of Rousseau, and conversely. The anticommercial attitudes of the Physiocrats are reviewed by Weulersse, *Le mouvement physiocratique,* 2: 36–92, 92–119. Not all the free trade advocates in France shared the anticommercial prejudices of the Physiocrats. The most important exception was Turgot, who had a horror of sects, who distanced himself from the "enthusiasm" of the Physiocrats, and who pointed out that the idea of free trade in grains was in any case borrowed by Quesnay from Dupin, Gournay, Herbert, and other economists-administrators. (For his comments on the Physiocrats, see *Œuvres de Turgot,* 3: 270, 474.) Turgot rejected the physiocratic denigration of manufacture, commerce, interest, and money. Indeed, his economic analysis attained a level of sophistication that had not been reached since Locke and was not equaled afterward until Adam Smith, who was acquainted with the man as well as his writings. Turgot's explication of market value, from the dual prospect of money and human psychology, is one of the most lucid in the economic literature. See his *Sur la formation et la distribution des richesses* and *Valeurs et monnais,* which may usefully be contrasted with Quesnay's *Dialogue sur le commerce* and *Dialogue sur les travaux des artisans.*

tivity by stimulating incentive was a central concept of liberal political economy.

Why did the eight-year trial period of free trade not produce the predicted results? Why were subsequent trials by Turgot unsuccessful? Quesnay had assumed that regulation suppressed or concealed a market in produce. Yet when restrictions were removed, the market that then appeared was not significantly different from the controlled market. What we call "the market" was actually hundreds of local markets, usually extending no more than a radius of ten miles. Many small farmers produced small amounts of grain. Most was sold to local buyers and was consumed within a few miles of its origin. Free trade did not alter this pattern, although it prompted panic buying and high prices wherever there were shortages. Stripping away regulation did not reveal a hidden regional market, let alone a national market in grains. Consolidation of production on larger plantations therefore did not occur.

These effects did not occur because the requisite for the formation of regional markets was missing: a system of inland water transport. The main cost factor for the movement of goods is weight. Since luxury goods have a high price-to-weight ratio, overland shipment had been feasible for centuries, despite poor roads. But grains are not luxury goods. They must be affordable by the people and their price-to-weight ratio is low. Overland transport was accordingly feasible only for light loads over short distances. Regional markets in grains could form only around a system of inland water transport.[11] This France did not have. The Loire was the principal waterway, forming the main link of the north and east with the Mediterranean. Its traffic was double that of the Seine and probably 20 percent more than the Rhône's. However, it was an unimproved river marred by sandbanks and irregular flow, which could cause delays of shipment from Nantes to Paris of six or eight months. The meandering Seine made sail almost impossible to use. The Rhône had many shallows and was subject to flooding; during the three-month dry season it was impassable. Its rapid current required a force of one horsepower to pull one ton, while the same power on the

11. A. P. Usher's study of the grain trade in France between 1400 and 1700 shows the close relation between grain markets and water transport. The patterns he discovered were that (1) market routes for long-distance transport followed rivers or entrepôt shipment by sea; (2) inland towns and cities dominated the markets in their neighborhood; (3) the conflict between consumers and producers was chronic—the *parlements* represented consuming centers, while intendants represented the producers; (4) the pattern of disorders and disturbances clearly revealed the local character of markets. See his *The History of the Grain Trade in France, 1400–1710*, 180–90, 223–68.

Rhine pulled seven tons. Although in 1770 France had about 1,000 kilometers of canals and 8,000 kilometers of navigable rivers, transport was
still too slow, costly, and irregular to support regional markets in
grains.[12] England, by contrast, did have a cheap and efficient system of
transport based on combined use of its many ports and canal linkages
between its deep-draught rivers.

Napoleon was the first to recognize this critical problem.[13] During
the Empire, the construction of roads, bridges, and canals was given

12. Roger Price, *The Economic Modernization of France*, 1–26; Edward W. Fox,
   History in Geographic Perspective: The Other France, 83–95; Shepard Bancroft
   Clough, *France: A History of National Economics, 1789–1839*, 82–86. Our transport deficiency thesis appears to be confirmed by Labrousse's study of price
   movements in grains. For example, during 1782–84, there was a slight contraction of cereals supply in the Dauphiné region, and cereals sold at high
   prices. But during the same period Languedoc and Montauban experienced
   good harvests and low prices. In general, Labrousse's study indicates that
   price fluctuated with supply, regulation notwithstanding. Diagnostic of
   transportation deficiency is the persistence of wide price differences from region to region in one and the same year, for they show that it was not possible to move grains about so as to create regional markets. See C.-E. Labrousse, *La crise de l'économie française à la fin de l'ancien régime*, 333–41,
   466–509, 579–83. Region studies also reveal this pattern; see Gaston Rambert, *Histoire du commerce de Marseille*, 4: 137–43, 331–90; 5: 535–41; Theophile Malvezin, *Histoire du Commerce de Bordeaux*, 2: 327–43. There is,
   however, another angle. Andrew B. Appleby argues from price fluctuations
   of grains that England escaped shortages owing to the practice of planting
   oats and barley as fallback crops in time of dearth. These spring grains prosper in weather unfavorable to wheat and rye. French peasants did not plant
   these grains because they were not favored in their diet. See Appleby, "Grain
   Prices and Subsistence Crises in England and France, 1590–1740," *Journal of
   Economic History* 39 (1979): 865–87.

13. The intendants, who bore local responsibility for securing the supply of
   grain, were aware that the improvement of roads and waterways was vital,
   but they did not focus their efforts here, probably because their powers were
   only local. They concentrated on controlling the destruction of crops by in-
   sect pests or by storage mildew. They recognized that if insects could be deprived of half their annual take, the problem of dearth would disappear. See
   Paul Ardascheff, *Les intendants de province sous Louis XVI*, 340–45, 355–58.
   Despite his intense study of the grains problem, Turgot did not appreciate
   the importance of transportation deficiency, although he refers to it. His free
   trade strategy hinged on the combined use of storage facilities and circulation, i.e. transportation of grains from areas of plenty to areas of dearth. He
   reasoned that storage of grain throughout the kingdom would solve the
   producers' problem of being compelled to sell cheaply during good seasons,
   and cheaply again during dearth. He did not say how storage facilities would

high priority for military and commercial reasons. The Continental System by which he meant to weld Europe into political-economic units was based on France's preponderance in population and agriculture. But as in so many other things, Napoleon's designs outran his performance. Inland transport did not create the proper conditions for regional markets until the building program of the 1830–48 period. During that time, 2,041 kilometers of canals were constructed, as against 921 during the Restoration and 518 during the Empire. This gave France 8,255 kilometers of navigable rivers and waterways. In 1848 there were 1,921 kilometers of railroads in use and 4,000 more under construction. Only on this basis was French agriculture brought under the stimulus of regional markets that terminated recurrent grain shortages. The same pattern occurred throughout Europe and the United States, the expansion of markets and production following the development of overland or water transport. Unhappily for French politics, grain shortages were for many years believed to be a moral problem—essentially a problem about inequity of distribution. Narrow and selfish farmers, grasping merchants, profiteering speculators, and treacherous politicians were at various times held to blame and sometimes executed. But the wicked of the world are numerous; any politics predicated upon their suppression faces a bleak future. In this case as in so many others, moralism disguised a technical and organizational problem, solved by steam technology.

Enlightened Despotism: Hobbism for Monarchs

Quesnay's plea for enlightened despotism gave a name to the politics already well established before he wrote. The long reign of Frederick the Great (1740–86) marked a revitalization of monarchy and largely defined its program. Frederick introduced economy into government, abolished serfdom and extended legal rights of commons, granted his

---

be capitalized and maintained from free market profits. His fullest statement is in his *Lettres sur la liberté du commerce des grains.* Quesnay also misjudged the transportation deficiency. He referred to it in a footnote of his article "Grains" for the *Encyclopédie,* where he said that it is "un grand obstacle à l'activité du commerce. Cependant, il semble qu'on pourrait y remédier en peu d'années: les propriétaires son trop intéressés à vente de denrées que produisent leurs biens pour qu'ils ne voulussent pas contribuer aux dépenses de la réparation de ces chemins" (*Œuvres économiques et philosophiques,* 241). Clearly, he had made no studied estimate of the costs of roads and waterways. After Napoleon's expansion of roads and canals, their critical role in the growth of French agriculture became obvious to economists. See, for example, J.-B. Say, *Letters to Thomas Robert Malthus,* 40n.

subjects the semblance of religious liberty and freedom of speech, relaxed censorship, made his court a refuge for philosophers, and threw the prestige of his throne behind the Enlightenment propaganda emanating from Paris, personified by Voltaire.

Frederick's remarkable combination of talents and ability to achieve orderly reform stirred the young Joseph II of Austria (1765–80) to emulate the Prussian example. In Tuscany, Joseph's brother Leopold I (1765–90) was animated by the same spirit. Frederick's reform model also took hold in Spain under Charles III (1759–80), in Sweden under Gustav III (1771–92), and in Russia under Catherine the Great (1777–96). Even the Papacy got into the act by dissolving, in 1773, the Society of Jesus, after it had been expelled from Portugal, Spain, and France. This was the extraordinary transformation that prompted Diderot's triumphant cry, "There is no prince in Europe who is not also a philosopher." It seemed a new day had dawned. Only a century before, the Treaty of Westphalia had terminated ruinous wars propelled by ancient prejudices and obsolete institutions. Now courts fell in with the political public on the march to a new order.

While details of reform varied from place to place, the basic program was everywhere the same. Reforms were predicated on the proposition that the strength of the throne depended upon the welfare and prosperity of subjects—a rationale that Frederick gave currency in his startling description of the Prussian king as the first servant of the people. This was the fundamental premise of Hobbes's enlightened despotism. We have seen that Jean-Baptiste Colbert's reforms in the reign of Louis XIV assumed the validity of Hobbes's basic premise. Frederick was acquainted with the writings of spokesmen for modernizing monarchies. But more important to him, no doubt, was the example of Colbert, whose policies made a deep impression on the chancelleries of the nations that opposed by arms Louis' aspiration to universal empire.

The Colbertian program, we have suggested, was the logical continuation of the impetus toward consolidated monarchy that had been set in motion by the medieval emperors in their struggle with the Papacy. Since the Emperor Frederick II, this politics had been more or less informed by political science. For Frederick, that meant Aristotle as expounded by Muslim philosophers. For Ludwig IV, it was Aristotle as expounded by Marsilius of Padua and William of Ockham. The replacement of Aristotle by Hobbesian doctrine marked an increase in the pretensions and potency of political rationalism. When Hobbes wrote, the Reformation had set the stage for the victory of Ghibelline politics by splitting religious orthodoxy into a babel of warring heterodoxies. German princes seized the opportunity and transformed ecclesiastical establishments in their territories into national churches whose bishops answered to the kings.[14] Hobbes executed the final step of this development by his root-and-branch demolition of the spiritual claims of all priests. Political science was then able to attend to the actual requirements of dominion, undistracted by the imagined requirements of supernatural salvation. What emerged were the Hobbes-Colbert specifications for further consolidation of the nation-state as a *dirigiste* rule-of-law regime informed by the insight that commerce and production were indispensable to national power.

Our examination of Colbert's reforms showed that they tended to collide with the institutions of France's military-aristocratic order. Great Britain's island position, by contrast, obviated the need of large land forces that all continental powers maintained. Its smaller, cheaper, seaborne force made it much easier to advance commercially without running afoul of the military-aristocratic order. The reform programs of enlightened despotism were attempts to modernize the feudal regime by reconciling the military-aristocratic order with the legal and social presuppositions of economic growth—growth mandated by the necessity to feed large populations and to maintain armies of 100,000 to 200,000 men. The ascendancy of Prussia in the nineteenth century was due to its success in reconciling dominance by the aristocracy of land and government with dominance by the commons of financial, commercial, and manufacturing institutions. France appeared for a time to have hit upon an alternative model of reform. In one thunderous burst of energy, the institutional drag of aristocracy was swept aside; a new despot then emerged to impose order on quarreling factions. Napoleon's military force was based on the formula of upward mobility for a free and equal citizenry—"careers for men of talent." But the first priority of the Continental System was not to enhance the economic growth of France or Europe; it was to ruin the trade of Great Britain. Events proved that this objective could not be achieved without depriving Britain of its command of the seas.

The reform program of enlightened despotism that Frederick initiated embraced

- the codification of civil, commercial, and penal law
- improvement of transport
- promotion of agriculture and commerce and selective elimination of trade restrictions
- placing state finance on a sound basis, rationalization of taxation, pruning the state bureaucracy of drones
- the abolition of serfdom

14. See above, chap. 3, 121n17, 123, 131–32.

- the introduction of some private liberties, particularly freedom of worship and abolition of judicial torture
- broadening primary and secondary education, and up-grading universities
- selective rehabilitation of ancient representative assemblies, or the introduction of new ones, composed to include the commons.

The program of enlightened despotism was the prototype of the Liberalism ascendant in the nineteenth century. We need but replace the despot by constitutional monarchy, broad electoral franchise, and party government, to arrive at the Liberal program. It is all the more significant, then, that the program of enlightened despotism specified what were perceived to be the objective requirements of a consolidated nation-state. Most of the projected reforms attempted to rectify the localism of rural societies dominated by patriciate and clergy. The abolition of serfdom, for example, gave peasants freedom of movement and certified their ownership of the land they worked. Improved transport combined with the abolition of tolls and other exactions on the movement of goods was meant to encourage productivity. The codification of law introduced uniformity in a legal system that previously had been a patchwork of local practices imposed by local patricians and bishops. Liberals touted these measures as essential to a humane and prosperous regime. Undoubtedly they are. But the political effect of equality, and freedom from arbitrary measures, was to smooth a patchwork of localisms into a uniform, coordinated system, where citizens become interchangeable parts in the complex social machinery. To be sure, the peasants, who suddenly discovered that their property rights were enforceable against the king, did not thereby acquire the capacity for agricultural entrepreneurship based on the latest crop improvement methods. Freeing the serfs was the prelude to their movement to industrial cities.[15]

Enlightened despotism superseded a style of monarchy that might be called harem despotism. Montesquieu's *Persian Letters,* a fable of the Bourbon court, described the malaise to a wide readership who believed he had hit the mark. Kings fixated on private indulgence drew public affairs into the seraglio with them, no matter how ministers might struggle to prevent the effect of personal lusts and private hatreds obtruding on the public business. The harem despot is extravagant, because his appetites recognize no bounds. He is cruel, because he resents

15. Frederick's reforms are detailed in Reinhold Köser, *König Friedrich der Grosse,* 1: 322–458.

any frustration. He draws his companions into the sinkhole with him, and they spread the blight. Fearing ministers who do not follow his example, he employs obscurantists to disguise his pettiness. Corruption spreads a torpor over the nation. Despite Montesquieu's warning, the Bourbons were unable to shake this extreme subjectivity; Louis XV was even worse than his father. When Joseph II visited Paris in 1774, he observed in his brother-in-law Louis XVI what Montesquieu had described fifty years earlier:

> The king is an absolute lord only in order to succeed from one slavery to another. He can change his ministers, but he can never become master of his business. . . . petty intrigues are treated with the greatest care and attention, but important affairs, those which concern the state, are completely neglected. The whole judiciary and all the nobility . . . constantly clamour against the rulers, asking for a change; but if an attempt were made to touch this loathsome form of monstrous despotism which each official exercises, then all would combine to prevent it, because everyone hopes to derive some advantage for himself.[16]

Similar observations could have been made of many European courts.

The personal style of enlightened despots was the reverse of all this. In Paris, the king conducted no business until the afternoon; Frederick rose at 5:30, and worked six days a week. Whereas Louis XV's ministers had to plead for action, Frederick set a fast pace that kept his ministers on the hop. Louis lived like a sultan in Versailles, sheltered from the external world. Frederick went among his subjects and knew their feelings. He inspected all aspects of government. He scrutinized accounts with an exacting eye impatient with wastage, intolerant of peculation. His intelligence network was probably the best in Europe; his public relations operations certainly were. In Frederick we see the organizational skill that was to make "German efficiency" a byword. This was polytechnic statecraft in the style of de Witt and Colbert.

The anguish of Maria Theresa stands as a commentary of feudal monarchy on Frederican reform. Mistress of Europe's oldest and most arrogant dynasty, pious to her toenails, heedless of economy, certain that distinctions of rank had been decreed from eternity, this redoubtable

---

16. Quoted by Saul Padover, *The Revolutionary Emperor*, 82. Unlike his father and grandfather, Louis XVI was not a harem despot. He was a somewhat puritanical, well-educated, and diligent king, despite his addiction to hunting. Joseph observed the aftereffects of Louis XV's reign.

woman struggled to save the Hapsburg monarchy from the infection of Enlightenment. Both sons, Joseph and Leopold, read Voltaire and modeled themselves on the Prussian king, even though he had removed territory from Austrian dominion. In the long struggle during their co-regency, she was mortified again and again by Joseph's desire to turn the kingdom on its head. "Petty reforms will not do," he declared. "The whole must be transformed. It is the foundation, the inner spirit and constitution, that must be changed." Like Frederick, he coined electrifying *bon mots* to give wide currency to the new spirit. "Being king is a profession," he declared. He turned a puritanical scorn on the pomp of rank and on bureaucratic torpor and evasion. He mingled casually with his subjects. Above all, Joseph's personal sympathy with the oppressed distinguished him from the enlightened despots who acted from expediency. On an inspection of Galicia, newly acquired in the partition of Poland, the misery of the peasants prompted in him the phrase that was to epitomize the Liberal reform sentiment: "My heart bleeds for them." He died regretting that he had been unable to transform the Austrian empire of 26 millions into a constitutional monarchy. Although he failed, Joseph cast the mold of the Liberal temper in Hapsburg politics.

Frederick and the Philosophes: Enlightenment as Power Politics

Frederick's father died a troubled man, apprehensive that his precocious son's flute-playing and literary pursuits might lose him the kingdom. As a youth Frederick attempted to run away to England; as crown prince he sighed in relief when he was allowed his own court, which he promptly made over as a French *salon*. He saturated himself in the enlightened philosophy and literature of the day. He made his literary debut with a tract, *Anti-Machiavel,* denouncing the thesis that the interests of princes are not consistent with the interests of their subjects. He drew Voltaire into correspondence, and maintained contact with the learned of the world. The father was so alarmed at these un-German tendencies that he pondered disinheritance. Yet when Frederick took the throne at age twenty-eight, he promptly put into action what was evidently a deeply laid plan. To the astonishment of everyone, he tore Silesia from Austria in a lightning war that established his credentials as a brilliant field general—a talent not suspected even by his intimates. In the diplomatic commotions that followed he was a match for the cunning men of foreign offices. This seeming dandy who could not endure to speak German, this critic of Machiavelli, was the prince who installed *ragione de stato* (*Realpolitik*) as the controlling principle of Prussian government. The true literary testament of his politics was not *Anti-Machiavel*, but von Clausewitz's *On War*, a Prussian general's manual for the rehabilitation of Prussian power in the wake of defeats in the Napoleonic wars. Clausewitz's study molded the thinking of two eminent practitioners of power politics, Otto von Bismarck and Vladimir Lenin. Friedrich Nietzsche attempted to recapture Frederick's combination of toughness and intellectuality in an age dominated by Josephan liberalism.

To Nietzsche, Bismarck was toughness without intellectual elevation, toughness in service to military-industrial domination. He turned to Frederick the Great hoping to riddle the beguiling synthesis of political will and intellectual dexterity, but apparently without success.[17] The prevailing view today, which was also Voltaire's view, is that Frederick's streak of meanness and cruelty was the dark side of a man unique among kings for his love of learning and progressive attitudes. On this view, Frederick's solicitude for the enlightened literati and the boost that he gave to Enlightenment stem from his taste and temperament. But Frederick's career reveals a man adept at distinguishing his subjective preferences from objective political requirements.

This may be the key to that strange combination of ruthlessness and intellectuality that Nietzsche attempted to fathom. Frederick was undoubtedly a skeptic; but he promoted toleration for reasons of state. He was undoubtedly a philosophe, but he courted the favor of the philosophical literati for reasons of state. Frederick wanted something from the literati—the public image as an enlightened, reforming king which he intended for use in a subtle foreign policy linked to his domestic reforms.

Frederick's opening to the literati was predicated on the new force that public opinion had acquired in modern politics. The philosophe Abbé Raynal put this point in his *The Revolution of America* (1782), which was itself a salvo in the struggle to dominate public opinion in France:

> Public opinion, which is becoming more and more informed, and which nothing has power to arrest or awe, has its eyes open upon nations and their courts. It penetrates into the cabinets where policy would lie hid. There is no longer a government in Europe but should stand in fear of its determinations.[18]

17. Nietzsche, *Beyond Good and Evil*, aphorism 209.
18. Abbé Raynal, *The Revolution of America*, 129.

In this grandiloquent depiction public opinion is omniscient and om- nipotent. Raynal openly menaced thrones while maintaining seemly si- lence about the trade secret of the literati: the all-seeing eyes of public opinion belonged to intellectuals, who scripted the events that dazzled the public.

The literati mingled in the power game on terms peculiar to them- selves. They exercised influence, sometimes decisive influence. They were often close to power; and yet, since they dealt in words rather than the substance of power, they did not themselves compete for the highest prize. The postures and motives of the intellectuals were formed by this peculiar relationship. Enjoying influence but not power, they could only be partisans of those who had power or who competed for it. They were, in the harsh language of power politics, only ideologues. Lacking political experience and responsibility, they were prone to play with pleasing but impractical schemes of government. Living as private men, the factuality of daily business did not prevent their mingling personal whims in their political ideas.

The literary character of the philosophes' conception of politics was apparent from their idea of their relation to politics. As publicists, they exaggerated the force and intelligence of public opinion, for in doing so they magnified their own importance. As thinkers, they imagined their office, in the Platonic manner, as that of philosopher-legislator contriv- ing schemes of government for a virtuous ruler to implement.

Politique that he was, Frederick spotted the fanciful quality of the philosopher-legislator idea. He also discerned how the naïveté betrayed in this conceit could be used to harness the literati to the Prussian chariot. Frederick wrote Voltaire flattering letters inviting him to Prus- sia, carefully timing them to coincide with the sage's exasperation with censors and other minions of the Bourbon court. Frederick declared himself lovingly as a "faithful friend" who invited the sage to disregard the trappings of titles and to close with him on terms of equality as a "zealous citizen." [19] He exhorted Voltaire to leave the tiresome, unwor- thy imbroglios of Paris and repair to the tranquillity of Sans-Souci, where his genius would have effect. Warming to this flattery, Voltaire began to celebrate the shining virtues of "the Solomon of the North." [20]

19. "I beg of you," Frederick wrote Voltaire, "See in me only a zealous citizen, a philosopher who is a bit skeptical, but a friend who is truly faithful. For God's sake, write to me only as a man, and join me in despising titles, names, and external glitter" (*Correspondance de Frederic II,* in *Œuvres de Frederic le Grand,* 10: 145).

20. Voltaire wrote of his thoughts at this time: "I did not fail to feel attached to

Largely because of Voltaire's praise, Frederick's court acquired its reputation as a haven for intellectuals.

Had Voltaire been privy to Frederick's confidential correspondence, he would have learned that the honeyed words were part of a well-laid plan to lure the plumed bird into an iron cage. "My intention," Frederick wrote Count von Rothenburg, "is to embroil Voltaire so thoroughly in France, that nothing will remain for him but to come to me."[21] At the moment when Frederick's letters to Voltaire deplored his harassment by Louis' mean-spirited functionaries, Frederick's Paris agents passed to court officers forged letters, purportedly by Voltaire, denouncing Louis XV. Thus did Frederick "embroil" Voltaire and entice him to the cold northern plains. And thus was the world amazed by the spectacle of the eloquent despiser of war and scourge of tyrants taking refuge with a king whose intricate use of force and deceit in foreign affairs had made him the most dangerous man in Europe. The French court was astonished that Frederick should want to import the French disease; the Prussian nobles were appalled by the same thought. Voltaire's friends were mortified that he should lend his prestige to a conqueror, in an act that seemed to repudiate the principles of humanitarianism. It was as if he had betrayed his class. No one appears to have sensed the political intention latent in the fact that Frederick's haven for intellectuals was reserved for political refugees who did not speak German.

The acerbic nightingale soon discovered that he had acquired a master, and a hard one. Voltaire was put through a program of browbeatings and insults, culminating in his public disgrace when he took sides against the president of the Berlin Academy in a scientific dispute. After two years of virtual captivity, Voltaire left Sans-Souci a shaken, if not wiser, man. Frederick had "squeezed the orange and discarded the peel": he had absorbed Voltaire's prestige and sent the sage away humbled. Yet there is no doubt that Frederick was personally fond of Voltaire, and continued to be so.

Although not a man to forgive insults, Voltaire never admitted to himself that he had been badly used. Nor did he learn caution in dealing with monarchs. Indeed he took the bait offered him by Catherine the Great, a close student of Frederick's reign. Catherine, born a German princess, took the Russian throne after her weak husband was murdered in the palace. To dispel odious suspicions, and to help promote her re-

---

him, for he had wit and charm, and what is more, he was king, which given human weakness, is always a great seduction. Ordinarily, we men of letters flatter kings; this one praised me from head to toe" (*Mémoires*, 1: 17).
21. *Correspondance*, 13: 46; letter of 7 August 1743.

forms of the nobility, she set out to recruit public relations support from the philosophes. Generous overtures were made to Voltaire and Diderot; both accepted. Voltaire dismissed the czar's murder as "a private family affair of no concern to me." That Voltaire was so easily recruited a second time indicates that his vanity forbade him to see that the sovereigns he magnified regarded him as a political tool. He imagined that Frederick desired him for his wisdom. But to his ministers Frederick abused Voltaire for having the "manners and malice of an ape," and declared that he had invited the poet only to improve his French.[22]

We do not reckon here with the personal weakness of one man, for the flaw lies in the literary conception of politics. Literati deal in praise and blame, in the subtleties of attitude. This they take to be wise and serviceable counsel. But advice is cheap. The poorest peasant will give it away. Politicians need studied policy and knowledge of the techniques of power. These competencies do not fall within the literary métier. To acquire them, the literati must acquire exact knowledge and technical proficiencies. But if they did that, they would cease to be literati; they would cease to attitudinize for public edification and private gratification.[23]

22. Gustave Desnoiresterres, *Voltaire et la société française au XVIIIe siècle*, 4: 93, 157, 415; see pp. 293–390 on the Berlin Academy dispute. Note as well Frederick's remark that he left some errors in the manuscript of his *Anti-Machiavel* in order to give Voltaire, whom he had asked to read it, the pleasure of correcting something (Desnoiresterres, *Voltaire*, 4: 112). Frederick's abuse of Voltaire to his ministers does not necessarily express his personal opinion: he was probably mollifying the resentment and incomprehension of Prussian nobles at his extravagant courtesies to a writer they thought dangerous. For the details of Voltaire's routine at Sans-Souci, see Köser, *König Friedrich der Grosse*, 1: 514–27.

23. As an example of the fanciful character of literary politics, consider this statement from Michelet's *Histoire de la révolution française:* "The revolution marched always with Rousseau and Voltaire at the head. The kings themselves follow in the train—Frederick, Catherine, Joseph, Leopold—this is the court of the two masters of the century. Reign, great men, true kings of the world! Reign, O my kings!" Here imagination transforms actual monarchs into courtiers, while literati become "true kings." This extravaganza overlooks the critical difference between programs or deliberation of any kind and action. This neglect of actual political reality is the chronic vice of literary politics, where everything is accomplished in imagination. Thus Chateaubriand, an admirer of Rousseau, claimed that *Émile* was "the famous book that precipitated our revolution." If, as is said, revolutions devour their children, it may be because the children entertain naïve notions about the relation between oratory and political power. The phrase "literary politics" seems to have been coined by Tocqueville in his *L'ancien régime et la Révolution,* where he reproached literati for substituting simple rational principles

Frederick's exploitation of intellectuals may have expressed malice; it certainly was intended to convert a liability into an advantage. In popularizing the modern program, the literati moralized it in a series of antitheses: liberty vs. tyranny, virtue vs. corruption, benevolence vs. cruelty, prosperity vs. poverty, reason vs. superstition. They made the program stand or fall, in the public estimation, according to its conformity to moral progress so conceived. Yet this moralization reestablished the moral illusion, which had to be deleted from the public agenda if enlightened politics was to succeed. Moralism condemns as tyrannical, inhumane, or corrupt the power techniques necessary to implement any political order, consequently the enlightened order as well. Intellectuals invented canards and jeremiads that moralized phenomena requiring objective reckoning, as Physiocrats did in the matter of free trade. They imagined that the system of enlightened self-interest they advocated could be achieved by humane means, even though the Hobbes-Locke doctrine stated that force lies at the base of political order. Frederick declared himself on this question in an anonymous review of d'Holbach's *La contagion sacrée*. D'Holbach had parlayed Hobbes's critique of superstition with Pierre Bayle's belief that an atheist society (China was the exemplar) might be achieved by patient teaching. Frederick disagreed; "rivers of blood" would inundate this path to utopia. That surmise was probably based on recognition that his own reforms could not be achieved without bloodshed. His good works were therefore subject to reproach by intellectuals. In a letter declining his offer of provisions, Rousseau reproached him:

> Sire:
> You are my protector, my benefactor, and I open my heart to acknowledge it. I want to acquit myself with you, if I can. You want to give me bread: are there then none of your subjects who lack it? Remove from before my eyes that sword which dazzles me and wounds me. It has had all too much service, and the scepter is abandoned. The career of kings of your stripe is great, and you are far from your limit. Change your heart, O Frederick! Are you resolved to rot to death without having been the greatest of men? I am able to see Frederick, the just and redoubtable, guarding in his realm a happy people of whom he is the father. And Jean-Jacques Rousseau, the enemy of kings, will die at the foot of his throne.[24]

---

for "complex and traditional jurisprudence." This is a Burkean criticism, quite distinct from Frederick's views.

24. The letter was written 30 October 1762, in the closing months of the Seven Years' War. Frederick's comment on it was: "He wants me to make peace.

The spectacular repertoire of postures packed into this paragraph is prodigious: bread, peace, reform of conscience, glory, heroic defense of liberty, morbidity, veneration—a catalog of the types of barriers to Enlightenment erected by intellectuals. Frederick's opening to the intellectuals was an attempt to impose a measure of control on the attitudinizing chaos. If they could be induced to identify Prussia as the model of reform, the chaos would find a center of gravity in an exemplar of actual enlightened politics.[25]

The good man does not know how difficult that is. . . . " Frederick had no very high opinion of Rousseau, despite the protection he extended. To Lord Keith he complained of Rousseau's paradoxes, and said: "I hold to Locke, to my friend Lucretius, and to my good Emperor Marcus Aurelius. They have said everything we can know. . . ." On the relationship between the two, see Emil Du Bois-Reymond, "Friedrich II und Jean-Jacques Rousseau," in *Reden*, 1: 333–80.

25. "Rest assured," Frederick wrote to Voltaire, "that if philosophers founded a government, at the end of half a century the people would have fashioned a new superstition for themselves and would have fixed their worship on some object or other that struck their fancy . . . [which would] triumph over the pure and simple cult of the Supreme Being. Superstition is a weakness of the human mind; it is innate in the creature" (13 September 1766). Frederick's challenge to the philosophes concerning the political consequences of their publicist activities went to the heart of literary politics. Their professional interest as writers on public questions mandated that they defend freedom of the press and attack despotism; professional interest further obliged them to maintain that the effects of religious enlightenment would be benign and salutary. Frederick's rivers-of-blood thesis demolished this assumption of the coincidence of public good with the private advantage of writers. It asserted in effect that he who wills Enlightenment in Europe's institutional setting promotes war and revolution, which were unlikely to have a salutary outcome if the Enlightenment party was unprepared for the hard consequences of its agitation. In denying the hard consequences that must follow, the philosophes put up a literary conceit that could only harm the long-term interest of enlightened government. By exposing their sham, Frederick indicated the danger of literary sensibility to politicians. This sensibility was exalted by the events of the Revolution into enthusiasm for terror. Testimony of the hold of this syndrome comes from Diderot, whose polemic against Frederick's thesis demonstrates even this enlightened man's incapacity to recognize the obvious flaw in literary politics. For Diderot's polemic against Frederick, see Anthony Strugnell, *Diderot's Politics*, 128–34. On the literary sensibility during the Revolution, see Pierre Trahard, *La sensibilité révolutionnaire*, especially chaps. 2, 6, 8; Bernard Faÿ, *L'esprit révolutionnaire en France et aux États-Unis*, 173–242.

Although Frederick held the "rivers of blood" thesis about the path of secularization, he nevertheless put himself at the head of a movement whose tendency was toward Deism and toleration. This he did because he discerned a critical difference between the capacity of Protestant and Catholic monarchies to absorb the secularization implied by the scientific component of modern institutions. In Catholic monarchies, the king with the aristocracy and clergy constituted the regime. For centuries it had been axiomatic in chancelleries that the removal of one of these constituents must unravel the whole fabric. This axiom did not hold in Prussia. There the Lutheran clergy was regulated by the Crown. The Church exercised no political control and was dependent on the Crown for revenues. Further, the Prussian nobility did not pursue ecclesiastical careers, whereas in Catholic lands the nobility monopolized the upper clergy. Consequently, the advance of Enlightenment must distress Catholic monarchies. Frederick's intelligence system kept him informed of the progress of this distress as appraised by leading men. Of the turmoils of 1749–53, ex-Foreign Minister Voyer d'Argenson said: "All the orders are discontent. The situation has become inflammable; a riot could become a revolt, and a revolt a *total revolution,* where veritable tribunes of the people, of committees and communes, will be elected, and the king and ministers will be deprived of their excessive power to harm." [26] Of this there was no hint in Prussia. Well might Frederick surmise that the storm of enlightenment could blow right through his kingdom leaving no more wreckage than a few neurotic pastors. Europe stood on the threshold of the consummation of five centuries of Ghibelline politics, and Frederick, who understood the legacy of his ancestors, was poised like an eagle to establish order in Europe when the houses of Bourbon and Hapsburg crumbled.

Frederick collected the first installment on his political investment in 1773, when Clement XIV dissolved the Jesuit order in the bull *Dominus ac Redemptor.* The Jesuits had been the linchpin of royal dominion in all Counter-Reformation lands. It had been their charge, among other things, to guard orthodoxy. But as enlightenment advanced, Jesuit intolerance became a liability compelling their expulsion and finally their suppression by Rome itself. This was a watershed event. Religious toleration must inevitably follow; yet it had been the most rigid of political dogmas that Catholic monarchies could not survive toleration.

Frederick's response to this momentous event shows how completely his deeply laid plan gave him leverage in European politics. Once again he baffled observers with an incomprehensible stroke: the prince of en-

26. Quoted by Félix Rocquain, *L'esprit révolutionnaire avant la révolution,* 146.

lightenment invited the defrocked princes of obscurantism to Prussia, and they accepted! By this Frederick proved much more than that the Prussian constitution could support religious toleration. He proved that his regime was sufficiently stable to digest the debris of crumbling Catholic monarchy. First he took the intellectuals, now the Jesuits, who happily brought with them their treasure.

Might not such a regime impose Pax Germanica? For a number of reasons this did not happen. But Frederick's renovated military-bureaucratic state vindicated his judgment during the post-Napoleonic recovery. Under its auspices Germany was united and displaced France as the leading continental power. It proved to be capable of ordering the changes wrought by the Industrial Revolution. The "rise" of the bourgeoisie and the formation of an industrial working class occasioned only a few riotous hiccups that never threatened the system. The regime collapsed only after its backbone, the officer corps, was decimated in World War I.

The Struggle between *Parlements* and the Crown

In 1774, Controller General A. R. J. Turgot advised Louis XVI: "Sire, the root of the evil is that the nation has no constitution." The difficulty was temporarily resolved fifteen years later with the dogma of the Republic, "The nation is the Third Estate."

The monarchy's constitutional problem was the incapacity of the court to integrate the nobility into its absolutist conception of the state. Under the legacy of Louis XIV, the nobility dominated the upper clergy, the Army, and the land; but government was to remain in the hands of ministers, assisted by a bureaucracy recruited largely from the commons but constituted as minor nobility.

The political institution reserved to the nobility was the regional *parlements,* which registered royal edicts.[27] The Crown interpreted the reg-

27. *Parlements* were courts hearing civil and criminal cases. They consisted of a *grand-chambre* headed by a first *président,* the *présidents à mortier,* and senior councillors. The *grand-chambre* heard pleas referred by lower courts. A number of subordinate courts operated under the supervision of the *grand-chambre:* the *chambres des requêtes,* the *chambres des enquêtes,* the *tornelle,* and the *chambres des vacations.* The officers of the courts were arranged in a hierarchy extending from the *président* to the *gens du roi* (the king's advocates) to a host of bureau chiefs and minor functionaries. They were busy and powerful institutions, not unlike superior courts today, which drew many political and commercial interests into their network of influence. *Parlements* were

istration function as a right occasionally to remonstrate concerning harmful consequences of edicts. But *parlements* tended to interpret registration as the right of judicial review. Between 1715 and 1750, the pretensions of *parlements* became the focal point of the old struggle between king and nobility. In France, as in England, the intellectual struggle took the form of a debate over the ancient constitution. The *thèse nobiliare* maintained that the ancient constitution enshrined seigneurial rights, and obliged the king to rule through the intermediary of noble councils.[28] The *thèse royale* held seigneurial rights to be feudal usurpations of Roman imperium, which was claimed as the certificate of legitimacy for royal prerogative.

In 1748, Charles Baron de Montesquieu published his *Spirit of the Laws* to expound and defend the *thèse nobiliare*. His was a modern de-

---

located at Paris, Toulouse, Grenoble, Bordeaux, Dijon, Rouen, Aix, Arras, Rennes, Pau, Metz, Colmar, Perpignan, Besançon, and Douai. The *parlement* was the registry of edicts and laws; royal ministers of intendants could act on no law that had not been duly registered. The *grand-chambre* in council might refuse to register a law, or remonstrate for its withdrawal. Since *parlements* were "sovereign," refusal to register could be overturned only by an act of king in council. This was the constitutional function that became increasingly important in the eighteenth century, and which Montesquieu rightly emphasized. See Bastard d'Estang, *Les parlements de France;* Henri Carré, *La fin des parlements;* and Franklin L. Ford, *Robe and Sword: The Regrouping of French Aristocracy after Louis XIV.*

28. The *thèse nobiliare* was argued by François Hotman (*Franco-gallia*, 1565), Étienne Pasquier, La Roche Flavin *(Treize livres des parlements de France,* 1621), Fénelon, Henri de Boulainvilliers (*Histoire de l'ancien gouvernement de la France,* 1727), and Montesquieu. The *thèse royale* was argued by Jean Bodin, Marquis Voyer d'Argenson *(Considérations sur le gouvernement ancien et présent de la France,* 1751), and Abbé Dubos (*Histoire critique de l'établissement de la monarchie française,* 1734). The *thèse nobiliare* was that the free Germanic institutions of the Franks replaced Roman institutions after the Romans were ousted by conquest. Fief rights were grounded in these conquests, as they were territories occupied by Frankish lords. For this reason they were not subject to tax. *Parlement* was held to be an ancient aristocratic council, which Boulainvilliers maintained was the cornerstone of liberty. On this view, the Capetian kings reintroduced the Roman imperium idea and corrupted the ancient constitution. The *thèse royale* denied that the Franks ever possessed free institutions and denied as well that Roman institutions were ever suppressed. Fiefs were not originally hereditary, and became so only by usurpation by the nobles. See Henri Seé, *L'évolution de la pensée politique en France au XVIIIe siècle;* and Franklin L. Ford, *Robe and Sword,* 222–52.

fense of aristocracy incorporating some basic principles of Lockean political science. He embraced Locke's minimal test for economic intelligence, that without commerce land must fail. He accepted the credit institutions entailed by commerce but so often made the object of aristocratic jeremiads. He was Lockean again in emphasizing that "sweet [or peaceful] commerce" acts as a check upon wars of honor, to which monarchies are prone. He accepted that a vigorous commercial interest supports political liberty and toleration. Walpole's Whig England was the constitution he held up for emulation. But Montesquieu understood that it was impossible to transfer the English model to France without drastic alterations. England was a sea power, France a land power. The implications of that difference made it appropriate for the English patriciate to engage in trade, but inadvisable for the French patriciate to do so. England had but one parliament, exercising a combination of legislative and judicial functions. Large France had fifteen *parlements* exercising a combination of judicial and executive functions locally. Montesquieu's defense of the *thèse nobiliare* hinged on a defense of local *parlements* as balance to the power of ministerial government. Their function in his scheme is analogous to judicial review in the American federalist scheme. It is essential to the scheme that the *parlements* were dominated by the *noblesse de robe*, with heritable rights to office. Their membership in the *noblesse* ensured their solidarity of interest with monarchy while at the same time affording them the necessary spirit of independence to oppose ministerial government when liberty was threatened or when legitimate interest might be damaged.[29]

The *thèse nobiliare* was burdened by a complication that Montesquieu wished could be conjured away. In the sixteenth-century civil wars, the *thèse nobiliare* had been associated with the cause of toleration for France's Protestants by François Hotman's *Franco-gallia* and *Protestation et défense*. The Huguenot Henry of Navarre defeated the Catholic armies and placed himself on the French throne as Henry IV. Believing that he could not hold the kingdom if he continued in the Protestant faith, he converted to Catholicism, but at the same time promulgated the Edict of Nantes, allowing freedom of worship to Protestants. The edict was hateful to the Jesuits, who led the Ultramontane party, and its revocation was a prime object of their policy. Assassins struck down Henry IV in 1610, but the edict remained in force until 1685, when Louis XIV accepted the Jesuit argument that republicanism, the *thèse nobiliare*,

---

29. For a discussion of Montesquieu's debt to Boulainvilliers balanced by awareness of Montesquieu's Lockean propinquity, see Thomas Pangle, *Montesquieu's Philosophy of Liberalism*, 291–303.

and religious toleration were all of a piece. The edict inaugurated Louis' second reign—the reign of harem despotism following two decades of enlightened policy. Two hundred thousand Huguenots, many prominent in commerce and finance, were driven from the realm by persecutions and confiscations. Louis' grand design was to bring England back to Catholicism as a client state of France. Charles II had secretly converted to Catholicism, according to the secret provisions of the Treaty of Dover; James II was the open Catholic who the Whigs believed would do what Charles had hesitated to do. The Revolution of 1688 confirmed to Louis the correctness of the Jesuit analysis. From that moment, the monarchy was heavily mortgaged to Jesuit enforcement of orthodoxy. With the Protestants banished, the Jesuits turned against their old enemies, the Jansenists, whose doctrine the pope had declared heretical some years previously. The Jansenists, they now said, were the "republican party in the Church and the State."[30] There was some substance in this allegation. The Jansenists espoused the Gallican Church, a legacy of French Ghibelline politics, for which Hotman had been an energetic spokesman. In religious doctrine the Jansenists emphasized the purity of will and the reform of conscience, as against Jesuit emphasis on the rites of the Church. Jansenists rejected the scholasticism guarded by the Jesuits; it was characteristic of them that one of their most powerful spokesman was the mathematician and scientist Blaise Pascal. Provincial universities, academies, and *parlements* were therefore the natural strongholds of Jansenism.

Since the Jesuits identified this modernizing movement as dangerous to the throne, Louis had to oppose it. Shortly before his death, he asked and received of Clement XI a bull that would settle the constitution of the Church entirely on Ultramontane principles. The pope obliged with *Unigenitus* (1713), whose doctrine of papal infallibility promulgated in the domain of opinion management a theory parallel to royal absolutism. The bull provoked violent reaction among clergy and laity alike, who identified it as a Jesuit machination to reduce France to papal vassalage in the manner of Spain, Portugal, and Italy.[31] Many *parlements* refused to register the bull, or registered it only with a rider declaring that nothing in the bull could be understood to conflict with the Gallican Church.

The effect of *Unigenitus* was to align the court of Europe's most enlightened nation with Europe's most obscurantist force. It crystallized a reform movement composed of *thèse nobiliare parlementaires*, Church re-

30. Rocquain, *L'esprit révolutionnaire*, 3.
31. Ibid., 1–15.

formers rallying around the moral writings of Fénelon, academics of provincial universities, and sundry intellectuals. But the court was not without partisans. The court party held that the defense of seigneurial rights, particularly privileges of office and exemption from taxes, was the foremost obstacle to reform. Some court nobles of ancient family, particularly the marquis d'Argenson and Turgot, believed it necessary to root out the aristocracy altogether. D'Argenson envisaged the Crown ruling directly in the interests of the broad mass—as enlightened despotism—while Turgot favored a representative legislature with broad powers. From about 1750, the institutional struggle of reform politics took shape as a duel between the *parlements* defending liberty against despotic encroachment and the court espousing equality against privilege. Spokesmen for these institutions realized that their struggle was watched by the nation. They courted public opinion and attempted to shape it. In their deliberations and declarations they used the idiom and endorsed the principles of modern political science, even though neither institution conformed to the principles invoked. The upshot was that the idiom of political science was embedded in institutions and in public discourse, and in such a way as to undercut the legitimacy of the aristocracy and monarchy. This drama provides an outstanding example of the unintended reformation of institutions by their legitimating rhetoric.

We may enter this drama at a critical juncture in 1761. Opinion management had been in the hands of the Jesuits for fifty years. This had burdened royal politics with a liability that must sooner or later be paid. The *parlements*, recognizing this liability, took aim at the Jesuits in an opportune moment, and drove them from the kingdom as "seditious destroyers of Christian morals, teaching a murderous and abominable doctrine, not only against the security and lives of citizens, but even against the sacred persons of sovereigns." [32] This daring defiance of royal sanction provoked public jubilation at the humiliation of the despised order. The Parlement of Paris was lionized as the defender of liberty, while Louis XV was immobilized, unwilling to incur further unpopularity by overturning the parliamentary decision.

This signal victory initiated a decade of parliamentary defiance and usurpations on royal authority. In 1763 the free trade reform administration of Bertin was instructed by the Parlement of Paris that its attempt to reassess property values and to tax property in office was contrary to the fundamental laws of the land. Intendants who attempted to enforce the tax decree were arrested by *parlements* in Toulouse and Grenoble. In

32. Ibid., 228.

the argumentation surrounding this sensational case, the Parlement of Paris promulgated numerous novelties recently discovered in the ancient constitution. The king's agents were found to be responsible not only to the king, but to "the nation and the laws," under "contracted engagements." The purpose of government was said to be the security of "liberty, honor and rights."[33] In a long constitutional disquisition, the Parlement reviewed French history and concluded that the sovereign commands by law. Louis yielded to this onslaught. He replaced his controller general and three offending intendants, and withdrew the tax edict.

In 1765 the Parlement of Paris declared void a ruling of the Assembly of the Clergy that no one would receive the sacraments unless he presented a certificate stating that he had been confessed by a priest in good standing (i.e. not a Jansenist). Further jousting with the court produced *parlement*-endorsed claims of the "autonomy" of defunct regional assemblies, as well as an unprecedented usurpation: the fifteen *parlements* associated themselves into a union and proclaimed themselves "the Parlement of France," which was "the one and only public, legal and necessary council of the Sovereign" as well as the "custodian and repository . . . of the political constitution of the state."[34]

Recognizing that the *parlements* were claiming equal power in legislation, Louis, in a dramatic appearance at the Palais de Justice, read to the startled Parlement of Paris a rebuke that vigorously asserted the absolute sovereignty of the Crown. It would not do, he said, for the *parlements* to declare it a crime to submit to his will, and to insinuate that "the whole nation groans to see its rights, liberty and security perish under a terrible power." Yet the *séance de la flagellation* had little effect, for the *parlements* continued to obstruct and remonstrate publicly, feeling secure in their hold on public opinion.

In 1770 Louis finally suppressed the *parlements,* and set up new courts staffed by salaried judges who had no property in office and who did not accept fees from litigants for decisions. At the same time, court jurisdictions were renovated to eliminate double jurisdiction and to facilitate trials. The fiscal reforms quashed by *parlement* resistance in 1763 were revived by the new controller general, Abbé Terray. The objective was to achieve an equitable distribution of the tax burden by levying tax in proportion to real income, irrespective of privileges and immunities honored in the past.

Parlement publicists responded with a barrage of pamphlets calling

33. Quoted by R. R. Palmer, *The Age of the Democratic Revolution,* 1: 91.
34. Ibid., 95.

the fiscal reforms "extortion" and attacking the new courts as royal puppets. There was much talk of citizens, their rights, representation, the constitution, and rule of law. Court writers responded with blasts against the grasping despotism of the "monstrous hereditary aristocracy." These struggles seemed always to end in a deadlock, or at least in the frustration of court attempts to reform the fiscal system. But in putting their cases, each side was drawn into idioms of legitimacy and institutional function peculiar to constitutional government. The court position implied the illegitimacy of aristocratic privilege, not merely in the name of absolutism, but under the banner of the public weal and of equality of citizen duties.

The *parlements* perceived this dangerous innovation and counterattacked in Montesquieu's political idiom, which attempted to support privilege on grounds of modern natural right. Thus, the Parlement of Paris declared, in rejecting Turgot's reforms in 1776: "The first rule of justice is to preserve for everyone what is due to him, a fundamental rule of natural right and of civil government, and one which consists not only in upholding rights of property but in safeguarding rights attached to the person and born of prerogatives of birth and estate."[35] The Parlement lashed out at the harm of establishing "an equality of duties" that would "overturn civil society, whose harmony rests only on the gradation of powers, authorities, preeminences and distinctions which holds each man in his place and guarantees all stations against confusion."[36] The nobles made defense of privileges a popular cause by espousing the privileges of various groups among the Third Estate, particularly craft guilds and small businesses, that were also threatened by reforms. Defense of privilege also led the *parlements* to defend the principle of public consent to taxation, freedom from arbitrary arrest, the irremovability of judges, and the liberties of provincial governments.[37]

The long struggle between court and *parlements* embedded maxims and principles of constitutional government in the public political discourse. Each protagonist defended a version of France's ancient constitution. *Parlementaire* resistance to the Crown aimed at a restoration of aristocratic participation in the legislative function, previously exercised through provincial assemblies of the Estates and through the Estates General. The *parlementaires* certainly did not intend to legitimate the equal participation of the Third Estate, or commons, in the constitu-

35. Ibid., 451.
36. Ibid.
37. Ibid., 456. On this dispute, see J. Q. C. Mackrell, *The Attack on "Feudalism" in Eighteenth-Century France*, 48–76.

tional monarchy they hoped to establish; nor did the Crown mean to legitimate the complete suppression of privilege in its attacks on the inequity of the tax burden. But these intentions were canceled by the logic of the available idioms of political discourse. As our quotations indicate, those idioms did not match the structures of the ancient constitution. They were the idioms of modern political science, based on principles of equality and self-interest incompatible with ancient forms of government. The *parlementaires* learned, belatedly and to their surprise, that what they intended in using the new idiom was not what they achieved: instead of preparing a revival of the ancient constitution, they gradually destroyed its legitimacy. They permeated institutional structures and public opinion with idioms legitimating the Declaration of the Rights of Man and a new constitution recognizing neither lords nor king. The *parlementaires* meant to use an enlightenment rhetoric to defend their power and advance their interests. But the fate that overtook theologians who attempted to appropriate the idioms of science also overtook patricians who attempted to appropriate the idioms of political science. They might use rationalism for a time, but in the end they were mastered by it.

The Causes of the French Revolution

This is not to suggest that mere words are decisive in government and politics. Disparities between legitimating rhetoric and practice need not cripple the political capacity—the American combination of the equality doctrine with slavery is an example. That combination occurred because the political will to independence crystallized long before there was a will to racial equality. The disparity between legitimating rhetoric and practice might in like manner have continued indefinitely in France in the absence of a political will to eliminate privilege and establish free constitutional government. When and how did that will originate?

When this question is put directly, some startling facts stand out in the chronology of the Revolution. The onset of the Revolution is often dated from the *révolte nobiliare,* which occurred in response to the May Edicts of 1788. The edicts were yet another ministerial attempt to put through the reform of fiscal policy whose defeat by the *parlements* had been the bone of contention for four decades. The edicts deprived the *parlements* of their power to verify taxes and legislation and lodged it in a new body, the Plenary Court. The public response was a fusillade of pamphlets, in every province, denouncing the Ministry and upholding the *parlements*. In June the Assembly of the Clergy met and refused to acknowledge the principle that its properties were taxable. The Assembly firmly supported *parlement* resistance. In September the Ministry bowed to opinion, withdrew the edicts, and restored the powers of the *parlements*. The prestige of the aristocracy had never been greater, nor that of the Crown lower, even though the former were defending privileges whose removal would benefit 26 million Frenchmen. This is one curiosity. Another is the rapidity with which this misrecognition of interest was rectified.

In September 1788, party or faction espousing republican government was nowhere on the political scene nor was it discernible behind the scenes to experienced observers. When the Estates General convened on 5 May 1789, such a party still was not visible, although its flag had been raised. The men who sat to represent the Third Estate had been elected in the first mass election ever held in France. The Estates General was not their show. The nobility had demanded it, determined its forms by consulting ancient records, and supervised the planning. The nobility appeared to have command of the situation, since they controlled not only the Second Estate (themselves), but also the First, the clergy. Yet from the first day the representatives of the Third Estate, who had for the most part never seen one another, refused to abide by the prescribed order of deliberating and voting separately by Estates; they demanded instead plenary sessions and voting by head. A deadlock ensued that numerous conferences could not resolve. It was broken on 17 June when the Third Estate, acting on a motion from Abbé Sieyès, declared itself the National Assembly and invited the other two estates to join. From that moment, events moved with remarkable speed:

- 19 June   The lower clergy join the National Assembly.
- 20 June   The Assembly resolves not to disband until the nation has a constitution (Tennis Court Oath).
- 23 June   Louis decrees that privilege cannot be abolished, but proposes to accept limitations on royal prerogative.
- 27 June   Louis revokes the decree of June 23.
- 1–7 July   30,000 troops assemble in and around Paris.
- 10 July   The Assembly addresses the king for the removal of troops.
- 14 July   National Guardsmen seize arms at the Invalids; the Bastille is taken; Marshall de Broglie withdraws troops from Paris.
- 15 July   Louis submits to the Assembly.
- 16 July   Bailly, president of the Assembly, is placed at the head of Paris municipal government; Lafayette swears

fealty to the people as commander of the National Guard.

- 17 July   Louis makes his will; journeys from Versailles to the Hôtel de Ville to confirm before the people the actions of the National Assembly. He wears the tricolor to signify his solidarity.
- 4 August   The Assembly abolishes the feudal order. All titles and privileges of birth are revoked; ecclesiastical offices are made elective.
- 26 August   The Declaration of the Rights of Man and Citizen is promulgated and published.
- 5 September   The Assembly resolves that government will be vested in a unicameral elective assembly, over which the king has a suspensive veto.

In four months, an assembly of some 600 men who had never before collaborated in government completely altered the political constitution of France. The aristocracy that had humbled the Crown was humbled in turn and then abolished. The nation was given the elements of a written constitution. The Assembly assumed the responsibility of government. The Army was quiet. The provinces stood behind the Assembly. There was little violence, although all parties perceived danger, and tactics of intimidation were used on all sides.

This performance is unique in modern history, at least for larger nations. Suddenly a political will appears, subdues the old regime with lightning speed, and shows itself, for a moment, able to govern. The American colonists needed eighteen months to produce a Declaration of Independence and a provisional government. The Revolution of 1688 is more comparable, for it also went with lightning speed. But the prime factor in that event was William's invasion with 15,000 troops. The men who met in the Convention Parliament to hammer out the Settlement (under William's protection) were experienced parliamentarians who had collaborated for years.

The usual explanations given for this phase of the Revolution do not explain these behaviors. Some authorities insist on the economic crisis, especially the imminent bankruptcy of the government and the hardship caused by the poor harvest of 1788. But this conjunction of circumstances had been recurrent for four decades. If they were enough to produce revolution in 1789, they should also have sufficed in 1749–53, 1763–66, 1774–77, and so on. It is true that from 1787, records of private conversations establish that experienced observers felt winds of revolution in the air. But again that perception does not distinguish 1787–89; in every previous crisis experienced observers remarked upon the imminence of revolution.[38] The most serious defect of the economic explanation, however, is its failure to articulate, let alone describe, the political dimension in which the economic question was argued. As we have seen, the Ministry, for four decades, took the view that the budget could not be balanced without invading the nobles' exemption. The fiscal policy carried political implications for the standing of privilege in the *ancien régime*. The nobility, acting through the *parlements*, represented the fiscal policy as royal invasion of rights and claimed that the proposed equalization of tax burden would be unnecessary but for court extravagance and corruption. The *parlements* turned the economic question into a power struggle in which, by 1789, they were prepared to concede the tax issue in return for institutionalized participation in the legislative function. This was, in effect, a demand for mixed monarchy on the English model—Montesquieu's program for reform of the constitution.

During this long struggle, public opinion sided with the *parlements*, while the ministers were often in odium. Louis XV and Louis XVI frequently dismissed ministers in response to public outcry; but the new ministries usually reverted to the policy of the predecessors. The ministries were frequently led by men who pursued the public interest, yet the public consistently supported the *parlements'* defense of privilege in the name of citizen rights. We need not read the tacit alliance between the Second and Third Estates against the Crown as blindness on the part of the Third Estate. By challenging the absolutist doctrine that law emanated solely from the will of the sovereign, they raised a constitutional question whose resolution in favor of the nobles could not but change the political fortunes of the Third Estate. Repeated retreats from absolute prerogative, in the form of withdrawn edicts after the firmest assertion of prerogative failed, proved that the *parlements*, with public support, were winning the struggle. By the time the Estates General convened, absolutism was a doctrine without force. It was then, and only then, that the Third Estate sided with the Crown against the nobility in demanding the recall of the dismissed Controller General Necker, who had backed the familiar tax reforms. This very articulate chain of events unfolded within the logic of France's political institutions and politics, and cannot be explained as stratagems of economic interest groups.[39]

38. Daniel Mornet, *Les origines intellectuelles de la révolution française*, 444–48.
39. Discussion of economic causes is perplexed by equivocal meanings of *revolu-*

The explanation by appeal to social class fares little better than the economic interpretation. The nobility who followed the lead of the *parlements* acted to advance a political interest at the cost of increased taxation. Since the Third Estate eventually outmaneuvered the king and nobility, one is tempted to equate the Third Estate with the bourgeoisie, who are conceived to have been in revolt against the aristocracy. But this explanation confuses a consequence of events from May to August with their cause. The bourgeoisie can be said to have made the Revolution only if the 600 men who were returned by elections to represent the Third Estate can be said to have represented a clear class interest. This condition did not hold subjectively or objectively. (1) The Third Estate took its program from Abbé Sieyès's pamphlet *What Is the Third Estate?*, published in January 1789. This pamphlet was the first unambiguous manifestation of the political will that six months later crystallized in the National Assembly.[40] (2) Sieyès's fundamental premise was that "the Third Estate is the nation." He argued his premise as a factual assertion

---

tion. Food shortages and other circumstances of widespread distress were often the spontaneous and immediate cause of riot, looting, and insurrection. If such actions are of sufficient magnitude, they may destroy a government; and this may be called a revolution. A second meaning of *revolution* designates the new programs introduced by the successor government. Revolution in this sense *cannot* be caused by mere riots, however large, because revolutionary government requires a program. The program of the National Assembly is not contained in the rhetoric of bread riots.

40. Sieyès's pamphlet appeared at the end of six months' intensive pamphlet discussion about the composition of the Estates General, in which the chief question was whether the estates should vote by head or by order. Sieyès himself had contributed two pamphlets during that time. His third pamphlet broke new ground by rejecting the legitimacy of the orders altogether; it was therefore the first unambiguous manifestation of a political will to fundamental constitutional change, or revolution. This is not to deny that there was a considerable body of opinion in favor of such a change. The celebrated *Mémoire au Roi* by the peers (6 November 1788) declared that "the state is in danger . . . a revolution in the principles of government is in preparation . . . some sacred institutions are reputed to be problematic and are decried as unjust . . . the rights of the two first orders divide opinion; the suppression of feudal rights has been proposed" (quoted by Henri Carré, *La noblesse de France et l'opinion publique au XVIIIe siècle*, 331). It was widely believed that the antinobility press campaign that commenced in the middle of 1788 was instigated by Louis' chief minister, Lomenie de Brienne, who the peers successfully demanded be dismissed. For a bibliography of the pamphlets of the second half of 1788, see Mitchell B. Garrett, *The Estates General of 1789*, 232–63.

by a simple arithmetical calculation showing that although the nobility (inclusive of the upper clergy) comprised only 0.7 percent of the total population, leaving the Third Estate with the remaining 99.3 percent, nevertheless the voting arrangements at the forthcoming meeting of the Estates General gave the nobility and clergy control of decision. Sieyès argued from this fact to the question of legitimacy, maintaining that it was absurd for a fraction of the nation to preponderate over the remainder. Transposing his argument into integers, he disregarded the 0.7 percent and declared that the Third Estate *was* the nation. Responding to the *parlementaire* program for a mixed monarchy along English lines, Sieyès blasted the English constitution as an accretion of accidents and compromises, which, imitated in France, would only place a veto in the hands of the nobility. The "true principles of political science," he maintained, mandated that the Third Estate should establish itself as the National Assembly representing "the nation," from which alone the constitution and law could legitimately emanate. "The Nation is the Third Estate" formula excised king, nobles, and clergy from government: this was the lean, hard rationalism that raised Burke's fury.

It is a singular fact, again probably unique in modern political history, that the delegates who assembled in Paris followed Sieyès's program to the letter. Although their belief that they represented the national will dominated their proceedings, they represented a fragment of interests numerically not much larger than the nobility. About 60 percent were lawyers.[41] Their preponderance is readily explained. Lawyers were uniquely placed in French national life at that moment. Provincial practice brought them in contact with a cross-section of the people and taught them the structures of local and national government. Pleading before the courts familiarized them with *parlementaire* constitutional doctrine and educated them in the reasoning of constitutional politics. As a professional group they understood *parlementaire* politics; indeed it was their own until the Revolution, when they democratized constitutionalism. That so many lawyers were returned in elections was partly due to their association, in the public mind, with *parlementaire* opposition politics; it was natural for lawyers to assume a leading role in preparing the *cahiers* of grievances that Louis requested from every parish as part of the documentation to be laid before the Estates General. Robes-

---

41. The vocational breakdown of the elected members of the Third Estate was as follows: nobles, 15; clergymen, 4; royal officials, 20; municipal officers, 204; merchants, bankers, and men of means, 130; physicians, 15; civil servants, 150; lawyers in private practice, 210; farmers, 40. These figures are given by Eric Thompson, *Popular Sovereignty and the French Constituent Assembly*, 1.

pierre, an attorney in Arras, was typical of these men. In helping farmers and tradesmen prepare their *cahiers,* he established a constituency.

While a persuasive class analysis does not require that factions align rigidly on class lines, the presence of deep cleavages within classes requires that class analysis be supplemented by other considerations. The French nobility were in fact unable to act as a class because they were divided into royalist and *parlementaire* factions. A noble seeking to optimize his interest in land, seigneurial rights, and privilege between 1750 and 1785 might choose between alternative positions. One defended his seigneurial rights, but forbade him to go into commerce. The other heavily invaded seigneurial rights, but enabled him to trade as he pleased. Both programs might seem to threaten aristocratic institutions by rejecting the charisma of noble blood as having any bearing on legitimacy claims, which were evaluated instead by rational analysis of the political and economic functions of all classes. Where did the objective interest of the nobility lie? There was no decision procedure to decide this question. But whichever faction a noble might support, he backed a program that made the aristocratic interest depend on its compatibility with other interests and requirements of the nation. This shows that in the actual situation, nobles did not and indeed could not act as a body to promote their class interest, because there was no political vehicle available for them to do so.

Inspecting events after May 1789, we are struck by the sudden collapse of the *parlementaire* initiatives that had been so strong until only six months before, and the defection of many nobles to the Third Estate. We underscored this turn of events by pointing out that a program for Third Estate politics did not appear until Abbé Sieyès's pamphlet was published in January. These statements must be qualified by noticing the influence of an isolated writer who long before had opened a third front between the *thèse royale* and *thèse nobiliare.* This writer was Gabriel Bonnot, Abbé de Mably, the son of a *parlementaire* of Grenoble. Mably's first political writing in 1740 was partially inspired by Montesquieu's work on the Roman Republic; it endorsed a commerce-nobility-monarchy arrangement similar to the one Montesquieu defended eight years later. But in his *Droits et devoirs du citoyen* (written in 1758, first published in 1789) and in *De la législation* (1765), Mably broke new ground. He argued that the stalemate between the Crown and the *parlements* had no remedy short of settling a new constitution on the nation. The Crown had no alternative, he maintained, but to convene the Estates General to settle the constitutional question. Mingling exhortation with prediction, the 1758 work projected that when the Estates assembled, they would transform themselves into a legislative assembly.

Mably even included a draft constitution in his work, and gloomily predicted that these good deeds, when they finally occurred, would be spoiled by haste and personal ambition.[42]

The force of Mably's position stirred the Crown and the Parlement of Paris to action against his publications. Yet it was the *parlementaires* who eventually pressed the Estates General on Louis XVI. In acceding to this demand, Louis was well aware of Mably's notion that a Crown–Third Estate alliance might turn the flank of the *parlementaire* opposition. When the Estates General finally convened, Mably's tracts were fashionable and his name was repeatedly mentioned in debates. His friend and literary executor, J. Mounier, was the author of the Tennis Court Oath, which in effect created the National Assembly from the Third Estate. Thus did events follow a script written long before events.

It would be gratifying if Mably's program articulated a class interest, and more gratifying still if it was the interest of commerce and finance; for then we could commend ourselves on discovering the bourgeois spokesman of the bourgeois revolution. Unfortunately, this noble ecclesiastic was a moralist whose model of a good political order was not progressive England but Lycurgus's Sparta—virtuous, egalitarian, communist Sparta. Mably believed that property induces avarice, pride, and ambition. His strictures against disparities of wealth, his yearning for a return to the original primitive communism which he thought obtained in the state of nature, were edifying to the "bourgeois" assembly that abolished feudalism in August 1789. But they also helped inspire some of the Revolution's worst atavisms.[43]

42. When Mably's disciple Mounier published the *Droits,* the public was so astonished by the author's prescience of events that many believed it must have been written by Mounier himself, sometime after 1788. More than any other author, Mably was responsible for injecting the word *revolution* into political discussion. It occurs frequently in his writings. Sometimes he used it as Aristotle did, as descriptive of the "mutations" of government. At other times it is associated with a moral content, where the oppression of rulers forces the people to break their chains. Since Mably's references are historical, he sighs or groans about their failed efforts. It is interesting to note that Mably was Louis XVI's favorite writer on politics and morals; and of interest also that Mably's *Phocion* was prized as a catechism of virtuous citizenship by many Jacobins.

43. The correlation between Jacobin radicalism and the Spartan ideal is so strong that one may almost say that Jacobinism was the attempt to recapitulate the Spartan polity. The most determined persecutors and uncompromising politicians, Billaud-Varenne and Saint-Just, constantly referred to Sparta in their speeches and defended it in *Les éléments du républicanisme* and

Among the nobility who went over to the Third Estate, it is difficult to find a common thread of class interest. Lafayette, who loved popularity, was the darling of the Paris crowd because of his manly endeavors on behalf of the American Revolution. Suspect at court for his republican principles, he was for that reason the Assembly's logical choice as commander of the National Guard. Mirabeau, son of the Physiocrat, was a déclassé profligate. But his combination of political astuteness and oratorical talent made him one of the masters of the Assembly until his death a year later. Le Peletier de Saint-Fargeau was among the wealthiest men in the kingdom. As president of the Parlement of Paris, he might have led the nobles. Yet his early desertion to the Third Estate struck a severe blow to *parlementaire* politics. He quickly gravitated to the radical wing of the Assembly and became one of several aristocratic leaders of the extreme "Mountain" faction. It is deeply unsatisfying to admit that an allegedly bourgeois revolution against the aristocracy was nevertheless led by nobles acting on a program designed largely by a priest of noble family. It rings with the same falseness as a proletarian revolution led by bourgeois intellectuals. The paradox is discharged by relinquishing the idea that the French Revolution was a bourgeois revolution.[44]

The class analysis of the French Revolution did not originate with the

---

Fragments sur les institutions républicaines. Marat was a spartiate, as were Babeuf and Buonarotti. For these men Sparta meant contempt of money and love of glory, equality, assemblies, collective decision, and the supremacy of oratory to political science. Mably, of course, was not the only forerunner to magnify the Spartan ideal; d'Argenson, Rousseau, Morelley, and even Helvétius espoused it. On the mania of the spartiates, see James Billington, *Fire in the Minds of Men*, 54–85; for a review of the spartiate literature of France, see Elizabeth Rawson, *The Spartan Tradition in European Thought*, 220–300.

44. The existence of an entrepreneurial, profit-oriented class who perceived their interests to be obstructed by the political influence of the nobility and the economic dominance of land is the minimum requirement of the social class interpretation of the Revolution. The search for such evidence was initiated by Jaurès and continued by Georges Lefebvre and others. The accumulated evidence, however, has falsified this assumption. Wealth in pre-revolutionary France was mainly wealth in land and offices, in which nobles and commons shared. In a review of this question, George V. Taylor declares that "what the emerging data have made impossible is to equate the identifiable leadership of the upper Third Estate—the 'revolutionary bourgeoisie'—with a social class that played a common role in the relations of production in an emergent capitalist economy" ("Noncapitalist Wealth and the Origins of the French Revolution," 494).

socialist and aristocratic historians who gave it currency; they merely took over an analysis originated by factional revolutionary leaders. While the political effectiveness of this analysis depended upon the emotional effects that could be obtained by invective against aristocrats, its root lies deeper in the practical vicissitudes of a theoretical concept dominating the constitutional thought of the Assembly. This concept was the idea of "the nation" or "the general will" as the legitimating source of law. Abbé Sieyès's formula, "the nation is the Third Estate," assumed "the general will" as the only legitimate source of law. His identification of the general will with the manifest interest of the Third Estate was implied by his calculations showing the disproportion between the number of the nobility (in the total population) and their political and economic power. The nation, Sieyès argued, could not will its domination by a few. Events confirmed him insofar as the representatives of the Third Estate—as well as opinion in Paris and the provinces—concurred that the people must have a voice in government. But the critical test was not whether the nation could concur in rejecting the *ancien régime,* but whether the general will could be effectively embodied in constitutional mechanisms. This was the question before the Assembly when it debated the merits of bicameral and unicameral legislative assemblies. Unicameralists, led by Sieyès and Condorcet (who chaired the constitution committee), maintained that the resolutions of a single representative chamber *were* deliverances of the general will. Bicameralists, led by Mounier, argued that such resolutions must in some cases be nothing more than momentary impetuosities, destructive of the public good. The compromise solution was a unicameral legislature tethered to a royal suspensive veto.[45]

Unicameralism is impaled on a double dilemma. (1) Legislative resolves either define the public good or they do not. If the former, political legitimacy drifts into a theology of parliamentary infallibility.[46] If

---

45. Thompson, *Popular Sovereignty and the French Constituent Assembly,* 49–70.
46. Publicists and politicians turned popular sovereignty into a doctrine comparable to the divine right and papal infallibility. For example, Anacharsis Cloots's proposed pledge of allegiance to the nation included the line "My profession of faith is as reassuring for the patriot as it is terrible for the treasonous: I BELIEVE IN THE INFALLIBILITY OF THE PEOPLE." Writers also described the National Assembly as a "temple" or as the "Vatican of Reason," while its deliverances were called "the evangel of the day." These attempts to fashion republican politics into a civil religion led to efforts to create a *volonté unique* in the nation by means of propaganda and indoctrination. Some even spoke of creating a "new race" of fanatical patriots. Le Peletier de Saint-Fargeau's proposal for public instruction would have taken

this notion is rejected, there must be other mechanisms, such as the veto or judicial review, to check parliamentary will. But then one rejects the basic argument for unicameral government and the system of balanced power follows through the breach. (2) The second dilemma arises when legislative resolve is weakened by faction and party. Unicameralism assumes that the legislature will discern and resolve upon the common good. Since factions weaken the will and obscure the common good, unicameralists cannot regard them with equanimity as the ordinary consequences of government. They can scarcely avoid regarding factions as private and perverse wills, saboteurs of the general will. But since each faction looks upon the others in this light, we are back to Hobbesian chaos. This result follows from the unicameral conception of a single assembly as sole representative of the public will. It yields a precise description of what actually began to happen from about October 1789. Perhaps the best political science would not have prevented *fraternité* becoming fratricide; but the Assembly's unicameralism blocked an institutional solution to the problem of faction. Unable to find the required organizational solution, the Assembly moralized the problem in the manic-depressive rhetoric of classical politics.

Here, in this underworld of nostalgic psychodramas, is the root of the class analysis of the French Revolution. The internal politics of the virtuous republic had been a perpetual struggle between patriciate and commons. Once the Assembly took the wrong fork in the road as it made its exit from the feudal order, it fell into the atavisms of Roman politics. Thus Marat, who thrilled at the thought of cutting off a hundred thousand, or better, half a million heads, urged the National Convention to adopt the Roman institution of elective dictatorship. "Gracchus" Babeuf, fancying himself in a toga, wrote in an article entitled "Tribune of the People": "What is the French Revolution? It is a declared war between the patricians and the plebeians [*plébéiens*], between the rich and the poor . . . democracy is the obligation of those who have much to provision those who have little . . . all deficit in the fortune of the latter proceeds from what the former have stolen . . . the terror is directed at no one, but to all."[47] And from Robespierre we hear that "the revolutions of the past three years have all been for the other classes of citizens, and almost nothing yet for the proletarians [*prolétaires*] whose only property is in their labor."[48] Tribunes, proletarians,

children from their parents at an early age and placed them in rigidly disciplined schools of virtue.

47. Quoted by Louis Villat, *La Révolution et l'empire*, 1: 353.
48. Quoted ibid., 240.

and blood: here is the psychodrama of the virtuous republic mired in the fever-swamps of political theater. To recognize the sanguinary opportunism parading here as zeal for the oppressed, we need only bear in mind that these utterances came four years after the Assembly had peacefully abolished seigneurial rights and sold the lands of the nobility. The consequence of furious zeal was what it had always been in Rome: ever more oppression and poverty following the carnage of civil war.

Hobbes had based his break with classical political thought partly on his insight that the factual truth of the virtuous republic was wars of conquest and a domestic oratorical politics that thrived on empty promises. The virtuous republicans of the French Revolution splendidly if cruelly confirmed his analysis by reenacting Roman politics. They manipulated the ancient canard that the poor could acquire bread by pillage and murder. This was all the more atavistic in 1795, when the real means of the relief of the people's estate, the steam engine, had been available for fifteen years.[49] But then, the steam engine belonged to a different political program of economic growth through the application of technical intelligence. The program did not appeal to the revolutionary orators because there was no room in it for the dramaturgy of class warfare and virtuous republics. The program required of its politicians not oratory and blood lust, but disciplined thinking and untheatrical work. The class analysis of the French Revolution is a Roman political superstition enjoying a posthumous existence thanks to cultural inertia and to the popular appeal of political theater.[50]

If economic crisis and class cannot describe the events of May through August, we are on much firmer ground with the American Connection. Two things distinguished 1789 from previous anticipations of revolution: the opportunity presented by convening the Estates General, and the example of a revolution freshly made against a great power that happened to be France's rival. These two things were not unrelated: Louis' final decision to convene the Estates General was prompted by Lafayette's insistence, and Lafayette was a leading Americanist among the nobility. But every level of French society was beguiled by the American drama. Autocrats in and out of government recognized in the rebellion a threat to British power and an opportunity for France, should the rebels succeed.[51] They still smarted from the defeats and territorial losses of

49. On revolutionary attempts to eradicate poverty, and their failure, see Alan Forest, *The French Revolution and the Poor*, 138–63.
50. The delinquencies of the class analysis of the Revolution have been criticized in exemplary fashion by François Furet, *Interpreting the French Revolution*.
51. Faÿ, *L'esprit révolutionnaire*, 30–36, 56–60, 67–70.

the Seven Years' War: now things had taken such a turn that the commercial empire of Britain was in jeopardy. France entered the American war slowly and with caution, owing to the strain of a new war on finances already distressed. But enter it did, and large numbers of the nobility repaired to the flag. Contrary to their usual practice, French officers and troops behaved with great courtesy and forbearance toward their allies: they paid for their stores, avoided damaging crops or property, and did not molest the women, under strict orders from the commander, the duc de Rochambeau. The officers and men who served in America provided fresh leaven for the strong pro-American current abroad in France. Crevecoeur's *Lettres d'un cultivateur americain* (1785) was a French nobleman's testimony to the virtues of the simple life of freedom and independence. The work's success among the nobility was evidence of their readiness to sacrifice some rank and privilege in exchange for participating in the rejuvenation of France along virtuous republic lines.[52]

The people also were captivated by America. Despite its cost, the American alliance was popular in France because it merged a patriotic struggle against an old rival with a fight for a new ideal. The embodiment of this ideal was the American envoy, Ben Franklin. Prior to hostilities, Franklin had become a symbol of the virtuous, unpretentious, sage agrarian democrat whose existence proved the possibility of regeneration. Once France allied with America, Franklin became a cult figure whose image was reproduced on millions of cameos, fans, signs, handkerchiefs, fabrics, and prints.[53] His words and deeds were high-impact charisma. When he appeared in Louis' court without a wig, it signified that the common man had penetrated the highest places on his

52. This group of nobles was associated with Brissot and Lafayette (Louis Gottschalk, *Lafayette Between the American and the French Revolution*, 279–80; Faÿ, *L'esprit révolutionnaire*, 187ff.).

53. Alfred O. Aldridge, *Franklin and His French Contemporaries*, 95ff., 212–34; Durand Echeverria, *Mirage in the West: A History of the French Image of American Society to 1815*, 45–52. John Adams, whose Paris mission overlapped with Franklin's, said of his popularity: "His reputation was more universal than that of Leibnitz or Newton, Frederick or Voltaire, and his character more beloved and esteemed than any or all of them. . . . His name was familiar to government and people, to kings, courtiers, nobility, clergy, and philosophers, as well as plebeians, to such a degree that there was scarcely a peasant or a citizen, a *valet de chambre*, a coachman or footman, a lady's chambermaid or a scullion in a kitchen, who was not familiar with it, and who did not consider him as a friend to human kind. *When they spoke of him, they seemed to think he was to restore the golden age*" (*Works*, 1: 660; italics added).

own terms. His laconic description of the progress of the Revolution—
"Ça ira!"—released reservoirs of political enthusiasm. This phrase,
which he pronounced in 1778, is good evidence that the popular emotions mobilized then were continuous with the emotions the people felt
a decade later, when it became the main slogan of the French Revolution.[54] Further evidence of the continuity is that when Franklin died in
1790, the National Assembly declared three days of mourning, eulogized
him from the rostrum, and erected a monument to the common people's
liberator from the oppression of tyrants and the terrors of gods.[55] No
other American envoy has ever exercised such public influence in a foreign nation. His success was only partly due to his public relations skills.
Franklin became an idol also because he exemplified nostalgia for the
republican simplicity valorized by writers, painters, poets.

Franklin was also the catalyst of the Americanist phase of the Enlightenment. He fit comfortably into the circle of the aging Turgot and
the younger Condorcet. He interpreted events and constitutional politics to these men, both of whom published works on American constitutions. Philosophes turned out pro-American propaganda, beginning
with Dubuisson's *Abrégé de la révolution de l'Amérique anglaise* (1778);
Abbé Raynal's *La révolution de l'Amérique* followed in 1781, and Condorcet added his *L'Influence de la révolution de l'Amérique sur l'Europe* in
1785. Dubuisson and Raynal upheld the American indictment of British
tyranny without any disruptive criticism. These tracts are interesting examples of how patriots may use a war alliance to inculcate maxims hostile to their own government: if Britain did not recognize the American
principles of popular sovereignty, the rights of man, republican government, and freedom of the press and commerce, the French monarchy
was even less advanced in that direction. These and other tracts magnified the American people as "the hope of mankind," as Turgot said, because they had shown that the principles advocated by enlightened men
could be made to prevail. Thus Condorcet wrote:

> This example [of the assertion of the rights of man], so useful for
> all nations able to contemplate it, might have been lost to the hu-

54. See above, 401–2.
55. The eulogies to Franklin in France were extravagant (see Aldridge, *Franklin
and His French Contemporaries,* 212–34). Franklin's view of the French Revolution only weeks before his death is telling: "Why I see nothing singular in
all this, but on the contrary, what might naturally be expected; the French
have served an *apprenticeship* to *Liberty* in this country, and now that they are
out of their time, they *have set up for themselves.*"

man race. Great nations despise the example of small ones, and England, which for a century has given so imposing an example, would only have confirmed by America's fall the opinion, so widespread, so dangerous and false, that laws have but slight influence on peoples, and polities are condemned to dissolution after a few brilliant moments. Had America been defeated by the British arms, despotism would have forged chains in the mother country, and England would have been like all republics that lose their liberty.[56]

This passage conveys the sense that events in America had brought human history to a turning point; a decisive and irreversible breakthrough toward a new humane and democratic dispensation had been made. This sense of the epochal character of political events imparted to the word *revolution* the distinctive meaning that it was to retain right through to Lenin. The Paris public was exposed to this notion by Chénier's tragedy *Charles IX,* a smash hit in 1789:

> This vast continent, surrounded by seas,
> Suddenly changed Europe and the Universe;
> It elevates for us, on the fields of America
> New interests, and another politics.

That the universe may be transformed by a revolution is doubtful. But Chénier was right about Europe: not only in England and France, but in the Netherlands, Sweden, portions of Germany, and Poland, factions appeared demanding constitutional change.[57] Frenchmen eventually claimed for themselves the vanguard role they previously had ascribed

56. *Œuvres de Condorcet,* 8: 12–14. Many intellectuals witnessed to the powerful impression made by the American example. Turgot said in 1778: "It is impossible not to hope that this people may attain the prosperity of which they are susceptible. They are the hope of mankind; they may well become its model." Louis Mercier surmised that "it is perhaps in America that the human race is to be recreated" (*De la littérature,* 1778). And Condorcet declared in his *Éloge de Franklin:* "Men whom the reading of philosophic books had secretly converted to the love of liberty became enthusiastic over the liberty of a foreign people while they waited for the moment when they could recover their own, and they seized with joy this opportunity to avow publicly sentiments which prudence had prevented them from expressing" (*Œuvres,* 3: 406–7).
57. Palmer, *The Age of Democratic Revolution,* 1: 239–82; Jan Nordholt, *The Dutch Republic and American Independence,* 70–112.

to America; but the idea remained the same, as we see with particular clarity from Condorcet's *Outline of an Historical View of the Progress of the Human Mind.*

A clear view of the Americanist phase of the Enlightenment resolves much of the debate about the influence of intellectuals on the Revolution. The traditional view held that the National Assembly deputies, as disciples of the philosophes, enacted their programs and declaimed in their idiom. This view has been criticized as simplistic or mythic, as in some versions it indeed is. We are reminded that the philosophes did not espouse revolution; that only one or two espoused popular sovereignty, and then only for small republics; that most preferred civilized despotism to democracy, and so on.[58] However, these sharp contrasts are obtained by pairing what a philosophe wrote in 1760 with what a disciple said in 1789; in this way, revolution principles are made to appear significantly discontinuous with Enlightenment political doctrine. But this method ignores the Americanist phase, when doctrine accelerated toward the principles of 1789. Thus, the younger generation of Physiocrats, particularly the du Ponts, abandoned despotism for republicanism under the influence of events in America. Raynal's *Histoire des deux Indes* was transformed from a description of colonial enterprises in the first edition (1770) to an indictment of colonialism in the third (1780).[59] Or again, the aged Diderot, who had taught Lockean political principles and monarchical allegiance throughout his life, became increasingly outspoken after the Declaration of Independence until he finally defended the right to revolution in 1780.[60] Condorcet's quite open embrace of American principles in 1785 shows that the legitimacy of the *ancien régime* had been largely destroyed among the intelligentsia.

That the new generation of philosophes carried the American Revolution into French politics may be ascertained by inspection of National Assembly leadership. The Declaration of the Rights of Man drew substantially on the Declaration of Independence and the Bill of Rights. The debates on the structure of government were conducted on the assumption that the American experience was a weighty authority. The bicameralists Mounier and Brissot argued from the U.S. Constitution and from Abbé Mably's writings. The unicameralist Condorcet, a political disciple of Franklin, espoused the unicameral system Franklin had

58. George V. Taylor, "Revolutionary and Nonrevolutionary Content in the *Cahiers* of 1789: An Interim Report," 479–80, 488–89.
59. Strugnell, *Diderot's Politics,* 208–9.
60. Ibid., 212–13.

devised for Pennsylvania (in effect until 1790).[61] Sieyès reinterpreted Rousseau in this new context, while others, such as Danton, reinterpreted Montesquieu.

The constitutional phase of the Revolution thus appears to have been dominated by the Americanist phase of the Enlightenment. The degree of this dominance can be estimated only by reference to the opinion of the constituents of the deputies: to what extent was there explicit electoral articulation of the constitutional program followed by the Assembly? The *cahiers de doléances,* prepared between March and May of 1789 for use by the Estates General, provide an unusually thorough measure of political opinion among the broad public at that time. Systematic studies of these 2,000 *cahiers* reveal that the reforms petitioned by the public bore little relation to the reforms actually given the nation by the Assembly: they do not demand a parliament, popular sovereignty, the abolition of feudalism, or the disestablishment of the Church; they do not mention the rights of man; they express local grievances in the political idiom of the ancient constitution; the commercial classes show no consciousness of themselves as the "revolutionary class" about to seize control of government.[62] The few exceptions to this general characterization—mainly in *cahiers* of some noble and urban groups—are just enough to prove that if the broad public had heard the intellectuals, they had not learned to speak their idiom.

The nearly complete absence of electoral articulation of the constitutional program of the National Assembly suggests that the dominance rating of the intellectuals on the Revolution must be somewhere close to 100 percent. How then are we to account for the broad public support of the National Assembly when the idioms of popular government began to ring out from Paris? Clearly the *cahiers* failed to register a certain stratum of sentiment that we must suppose existed.

That stratum is identified through the pamphlet literature on the convening of the Estates General. In these writings one finds that the literate public was well aware of a constitutional struggle between the Crown and the aristocracy, and between the aristocracy and the Third Estate.[63] The illiterate public was possessed of a stock of images and revolutionary emotions imparted by Dr. Franklin and the American Revolution. Finally, we should take note of Condorcet's remarks, read

61. Faÿ, *L'esprit révolutionnaire,* 179–87.
62. Taylor, "Revolutionary and Nonrevolutionary Content in the *Cahiers* of 1789: An Interim Report," 489–500.
63. See n. 39 above.

from the rostrum on the occasion of Franklin's eulogy, about how ideas were translated into practice:

> Men whom the reading of philosophic books had secretly converted to the love of liberty became enthusiastic over the liberty of a foreign people while they waited for the moment when they could recover their own, and they seized with joy this opportunity to avow publicly sentiments which prudence had prevented them from expressing.[64]

Condorcet's view of the origin of the revolutionary will was again officially endorsed in 1794, on the occasion of the gala reception of the American envoy, James Monroe. The president of the Assembly, Merlin de Douai, declared to a throng of 10,000 spectators:

> The French people have not forgotten that it is to the American people that they owe their initiation into the cause of liberty. It was in admiring the sublime insurrection of the American people against Britain, once so haughty, but now so humbled; it was in cementing your independence by the blood of our brave warriors, that the French people learned in their turn to break the scepter of tyranny, and to elevate the statue of liberty on the wreck of a throne supported during fourteen centuries only by crimes and by corruption.

64. *Œuvres de Condorcet*, 3: 406–7.

chapter 11

The Formation and Reformation of Government (United States)

The New Political Science of *The Federalist*

When the U.S. Constitution became fundamental law in 1789, it was an open question whether the new nation would endure under its auspices. One of the Constitution's ablest expositors and exponents, Alexander Hamilton, privately called it a "frail and worthless fabric," for he believed that its executive was too weak to support stable government. James Madison, who in *The Federalist* praised the "wholly popular republic" that the Constitution gave the nation, nevertheless envisaged at the Philadelphia Convention that in the course of time most citizens would forfeit their property to manufacturers and would "become tools of opulence and ambition."[1] Ben Franklin, apprehensive that the bicameral system would realize Madison's projection, endorsed the Constitution with misgiving.

Such sober assessments were typical of those who contrived American government. Their vision of the future was tempered by awareness of the vulnerability of the new government to internal dissentions and foreign intervention. Nevertheless, a century after the founding, the United States remained a "wholly popular republic." It had attracted hopeful immigrants by the millions. A continent had been tamed in four generations. Despite a short but bloody civil war, despite unprecedented growth and change, government was stable. It was also demo-

---

1. Max Farrand, *Records of the Federal Convention*, 2: 203–4.

cratic. The people had not been dispossessed by oligarchs. Their liberties were secure and expanding; they owned the land and bought shares in corporations. The "frail and worthless fabric" had accumulated capital with a velocity unmatched anywhere, anytime, and it was immune to military threat. The American people had not only escaped the worst-case scenarios considered by the Founders; the intention to found a democratic republic had succeeded beyond their most sanguine hopes.

Caution was warranted because the American system of government introduced significant novelties. Never before had a wholly popular republic—one without an aristocracy—been tested, unless the colonial experience under monarchical auspices was such a test. Another innovation was America's territorial size. The received wisdom, much debated at the Constitutional Convention, declared that a large republic was incompatible with liberty. The political experience of the ages seemed to confirm that maxim. But the Convention accepted the new argument that the nation's large extent was one of its best guarantees of liberty. Yet another innovation concerned religion. There was no record of a polity lacking a national religion; even tolerant Holland retained the Reformed Church. Nevertheless, the Constitution did not create an ecclesiastical establishment; indeed, it did not formally commit itself even to Christianity. The federal system was also unprecedented. Confederations such as the United Provinces were partial unions lacking the power to make law for their member states except by consent. The federal system, by contrast, created the national government as sovereign over citizens yet left broad concurrent powers to states. A further innovation concerned the arrangement and balance of power. Constitutional balance ideas had been central to republican political thought. But prior to the American founding, investigations of balance presupposed a landed aristocracy and a monarch. Since these institutions were prohibited from the American polity, the framers developed an intricate system of powers and jurisdictions enabling the government to execute public business, but in a way that controlled the tendency of confined power to encroach.

The authors of the Constitution entertained explicit views about the warrant for these novelties: they were "improvements" in the design of that form of government most wished for but historically weakest in performance. These improvements were said to stem from the progress of the arts and sciences, especially political science. Thus *The Federalist* declared:

> The science of politics . . . like most other sciences has received great improvement. The efficacy of various principles is now well

understood, which were either not known at all, or imperfectly known to the ancients. The regular distribution of power into distinct departments—the institution of courts composed of judges, holding their office on good behaviour—the representation of the people in the legislature by deputies of their own election—these are either wholly new discoveries or have made their principal progress toward perfection in modern times.[2]

The confidence that political *science* exists and that its precepts are embodied in the American system of government received its classic expression in *The Federalist*. John Adams asserted the same view in his *Defense of the Constitutions of the Government of the United States* (1787) against criticisms stemming from what he believed to be the defective political science of the philosophes;[3] other examples are numerous. But *The Federalist* has a special claim to attention because here the principal architects of American government provided a comprehensive explanation of its mechanics.[4]

2. *Federalist,* no. 8/51. (The Jacob Cooke edition pagination is cited.) Science and political science are also discussed in nos. 14/84, 31, 37/235. In his Helvidius Letters, Madison remarked of political science that "writers, such as Locke and Montesquieu, who have discussed more the principles of liberty and the structure of government, lie under the same disadvantage, of having written before these subjects were illuminated by the events and discussions which distinguish a very recent epoch. Both of them, too, are evidently warped by a regard to the particular government of England, to which one of them owed allegiance; and the other professed an admiration bordering on idolatry. Montesquieu, however, has rather distinguished himself by enforcing the reasons and the importance of avoiding a confusion of the several powers of government, than by enumerating and defining the powers which belong to each particular class" (*Letters and Other Writings of James Madison,* 4: 474–75).

3. In the *Defense,* Adams delineated three recent periods of political science and named his authorities. They were Machiavelli ("The great restorer of true politics"); John Ponet, whose *Short Treatise* (1556) "contains all the essential principles of liberty, which were afterwards debated on by Sidney and Locke"; Harrington, Milton, Hobbes, Sidney, Locke, Hoadley, Trenchard, Gordon, and Neville (*The Works of John Adams,* 6: 4 ff.). The crux of political science for Adams was the balance and separation of powers based on Hobbesian anthropology.

4. *The Federalist* was composed to answer objections to the Constitution, which began to appear in newspapers immediately after it was proposed by the Philadelphia Convention on 17 September 1787. Alexander Hamilton solicited and received collaboration by James Madison and John Jay; Robert Morris and William Duer were also approached, but they did not contribute. The

The Federalist espoused a political science based on experience. For its immediate purposes, the most important experience was the colonists' efforts to contrive constitutions and govern under their aegis. *The Federalist* pictured this period as a clumsy overture to mature institutional design. State constitutions were repeatedly instanced to show how design faults had led to ineffective or dangerous practice.[5] This same imperfect knowledge contrived the Confederation, whose defects were then universally acknowledged and whose brief career was to be terminated by adoption of the Constitution. *The Federalist's* confidence that the Constitution represented the first fully scientific design of republican government—or any government—signals the freshness of the latest scientific advance. The knowledge was so new, and qualitatively so distinct from precepts that theretofore had guided Americans, that a faction collected around the older wisdom to oppose the Constitution as dangerous to liberty. This faction was the Antifederalists. Their precepts were drawn from a mixture of Court and Country Whig authors, supplemented by certain continental authors, chiefly Montesquieu. The "Court" orientation of the Constitution sent the Antifederalists, led by John Taylor of Caroline and Governor George Clinton of New York, flying to the Country armory.[6]

The Federalist adopted a disdainful attitude toward the "counterfeit zeal" and "incoherent dreams of delirious jealousy" that it purported to discern in Antifederalist criticism. It was obliged to dismember all the Country shibboleths: violent opposition to standing armies, extreme jealousy of the taxing power and extreme suspicion of the executive power, blindness to the despotic potential of popular assemblies, and unshakable faith in the virtuous republic.[7]

---

first essay, by Hamilton, was printed in *The Independent Journal* on 27 October 1787. From about that date until March 1788, the authors were all in New York City, where the remaining eighty-four essays were written.

5. See particularly *Federalist*, no. 47; also nos. 7/42, 21/131, 26/166.

6. Antifederalist authors were generally agreed that the Confederation was too weak to conduct foreign policy, but they took no single alternative position. Some proposed regional alliances, a view especially popular in New England. Others would go it alone. Rhode Islanders were the main exponents of this position; the state did not even send delegates to the Convention. The largest group, however, wanted a confederation strong enough to conduct foreign policy but deprived of domestic powers, particularly direct power over individuals. *The Federalist* directed its persuasion primarily to this body of sentiment. See Jackson Turner Main, *The Antifederalists*, 184 ff.

7. Three entire essays (nos. 24–26) are devoted to standing armies. In no. 26, *The Federalist* traced the source of this dogma to Whig reaction to James II's

The perspective of *The Federalist,* however, was not limited to American experience. The whole body of "celebrated authors, whose writings have had a great share in forming the modern standard of political opinion," was placed under review and winnowed. This prepared the discovery of the dynamics and architecture of a wholly new type of polity, which Madison styled the "unmixed and extensive republic." Elaborating on a discovery never imagined "in the theories of the wildest projectors," Madison explained that modern political science was confused by imperfect emancipation from the prestige of traditions (*Federalist,* no. 14). Authors either fastened on ancient politics and investigated unmixed but small republics (Mably, Rousseau), or else like Hume and Montesquieu they investigated large republics that mixed popular representation with aristocracy and kingship. The possibility of a large republic unmixed with aristocracy or king, "deriving all its powers directly or indirectly from the people," had been conceived only to be rejected out of hand (no. 39/351). When Antifederalists invoked the well-known opinion of Montesquieu to this effect, *The Federalist* responded that while extensive territory was indeed incompatible with republics constituted for direct participation of citizens in legislation, large population and territory were *indispensable* for a republic based on representation.[8]

The force of this argument becomes apparent as *The Federalist* clarifies its position vis-à-vis the received political science. Previously we have identified two major stands in modern political thought. The scientific stand was initiated by Hobbes, developed by Locke, polished by Hume and Montesquieu. This stand rejected classical republicanism because of its instability and martial character, deficiencies that were traced to the specious notion of virtue and to the barbarism of Greece and Rome. Modern republics were to be based on the new dispensation of produc-

---

increasing his army. It may be noted that Country Whig opinion did have its way about one old dogma—placemen. The Constitution excludes elected federal officers from executive appointments. This separation was partially mended by consolidation of opinion around electoral parties—a process that began even before the first presidential election. Antifederalist objections are catalogued by Main, *The Antifederalists,* 119–67.

8. Ibid., no. 47; also nos. 14/88, 9/54. The authority of Montesquieu carried great weight in deliberative assemblies, and his opinion on small republics frequently was invoked by Antifederalists (see Paul Spurlin, *Montesquieu in America, 1760–1801,* 181–257). The Antifederalists misunderstood Montesquieu; for he, together with Hume, pioneered the idea that republics could be large provided that their principle was commerce rather than virtue.

tion, commerce, and improved knowledge stemming from the progress of the arts and sciences (*Federalist*, no. 6/35). John de Witt and Locke had argued that greater emphasis on accumulation would help calm the acrimony of religious faction. Hume and Montesquieu expanded this horizon to project a gradual pacification of nations as commercial civilization softened aristocratic military traditions and as commercial interests increased their influence on foreign policy. The most recent expression of scientific politics was the free trade doctrine, whose object was, in part, to prevent the use of economic weapons as auxiliary to aggressive foreign policy. In the *avant-garde* of optimism, a string of weighty authors began to canvass the possibility of "perpetual peace" as the next stage of progress.[9]

The other strand of political thought espoused the virtuous republic. Its posture was nostalgic and moral, since no program could be generated from virtue. Exponents could usually be found favoring civil religion but opposing ecclesiastical establishments. They preferred the simple life to accumulation and the country to the city. They were nearly always hostile to the modern commercial dispensation. They tended to dislike the effects of the influence of science and enlightenment on opinion. Their views on the patriciate were of the most varied kind.

The Federalist rejected the virtuous republic with such energy that a side effect was an unexpected casuality: it dismissed as a "deceitful dream" the view that commercial republics tended toward the increase of benevolence, the softening of manners, and the reduction of force in international relations. After a fast-paced review of the course of politics under the commercial dispensation, *The Federalist* gave it out as "solid conclusions drawn from the natural and necessary progress of human affairs" that the actual tendency of such politics was not toward peace and liberty, but toward war and despotism (no. 6/35).

We pause before this staggering conclusion, so at cross-purposes with the advanced political thought of the day. Turgot and Kant did acknowledge that perpetual peace might need centuries to establish, but they were convinced that the elimination of despoilers by popular government must eventually bring the masses to recognize their true interest in peace. Avant-garde confidence was unreservedly affirmed by Condorcet in his *Outline of an Historical View of the Progress of the Human Mind* (1793), which portrayed the tendency of history as moving toward the elimination of war, despotism, national jealousies, slavery, inequality

9. For a discussion of this aspect of eighteenth-century political thought, see Elizabeth Souleyman, *The Vision of World Peace in Seventeenth and Eighteenth Century France.*

(including inequality of the sexes), poverty, and even death. Something akin to that ebullient confidence entered the American ethos, and *The Federalist's* demurrer was forgotten. Nevertheless, the demurrer signals a theoretical scission in the politics of progress, antedating by five years the onset of two decades of warfare that cost about 8 million lives.

As mentioned, *The Federalist* arrived at its sobering judgment in the course of dispelling the delusion that American states were virtuous republics. Local opinion, enthusiastically endorsed in Paris, held that Americans had thrown off the corruption and avarice of the Old World. Here the human race had begun to regenerate itself. Pretension and opulence were replaced by simplicity of manners and equality of fortune. The pomp and arrogance of courts were replaced by free men assembling on an equal footing to deliberate the public weal. Virtuous-republic notions converged with progress-toward-benevolence ideas to affirm that peoples who were circumstanced as Americans were must surely make their rational interest in peace prevail. This belief in the special providence of America was the background of Antifederalist opposition to the Constitution, on the ground that a federal government would introduce standing armies, banks, a powerful executive, and at length despotism.

The Federalist hammered these notions:

A man must be far gone in Utopian speculations who can seriously doubt, that if these States should either be wholly disunited, or only united in partial confederacies, the subdivisions into which they might be thrown would have frequent and violent contests with each other. To presume a want of motives for such contests, as an argument against their existence, would be to forget that men are ambitious, vindictive and rapacious. To look for a continuation of harmony between a number of independent unconnected sovereignties, situated in the same neighborhood, would be to disregard the uniform course of human events, and to set at defiance the accumulated experience of the ages.[10]

10. *Federalist*, no. 6/28. Rejection of the virtuous republic and its anthropology was a hallmark of Federalist politics. In his *Defense of the Constitutions of the Government of the United States,* John Adams reproached the virtuous-republic illusion: "How long will republicans be the dupes of their simplicity? How long will they depend on sermons, prayers, orations, declamation in honor of brotherly love, and against discords, when they know that, without human means, it is but tempting and insulting Providence, to depend upon them for the happiness of life, of the liberty of society." He emphasized that all men are acquisitive and "a free people are most addicted to luxury of any.

The premise correcting the new moral illusion is the equality doctrine: Americans are men, and therefore bear in themselves the ambition and rapacity that idealists imagined to be the preserve of courts. This thesis was supported by a review of recent disputes between various states, wherein it appeared that the opprobrious terms "ambition" and "rapacity" were interchangeable with the respectable pleading of "right of first occupation," "sovereignty," "territorial claim," "commercial rights," "redress of grievance." Commenting on this interchangeability of names, *The Federalist* declared: *"We should be ready to denominate injuries those things which were in reality the justifiable acts of independent sovereignties consulting a distinct interest"* (no. 7/40). The future of thirteen sovereign virtuous republics could be projected from their current disputes. It would be a future of war and oppression, of shifting alliances and conquest, until the underlying political-economic forces asserted themselves in the formation of a northern and southern confederation (no. 5/25ff.). This said, *The Federalist* addressed the Hume-Montesquieu position:

> The genius of republics (say they) is pacific; the spirit of commerce has a tendency to soften the manners of men and to extinguish those inflammable humours which have so often kindled into wars. Commercial republics, like ours, will never be disposed to waste themselves in ruinous contentions with each other. They will be governed by mutual interest, and will cultivate a spirit of mutual amity and concord. (no. 6/31)

The Federalist came down very hard on this opinion, calling it "visionary," "idle theory," "the deceitful dream of a golden age." The men who operate commercial republics are still men, subject to the same impulses, jealousies, and fears as everyone. They cannot avoid evils "incident to society in any shape." Commerce does not change human passions; it merely directs them to other objects. *The Federalist* supported this statement by reviewing the records of Athens, Carthage, Holland,

---

That equality which they enjoy, and in which they glory, inspires them with sentiments which hurry into luxury." In a discussion of Roman austerity, he cited an anecdote that tells that in the early days of the republic, possession of more than seven acres was thought to betray avidity. Adams snorted: "What American would agree to a law to limit their possessions to seven acres?" However, one could cite many passages in which Adams expressed the traditional view that austere virtue was necessary to the maintenance of republics. This inconsistency is unresolved in his writings and probably is the testimony of his heart.

and England to show that they engaged in wars almost without interruption. Moreover, these wars sprang from commercial considerations—"the desire of supplanting and the fear of being supplanted either in particular branches of traffic or in the general advantages of trade and navigation" (no. 6/34). I have quoted at length so that readers may recognize the theoretical locus of *The Federalist*'s new political science. The idioms and emphasis have a familiar ring and seem to describe an animal known to cruise the seas of political science: is it not the great whale Leviathan? That Hobbist views were not voiceless at the Philadephia Convention is a point taken by historians. But the prospect before us is that the science embodied in the Constitution sprang from a return to Hobbes and to the original principles of political science.[11] If so, we seem to be pinched by a certain cognitive dissonance. Hobbes, the exponent of indivisible sovereignty, opposed all notions of balance and separation of powers. Yet the new political science of *The Federalist* unquestionably pivots on its fresh analysis of balanced constitutions.

An exit from the paradox is accessible by following the trace marked in *The Federalist*. When the Founders came seriously to consider a new frame of government, they were obliged to invent some new science because the Montesquieu-Hume theory provided no concrete guidance for the innovative step they were about to take—the founding of a republic unable to draw on the stability provided by aristocratic and ecclesiastical establishment. They were obliged to think anew about how political balance could be made to work in a condition of political equality. Reflection on human equality brought them back to the modern master of this question, Thomas Hobbes. He had anchored equality in the striving of men for power after power, but especially the power impulse to life, liberty, and the means of life. It followed that distinctions drawn from morality, religion, or honor are illusions used by designing men to promote their own power. The trace of this reflection is stamped deeply in *Federalist* nos. 1–8, which vigorously reassert the constancy of human nature and the war of all on all (no. 51/349).

By reopening the problem of government at the ground level, the avenue for finding a substitute for aristocracy was at hand. On Hobbes's premise, political relations are power relations; hence, the stability pro-

---

11. Since *The Federalist*'s authors did not document their sources, direct evidence of their having read Hobbes is wanting. However, they need not have read him at all, since the essentials were in Adams's writings on the Constitution. Adams, who did document his sources, included Hobbes among his authorities. His *Discourses on Davila*, especially, restates the Hobbesian anthropology in crisp and compelling prose. See *Works of John Adams*, 6: 237–65.

vided by aristocracy could be obtained by discerning how aristocracy functioned and by replicating those functions in democratic institutions. Hume and Montesquieu had been clear about the first part. Aristocracy imparts stability thanks to its standing *interest* in its own political and social dominance. Popular republics cannot count on a small, homogeneous class whose abiding social interest translates into political institutions; but a similar effect can be achieved by so constructing political institutions that a *standing interest is built into them, regardless of changes of personnel.*[12] The art of "inventions of prudence," then, is to take maximum advantage of the fact that institutions of government themselves generate standing interests that may be made to impose order on the flux of a society unstructured by class deference.

The same insight enabled the Founders to criticize Hobbes's axiom that sovereignty is indivisible. He meant that all authority lodged in courts, councils, commanders, and other functionaries is authority delegated at the pleasure of the sovereign, and therefore can be recalled at pleasure. The sovereign is therefore the supreme legislator, judge, executor, and commander.[13] This axiom recommended itself to Hobbes not as a description, but as a logical presupposition of order; for single and indivisible sovereignty yields an airtight decision procedure for all disputes, namely, the sovereign will. The political form answering to this axiom is a pyramidal command structure, i.e. absolute despotism. But how does the sovereign maintain position at the peak of the pyramid? Since the sovereign cannot use balanced power, the only remaining means is military force. This reflection indicates that every government except military despotism depends on some sharing of power between political institutions. But on Hobbes's principles, the moment power is divided, sovereignty is split.

Following through this observation, the Founders arrived at a novel means of dealing with sovereignty, which they called the federal system. The idea is to create numerous institutional loci capable of exercising the power of government; but institutions are so arranged that the whole sovereign power rotates through the loci without ever reaching a final position. To illustrate: the whole legislative power is located in Congress; but concurrent with that power is the whole power of sovereignty located in presidential veto; Congress may reclaim its power by

12. Sovereignty became a fundamental question in America owing to the need to reconcile the states to a federation. Sovereignty was also central to French political thought at the same moment, as thinkers sought to transfer legitimacy from the Crown to the nation.

13. See Hobbes, *Leviathan*, chaps. 19, 20.

overriding the veto; but then another location of the whole power of sovereignty appears in judicial review; that whole power may again be seized in another location, the amending power of the Constitution, or by impeachment of judges. Again: the president enjoys supreme power as commander-in-chief; but he has no power to declare war or make treaties without Senate consent; nevertheless, the president is not prohibited from fomenting a war; but if he foments clumsily, he may be impeached. The system contrives to impart energy to government while yet preventing the collection of all power at one location. It is managed by lodging the whole sovereignty in many locations and marking out a routing procedure that enables the power located at one point to rotate into another and obliterate a particular action but not institutional power.[14]

The character of the system is not adequately described without remarking the relation between power and force. Hobbes had emphasized that government originates in force and depends perpetually upon its application through courts in domestic affairs and through military establishments in relation to other states. He nevertheless distinguished between force applied in war and force that forms government; for in the latter case, citizens consent to have government settled upon them. Locke took over this view, but emphasized the consent element. Hume, believing that modern publics were progressing toward greater humanity, declared that government depends ultimately on opinion. *The Federalist*'s many discussions of external threats, Indian wars, insurrections, and animosities between states impress the reader with the ubiquity of force. How does the Constitution relate the powers of government to force?

The most expansive warrant for the use of force by one branch of government against another stems from the subordination of the states to federal powers. A second capacity to use force reposes in the impeaching power. But the three branches of federal government are remarkably free from warrant to use force. The Congress is wholly uncontrolled; the judicial and executive powers are residually controlled by impeachment. The branches of government are thus armed with that crucial ingredient of sovereignty, immunity or near immunity from force. The federal government as a whole therefore has the character of an absolute sovereign, whose force is exercised against citizens through courts and through control of the military.

The actual exercise of despotic force is constrained by public opinion,

14. *The Federalist* expressed this conception in the language of "concurrent jurisdictions" or powers. For a particularly apt statement, see *Federalist*, no. 82.

especially as it expresses itself in the requirement of frequent elections. And should newspapers and the ballot box fail, an armed citizenry may answer force with force: the "federals" are countervailed by thousands of muskets hanging over fireplaces. The effect of the system is to reduce the use of domestic force almost to the execution of judicial decisions. This is the ultimate in civilian government: a power system operating within the limits of law.

Governing by Interests

Hobbesian political science rested on a political anthropology asserting that people, naturally sundered by their passions, are united artificially by their interests. The divisive passions are competitions for life, liberty, and the means to life; above all, men are sundered by their restless striving for domination, by love of glory and distinction. These impulses or "passions" are unreasonable when they defeat their own purpose by disturbing public order. Moral suasion or strict upbringing do not effectively control them. Only a standing threat of punishment operating through law can countervail these impulses. Government compels publics to behave by bringing to bear a network of institutions that enable them to express their reasonable interests in peaceful activities. But this network is artificially constructed and depends ultimately upon force, even if it draws strength from the interest people may take in the stability of institutions.

We have seen that political economists embroidered this theme by arguing that the impulse to self-preservation could be harnessed to government in a new and more solid way by encouraging the acquisitive interest. The acquisitive interest is a standing expectation of improvement, and labor is directed to improvement of one's condition. Its presupposition is the growth economy that gradually increases the national wealth.[15]

Despite this extension of the Hobbesian program, Hume raised an important objection to its anthropology. He denied that man's self-regard sunders him from his fellows quite so entirely as Hobbes thought. In the bond between the sexes, and in parental care for offspring, Hume urged, one recognizes passions that aggregate human beings. Such natural filiation shows that "society" has a natural foundation.[16] But this

15. *Enquiry concerning the Principles of Morals*, § 4.
16. Throughout his writings Hume equivocated on the state of nature doctrine. In the *Treatise of Human Nature* the state of nature was dismissed as a "mere philosophical fiction" (bk. 3, pt. 2, par. 2). Yet he accepted the implications

observation was inconclusive, since the question is not the naturalness of familial "society," but the naturalness of political association. Hume accordingly looked for evidence of wider affiliative bonds, and he found it in the mechanism he called "sympathy." Sympathy is a mechanical or compulsive reactivity to the emotions of others. Laughter and tears, even on the stage, move men to a similar emotion; fads, crazes, and moods sweep through a group and tune feelings to a common chord. Such spontaneous sympathetic feelings show that man is sociable to a high degree; it is in these common passions that men achieve solidarity. Having reestablished man's natural sociability, Hume made sympathy the basis of the moral sentiment of benevolence. Combining benevolence with his notion that the passions may be domesticated by the long-term effects of increased refinement induced by progress in the arts and sciences, he cautiously projected moral progress under the aegis of commerce.

Such was the progressive commercial republic concept that reached the authors of *The Federalist* from Hume and his disciple, Adam Smith. They also knew more sanguine versions emanating from France. Those philosophes who viewed man as a creature of habit claimed that antisocial passions were to be attributed to peculiarities of social milieu; sociability could be increased indefinitely by appropriate manipulation of education and social environment. Utopia began to take shape on this horizon, and Condorcet heralded its approach.

Rejection of the peaceful commercial republic signals *The Federalist*'s return to Hobbes's thesis of the constancy of human nature. The progress presupposed by American institutions will not be the moral progress of individuals; no institutional reliance is to be placed on benevolence. However, the Hume-Smith study of sympathy enabled *The Federalist* to sharpen its concepts of factions and interests. Such aggregations are held together by sympathetic bonds, that is, they are "united and actuated by some common impulse of passion, or of interest." Nevertheless, the impulse of faction cannot become cosmopolitan and benevolent since its character is determined by what it opposes. Men enter into political combinations not because they are gregarious, but because individually they are weak:

---

that Hobbes and Locke drew from the doctrine, namely, that justice and political association are inventions based on calculation of public interest or utility. Should these inventions fail, "everyone must fall into that savage and solitary condition, which is infinitely worse than can possibly be supposed in society" (ibid.; also bk. 3, pt. 2, par. 7). This ambivalence was repeated in the essay "Of Original Contract," and in the *Inquiry*.

The reason of man, like man himself, is timid and cautious when left alone, and acquires firmness and confidence in proportion to the number with which it is associated. . . . in a nation of philosophers, this consideration ought to be disregarded. A reverence for the laws would be sufficiently inculcated by the voice of enlightened reason. But a nation of philosophers is as little to be expected as the philosophical race of kings wished for by Plato. (*Federalist,* no. 49)

Hobbes's political anthropology picturing selfish men competing for riches and power is replaced in *The Federalist* by an anthropology of selfish collectivities (factions and interests) competing for riches and power. How can the public good be made to prevail in a system whose constituent publics are assumed to be partial to particular advantage? In a passage celebrated as a high moment of realism in modern political thought, Madison displayed the daunting magnitude of the problem:

So strong is this propensity of mankind to fall into mutual animosities, that where no substantial occasion presents itself, the most frivolous and fanciful distinctions have been sufficient to kindle their unfriendly passions and excite their most violent conflicts. But the most common and durable source of factions has been the various and unequal distribution of property. Those who are creditors, and those who are debtors, fall under a like discrimination. A landed interest, a manufacturing interest, a mercantile interest, a moneyed interest, with many lesser interests, grow up of necessity in civilized nations, and divide them into different classes, actuated by different sentiments and views. *The regulation of these various and interfering interests forms the principal task of modern legislation, and involves the spirit of party and faction in the necessary and ordinary operations of the government.* (no. 49)

Madison suggested that political contention is analytically divisible into an emotional component, excitable by frivolous, insubstantial causes, and an interested component, deriving from property. The emotional component is more dangerous. It is fueled especially by vanity, i.e. desire for distinction or hatred of invidious distinction. Once aroused, it can lead men into actions destructive of their substantial interest, property. Property is a reasonable interest because it is necessary to support life and liberty. Interest in property also tends to make men reasonable by fixing attention on concrete realities and on the longer view. Optimizing property interest thus dampens the intransigence of conflicts over frivolous distinctions. But by itself it is no remedy, since property distinctions may also be occasions for violent animosities, particularly when they involve vanity, i.e. the competition for distinction. *The Federalist*'s well-known solution to this problem was the combination of the representative principle with diversity of interests. Representation ensures that aroused popular passion will register at once upon government, thereby gratifying part of its desire to assert itself. But on entering the legislative chamber or other department of government, popular passion confronts a variety of other interests that automatically evaluate claims relative to their compatibility with established interests. If factional voices threaten established interests, they risk isolation or defeat by arousing an opposing faction. Representation of multitudes of interests thus exerts a constant pressure on factions and interests to refine and moderate their political objectives so that they may be, or least seem to be, compatible with the common interest in property as well as the interest in private rights. The crucial supposition here is that the multitude of property interests are in fact compatible and even complementary in some comprehensive sense, notwithstanding numerous smaller conflicts. For without that compatibility, there would be no objective common good to which the contending interests might refer; and interest politics would soon degenerate into factional struggles for power, struggles revolving about the opposition of colliding vanities.

The new frame of government and the new political science evidently presupposed a definite political economy only hinted at by *The Federalist* in its characterization of America as "commercial republic." When Hamilton specified that political economy in his reports to Congress on public finance and manufactures, it contained a supplement to the political anthropology of *The Federalist*. Indeed, it pierced the barriers of the commercial phase of modernity, summarized in *The Wealth of Nations,* and opened a political perspective on the high technology manufacture that was to dominate the next century.

Hamilton's political economy was a growth economics animated by insight into the distinctively modern sources of growth. The first of these sources is "the artificial force brought in aid of the natural force of man," that is, the exponential growth of productivity achieved by the mechanization of manufacture. The "immense progress which has been so suddenly made in Great Britain" is due to the "prodigious effect" of mechanization.[17] With the advent of machine production, the second source of growth, "the activity of the human mind," attains a hitherto unknown degree of fecundity through the release of untapped talents:

17. Alexander Hamilton, *Industrial and Commercial Correspondence,* 258.

The results of human exertion may be immensely increased by di-
versifying its objects. When all the different kinds of industry obtain in a community, each individual can find his proper element,
and can call into activity the whole vigor of his nature. And the
community is benefited by the services of its respective members,
in the manner in which each can serve *with most effect.* (*Industrial
and Commercial Correspondence,* 260)

By multiplying the objects of men's exertions, high technology manufacturing stimulates the useful and prolific "spirit of enterprise"; "every
new scene which is opened to the busy nature of man to rouse and exert
itself, is the addition of a new energy to the general stock of effort"
(261).

Hamilton's anthropology may be usefully contrasted with that of
Adam Smith and Condorcet. Smith pictured intelligence as a passive
faculty led by the passions, for he adopted the human psychology in
which reason is "the slave" of the passions. This model dominated his
economics, whose dynamic elements are "the tendency to improve" and
consumer demand. The long secular trend of economic growth since
the Middle Ages was due to the operation of these passions; reason, in
the shape of fiscal policy or mercantilist political economy, Smith would
not allow to have contributed anything. In the same manner, he imagined that mechanical improvements were due to mere association of
ideas, not to methodical search for improvements. He did not register
the industrialization that unfolded before his eyes, and his economics
provided no description of the new supply market.[18]

18. See above, 349–56. Smith's theory of value was predicated upon a description of labor that Hamilton rejected. His unit of value was equal labor over
equal times. While recognizing that such a unit is notional only, Smith nevertheless thought it sufficiently exact to assume as a basic measure. Yet it obliged
him to treat labor as expenditure of animal energy and to suppose that labor
is onerous. Thus he contrasted work as "toil and trouble" and "toil of the
body" with man's "ease, his liberty, and his happiness" (*Wealth of Nations,*
I, v). While this may or may not be a satisfactory description of physical
labor, it overlooks the human delight in activity per se and in "interesting"
work. While productive necessity is the objective basis for work in civilized
societies, interesting work is probably the subjective ground for the obsession with work characteristic of civilized life, irrespective of rewards. One
sees this, for example, in the high attainments of artisanal skill. This motiva-
tional difference correlates with the great difference between the productive
value of skilled and unskilled labor, even when skilled labor is dedicated to
the production of luxuries. It is also to be remarked that Smith's concept of

It might be supposed that the scientist Condorcet would have placed the effects of polytechnic intelligence in the forefront of his description of the final stage of progress. Yet it appears as a secondary effect in a utopia from which suffering, deprivation, and all forms of domination have been removed. Human beings have nothing left to do but enjoy the blessings of progress. Hamilton, by contrast, characterized his active principle independently of moral norms or utopian goals. While its public recommendation is that it contributes to the common good by promoting material advantage and diversity of talent, his *Report on Manufactures* did not project a utopia. It projected a comprehensive program of national development geared to appropriate manufacturing technology as a new force to expand trade and agriculture, and as a tool for the exploitation of the wilderness. The construction of railroad systems is an eminently Hamiltonian project.

This anthropology supports a program whose goal in the first instance was to make the nation self-sufficient in manufactures and to create a larger domestic market for agricultural produce. The *Report* began with a rebuttal of the physiocratic doctrine that manufacture is not productive, followed by a rebuttal of Smith's view that manufacture, while productive, is decidedly less productive than land. Manufacture is at least as productive as land, the *Report* asserted. But Hamilton stated that an agricultural economy is decidedly weaker economically and politically than an economy with a vigorous manufacturing sector.[19] Manu-

---

labor value abstracts entirely from technical, entrepreneurial, and managerial skills, even though they are the source of great productive leaps.

19. Although Hamilton quoted Smith and evidently had studied *The Wealth of Nations,* he was not a disciple, as his marked departures show. Hamilton agreed with Smith, against the Physiocrats, that commerce and manufacture are productive. But he denied Smith's thesis that agriculture is more productive than manufacture; this was because Hamilton had the concept of exponential economic growth while Smith did not. Smith espoused free trade and the peaceful republic; Hamilton was a mercantilist and expected war. Whereas Smith condemned government promotion of manufacture as forcing the economy out of the track of natural development, Hamilton's program hinged on promotion of manufacture.

Hamilton was endorsed by the founder of the influential Historical School, Friedrich List. List's *National System of Political Economy* (1844) takes Adam Smith as its polemical object; and each disagreement with Smith marks an assertion of Hamiltonian economics. Thus List rejected the "cosmopolitan" system of free trade and its unreal supposition of international peace. He favored protective tariffs on grounds of national interest. His anthropology was in agreement with Hamilton's preference of urban to agrar-

facturing adds diversity to the sources of wealth, thereby avoiding dependency on a single type of export while reducing dependency on imports. To the objection that the promotion of manufacture favored northern states, Hamilton responded that since manufacture and agriculture are economically reciprocal, any short-run advantage would be outweighed by the political advantage gained by enhancing the reciprocity of northern and southern interests.[20]

In proposing the enhancement of manufacture by a system of bounties, premiums, tariff protection, and other devices, the *Report* ran headlong against the authority of Adam Smith, which at that time was considerable.[21] Insofar as Smith's strictures were directed against fettering trade and productivity by purchase of privilege, Hamilton was in accord with him: this much of free trade doctrine he emphatically endorsed. But Smith was critical also of Colbertian attempts to foster manufactures by artificial means as an instrument of state policy. This forced economy out of its "natural" track, that is, out of the courses established by demand and efficiency of supply. Here Hamilton disagreed; and his reasons nicely exhibit the unity of the two economists' respective economics and anthropology. Hamilton would not passively await the advent of manufacture because, as an enterprising spirit, his eye had fastened on growth—on "the immense mass of improvable matter" possessed by the nation. The *Report* identified two things needed to facilitate this improvement: capital and labor.[22] Domestic capital was to be mobilized by the funded debt and hard money banking. This system was created in 1790 as a consequence of Hamilton's *Report on Credit*. The immediate result was a strong flow of foreign capital to purchase U.S. securities. He now surmised that "sagacious capitalists" abroad would take note of the "infinite fund of resources yet to be unfolded" in America.[23] A national policy of economic growth emphasizing sound currency, firm public credit, stable government, and ports open to all

ian values and with his firm assertion that human intelligence, especially as applied in manufactures, is the chief vehicle of capital accumulation. Smith's dictum that capital could be increased only by savings seemed to List a mere accountant's concept (see especially chapters 17 and 19 of *National System*). List came upon Hamilton's writings during his sojourn in the United States, where he associated with Henry Clay and other heirs of Hamilton's legacy. See Hiram Caton, "The Preindustrial Economics of Adam Smith."

20. Hamilton, *Industrial and Commercial Correspondence*, 286.
21. The Smithian economic basis of Republican ideology is discussed in note 65 below.
22. Hamilton, *Industrial and Commercial Correspondence*, 269–77.
23. Ibid., 273.

nations would attract capital and labor to work upon the "immense mass."

The *Report* had two further political implications that Hamilton did not stress. The addition of a manufacturing interest and the diversity of talents it fosters would tend to multiply the diversity of property and interest that *The Federalist* postulated as its economic remedy for the excesses of faction. The opposition that his banking and credit measures encountered in Congress persuaded Hamilton that "the headquarters of faction" was the State of Virginia, whose dominant agrarian interest might destroy the Union were it not checked.[24] Hamilton might reasonably hope that the growth of manufactures would in the long run dilute the influence of rural interests and the dangerous localisms of husbandmen. Linked with the growth of cities was an increase in the numbers of professionals. In *The Federalist* Hamilton speculated that "the learned professions" might mediate or moderate the contention of interests, for the professions comprised no distinct economic interest and their labor brought them into contact with all. Their neutrality might enable them to be, and be seen to be, "impartial arbiter[s] between [interests], ready to promote either, so far as it shall appear to [them] conducive to the general interests of society" (no. 35). Political science, political economy, and law were the fields of learning frequently invoked by *The Federalist* as the knowledge resources for objective deliberation about the matters of high importance that were before the nation. Tocqueville subsequently glossed this passage by noting that one branch of government, the judicial, was manned by a single profession. Lawyers did indeed fulfill Hamilton's projection by making the higher courts a potent and august part of government largely independent of momentary political passions.

Hamilton's program evidently mandated a foreign policy that placed a premium on peace. The Confederation expended about $160 million for the war of independence; and the Federalist politicians were keenly aware that another war in the early years of the republic could sink politics under the weight of debt. Yet according to *The Federalist*, the peaceful commercial republic idea was a chimera. How were these discrepancies to be resolved? Closer inspection of *The Federalist* (no. 36) reveals a subtle, differentiating assessment of forces tending toward war or peace. The power of the purse and the war-making power are both lodged in Congress on the ground that the cost of war in life and treasure creates a presumption against war in the public, who must bear the cost. But when interests come absolutely into competition, war is unavoidable.

24. John C. Miller, *The Federalist Era*, 52.

In the Indians, the new nation had one such competitor. Since there will always be absolute competitions, commercial republics are not exempt from the necessity of war. They are also not exempt from the sensitivities of national honor or ambition that most frequently lure nations into war. Montesquieu and Hume reasoned badly in imagining that the attitudes and interests fostered by commerce would make a substantial difference in international relations. The idea is chimerical in its assumption that passions that incline men to peace will somehow displace passions that incline to war, whereas in reality the only effective control upon war is reason. Reason exerts itself by institutional design that tends to remove absolute competitions and to frustrate political expression of war power. According to *The Federalist*, the greatest danger of war to the newly independent Confederation was the sovereignty of the states; the remedy was federation. Events confirmed both the diagnosis and remedy. Jealousy of state sovereignty was a major cause of faction and turmoil in the new republic; yet in the first century of its existence, there were only four years of war over that matter. In the same period, the nation was at war with external foes only four years, not counting the usually ill-defined conflicts with Indians. Not the commercial republic as such, but the rationally designed republic is peaceful.

The Construction of Government, 1789–1800

That the whole frame of government may be constructed *ab initio* is today a fact writ large in modern political experience. The idea that the thing could be done without the superior force of a conqueror entered the world from the American experience. Presumptions against an undertaking so audacious were registered not only by Edmund Burke; the Founders themselves were skeptical. There was general agreement in 1789 that there would be no second chance if the new contraption did not work on the first try. Its near dereliction during the first decade of the new republic therefore surprised few Federalists, who tended to agree with Madison that the "centripetal force" lodged in the national government could scarcely balance the "centrifugal force" of the states. Nevertheless, the machine did work; and the idea that it was feasible to contrive engines of government geared to designated social and political objectives became a postulate of progressive politics.

The start-up period of American government bears some resemblance to the troubled experiences of new nations in recent years. There was the problem of the old regime, which would not go quietly to oblivion. The old regime in this case was state sovereignty. Although the states had enjoyed sovereignty only since 1776, they had been political units for a much longer time. In each state there was a settled order of interests, an ethos, and a jealousy of local power. These localisms had been the bane of the Confederation; and *The Federalist* correctly forecast that their persistence would pose the most serious challenge to the new order.

The first national factions, Federalists and Antifederalists, were aroused by the contest over ratification of the Constitution. They were not wholly new; the interests they espoused and the rhetoric they deployed had developed during the difficult period of the Confederation. Well-organized Federalists pushed ratification through state legislatures despite the strenuous resistance of Antifederalists. Ratification undermined the legitimacy of overt opposition to federation, but it scarcely changed the attitudes supporting the old regime. Those attitudes asserted themselves as a minority faction in the heavily Federalist first Congress, which assembled in New York in 1790. For several years the faction had no name—the Federalists called them "the Antis"—nor any program; but they did have a rhetoric and an opposition strategy. Late in 1792 they acquired a name, "Republican"; France's declaration of war on Great Britain in 1793 handed the Republicans a great issue to dramatize their cause in a struggle over foreign policy. For the next seven years, domestic politics became a battle between Republicans favoring alliance with a revolutionary government purporting to espouse the cause of mankind and Federalists favoring neutrality between the superpowers while yet seeking to maintain trading relations with the nation's enemy in the war of independence. France intervened on the side of the Republican faction hoping to throttle the Jay Treaty with Britain. These struggles violently shook the nation. Republicans were reprobated as Jacobins while Federalists were scorned as "monocrats" conspiring to impose the wicked British system on virgin America.

These traumatic events produced a correspondingly exaggerated partisan mythology. When his Republican party swept to power in 1800, Jefferson deemed it a "revolution." The party's subsequent three-decade control of government deeply impressed that hyperbole upon the popular perception of events.

It is not easy to free history from the glamorous distortions of partisan rhetoric. American historians no longer quite accept the myth that the Federalists meant to bury American liberties under a British bank. But they have not entirely rejected it either.[25] If they were to do so,

---

25. The Jeffersonian bias of Federalist era historiography is marked. Often it is explicit, as in John C. Miller's *Crisis in Freedom: The Alien and Sedition Acts* and Joyce O. Appleby's *Capitalism and a New Social Order: The Republican*

Jefferson's reputation as the savior of popular liberties would need to come down a notch or two from its present high standing; for if there was no threat to liberty, there was nothing to salvage from danger. What seemed to Jefferson a "revolution" was merely a change of personnel in government, not a change of government. Historians indeed have on the whole endorsed the image of Jefferson as a great libertarian and exponent of strict limits on government, even though a comparison of his behavior in office with his pronouncements exposes stunning discrepancies that suggest an evaluation of his politics somewhat less exalted than that now current.

An objective account of the nation's first decade demands an unobstructed view of the dynamics of faction and interest as they penetrated the structures of the new government and set them in motion. The needed correction upon partisan hyperbole may be obtained by matching up programs and alliances of interests with behavior. One element of that dynamics is gratifyingly easy to locate: *the* factional question between 1787 and 1789 was the sovereignty of the federal government over the states.[26] This question was not eliminated from politics by ratifica-

---

Vision of the 1790s. More frequently it comes through obliquely as a result of what seems to be an ideological entrapment. Gordon Wood's *The Creation of the American Republic* may serve as an example. Wood supports the thesis, central to Republican doctrine, that the Federalists betrayed the democratic principles of the Declaration (*Creation,* 562). They did so by attempting to implant a natural aristocracy as a political class to whom the people were to defer, while the Republicans espoused what the reader assumes to be sound democracy (485, 502). However, in his "Rhetoric and Reality in the American Revolution" Wood admits that there was precious little reality in revolutionary rhetoric, particularly concerning the allegations of British tyranny; and he also admits that the leveling rhetoric of the Republicans went so far that "ability, education, and wealth were becoming liabilities . . . in attaining public office" (*Creation,* 493). He is aware of the "economic" interpretation (n. 28 below) that characterizes Republican rhetoric as demagoguery. With this characterization he both agrees (494) and disagrees (484). He neglects to remark that Republican writers, despite the leveling talk, are on record as being quite as much alert to and opposed to majority tyranny as Federalists. He reviews Antifederalist objections to the Constitution without remarking that annual elections, the power of recall of representatives, and so on, if implemented, would have crippled government. In his summary he alleges that Federalists "appropriated and exploited the language [of democracy] that more rightly belonged to their opponents" (562). The fact is that the Federalists invented a new language of democratic politics (vide *The Federalist Papers*) and inserted a new institution (representative democracy), which the Republicans were obliged to imitate despite themselves.

26. The Republicans were continuous with the Antifederalists in personnel and

tion, but continued to influence domestic politics and foreign policy until it led to the dissolution of the Union in 1861. An adequate account of events must accordingly lay bare the dynamics of this primary factional division. But other factional drives crisscross and complicate this one. According to *The Federalist,* the "most common and durable source" of faction is the various kinds of property and their unequal distribution. *The Federalist*'s discussion of the dynamics of property, interest, and faction is flawed by a singular omission: the political effects of property in human beings. This silence was not due to oversight or unconcern; *The Federalist*'s silence respected the tacit agreement not to make slavery a partisan issue. The agreement was publicly avowed in 1790 when a Quaker memorial proposing abolition was rejected by the House with only one dissenting vote. In 1793, Congress passed the Fugitive Slave Act by a large majority that included members active in abolition for their own states. Acquiescence to the "domestic institution" of the South was the price of Union. Here, then, we locate a second element of the dynamics of faction. Artificially suppressed in the early years, it became increasingly prominent as southern spokesmen demanded the extension of slavery into new territories, finally to emerge as the second great issue that dissolved the Union. Southern opponents of "consolidated government," as they called it, emphasized a connection between their fear of strong government and their interest in human property: a strong government might implement the equality doctrine that was supposed to be among the nation's founding principles. The means of

---

motive. Madison very early captured the spirit of the movement when he wrote to Tench Coxe (20 July 1788) that "the real object of their zeal in opposing the [Constitution]" was to maintain "the supremacy of the state legislatures" with a view to financial manipulation in the interest of debtors. Madison is an important witness because Virginia was dominated by this faction. Under Patrick Henry's leadership, it hoped to make the new federal government "commit suicide" (Hamilton) by sending Antifederalists to Philadelphia. Madison himself was targeted for destruction but escaped by his wits (n. 33 below). Subsequently the Virginia House passed resolutions contesting the legality of the assumption of state debts, the legality of suits by foreign creditors to win judgments, the legality of the Jay Treaty, and so on until the Virginia Resolves that laid down a doctrine for secession from the Union. On the Antifederalist-Republican continuity, see Main, *The Antifederalists,* passim; Albert J. Beveridge, *The Life of John Marshall,* 2: 66–67, 83–84, 89; Richard Kohn, *The Eagle and the Sword,* 197ff., 450–55; Lance Banning, *The Jeffersonian Persuasion,* 114; Gordon Wood, *The Creation of the American Republic,* 484–85; 494–502, 522–23; Robert E. Shalhope, *John Taylor of Caroline,* 4, 73–74, 103; Charles Beard, *Economic Origins of Jeffersonian Democracy,* chap. 4.

keeping the federal government weak was to obstruct the exercise and extension of its powers. This strictly interested behavior they supported by interpretations of the Constitution that vaunted the power of states as the bulwark against despotic national government.[27]

If the two roots of war in 1861 are identified with the roots of faction in 1789, we obtain a grip on the problem of faction in the period under scrutiny. Federalists drew their electoral support mainly from urban areas, north and south, while the Republican party was led by southern planters, especially the Virginians. Yet this slave-owning interest not only captured the northern urban electoral bastions of the Federalists, they drove them out of politics under the infamy of conspiring to impose an aristocracy.[28] This was a dexterous feat indeed. Analysis of fac-

27. The most consistent advocate of Republican politics as a defense of "the Virginia gentry style of life as right and good" was John Taylor of Caroline. Taylor was equipped with a rhetoric directed against "capitalists," whom he identified as lords of finance and commerce who oppressed agriculture. From Adam Smith and physiocracy he had imbibed deeply from the cup of free trade and small government; indeed, Taylor believed that Smith had left too much to government. Taylor did not, like the national politicians of the South, equivocate on the matter of slavery. He defended the excellence of the institution, and denounced emancipation schemes as stupidity (see Shalhope, *John Taylor of Caroline*, 103–4, 114, 124, 135, 142–43).

28. Main, *The Antifederalists*, 28ff., 104–5, 111, 133, 190–200, 236–42, 288. Main's findings about Antifederalist combinations are confirmed by Rudolph M. Bell's study of voting patterns in Congress (*Party and Faction in American Politics*, 20–26). Main's study continued the pioneering scholarship of Charles Beard's *An Economic Interpretation of the Constitution of the United States* and his *Economic Origins of Jeffersonian Democracy*. The "economic" interpretation is a rebuttal to the "ideological" interpretation of Federalist era party politics. The ideological interpretation is a version of the view that the fundamental issue concerned the kind of democracy that the new nation was to have—in the blunt Republican formulation, aristocracy vs. the popular will. Beard's research shows that the chief spokesmen for both sides, in their deeds and their most considered statements, held that ideological contention revolved about a fundamental contest between two types of property, finance capital and land. "Aristocracy" did not mean a class entrenched by inherited privilege, or even a class of "betters" enjoying the deference of "the meaner sort," but the domination of government by an oligarchic few exercising power through the machine of "paper and patronage," i.e. the Walpole system. This system was held to be a subtle but emphatic subversion of democratic government which robbed the people of the fruits of their labor through high taxes raised to pay the national debt. In the Federalist version of the contest, the credit system was essential to the prosperity of all citizens. Agrarian opposition to the credit system was ascribed to the debtor's desire

tional politics in the nation's first decade reveals how this improbable outcome was obtained.

Since America was a representative democracy, we must begin with a description of the distribution of Federalist and Antifederalist electoral strength as it appeared during the ratification struggle. The broad pattern was for urban centers, dominated by financial and commercial interests, to favor Federalists, while agrarian interests were Antifederalist. But this generalization is useless without qualifying descriptive detail. Urban centers included artisans, who were substantially Federalist in 1789 but who went Republican after 1794. Massachusetts was evenly split in 1789, with both parties drawing support from the entire range of interests; but the state went solidly Federalist in 1790 and remained so. New York and Pennsylvania were quite different. In both states old factional divisions set commercial and financial interests against a combination of rural, commercial-urban, and artisanal interests. Philadelphia and New York City were Federalist by four to one; but the backcountry opposition, centering in Albany and Pittsburgh, was so strong that both states narrowly ratified. Republicans were later to capture these states by retaining their backcountry support while increasing their urban support. Agricultural interests in the South divided into planters producing for export and small farmers producing for local markets. Export agriculture was confined to the tidewater and riverine areas; as the nation's chief export industry, it was the single most important economic interest. In South Carolina this interest, centered in Charleston, was two-to-one Federalist. In Virginia, it split about evenly. Ratification was narrowly achieved when Federalists persuaded west-

---

to maintain the supremacy of state legislatures, with its advantages of debt liquidation through printing money and violating contract. For Beard's citations, see *Economic Origins*, 168–73 (Jefferson), 198ff., 327ff. (John Taylor), 242–44 (Fisher Ames), 237–42 (John Marshall), 13ff., 113ff. (Hamilton). Beard shows in detail that the popular will catch-cry did not imply any difference in principle about the inviolability of real property and the property qualification for suffrage. In this sense their leveling rhetoric was just talk. "Jeffersonian democracy," he says in summary, "simply meant the possession of the federal government by the agrarian masses led by an aristocracy of slave-owning planters, and the theoretical repudiation of the use of the Government by any capitalistic groups, fiscal, banking, or manufacture" (487). The present interpretation is concordant with Beard's findings. I note Beard's tribute to *The Federalist* as "the finest study in the economic interpretation of politics that exists in any language; and whoever would understand the Constitution as an economic document need hardly go beyond it" (*An Economic Interpretation of the Constitution*, 153).

erners that the federal government would improve roads and water-ways. Generally in the South, Antifederalist electorates tended to be comprised of small farmers, westerners, and debtors; typically, the state dominated by these interests, North Carolina, was three-to-one Anti-federalist and did not ratify until 1790.[29]

The bedrock Antifederalism of the small farmers expressed their an-cient antagonisms against townsmen. Farmers were the principal debt-ors to merchants and bankers. In state politics they often espoused rapid-depreciation emissions enabling them to pay a debt of $100 with paper money whose market value might be half or a quarter its face value. This interesting mechanism was the democratic version of the royal game of milking the public by debasing the coinage. The electoral strength of American farmers enabled them to use this debt liquidation mechanism repeatedly, with the result that the antagonism between hard money creditors and soft money debtors was and remained a prominent feature of American politics for more than a century. Farm-ers also resented the opulence and arrogance of townsmen and their domination of government. Many viewed government as an engine of oppression constructed to squeeze tax monies from poor farmers so that they might be spent to enhance urban splendor. Such attitudes springing from rural interests and resentments generated the Anti-federalist rhetoric espousing small government, casting suspicion upon the despotic tendency of all government, decrying tax collectors and other vexatious government agents, extolling rural freedom and inde-pendence, and reprobating those "blood suckers," land speculators, and creditors of all stripes. This was the small-government, antioligarchy popular sentiment that Republicans were about to appropriate as the electoral foundation of their party.

Antifederalists anticipated the creditor bias of the new government. The most important achievement of the first Congress was to enact Hamilton's proposals to eliminate credit and monetary chaos by setting up the system of public credit prevailing in trading nations. The system consisted of three main parts. Congress chartered the Bank of the United States to coin money and to regulate private and state banks. It rescued the derelict credit of the Confederation by honoring its issues of securities at par. Creditors who had written off these securities as losses suddenly found that they had recouped their capital plus interest. As a result, U.S. securities leaped in overseas markets from discounts up to 90 percent to values above 100 percent, even though the new securities bore only 3 percent interest. The national debt of $78 million was there-

29. Main, *The Antifederalists*, 120–38.

fore successfully funded by a massive infusion of foreign capital. The third component of the package was federal assumption of debts contracted by states to fund the war, a measure Federalist leaders believed essential to their global aim of stabilizing credit structures and creating in many citizens a potent private interest in the national government.[30]

In this first test of government, Antifederalist opinion asserted itself, and the initiative came from Virginia planters. Attorney General Edmund Randolph and Secretary of State Jefferson advised President Washington that the Bank was unconstitutional because Congress had no authority under the Constitution to charter corporations. The effect of this opinion was to reserve to the states an essential power of sovereignty. Hamilton replied to these submissions with his doctrine of "implied powers," according to which a power delegated in the Constitution implied all powers necessary to its exercise. Seizing mischievously on the clause of the Preamble that sets the "general welfare" as one of the objects of government, Hamilton claimed that the power to charter corporations was implied by this phrase. Jefferson was shocked by the immense gate Hamilton had opened for the expansion of federal power, and from that moment, if not before, he became a determined foe of "consolidated" federal government.

The center of controversy, however, was the House. There another Virginian came forward to assume leadership of the opposition that during the next decade attempted to thwart virtually every Federalist measure, beginning with funding the debt. That leader was the ex-Federalist James Madison. The genius he had set to work designing the architecture of federal government was now employed to shackle its power in the toils of legal casuistry and political insinuation. The organizational skill that he had devoted unreservedly to bringing the nation together was now put in reverse gear. Madison enjoys the unique distinction of having been the principal architect of the nation's institutions, as well as the principal architect of their antithesis, the doctrine of states' rights; moreover, he was a moving spirit of *both* the nation's factions. Since this stunning fact was obliterated by Republican mythology, which denied Madison's Federalist past, we must dwell on it a little.

Prior to 1789, Madison was no mere Federalist; he was the arch Federalist. At the Constitutional Convention he unsuccessfully advocated several design features as essential to consolidated federal government. One, "absolutely necessary" in his opinion, was to give Congress a negative on all state laws. This was no mere review power, but one that

---

30. E. James Ferguson, *The Power of the Purse*, 297–305; Bray Hammond, *Banks and Politics in America*, 106–12.

made Congress integral to state legislation, conceived on analogy to Privy Council's power to negative or prohibit specific legislation in the colonies. This subordination of state to national legislation was required because "turbulent assemblies" in the states produced a mass of ill-considered, demagogic law; Madison was particularly exercised by the folly and destructiveness of soft currency emissions, which attacked property by placing credit in hostage to monetary alchemy. Madison believed that without this provision in the Constitution, the union would be an erratic "feudal system of republics."[31] He also urged, again unsuccessfully, that the Constitution should contain a clause expressly empowering the president to use force to oblige state compliance with federal law. Within the federal government, he favored an executive much stronger than the one that emerged; he believed that the president's liability to impeachment by the House seriously weakened such powers as he did possess.[32] At the Constitutional Convention Madison thus went as far toward consolidated government as it was possible to go.

Like other Federalists, Madison used his influence to secure ratification of a contrivance of government that did not enjoy his entire confidence. He was instrumental in securing ratification in Virginia against strong opposition from Antifederalist planters by winning support from western farmers. But the "Antis," angered by their defeat, were strong enough to hand Madison a sharp rebuke and warning. His candidacy for the U.S. Senate was defeated in the House of Burgesses, and he was assigned to a heavily Antifederalist congressional district in anticipation that he would lose the election.[33] This defeat showed that his

31. Madison's arguments have been reviewed by Charles F. Hobson in "The Negative on State Laws: James Madison, the Constitution, and the Crisis of Republican Government"; see especially 219, 234. For Madison's criticisms of paper emissions, see *The Federalist,* no. 44, and Hammond, *Banks and Politics in America,* 115–16. Madison declared that the object of the Antifederalists in opposing the Constitution was to uphold "the supremacy of state legislatures," and the twin uses thereof, printing money and violating contract (Madison to Tench Coxe, 20 July 1788).

32. Farrand, *The Records of the Federal Convention of 1787,* 2: 612.

33. Miller, *Federalist Era,* 35, 41. Madison's desertion to Antifederalist politics is documented in *The Madison Papers,* 10: 26, 40, 45, 55–56, 59–60, 62, 64, 67, 79. See also Beveridge, *The Life of John Marshall,* 2: 49–50; Alexander Hamilton, *Works,* 9: 513–35. The Virginia House passed a resolution against the assumption of debts which claimed that the act was meant to "erect and concentrate and perpetuate a large monied interest in opposition to the landed interest." This would "prostrate agriculture at the feet of commerce," which would in turn be "fatal to the existence of American Liberty." Hamilton re-

best powers of eloquence could not prevail against hustings prejudices, thereby adding a confirmation to his apprehensions about the success of the Union. But whatever his private thoughts on this occasion might have been, Madison from that moment exchanged his Federalist politics for Virginia localism, and demonstrated by his subsequent behavior the power of electoral opinion to subdue high-minded but unpopular statesmanship.

This *volte-face* is clearly marked in his opposition to Hamilton's Bank and debt funding system. Madison was knowledgeable in fiscal matters. His views on the requisites of public finance, voiced at the public debate, were now incorporated in Hamilton's *Report on Credit,* on which Hamilton had consulted him. There was every reason to expect that Madison would be a foremost spokesman for this plan. Instead, the converted Madison proved to be its most formidable opponent, prolific in the invention of specious arguments and contentious distinctions.[34] His erstwhile Federalist colleagues were aghast when his unyielding opposition deadlocked Congress for four months and fanned the embers of faction. Hamilton called it "a perfidious desertion of principles which he was solemnly pledged to defend."[35] But Madison knew what he was

---

marked on the resolution that "this is the first symptom of a spirit which must either be killed or it will kill the Constitution of the United States." Quotations are from Beveridge, 2: 66, 68.

34. Ferguson, *The Power of the Purse,* 297ff., 325; Hammond, *Banks and Politics in America,* 115–23; Forrest McDonald, *Alexander Hamilton,* 163–88; Paul A. Rahe, *Republics Ancient and Modern,* in press. The reason often given for Madison's *volte-face*—that speculation in government securities, in anticipation of assumption of debts, had created a new situation of sinister creditor influence—will not do. There had been speculation in state government securities throughout the Confederation period, and Madison had been an opponent of debt repudiation through currency depreciation and in particular of the discrimination proposal that in 1790 he began to espouse. According to the discrimination scheme, securities sold by their original holders would not be paid at par, but at their highest market value prior to 1789, the balance of par to be issued in federal stock to the *original holders.* The scheme was based on the popular belief that speculators had plunged in securities (anticipating funding at par), and had bought them from original holders who were unaware of the appreciation that their stock was about to undergo. This scheme was demagogic, but it was backed by the Virginia magnates and Madison probably could not have resisted its force had he wished. On Madison's role in activating the engines on anti-Walpole jeremiads against the Federalists, see Drew R. McCoy, *The Elusive Republic,* 137ff.

35. Alexander Hamilton, *Works,* 9: 513ff.

doing. Eighty percent of the creditors of the national debt were in northern states. The counterargument that sound public credit would benefit everyone availed little against the promptings of envy. The final vote reflected this sectional split: 33 of 39 ayes were from states north of the Potomac, whereas 15 of 20 nays were from Virginia, the Carolinas, and Georgia. Even this measure of agreement was reached thanks only to a backstairs deal that Hamilton made with Madison and Jefferson: in return for acquiescence, Federalists would agree to locate the new capital on the Potomac.[36]

Madison's arguments against the Federalist public credit scheme articulated in a more genteel way the fierce declamations of his Virginia colleagues. Richard Henry Lee thundered that he would prefer the dissolution of the Union to "the rule of a fixed insolent northern majority" that the Bank would establish.[37] John Taylor and Patrick Henry unlimbered the old Country Whig impetuosities that had served John Trenchard so well eighty years previously. "When the systems of the vilest and most corrupt government," Henry asked rhetorically, "find advocates in the councils of America, shall we dare any longer say that America is the land of freedom?" The answer was negative as far as the Virginia aristocracy was concerned: "Not satisfied with a majority in the legislative councils," Henry railed, "they must have all the property . . . this is a contest for money as well as for empire." The specter of Walpole now became an urgent requirement of the mythology that southern planters were about to foist on the nation: liberty was endangered by a coterie of corrupt politicians and speculators responding to strings pulled by a new Walpole, Alexander Hamilton.[38]

36. Miller, *Crisis in Freedom*, 48.
37. Quoted ibid., 47, 50–51.
38. Two studies by Drew McCoy and Lance Banning contribute substantially to the description of Country Whig politics and political economy in the period 1770–1815. McCoy's *The Elusive Republic: Political Economy in Jeffersonian America* emphasizes the physiocratic and Scottish additions to the mainstream Harringtonian inheritance in America; he also nicely describes the revival of the Walpole bogey in 1792. Banning's *The Jeffersonian Persuasion: Evolution of a Party Ideology* emphasizes the continuity between Antifederalists and Republicans and the political significance of the conspiracy allegation Republicans laid against Federalists. Both authors are perhaps too passive toward the fact, which they recognize, that Republican agrarianism was the ideology of a sectional interest. Toward the end of his book, McCoy allows Jefferson to forfeit his political dignity by ascribing to him a "frantic retreat to a sectional, narrowly agrarian outlook . . . fueled by a volatile mixture of fear, bitterness, and paranoia" (*The Elusive Republic*, 249). The retreat did

The declared sectional bias evident in these versions of Country rhetoric rendered it unfit for service beyond southern hustings. Political finesse was needed to transform it into an ideology able to draw crowds in the North. Again it was Madison who supplied this delicate and vital touch. In September 1792, he issued the manifesto of the Republican faction to which he now gave the name. Writing in an early number of the *National Gazette*, which he and Jefferson set up to oppose the Federalist *Gazette of the United States*, Madison described national politics as divided between republicans and "anti-republicans." Republicans he credited with belief in the capacity of mankind to govern themselves, and with hating hereditary power as "an insult to reason and an outrage to the rights of man. . . . [Republicans] are offended at every public measure that does not appeal to the understanding and to the general interest of the community." "Anti-republicans" were those who "having debauched themselves into a persuasion that mankind are incapable of governing themselves . . . [believe] that government can be carried on only by the pageantry of rank, the influence of money and emoluments, and the tenor of military force." [39] Northern Federalists were stunned by

---

not occur, as he suggests, after Jefferson left office; his own study shows that it always had been an element of Jefferson's politics.

The continuity of the Virginians' political rhetoric with Country Whig conceptions is most conspicuous in the writings of their chief publicist, John Taylor of Caroline. Taylor borrowed freely from *Cato's Letters* and *The Craftsman;* he had no difficulty recognizing in Hamilton's credit system its British model, and he declaimed that Walpole's device for ensnaring liberty in the chains of debt was being repeated in virtuous America. All this assumed, of course, the myth of British tyranny and corruption. Jefferson identified his own position when he wrote that "Colonel Taylor and myself have rarely, if ever, differed in any political principle of importance" (*Writings of Thomas Jefferson*, 12: 176). See E. T. Mudge, *The Social Philosophy of John Taylor of Caroline;* E. A. J. Johnson, *The Foundations of American Economic Freedom*, 105–14; Lance Banning, *The Jeffersonian Persuasion*, 114–15, 128f.; J G. A. Pocock, *The Machiavellian Moment*, 528–43; Shalhope, *John Taylor of Caroline*, 74–75, 103; Rahe, *Republics Ancient and Modern*.

39. James Madison, *The Mind of the Founder*, 247. The constitutional doctrine Madison stated in this and related essays of this period comes straight from Antifederalist manifestos of the 1788–90 period, e.g. the Statement of the Albany Antifederalists of 10 April 1788. One of the links between Antifederalist and Republican opposition is the distinction between "consolidated" and "federal" government common to them. Antifederalists reproached the Constitution for giving unlimited power of the purse and of the sword to the federal government, which thereby "consolidated" it, i.e. made it sovereign over the states. Madison was the apostle of consolidation

the boundless imposture of Madison's gambit: slave owners the champions of human rights; aristocratic levelers; proud men reprobating military force. It was too much, as we see in Oliver Wolcott's letter to his father sitting in Congress:

> The papers printed [in Hartford] contain much insufferable cant about aristocracy—this political vice is supposed to prevail in New England, but especially in Connecticut! . . . will it be possible for the Southern people to make the opinion prevail?[40]

The next three years were to tell. Federalist politicians found their electorates invaded by a revised version of Country Whig rhetoric. To the old allegation about corrupt and corrupting credit systems was added a damnation by epithet, "British made." The alleged British provenance of this engine (the Old Whigs knew it came from corrupt Holland) was adduced as evidence of a conspiracy by monocrats to impose the British political system on the nation. Certain Republican leaders, Jefferson foremost among them, undoubtedly believed this nonsense. But it took the political genius of Madison to realize that precisely the intransigent obtuseness of the Country rhetoric preadapted it for use as a factional tool of southern interest.

   1. Southern jealousy of northern financial and commercial dominance was moralized in a jeremiad against sinister financial interests. In this form, the southern gambit could and did appeal to debtors everywhere.

   2. By imputing aristocratic and monarchist sympathies to Federalists, the planters distracted attention from the terrible accusation against slavery implied by the equality doctrine. It was essential for these men to find some extraordinary means to parry an accusation potentially so dangerous. The means was to fan popular discontent in northern electorates while cementing the deferential hierarchy peculiar to the South. Planters achieved solidarity with small southern farmers thanks to their shared resentment of finance and their common reverence for the white race.

   3. Imputation of conspiratorial intention is a common means of arousing fear and suspicion. It had been used effectively against the North government between 1772 and 1776. It was used against the Fed-

---

in 1788; by 1791 he was denouncing it. For Antifederalist manifestos, see Arthur Schlesinger, *History of U.S. Political Parties*, 1: 175–216.
40. George Gibbs, *Memoirs of the Administrations of Washington and John Adams*, 1: 87.

eralists to destroy their image as the party of patriots and as the true heirs of the political legacy of '76.[41]

4. Congressional Republicans would not countenance funding even a miniscule land or naval force, alleging against it the tired complaints about standing armies and multiplication of employment.[42] (Madison faithfully repeated this line even though he had formerly urged that the federal government be empowered to impose obedience on states by force.) Yet in plain fact the southern gentlemen, far from despising military despotism, exercised one over 800,000 blacks. They opposed federal control of state militias and their absorption into a federal army because state militias were the key instrument for enforcing slavery.

5. Virginia planters chafed under debts to British merchants: fully £2 million of the total £4 million owed by private citizens to British

41. The undertow in Country Whig thought that led writer upon writer to a conspiracy theory was the inordinate weight laid upon corruption. Corruption dislikes the light of day; it advances stealthily by bribery, closet deals, anonymous betrayals, and the like. Open debauchery and licentiousness thus appear as the visible fragment of a vast hidden intention to stifle liberty. Lance Banning emphasizes the prominence of conspiracy notions in Country Whig, Antifederalist, and Republican thought (*The Jeffersonian Persuasion*, 14, 92–93, 121–22, 151ff., 190ff., 205–6). The chief source of conspiratorial thinking in America was James Burgh's *Political Disquisitions,* an indictment of court politics whose appearance in 1774 was like a match set to powder. Jefferson was wholly committed to the conspiratorial interpretation of Federalist intentions, as evidenced by numerous letters and the celebrated "Anas" statement on American factions. He declared of Hamilton that he was "a man whose history from the moment at which history can stoop to notice him, is a tissue of machinations against the liberty of the country which . . . has heaped its honors on his head." What Banning does not notice, or at any rate does not emphasize, is that the conspiracy allegation authorizes the transformation of a party into a righteous sect whose primary mission to save liberty entails the complete destruction of the opposing party. At this point fanaticism enters the picture.

42. That the new federal government must have the power to raise and keep armies was imperative to the men of the Constitutional Convention, for nothing frustrated the war effort under the confederation more than the lack of this power. Elbridge Gerry's attempt to set constitutional limits on the size of standing armies got no support. *The Federalist* reflected this rejection of the Country Whig horror of standing armies, devoting no less than three numbers to the subject. During ratification, Antifederalists violently attacked this provision; and Madison as leader of the opposition duly fought every attempt to raise the military force that as a Federalist he had deemed necessary. See Kohn, *The Eagle and the Sword,* 74–84, 128–38, 174–92.

creditors were debts contracted by Virginians to support their opulent living.[43] It was therefore profitable to foment hatred of everything British, except their own ideology, for the debtors might hope that a deterioration of relations between the United States and Britain would lead to repudiation of debts recognized in the peace treaty of 1783.

Ingenious as this marriage of Virginian interests to ancient prejudices might be, something extra was needed to dramatize it, to give it an apparent plausibility, to lock it into the gut responses of the average man. France handed the Republicans that drama by declaring war on England in January 1793.

Foreign Influence on Faction

In *The Federalist* Hamilton observed that foreign affairs had played a disproportionately large role in the domestic politics of republics because factions often yielded to the temptation to augment their strength by allying with interested foreign powers. The converse of this proposition is also true. The play of factions allowed in republics makes them liable to open or covert influence from abroad.

Hostilities between Britain and France display the influence of a struggle between superpowers on a weak republic remote from the main theater of war. For about six years domestic politics was strained by the Republican effort to use popular enthusiasm for the French cause to drive a wedge between the government and the people. Not until the Civil War were citizens again to become so violently agitated against one another. To Republicans, the Jay Treaty with Britain seemed to injure the nation's trading interests, offended moral and treaty obligations to France, and provided new evidence for the alleged Federalist conspiracy against the Constitution. Federalists believed that peace with Britain must have the highest political priority. The nation had no forces to answer Britain's potent Navy and Canadian troops; coastal cities might be sacked at will. War would drive the nation into military alliance with France in panic conditions conducive to the Jacobinization of the na-

43. Federalist opinion traced Republican agitation to these debts; thus Oliver Wolcott wrote in February 1793: "The best solution which I can give to this disquiet is the pressure of the foreign debts due from the Virginia planters; these, they imagined, had been thrown off. The effect of the treaty and of the Constitution is to make them responsible; . . . the prospect of poverty and dependence to the Scotch merchants is what they cannot view with patience. They seem determined to weaken the public force, so as to render the recovery of these debts impossible" (quoted by Gibbs, *Memoirs of the Administrations of Washington and John Adams*, 1: 85–86).

tion. Both factions believed that the fate of domestic politics turned upon foreign alliance.

The broad aims of Britain and France on the North American continent varied little until Napoleon sold the Louisiana Territory in 1803. They were also very similar. Both believed that much more was to be lost than gained by war with the United States. Each was eager for American trade and determined to deny it to the other. They respected the integrity of the United States, but they prepared contingency plans in the event of its dissolution. Both wished to contain American expansion east of the Mississippi; they agreed that control of the Mississippi River valley was the key to the geopolitics of North America. France wished to recover Louisiana from Spain to make it the base for the reconstruction of French colonial power in the Western Hemisphere. Britain wished to frustrate that ambition, if necessary at the cost of throwing Louisiana to the United States.[44] These broad lines of French policy originated with Vergennes in 1778 and varied little over the next two decades despite all changes of government. It was compatible with massive interference in U.S. domestic politics between 1793 and 1796, to oblige the Washington administration to adhere to the French interpretation of the Consular Convention of 1788 and, subsequently, to abort the Jay Treaty.

At the outbreak of hostilities between France and England, the Cabinet began to discuss how neutrality might be preserved in light of the Convention, which gave France the right to bring prizes to American ports and to outfit privateers and warships in these ports. Federalist and Republican views on the matter soon took shape. Hamilton argued that the Convention accorded these rights only in a defensive war; but since France had opened hostilities against England, the Convention was inoperative. He and his colleagues in Cabinet urged that the president proclaim American neutrality, suspend the Convention, and refuse to receive the new French emissary. Republicans, led by Jefferson, looked beyond the letter of the Convention to wider implications. They doubted the president's authority to proclaim neutrality. They suggested that neutrality should be used to bargain advantages from the belligerents. Washington split these differences in his 19 April proclamation. The United States would pursue "a conduct friendly and impartial

44. On French and British policy in North America, particularly concerning Louisiana, see E. Wilson Lyon, *Louisiana in French Diplomacy, 1759–1804*, 109–26; Frederick Jackson Turner, "The Policy of France toward the Mississippi Valley in the Period of Washington and Adams," 252–53, 255–56, 258; E. Wilson Lyon, "The Directory and the United States," 515–16, 256.

toward the belligerent powers," he said; the crucial issue for neutrality, the Consular Convention, was evaded by silence. But Washington received Ambassador Genêt, making the United States the first nation to recognize the regicide French government.

This decision was influenced by the emphatic expression of pro-French feelings in response to news of the war and the execution of the king. Citizens displayed the cockade and the tricolor, hailed revolutionary heroes in the press, and organized civic festivities to celebrate victories of French armies over "the despots of Europe." Into this auspicious atmosphere stepped the young, brilliant, well-born, impetuous new envoy, Citizen Edmund Genêt. On his arrival in Charleston on 19 April aboard the frigate *L'Ambuscade*, he was the toast of the town during ten days of banquets and festivities at which "cowardly conservatives, anglomen, and monarchists" were roasted and the noble French republic held up for veneration. That great predatory slogan—"Enemies of equality, reform or tremble!"— burst the air at public celebrations, without any apparent feeling of uneasiness about what those brave words might mean to the shackled blacks.[45] These scenes were repeated as Genêt made his way by land to Philadelphia, where the dignitaries of the city and state received him in a wildly enthusiastic public demonstration. The entire nation, it seemed, was in a frenzy for the progress of liberty; and if France was the beneficiary, Federalist policy was the goat. "The cause of France," declared the Pennsylvania Republican Breckenridge, "is the cause of man, and neutrality is desertion." Secretary of State Jefferson castigated Washington's proceedings "towards the conspirators against human liberty [the British] and the asserters of it, [which are] unjustifiable in principle, in interest, and in respect to the wishes of our constituents."[46]

Once installed in Philadelphia, Genêt set out to milk full advantage from the popular solidarity of feeling with France and the divisions in government councils. He encouraged the establishment of francophile political clubs known as Democratic-Republican Societies. Within weeks dozens of these clamorous clubs sprang up. They functioned

45. Charles D. Hazen, *Contemporary American Opinion of the French Revolution,* 175–76.

46. Ibid., 180. Genêt's euphoric descriptions of his triumphal progress are contained in the *Correspondence of the French Ministers to the United States, 1791–1797,* 212–20. For a review of the "inflammatory and outrageous language" of this period, inclusive of conspiracy accusations from both sides, see two articles by Marshall Smelser, "The Jacobin Phrenzy: Federalism and the Menace of Liberty, Equality and Fraternity," *Review of Politics* 13 (1951): 457–82, and "Jacobin Phrenzy: The Menace of Monarchy, Plutocracy and Anglophobia, 1789–1798," *Review of Politics* 21 (1959): 239–58.

much as Committees of Correspondence had prior to the Revolution. They disseminated information, organized petitions, marches, and rallies, and menaced outspoken Federalists.[47] The importance of the clubs as rapid-development agitprop squads became apparent when Genêt began to organize American bases for French military activity. From the moment of his arrival in Charleston, he began recruiting a mercenary army, the Armée du Mississippi, to wrest Florida and Louisiana from Spanish control.[48] He issued letters of marque to American privateers to raid British shipping. He authorized French war vessels to bring British prizes to American ports, where French consuls condemned them and sold them to cheering crowds singing the *Marseillaise*. These extraordinary powers Genêt claimed under the Consular Convention of 1788. He was able to exercise them because partisan crowds on the docks and in the streets prevented government agents from carrying out orders to seize British prizes from privateers. Any doubt that these crowds were organized disappeared when their campaign of intimidation escalated to pulling guillotines through the streets of Philadephia, New York, and Boston, to shouts of "Ça ira!" Recalling these stormy days in a letter to Jefferson years later, John Adams declared:

> You certainly never felt the terrorism excited by Genêt in 1793 when ten thousand people in the streets of Philadelphia day after day *threatened to drag* Washington out of his house and effect a revolu-

47. The first Democratic Society was organized in Philadelphia shortly after Genêt's arrival; it in turn began to organize affiliate groups in all states. That they were French controlled is evident from their rhetoric ("We most firmly believe that he who is an enemy to the French Revolution cannot be a firm republican") and from the fact that their chief object was to undo Washington's neutrality policy. See Hazen, *Contemporary American Opinion of the French Revolution*, 188–209; Kohn, *The Eagle and the Sword*, 199–200.
48. Genêt appointed the adventurer and Indian fighter George Rogers Clark as major general of the "Independent and Revolutionary Legion of the Mississippi." He was acting on instructions of his government to free Spanish America, to open navigation of the Mississippi to Kentuckyians, to detach Louisiana from Spain, and to add Canada to U.S. territory (*Correspondence of the French Ministers to the United States, 1791–1797*, 204). Genêt carried out this mission and described his covert operations in diplomatic dispatches: "J'excite les Canadiens à s'affranchir du joug de l'Angleterre; j'arme les Kentukois, et je prépare par mer une expedition secondera leur descente dans la nouvelle Orléans"; and "j'ai préparé la révolution de la nouvelle Orléans et du Canada . . ." (ibid., 217–18, 232). Governor Moultrie of South Carolina and Jefferson were parties to Genêt's New Orleans military adventure (ibid., 219, note *d*; 220–21).

tion in government or compel it to declare war in favor of the
French Revolution and against England.[49]

Jefferson did not feel the terrorism because he was probably among
its directors. He and other high-level Republicans were on intimate
terms with Genêt and kept him informed on privy deliberations of
the Cabinet and on shifts of opinion in Congress. These "Republican
friends of France," as Genêt styled them in his diplomatic reports, were
and remained crucial to the diplomatic offensive in the United States.
Impetuous though he was, Genêt would scarcely have dared such encroachments and defiance of U.S. sovereignty without the agreement of
high-level Republicans.[50]

By August, Genêt was sufficiently confident of his influence that he
played his big card: he challenged Washington to convene a special session of Congress to judge their differences about the government's neutrality policy; if he would not, Genêt threatened to take his case to the
people. This audacity proved to be ill timed and ill coordinated. An investigation by the South Carolina legislature of Genêt's recruitments to
his mercenary army turned up some evidence of a plan to land a French
force in Charleston and arm the blacks.[51] This intelligence somewhat
cooled the ardor of the planter Jacobins. Sensing the danger, Jefferson,
Madison, and Randolph shut down their unofficial channels to Genêt
and ducked for cover.[52] In December Congress in regular session ap-

49. Quoted by Hazen, *Contemporary American Opinion of the French Revolution*,
    186. I have been unable to confirm Adams's report from another source.
50. The Franco-Republican collaboration antedates the neutrality proclamation:
    by mid-1792, Jefferson called French alliance "the polar star" of policy (*Writ-
    ings*, 1: 212). Amidst the anti-French reaction in 1798 he urgently advised the
    Directory that reconciliation with America was necessary to save the Repub-
    lican party (Lyon, "The Directory and the United States," 529). French dip-
    lomatic correspondence shows that all French envoys between 1792 and 1798
    consulted confidentially and intimately with Republican leaders. The earliest
    evidence of an axis between French diplomats and Republican officeholders
    is Ternant's communication of 8 April 1792 about his long confidential dis-
    cussion with Jefferson concerning a trade agreement with France (see *Corre-
    spondence of the French Ministers*, 108ff., 215, 245, 407ff., 450–51). Genêt's re-
    ports boast of his influence on public opinion; clearly he was hoping for a
    signal from Paris to "revolutionize" the country, which he would have done
    without depending on Jefferson, whom he came to regard as cowardly
    (ibid., 216–17, 235, 241–48; see also Kohn, *The Eagle and the Sword*, 199–213,
    for a résumé of Franco-Republican activity from 1792 to 1800; and Miller,
    Crisis in Freedom, 131–37).
51. Turner, "The Policy of France toward the Mississippi Valley," 263.
52. Jefferson began backtracking from Genêt late in June. On 7 July he wrote

proved Washington's proposal to request Genêt's recall. The new Jacobin government, realizing that Genêt had overplayed his hand, complied with Washington's request and announced that the envoy would be tried on his return to Paris. Genêt decided not to put his head in the guillotine. He requested and received political asylum, and moved to New York, where he married the daughter of Republican kingpin Governor George Clinton.

During this heady period, the harassed but sturdy British consul had protested every violation of American neutrality by Genêt and his agents. In December 1793, Privy Council superseded diplomacy by a demonstration of its power to dispose as it pleased of American shipping. A dragnet was thrown across the Caribbean, capturing about 250 merchant vessels, which were taken to West Indian ports, condemned, and sold down to the keels. This awesome cleansing of the seas was meant to demonstrate the error of the Republican argument that America could use its commercial might to oblige the British to accept American neutrality on American terms. But public opinion did not register the sobering thought that the draconian visitation was meant to suggest. Anti-British feeling swept through the country. Throughout the spring of 1794, there was talk of war. In March, Congressman Jonathan Dayton proposed that the £4 million in private American debts to British creditors be sequestered. By May, debate over the direction of foreign policy had produced such deep divisions that there was talk of splitting the Union into northern and southern confederations. In this turbulent atmosphere, Washington dispatched Chief Justice John Jay as special envoy to Britain with instructions to reach agreement on a commercial treaty that respected American neutrality.

Congressional Republicans had for several years renewed the colonial tactic of frustrating government by opposing taxes as the arm of despotic ambition. Antitaxation slogans were now heard in the western districts of Pennsylvania, where the excise tax on whiskey, long a local irritant, became the cause of an insurrection. The president's demand that the rebels lay down their arms was met by a boast that, having subdued Pittsburgh, they would now march on Philadelphia. This test of political will was met when Washington's call-up of New Jersey and Virginia militia brought a force of 13,000 troops. When Washington marched into the rebel territory, the rebels dispersed without a fight.

Meanwhile Washington's attempt to conduct a bipartisan government was foundering. He dispatched the ardent francophile James

---

Madison that Genêt's appointment had been calamitous and noted that if his communications to the government were laid before Congress or the public, "they will excite universal indignation" (*Writings*, 6: 238).

Monroe to Paris shortly after Jay's departure for London. On his arrival, Monroe delivered a strongly worded pro-French speech before the National Assembly and a throng of 10,000 cheering Parisians. Although this raised eyebrows in London, Jay successfully negotiated his treaty. It provided for American shipping limited access to West Indian ports, and free access to all North American ports, but imposed the onerous provisions of the Navigation Act on American exports to Britain and Europe, viz. that they be carried in British bottoms. The British undertook to withdraw troops from lands ceded by the peace treaty of 1783. A commission was established to handle claims of British creditors, thus removing them from the jurisdiction of U.S. courts. American claims to compensation for slaves taken during the revolutionary war were not pressed by the abolitionist Jay.

The Jay Treaty was the outcome of Hamilton's careful preparatory diplomacy and close collaboration between him and Jay on the negotiation of articles. Its terms reflected the political realism distinctive of the Federalists. The principal gain for the United States was peace—peace on the seas and peace on the frontier, where Britain had steadily applied pressure by fomenting Indian wars. Its terms clearly reflected Britain's commercial and military preponderance during a period when the regulation of commerce by force of arms had become the norm.

Aware that the treaty would enrage Republicans, Washington kept it on his desk for four months before sending it to the Senate for debate in secrecy. Copies of the treaty leaked, and it was published by the Republican newspaper *Aurora*. Furious mobs took to the streets and burned Jay in effigy daily, while the press kept up a drumfire of invective against the cowardly capitulation to Britain. Although the Senate had approved the treaty, Washington now hesitated to sign it into law. The British consul changed his mind by passing to him secret correspondence between Secretary of State Randolph and Ambassador Fauchet, intercepted on an American vessel. This correspondence was the first tangible evidence that Cabinet officers were passing state secrets to the French. It also revealed that Fauchet and Randolph had been involved in the Whiskey Rebellion.[53] Washington recognized the gravity of this

---

53. The passage of Fauchet's dispatch implicating Randolph is too long for quotation here. It connects Randolph with the Democratic Societies—which Washington had suspected of fomenting the rebellion—and refers to Randolph's suggestion to Fauchet that he bribe certain traders in western Pennsylvania to testify that the rebellion was incited by the British. Of this Fauchet declared: "Ainsi avec quelques milliers de Dollars la République aurait décidé ici sur la Guerre Civile ou sur la paix! Ainsi les consciences des

evidence. He had believed that the Democratic-Republican Societies were instrumental in fomenting the Whiskey Rebellion. Now this letter suggested that the publicly visible affinities between the Republicans, the Democratic clubs, and French envoys were coordinated by confidential attachments leading into his own Cabinet. Furthermore, Randolph was closely allied with Jefferson, Madison, Monroe, and William Branch Giles, who composed the core of the Virginia opposition making life difficult for his administration. If Randolph was a mole, what of the others? Washington never saw the diplomatic correspondence establishing Jefferson's key role in the French-Republican network;[54] but what he had seen was enough to convince him that his attempt to run a bipartisan Cabinet had miscarried. Washington assembled his Cabinet and placed the correspondence before Randolph, who recognized in it a demand for his resignation. Back in Virginia he wrote a vindication of himself in which he accused Washington of character assassination.[55] Washington promptly signed the Jay Treaty into law.

    Yet this was not the end of the matter, for the treaty came before the House in the form of an appropriations bill to fund the claims commission stipulated by the treaty. Madison and his colleagues, determined to defeat the treaty at any cost,[56] spun webs of casuistry arguing from the House's exclusive power to declare war to the conclusion that

---

prétendus Patriotes en Amerique ont déjà un tarif!" (*Correspondence of the French Ministers*, 451). Fauchet's astonished disillusionment is a commentary on the nature of the Virginians' attachment to France: it was a weapon in a domestic power struggle.

54. Ibid., 215, 245, 948, 975.

55. The dispatch that implicated Randolph also commented on other Virginian francophiles in a manner that could not have pleased Washington. Irving Brant, Madison's biographer, has attempted to exonerate Randolph ("Edmund Randolph, Not Guilty!," *William and Mary Quarterly*, 3d ser., 7 [1950]: 180–98). The effort is unconvincing because it ignores the French diplomatic correspondence as a whole, which establishes Franco-Republican collusion. Brant's interpretation of the damning passage of Fauchet's letter, which is tendentious at best, is nonsense in light of the collusion (p. 405 of his article). The article is not devoted to canvassing evidence but to describing circumstances surrounding Randolph's resignation.

56. In a corrective gloss on earlier scholarship, Jerald Combs writes: "The idea that Madison and the Republicans in the House were not determined to overthrow the treaty arose from a gross misunderstanding of Republican tactics in the Congressional debates. A close examination of the House fight will demonstrate that Madison and the Republicans were dead serious in their attempt to destroy the treaty" (*The Jay Treaty*, 172).

the House alone could make foreign policy. The executive's power to make treaties was interpreted to imply only a "permission" to execute House directives. These arguments need not detain us, except to observe that in the history of jurisdictional struggles few can match the brazenness of this attempt to create a new power by obliterating a power clearly ascribed.[57] The attempt failed only on the casting vote of House Speaker Muhlenberg.

When the last effort to defeat the treaty expired in April 1796, its commercial provisions had been informally observed by the two governments for over two years. Its effect on the economy was instant; a boom began thanks to the greatly increased security of passage. Moreover, one of those "inventions of ingenuity," the cotton gin, had transformed cotton from a marginal to an export commodity. Exports rose from 3 million pounds in 1793 to 6 million in 1796, and from there to 20 million in 1801, nearly all of it shipped to English mills. In view of this prosperity clearly traceable to the cause, how could Republicans continue as late as 1796 to oppose the treaty as injurious to the nation's interests?

Republican ideology was tied to a peculiar dogma that made its appearance in the first session of Congress when Madison proposed his discriminating tariffs in order to extract better trade agreements with Britain. It thereafter operated as an unchallengeable opinion among Republicans until it bore fruit in the Embargo Act of Jefferson's administration. The opinion was that the dependency of the British economy on the export trade to America made Britain vulnerable to various demands in return for trading privileges. The Embargo Act was expressly based on this reasoning: the damage done to the British economy by closing American ports to its goods would compel Britain to meet American demands, in that case for freedom of the seas. The validity of that view is easily assessed from the actual consequences of the embargo. It produced barely a ripple in the British economy, whose exports to America were only 7 percent of the annual total. Its effect domestically was the reverse: mercantile New England was brought to its knees and southern commodity exports were badly damaged.

This illusion that the tail could wag the dog took root in the 1770s, when colonists believed that their nonimportation agreement would oblige Privy Council to meet their political demands. Although the stratagem was as barren then as later when Jefferson revived it, belief that American markets provided a decisive leverage over British foreign policy became a doctrine for the Republican faithful. It was accompanied by another illusion, the half-sister of the first, to the effect that the

57. Edward Corwin, *The President, Office and Powers*, 219.

American military capacity, suitably allied, could challenge the British. This illusion accounts for the readiness of Republicans throughout the 1790s to declare war on Britain. When the war hawks finally had their day in 1812, His Britannic Majesty's cruisers sailed up the Potomac, put the government to flight, and burned the capital.

The partisan function of these two illusions was to obfuscate the Federalists' clear and distinct conception of the national interest as peaceful trade with Britain. The interplay of interest and faction during the 1790s cannot be understood without a clear grasp of the necessity of these illusions to the Republican bid for power. For if the Federalists were correct, then the British orientation of their foreign policy might not be a sinister attempt by monocrats to anglicize America, but merely the prosaic calculation of the nation's self-interest. Republicanism, however, was a faith—a sectarian democratic faith—requiring icons of good and evil to mobilize the frenzy of self-righteousness. This was the potent spiritual value championed by the Republicans. It explains why Republicans nurtured goals out of joint with present and foreseeable interests; why they persevered in those goals despite the ruin they caused; why Republicanism assumed the character of an orthodoxy; and why the Republicans were able to drive the Federalists from office once they expropriated from the Federalists their emotional bond with the people, patriotism.

To resume our narrative, the new French envoy, Adet, had used all his influence to secure the House defeat of the Jay Treaty. Once this effort collapsed, the Directory in Paris informed Ambassador Monroe that it would recall Adet and proceed forthwith to revolutionize America until a government acceptable to France was installed. Monroe persuaded the Directory to stay its hand until the next presidential election.[58] On the basis of this understanding, Adet intervened in the election by publishing proclamations announcing the suspension of full diplomatic relations and a tough policy toward American shipping, while blaming the deteriorated relations between France and the U.S. on the Federalists. Adet's candidate, Jefferson, ran second in the race to John Adams. The Directory then began to execute its threats, beginning with depredations of American shipping in the West Indies. Adams, believing that reconciliation was possible, sent a mission to Paris with instructions to mend the breach. Foreign Minister Talleyrand declined to receive the envoys unless they agreed to pay a $250,000 bribe and advance a loan of $12 million to the Directory. Since this was Talleyrand's usual way of doing business, the envoys agreed, provided that their credentials be ac-

58. Miller, *Crisis in Freedom,* 192.

cepted. Talleyrand refused, and the envoys returned to Philadelphia to report. The Senate ordered the correspondence stating the bribe and loan conditions to be published. The effect was to make the Federalists the beneficiaries of patriotism for the first time in a long while. "Millions for defense, but not one cent for tribute!" became the catch-cry. President Adams was the darling of crowds, and France became the goat of public opinion.

This wave of good feeling, the first they had experienced after a long drought, emboldened the Federalists to strike at the francophile menace through the Alien and Sedition Acts (1798). These acts made French, French West Indian, and English political activists liable to deportation by administrative discretion; they also enabled the attorney general to prosecute seditious or libelous utterances. Republicans interpreted these acts as an attempt to suppress their party, the Democratic clubs, and freedom of speech generally. After a half-dozen prosecutions Jefferson declared that the Federalists had initiated a "reign of terror." Republicans unleashed their own terror—surly mobs roaming the streets in search of victims. President Adams felt so menaced by them that he quietly armed his household. Meanwhile Vice-President Jefferson and Madison retired to Virginia to prepare their grand riposte: drafts of what became the Virginia and Kentucky Resolutions after they were passed by the legislatures of those states in 1799. These declarations denounced the Alien and Sedition Act as unconstitutional, not because they violated the First Amendment guarantee of free speech, but because they usurped states' rights. The political sense of these resolutions is missed when they are read as a defense of civil liberties. By resting their argument on states' rights, Madison and Jefferson implied that the act, if passed by states, *would be legal.*[59]

Madison and Jefferson avoided a civil liberties appeal. Had that been their intention, Madison at least might have publicly taken that stand. Instead, they worked secretly, their authorship of the resolutions known to but a few. Their political intention becomes apparent in the new constitutional doctrine that they announced as a corollary of the alleged

59. Jefferson approved prosecutions for libel under the common law in state courts, and in fact a number of such prosecutions were brought by Republican prosecutors with dire consequences for accused Federalists (see Leonard W. Levy, *Jefferson and Civil Liberties: The Darker Side*, 45, 48, 56, 59; Miller, *Crisis in Freedom*, 231). As Miller points out, the few prosecutions brought under the act bore no relation to the political capital that Republicans were able to make of its spirit of persecution. It is doubtful that the act was of any restraining influence at all.

usurpation of states' rights: states have the right to nullify congressional legislation. Madison certainly knew that the Supreme Court was the sole judge of the constitutionality of legislation; and seven state legislatures, responding to the Virginia and Kentucky Resolutions, drew attention to that fact. But the nullification doctrine, which was subsequently to dissolve the Union, served to bolster talk in Virginia of secession. Vice-President Jefferson began to disparage the federal government as a "foreign jurisdiction" and revived the Antifederalist complaint that the excise tax and the Bank were unconstitutional. Madison for his part recirculated the old canard that Federalist politicians wished to form a "consolidated government" on the ashes of "state sovereignties [*sic*]." This talk was accompanied by stockpiling of magazines and a militia call-up to resist a march through Virginia by federal troops.[60] President Adams, however, had no heart for a display of federal sovereignty that might lead to armed resistance, and he completed his term with his party split over what should be done about the Virginians. When the Federalists failed to compose their quarrel in time for the election, the Virginians took command of the presidency for the next quarter-century.

60. Between January and April of 1799, the Virginia legislature voted to raise taxes, reorganize the militia, and construct an armory. The prominent Virginian St. George Tucker declared that as many as 100,000 Americans, himself among them, were prepared to join a French army of invasion. Manifestations such as these, not mere hysteria, led Federalists to view the Virginia and Kentucky Resolutions as the tocsin of insurrection (see Kohn, *The Eagle and the Sword*, 216, 213, 251). The Alien and Sedition Acts were not what aroused the Virginians. They were excited by Congress's approval, after years of effort, of a bill to establish a professional army of 20,000 men under Hamilton's control. Republicans maintained that since France, the alleged threat, lacked the capacity to invade, these troops had no other purpose than to impose "consolidated government" on refractory Republicans. This assessment rings true. British naval victories in 1798–99 destroyed the French capacity to move a large force to the West Indies or to Louisiana. Hamiltonians wanted a war with France in order to destroy the credibility of the Republican party. If the Kentucky Resolution was the tocsin of insurrection, the Alien and Sedition Acts were the prelude to a showdown with Republicans; the issue was not civil liberty but civil war. President Adams saved the day by frustrating the army buildup and by successfully negotiating an accord with France. Hamilton, frustrated in his ambition, violently attacked Adams for destroying what appeared to be the decisive stroke against Republicans; this breach crippled the Federalists.

The Virtuous Republic in Action

The Republican victory of 1800 was a sweep; besides the presidency and the House, the party dominated all but four state legislatures. Such plenitude of power affords ample scope to compare the promise of virtuous government to performance.

A reorientation of foreign policy was preempted by Adams's most important service to his country, peace with France. In Britain, a judicial definition of neutral goods removed most of the ambiguity unresolved by the Jay Treaty, and did so to the advantage of the United States. With neutrality acknowledged by Britain and France, the reexport trade boomed. President Jefferson, ever the man of all seasons, adapted to the new mood by praising Britain as the "bastion of liberty" and suggesting that a Bourbon restoration would be a blessing to France. The Louisiana Purchase of 1803 eliminated the contest of foreign powers in the West and settled on the nation a manifest destiny of expansion. Foreign policy continued to be Federalist until the British and French effort to control neutral shipping provoked the Embargo Act.

Republicans had inveighed so long and hard against the despotism of finance capital that Federalists expected to see the Bank of the United States burned on the altar of liberty. But to the surprise of many and the delight of Hamilton, Jefferson's inaugural address embraced the engine of credit in its ecumenical declaration that "We are all Federalists, we are all Republicans." His treasurer, Albert Gallatin, successfully defended the Bank against fitful attempts to bring it low. Jefferson's blow to the system consisted of reducing the national debt by half during his administration. However, when the Bank's charter expired in 1811, financial interests represented by congressional magnates scuttled the Bank so that private banks could expand their activities. This they promptly did with numerous unregulated paper emissions and overextensions of credit. The resulting monetary chaos and bankruptcies brought cries for remedy and revenge. The virtuous republicans could think of no other remedy than to recharter the Bank.[61] President Madison, the original bank-buster, signed the bill and vouched for its constitutionality. This experience might have terminated antibank politics had Republican rhetoric not embedded itself so deeply in popular political demonology. When internal quarrels stressed the party in the 1820s, antibank jeremiads once more rolled into electoral politics. Andrew Jackson's splinter Democrats seized this issue and rode a new wave of populism to power. Once again the familiar cycle of bank bashing,

61. Hammond, *Banks and Politics in America*, 209 ff.

chaos, and recharter was run through. In this instance it was not, as previously, a matter of private interest prevailing over public; Jackson was a simple man of vigorous prejudices, who believed that the South Seas Bubble exposed the fraudulence of banks.[62]

Nothing exercised Republicans so much as the use of patronage and favor to form party cadres. This was the worst Walpolean vice because it struck at the roots of free government as Country Whigs and Republicans imagined it: if a man's vote, or deliberations, or executions as a ministerial servant were influenced by favors received or expected, then he was not free; he was the lackey of men who made subservience a system. The Federalists' ample use of patronage, which they defended as necessary to government, had been instanced as a major proof of Federalist intention to subvert the government to monarchy. From the Republicans, then, a reformation was to be expected. However, the election of 1800 was a tight race, and Jefferson found it expedient to accept the vote of the South Carolina legislature in return for promises of choice appointments (which he kept). Once in office, Jefferson was determined to cleanse the temple of liberty; he replaced "the enemy" with Republicans who had been loyal to him in the presidential contest. Nor did he stop at the federal level; he pursued the system of party dominance of jobs down to the last precinct in remote Ohio.[63]

Jefferson was the first president to be also his party's chief; that combination, together with his control of patronage, suddenly altered the relation between the executive and legislative branches. Republican doctrine minimized executive power by interpreting executive functions narrowly and legislative functions broadly. But the completeness of their victory fastened upon Republicans the paradox that party attachments threw a bridge from the executive to the legislative branch and made the president, as party leader, all-powerful. It was Hamilton's dream come true: a consolidated government capable of energetic action. But consolidated government was what Republicans had for a decade decried as monarchy. The paradox was extreme; the collision between declared intention and actual outcome was complete. On the Republican theory, the liberties of the people were gravely jeopardized by the mere collection of so much power. What were Republicans to do with it?

The answer suggested by Jefferson's first inaugural address was—very little. The address reviewed the principles of government in a broad, conciliatory manner that might reassure any who feared a Jacobian onslaught. He affirmed his commitment to equal justice for all, peace

62. Ibid., 374–92.
63. Henry Adams, *The History of the United States of America*, 1: 292–315.

with no entangling alliances, preservation of the federal government and credit system, strength to state governments as the "bulwarks against anti-republican tendencies," freedom of religion and of the press. These affirmations were common pieties. But the address also included what subsequent tradition singled out as his most succinct statement on the functions of the federal government:

> With all these blessings, what more is necessary to make us happy and prosperous people? Still one thing more, fellow-citizens,—a wise and frugal government, which shall restrain men from injuring one another, which shall leave them otherwise free to regulate their own pursuits of industry and improvement, and shall not take from the mouth of labor the bread it has earned. This is the sum of good government, and this is necessary to close the circle of our felicities.[64]

The sum of good government assigns only one positive function—the police function—and sets two limits, tending to the advantage of individual liberty. There is no trace of a program in this or any of Jefferson's presidential statements. Programs were Federalist devices; they smacked of energetic government. What Jefferson proposed as the task of his administration was the nurture of a moral ideal—to preserve the innocence of the American people against the corruption of government so vividly displayed in Europe. That ideal, agrarian democracy, mandated opposition to the requisites of modern states, pithily conveyed by his dictum "Banking establishments are more dangerous than standing armies."

Jefferson's accession to the presidency represented the victory of agrarian ideology fortified by laissez-faire economics,[65] but tempered by the Virginian's instinct for the middle ground. His administration traced a zigzag path between pragmatism and ideology, as well as be-

---

64. Ibid., 202.
65. Joyce Appleby maintains that the Jeffersonian agrarians were not nostalgic patricians, but acquisitive (or capitalist) and democratic. She also maintains that Adam Smith's conception of the self-regulating market embracing all individuals was an important element in the theoretical formulation of this conception (see *Capitalism and a New Social Order*). But she does not document that *The Wealth of Nations* was an important source for Republicans, as it probably was, or that Smithian economics favors agriculture, as it does. For a criticism of Appleby's study and an assessment of the relation of *The Wealth of Nations* to Republicanism, see Hiram Caton, "The Second American Revolution."

tween declared intentions of Republican rhetoric and its true purport. The result was a spectacular record of inconsistencies. Thus, to protect the Republican victory, he commenced a purge of Federalist judges from the courts; that initiated a long assault on the institutions of government and on the liberties and property of citizens unmatched by any subsequent peacetime president.[66] The champion of states' rights drove two states to the verge of armed resistance. The laissez-faire exponent forced the most extreme commercial regulation on the nation—a total stoppage of international trade. The benign moralist who promised not to take bread from the mouth of labor brought economic ruin to half the nation. The Country Whig thinker who abhorred standing armies asked for an army of 50,000, not to repel an invader, but to force a hated law on his own people.[67] The apostle of civil liberties used every means at his disposal, including defiance of a Supreme Court order, to impose on the courts his private certainty of a man's guilt. The democrat who pledged "absolute acquiescence in the decisions of the majority," and who recommended a little rebellion now and then, condemned as "parricides" those whom his measures made desperate to the point of disobedience. The enemy of tyrants accepted without demurrer extraordinary powers that his own Cabinet deemed "most arbitrary." The statesman who dreaded the corrupting influences of war brought the nation to the brink of war with Britain and France simultaneously. This congeries of inconsistencies, and the thinking that sponsored them, are epitomized by the politics of the Embargo Act.

The act, in force during the last fifteen months of Jefferson's second term, was a response to the effects on American commerce of the economic war between Britain and France. In 1807, Napoleon had closed all continental ports to British goods and prohibited neutral ships from carrying contraband goods to Britain, with the avowed aim of ruining British trade and starving the island. Britain required all neutral European trade to pass through its ports and pay customs, and Orders in Council were about to declare the blockade of France. The exigencies of total war had destroyed the idea of neutral shipping. Nations attempting to defend neutrality by arming their vessels were taught harsh lessons, as when a British squadron set Copenhagen to the torch.

Depredations against American shipping committed by both nations aroused public resentment. But Napoleon's empire had cast down France, in American opinion, from its former exalted position as champion of liberty. In that climate, the old Federalist argument for a commer-

66. Levy, *Jefferson and Civil Liberties*, 18, 59, 86, 109, 130ff., 139.
67. Ibid., 109.

cial pact with Britain retained its plausibility: the might of the British Navy, British bases in Canada and the Caribbean, the profusion of British markets, France's naval weakness, all counseled making as good a bargain as the British would condescend to make. President Jefferson and Secretary of State Madison orbited indecisively during negotiation over restitution concerning a violation of national honor. The British were prepared to disavow the offending act, but Jefferson defeated the negotiations because he desired war. When his Cabinet would not support his war resolution, he resolved on an embargo of all foreign trade.[68]

Everything about the embargo was extraordinary. Legislation was sent from the Cabinet to both houses on 17 December 1807 for secret debate. When Jefferson signed the act into law on 22 December, he presented the public a decree of which they had no prior warning. The act contained no provision to compensate the thousands who would be put out of work or forced to bankruptcy. Citizens were abruptly informed that, to protect American property from foreign depredations, it would be kept at home. Supplementary acts soon followed. They stopped overland trade with Canada and Florida; they required heavy bonds and threatened excessive penalties upon fishing vessels in cases of trading in foreign merchandise; finally, they exercised that "most arbitrary" power, as Gallatin styled it, enabling federal officers to search and detain persons and goods on suspicion of illicit traffic. When it was suspected that the many coasting vessels carrying domestic traffic on the East Coast were engaging in illegal traffic, Jefferson demanded and received the power to require all vessels to seek permits for any movement at all, as well as the power to seize any vessel summarily. Thus in the virtuous republic it became a crime for a New York farmer to sell a pig to an Ontario merchant.[69]

In the initial phase, the American jealousy of liberty was strangely silent. Jefferson read with satisfaction messages of support from state leg-

68. Burton Spivak, *Jefferson's English Crisis: Commerce, Embargo, and the Republican Revolution*, 88–94, 111–13.
69. Madison was the architect of embargo politics. He supposed that it would compel Britain to acknowledge reciprocity, since he believed that the West Indies could not be provisioned save by access to American ports. He was willing to threaten what he believed to be an essential interest even though he acknowledged that American arms could not repulse a British invasion. Madison and Jefferson imagined, however, that this disadvantage—a British Navy of 6,000 vessels as against 16 U.S. vessels—was somehow offset by the prospect of an easy American conquest of Canada (J. C. S. Stagg, *Mr. Madison's War: Politics, Diplomacy and Warfare in the Early American Republic*, 20–22).

islatures, from municipalities, even from some merchants. But as the weeks turned to months, the "experiment in peaceable coercion" of European powers turned into a trial of violence against the American people. Property was seized, offenders were jailed, smugglers were massacred, mobs fired upon. These events did not suggest to Jefferson that tyranny might be loose in the land. Those who complained of deprivation he branded luxury-loving malcontents; those who conspired to trade were "enemies" and "parricides." These categories were manufactured by a mind that had always believed that anyone who opposed its moral will was a demon bent on destroying the virtuous republic. So it was that disobedience and petitions for redress only strengthened his resolve to turn the screws yet tighter: the embargo was now extended indefinitely, and another 10,000 troops were outfitted to enforce it. After six months, the wreckage was universal. The Virginia tobacco harvest could not be sold; South Carolina kept its cotton and rice; in New England shipping was at a dead stop; bankruptcies ruined hundreds of merchants and tradesmen.[70] After twelve months, Massachusetts and Connecticut began moves to secede from the Union and invoked Jefferson's own constitutional doctrine of the Kentucky Resolution to justify their threatened action. Still he would not relent, saying that the "experiment" had not yet had time to be proved right.

The rationale for this policy was stated by Madison immediately after the embargo's enactment. Like the nonimportation agreement of 1773, the embargo was meant to make Britain recognize America's neutral rights by pressuring its economy. The argument was that Britain must be the great loser in this struggle, because it imported from America foodstuffs and raw materials, which were necessities, whereas America imported manufactured "superfluities." Further, since America imported goods at a value nearly ten times its exports to Britain, the loss of markets together with the loss of foodstuffs would be crippling.

Federalist remnants objected that no experiment was necessary to refute this argument. Whereas the embargo shut down American trade completely, Britain was free to supply its wants elsewhere; and the loss of an export market that amounted to only 7 percent of its total was scarcely more than a pinch. The embargo was a self-inflicted wound that the Canning government viewed with bemused contempt while Britain suffered some dislocations.[71]

70. W. W. Jennings, *The American Embargo*; Leonard D. White, *The Jeffersonians: A Study in Administrative History, 1801–1829*, 424–33.
71. In the embargo's first year, exports dropped from $108 million to $22 million. Figures for all financial losses are given by Jennings, "The Embargo,"

That this objection made no impression on the administration indicates that Madison's second rationale for the embargo was decisive. He proposed that the embargo would put the nation back on course to the virtuous republic. Trade with corrupt nations had introduced their corruptions into the pure land. A dependency on foreign luxuries and an unwholesome desire for wealth had insinuated itself into the nation. Embargo would oblige the people to return to the habits of frugality; it would suggest to many idle and desperate townsmen a return to the soil and its self-sufficiency; and it would encourage cottage manufacture of coarse but honest materials to replace the unnecessary refinements of Britain.

The commercial men of the North were in fits about this "Spartan" or "Chinese" political economy of isolation, rustic barbarism, and slovenly indifference. Embargo, they claimed, was the visionary Jefferson's revenge upon the commercial North, whose politics and prosperity he had attempted to frustrate for twenty years. The press rehearsed all the arguments of Hume and Smith about the civilizing influence of trade; and Noah Webster cut close to the bone when he thundered that "no nation but *barbarians* and *slaves*, have ever been without commerce." Jefferson's experiment proved what Federalists had all along suspected: the Virginian vision of liberty, framed to accommodate 800,000 black slaves, now required that the northerner be driven into poverty at bayonet point.

Jefferson was able to visit sublime and ridiculous absurdities on the nation because Federalists compromised the principle of equality by agreeing to countenance slavery. This was the root cause of the mendacity that took political life in its grip. A political culture whose logic system was wired to accept slave owners as spokesmen of liberty would probably exhibit a certain invincible ignorance about the elementary facts of national life, and a certain indecisiveness in affirming the basic conditions of modern political existence—a national government, an army and navy, roads and waterways, banks, education, protection for patents. As the nation grew, the Virginian elder statesmen became ever

---

204–15. Spivak (*Jefferson's English Crisis,* 107) writes that the embargo "honored none of the precepts of Jeffersonian economic coercion. It destroyed much of the foreign market for American agriculture. It supported England's quest for monopoly of the world's carrying trade. When one considered whom it rewarded and whom it punished, the embargo caricatured the Republican tradition of economic retaliation." Spivak means the traditional goals of Republican policy, as distinct from successful practice, of which there was no tradition.

more eccentric and narrowly sectional. Madison and Jefferson resolved to install the "southern creed" in the University of Virginia Law School; they agreed on the exclusion of *The Federalist Papers* from the syllabus.[72] They had fixed their hopes for the virtuous republic on thousands of uncontrollable small farmers settling western lands. When the farmers' liberty came into conflict with the extension of slavery into the territories, Jefferson saw in their demands a new Federalist plot to build a coalition of free states that would impose consolidated government.[73] Madison headed a movement to transport all the slaves back to Africa. Jefferson did some calculations and concluded that the resettling costs would be about $1 billion, if it succeeded; but it couldn't succeed because the fertility rate was greater than the maximum feasible resettlement rate.

The presence of slaves obliged Jeffersonians and Jacksonians to obfuscate the equality doctrine with the rhetoric and practice of "leveling." Property-rich but mortgaged planters entered a combination with small farmers and artisans to keep the high flyers of finance and commerce down. By this means they delayed the diversification of talents and vocations, the development of intelligence and culture, that did eventually supersede the sensual prejudices of the agrarian mind. After force had established a consolidated government, it became possible to distinguish between equality of persons under law, and differences arising from the diversity of vocational competencies.

72. Levy, *Jefferson and Civil Liberties*, 155.
73. John C. Miller, *The Wolf by the Ears: Thomas Jefferson and Slavery*, 158ff.

chapter 12

Industrialization and
Its Liberal Interpretation

The Spirit of the Age

When Parliament sanctioned the Reform Bill (1832) that modestly expanded the electorate, it added to the many advantages that seemed to place the British people among time's fortunate few. From external threats there was little to fear. The Treaty of Vienna continued to enjoy the confidence of the great powers, and Britain's navy of 1,100 ships assured its mastery of the seas. A merchant fleet of 2.4 million tons' burden carried annual exports worth about £34 million, and imports of even higher value to and from every continent. Since 1790 the economy had averaged an annual growth of 2.6 percent, largely because Britain's agriculture and manufactures were the pacesetters of productive efficiency.[1]

Effects of the new economy of growth and technological innovation were everywhere discernible. Gas streetlights, paving, sewerage, and public health measures improved the quality of urban life. Train rides and balloon flights added new dimensions to recreation, already much diversified by a great variety of reading matter and other familiar forms of enjoyment. Wages rose at the same time that the length of the workday contracted. A cotton spinner in Birmingham earned £2.6s. per week; skilled laborers in the engineering and metallurgy industries brought home twice that amount. The demand for British labor throughout

1. Walter G. Hoffman, *British Industry, 1700–1950*, 50–51.

Europe was so strong that a working man might earn £400 per year by taking a supervisory position abroad. The opportunities for entrepreneurship seemed bounded only by imagination; some political economists even projected indefinite progress and expansion for the industrial economy.

The professions too were expanding. British science had unobtrusively undergone professionalization. Chemists, geologists, civil and mechanical engineers were integrated into the high-technology manufacture that was now the wonder of the age. When the British Association for the Advancement of Science was founded in 1834, it drew 200 members from Manchester alone. While aspiring scientists still could not enroll in an equivalent of the École polytechnique, the founding of the University of London (1826) and the growth of a variety of teaching institutions in the Midlands and Scotland placed them more favorably than a few decades earlier.

These and like indices might induce us to anticipate that public life would be imbued with a corresponding sensibility: a sense of exaltation in the discovery of human powers and exhilaration in their exercise; a sense that the prospect of unlimited productive increase rendered all previous class societies obsolete; a sense of delight in the boundless possibilities opened by the maturation of polytechnic intelligence. This sensibility was indeed abroad in England as elsewhere. It had achieved the status of public doctrine, pregnant with policy implications. The doctrine was celebrated on suitable occasions, as when the prime minister, manufacturers, and scientists assembled in 1819 to unveil a memorial to James Watt. On that occasion, Lord Jeffery, editor of the *Edinburgh Review*, declared:

> [The steam engine] has increased indefinitely the mass of human comforts and enjoyments, and rendered cheap and accessible, all over the world, the materials of wealth and prosperity. It has armed the feeble hand of man, . . . with a power to which no limits can be assigned; completed the domination of the mind over the most refractory qualities of matter; and laid a sure foundation for all those future miracles of mechanic power which are to aid and reward the labours of after generations.[2]

While this sensibility prevailed in the century of liberalism's dominance, there was opposed to it a quite different spirit. Two of England's most widely read authors, William Cobbett and Thomas Carlyle, as-

2. Quoted by D. F. J. Arago, *Historical Eloge of James Watt*, 176–77.

sailed the new industrial order, claiming that manufacture and commerce despoiled the nation and ruined its people. Laissez-faire, competition, foreign trade, wage labor, the pursuit of wealth, the factory system, and economic growth were all pronounced monsters begotten by grasping Whig lords. The Owenite movement concurred in most of these sentiments, but heralded the advance to a new rational society where the shackles of marriage, religion, and competition would be replaced by cooperation and free love. The combined voices of Tories, Owenites, and Chartists made it seem that the workingman, far from enjoying unexampled prosperity, lived from day to day in the margins of life whose quality steadily deteriorated. The Whigs, competing with the Tories for popular favor, aspired to lead the campaign for electoral reform and lashed out at monopolies, restrictive legislation, and the selfish indolence of the landed interest. Benthamites demanded that the old system of patronage be replaced by a professional civil service and urged the codification of laws. British science, to all appearances flourishing as never before, was nevertheless found to be dangerously decayed by the mathematician Charles Babbage. This was the beginning of a campaign for expansion of educational facilities—a campaign that was to assume harsh political overtones in pronouncements to the effect that "scientific knowledge is rapidly spreading *among all classes* except the higher, and the consequence must be, that that class *will not long remain* the higher."[3] These and like disputes so fragmented British politics that between 1815 and 1870, nineteen governments were formed and dissolved.

A diagnosis of these discontents appeared in 1831 under the title "The Spirit of the Age." It was written by the young John Stuart Mill for *The Examiner* as part of the campaign for the Reform Bill. Mill was then fresh from a sojourn in France, where he had met the Saint Simonians. His essay borrowed their description of the times as an "age of transition" from an old order that no longer enjoyed the allegiance or faith of the people to a new order as yet unestablished (*"The Spirit of the Age,"* 6). This in-between state, Mill claimed, was the central fact of the times. The old shibboleths and certainties clattered like hollow pots across the corrugated surfaces of public life, producing noise but no conviction. New and contrary doctrines arose, but they were at odds with one another as well as with the old; so again there was wanting a basis for consensus on a public philosophy. This unsettled state prompted in the public mind the common view "that the times are pregnant with change; and that the nineteenth century will be known to posterity as the era of one of the greatest revolutions of which history has preserved remem-

---

3. Quoted by Robert Kargon, *Science in Victorian Manchester,* 77.

brance, in the human mind, and in the whole construction of human society" (2).

The revolutionary motion tended toward what Mill called the "natural state" of society. Society in its natural state imparts to institutions a sense of rightness, and to persons a sense of place and direction. In these circumstances, opinion assumes a gravity enabling men to act decisively. The crucial ingredient for the natural operation of society is that power and fitness for power coincide in the ruling classes. The ruling classes of Europe's old regime, the aristocracy and the clergy, had been once fit to rule because they knew how to impart authority to the institutions they dominated. But they gradually lost that fitness, as they also lost power and wealth to new men who did not know how to imbue with authority the power they acquired. This process of erosion and accumulation continued "until power, and fitness for power, have altogether ceased to correspond; and . . . this is one great cause . . . of the general dissatisfaction with the present order of society, and the unsettled state of political opinion" (44). The parvenus could not imbue their power with authority because they had achieved power by destroying the credibility of deference and tradition, the chief means used by the old regime to make its power authoritative; having destroyed these means, they had no new ones to set in their place (68).

The discontent and "intellectual anarchy" of the new age were consequences of this condition. There were no firm and settled convictions. All opinions were tentative, because tomorrow they might seem false. It was no help, Mill argued, to say that clamorous opinion was merely the surface agitation of a fundamental phenomenon—the replacement of ancient prejudices by enlightened knowledge. That public opinion had been improved by enlightenment, Mill conceded, but he insisted that it had not achieved a consensus, nor had it imparted certainty to action: "The grand achievement of the present age," he said acidly, "is the *diffusion* of superficial knowledge" (10). He welcomed the fact that many now discussed and judged of public questions. But the superficiality of enlightenment teased public opinion with the dazzle of imposture. The fruit of enlightenment was anarchy and humbug.

"The Spirit of the Age" promised a sequel discussing the new dispensation lying in the immediate future, but Mill abandoned that project. As a writing ostensibly favoring the Reform Bill, it is ambiguous to the point of indecision. The old regime, with its insignia of throne and altar, was repudiated; but Mill did not endorse the attenuated Whig alliance of workingmen with manufacturers. Thomas Carlyle's enthusiasm for the essay—on reading it he rejoiced that he had "found a new mystic"—suggests that its ballast is the Tory doctrine that the new era of free discussion and electoral politics could not (and should not) endure. Liberalism was a phase in the transition to some future version of the natural or organic society, which would integrate power with authority in a hierarchy of rank.

This of course is the opposite of the archliberal argument of *On Liberty* (1859), where Mill legitimated fragmented opinion as a check against majority tyranny exercised through consolidated public opinion. The unwritten sequel to "The Spirit of the Age" could only have been a prospectus for a Saint-Simonian organic society, i.e. socialism. It remained unwritten because the liberal voice in Mill rejected an essential assumption of socialism—that society, especially modern society, *can* have a single, moral goal ordering all institutions and beliefs around a hierarchy of values. Thus the young Mill's inability to settle on a firm view marked him as one of those sons of the age described in his essay. Yet the liberal in Mill soon after gained the upper hand and penned all his most important works. But the socialist in Mill did not expire; he merely retired to the drawing room to converse with Carlyle. Saint Simon and his disciple Comte always held a fascination for him, despite their bizarre sectarianism. In the last years of his life, John Stuart Mill, the scholarly and eloquent liberal, began that adaptation of liberal economics to socialist sentiment that was to prevail in the next century.

Tocqueville's *Democracy in America* (1834), which Mill praised as the authoritative study of modern democracy, framed the concept of transition in somewhat different terms. The old regime was the aristocratic monarchy; the new, democracy. France was stalled midway between these regimes, and was suffering the traumas of transitional men. Americans by contrast enjoyed robustness because they had made the leap to democracy—or nearly had, for Tocqueville did not forget slavery. Frenchmen suffered because they lost the advantages of aristocracy before they gained the advantages of democracy; their anarchy of opinion Tocqueville described in this way:

> The democracy of France, hampered in its course or abandoned to its lawless passions, has overthrown whatever crossed its path and has shaken all that it has not destroyed. Its empire has not been gradually introduced or peacefully established, but it has constantly advanced in the midst of disorders and the agitations of a conflict. In the heat of the struggle each partisan is hurried beyond the natural limits of his opinions by the doctrine and the excesses of his opponents, until he loses sight of the end of his exertions, and holds forth in a way which does not correspond to his real sentiments or secret instincts. Hence arises the strange confusion that

we are compelled to witness. I can recall nothing in history more worthy of sorrow and pity than the scenes which are passing before our eyes. It is as if the natural bond that unites the opinions of man to his tastes, and his actions to his principles, was now broken; the harmony that has always been observed between the feelings and the ideas of mankind appears to be dissolved and all the laws of moral analogy to be abolished.[4]

Here is a piquant description of the much discussed nineteenth-century "alienation." The vast accession of new ideas around 1800 would have embarrassed many minds in the best of circumstances; but among the new ideas were revolutionary doctrines that, hurling down the old regime, unhinged all ideas from their natural setting in custom and institutions. Charged emotions and big ideas became free-floating compounds that might combine, contrary to the instincts of those who mouthed them, into bizarre silliness, as when we hear that marriage is prostitution and that property is theft. The tensions of this transitional age exercised a cruel dominion over some who approached them too closely, or insufficiently prepared. Saint Simon was at once imperious and suicidal. Comte, Herbert Spencer, Nietzsche, and Weber suffered from depressive psychosis. Mill recovered from his early depression only to withdraw again into a recluse existence. Marx, also recluse, was subject to fits of rage. Robert Owen required his followers to believe that he was the only sane man living, while Hegel delivered his "absolute knowledge" in language most obscure. We do not find, in the nineteenth century, many intellectuals who combined equanimity with breadth of vision and penetration into the human predicament. This proneness to imbalance and eccentricity was not confined to intellectuals, however. By 1880, the newly arisen clinical neurology surveyed what seemed an epidemic of hysteria, schizophrenia, depression, degeneration, and suicide. Talk of the sick psyche and of cultural decadence became fashionable; Nietzsche and Freud parlayed those perceptions into a new style of psychological analysis.[5]

4. Tocqueville, *Democracy in America*, lxxviii.
5. Historians commonly make no attempt to integrate the known facts of subjects' mental illness with studies of their thought—no doubt for the good reason that hitherto methods have been wanting. As a result, the high incidence of depressive neurosis among nineteenth-century writers on politics has not been noticed. I have attempted to bring the refractory domain of "psychohistory" under the discipline of method in two essays, "Pascal's Syndrome: Positivism as a Symptom of Depression and Mania" and *A Method for the Analysis of Neurotic Political Thought*.

Important as they were, the tensions between the old and new orders, and between liberalism and socialism, convey no adequate sense of what was unquestionably the fundamental novelty of the nineteenth century: the transition to high-energy civilization sustained by polytechnic rationality, institutionalized mainly in manufactures. The capacity to convert water, coal, and petroleum into any required amount of power, and to any desired motion, was more than an improvement in productive technology. It inaugurated a new stage in the development of civilization from its beginnings in primitive pasturage and agriculture about 10,000 B.P. The previous stages had all been irreversible in the sense that their capacity to support progressively larger populations had compelled, on pain of distress and starvation, the continuation of productive technologies once they were applied. This "law of progress" held equally for the new high-energy technology. But the character of the new technology altered all previous relationships between population levels, social organization, and productive technique. Owing to the combination of absolute numbers and increased rates of population growth, feedback between population levels and productive technologies operated on much shorter time scales than previously; accordingly, the deployment of new technologies over *very short times* became necessary to maintain the rapidly growing population.[6]

Prime examples of this feedback were the development of railroads that brought to market agricultural products greatly increased by the mechanization of agriculture, as is indicated by table 12.1.

During the 1815–41 period, the population of France increased from 29,380,000 to 35,630,000 (1850 census), or 14 percent. The substantial difference between population growth and wheat and potato production means that per capita consumption had increased by factors of 3 to 5. Evidently, then, a Malthusian population pressure against food supply was not driving these increases; it was, instead, the appetite for abundance ("the revolution of rising expectations").

We see, then, that whereas in previous ages the feedback between technological innovation and population growth involved a response interval too long to be discerned, from about 1700 the interval contracted to quarter-centuries and finally to decades or even less, despite large mi-

---

6. It is only within the last four decades that economists have begun to develop data and models for macroeconomic evolution; for a review, see Nathan Rosenberg, *Inside the Black Box: Technology and Economics*, chap. 1. The study of this critical component of recent history must eventually be integrated into an evolutionary scenario, an exemplar of which is sketched in the introduction of this work.

Table 12.1. Wheat and Potato Production in France, 1815–41

	1815–24 annual yield	Efficiency	1825–41 annual yield	Efficiency
Wheat	51,719,000[a]	10.78[b]	79,590,000	50%
Potatoes	28,755,000[a]	—	71,329,000	150%

a. Hectoliters.
b. Hectoliters production per hectare.
SOURCE: *Annuaire statistique* 25 (1905): 10, 32–33.

grations from Europe. This contraction entailed the expenditure of far more energy in equal times than previously; the "pace of life" increased from a leisurely walk to a jog. Efficient organization of that energy expenditure required time-tabling production according to schedules of machines. This circumstance was the backbone of the factory system, and its consequences imposed time-and-money measurements right through the social system. High-energy civilization was grounded upon mechanical organization of expansive, hyperactive, mobile, productive energies, human and inanimate. Work time and the workplace became sharply distinguished from leisure time.

So great a transformation was bound to provoke a range of negative responses; and those that came down to us are so charged with pathos and dismay that it is not easy to rid inquiry of their distorting influence. For example, the accusatory literature circa 1830 leaves the impression that factory masters had slammed virtually the entire "working class" into iron cages; yet factory laborers in Britain at that time numbered about 350,000, or 2.5 percent of the total population and 10 percent of the work force. By 1870, factory laborers numbered about 850,000, or 16 percent of the work force. (These ratios were comparable in other countries.) Had the factory workers of the world united, they would have found themselves a decided minority. The accusatory literature also leaves the impression that its *cri de cœur* expressed the feelings of workers, not the reporter-intellectuals. While in some cases this is so, inquiry must begin with documentation of what laborers thought, independent of commentary or embroidery by others who were not in the workplace. When this is done, it turns out that the workingman's notion of his condition had little in common with what intellectuals attributed to him. Not only did they not quail in terror at the factory door, they often sought out factory employment in preference to other forms of employment, particularly domestic service. Their actual complaints were very particular and were innocent of metaphysical distress and ideas of political apocalypse.[7]

The labor question in the nineteenth century is really two questions. On the one hand, we would see the growth of the labor movement, agitating for a larger share of wealth and political power, as the natural out-

7. This point has been emphasized by John Clarke in his study of William Cobbett, whose *Political Register,* selling 40,000 copies weekly, was popular among laborers. There is little evidence, for example, that workers felt dehumanized by machines, but abundant evidence that they enjoyed building and manipulating them. Machines were smashed but once during the course of England's industrialization, and that was by weavers who were being displaced. It is notable that the Luddites pointedly abstained from smashing machinery that did not reduce the number of their jobs. Clarke further observes that middle-class writers turned the fact that servant women preferred factory employment to domestic employment into the accusation that the factory system depraved their morals. The truth was that factory employment greatly increased their disposable income and reduced their supervision by employers. Many writers, including Friedrich Engels, were shocked by the independence that wage labor gave women, and even more by the role reversals stemming from the phenomenon of the employed wife and unemployed husband. See Clarke, *The Price of Progress,* 123–29, 136.

Historians of labor sometimes fleetingly suggest that working-class opinions and middle-class representations of these opinions are to be distinguished. There is an instructive example in Harold Perkin's *The Origins of Modern English Society,* where he summarizes "the working-class ideal." Observing that the sources he cites for the ideal were authored by nonlaboring intellectuals and publicists, he assures readers that "this is not to say that this motley collection of 'social cranks' invented the ideal and foisted it on the working class. At best they formulated it in striking form and 'spoke to their condition'" (235). There are two ways to show that what is supposed not to have happened assuredly did happen. One is to trace the origin of what Perkin identifies as the elements of the ideal. For example, that key doctrine, the labor theory of value interpreted in a way that denies the productive value of entrepreneurship and investment, was authored by François Quesnay and seconded by Adam Smith. Subsequent claims to the "whole fruit of labor" stem from these sources. Again, the ideal of cooperation, to the exclusion of competition, is a perennial notion independent of class or historical time. The second source of evidence is a direct examination of surviving records of working-class opinion, which show traces of the working-class ideal together with traces of the entrepreneurial ideal; affirmation of the aristocratic ideal together with its cynical denial; strong doses of Anglican and evangelical piety together with their denial. Examination of the opinions of any other class during a period of social change would probably reveal a similar fragmentation. It is a telling point about origins that while 75 percent of factory

come of the creation of a wage-labor interest group. That is the nub of the matter. Then there are the intellectuals who inflated this ordinary competition into cosmic dramas whose outcomes would decide the cultural fate of mankind. Since those cosmic scenarios were not composed by worker-intellectuals, the anxieties they projected upon the working class are best read as displacement of the anxieties of leisured intellectuals. What were these anxieties? Our main clue will be "Tory socialism," or the interesting fact that there was a conservative revolt against the new mechanical civilization animated by a pathos quite as cosmic as may be found on the Left. These kindred spirits inveighed against many of the same iniquities, and in similar language. Their disciples may be pardoned if they sometimes lost sight of the boundaries chalked between Left and Right. Who could tell from which side of the line this thunderbolt was hurled?

> If men had lost belief in a God, their only resource against a blind No-God, of Necessity and Mechanism, that held them like a hideous World Steam-engine, like a hideous Phalaris' Bull, imprisoned in its own iron belly, would be, with or without hope,—*revolt*. They could . . . by a "simultaneous act of suicide," *depart* out of the World Steam-engine; and end, if not in victory, yet in invincibility, and unsubduable protest that such World Steam-engine was a failure and a stupidity.[8]

This swelling accusation resonates in the writings of Saint Simon, Proudhon, Comte, Marx, Tolstoi, Dostoevski, Nietzsche, Tönnies, Weber.[9] It was authored by Thomas Carlyle in his impassioned defense of England's first working-class combination, Chartism, whose goal was universal suffrage. Carlyle's essay eloquently damned the main items on the liberal agenda, among them the parliamentary democracy that the Chartists sought. Carlyle was a Tory socialist, but his contempt of parliamentary democracy was shared by many on the Left. He never set foot in a factory, and the steam engine was for him a metaphor signifying the new polytechnic mechanics, whose sudden rise challenged the

---

labor during the initial phase of the Industrial Revolution were women and children, what publicists of the time established as the working-class view does not reflect the specific interests of women and children. For working-class opinion, see J. Burnett, D. Vincent, and D. Mayall, eds., *The Autobiography of the Working Class;* J. Burnett, ed., *Useful Toil: Autobiographies of Working People from the 1820s to the 1920s.*

8. Thomas Carlyle, *Works,* 4: 62.

9. See above, n. 5.

cultural dominance of philosophers and literary men. This suggests that doctrinal socialism was the new expression of the ancients' struggle against the moderns, of Country against Court, of literary politics against political science and economics.[10]

Political Economy and Market Value

Political economy was the touchstone of nineteenth-century liberalism. This "science," as it was called, described the production and distribution of wealth and explained why a clear view of these processes was the presupposition of enlightened politics. The centrality of economy to politics had been a key insight since the principles of political science were laid down in *The Interest of Holland* and *Leviathan*. But economics could not move to front position, as it did in the nineteenth century, until certain conditions were satisfied. One of these was the maturation of economics. We need only compare physiocratic errors with the amplitude of *The Wealth of Nations* to appreciate the watershed that Smith's work represented. He placed a vast array of activities and data under descriptive concepts and principles. If he did not transform antecedent theories into science, he did establish economics as a distinct field directed to a well-defined subject matter.

We previously mentioned that the breakthrough to new productive technologies falsified some basic suppositions of Smith's model of pre-industrial, commercial economics. Economists writing under his immediate influence, notably Bentham, Ricardo, Malthus, and Sismondi, did not perceive this fact; but Jean-Baptiste Say did, perhaps because the physiocratic legacy he combated in France incorporated extreme forms of Smith's errors.[11] Say published his new principles in his *Treatise on Political Economy* in 1803, but it was not until the "general glut" controversy of 1819 that classical economists were obliged to grapple with the new industrial economics. Say viewed gluts not as overproduction, but as a disequilibrium created by underproduction; and this he argued from an axiom that came to be known as Say's Law—that supply generates demand. Say clearly had struck at the heart of classical economics, where it is axiomatic that supply follows demand. After fifteen years of

---

10. This point is discussed below, 542–55.
11. But as Elie Halévy observes, physiocracy also incorporated a concept of deductive rigor missing in *The Wealth of Nations*. He argues that the element of rigor introduced into classical economics by Say was decisive for the development of economics from Ricardo onward. For Halévy's penetrating comments on Say's relation to Smith, Malthus, and Ricardo, see his *Growth of Philosophic Radicalism*, 268–82.

debate, Say's Law triumphed and classical economics underwent a conceptual revision that brought it more in line with the industrial economy. The only notable economist of the nineteenth century to repudiate Say's Law was Marx; otherwise, renovated classical economics was supreme in the business community as well as the government. However, it did begin to unravel in the hands of Alfred Marshall, and it was overturned by John Maynard Keynes as he sought strategies for recovery from the Depression. Keynes restored Smith's orientation on the market, and therefore on demand and credit; "supply," he once remarked, "can take care of itself." Under the new dispensation, there was no way to articulate what had been the fundamental phenomenon of the nineteenth-century economy—exponential growth. Growth was placed in a black box marked "supply," which agreeably churned out commodities in response to demand. But to Say, the items in the box—technological innovation, entrepreneurship, and the organization of labor— were the distinctive features of the modern economy.[12]

The worldwide glut of 1818–19 was diagnosed in various ways by classical economists. Sismondi believed that mankind had begun to produce in excess of its wants. Malthus, a great worrier even in boom years, trotted out the maxims of gloom. He detected an "indisposition to consume," meaning that savings withdrawn from commodity purchases had created the glut. If these savings were not being hoarded, then they were invested as capital for production or for commercial enterprise. On either alternative the glut must intensify. Thus, the capital surplus dilemma that Smith had written into his forecast of the decline phase of commercial capitalism had been reached, Malthus believed, by 1818! Fearful that "this stagnation must throw the rising generation out of employment," Malthus thought it needful to stimulate artificial wants for luxuries in order to revive the market.[13]

For Say, all this was fanciful. While particular markets might be saturated temporarily, neither European nor overseas markets were anywhere near saturation; and to speak of a *general* glut stemming from supply in excess of wants was nonsense. Human wants are boundless and therefore potential demand is also boundless; consequently, there can be no surplus of capital, and there will scarcely be surpluses of any commodity, given a world market.[14]

The prospect of unlimited markets servicing man's boundless capacity

---

12. Rosenberg, *Inside the Black Box;* Hiram Caton, "The Preindustrial Economics of Adam Smith."
13. Say, *Letters to Thomas Robert Malthus,* 32ff.
14. Ibid., 27. Say assumes the frictionless movement of goods and services, which of course is contrary to fact.

to consume replaced the gloom of classical economics by the rosy prospect of unlimited growth. But wants are bounded by consumer purchasing power; and this Say defined not as a monetary resource (as it was for Smith and Keynes), but as a deficiency of production. If merchants cannot sell their worsted in Boston nor their calico in Brazil, it is because consumers there have not produced goods with which to purchase these commodities (*Letters to Malthus*, 28–29). For produce, including specie or money, is always purchased by other produce; and one cannot buy to greater value than one has produced. Production, then, not trade or capital or credit, is the key to wealth.

Having laid down this axiom, Say began to pick the bones of classical economics. "The doctrine of production," he declared, "Smith has neither understood, nor entirely described" (22). Smith interpreted profit as interest on investment capital, but this fails to differentiate wages paid to risk from wages paid to entrepreneurship and management. Smith believed that profits are the only source of capital, whereas for Say profits are merely money purchased with goods derived from human productive powers, which are the real "revenue of mankind" (16). Smith taught that declining price must be at the expense of profits, which had been falsified already when *The Wealth of Nations* was published. Four decades later Malthus still clung to this idea despite continuous price declines for every commodity produced by machines. Ricardo and Sismondi, for their part, feared that machines would generate unemployment despite the stupendous growth of industrial employment.[15] Irritated by these obsolete anxieties, Say protested that

> The perfection of our tools, Sir, is connected with the perfection of our species. It is that which makes the difference which is observable between us and the savages of the South Seas, who have axes of flint and sewing needles of fish bones. It is no longer admissible, for any one who writes upon political economy to endeavor to circumscribe the introduction of the means which chance or genius may put into our hands, with a view to preserving more work to our laborers; such a one would expose himself to have all his own arguments made use of to prove to him that we ought (retrograding instead of advancing in the career of civilization) successively to renounce all the discoveries we have already made, and to render our arts more imperfect in order to multiply our labor by diminishing our enjoyments. (*Letters*, 59)

15. Say himself held this view in his *Treatise on Political Economy* (see bk. 1, chap. 8), but abandoned it as the record came in.

This sharp rebuke was probably deserved. Here were healthy adult males, purporting to be economists, but unable to comprehend the greatest revolution of productivity in human history. Say's reproaches were expanded about a decade later when Andrew Ure discarded as obsolete the principle that classical economists, following the master, believed to be the backbone of manufacture—the division of labor:

> The division, or rather the adaptation of labor to the different talents of men, is little thought of in factory employment. On the contrary, wherever a process requires peculiar dexterity and steadiness of hand, it is withdrawn as soon as possible from the cunning of the workman, who is prone to irregularities of many kinds, and it is placed in charge of a peculiar mechanism, so self-regulating, that a child may superintend it. . . . The principle of the factory system then is to substitute mechanical science for hand skill, and the partition of a process into its essential constituents, for the division or gradation of labor among artisans. On the handicraft plan, labor more or less skilled was usually the most expensive element of production—*Materiem superabat opus;* but on the automatic plan, skilled labor gets progressively superceded, and will, eventually, be replaced by mere overlookers of machines.[16]

Machines do not divide labor, they consolidate it. In 1770, a single spinner spun one thread at a time, but in a Manchester mill in 1830 she could superintend the spinning of about 2,000. This was done with little exertion because the force to drive the machine was supplied by a steam engine.

Smith and his disciples also did not understand labor, for they conceived it as the exertion of mere animal energy (*Letters,* 25). If this were a correct reading, workers who exert the greatest energy ought to receive the highest wages, whereas skilled labor generally commands the highest wages, owing to its investment in skill and its relative scarcity. For Say, labor was any application of the powers of mind or body that creates values; he called it "productive service" (*industrie*) to indicate

16. Andrew Ure, *The Philosophy of Manufactures,* 19–20. Ure said that the division of labor was a "scholastic dogma exploded by enlightened manufacture" (23–24). That Ure's observation was not obvious to everyone may be seen in Charles Babbage's *On the Economy of Machines and Manufacture* (1832), where Smith's view that machines are based on the division-of-labor principle is repeated (211–15). Nevertheless, Babbage had a firm grip on the relationship between output and power, and this fact made most of his analysis pertinent.

this broad signification (*Treatise*, bk. 1, chap. 8). The labor or productive service that creates values is itself valuable. Generally speaking, it is the source of *all* revenue; but any particular labor is valuable in proportion as it multiplies equal output in equal times (*Letters*, 16, 26). Production is constrained by the laws of nature, and "it is by obeying nature," said Say, quoting Bacon, "that we learn to command it." The fundamental law of all human production is the conservation principle, according to which matter is neither created nor destroyed in any natural process; human production merely rearranges or transforms materials (68ff.). What human art adds in production is therefore "immaterial"—it endows the product with *value*. Such values are wealth, Say maintained, against Ricardo; and knowing the conditions of the production of wealth, political economy arrives at its "greatest discovery," that "everything may be converted to wealth" (69). The most valuable labor is the work of minds discovering the many ways to convert "everything" into wealth, and applying that knowledge: it is the work of entrepreneurs, engineers, inventors, scientists.[17]

By understanding industrial production as the labor of polytechnic skill, Say dispelled the mystery surrounding industrial economy. Classi-

17. Say, *Letters to Malthus*, 71–74. This argument has been little noticed by economic historians. Joseph Schumpeter supposed that Say's notions concern entrepreneurship only, and that they were borrowed from Chantillon! In a recent study of Say, Thomas Sowell promptly reduces Say's critique of classical economics to a market formulation, and therefore overlooks Say's criticism of key classical assumptions. It is curious that a study focusing sharply on the general glut controversy should ignore Say's contribution to that debate (the *Letters to Malthus*), to concentrate instead on the *Treatise*, which was written fifteen years earlier (Sowell, *Say's Law: An Historical Analysis*, 12–20). Michael James contracts Say's argument about the productivity of entrepreneurship and technical skill to an argument for creating a new budget line, which argument he declares to be "disappointingly obscure and unconvincing" ("Pierre-Louis Roederer, Jean-Baptiste Say, and the Concept of *Industrie*," 469). This is further testimony to the tendency of market-oriented economics to obliterate recognition of production mechanisms. Say's grasp of industrial economics is probably due to the work and writings of Jean-Antoine Chaptal, an industrial chemist who was minister of interior from 1800 to 1804. Chaptal's *Essai sur le perfectionnement des arts chimique en France* (1800) presents a lucid description of the productive power of technology. This work was highly regarded throughout Europe. Chaptal's *L'industrie française* (1819) covers commerce, agriculture, industry, and industrial administration. When Lujo Brentano discovered Chaptal around 1900, he thought that he had made a major historical find; but I have located no other economic historian who mentions him.

cal economics had no means of interpreting the unprecedented behavior of the industrial market. The price of labor increased simultaneously with a commodity price decline. Smith's formula for price is

$$\text{Rent} + \text{Wages} + \text{Profit} = \text{Price},$$

where profit is interpreted as the reward of investment capital.[18] Price declines could therefore only cut away at profit (assuming wages at subsistence). Yet profits increased. In addition to this enigma there was the puzzle that the more labor was eliminated by machines, the larger the industrial work force became. The enigmas disappear the moment intelligence is conceded its role in production. The whole secret of the industrial economy, Say repeatedly emphasized in this debate, is volume production at falling costs per unit produced. Mechanical ingenuity and managerial expertise contrive the "impossible" feat of increasing profit by reducing price.[19]

18. *Wealth of Nations,* ed. Campbell and Skinner, I, ix, m, 1–7; I, ix, o, I. Smith's assessment of costs in manufacture was remote from the facts. Building capitalization and maintenance, depreciation, purchasing, marketing, transportation, personnel servicing, accounting, and management salaries are all aggregated under "rent" and "wage." This aggregation is the budget line expression of his insistence that profits were regulated by the value of stock employed and bore "no proportion to the quantity, the hardship or the ingenuity of this supposed labor of inspection and direction." In other words, the "supposed" labor of management and entrepreneurship is no labor at all; consequently, profit is the wages of investment only. This spectacular omission is the ultimate target of Say's attack. It is probably connected with Smith's prejudices against merchants, inventors, and entrepreneurs, whom he denounced as cheats and scoundrels (on this "problem," see A. W. Coats, "Adam Smith and the Mercantile System"). This is not very far from the belief that the hard work of laborers, to the exclusion of mechanics, foremen, etc., is alone productive. This belief was argued by a number of self-designated Smithian political economists, e.g. Thomas Hodgskin, Patrick Colquhoun, and indeed Ricardo and Malthus. See Perkin, *Origins of Modern English Society,* 233–34.

19. Say, *Letters to Malthus,* 53, 57, 61, 64. Among the economists who partially or inconsistently assimilated Say's correction of classical economics was Thomas Hodgskin, whose *Popular Political Economy* (1827) devotes a chapter to the subject of the productive value of polytechnic intelligence. To illustrate Say's point, he gives the following statistics. The total (stationary and marine) horsepower of Great Britain was 320,000, equivalent to the labor of 2,240,000 men. The work performed by 350,000 industrial workers was equivalent to 53 million men working without engines. The annual "savings"

Machine production, Say believed, made market price the sovereign arbiter of values. Smith had distinguished use value from exchange value, and market value from natural value, but Say discarded these distinctions as baseless.[20] The value of productive service and commodities is their exchange value at current price, and nothing else. The market derives its authority from price competition, in which the largest rewards go to entrepreneurs who discover technical means of reducing production costs. A preindustrial, commercial economy cannot experience more than sporadic price competition because production costs and sales volume are inelastic. Such economies invariably develop restraints on competition (monopolies, guilds, grain laws, duties) to maintain price at levels acceptable to the social requirements and technological proficiencies of interested groups. Only an industrial economy provides a steady and uniform incentive to increase profits by price competition. Only there do the doctrines of free trade and open markets make economic sense.

Say's exuberant discovery that "*everything* may be converted to wealth" means that everything is marketable, including especially human talents. Here Say's political economy links with the anthropology of Hamilton's *Report on Manufactures*. Not merely restraints on trade, but restraints on the exercise of human productive talents must be removed so that they may be brought to the market, where their values are determined. Clearly the market must place the highest value on managerial, financial, marketing, and technological skills.

The development of a robust market in skills culminated the transvaluation of values whose opening shots were fired in *The New Organon*, *The Discourse on Method*, and *Leviathan*. There religious and literary talents were deprecated at the expense of "reason." That value judgment now found objectification in the great power of the market, which raised new men from factory floors into social competition with the fading old regime. Literary men who contemplated the new hierarchy of market values found little encouragement—a point that Say made when he wondered what might be the value of clergymen if they lost their state subsidies.

---

on the wage bill by using machines was £700 million. The productive capacity of Great Britain was four times that of all other continents combined (Europe excepted), and 2,500 times the productive capacity of ancient Egypt.

20. Ibid., 71. This follows, of course, from rejection of the labor theory of value, where labor is understood to be animal energy, whose subsistence is calculated as the base line for cost and for use value.

Certainly a far-reaching transvaluation of values was in the making. Preindustrial societies rewarded religious and literary skills with high prestige, if not with high wages. Their wages were paid by institutions dependent on prestige, the court and the Church. In the new democratic industrial order, prestige was devalued and tended to flow to the men who "proved their worth" by accumulating fortunes. We have seen that the rise of finance capital, its new men and new values, inflicted great distress on the literary-landed intelligentsia.[21] Now came the manufacturers, with their notion that market value objectively measured a man's worth as a wealth-producer. Here the progeny of Baconian philosophy ran hard on the literary intelligentsia. The reaction was violent. They unleashed a jeremiad whose vehemence has scarcely an equal. In the struggle that followed, they abominated "the demon that smokes and thunders" and vilified the new men as hangmen of the human race, whose greed drove them to the foulest crimes.

This violent accusatory legend organizes nineteenth-century history as the martyrdom of labor to capital. Its opposing legend valorized the new men as giants of industry, who raised themselves and the common man from wretchedness by creating abundance; as heroes of invention, who transformed the world with new sights, sounds, and comforts; as the masters of nature, whose magical dexterity placed in human hands powers too great for the imagination to comprehend. These two legends rooted themselves in the mind as a manic-depressive fantasy. Nowhere is their effect on historiography more apparent than in the discord about the character and effect of the factory system.

The Factory System

The men who founded British industry were a mixture of ancient families and new men. Mining and canal building had long been the favored activities of entrepreneurial aristocrats because of their association with land ownership. During the eighteenth century, these high-technology industries brought peers into business association with engineers and other technicians. Late in the eighteenth century, a few entrepreneurial peers branched into iron foundries from mining interests. But that unique method of mass production, the factory system, was the creation of new men alone.[22] Once it was established, aristocrats took little interest in acquiring firms or beginning their own. The new men thus main-

---

21. See above, 298–312.
22. P. L. Payne, *British Entrepreneurship in the Nineteenth Century*, 24ff.

tained their dominance of this economic sector throughout the period of its growth and greatest financial success.

The invention of the factory system is traditionally attributed to Richard Arkwright, who devised a new organization of labor around the operating requirements of the water-frame spinning machine. The growth of the textile industry under this system set off a chain reaction in the renovation of old industries and the creation of new ones, so that by 1835 British industry had acquired the essential features of the modern industrial complex. The crucial growth symbiosis, in the early phase, was between factories and steam engines. Profits accruing from textile sales were sufficient to support the development costs of metallurgy and machine tool industries required by the high-pressure steam engine. The capacity of the latter industry to fabricate to exact specifications made possible the economy of interchangeable parts. Coal to drive the engines and efficient transport to move heavy burdens gave enormous impetus to mining and transportation. One outcome of the interplay between these industries was railroads, whose construction required financing on a new scale of magnitude. Between 1820 and 1850, £240 million were invested in this new mode of transportation. Numerous service industries grew up to accommodate new requirements. Industrial architecture became a distinct field of engineering. Industrial chemistry, which from its early days had embraced processes as remote as fermentation and oxidization, now included product creation and pollution control. The manufacture of prime movers and associated equipment for the transfer of power from engines to machines demanded technicians conversant in the physics of heat, gearing, and materials.

This was the economic base that generated Britain's polytechnic intelligentsia and their institutions. The research and development departments of industrial firms were the most important locus for the selection and education of these men until well into the century. But from the time of the founding of the Manchester Literary and Philosophical Society (1782), textile manufacturers recognized the need to establish a variety of institutes to provide the technical and commercial education required by the industrial economy. The Manchester men founded a mechanics institute to teach mathematics and engineering physics. The British Institution, established in 1800, supported a somewhat incoherent array of teaching and research activities. The University of London, the Statistical Society, the British Association for the Advancement of Science were all responses to this growth.

The new industrial elite stepped onto the political stage with an ideology styled "liberalism." Its dogmas were the teachings of political economy; its political program was Whig and, later, Liberal party reform politics; its social outlook was the prospect of continuous "improvement" and "amelioration" of the human condition based on the progress of science and industry.

Andrew Ure's *Philosophy of Manufactures* (1835) is a vigorous apology for that elite, of which he was a prominent member and a recognized spokesman. He was an industrial chemist, a technical writer on manufactures, a publicist, and a scientist on the staff of the British Institution.[23] His firsthand acquaintance with factories and personnel equipped him to compose this defense, which he subtitled *An Exposition of the Scientific, Moral, and Commercial Economy of the Factory System*. It would be difficult to find an apologetic work whose author's private interest coincided more exactly with the system defended. That coincidence was no embarrassment to Ure; for the basis of interest politics was the consistency of competing interests within the horizon of political economy; and Ure meant to show that the prosperity of British industry, then under heavy political attack from a combination of Tories, socialists, and workingmen, was the engine for the improvement of all Englishmen and indeed all mankind. Industrial production, he maintained, was the greatest instrument of "philanthropy" ever placed in the hands of man.

The spiritedness of Ure's rebuttal to the Tory-socialist accusations made him notorious in those circles, and the odium eventually took the man and his book out of circulation in the marketplaces of ideas. This bias has not been notably rectified by social historians, who tend to neglect the entrepreneurial ideology, or to assume that it is adequately covered as liberal politics and political economy.[24] But from Ure's point

23. After taking his M.D., Ure's first appointment was to the chair of chemistry in the Andersonian College, Glasgow (1804). He subsequently conducted significant laboratory studies on the specific gravity of sulfuric acid, and on electro-physiology. He became an associate of the British Institution in 1820 and was elected a fellow of the Royal Society in 1822. His major publications were *Dictionary of Chemistry* (1821), *The Cotton Manufactures of Great Britain* (1836), and the two-volume *Dictionary of Arts, Manufactures and Mining* (1839), which went through many editions. He died in 1857.

24. The identification and partial correction of this bias is the theme of Frederick Hayek's edited volume *Capitalism and the Historians*. One historian who did not forget Ure is E. P. Thompson, who preserves him in the satanic majesty bestowed upon him by the original conservative critics. But Thompson, who has also imbibed the Weber historiography, promptly

of view, liberals such as Gladstone and J. S. Mill were half-conservative, since they conceded that the factory system was a moral burden at best and a great iniquity prior to successive legislative and civic reforms. This was not the point of view of the manufacturing interests, which maintained that the factory system, including the factory as a workplace, had been a boon to workers from its inception, not only by improving their material circumstances but also by improving them morally. The factory system, in a word, was not only a great productive instrument; it was also a great humanitarian instrument.

Ure's defense of the factory system required a description of what it was. He was at pains to show that it was something completely new. Its basis was a union of laborer and machine made possible by a new kind of machine that he styled "self-acting" and "automatic." Such machines had an unusual property: although they consisted of inanimate materials arranged according to mechanical laws, the effect was like the action of an animal. The thousands of parts of automatic machines were so many "organs and members . . . infusing into forms of wood, iron, and brass an intelligent agency" (*Philosophy of Manufactures*, 2). Mechanicians had discovered "innumerable means" to "give to portions of inert matter precise movements resembling those of organized beings." Ure's animal analogy was the device commonly used to express a concept known today as the servomechanism, which enables machines to change their own states by information feedback from effects they produce. The steam engine governor, invented by Watt, was the first true servomechanism. Numerous servomechanisms were subsequently introduced on the bobbin and fly frame, the throstle frame, the continuous carding machine, on power trains, and on automatic loading equipment. The technology of servomechanisms led in the twentieth century to automation. For Ure, it was, together with steam power, the distinguishing technological feature of factory production. Nevertheless, the machines were not completely automatic; they required human beings to tend them. Machines and their human superintendents made up the technological and human components of the factory system, which

> involves the idea of a vast automaton, comprised of various mechanical and intellectual organs, acting in uninterrupted concert

likens his Satan to the Puritan divine Richard Baxter, thereby suggesting a theological inversion of indistinct character (Thompson, *The Making of the English Working Class*, 359, 362).

for the production of a common object, all of them being subordinated to the self-regulated moving force [of the power plant]. (13)

On Ure's definition, the relation of workers to machines is not that of "operatives," as they were called. Workers do not steer or direct the machine in any way; nor do they set its pace. Their function is to superintend the operation of a machine that imperfect technology has not yet succeeded in automating. They are, in effect, living servomechanisms of the machines they tend. Their relation to the machine is therefore wholly different from the relation of the craftsman to his tools. Whereas the craftsman uses his tools to make an artifact, the factory system uses the human sensing capacity as the substitute for a mechanical servomechanism not yet invented. The worker is functionally a part of this "vast automaton." Perhaps now we begin to see why the factory system produced so great a trauma upon the imagination of the humanist intelligentsia.[25] In this, Homo sapiens's first intimate and extensive encounter with machines, the worker functions as the *organ of a machine,* as a "component of a mechanical system."

Ure maintained that the factory system altered the nature of work. Traditionally, unskilled labor consisted in the application of animal energy to some task; agricultural labor was largely of this description. But the factory worker's labor is light, because the machine receives its impulse from the prime mover. Skilled labor, on the other hand, traditionally combined some physical exertion with dexterous routines, as in weaving. But the principle of the factory system is to build skill into the machines so that it becomes unnecessary to rely on the "imperfections" and "irregularities" of the artisan. Work is de-skilled because hand skills cannot approach the perfection attained by machines:

25. E. P. Thompson's reaction to Ure illustrates the response. He does not examine Ure's technical analysis of the relation between machine and labor; instead he interprets these statements as a diabolic-Methodist-Calvinist theological metaphor for a guilt and salvation cycle; he attributes to Ure the view that "God's curse over Adam . . . provided irrefutable doctrinal support as to the blessedness of hard labour, poverty, and sorrow 'all the days of thy life'" (*The Making of the English Working Class,* 365). But Ure's express view on the curse is the exact opposite: the factory, he said, "in some measure . . . repeals the primeval curse on the labour of man" (*Philosophy of Manufactures,* 17). Contemporary reactions to Ure's book may be found in Phillip Gaskell's *Artisans and Machinery,* which devotes a chapter to refuting Ure's claims that the factory system was benevolent; and John Fielden's *The Curse of the Factory System,* which violently attacked Ure. Neither author noticed a theological underpinning to Ure's philosophy of work.

By the infirmity of human nature it happens, that the more skilled the workman, the more self-willed and intractable he is apt to become, and, of course, the less fit a component of a mechanical system, in which, by occasional irregularities, he may do great damage to the whole. The grand object therefore of the modern manufacturer is, through the union of capital and science, to reduce the task of his work-people to the exercise of vigilance and dexterity,—faculties which, when concentrated in one process, are speedily brought to perfection in the young. (*Philosophy of Manufactures*, 20–21)

From the experience of automation and robotics, we know that the process Ure described leads to the elimination even of this superintending role. He had grasped the trend himself: "It is, in fact, the constant aim and tendency of every improvement in machinery to supercede human labour *altogether* . . ." (231). In this process Ure could detect only benefits for workers, who are relieved of drudgery as well as the strain and exhaustion of repetitive but exacting routines of skilled labor. He celebrated this humane triumph of "scientific research and human ingenuity" as the beginning of the revocation of Adam's curse:

> If then this system be not merely an inevitable step in the social progression of the world, but the one which gives a commanding station and influence to the people who most resolutely take it, it does not become . . . a denizen of this favored land, to vilify the author of a benefaction, which, wisely administered, may become the best temporal gift of Providence to the poor,—a blessing destined to mitigate, and in some measure to repeal the primeval curse pronounced on the labour of man, "in the sweat of thy face shalt thou eat bread." (17)

This is Ure's answer to the accusation that machine production destroyed the crafts. The benefactor meant here is Richard Arkwright, whose home was besieged by cottage spinners alarmed that his waterframe spinning engine would put them out of work. This episode was subsequently repeated many times. The king-and-church rioters of Birmingham (1791) burned to the ground the home and laboratory of Joseph Priestley, the dissenting clergyman, "Jacobin," and industrial chemist who was closely associated with manufacturing establishments that were also attacked or menaced at that time. In France, the *sansculottes* demanded and got the abolition of the Académie des sciences, whose members had supported the law abolishing craft guilds as impediments upon industrial innovation. The Luddites of Nottingham, composed of technologically superseded weavers, destroyed machines to the value of £80,000 in two years of arson and looting. Here were craftsmen in arms against the "expropriation" of their skills by the polytechnic factory men.

Ure's response was that the ex-craftsmen had never had it so good. The fear of unemployment was baseless, for the spinners and weavers were taken on as factory hands. Instead of the 6s. per week that they earned as independent craftsmen, they now earned 26s. and more. Instead of working in cold, damp cottages or filthy hovels, they enjoyed the factory environment—the marvel of modern architecture, featuring fireproof, scientifically ventilated, gas-illuminated structures, more wholesome beyond compare than the cottage. On exhibiting these fair specimens of improvement, Ure declared triumphantly that "the constant aim and effect of scientific improvement in manufactures are philanthropic" (8).

But into every worker's paradise a little rain must fall, and Ure acknowledged that factory hands did chafe at the routine imposed by machine superintendence. The work discipline problem was well attested from many sources. Artisans who entered factories were accustomed to labor in their cottages at a fearful pace for three or four days at a stretch; then, collecting their earnings, they caroused, gamed, or slept for two or three days, when the cycle recommenced. This habit, common to both sexes, was cherished as something close to a birthright. Although they might have doubled their earnings by working a steady pace for six days a week and practicing sobriety, many preferred the old way. These habits were incompatible with the factory system, which required that the whole work force be in place when the morning whistle blew and remain there until the machines were quiet. Every factory had a long list of work rules meant to assure the presence of sober workers at their machines promptly at 5:30 A.M. The rules were enforced by fines, threats, or dismissal.[26] So much weight did Ure lay on this obstacle that he credited Arkwright with founding the factory system by overcoming it:

> It required . . . a man of Napoleonic nerve and ambition to subdue the refractory tempers of work-people accustomed to irregular paroxysms of diligence, and to urge on his multifarious and intricate constructions in the face of prejudice, passion, and envy. Such was Arkwright, who, suffering nothing to stay or turn aside his progress, arrived gloriously at this goal, and has for ever fixed his name to a great era in the annals of mankind—an era which has laid open

26. Fitton and Wadsworth, *The Strutts and the Arkwrights,* 232–42.

unbounded prospects of wealth and comfort to the industrious, however much they may have been occasionally clouded by ignorance and folly.[27]

Factory masters found a more elegant means than "Napoleonic nerve" to whip the work force into line: they maximized the employment of more docile females and youths. This system was perfected in the famous Lowell Mills at Waltham, Massachusetts, which employed exclusively women between the ages of sixteen and twenty-two. These mills were at the time touted as a model of the moral and political economy of the factory system. The young women were housed in prim dormitories, received instruction in domestic arts, and attended Sunday school without fail. At the age of exodus, each had accumulated a dowry, in some cases in excess of $1,000. Meanwhile management was content with a turnover that gave a fresh supply of able-bodied workers whose short tenure kept labor-management frictions within easy bounds. In Britain, this optimum was only approached. Out of a factory work force of 344,000 (in 1832), only 26 percent were males over eighteen. Females over eighteen comprised 30 percent, while males and females under eighteen made up the remaining 44 percent.[28] In addition to the management advantage of these ratios, there was the clear advantage on the account books, for females were paid at about half the rate paid to males.

Such discipline and employment practices illustrate what Ure called

27. Ure, *Philosophy of Manufactures*, 16. Fitton and Wadsworth's study of the Arkwright establishment does not sustain Ure's belief that Arkwright effected a dramatic transformation of management practice. The twelve-hour day and child labor had been standard practice in silk manufactories for a century, and this system was simply transferred to spinning cotton (Fitton and Wadsworth, *The Strutts and the Arkwrights*, 225ff.). S. D. Chapman's study *The Early Factory Masters* confirms Fitton and Wadsworth. The factory system was put into operation at the Derby silk mill around 1721. This mill, which was water-powered, employed 300 persons. Chapman denies that Arkwright was mechanically gifted; he merely put the finishing touches on the Wyatt-Paul jenny. Arkwright's genius was entrepreneurial drive (40–41, 62–77).

28. Ure, *Philosophy of Manufactures*, table, n.p. Ure's estimate is the highest given by various authorities. Edward Baines in his *History of Cotton Manufacture* gave the lowest estimate, 237,000; but the *Victoria County History for Lancashire* put the number of factory hands in that county alone at 218,000, of whom half were female and 13 percent were children under thirteen years of age. See Ursula Henriques, *The Early Factory Acts and Their Enforcement*, 3.

the "moral economy" of the factory system. Management attitudes toward the work force during the 1785–1830 period were predicated on two beliefs. One was that workers would tend to dissipate their earnings on leisure and drink unless prevented by factory discipline and Methodist preaching in Sunday schools. The second was that factory labor gave the poor their first opportunity ever to accumulate, or even to step up the social ladder by achievement in the workplace. These two beliefs combined in the preachment that sobriety and hard work were the means to escape misery. While this doctrine served the requirements of the factory system admirably, it came naturally to a class of men who had themselves lived austerely until success was secure. This observation suggests a distinction between the work discipline mandated by the nature of productive technology and the moral economy that displayed the benign results of austerity and perseverance. This "work ethic" was not an ideological smokescreen; in it the factory masters transmitted to workers the success formula they themselves had followed. Richard Arkwright is said to have worked sixteen hours a day after his fortune was secure; and in general, factory management was a high-stress, work-intensive vocation demanding men obsessed with their work.

This obsession with work, as the production of prodigious effects through technology, is central to the attitudes and outlook of the manufacturing leadership. Its popular expression was the "philosophy of self-help," an industrial variety of Ben Franklin's "way to wealth." Samuel Smiles's studies in industrial biography created for popular consumption a new manic icon—the heroic conquest of low birth and social stigma, of poverty and adversity, of ridicule and disbelief, by the demonic powers of polytechnic intelligence operating on nature to create machines. The myth-generating components of Smiles's biographies were not the fabrication or suppression of facts. On the contrary, the verisimilitude of his portraits of men who were still in the memories of the living was an ingredient essential to their persuasiveness. Their falseness stemmed from an error prompted by class consciousness. The low birth and mechanical occupations of the Watts and Maudsleys were touted by Smiles as vindications of the common man, certifying their power to improve their condition by self-reliance despite penalties and obstructions encountered in an aristocratic order. This solidarity between the common man and heroes of technology is the nerve of the myth; for the heroes were men of uncommon talents, whose performance could be imitated by very few. The error duplicated, in other words, the prejudice that birth determines class. Napoleon got it right when he recognized that the new men constituted a distinctive new elite of polytechnic talent that could perpetuate itself only through institutional recruitment.

Of course Smiles knew, as his many thousands of working-class readers knew, that it was not within every mother's son to become a Watt or Faraday. But between the Olympian heights and the low-lying plains were many degrees and stations of skilled labor to which lesser talents could help themselves. This chain of vocational rank established a more realistic picture of the solidarity in ambition between the highest and the lowest. It remains to this day the image of upward mobility essential to a classless but stratified, technologically advanced democracy. But in the period under investigation, two factors at least prevented its effective operation. One was the phenomenon called "the labor aristocracy," consisting of more highly paid skilled labor. Skilled labor had always distinguished its interests from those of semiskilled and unskilled labor and had used guild rules to prevent free entry into their trades. Guilds were no sooner abolished by law in Europe than they were replaced by unions, effective despite their illegality, which promptly reverted to the old practices.[29] Self-help alone, then, was not enough to rise.

The second impediment to working-class imitation of the factory masters was the paucity of avenues for accumulation. In this point there was a significant contrast between European nations and the new worlds of North America and Australia. There abundance of land put ownership within the reach of most. Three generations of immigrants worked in factories on the East Coast, saved, and moved west to farm or entered small business in the towns and cities. In this way many millions, working upon the "immense mass of improvable matter," assured their progress by homeownership and possession of durable goods. Indeed, homeownership by tradesmen was common in America from the earliest days. But the high cost of land and building materials prevented this avenue opening in Europe, certainly for factory labor. Workers in the 1830s and 1840s might easily save from family earnings that could top 50*s.* per week. But the savings possible were insufficient to invest in anything that would appreciate in value: they could not capitalize. Consequently they spent on consumer goods and alcohol. The impasse was in some manner mitigated by cooperative societies and savings societies. Cooperative societies were established initially not as investment propositions but to short-circuit the truck system (or company store). These retail outlets quickly became joint stock companies with very expansive trade. By 1850, co-ops were valued at £10 million.

29. Perkin, *Origins of Modern English Society,* 393ff.

Ure's discussion of labor-management relations registers management's attempt to reassert the solidarity of labor-management interest in the teeth of trade union arguments to the contrary. It is a mark of the maturity of British industry that the arguments and agenda on both sides had by 1835 taken the shape they were long to retain.

Unions, and particularly the strike ("call-out"), Ure represented as harmful to management and labor. Their common interest in avoiding that harm is the baseline of labor-management solidarity: "workers cannot prosper unless the mills do" (*Philosophy of Manufactures*, 363, 329). Strikes are severe for mills because overheads on equipment and capital continue although there is no income; because equipment deteriorates without maintenance; because markets are lost. Workers for their part lose wages that are never recovered by wage increases. Ure therefore denied that wage increases were the real reason for strikes, whatever workers might say. Nevertheless, he ran through management's list of wage arguments: manufacturing wage scales were high compared with other economic sectors and with overseas manufacturing wage rates; wages must be tied to productivity; the wages-to-productivity ratio was in fact advanced in labor's favor (281, 317, 320, 325). Similar arguments were brought out to rebut labor's claims to better working conditions and shorter hours. From 1810 to 1820, workers had opposed shorter hours, even when initiated by management, because it cut their earnings. But in the 1820s the idea arose that workers should be rewarded at the same rate for shorter hours. To Ure this was a most disastrous notion. It uncoupled wage increases from productivity and opened the door to a series of actions that would inflate the wage bill. As for working conditions, Ure claimed them as a strong card for management. Scientifically designed factories provided "salubrious" work environments, superior to the farm, and in another universe from the dangerous and toilsome work of mining.[30] In sum, unions and strikes are unnecessary because benevolent management will pass on benefits as soon as the firm can afford them.

In the context of 1835, all this had about it an air of unreality. The solidarity of interest and feeling between management and labor, of which Ure made so much, had indeed once existed in not a few textile firms, and the ideal was not dead even then. But the dominant industrial reality at that time was the adversary posture that labor and management had assumed. At every turn of his argument, management intran-

---

30. Original architectural drawings of scientifically designed factories that were built and used are reproduced by Jennifer Tann in her *The Development of the Factory;* see especially pp. 4, 38, 59.

sigence punctured the ideal of solidarity. Strikes, he said, are calamities, but he attributed them exclusively to the rashness of a few agitators. He did not observe that it takes two to make a strike; and if it is unprofitable for workers to go out, how much more unprofitable must it be for the firm? Why is it not good political economy to negotiate and save the costs, in money and good will, of strikes? Why not even introduce profit-sharing plans (as some firms did) to regularize the wage-bargaining process?

Ure thought in terms of strike-breaking rather than negotiation because his first priority was protection of management control of wages and working conditions. Wage bargaining was not consistent with his notion of management control. From this perspective he presented the management case against unions (still illegal then) and labor organizers. "Mutinous" attitudes among workers were fomented by the top wage earners, who had least cause for complaint. That their attitudes were not shared by the great majority of workers was proved by their criminal methods of organization. They used threats, beatings, and acid-throwing to prevent those willing to work from crossing the line. These conspirators were in an unholy alliance with Tory landed interests, who were jealous and afraid of the new men. Together they contrived a campaign of vilification against the factories and their owners (*Philosophy of Manufactures,* 290–91, 277, 287, 336, 434).Ure's statement of the management case is classic in the sense that it enunciated a position that industrialists were to hold for another century: Strikes are no proof of labor disaffection; they are caused by agitators who gain control of workers' behavior by using criminal means to intimidate them. Left to themselves, workers would stay on the job because it is in their interest to do so; accordingly, management resistance to union demands is no sign of intransigence or ill will toward employees. On the contrary, it is a public-spirited defense of the common good against tyrannical union leaders. This line may be styled the legend of wicked unions. While he did not invent it, Ure more than any other writer gave it currency. The legend did not explain the origin or reasons for the antagonism between labor and management. Rather, the legend was adopted as a weapon of struggle *after* the antagonism had hardened. It was used to counter another legend—the legend of wicked capitalism.

The Legend of Wicked Capitalism

The dead-end policy apparent in Ure's book faithfully replicated the incapacity of industrial management at that time to move off its posture of laissez-faire intransigence toward some sensible formula of industrial peace. Controversy over the Factory Acts of 1819 and 1832 had put management in a defensive posture; indeed the factory system had by that time acquired a certain infamy. The thirteen-hour day and child labor had taken shape as a public legend of cruelty and inhumanity. "Factory master" and "capitalist" were associated with the horrific image of children crucified on iron jennies in the name of progress and profits; of hussars martyring peaceful protesters on the commons of Peterloo. Such icons of suffering had uncoupled the new modes of production from benevolence and linked them with oppression, misery, and metaphysical distress. The legend of wicked capitalism had appeared, and it was destined to become historical orthodoxy.

Orthodoxy declares that the original manufacturing capitalists were motivated solely by the desire to make money, however energetic and gifted they may have been as organizers. The profit motive is construed as the original sin or tragic flaw of a hero whose gargantuan deeds cast a plague of oppression upon the earth.[31] The tragedy's sequel features a rally by the oppressed, comprised of workers assisted by intellectuals, who subdue the ravenous beast with the institutions of the welfare state; or, in another scenario, they slay the beast in an apocalyptic revolution. This is a fine story. Its persistence indicates that it serves a cluster of partisan functions and psychological needs. But it is a legend.

The facts, summarily stated, are these. The legend of wicked capitalism was the successor of the *original* legend of benevolent capitalism, which Ure continued to purvey. The latter expressed the ideology of the Midlands manufacturers circa 1780—the Baconian program of progress and enlightenment. The Lunar Society of Birmingham, the Manchester Literary and Philosophical Society, the Andersonian College of Edinburgh were their institutions; high-technology modes of production were their proud achievement. Whig in politics, Unitarian in religion, strongly sympathetic to the American and French revolutions, they fancied themselves to be the progressive vanguard, while Tories and Old Whigs like Burke despised and feared them as upstarts espousing dis-

31. The orthodoxy is put succinctly by Paul Mantoux: "Industrial entrepreneurs deserved admiration for their initiative and activity, their power of organization and their gift of leadership. But their one aim was money, men and things alike being only tools for the attainment of this single object. . . . The consciousness of power made them tyrannical, hard, and sometimes cruel: their passions and greed were those of upstarts" (*The Industrial Revolution*, 388). The nonsense is not that this is false; it lies in the implication that only one category of men were subject to a flaw observable in every social class and vocation.

ruptive leveling doctrines.[32] From 1810 to 1820, these former "Jacobins" took the name "Radicals," after Bentham's proposal for "radical reform" of Parliament.

The wicked capitalism legend had a prototype that is important to note because of the light it throws on the phenomenon of the Tory radical. It was the creation of the publicist William Cobbett, who from about 1800 to his death in 1835 regaled his large following with John Bull diatribes. His initial position was strong support for the Pitt ministry against the perils of Jacobins, nonconformity, Catholic emancipation, and new men. But he came to be the most vehement and colorful critic of the Pitt war policy because he was more British than the Court party. The source of his subsequent radicalism appears in the reasons for this opposition. Pitt's policy assumed the pattern familiar with mercantile nations. It meant to optimize the advantages of the fleet and of financial resources while minimizing the commitment of British land forces. When this strategy failed to subdue Napoleon, Cobbett blamed the reliance on money in preference to patriotism and discovered incompe-

32. Prominent among these men were the Strutts, the Oldknows, Davison and Hawksley, Robert Denison, Charles Morley, Henry Hollins, William Smith, Elihu Fellows, Samuel Unwin, John Bacon, the Churchhills, Major Cartwright, Coltman and Whetstone, all of whom were members of the High Pavement Unitarian Chapel (Chapman, *Early Factory Masters*, 196). Robert Schofield covers the policies of the very influential Lunar Society in *The Lunar Society of Birmingham*, 328–68. These two studies exhibit the popular and the aristocratic bias against these dissenters and innovators. A piquant expression of these biases appears in Mary Cartwright's memoir of her father, Edmund Cartwright, the clergyman whose invention of the power loom led him to a career in manufacturing and science: "Nor was Mr. Cartwright's new position in society altogether without its trials. By the upper class of the inhabitants of a provincial town, proud of their exemption from commerce and manufactures, his proceedings were viewed with no small degree of distrust. . . . he was considered as having deserted his *caste*. . . . With the poor of the place, however, his establishment was far from being equally unpopular. . . . his name is still venerated by the descendants of his ancient workmen. . . . at the time when he first commenced his mechanical career, there was a considerable class of persons, who, dreading the advance of every degree in society below themselves, deprecated the progress of machinery, as being the means of supplying the poor with indulgences heretofore confined to the rich, and consequently tending to raise them higher in the scale of refinement than was compatible with the due subordination of society" (*A Memoir of the Life, Writings, and Mechanical Inventions of Edmund Cartwright*, 84–86).

tence in the officer corps. Tom Paine's *The Decline and Fall of the English System of Finance* opened his eyes to the corruptions of "THE PITT SYS-TEM," which was of course the Walpole system and the Hamilton system; Cobbett thundered his denunciations in article series whose titles indicate their contents: "Stock-Jobbing Nation," "Paper Aristocracy," "Perish Commerce." Britain was to relinquish financially and morally ruinous foreign trade and revert to agrarian self-sufficiency. Advocating a return to pristine British virtue at a time when the Court party had long since accepted the commercial dispensation made Cobbett a radical Tory, that is, a man with a deep animus against the establishment, including its corrupted great families. It will be understood, then, that the invasion of the quiet countryside by manufacturing aroused Cobbett's intense loathing; and it was natural for him to join the antifactory contingent in Parliament on his election in 1828.[33]

But the legend of wicked capitalism originated in a completely different quarter—from a quarrel among manufacturers about labor policy. The quarrel began in 1816 when the Tory manufacturer Robert Peel introduced legislation to regulate child labor. Peel's bill raised the question whether management should develop a policy of industrial paternalism, or whether it should opt for market values in labor. Until then it was not clear that these alternatives were mutually exclusive. Nearly all manufacturers supported free trade in goods, while many practiced various degrees of paternalism in their establishments. Free schools, and a concern for the literacy of employees, were perhaps the best-known expression of that impulse. But the concept of the planned industrial community had put in its appearance around 1800. Robert Owen's model community at Lanark, Samuel Oldknow's establishment at Mellor, and the Gregs' innovative community at Styal were exemplary of this trend.[34]

33. Daniel Green, *Great Cobbett: The Noblest Agitator,* 228–58. Green says of Cobbett: "It would always be difficult to credit Cobbett with anything that resembled a coherent political philosophy, for he was a politician of the belly" (133).

34. The Oldknow establishment has been described by Unwin in *Samuel Oldknow and the Arkwrights.* The Strutts of Derbyshire were typical of mill owners who thought of themselves as social improvers without going so far as to undertake experiments in community arrangements. In 1816, the Strutts wrote to Peel's Select Committee that "it is well known in this neighborhood that *before* the establishment of these works the inhabitants were notorious for vice and immorality, and many of the children were maintained by begging; now their industry, decorous behavior, attendance on public worship, and general good conduct, compared with the neighboring

In these associations, employees were not regarded as wage labor simply, but as dependents of a master who bore broad obligations for their well-being. This relationship obviously reiterated the squire-tenant relation. But the difference between squires and the new men showed itself in their taste for social experimentation as an expression of heterodox advanced opinions as well as polytechnic skill.

While total welfare communities were exceptional, they were based on ideas widely shared and practiced, namely, solidarity of interest and feeling between master and dependent. This impulse led to numerous welfare measures, such as the provision of regular medical care for employees, improvements of factory design to enhance safety and comfort, periodic largesse and town festivities hosted by the master, municipal improvements, and reductions in the hours of work. By 1813, there was a trend among such masters to cut the workday to ten or eleven hours. But those who followed this trend were exposed to competition from masters who worked their laborers thirteen or even fourteen hours per day. A number of these spoilers jumped into textiles after the war; although they were usually small operators, they could hurt big firms in a highly competitive business. The benevolent masters did not like this development, for reasons easily understood. To illustrate with a typical case, the Fieldens of Todmorden employed some 2,000 workers. In twenty years they had raised themselves from poverty and obscurity to become lords of their community. They were trusted and beloved by their employees, because the Fieldens had given many proofs of their benevolence. The legitimacy of their power was certified in the eyes of workers who had witnessed their rise. The Fieldens' low origin and benevolent practice had generated an organic solidarity with their work force. But now the competitive effects of the spoilers obliged the Fieldens to go to their employees to say that it would be necessary to increase the workday from ten to twelve hours.[35] This was a humilia-

---

villages, where no manufactures are established, is very conspicuous" (quoted by Chapman, *Early Factory Masters,* 197–98).

35. Fielden was explicit about this: "Here, then, is the 'curse' of our factory system: as improvements in machinery have gone on, the 'avarice of masters' has prompted many to exact more labour from their hands than they were fitted by nature to perform, and those who have wished for the hours of labour to be less for all ages than the legislature would even yet sanction, have had no alternative but to conform more or less to the prevailing practice, or abandon trade altogether. This has been the case with regard to myself and my partners" (*Curse of the Factory System,* 34–35). On the Fielden establishment, see J. T. Ward's introduction to *The Curse of the Factory System,* viii–xi.

tion: a master unable to protect his dependents. The response of the benevolent masters was to curb the spoilers by restrictive legislation.

Such was the origin of Robert Peel's bill, introduced in 1816, to ban children under nine years of age from the factories, and to restrict the workday for those aged nine to sixteen to eleven hours. However, the benevolent manufacturers had not prepared the ground for their bill by lobbying manufacturers who shared their feeling about the spoilers but whose commitment to laissez-faire doctrine made them reluctant to accept restrictive legislation as a means of putting a stop to spoiler practices. Consequently, the bill split the manufacturing interest and unleashed a three-year battle between the manufacturing exponents of regulation and those of laissez-faire. This struggle culminated in the Factory Act of 1819. During its course, the regulation party hit its opposition with a polemic so damaging that by 1819 the albatross of child labor hung from the factory chimney. Such was the origin of the legend of wicked capitalism.

The subsequent mutations and career of the legend makes its origin seem quite incredible. How could manufacturers have originated the great accusation against the factory system that finally destroyed public trust in the good will of manufacturers? Obviously, in the first real test of their leadership as an interest group, the manufacturers blew it. But the facts are unequivocal. Not only did the struggle over the Factory Act of 1819 pit opposed manufacturing factions, but this struggle continued for the next two decades under their leadership. Tories, and subsequently labor, leaped into the struggle under the flag of regulation borne by that party's leaders, Peel, Fielden, and Owen foremost among them. Owen invented and was the first to use a number of labor weapons, including the general strike and the national organization of trade unions. Fielden led the campaign for the ten- and then the eight-hour day, and he authored that bitter and intransigent tract, *The Curse of the Factory System*. The first Englishman to advocate throwing down the entire system of religion and property, and its replacement by communism, was not a desperate Luddite; he was Robert Owen, owner of Lanark Mills. The original radical attacks on the factory system came from manufacturers because they *were* the vanguard of progressive benevolence and enlightenment.[36]

36. The combination of Tories and radicals into Tory socialism—and after 1841, conservatism—was a European movement taking its impetus from the Saint Simonians. The combination was obtained when avant-gardists looked at the obverse of the liberal coin of liberty and found confusion and disorienta-

By stripping back the legend of wicked capitalism, we expose to view the nerves and fibers of a controversy whose significance in the progress of modern politics can scarcely be exaggerated. It was the watershed for what was to become the bitter opposition, labor vs. capital. But at this point the quarrel was an in-house fight between manufacturers, in which paternalistic benevolence protested the iron in the heart of laissez-faire economics.

Superficially, there was not so much in Peel's legislation to raise controversy. The precedent for protective labor legislation had been set by the Apprentices Act (1802), brought in by the elder Robert Peel, which regulated the influx and treatment of child employees who did not come to the factory under the supervision of a working parent. Many factory masters preferred not to have children under nine in any case—it seems that they misbehaved.[37] The act would have affected about 3,000 children under nine, but a much larger number aged nine to sixteen.

The initial sticking point concerned this second category of children. If they went off the job after eleven hours, their parents would have to go with them, and the factory would shut down. For the jobs of the spinner parents and the piecer children were coordinate: no piecing, no

---

tion; and when the competitive ideal was seen as a forcing house subordinating all human qualities to selfish conflict. These discoveries activated the ideal of moral community among the avant garde. But moral community had always been the core of throne and altar, as Saint Simon and other avant-gardists fully appreciated; hence their openness to religion or attempts to renovate Christianity. In England the conservative cause centered around opposition to Catholic emancipation, the Reform Act, and the Anti–Corn Law League, and advocacy of industrial regulation and Poor Law reform. Its parliamentary leaders were Peel, Lord Ashley, and Disraeli. Its ecclesiastical leaders were the Oxford Tractarians. These groups made a frontal assault on liberal doctrine, particularly laissez-faire and the concept of the primacy of institutions, and wanted to substitute a return to the bonds of service and obligation, à la Carlyle. As Disraeli put it: "I see no other remedy for that war of classes and creeds which now agitates and menaces us but in an earnest return to a system which may be described generally as one of loyalty and reverence, of popular rights and social sympathies." See George Kitson Clark, *Churchmen and the Condition of England, 1832–1885,* 59–63, 76ff.; and *Peel and the Conservative Party,* 444–94, by the same author.

37. Richard Arkwright, giving evidence to Peel's Select Committee, said that he had excluded children under ten for a decade, and remarked of boys in factories, "I see them often running about, and in mischief" (Fitton and Wadsworth, *The Strutts and the Arkwrights,* 227).

spinning. This effect was not in dispute; Owen suggested that the problem could be met by working children in relays.[38] But relays had a disadvantage. For half of every day, parents would be supervising children not their own. Such a disruption of the parent-child supervisory relationship was thought to jeopardize the whole system; consequently, manufacturers viewed the bill as a piece of quixotic philanthropy.[39] They escalated the debate by climbing the ramparts of free trade to argue that the market alone should decide at what hours and ages children should work. Peel agreed that the market should determine the price of labor, but urged that minor children were not free labor. Then came the response that the children were not engaged by the factory but by parents, their lawful guardians, who alone were entitled to judge the suitability of employment for their offspring. The proposed legislation, they maintained, not only violated the most sacred tie of parent and child, but contained the implied slander that the good working people of England would sacrifice their children to their avarice.[40]

A laissez-faire man himself, Peel realized that something big was needed to counter weighty arguments drawn from the science of political economy. The big thing he found was the contrary voice of another

38. Maurice Thomas, *The Early Factory Legislation*, 21.
39. The anonymous author of *An Inquiry into the Principle and Tendency of the Bill Now Pending in Parliament for Imposing Certain Restrictions on Cotton Factories* (London, 1818) wrote: "Late years have been wonderfully prolific of ostentatious and useless schemes of philanthropy, from humble Evans and his nation of happy landholders, to Mr. Owen with the millennium dawning over the ruins of Christianity in a cotton-mill; not quite the spot, and not quite the circumstances, in which the beginnings of that blissful period were to be expected. Of all these schemes the present is one of the strangest. . . . for it would be difficult to imagine a plan, in which the means are more oddly adapted to the ends. Here is a philanthropy which professes to remedy the miseries of the poor by making them still poorer" (311). This tract is hereinafter cited as *An Inquiry.*
40. Thomas, *Early Factory Legislation*, 26–27. The author of *An Inquiry* addressed this point in the following laissez-faire deliberation: "for it was hazardous in the extreme to charge a great proportion of the manufacturing laborers with such a want, not merely of natural affection, but of common humanity, as was involved in the supposition that they voluntarily sacrificed the bodily and mental health of their children, to supply funds for their own debaucheries. This charge . . . is virtually made by the bill; for it proceeds in the supposition that cotton factories, as they are at present managed, are equally fatal to health and morals; while no man denied . . . that young children are received, not to promote the interest of their employer, but solely to gratify the wishes of their parents" (23).

science. On 25 April 1816 his Select Committee began hearing testimony on whether factory employment adversely affected the health and well-being of children.[41] Science was represented by eight physicians, who testified unanimously that such long hours of confinement and work must stunt the growth and affect the health of children; and one physician opened the prospect of far-reaching change when he surmised that the thirteen-hour day must distress the health of adults, let alone children.[42]

This testimony carried grave implications against laissez-faire. If medical opinion was relevant to employment practices, then rigid appeal to market factors could not be maintained. The implications went further. When employers claimed that parents alone could rightfully judge the suitability of employment for their children, they appealed explicitly to law and implicitly to the utilitarian principle that the individual alone is competent to judge what is good for himself. This principle was fundamental to the anthropology of laissez-faire, which assumes that each individual's freedom to buy and sell guarantees that each acts to maximize his happiness (or utility). But now it appeared that he might make serious mistakes, in ignorance of relevant facts. Or, knowing the facts, he might persist in a choice that could be known *not* to enhance his "utilities," however much he might enjoy them.

It would be an exaggeration to say that Peel's call upon expert testimony was the watershed for all subsequent industrial politics in Britain. But it would not be a gross exaggeration. Political economy was challenged to its roots: this we must see to appreciate the vehemence of employer reaction. Medical testimony broached the possibility that the architectonic perspective on production was not economics, but some more comprehensive view of human weal and woe. Mercantilism was the old opponent here; but by 1816, manufacturers had become aware of a new comprehensive approach, called socialism, gotten up by one of their own, Robert Owen. They registered their apprehension by asking where regulation would end if so drastic a measure as Peel's bill were

41. Robert Peel's concern with factory regulation stemmed from the "factory fever" that struck his employees in 1792. His firm was visited by Dr. Thomas Percival, a civic leader in Manchester and first president of the Manchester Literary and Philosophical Society. That visit also had an enduring effect on Percival, who became an advocate of health regulations and restrictions on working hours. On his initiative the Manchester Board of Health was set up in 1795 to oversee municipal health regulations. Thus, when the younger Robert Peel called expert medical testimony, he merely retraced the steps that had originally persuaded his father of the need for regulation.

42. Thomas, *Early Factory Legislation,* 20.

acceptable.[43] Nor was that all. The physicians' testimony placed on the public agenda what until then had been the troublesome private opinion that child labor was an insupportable practice. Therewith the Dickensian apparition of the work-broken child made its appearance; it had not yet become the terrible accusatory icon of the child ruthlessly exploited for profit. But Peel had put the laissez-faire manufacturers on the defensive, and they knew it.

They were at a crossroad. They could accept regulation and disburden themselves of child labor; or they could fight to retain owner control and attempt to shift responsibility for child labor to parents. They chose to fight. The bill finally enacted did not represent a clear-cut victory either way. It did reaffirm the legitimacy of regulation and banned employment of children under nine. In this sense it was a victory for regulation. But the real objective had been to cut the hours for adult laborers by cutting to eleven the permissible number of hours for the critical nine-to-sixteen age group. Here they failed; the act "restricted" their labor to thirteen-and-a-half hours per day. This meant that the benevolent masters got no relief from the spoilers, who were compelling them to work their people twelve or thirteen hours a day in order to compete. Consequently, the act was merely the opening shot of the next, more bitter campaign to reduce the hours of the workday. The free trade men had opted for a war that they could not win. For the next thirty years the struggle went on, pouring bitterness into the workplace and spoiling the tone of public life. The Chartist movement succeeded Owen's original labor movement; at the peak of its agitation in 1848, when revolution broke across Europe, the duke of Wellington was needed to restore the queen's peace.

Today the tenacious opposition of the free traders—or liberals, as they were called—is taken as evidence of insatiable greed and heartless exploitation. To view events in this way is to view them through the spectacles fashioned by Fielden and his allies: "Mammon or Mercy!" was the slogan of reproach to their opponents. This makes a good war cry, but it is no explanation of behavior. There were reasons, beyond those already mentioned, why manufacturers took the stance that they did.

One is related to the syndrome known as entrepreneurial anxiety. Legends of rapidly accumulated fortunes suggest the image of the idle rich bathing in the sybaritic pleasures of Europe's watering places. But pleasure gardens were the road to ruin in a highly competitive business that visited bankruptcy on those who fell behind or made poor judgments. The failure rate of industrial enterprises from 1819 to 1835 was

43. John Fielden, *The Curse of the Factory System*, 40–45.

about 30 percent.[44] The difference between safety and danger was tested daily in an enterprise where success went to those who reduced the price per unit on mass-produced goods. Even for large firms there was no such thing as assured success. The orientation and organizational goals of industrial manufacture were distinct from innovative commercial firms of the eighteenth century. Whereas the merchant attempted to buy cheap and sell dear, the industrialist had to produce cheap to sell more cheaply in a market of declining price and increasing volume. The merchant had to make his fortune against the hazard of corsairs, storms at sea, surplus inventories, and fickle markets. But industrialists had to juggle large wage costs, debt servicing, plant maintenance, inventories, transportation, and technological innovation to come up in the black. In this milieu, loss of control over labor seemed to throw an intolerable uncertainty into a business where short margins were the rule.

Second, the behavior of the manufacturers cannot be understood without appreciating the facts about child labor. The idea of six-year-old children working thirteen hours a day, year after year, is difficult to credit in either a physical or moral sense. Common sense denies that children have the stamina for it, quite apart from the seeming impossibility of repressing their playful spirits. Morally, one is staggered that a population not at war or in the grip of calamity could sanction this enormity. To a child, a thirteen-hour day is indistinguishable from permanent captivity; but unlike the agricultural slave, Manchester children had no control over the pace of their work.[45] It is therefore with difficulty that we insert ourselves into a context that had accepted but was attempting to reject child labor.

The common-sense notion that children of six cannot work thirteen-hour days yields to factual documentation to the contrary. They worked that regimen and did not drop like flies from shock, exhaustion, or autism. Many became parents of second-generation factory children. The system was so ingrained in the experience of textile workers that they did not join the campaign against child labor until 1830, fifteen years after Peel raised the matter in Parliament for the first time. That children entered factories at all is due to an improbable coincidence of cottage work practices and the technology of machine production. It was the custom of cottage spinners and weavers to involve their children in their

---

44. Hoffman, *British Industry, 1700–1950,* 154–55.
45. The analogy of the thirteen-hour day to slavery was vigorously pressed by the Tories as an obvious riposte to the leveling tendencies of the liberals. See Fielden, *The Curse of the Factory System,* 42–43; Gaskell, *Artisans and Machinery,* 228–29.

work from an early age. On the farm it was no different. Children were expected to contribute to the meager household economy. Consequently, the entry of children into factories with parents represented the *continuity* of established practice, not a new departure; and this was the basis of its original legitimacy in the eyes of workers and masters alike.[46]

Had this labor been ruinous, medical testimony to that effect would have been superfluous. But in the event, the unanimous testimony of Peel's eight physicians turned out to be a minority opinion. He might equally well have called eight physicians, long in practice among industrial labor, to testify that the health of factory children was as good as, and indeed better than, that of agricultural labor populations. Most physicians who testified before the Sadler Committee of 1830 took an agnostic position as to the capacity of medical science to prove that long hours, long intervals of standing and walking, or lint in the air caused stunted growth, tuberculosis, and other harmful effects alleged by some physicians. Much to the annoyance of the Sadler Committee, doctor after doctor, including some who were active against child labor, testified that the state of medical knowledge and clinical evidence did not warrant a conclusion either way. Repeatedly they acknowledged holding an opinion while denying that it had a foundation in fact. They were not prepared to make suggestions toward the formulation of protective legislation on the basis of opinion. The reason was simple: since their opinions were contradictory, nothing conclusive could be milked from them.[47]

46. See n. 27 above.
47. Attempts to form an accurate impression of the health of factory laborers and the effects of the factory environment and long hours are frustrated by the unevenness of the data. The most comprehensive documentation is contained in *The Chadwick Report on the Sanitary Condition of the Labouring Population with Local Reports for England and Wales, 1837–42*, prepared for the Poor Law commissioners. Its data consist largely of depositions by public health officers, usually physicians, and the testimony of working people. The medical opinion was undisciplined by sampling techniques; cases were described in an impressionistic manner; no attempt was made to arrange data statistically. Certain frequently occurring descriptive terms ("looks weak," "appears sickly") are without medical value. The testimony of working people was wholly anecdotal. It is curious that the parties to the dispute did not organize a medically and statistically sound investigation of factory populations, as they might easily have done. Today it is known that the cholera epidemic of 1831–33 was not due to unsanitary conditions or overcrowding, although the mistaken belief to the contrary was a stimulus to the promotion of public sanitation. Textile workers were and are subject to res-

Manufacturing spokesmen made a great deal of the inconclusiveness of medical opinion: medical science did not after all contradict political economy. They complained that Peel's Select Committee, and later the Sadler Committee, had stacked the deck by calling on expert witnesses of whom it was known in advance that they would give the opinion needed to slander manufacturers. Among those who shared this view was an advanced Owenite and rebellious son of a textile manufacturer, Friedrich Engels, who stated in *The Condition of the Working Class in England:* "[The Select Committee Report] is a very partisan document, which was drawn up by enemies of the factory system for purely political purposes. Sadler was led astray by his passionate sympathies into making assertions of the most misleading and erroneous kind."[48] If Engels saw it this way, it is not to be wondered that the manufacturers believed themselves to be victims of a campaign of infamy. Today we know that the most widely circulated of all factory atrocity stories, *The Memoir of Robert Blincoe,* was largely a fabrication.[49]

With these circumstances in mind, we may attempt a more balanced appraisal of what this controversy was about. In 1800, child labor was an accepted institution. Poverty, hunger, and drink were the recognized

---

piratory disease (brown lung), as was believed; and it is possible that stunted growth, so widely alleged, could have resulted from factory labor (through inhibition of growth hormone synthesis). Overall, however, the English of 1830 were a healthier, better-fed, and more fertile population than their great-grandparents. M. C. Buer sums his findings to this effect in these words: "Man develops an extraordinary moral resistance against accustomed ills so that new evils really cause more acute suffering simply because they are new. Hence the universal tendency to deprecate the present. . . . It is not claimed, therefore, that the new conditions did not cause suffering. . . . But it is claimed that, on balance, material conditions improved enormously for the people as a whole between 1760 and 1815" (*Health, Wealth and Population in the Early Days of the Industrial Revolution,* 241; see also N. L. Tranter, *Population since the Industrial Revolution*). For excerpts of medical testimony before Peel's Select Committee, where physicians abstained from expressing an opinion on the effects of factory labor, see *Observations &c. as to the Ages of Persons Employed in the Cotton Mills in Manchester,* 36–44; and *Reasons in Favour of Sir Robert Peel's Bill,* 20–25.

48. Friedrich Engels, *The Condition of the Working Class in England,* 192. Like Engels, Sadler was the son of a textile manufacturer. Engels's criticism of Sadler may also be made of Engels's *Condition.*

49. Chapman, *Early Factory Masters,* 199–209. Chapman also shows that accusations made against Davison and Hawksley, proprietors of Arnold Mill, were baseless (see 179–96).

scourges of society's bottom dwellers, but the working class, in regular employment, were supposed to have attained a state of relative well-being. By 1835, child labor was odious, and for the first time in history, the regular pay and employment of workers was recognized as a distinct "problem," styled "the condition of the working class." Evidently English people had undergone a rapid change of sensibility. During that same time, those who benefited from that change, industrial laborers, developed into an organized political force. By opposing this development at every step, the liberal manufacturers made themselves indistinguishable from the spoilers and acquired the infamy of every group that loses a legitimation struggle.

Insofar as the legend of wicked capitalism identifies child labor and the long workday as barbarous practices, it is no fairy tale. The pathos of the legend is compelling; and that pathos is probably the reason for its enduring power. But there are also reasons why it should be compelling to recipients of modern political science. The factory system offended against the principle of equality and against what Hobbes called "a life that is not miserable." The Declaration of Independence and Jeremy Bentham substituted for this phrase the word "happiness." Hobbes was more circumspect. Human beings may pursue happiness, but a measure of discontent is the lot of everyone. However, it will not do to have one portion of the population suffer miserable circumstances while the remainder are unaffected.

While right is founded on every person's necessary revulsion from misery, its exercise is by no means guaranteed by the ordinary course of things. For most of human history, the ordinary course of things has regularly placed large numbers among the miserable, and has locked them up under the seal of necessity. The escape route from misery, Hobbes taught, is not revolt but work intelligently directed to mend nature's niggardliness. The workers performed their part of the social contract; it was imperative for the factory masters to comply with their obligation. Specifically, the situation called for a renovation of labor-management relations that would make labor in some measure a firm partner. The ground floor for such a policy was recognition of bargaining position and some profit-sharing scheme and/or a system of benefits to absorb the shock of unemployment. This was not advice offered gratuitously from hindsight, for such ideas were abroad among the paternalist manufacturers; indeed, they were practiced informally in a number of establishments. Moreover, the Poor Law system was ripe for comprehensive reform. Britain in 1820 was paying out about £7 million annually for poor rates. The Speenhamland Law (1795), however wretched its consequences, was based on the proposition that persons unable to provide assistance for themselves had a claim upon the public purse. The rudiments of a sound employment policy were therefore available. But instead of accepting this interesting challenge, the manufacturing leadership made a total mess of it. While the Owenites flew off to utopia on the wings of hot air, the liberals cried, "Let it be!" when clearly the matter was not to be left alone.

The root of the problem for the liberals was that their system of prudence, political economy, contained no organizational teaching. This is nowhere more apparent than in the chapter of political economy dealing with labor relations. Its deliverance on this critical topic is reducible to a sentence: Let the market determine the price of labor. No liberal political economist of this period came forward with an economically grounded labor relations policy. J. B. Say, whose sound concept of productivity placed him in a strong position to make headway, gave it little thought. He deferred to the presiding genius of "Radical Reform" liberalism, Jeremy Bentham. To understand better the baffling failure of this stage of enlightenment to respond to *the* problem of the times, we examine Bentham more closely.

Bentham's Liberalism

Liberalism was the child of multiple births in the last quarter of the eighteenth century. In France it issued from the circles of Turgot and Helvétius, and took its mother's milk from the drama of the American Revolution. In England Adam Smith made the "generous and liberal system" of Quesnay fundamental doctrine for liberal political economy. In book 4 of *The Wealth of Nations*, Smith took the "colonial disturbances" as paradigmatic of the struggle between unregenerate Old World mercantilism and vital New World democracy, small government, and agrarian capitalism. The doctrines of agrarian capitalism were spread in the colonies by the man who cross-fertilized American and French thought, Ben Franklin. In England liberalism was the creed of the dissenters and later "Jacobins" who composed the Lunar Society of Birmingham, the Constitutional Societies, and similar organizations in the Midlands devoted to industrial entrepreneurship and politics. It was natural that when war with France inhibited their activities, some would seek refuge in America and close ranks with the Jeffersonians.[50]

50. Halévy's description of the French and English roots of liberalism still commends itself despite the wealth of research published in the intervening sixty years; see especially his *Growth of Philosophic Radicalism*, 120–80. Albert Goodwin's fine-grained study of English democratic societies, *The Friends of*

The representative figures of the first wave of liberal theory were Condorcet and Jeremy Bentham. They were warmly attached to the American and French revolutions. They were ardent democrats and staunch constitutionalists, and both poured their energies into drafting legal codes, constitutions, and legal reforms. They advocated representative democracy and the unicameral system. They opposed slavery, the subordination of women, colonialism, war, and the death penalty. Bentham invented the term "international law" and drew up a list of schemes for world peace under the auspices of an international "fraternity of nations." These schemes called for complete disarmament and divesting of colonies. Condorcet and Bentham had enormous faith in the power of education to reform manners and morals. They were confident of the superior humanity of their age, as they were also confident that future generations would be yet more humane. Public affairs they believed would fall increasingly under the influence of public opinion, which they expected intellectuals to dominate.

Such was the liberal outlook circa 1830. It was evidently derived from the seventeenth-century initiation of political science. The equality doctrine was now broadened to include women and colonial peoples. The aspiration to world peace flowed from the identification of civil war as the greatest misery. Ameliorating the human condition by stable government and economic growth now became the means of making all citizens happy and fulfilled. However, these extensions were obtained only by repudiating some of the essential elements of the original program. The concept of unchanging behavioral traits was replaced by the concept of the malleability of behavior by social institutions. If this were so, then the life-and-death conflict situation that lies at the basis of Hobbesian political science might be replaced by new notions, such as Bentham's greatest happiness principle, characterized by the absence of life situations requiring forced sacrifice.[51] However, the real world had

---

Liberty: The English Democratic Movement in the Age of the French Revolution, indicates in gratifying detail how liberalism was diffused in England and from what intellectual sources it took its bearings. On the matter of sources, Isaac Kramnick's "Republican Revisionism Revisited" may be consulted with profit. Peter Gay's *The Party of Humanity* is a useful study of preludes to French liberalism, while R. R. Palmer's *The Age of Democratic Revolution* is essential for a comprehensive picture of liberal politics in its initial phase, which, as this study shows, stretched from Russia to Latin America. Guido de Ruggiero's widely read *History of European Liberalism* is weak on this critical period. Harold Laski's *The Rise of European Liberalism,* published in 1936, reads today as a classic statement of the then prevailing liberal view of the origins of liberalism.

51. Malthus's population speculations or Ricardo's doctrine of wages might ei-

not reached this state of blessedness; and the tension between the ideal and the real, for a doctrine purportedly realistic, made liberalism liable to surprising mutations. One was reversion to the moral community, common to Tory socialists and Saint Simonians. The theorist who transmitted this mutation was J. S. Mill. Another variation would fully exploit the potential of human science and human perfectibility in a benevolent program to make people happy by social conditioning. This variation is latent in the theory of Bentham.[52]

Bentham's system is single-mindedly devoted to benevolence, and

---

ther have been sufficient to arouse liberals of this period to a sharp perception of essential conflict native to the original position of modern political science. Yet this did not happen. J. S. Mill managed to find a basis for moral optimism in both doctrines. For a discussion, see Ruggiero, *History of European Liberalism,* 109–12.

52. It is to be hoped that someone will make a study of nineteenth-century variations of liberalism. In his examination of what he calls "modern liberalism," Gerald F. Gaus lumps J. S. Mill, T. H. Green, Bosanquet, Hobhouse, Dewey, and John Rawls together in virtue of their common sustained effort to engraft some concept of moral community onto classical liberal individualism in its economic and rule-of-law modes (*The Modern Liberal Theory of Man,* 1–9). Gaus is justified in dating this reconciliation attempt to the 1830s, seventy years before it found a potent electoral voice. He mentions James Mill and Hayek as exponents of classical liberalism. But the yardstick of classical nineteenth-century liberalism is undoubtedly Herbert Spencer, whom Gaus doesn't mention. The point is important because Spencer lived to witness the ground-swell for modern liberalism, with its economic collectivism and moral community notions for the achievement of social equality; and he denounced it as betrayal of liberty. This split goes sufficiently deep that classical and modern liberals do at times regard one another as reactionary, or, in polite language, conservative. A split of equal significance occurred when Burke, who was comfortable with the politics of American independence, set his face against the French variation lest the English radicals dismember the British constitution. (The Burkean heritage informs a recent outstanding essay pertinent to these remarks, *That Noble Science of Politics: A Study in Nineteenth-Century Intellectual History,* by Stefan Collini, Donald Winch, and John Burrow.) The Burkean legacy is liberalism of a conservative stripe, which fosters individuality within a moral community defined as national tradition. Tocqueville's political sociology marks yet another type, and so on. I hope these observations will make the variations discussed in this text seem less improbable than otherwise they might. Thomas A. Spragens has attempted to diagnosis the whole career of liberalism from the perspective of its "quiet demise," and identifies the cause of death as the incoherence among the principles of purportedly rational political science (*The Irony of Liberal Reason,* 311–56).

that feature won him a degree of celebrity and prestige among the political public scarcely rivaled by any other thinker. Two American presi-
dents, the National Convention, the czar of Russia, prime ministers,
Latin American revolutionary heroes, kings, and dukes paid homage to
his genius and set him to work at his favored activity, drawing up legal
codes. Curiously, Bentham did not capitalize his fame into worldly influence. His most enduring mark was on the Reform Bill of 1832 and on
British jurisprudence.

The uneasiness one feels in comparing the pretension with the achievement also arises on considering the rhetoric of Bentham's advocacy. His
conviction of the harmony of utilities and of human desires made him
neglect the great life conflicts that impart elevation and gravity to ethics.
The elimination of self-discipline and high striving in favor of benevolence practiced in a benign environment places a stamp of abstraction
on his ethical writings, however incisive he might have been as a legal
technician.

The abstract character of Bentham's doctrine goes some way toward
explaining why he uttered not a syllable about labor relations, even if his
disciples did serve on the Poor Law Commission that administered factory legislation. The operation of Bentham's abstract, benevolent rationalism is clearly articulated in this statement on laissez-faire:

> The more we become enlightened, the more benevolent shall we
> become; because we shall see that the interests of men coincide
> upon more points than they oppose each other. In commerce, ig-
> norant nations have treated each other as rivals, who could only
> rise upon the ruins of another. The work of Adam Smith is a
> treatise upon universal benevolence, because it has shown that
> commerce is equally advantageous to all nations—each one profit-
> ing in a different manner, according to its natural means; that na-
> tions are associates and not rivals in the grand social enterprise.
> (*Works*, 1: 563)

Free trade negates the mercantilist system of national economy, whose
objective is to maintain a trade advantage vis-à-vis other nations by
using a repertoire of tariffs, bounties, monopolies, state enterprises,
fiscal policy, and war to assure a favorable balance of trade and political
leverage. Free trade as an economic system replaces the mercantilist perspective of national power with a transnational perspective of mutually
beneficial cooperation in the "grand social enterprise" of improving the
human condition. Open international trade—restrictions on movements of goods—replaces national self-sufficiency by international mu-

tual dependency; so that local political interest and rising expectations conspire to impel national governments to international cooperation (*Works*, 2: 538–50).

None of this was original to Bentham. The physiocratic originators of free trade were explicit about its tendency to undermine the capacity and the desire of governments to wage wars of aggrandizement. Adam Smith took these notions with him from France and perpetuated them in *The Wealth of Nations*.

To liberals, Napoleon's continental system was the crowning proof of their doctrine. The continental system was mercantilism *in extremis,* imposed by a despot whose declared object was to ruin a rival nation. The system was undone by smugglers, those intrepid free traders who arrive on the scene whenever governments try to interfere with natural market movements by excessive duties and prohibitions.

Andrew Ure also endorsed these ideas. He identified free trade with "the liberal system" and mercantilism with "illiberal policy" (*Philosophy of Manufactures,* 451, 453). As his readers no doubt expected, Colbert and Napoleon were marched past for flagellation:

> Colbert's avowed purpose was to render France as much the mistress of the civilized world in manufacturing as he thought her to be in military glory; . . . his was indeed the vainest of projects, for it aimed at nothing less than controlling and turning the wayward streams of industry, flowing from the wants, tastes, and caprices of millions of individuals, into a few artificial channels scooped out by the state. (459)

Free trade was believed to serve the greatest good for the greatest number in many ways. By eliminating protection, it eliminates the futility of producing goods at higher than free market price. By cheapening price, it makes more goods available to more consumers at lower price. In allowing popular taste to list as it will, it constitutes a decision procedure enabling individuals to make their own effective decisions about what most contributes to their happiness. Free trade, utilitarianism, and universal benevolence were made for one another. If a consequence of free trade is that no nation is self-sufficient in war materiel and manufactures, so much the better.

The protectionist riposte to free trade was that large numbers of producers may be, or rather, certainly will be wiped out by competition. Free traders responded that those who cannot produce at a profit on the free market are a burden on those who pay artificially high prices for their protected products; the utility criterion of the greatest good for the greatest number—all mankind—demands that they produce something which *is* competitive in the free market. Free trade is benevolent.

Let us consider how it worked. Within a few years of the mechanization of spinning, cottage spinning was eliminated. The artisan's solitary labor over his ancient wheel was no match for machine productivity. Cottage spinners moved into the factories, and earned more than they had as self-employed artisans. Here everyone benefited, as the liberal scenario required. Then came the mechanization of weaving, which took longer to perfect because of the complexity of the operation; the weavers were not faced with the sudden-death situation of the spinners. They could try to hold out, or, reading the signs, exchange the cottage for the factory loom. There were some 200,000 of these artisans in the Midlands, traditionally proud of their skill and jealous of their "private enterprise." Most of them tried to hold out. But the machine was not to be denied. Their wages fell from 25 s. in 1800 to 8 d. 6 d. in 1820 and finally to starvation at 5 s. 6 d. in 1829.[53] Considering now the distress of tens of thousands of stubborn weavers, is free trade still benevolent? Yes, says the Benthamite. The weavers exercise a market option, purchasing the greater happiness of independence at the cost of declining wages. Only the individual exercising this option can know when the cost of misery tips the scales against the happiness of independence. When that happens, the weaver will make peace with the machine and beat a path to the factory door. But no one can make that decision for him; only the individual can judge his pleasures and pains.[54] This is well so long as the weavers agree to confine their options to market transactions. As it happened, they saw a third possibility: smash the machines. This was the Luddite movement of 1811–12, which used arson and vandalism to destroy the stocking frames and looms that were depriving them of their livelihood.

Bentham's system covered contingencies of this kind by the penal code. Once the hapless Luddite was sentenced to hard labor, he was subtracted from the free labor market and added to the state system of penitential labor. At that point the organization and use of labor became a legitimate concern for the laissez-faire economist and codifier. Bentham made up for his silence on the factory system and labor-management relations by the effort he put into reforming the rationale of imprisonment and the design of prison regimes and penal institutions.

When Bentham arrived on the scene, the object of imprisonment was to deter crime by punishment. The usual punishment in law was hard

53. Perkin, *Origins of Modern English Society*, 145.
54. Bentham defended this position in his *In Defense of Usury*, letters 2–5.

labor, reinforced by a system of deprivations, humiliations, and terrors. This orientation, Bentham decided, was mistaken in its assumptions about human motivation;[55] it was also mischievous in its effects. Deterrence by punishment assumed in the felon a fixed disposition toward crime that could be checked only by what Benthamites of a later era were to call "schedules of negative reinforcement," i.e. pains. By dropping the assumption of a fixed disposition, Bentham arrived at the enlightened notion that the object of confinement should be rehabilitation ("reformation"). This change of heart, or moral discipline, may be effected by a well-designed system of positive reinforcements, or inducements, that prepare the felon for return to civilian life as a useful citizen.

Once the problem is grasped from this end of the stick, a quite remarkable transformation of penal practices follows. It now appears that the fundamental punishment, hard labor, is in every way misguided; in the first instance because it gives labor an infamous color, whereas to rehabilitate the prisoner requires that he be habituated to the idea that "industry is a blessing" because it is "the parent of wealth" (*Works of Bentham*, 4: 144). Second, the hard labor exacted of prisoners is useless to the prisoners and to the state, whereas it is desirable to set prisoners to work at trades of their own choice, provided that they are practiced in civil life. Third, prisons as then constituted were a financial burden, whereas under Bentham's conception, they should aim at economy in their operation as well as at making inmates proficient in work. Economy is indeed the key to the whole reformed penal system. Economy mandates that prison labor should be not for labor's sake "but for profit" (*Works*, 4: 153). Prisoners should be allowed to accumulate wages on their labor. Economy mandates the mixture of leniencies and severities that would maximize output while constantly reminding prisoners of their punitive state.[56] And economy recommends that prison management be contracted out to private entrepreneurs who are expected to optimize production for the sake of the commission they are to receive on prison commodities (*Works*, 4: 125–47).

55. In his *A View of the Hard Labour Bill* (1778), Bentham endorsed almost all the logic and specific measures of Mr. Howard's bill, which was based on the premise that punishment effectively deterred crime only if it were exemplary, i.e. cruel. But when *Panopticon* was published in 1787, he had arrived at his new system.

56. Thus, Bentham would allow inmates to eat their fill; but the diet was to consist only of plain, cheap fare and the menu was not to vary. However, inmates would be allowed to purchase food from their earnings.

The founding idea of Bentham's penitentiary system is the belief that the rehabilitation of felons is accomplished by making them sensible of the efficacy of well-directed work; consistent with this objective, he wanted the prison governor to combine security, reform supervision, and business entrepreneurship in one office. The belief that work induces good morals while leisure encourages mischief was common among factory masters. Ure expressed a common view when he argued that the long workday was a prop to morality in no small measure because, by reducing leisure to a fragment, it kept the workingman out of mischief. Bentham's prison rationale and regime duplicated this idea: long hours and small but steady and tangible rewards were the regiment of the reformation of felons, who, he noted, came almost entirely from the working class. This suggests that Bentham's interest in penal institutions was the laissez-faire economist's way of addressing the labor problem, especially when we discover that he would transfer prison management to the free market.

We need not leave it at a suggestion. Bentham put forward his ideas on prisons as a special case of the general problem of the management of labor. Its architectonic concept was an establishment called Panopticon, a building whose remarkable properties made it applicable to the organization and management of "penitentiary houses, prisons, houses of industry, work houses, poor houses, manufactures, lazarettos, hospitals, and schools." [57] What do these very diverse institutions have in common, that a single plan of spatial design suits them all? Panopticon, Bentham claimed, was the most economical maximum-security "inspection house" possible. It was a circular building whose geometry was determined by the requirements of the inspector and the inspected. On the circumference of the circle were situated the individual quarters of the inspected, stacked in a tier of four floors. At the center of the circle was the inspection tower, manned by benevolent improvers. This geometry enabled a few improvers to keep an eye on the inmates twenty-four hours a day. Actually—and here was one of its many economical virtues—only a few pairs of eyes were needed for this purpose. It would not be necessary to watch all inmates at all times. The effect of constant watching was achieved if the inmates could not tell when they were not being watched. [58]

57. From the title page of *Panopticon*. These applications are discussed in *Works of Bentham,* 4: 60–66.
58. It was also part of the plan that Panopticon would be open to the public, whose prison visits were meant to have a deterrent effect. Thus, these many eyes would also be turned on the inmates. The prison governor, incidentally,

The inspected were watched for their conformity to the institutional regimen, which was scientifically designed to reform the class of inmates housed in a given Panopticon. When deviations from the regimen were detected, an inspector promptly called the straying inmate back to the norm. Assuming that behavioral conformity might be achieved in this way, what reason was there to believe that the system would effect the intended rehabilitation? Why might not hatred or paranoia come of it just as easily as rehabilitation? Bentham saw no problem here. His system was not for incorrigibles, but for delinquents:

> Delinquents are a peculiar race of beings, who require unremitted inspection. Their weakness consists in yielding to the seductions of the passing moment. Their minds are weak and disordered, and though their disease is neither so clearly marked nor so incurable as that of idiots and lunatics, like these they require to be kept under restraints, and they cannot, without danger, be left to themselves.[59]

This opinion may probably stand as Bentham's considered view on the reason for the liability of the poor to crime, drink, and negligence.

These observations may go some way toward explaining why the benevolent Czar Alexander I engaged Bentham to advise on legal reform, why certain French revolutionaries were so excited about Panopticon, and why admirers in many lands hailed him as the greatest lawgiver of all times: Bentham had invented machinery for improving forlorn individuals previously dealt with by ruthless suppression. These "two great engines," reward and punishment, could be used scientifically to alter behavior. To many it appeared that Bentham had discovered the key not merely to law, but to the reformation of society by what subsequently was called "social conditioning." Although he lacked a terminology for it, he surely had the concept of behavioral engineering.[60] The "immense mass of improvable matter" presented by nature now expanded to in-

---

was also subject to inspection not only by his Board, but by any interested citizen. His Public Opinion Tribunal was yet another inspection agency in politics. This scheme of total inspection was to have a future among other benevolent improvers.

59. *Works of Bentham,* 1: 499; also 1: 40, 174–75. Bentham was conscious of the similarity between the function of his inspection tower and the omnipresent divine eye of conscience (1: 45, 38n).

60. The main inspiration of Bentham's thought on the modification of behavior was Helvétius, whose writings were also the mainspring of the French behavioralist school, the Ideologues, led by Cabanis.

clude "the whole mass of the now existing and suffering multitude." This is a big idea. That he had hit upon it is not widely appreciated, no doubt partly because of its incompatibility with Bentham's commitments to representative democracy and to laissez-faire economics. But his commitment to the Panopticon project as machinery for improving human beings in prisons, schools, and the workplace is unambiguous.[61] It is equally clear that his analysis of penal law and practice is founded on rigorous instrumental application of skillfully devised rewards and punishments to achieve well-defined behavioral changes. Modern penal thinking begins here.[62] So does behaviorism, for Bentham recognized that his system must be applicable in many institutional settings.

If prison and factory are interchangeable sites for the operation of the benevolent improvement machine, Panopticon, we should expect to find Bentham involved with some benevolent factory master. And indeed he was. In 1813, after Robert Owen had shed partners reluctant to fund his social experimentation at New Lanark, Bentham and five other progressives joined him as partners. The deed of partnership stipulated that "all profits made in the concern beyond five percent per annum on the capital invested shall be laid aside for the religious, educational, and moral improvement of the workers, and of the community at large."[63] Unfortunately, the record of what passed between these two men during their meetings is sparse. There is no evidence that Owen invited, or that Bentham proposed, to collaborate actively.[64] Even so, the two men

61. Bentham espoused Panopticon for forty years. He spent his own money building a pilot structure, in the hope of persuading Parliament to take over the project, which at one time seemed likely. These projects failed. But Panopticons were built in France and the United States, exactly copying Bentham's plan, as recently as 1930.

62. John Austin was the first important utilitarian jurist. Sir Henry Maine, A. V. Dicey, Coleman Phillipson, and William H. Alexander have all emphasized Bentham's impact on law. See Coleman Phillipson, *Three Criminal Law Reformers,* and William H. Alexander, "Jeremy Bentham, Legal Philosopher and Reformer" (*New York University Law Quarterly Review* 7 [1929]), who said that Bentham's *Principles of Penal Law* "may even today be the most lucid and penetrating single work ever written on the subject."

63. G. D. H. Cole, *The Life of Robert Owen,* 206.

64. Owen's anecdote about his first meeting with the excitable Bentham is recounted ibid., 148. In his memoirs, Bentham appraised Owen in these terms: "Robert Owen begins in vapour, and ends in smoke. He is a great braggadocio. His mind is a maze of confusion, and he avoids coming to particulars. He is always the same—says the same things over and over again. He built some small houses; and people, who had no houses of their own, went to live in those houses—and he calls this success" (*Works of Bentham,* 10: 570–71).

shared important ground. In the same year the partnership was formed, Owen published his *Report to the Committee of the Association for the Relief of the Manufacturing and Labouring Poor,* which urged Parliament to a fresh consideration of the entire problem of the employed and unemployed poor, in light of the costly ineffectiveness of the poor rate and the economic effects of factory production.[65] His exhortation appealed to the good news from his Lanark experiments, that the self-destructive behavior of the poor was remedial. If children were placed in a favorable environment, insulated from the influence of vicious parents, they acquired firm moral characters. Subsequently Owen developed this insight (which he knew had been confirmed by the experience of many religious communities) into the great dogma of hope: that character and behavior are not made *by* the individual; they are made *for* the individual by environment and circumstances. This was the new rational doctrine. But Owen formed a sect to propagate the gospel of utopian communism, to be created by reordering society to eliminate competition, religion, and marriage. Thus "the only sane man living," as he styled himself, the prophet of "the rational system," cast himself into the Messiah role and attracted the hopes of numerous believers. Owen ended his days in the seance chambers of spiritualists.

Panopticon and experimental communities were engines of moral improvement erected by the benevolent imaginations of social welfare entrepreneurs. These contraptions did not work. They raised hopes and

65. The reform plan Owen presented in 1813 carried a high price tag. His scheme was to settle the poor in a series of cooperative villages engaged in agriculture and light manufacture. The capital outlay for each village of 1,000 persons he estimated at £60,000 minimum. Thus, to settle 100,000 persons would have required a capital outlay of £6 million at a time when the national debt stood at £600 million. Yet the plan was not unfeasible. Parliament was then paying out between £6 million and £8 million annually on poor rates. If these monies could have been capitalized to liquidate the recurrent expenditure by eliminating poverty, economy would have lain on the side of relief. Moreover, Owen's plan permitted a stepwise progressus that could be modulated to available capital. Unable to engage Parliament or the Church to underwrite his project, Owen founded New Harmony at his own expense. For a time it was a moderate success, but it did not become the critical mass touching off a chain reaction despite its many imitations outside England. Actually, community planning for the poor at very low capital cost was an enormous success at that time—in the United States. This interesting and instructive example never attracted Owen's eye because these unplanned communities gave no scope to social messiahs, which was the role he craved. His engagement with this role was the reason why Owen "went a little mad in 1817, and he went on getting madder to the end of his days" (Cole, *Life of Robert Owen,* 197).

propagated errors. In 1841 Sir Robert Peel took government under the banner of the newly formed Conservative party and in 1848 the liberal-radical combination was defeated throughout Europe. Nevertheless, liberalism in one or another of its variations would dominate the politics of the remainder of the century.

afterword

IT IS well that historians of political thought have been admonished by one of their number about the hazards of "obsession with liberalism." The measure of enlightenment that history may provide is shortened when study is tightly yoked to finding in the past the genealogy of some problem or impasse that exercises us today. Studies so highly purposive usually succeed in finding what was sought, but at the cost of imposing the investigator's priorities upon the thought and action of the past.

The present study has been concerned primarily with thought and action that has long since been assigned to the canon of liberalism. However, it has not been my purpose to identify a liberal Ur-type and trace its development. I have attempted to describe the expansionist dynamic of modern states regardless of whether the designation "liberal" could be aptly applied to a particular configuration of thought or political organization. Liberalism, in perspective of the present study, is but one element, or, more accurately, succession of elements, in the repertoire of modernity. When it appeared in the last quarter of the eighteenth century, liberalism was the creed of publicists and intellectuals whose doctrines were rapidly overtaken by war and by rival political creeds.

In this afterword I will indulge the obsession with liberalism so far as to reflect briefly on the contemporary implications of its legacy. In doing so I take note of a widespread disaffection from liberalism which the disaffected express as its alleged decline, collapse, incoherence, and other metaphors of decrepitude. While the disaffection is an indicator

567

of political change, one may doubt that the recently changed political fortunes of liberalism pertain to basic philosophy. The conservative and social democratic theories being offered by critics do not match the scope of liberal theory and often differ from liberalism more in temper and priorities than in basics; so, at any rate, one might conclude from observing the banner of Adam Smith unfurled over the New Right bastions, or from listening to the protestations of neoconservatives that they are really liberals concerned to correct liberal excesses. Certainly liberalism is easily criticized; its problems of theory and practice have long been recognized. But if the existence of acknowledged problems were sufficient grounds for dismissing a normative or descriptive political theory, we should have to dismiss them all. As it happens, liberal beliefs are so deeply entrenched institutionally that probably nothing short of a complete change of legitimacy is likely to dislodge them. In this sense liberalism is a political fatality and we must attend to it.

As representative liberals we may take Adam Smith, the marquis de Condorcet, and Alexander Hamilton. They shared commitment to constitutional government founded on basic theory of human action, and a projection of a dynamic future based upon a long view of the past and of basic theory. Smith and Condorcet were heirs of physiocracy; Hamilton updated and modified Smithian economics while assimilating it. Condorcet and Hamilton were politicians as well as theorists. Although Smith was not active, his criticism of colonialism and vindication of agrarian capitalism helped establish the foreign policy positions of the "Little England" Whigs and the Jeffersonians.

Liberalism means generosity. Liberal theory was distinguished from antecedent political doctrines by its promise of liberty. The *ancien régime* in Europe applied the discipline of class subordination and religious prescription. Hobbesian doctrine removed these encumbrances upon the release of human potential, but imposed the rigorous artificial force of the state to keep those energetic potencies within the limits of institutional order. To propound a doctrine more liberal than the Hobbesian, one needed to find a mild, "natural" solution to Hobbes's problem—the tendency of natural impulse to turn feral in the civilized condition. Condorcet, Smith, and Hamilton each provided a new solution.

Building on the much enlarged historical perspective that had been won through the encyclopedists' work in comparative history, Condorcet discerned an epochal progression of enlightenment that coordinated with increasing refinement of the arts and growth of knowledge. As civil life became more intellectual, manners were refined and the wildness in man was progressively tamed. Hobbes's problem is solved by rejecting, on the basis of historical evidence and Lockean psychology, the thesis of the fixity of human traits relevant to civil life. With the horizon of change so radically open, Condorcet projected a future in which all the doctrinal postulates of Hobbesian doctrine were fulfilled. Equality encompassed racial and sexual equality; the peace postulate was to be perfected by the abolition of war and oppression; and so on. The mechanism of this change was the incremental transformation of institutions and manners by the infusion of ever-increasing knowledge. National and individual competition, which for Hobbes was the ineluctable impediment to such an outcome, was removed in Condorcet's future, thanks to boundless abundance.

Smith also adopted the encyclopedists' conception of the stages of civilization, but gave it an economic interpretation that derived directional change as the imperceptible and unintended residue of the constant striving of everyman to improve his condition. This abstract idea was given political effect by embedding it in a description of market forces which exhibit the market as the expression of countless exchanges by ordinary people that aggregate into a continuous objective measure of the value of commodities. This is the scientific description of the great democratic vision that Smith's friend Ben Franklin put into homespun prose.

The vision had not been available theretofore because the vision's realization depended on the coincidence of two contingent events. The first was that everyman's striving for improvement had to result in individual accumulation; that would happen only when new lands were being brought under tillage. The discovery of the New World made widely distributed economic growth likely for the foreseeable future. The second condition was that the market had to be large enough to absorb local distortions created by cheating and collusion; and rewarding enough to create an interest in preserving it against relapse into the system of armed merchants for whom theft, pillage, and extortion were honorable modes of exchange. The monarchs of Europe had displaced the freebooters, but in doing so had appropriated their devices under the names of mercantilism and foreign trade. Hence the catch-cry of economic liberals that the true welfare of the masses is served when the market is not disturbed by the intervention of governments and monopolies enjoying government privilege; and when government, which consumes but does not produce, is kept small.

Smith's system, like Condorcet's, pictures the gradual taming of wildness; it also describes a trend toward international peace by debunking the doctrine of national markets upon which the balance-of-trade worries depended. But it will not endorse Condorcet's vision of emancipation because it identifies irremovable natural limits on the production of wealth. The social consequence of these limits on competition is permanent. It is from concern about the political effects of competition that Smith would have his agrarian capitalists renounce the splendor of empire.

Hamilton's political thought reasserts the constancy of human nature. Believing that men were as wild as ever, he advocated strong government. Nevertheless, there was greater scope for unfettered endeavor than Hobbes allowed. That great mass of improvable matter, the wilderness, could absorb human wildness and tame it in the process of being tamed itself. Further, the advent of industrial production opened up new possibilities for the creation of wealth, and—no less important— an abundance of new opportunities for the release of talents. The wilderness and industrial technology, then, were two new "states of nature" upon which humankind could exercise its energies while yet maintaining political order. The conception of that order accordingly changed. Whereas the *Leviathan* exhibits the polity held to a static condition by sovereign power, *The Federalist Papers* exhibit the dynamics of active wills operating in the expansive structures of a large democratic republic.

It is one of the ironies of liberalism that its doctrine of peace, freedom, and prosperity was implanted in the hearts of millions by the dramaturgy of revolution and war. French liberalism was connected with revolution in an erratic manner. The early phase, which peaked with the Declaration of the Rights of Man, was under liberal auspices; but the Revolution hastened to its neoclassical phase and finally came to rest in neo-Caesarism. Liberals of the Empire regarded the termination of the Bourbon dynasty as a watershed toward progress, but yearned for the political liberties enjoyed by Englishmen even as Napoleon's victories spread the liberal doctrine of rights.

In America there was no such ambiguity. The uprising against the British "oppressor" was the event that midwifed the founding of the polity on liberal principles. Thus revolution, which Hobbes dreaded as the most destructive war politically, became a fundamental signifier and validating example for the expression of liberal liberty. As such it has been invoked repeatedly to legitimate domestic reforms as well as world-improving foreign policy. In this way the political program that aimed at subduing wildness to stability and prosperity came to inscribe the symbols of untamed heroic action on its banners. This is not so much an irony as a paradox.

A similar fate befell the factory system. The system was devised and implemented by the progressive new men who viewed it as a great instrument for the moral improvement of the underclass from which they themselves had risen. The intended improvement was a model of rational economic choice. High wages increased purchasing power; the work routine imposed regularity on the labor force; competition prompted continuous innovation resulting in market expansion. Yet this paradigm of docile, disciplined work became a new symbol of oppression. Escape from the oppression was not pictured as an alternative mode of production, but as heroic rebellion. Despite the appropriation of this imagery by a variety of political movements, no revolution was ever made under its auspices in an industrial nation. But there is one telling instance of its impact on political consciousness—the European response to the commencement of the Great War. The war dread and pacifism that had been widespread since 1900 disappeared in an outburst of popular war enthusiasm in all belligerent nations. Roland Stromberg's cross-national study of the response of intellectuals shows that they also experienced these feelings.[1] The war was greeted as a revitalizing and purifying event. Liberals concurred with socialists, anarchists, and conservatives in reprobating the stultification of spirit that the era of commercial regularity had induced. "Narrow self-interest," i.e. rational economic choice, was suddenly set at naught as the flower of each nation's youth marched off to make the supreme sacrifice. National consciousness was revitalized. A moving sense of a single national will and of solidarity of the people in adversity replaced the selfish interest and factionalism that had held sway in public life. The long reign of civilian "materialism" was terminated by an ecstasis of martial idealism. For a brief moment (lasting perhaps a year) liberal Europe disburdened itself of prosaic liberal modes of thought to celebrate the poetic festivals of heroic splendor.

Heroism is the name that the unenlightened consciousness gives to what the enlightened language of Hobbesian philosophy calls the endeavor for power that seeks to dominate other men. Despite the tremendous debunking that heroic action underwent in the anthropology of Hobbes and his successors, despite all attempts to replace heroism by self-interested action directed toward obtainable ends, liberals were unable to prevent their doctrine acquiring the emblems of heroic legitimation in its uptake by democratic publics. The Hobbist may regard this phenomenon as a confirmation of the constancy of human nature. Smith seems to have thought that a world without heroes would be the poorer for it, while Hamilton's actions as commander, politician, and intellectual were of heroic dimensions.

Heroes smack of inequality. Liberalism's equality requirement was

1. Roland Stromberg, *Redemption by War: The Intellectuals and 1914* (Lawrence, Kansas: Regents Press of Kansas, 1982).

preached to the millions as an ethical duty. But its theoretical basis is purely utilitarian. The equality prescription is a way of saying that political order reaches its optimum when citizens orient their action upon the grid of enlightened self-interest. Public law can then treat individuals equally because they are identical or at least commensurate in the decisive respects.

The initial polemical objects of the equality doctrine were distinctions based on social rank and religious beliefs. The unexpressed message of the equality text indicated that white adult males were meant. The effective extension of equality to other races was arduous. Its extension to females has yet to establish its viability. Regardless of how this interesting experiment may turn out, it is to be noted that neither liberal theory nor its Hobbesian predecessor has the conceptual resources needed to identify and describe the psycho-social implications of sexual equality.

Hobbes took the monogamous family for granted. Subsequent writers remarked the assumption; but apart from an inconclusive effort by Rousseau, none investigated it. By mid-nineteenth century J. S. Mill was thinking seriously about sexual equality, but he initiated no study of the bearing of family and kinship on social structure. Socialists of various hues called for the abolition of the family; but they did so mechanically, registering it as yet another institution ripe for riddance.

The attempt to abolish the family has failed on every trial. Today self-styled Marxist governments are firm supporters of the family, which they shield from "decadent" western influences. For their part liberal theorists have as yet been unable to focus the sexual equality question in terms other than rights claims. This is, of course, tautologically correct within liberal theory: when the problem is conceived to be the extension of equality, the solution clearly lies in the effective delivery of rights.

However, this does beg the question. We recall that from Hobbes onward the individuals who were to be equal were implicitly white adult males. Heroism was excluded from the individual concept because it is the male trait that most endangers public safety by blinding heroes and their following to cautious self-interest. The removal of heroic legitimation from the polity, and reduced incidence of heroic temperaments, was the formula for the taming of natural wildness. This reflection may assist in recognizing that the application of the individual concept to females requires that their distinguishing feature, the reproductive function, be left out of account. In law and employment, they must be treated "like anyone," i.e. like nonheroic men. However, men do not have babies and do not at present have the primary nurturing responsibility. To treat mothers on a parity, whether in contract or employment, is thus to disadvantage them. This perceived outcome is meant to be remedied by "affirmative action" to compensate the "disadvantages" of childbearing, although the childbearing capacity is inherent in female individuality. The quandary may be reduced to the observation that when mothers are measured by performance norms fashioned by males for application to males, they don't measure up. This unsurprising result might suggest that the error lies in applying such a standard. If so, it is not an error easily corrected because the liberal polity is imperiously directed to equality. The delegitimation of heroic action led at length to the wimpdom of muddling through by committee. The delegitimation of motherhood may lead to harvesting babies in the laboratory. One of the fascinations of the future will be the fate of that liberal mutant, the biocracy that aspires to control human evolution. Will wimp biocrats destroy motherhood in their endeavor to improve the quality of life by nurturing it in a controlled, sterile environment? This question cannot arise as a serious political question in a wholly liberal polity. That it is serious today and promises to be more serious tomorrow is an indication that the biocratic mutant is behaving like the successor to liberalism.

bibliography

THIS BIBLIOGRAPHY substantially condenses the working bibliography assembled for this study. The working bibliography consists of about 600 titles of original sources, 2,000 titles of secondary literature, and 1,100 titles in biosocial science.

For works cited in the footnotes by author and title alone, full publishing information is given in this bibliography. Some works cited in the footnotes are not included in the bibliography; for these, publishing information appears in the note. For material quoted repeatedly from original sources, citations are often inserted into the text.

The principal bibliographic tool for contemporaneous sources was the *Goldsmiths'-Kress Library of Economic Literature: Consolidated Guide to Microfilm Collection*. It lists some 50,000 titles in the Goldsmiths'-Kress Collection, which includes materials printed in seven European languages from 1500 to 1800. Study of the guide was indispensable to the formation of my estimation of the levels of economic and political understanding achieved at various times in Europe during the period under investigation. I studied the microfilm collection loaned from the Australian National Library and the originals held at Harvard University and the University of London when from time to time I was in those precincts. It was my intention to describe, in the notes, the methods used to derive evaluations from this collection. The intention was abandoned when it became apparent that its execution required a methodological essay. This I hope to supply sometime in the future in the form of a guide to the *Guide*. Suffice it that my approach was populational, taking aggregates of titles under assigned classifications. For this reason it was to no effect to cite individual titles; consequently this dimension of the study has not been documented. The excluded documentation supports a major contention of this study, that economic wisdom flowed into European fiscal and economic institutions through various elites, some representatives of which I have discussed.

In working through the secondary literature, it was my practice to assemble bibliographies on particular subjects that covered the entire period of modern historical writing. This device was adopted to guard against undue acceptance of contemporary Anglo-American prejudices. The protestations of several referees of the manuscript suggest that the procedure has not been without effect. The procedure also exhibited the wonderful range of historical description and documentation. This immersion in historiographic variety no doubt accounts for the author's irreverence toward certain supposed rules of historical representation: if they are rules, they have been ignored by numerous historians past and present. The temptation to enter upon historiographic discussions has been severely suppressed lest the study become entangled in second-order considerations at the expense of narrative. Those interested in shop talk are referred to J. H. Hexter's *The History Primer,* in my estimation the most accurate and concise description of what most narrative historians actually do. His study and J. G. A. Pocock's criticism of the philosophic history of ideas have been invaluable guides for those aspects of the present work that remain within conventional historical method.

The scientific literature supporting the study covers human evolution, prehistory, animal and human ethology, sociobiology, physical anthropology, endocrinology, experimental psychology, and psychobiology inclusive of psychopathology. Some 2,500 titles have been published as *A Bibliography of Biosocial Science.* The assembly of this material was meant to furnish an independent view about human behavior, about which historians make many assumptions and not infrequently tell tales. An independent view was deemed necessary because reflection and disputation about the nature of man and human society is central to my theme, and I had no wish merely to rehearse familiar opinions doxographically. The introduction sets out the one explicit application of behavioral biology to historiography contained in this study. Some half-dozen such applications were originally intended, as demonstrations of the new biosocial historiography. The plan was abandoned lest the weight of that innovation, added to the others, drag the book into the oblivion that awaits studies that venture too far from received conventions. Instead I am making a systematic application in a short study of one topic, the revolutionary idea in modern Europe.

Sources

Académie des Sciences. *Machines et inventions approuvées par l'Académie royale des sciences.* Vols. 1–7, 1666–1701. Paris: G. Martin, 1735–77.

Adams, John. *The Works of John Adams.* Edited by Charles Francis Adams. 12 vols. Boston, 1851. Reprint. New York: AMS Press, 1971.

Adams, Samuel. *The Writings of Samuel Adams.* Edited by H. A. Cushing. 4 vols. New York: Putnam, 1904–1908.

Arago, D. F. J. *Historical Eloge of James Watt.* 1839. Reprint. New York: Arno Press, 1975.

Argenson, Marquis d'. *Journal et mémoires.* Edited by E. J. B. Rathery. 14 vols. Paris: Renouard, 1859.

Aubrey, John. *Aubrey's "Brief Lives."* Edited by Oliver Lawson Dick. London: Secker and Warburg, 1949.

Babbage, Charles. *On the Economy of Machines and Manufactures.* 4th ed. (1835). Reprint. New York: Kelley, 1963.

Bacon, Francis. *The Works of Francis Bacon.* Edited by James Spedding, Robert Leslie Ellis, and Douglas Heath. 11 vols. London: Longman, 1858.

Baillet, Adrien. *Vie de Monsieur Descartes.* 2 vols. Paris: Horthemels, 1691.

Baxter, Richard. *Richard Baxter and Puritan Politics.* Edited by Richard Schlatter. New Brunswick, N.J.: Rutgers University Press, 1957.

Bell, William. *A Dissertation on 'What Causes Principally Contribute to Render a Nation Populous, and What Effect Has the Population of a Nation on Its Trade.'* Cambridge, 1756.

Bentham, Jeremy. *The Works of Jeremy Bentham.* 11 vols. Edinburgh, 1843.

Bolingbroke, Henry St. John. *The Works of Lord Bolingbroke.* 4 vols. London, 1841.

———. *The Works of the Late Right Honourable Henry St. John, lord viscount Bolingbroke.* 8 vols. London, 1809.

[Anon.] *A brief history of trade in England. By a merchant.* London: E. Baldwin, 1702.

Burnet, Gilbert. *History of His Own Times.* Edited by M. J. Routh. 6 vols. 1856. Reprint. Heidelsheim: Olms, 1969.

Carlyle, Thomas. *The Works of Thomas Carlyle.* 26 vols. Boston: Estes, 1899–1901.

Cartwright, Mary S. *A Memoir of the Life, Writings, and Mechanical Inventions of Edmund Cartwright.* London: Saunders and Otley, 1843.

The Chadwick Report on the Sanitary Condition of the Labouring Population with the Local Reports for England and Wales and other related papers, 1837–42. Vol. 33 of *British Parliamentary Papers.* Shannon: Irish University Press, 1971.

Child, Sir Josiah. *A discourse about trade.* London, 1690.

Choix de rapports, opinions et discours prononcés à la Tribune nationale depuis 1789 jusqu'à ce jour, recueillis dans un ordre chronologique et historique. 21 vols. Paris: Eymery, 1818.

Colbert, Jean Baptiste. *Lettres, instructions et mémoires.* Edited by Pierre Clément. 7 vols. Paris, 1861–73.

Condorcet, M. J. A. Marquis de. Œuvres complètes. 12 vols. Paris, 1847.

The Constitutional Documents of the Puritan Revolution 1625–1660. Edited by S. R. Gardiner. Oxford: Clarendon Press, 1927.

Correspondence of the French Ministers to the United States, 1791–1797. Seventh Report of the Historical Manuscripts Commission. Edited by Frederick Jackson Turner. Washington: U. S. Government Printing Office, 1904.

The Craftsman [Caleb d'Anvers, pseud.]. 14 vols. London: R. Franklin, 1731–37.

Craig, John. Theologiae Christiania principia mathematica. London, 1699.

Daire, Eugène, ed. Physiocrates: Quesnay, Dupont de Nemours, Mercier de la Rivière, l'Abbé Baudeau, le Trosne. 1847–48. Reprint. Geneva: Slatkine, 1971.

d'Alembert, Jean. Preliminary Discourse to the Encyclopedia of Diderot. Translated by Richard N. Schwab. Indianapolis: Bobbs-Merrill, 1963.

Davenant, Charles. England's treasure by forraign trade. London, 1694.

———. An Essay Upon the Probable Methods of Making a People Gainers in the Balance of Trade. London, 1700.

———. Essays Upon the Ballance of Power, the Right of Making War, Peace and Alliances, Universal Monarchy. London, 1701.

———. The True Picture of a Modern Whig. London, 1701.

Defoe, Daniel. An Essay upon projects. London, 1697.

[de la Court, Pieter.] The True Interest and Political Maxims of the Republic of Holland and Westfriesland. 1662. Reprint. Translated by John Campbell. London, 1743.

Desaguliers, J. T. A Course of Experimental Philosophy. 2 vols. London, 1734–44.

Descartes, René. Œuvres philosophiques. Edited by F. Alquié. 3 vols. Paris: Garnier, 1963–73.

Diderot, Denis, and d'Alembert, Jean le Ronde. Encyclopédie, ou dictionnaire raissonné des sciences, des arts et des métiers. 35 vols. Paris: Briasson, 1751–65.

Dossie, Robert. Memoirs of Agriculture and Other Œconomical Arts. Vol. 1. London, 1768.

[Anon.] The Dutch Drawn to Life. London, 1664.

Engels, Friedrich. The Condition of the Working Class in England. Translated by W. O. Henderson and W. H. Chaloner. 1844. Reprint. Oxford: Blackwell, 1958.

Evelyn, John. The Diary of John Evelyn. Edited by H. B. Wheatley. 4 vols. London: Bicker, 1879.

Farrand, Max, ed. The Records of the Federal Convention of 1787. 4 vols. New Haven, Conn.: Yale University Press, 1966.

The Federalist. See Hamilton, Alexander, et al.

Fielden, John. The Curse of the Factory System. 2d ed. 1836. Reprint. New York: Kelley, 1969.

Fletcher, Andrew. Discourse of Government with Relation to Militias. London, 1732.

Fontenelle, Bernard le Bovier de. A Conversation on the Plurality of Worlds. To which is added Mr. Addison's Defense of Newtonian Philosophy. London, 1777.

———. Œuvres de Fontenelle. 5 vols. Paris: Salmon, 1825.

Franklin, Benjamin. The Complete Works of Benjamin Franklin. 3 vols. London: Johnson, 1806.

Frederick the Great. Œuvres de Frederic le Grand. 30 vols. Berlin, 1846–56.

Gaskell, Phillip. *Artisans and Machinery*. London: Parker, 1836.

Gassendi, Pierre. *The Mirrour of True Nobility*. London, 1657.

Gilchrist, John T., and Murray, W. J., eds. *The Press in the French Revolution. A Selection of Documents, 1789–1794*. New York: St. Martin's Press, 1971.

Gunn, J. A. W., ed. *Factions No More: Attitudes to Party in Government and Opposition in Eighteenth-Century England*. London: Frank Cass, 1972.

Hamilton, Alexander. *Industrial and Commercial Correspondence of Alexander Hamilton*. Edited by A. H. Cole. Chicago: A. W. Shaw, 1928.

Hamilton, Alexander; Madison, James; and Jay, John. *The Federalist*. Edited by James E. Cooke. Middletown, Conn.: Wesleyan University Press, 1961.

Harrington, James. *The Political Works of James Harrington*. Edited with an introduction by J. G. A. Pocock. Cambridge: Cambridge University Press, 1977.

[Hartlib, Samuel?] *A description of the famous kingdom of Macaria*. London, 1641.

Hobbes, Thomas. *The English Works*. Edited by Sir William Molesworth. 11 vols. London: J. Bohn, 1839–45.

———. *Leviathan, or the Matter, Forme and Power of a Commonwealth Ecclesiasticall and Civil*. Edited by M. Oakeshott. Oxford: Blackwell, 1960.

———. *Opera Latina*. Edited by Sir William Molesworth. 5 vols. London: J. Bohn, 1839–45.

Hodgskin, Thomas. *Popular Political Economy*. London: Tait, 1827.

Hume, David. *Essays, Moral, Political and Literary*. 4 vols. London: World's Classics, 1903.

———. *The Letters of David Hume*. Edited by G. Y. T. Greig. 2 vols. Oxford: Clarendon Press, 1969.

———. *The Philosophical Works of David Hume*. Edited by Thomas Hill Green and Thomas Hodge Grose. 4 vols. 1882. Reprint. Aalen, West Germany: Scientia Verlag, 1964.

———. *Writings on Economics*. Edited by Eugene Rotwein. Madison: University of Wisconsin Press, 1970.

Huygens, Christiaan. *Œuvres complètes*. 22 vols. The Hague, 1888–1950.

Jefferson, Thomas. *The Papers of Thomas Jefferson*. Edited by Julian P. Boyd. 19 vols. Princeton, N.J.: Princeton University Press, 1950–82.

———. *The Writings of Thomas Jefferson*. Edited by P. L. Ford. 10 vols. New York: Putnam, 1893–99.

Law, John. *Money and trade consider'd*. Edinburgh, 1705.

List, Friedrich. *The National System of Political Economy*. 1841. Reprint. London: Longmans, 1909.

Locke, John. *The Correspondence of John Locke*. Edited by E. S. de Beer. 8 vols. Oxford: Clarendon Press, 1979.

———. *John Locke: Two Treatises of Government*. Edited by Peter Laslett. Cambridge: Cambridge University Press, 1960.

———. *The Works of John Locke*. 9 vols. 12th ed. London, 1824.

Louis XIV. *Œuvres de Louis XIV*. Paris and Strasbourg: Treuttel et Wurtz, 1806.

Machiavelli, Niccolò. *Opere*. Edited by Mario Bonfontini. Milan: Ricciardi, n.d.

———. *The Works of the Famous Nicolas Machiavel*. [Edited by Henry Neville.] London, 1675.

Madison, James. *The Complete Madison: His Basic Writings.* Edited by Saul K. Padover. New York: Harper, 1971.

———. *Letters and Other Writings of James Madison.* 4 vols. New York: Lippincott, 1865.

———. *The Mind of the Founder: Sources of the Political Thought of James Madison.* Edited by Marvin Meyers. Indianapolis: Bobbs-Merrill, 1973.

Mandeville, Bernard. *An Enquiry into the Origins of Honour and the Usefulness of Christianity in War.* Edited by M. M. Goldsmith. London: Cass, 1971.

Marsilius of Padua. *The Defender of Peace.* Translated with an introduction by Alan Gewirth. New York: Harper & Row, 1967.

Mill, John Stuart. *The Principles of Political Economy.* 2 vols. Rev. ed. New York: Cooperative Publication Society, 1900.

———. *"The Spirit of the Age."* Chicago: University of Chicago Press, 1942.

———. *A System of Logic, Ratiocinative and Inductive.* London: Longmans, 1961.

Molesworth, Robert. *The Principles of a Real Whig.* 1711. Reprint. London, 1775.

Montesquieu, Baron Charles Secondat. *Considerations on the Causes of the Greatness of the Romans and Their Decline.* Translated by David Lowenthal. New York: The Free Press, 1965.

———. *Œuvres complètes.* 2 vols. Paris: Gallimard, 1949–51.

More, Henry. *A Collection of Several Philosophical Writings of Dr. Henry More.* 4th ed., corrected and enlarged. London: Downing, 1712.

Mun, Thomas. *England's Treasure by Forraign Trade.* London, 1664.

[Anon.] *Observations, &c. as to the Ages of Persons Employed in the Cotton Mills in Manchester. With extracts of evidence against Sir Robert Peel's Bill taken before Lord's committees.* Manchester, 1819.

Owen, Robert. "Report to the Committee of the Association for the Relief of the Manufacturing and Labouring Poor." In *A New View of Society.* London, 1818.

Parker, Henry. *Of A Free Trade: A Discourse Seriously Recommending to Our Nation the Wonderful Benefits of Free Trade.* London, 1648.

Pepys, Samuel. *The Diary of Samuel Pepys.* Edited by Henry B. Wheatley. 8 vols. London: Bell, 1952.

Perrault, Charles. *Mémoires de ma vie.* Paris: Librairie Renovard, 1909.

Poitevin, Citizen. *Catéchisme républicain, suivi de maximes de morale républicaine, propre à l'éducation des enfants de l'un et de l'autre sexe.* Paris: de Millet, 1791.

Quesnay, François. *Œuvres économiques et philosophiques.* New York: Burt Franklin, 1969.

[Ralph, James.] *Of the Use and Abuse of Parliaments. In Two Historical Discourses.* 2 vols. London, 1744.

Raynal, Guillaume Thomas. *A Philosophical and Political History of the Settlements and Trade of the Europeans in the East and West Indies.* 6 vols. Edinburgh, 1782.

———. *The Revolution of America.* 2d ed. Edinburgh, 1782. Reprint. Boston: Gregg Press, 1972.

[Anon.] *Reasons in Favour of Sir Robert Peel's Bill, for Ameliorating the Condition of Children Employed in Cotton Factories.* London, 1819.

Recueil des documents relatifs à la Convocation des États généraux de 1789. Edited by Armand Brette. 3 vols. Paris, 1894.

Register of Premiums and Bounties Given by the Society from 1754 to 1776 inclusive. London: Society for the Encouragement of Arts, Manufactures and Commerce, 1778.

Résumé général ou extrait des cahiers des pouvoirs, instructions, demandes et doléances remis par les divers bailliages, sénéchaussées, et pays d'états du royaume à leurs députés à l'Assemblée des États Généraux ouverts à Versailles le 4 mai 1789. Par une Société de gens de lettres. 3 vols. Paris, 1789.

Ricardo, David. *Works and Correspondence.* Edited by Piero Sraffa. 9 vols. Cambridge, England: Royal Economic Society, 1951–62.

Robespierre, Maximilien. *Œuvres de Robespierre.* Edited by A. Vermorel. Paris: Cournal, 1866.

Robinson, Eric, and Musson, A. E., eds. *James Watt and the Steam Revolution, A Documentary History.* New York: Kelley, 1969.

Rousseau, Jean-Jacques. *The First and Second Discourses.* Edited by Roger D. Masters. New York: St. Martin's Press, 1964.

————. *Œuvres complètes.* 3 vols. Paris: Gallimard, 1964.

Savile, George, First Marquess of Halifax. *The Complete Works of George Savile.* Edited by Walter Raleigh. Oxford: Clarendon Press, 1912.

Say, Jean-Baptiste. *Letters to Thomas Robert Malthus on Political Economy and Stagnation of Commerce.* 1820 (first French ed.). Reprint. London: George Harding, 1936.

————. *A Treatise on Political Economy; or the Production, Distribution and Consumption of Wealth.* 1803. 4th ed. Philadelphia, 1830.

Schlatter, Richard, ed. *Richard Baxter and Puritan Politics.* New Brunswick, N.J.: Rutgers University Press, 1957.

Shaw, William A., ed. *Select Tracts and Documents Illustrative of English Monetary History, 1626–1730.* London: George Harding, 1896.

Sieyès, Abbé. *Qu'est que le tiers état?* Edited by Edme Champion. Paris, 1888.

Smiles, Samuel. *Industrial Biography: Iron Workers and Tool Builders.* Baltimore, 1863.

Smith, Adam. *An Enquiry into the Nature and Causes of the Wealth of Nations.* Edited by Edwin Cannan. 1776. Reprint. Chicago: University of Chicago Press, 1976.

————. *An Inquiry into the Nature and Causes of the Wealth of Nations.* Edited by R. H. Campbell and A. S. Skinner. 2 vols. 1776. Reprint. Oxford: Oxford University Press, 1967. Indianapolis: Liberty Classics, 1981.

[Somers, John Lord.] *Anguis in Herba or the fatal consequences of a treaty with France.* London: A. Baldwin, 1702.

[Somers' Tracts.] *A Collection of Scarce and Valuable Tracts.* Edited by Walter Scott. 14 vols. 2d ed. London, 1815.

Spinoza, Benedict de. *Chief Works.* 2 vols. New York: Dover, 1951.

Sprat, Thomas. *History of the Royal Society.* 1667. Edited with critical apparatus by Jackson I. Cope and Harold Whitmore Jones. London: Routledge, 1959.

Stevin, Simon. *Principal Works of Simon Stevin.* Edited by E. J. Dijksterhuis. 6 vols. Amsterdam: Zeitlinger, 1955.

Stewart, Dugald. "Account of the Life and Writings of Adam Smith." In *Essays on Philosophical Subjects,* by Adam Smith. 1795. Facsimile. New York: Garland, 1971.

Strauss, Gerald, ed. *Manifestations of Discontent in Germany on the Eve of the Reformation: A Collection of Documents.* Bloomington: Indiana University Press, 1971.

Swift, Jonathan. *The History of the four last years of the Queen.* Edited by Herbert Davis. 1715. Reprint. Oxford: Blackwell, 1951.

———. *The Works of the Reverand Dr. Jonathan Swift.* 20 vols. Dublin: George Faulkner, 1772.

Tann, Jennifer, ed. *The Selected Papers of Boulton and Watt.* Vol. 1. Cambridge: M.I.T. Press, 1981.

Temple, William. *Observations upon the United Provinces of the Netherlands.* London, 1673.

Temple, William. *A Vindication of Commerce and the Arts, Proving that they are the source of the greatness, power, riches and populousness of a state.* London, 1758.

Tocqueville, Alexis de. *Democracy in America.* 2 vols. 1834. Reprint. New York: Schocken, 1967.

Toland, John. *Christianity not Mysterious: or, a Treatise Showing that There is Nothing in the Gospel Contrary to Reason, Nor Above It.* London, 1696.

Trenchard, John. *Some Considerations upon the State of our Publick Debts.* London: S. Peele, 1723.

Tucker, Josiah. *Four Tracts on Political and Commercial Subjects.* Gloucester, 1774.

Turgot, Anne Robert Jacques. *Œuvres de Turgot.* Edited by Gustave Schelle. 6 vols. Paris: Alcan, 1923.

Ure, Andrew. *Philosophy of Manufactures.* London, 1835.

Volney, C. F. *Œuvres de C. F. Volney.* 8 vols. 2d ed. Paris: Parmantier, 1825.

Wharton, Francis, ed. *State Trials of the United States during the Administration of Washington and Adams.* New York, 1849. Reprint. New York: Burt Franklin, 1970.

Wood, Anthony à. *Athenae Oxonieses.* Edited by Philip Bliss. 4 vols. London, 1813–20.

Worsley, Benjamin [Philopatris, pseud.]. *The Advocate: or a Narrative of the state and condition of things between the English and Dutch Nation . . . as it was presented in August 1651.* London, 1652.

Wren, Matthew. *Monarchy Asserted, or the State of Monarchicall and Popular Government.* London, 1659.

Secondary Works

Acomb, Frances. *Anglophobia in France, 1763–1789. An Essay in the History of Constitutionalism and Nationalism.* Durham, N.C.: Duke University Press, 1950.

Acton, John E. E. D., 1st Baron. *Lectures on Modern History.* New York: Macmillan, 1906.

Adams, Henry. *History of the United States of America.* 9 vols. New York: Scribner's, 1890.

Advielle, Victor. *Histoire de Gracchus Babeuf et du Babourisme d'après de nombreux documents inédits.* 2 vols. Paris: Chez l'autour, 1884.

Aldridge, Alfred O. *Franklin and His French Contemporaries.* New York: New York University Press, 1957.

Allen, D. G. C. "The Society of Arts and Government, 1754–1800." *Eighteenth-Century Studies* 7 (1974): 434–52.

Allen, Don C. *Doubt's Boundless Sea: Skepticism and Faith in the Renaissance.* Baltimore: Johns Hopkins University Press, 1964.

Allen, Phyllis. "Scientific Studies in the English Universities of the Seventeenth Century." *Journal of the History of Ideas* 10 (1949): 219–53.

Anderson, F. H. *The Philosophy of Francis Bacon.* Chicago: University of Chicago Press, 1948.

Appleby, Joyce Oldham. *Capitalism and a New Social Order: The Republican Vision of the 1790s.* New York: New York University Press, 1984.

———. *Economic Thought and Ideology in Seventeenth-Century England.* Princeton, N.J.: Princeton University Press, 1978.

———. "Locke, Liberalism and the Natural Law of Money." *Past and Present* 17 (1976): 43–69.

Arblaster, Anthony. *The Rise and Decline of Western Liberalism.* Oxford: Blackwell, 1984.

Ardascheff, Paul. *Les intendants de province sous Louis XVI.* Paris: Alcan, 1909.

Aronson, Jason. "Shaftesbury on Locke." *American Political Science Review* 53 (1959): 1101–4.

Artz, Frederick B. *The Development of Technical Education in France, 1500–1850.* Cambridge: M.I.T. Press, 1966.

Ashcraft, Richard. "Locke's State of Nature, Historical Fact or Moral Fiction?" *American Political Science Review* 62 (1968).

———. "*The Two Treatises* and the Exclusion Crisis: The Problem of Lockean Political Theory as Bourgeois Ideology." In *John Locke.* Papers read at Clark Memorial Library seminar, Los Angeles, 1980.

Ashley, Maurice. *Financial and Commercial Policy under the Cromwellian Protectorate.* 1934. Reprint. London: Case, 1962.

Atherton, Herbert M. *Political Prints in the Age of Hogarth: A Study of the Ideographic Representation of Politics.* Oxford: Clarendon Press, 1974.

Bailyn, Bernard. *The Ideological Origins of the American Revolution.* New York: Knopf, 1968.

Baker, Keith Michael. *Condorcet: From Natural Philosophy to Social Mathematics.* Chicago: University of Chicago Press, 1975.

Banning, Lance. *The Jeffersonian Persuasion: Evolution of a Party Ideology*. Ithaca, N.Y.: Cornell University Press, 1978.

Baron, Hans. "Franciscan Poverty and Civic Wealth as Factors in the Rise of Humanistic Thought." *Speculum* 13 (1938): 1–37.

Baruzzi, Arno, ed. *Aufklärung und Materialismus in Frankreich des 18. Jahrhunderts*. Munich: List Verlag, 1968.

Baxter, Stephen B. *William III*. London: Longmans, 1966.

Beard, Charles A. *An Economic Interpretation of the Constitution of the United States*. New York: Macmillan, 1960.

———. *Economic Origins of Jeffersonian Democracy*. New York: Macmillan, 1915.

Becker, Carl. *The Declaration of Independence: A Study in the History of Political Ideas*. New York: Knopf, 1942.

Belin, J.-P. *Le commerce des livres prohibés à Paris de 1750 à 1789*. Paris, 1913. Reprint. New York: Burt Franklin, n.d.

Bell, A. E. *Christian Huygens and the Development of Science in the Seventeenth Century*. London: Edward Arnold, 1947.

Bell, Rudolph M. *Party and Faction in American Politics: The House of Representatives, 1789–1801*. Westport, Conn.: Greenwood Press, 1973.

Beloff, Max, ed. *The Debate on the American Revolution, 1761–1783*. 2d ed. London: Adam and Charles Black, 1960.

Ben-David, Joseph. *The Scientist's Role in Society: A Comparative Study*. Englewood Cliffs, N.J.: Prentice-Hall, 1971.

Berthold, Otto. *Kaiser, Volk und Avignon*. Berlin: Rutten & Loening, 1960.

Bertrand, Joseph L. F. *L'Académie des sciences et les académiciens de 1666 à 1793*. Paris: J. Hetzel, 1869.

Beveridge, Albert J. *The Life of John Marshall*. 2 vols. Boston: Houghton Mifflin, 1916.

Bigelow, Jacob. *Elements of Technology*. 2d ed. Boston: Hilliard, Gray, Little and Wilkins, 1831.

Billington, James H. *Fire in the Minds of Men: Origins of the Revolutionary Faith*. New York: Basic Books, 1980.

Biver, Marie-Louise. *Fêtes révolutionnaires à Paris*. Paris: Presses universitaires de France, 1970.

Blaas, P. B. M. *Continuity and Anachronism: Parliamentary and Constitutional Development in Whig Historiography*. The Hague: Martinus Nijhoff, 1978.

Boissonade, P. *Colbert et le triomphe de l'étatisme*. Paris: Marcel Rivière, 1932.

Bordas-Demoulin, Jean Baptiste. *Le Cartésianisme; ou la véritable rénovation des sciences*. Paris: Huet, 1843.

Borg, Maxine. *The Machinery Question and the Making of Political Economy, 1815–1848*. Cambridge: Cambridge University Press, 1982.

Bouwsma, William J. *Venice and the Defense of Republican Liberty*. Berkeley: University of California Press, 1968.

Boyd, J. P. *Number 7: Alexander Hamilton's Secret Attempts to Control American Foreign Policy*. Princeton, N.J.: Princeton University Press, 1964.

Bradley, Margaret. "Scientific Education for a New Society: The École polytechnique 1795–1830." *History of Education* 5 (1976): 11–24.

Brisco, Norris A. *The Economic Policy of Robert Walpole*. New York: Columbia University Press, 1907.

Brocard, Lucien. *Les doctrines économiques et sociales du Marquis de Mirabeau*. Paris: Giard et Brière, 1902.

Brown, Harcourt. *Scientific Organizations in Seventeenth Century France*. New York: Russell and Russell, 1967.

Brunt, P. A. *Italian Manpower 225 B.C.–A.D. 14*. Oxford: Oxford University Press, 1971.

Buckley, George T. *Atheism in the English Renaissance*. Chicago: University of Chicago Press, 1932.

Buel, Richard, Jr. *Securing the Revolution: Ideology in American Politics, 1789–1815*. Ithaca, N.Y.: Cornell University Press, 1972.

Buer, M. C. *Health, Wealth and Population in the Early Days of the Industrial Revolution*. London: Routledge, 1968.

Burke, Peter. *Venice and Amsterdam: A Study of Seventeenth-Century Elites*. London: Temple Smith, 1974.

Burnett, John, ed. *Useful Toil: Autobiographies of Working People from the 1820s to the 1920s*. London: Allen Lane, 1974.

Burnett, J.; Vincent, D.; and Mayall, D., eds. *The Autobiography of the Working Class: An Annotated Critical Bibliography, 1790–1900*. Brighton: Harvester, 1985.

Butler, Dom Cuthbert. *The Vatican Council 1869–1870*. London: Collins and Harvill, 1961.

Buxbaum, Melvin H. *Benjamin Franklin and the Zealous Presbyterians*. University Park: Pennsylvania State University Press, 1975.

Caldwell, Lynton K. *The Administrative Theories of Hamilton and Jefferson*. New York: Russell and Russell, 1964.

Capp, Bernard. "Godly Rule and English Millenarianism." In *The Intellectual Revolution of the Seventeenth Century*, edited by Charles Webster. London: Routledge, 1974.

Carlyle, R. W., and Carlyle, A. J. *A History of Medieval Political Theory in the West*. 6 vols. London, 1903–36.

Carnegie, Andrew. *James Watt*. New York: Doubleday, 1933.

Carré, Henri. *La noblesse de France et l'opinion publique au XVIIIe siècle*. Paris: Champion, 1920.

Carswell, John. *The Old Cause: Three Biographical Studies in Whiggism*. London: Cresset Press, 1954.

Cartwright, W. C. *The Jesuits: Their Constitution and Teaching*. London: Murray, 1876.

Caton, Hiram. "Analytic History of Philosophy: The Case of Descartes." *Philosophical Forum* 12 (1981): 273–94.

———. "Descartes' Anonymous Writings: A Recapitulation." *Southern Journal of Philosophy* 20 (1982): 299–312.

———. *A Method for the Analysis of Neurotic Political Thought*. Brisbane: St. Albans Press, 1987.

———. "On the Basis of Hobbes' Political Philosophy." *Political Studies* 22 (1974): 414–31.

————. *The Origin of Subjectivity: An Essay on Descartes.* New Haven: Yale University Press, 1973.

————. "Pascal's Syndrome: Positivism as a Symptom of Depression and Mania." *Zygon* 21 (1986): 319–51.

————. "The Preindustrial Economics of Adam Smith." *Journal of Economic History* 45 (1985): 833–53.

————. "The Second American Revolution." *Journal of Eighteenth Century Studies* 28 (1987): 69–83.

————. "Tory History of Ideas." *Independent Journal of Philosophy.* In press.

————. "Toward a Diagnosis of Progress." *Independent Journal of Philosophy* 4 (1983): 1–14.

————. "Whingeing." *Quadrant* 26 (January–February 1982): 45–49.

Censer, Jack Richard. *Prelude to Power: The Parisian Radical Press, 1789–1791.* Baltimore: Johns Hopkins University Press, 1976.

Champion, Edme. *J.-J. Rousseau et la Révolution Française.* Paris: Armand Colin, 1909.

Chapman, S. D. *The Early Factory Masters: Transition to the Factory System in the Midland Textile Industry.* London: Newton Abbot, 1967.

Clarke, John. *The Price of Progress: Cobbett's England, 1780–1835.* London: Hart-Davis Macgibbon, 1977.

Clément, Jean Paul. *Histoire de Colbert et de son administration.* 2 vols. 3d ed. Paris, 1892.

Clough, Shepard Bancroft. *France: A History of National Economics, 1789–1939.* New York: Octagon, 1964.

Clow, A., and Clow, N. *The Chemical Revolution.* London: Batchworth Press, 1952.

Coats, A. W. "Adam Smith and the Mercantile System." In *Essays on Adam Smith,* edited by A. S. Skinner and Thomas Wilson, 219–36. Oxford: Clarendon Press, 1975.

Cobban, Alfred. *Historians and the Causes of the French Revolution.* London: The Historical Association, 1958.

Colbourn, Trevor, ed. *Fame and the Founding Fathers: Essays by Douglass Adair.* New York: W. W. Norton and Company, 1974.

————. *The Lamp of Experience: Whig History and the Intellectual Origins of the American Revolution.* Chapel Hill: University of North Carolina Press, 1965.

Cole, C. W. *Colbert and a Century of French Mercantilism.* 2 vols. Hamden, Conn.: Archon, 1964.

Cole, G. D. H. *The Life of Robert Owen.* London: Archon, 1966.

Combs, Jerald C. *The Jay Treaty: Political Battleground of the Founding Fathers.* Berkeley: University of California Press, 1970.

Comte, Auguste. *The Positive Philosophy of Auguste Comte.* Translated by Harriet Martineau. 2 vols. London: John Chapman, 1853.

Conner, Paul W. *Poor Richard's Politics: Benjamin Franklin and His New American Order.* New York: Oxford University Press, 1965.

Corwin, Edward S. *The President, Office and Powers 1787–1968: History and Analysis of Practice and Opinion.* New York: New York University Press, 1968.

Cox, Richard H. *Locke on War and Peace*. Oxford: Clarendon Press, 1960.

Coxe, William. *Memoires of the Life and Administration of Sir Robert Walpole*. 3 vols. London, 1798.

Cragg, G. R. *From Puritanism to the Age of Reason: A Study of Changes in Religious Thought within the Church of England, 1660 to 1700*. Cambridge: Cambridge University Press, 1950.

Cranston, Maurice. *John Locke: A Biography*. London: Longmans, 1957.

Cropsey, Joseph. "Adam Smith and Political Philosophy." In *Essays on Adam Smith*, edited by A. S. Skinner and Thomas Wilson, 132–53. Oxford: Clarendon Press, 1975.

———. *Polity and Economy: An Interpretation of the Principles of Adam Smith*. The Hague: Nijhoff, 1957.

Crosland, Maurice. *Gay-Lussac: Scientist and Bourgeois*. Cambridge: Cambridge University Press, 1978.

———. *The Society of Arcueil. A View of French Science at the Time of Napoleon I*. Cambridge: Harvard University Press, 1967.

Currey, Cecil B. *Road to Revolution: Benjamin Franklin in England, 1765–1775*. Garden City, N.Y.: Anchor Books, 1968.

David, Paul A. *Technical Choice, Innovation and Economic Growth. Essays on American and British Experiences in the Nineteenth Century*. Cambridge: Cambridge University Press, 1975.

Davidson, Philip. *Propaganda and the American Revolution, 1763–1783*. Chapel Hill: University of North Carolina Press, 1941.

Davis, Ralph. *The Rise of the Atlantic Economies*. London: Weidenfeld & Nicolson, 1973.

———. "The Rise of Protection in England, 1689–1786." *Economic History Review* 19 (1966): 306–17.

Delvaille, Jules. *Essai sur l'histoire de l'idée du progrès jusqu'à la fin du XVIIIᵉ siècle*. Paris: Alcan, 1910.

Denis, Jacques. *Sceptiques ou libertins de la première moitié du XVIIᵉ siècle. Gassendi, Gabriel Naudé, Gui-Patin, La Mothe Le Vayer, Cyrano de Bergerac*. Caen: Blanc Hordel, 1884.

Dent, C. M. *Protestant Reformers in Elizabethan Oxford*. Oxford: Oxford University Press, 1983.

Desnoiresterres, Gustave. *Voltaire et la société française au XVIIIᵉ siècle*. 8 vols. Paris: Didier, 1870.

Dickerson, Oliver M. *The Navigation Acts and the American Revolution*. Philadelphia: University of Pennsylvania Press, 1951.

Dickinson, H. T. *Bolingbroke*. London: Constable, 1970.

———. *Walpole and the Whig Supremacy*. London: English University Press, 1973.

Dickson, P. G. M. *The Financial Revolution in England: A Study in the Development of Public Credit 1688–1756*. London: Macmillan, 1967.

Digard, G. A. L. *Philippe le Bel et le Saint-Siège de 1258 à 1304*. 2 vols. Paris, 1936.

Dolberg-Acton, J. E. E. *Lectures on Modern History*. Edited with an introduction by J. N. Figgis and R.V. Laurence. London: Macmillan, 1952.

Donoughue, Bernard. *British Politics and the American Revolution: The Path to War, 1773-75.* London: Macmillan and Company Ltd, 1964.

Dorter, Kenneth. "Science and Religion in Descartes' *Meditations.*" *The Thomist* 37 (1973): 313–40.

Dowd, David L. *Pageant-Master of the Republic: Jacques-Louis David and the French Revolution.* Lincoln: University of Nebraska Press, 1948.

Du Bois-Reymond, Emil. "Friedrich II und Jean-Jacques Rousseau." In *Reden.* 2 vols. Leipzig: Von Veit, 1886.

Dunn, John. *The Political Thought of John Locke.* Cambridge: Cambridge University Press, 1969.

———. "The Politics of John Locke in England and America in the Eighteenth Century." In *John Locke: Problems and Perspectives,* edited by John W. Yolton. Cambridge: Cambridge University Press, 1969.

Dussinger, John A. "'The Lovely System of Lord Shaftesbury': An Answer to Locke in the Aftermath of 1688?" *Journal of the History of Ideas* 42 (1981): 151–58.

Echeverria, Durand. *Mirage in the West: A History of the French Image of American Society to 1815.* Princeton, N.J.: Princeton University Press, 1957.

Eisenach, Eldon. *Two Worlds of Liberalism: Religion and Politics in Hobbes, Locke, and Mill.* Chicago: University of Chicago Press, 1981.

Ekirch, Arthur Alphonse, Jr. *The Idea of Progress in America.* New York: Peter Smith, 1951.

Eliot, T. D. "The Relation between Adam Smith and Benjamin Franklin." *Political Science Quarterly* 29 (1924): 67–96.

Elosu, Suzanne. *La maladie de Jean-Jacques Rousseau.* Paris: Fischbacher, 1929.

Eltis, W. A. "Adam Smith's Theory of Economic Growth." In *Essays on Adam Smith,* edited by A. S. Skinner and Thomas Wilson, 426–54. Oxford: Clarendon Press, 1975.

Elton, G. R. "Constitutional Development and Political Thought in Western Europe." In *New Cambridge Modern History,* 2: 438–63. 14 vols. 2d ed. rev. Cambridge: Cambridge University Press, 1967.

———. *Reform and Renewal: Thomas Cromwell and the Common Weal.* Cambridge: Cambridge University Press, 1973.

Ewald, A. C. *Sir Robert Walpole.* London: Chapman and Hall, 1878.

Fabro, Cornelio. *God in Exile: A Study of the Internal Dynamic of Modern Atheism, from Its Roots in the Cartesian Cogito to the Present Day.* Westminster, Md.: Newman Press, 1968.

Faÿ, Bernard. *L'esprit révolutionnaire en France et aux États-Unis à la fin du XVIIIᵉ siècle.* Paris: Champion, 1925.

Fay, C. R. "Locke versus Lowndes." *Cambridge Historical Journal* 4 (1932–34): 143–55.

Fèbvre, Lucien. *Le problème de l'incroyance au XVIᵉ siècle: la religion de Rabelais.* Paris: Michel, 1962.

Ferguson, E. James. *The Power of the Purse.* Chapel Hill: University of North Carolina Press, 1961.

Feuer, Lewis S. *The Scientific Intellectual: The Psychological and Sociological Origins of Modern Science.* New York: Basic Books, 1963.

Figuier, Louis. *Les merveilles de la science, ou description populaire des inventions modernes.* 4 vols. Paris: Furne, Jouvet, and Co., 1867–69.

Fischer, David Hackett. *The Revolution of American Conservatism: The Federalist Party in the Era of Jeffersonian Democracy.* New York: Harper and Row, 1965.

Fitton, R. S., and Wadsworth, A. P. *The Strutts and the Arkwrights 1758–1830: A Study of the Early Factory System.* Manchester, England: Manchester University Press, 1958.

Flower, Milton. *John Dickinson, Conservative Revolutionary.* Charlottesville, Va.: Friends of the John Dickinson Mansion, 1983.

Foord, Archibald. *His Majesty's Opposition, 1714–1830.* Oxford: Oxford University Press, 1964.

Forbes, Duncan. *Hume's Philosophical Politics.* Cambridge: Cambridge University Press, 1975.

———. "Sceptical Whiggism, Commerce and Liberty." In *Essays on Adam Smith,* edited by A. S. Skinner and Thomas Wilson, 179–201. Oxford: Oxford University Press, 1975.

———. "Scientific Whiggism, Adam Smith and John Millar." *The Cambridge Journal* 7 (1954): 643–70.

Ford, Franklin L. *Robe and Sword: The Regrouping of the French Aristocracy after Louis XIV.* Cambridge: Harvard University Press, 1953.

Forest, Alan. *The French Revolution and the Poor.* New York: St. Martin's Press, 1981.

Forster, Winfried. "Thomas Hobbes und der Puritanismus." In *Hobbes-Forschungen,* edited by Reinhart Koselleck and Roman Schnur, 84–102. Berlin: Duncker and Humblot, 1969.

Fox, E.W. *History in Geographic Perspective: The Other France.* New York: Norton, 1972.

Fox Bourne, H. R. *The Life of John Locke.* 2 vols. London, 1876.

Fox-Genovese, Elizabeth. *The Origins of Physiocracy.* Ithaca, N.Y.: Cornell University Press, 1976.

Frank, Robert G., Jr. "Science, Medicine and the Universities of Early Modern England." *History of Science* 11 (1973): 239–69.

Freudenthal, J. *Spinoza: Leben und Lehre.* 2d ed. Heidelberg: Winter, 1927.

Furet, François. *Interpreting the French Revolution.* Cambridge: Cambridge University Press, 1981.

Gardiner, S. R. *The First Two Stuarts and the Puritan Revolution, 1603–1660.* London: Longmans, 1893.

Garrett, Mitchell. *The Estates General of 1789: The Problems of Composition and Organization.* New York: Appleton Century, 1935.

Gascoigne, John. "'The Holy Alliance': The Rise and Diffusion of Newtonian Natural Philosophy and Latitudinarian Theology within Cambridge from the Restoration to the Accession of George II." Ph.D. dissertation, Cambridge University, 1980.

Gaus, Gerald F. *The Modern Liberal Theory of Man.* London: Croom Helm, 1983.

George, Albert J. "The Genesis of the Académie des Sciences." *Annals of Science* 3 (1938): 372–90.

Geyl, Pieter. *History of the Low Countries: Episodes and Problems.* London: Macmillan, 1964.

————. *The Netherlands in the Seventeenth Century.* Part 1, 1609–48. London: Ernest Benn, 1961.

————. *Orange and Stuart, 1641–1672.* New York: Scribner's, 1969.

Gibbs, George. *Memoirs of the Administrations of Washington and John Adams.* 2 vols. New York, 1846.

Gillispie, Charles C. "The Natural History of Industry." In *Science, Technology and Economic Growth in the Eighteenth Century,* edited by A. E. Musson, 121–35. London: Methuen, 1972.

Goldgar, Bertrand A. *Walpole and the Wits: The Relation of Politics to Literature, 1722–1742.* Lincoln: University of Nebraska Press, 1976.

Goodwin, Albert. *The Friends of Liberty: The English Democratic Movement in the Age of the French Revolution.* Cambridge: Harvard University Press, 1979.

Gottschalk, Louis R. *Jean-Paul Marat: A Study in Radicalism.* Chicago: University of Chicago Press, 1967.

————. *Lafayette Between the American and the French Revolution (1783–1789).* Chicago: University of Chicago Press, 1950.

Goubert, Pierre. *Louis XIV and Twenty Million Frenchmen.* New York: Vintage, 1972.

Gough, J. W. "James Tyrrell, Whig Historian and Friend of John Locke." *Historical Journal* 19 (1976): 581–610.

————. *John Locke's Political Philosophy, Eight Studies.* Oxford: Oxford University Press, 1950.

Grassby, R. B. "Social Status and Commercial Enterprise under Louis XIV." *Economic History Review* 13 (1960): 19–38.

Greaves, R. J. "Puritanism and Science: The Anatomy of a Controversy." *Journal of the History of Ideas* 30 (1969): 345–68.

Green, Daniel. *Great Cobbett: The Noblest Agitator.* London: Hodder and Stoughton, 1983.

Greene, Jack P. "The Seven Years' War and the American Revolution: The Causal Relationship Reconsidered." In *The British Atlantic Empire before the American Revolution,* edited by Peter Marshall and Glyn Williams, 85–105. London: Peter Cass, 1980.

Gruber, Alain-Charles. *Les grandes fêtes et leurs décors à l'époque de Louis XVI.* Paris: Droz, 1972.

Gruen, E. S. *The Last Generation of the Roman Republic.* Berkeley: University of California Press, 1974.

Gwyn, Julian. "British Government Spending and the North American Colonies, 1740–1775." In *The British Atlantic Empire before the American Revolution,* edited by Peter Marshall and Glyn Williams. London: Peter Cass, 1980.

Hägglund, Bengt. *Theologie und Philosophie bei Luther und in der Occamistischen Tradition.* Lund: Gleerup, 1955.

Hahn, Roger. *The Anatomy of a Scientific Institution: The Paris Academy of Sciences, 1666–1803*. Berkeley: University of California Press, 1971.

Halévy, Elie. *The Growth of Philosophic Radicalism*. 2 vols. London: Faber & Gwyer, 1928.

Haley, K. H. D. *The First Earl of Shaftesbury*. Oxford: Clarendon Press, 1968.

Hall, A. R. "Merton Revisited, or Science and Society in the Seventeenth Century." *History of Science* 2 (1963): 1–16.

―――. "The Scientific and the Puritan Revolution." *History* 50 (1966): 332–37.

Hallam, Henry. *The Constitutional History of England*. 3 vols. London, 1870.

―――. *View of the State of Europe during the Middle Ages*. 2 vols. London: Murray, 1818.

Haller, William. *The Rise of Puritanism: or, The Way to the New Jerusalem as set forth in pulpit and press from Thomas Cartwright to John Lilburne and John Milton, 1570–1643*. New York: Columbia University Press, 1938.

Hammond, Bray. *Banks and Politics in America from the Revolution to the Civil War*. Princeton, N.J.: Princeton University Press, 1957.

Hans, N. *New Trends in Education in the Eighteenth Century*. London: Routledge and Kegan Paul, 1951.

Haraszti, Zoltan. *John Adams and the Prophets of Progress*. Cambridge: Harvard University Press, 1952.

Hargreaves, E. L. *The National Debt*. London: Cass, 1965.

Hartley, Harold, ed. *The Royal Society, Its Originators and Founders*. London: Royal Society, 1960.

Havens, George R. "Diderot and the Composition of Rousseau's First Discourse." *Romantic Review* 30 (1939): 369–81.

Hazard, Paul. *The European Mind: The Critical Years 1680–1715*. New Haven: Yale University Press, 1953.

Hazen, Charles D. *Contemporary American Opinion of the French Revolution*. Baltimore: Johns Hopkins University Press, 1897. Reprint. New York: Peter Smith, 1941.

Heckscher, Eli F. *The Continental System: An Economic Interpretation*. 1922. Reprint. Gloucester, Mass.: Peter Smith, 1964.

Heilbroner, Robert L. "The Paradox of Progress: Decline and Decay in *The Wealth of Nations*." In *Essays on Adam Smith*, edited by A. S. Skinner and Thomas Wilson, 524–39. Oxford: Clarendon Press, 1975.

Henriques, Ursula R.Q. *The Early Factory Acts and Their Enforcement*. London: The Historical Association, 1971.

Hervier, Marcel. *Les écrivains français jugés par leurs contemporains*. 2 vols. Paris: Mellottee, n.d.

Hexter, J. H. *The Reign of King Pym*. Cambridge: Harvard University Press, 1941.

Hills, Richard L. *Power in the Industrial Revolution*. Manchester, England: Manchester University Press, 1970.

Hirschfield, J. M. *Académie Royale des Sciences (1666–1683): Inauguration and Initial Problems*. Chicago: University of Chicago Press, 1957.

Hobson, Charles F. "The Negative on State Laws: James Madison, the Constitution, and the Crisis of Republican Government." *William and Mary Quarterly* 36 (1979): 215–35.

Hoerder, Dirk. *Crowd Action in Revolutionary Massachusetts, 1765–1780.* New York: Academic Press, 1977.

Hoffman, Walter. *British Industry, 1700–1950.* Translated by W. O. Henderson and W. H. Chalmer. Oxford: Blackwell, 1955.

Holmes, Geoffrey. *The Trial of Doctor Sacheverell.* London: Eyre Methuen, 1973.

Holmes, Geoffrey, and Speck, W. A. *The Divided Society: Parties and Politics in England, 1694–1716.* London: Edward Arnold, 1967.

Howe, John R., Jr., ed. *The Role of Ideology in the American Revolution.* New York: Holt, Rinehart and Winston, 1970.

Hubert, René. *Les sciences sociales dans l'Encyclopédie.* Paris: Alcan, 1923.

Hudson, Derek, and Luckhurst, Kenneth W. *The Royal Society of Arts, 1745–1954.* London: John Murray, 1954.

Hufton, Olwen. *The Poor in Eighteenth-Century France, 1750–1796.* Oxford: Oxford University Press, 1974.

Humbert, P. *Un amateur: Peiresc, 1580–1637.* Paris: Desclee, de Brouwer et Cie., 1947.

Hutchins, B. L., and Harrison, A. *A History of Factory Legislation.* 3d ed. London: Cass, 1966.

Inglis, Brian. *Poverty and the Industrial Revolution.* London: Hodder and Stoughton, 1971.

Jacob, J. R. "Restoration Ideologies and the Royal Society." *History of Science* 18 (1980): 25–38.

Jacob, Margaret C. *The Newtonians and the English Revolution, 1689–1720.* Ithaca, N.Y.: Cornell University Press, 1976.

James, Michael. "Pierre-Louis Roederer, Jean-Baptiste Say, and the Concept of Industrie." *History of Political Economy* 9 (1977): 455–75.

Jennings, W. W. *The American Embargo.* University of Iowa Studies in Social Sciences, 1921–29, 8: 4–242.

Johnson, E. A. J. *The Foundations of American Economic Freedom: Government and Enterprise in the Age of Washington.* Minneapolis: University of Minnesota Press, 1973.

Jones, J. R. *Country and Court: England 1658–1714.* London: Edward Arnold, 1978.

————. *The First Whigs: The Politics of the Exclusion Crisis, 1678–1683.* London: Oxford University Press, 1961.

Jones, R. F. *Ancients and Moderns: A Study of the Rise of the Scientific Movement in Seventeenth-Century England.* 2d ed. Berkeley: University of California Press, 1961.

Jordan, W. K. *The Development of Religious Toleration in England: Attainment in the Theory and Accommodation in Thought and Institutions (1640–1660).* 2 vols. 1932. Reprint. Gloucester, Mass.: Peter Smith, 1965.

————. *Men of Substance: A Study of the Thought of Two English Revolutionaries, Henry Parker and Henry Robinson.* Chicago: University of Chicago Press, 1942.

Jourdain, Charles. *Histoire de l'Université de Paris au XVIIe et au XVIIIe siècles.* 2 vols. Paris: La Hachette, 1862–66.

Kallich, Martin, and MacLeish, Andrew, eds. *The American Revolution through British Eyes.* Evanston, Ill.: Row, Peterson, 1962.

Kargon, Robert. *Science in Victorian Manchester: Enterprise and Expertise.* Baltimore: Johns Hopkins, 1977.

Kemp, Betty. *King and Commons, 1660–1832.* London: Macmillan, 1957.

Kennington, Richard. "René Descartes." In *History of Political Philosophy,* edited by Joseph Cropsey and Leo Strauss. 2d ed. Chicago: Rand McNally, 1972.

Kenyon, J. P. *Revolution Principles: The Politics of Party, 1689–1720.* Cambridge: Cambridge University Press, 1977.

Kindleberger, C. P. "The Historical Background: Adam Smith and the Industrial Revolution." In *The Market and the State,* edited by A. S. Skinner and Thomas Wilson, 1–21. Oxford: Clarendon Press, 1975.

King, James E. *Science and Rationalism in the Government of Louis XIV.* Baltimore: Johns Hopkins University Press, 1949.

Kitson Clark, George. *Churchmen and the Condition of England, 1832–1885.* London: Methuen, 1973.

———. *Peel and the Conservative Party: A Study in Party Politics 1832–1841.* 2d ed. Hamden, Conn.: Archon, 1964.

Koch, Adolph. *Jefferson and Madison: The Great Collaboration.* New York: Oxford, 1964.

Kohn, Richard. *The Eagle and the Sword: The Federalists and the Creation of the Military Establishment in America, 1783–1802.* New York: Free Press, 1975.

Kors, A. *D'Holbach's Coterie: An Enlightenment in Paris.* Princeton, N.J.: Princeton University Press, 1975.

Köser, Reinhold. *König Friedrich der Grosse.* 2 vols. 2d ed. Berlin: Gotta'sche Buchhandlung, 1901.

Köstlin, Julius. *Life of Luther.* 2d ed. London: Longmans, 1898.

Krailsheimer, A. J. *Studies in Self-Interest: From Descartes to La Bruyère.* Oxford: Clarendon Press, 1962.

Kramnick, Isaac F. *Bolingbroke and His Circle: The Politics of Nostalgia in the Age of Walpole.* Cambridge: Harvard University Press, 1968.

———. "Republican Revisionism Revisited." *American Historical Review* 87 (1982): 629–64.

Krieger, Leonard. *Kings and Philosophers, 1689–1789.* New York: Norton, 1970.

Labrousse, C-E. *La crise de l'économie française à la fin de l'ancien régime et au début de la révolution.* Paris: Presses universitaires de France, 1943.

Lachterman, David L. "Descartes and the Philosophy of History." *Independent Journal of Philosophy* 4 (1983): 31–44.

Lagarde, Georges de. *La naissance de l'esprit laïque au déclin du Moyen Age.* 2 vols. 2d ed. Paris: Nauwelaerts, 1958.

Landes, D. S. *The Unbound Prometheus: Technological Change and Industrial Development in Western Europe from 1750 to the Present.* Cambridge: Cambridge University Press, 1969.

Lange-Eichbaum, Wilhelm. *Genie, Irrsinn und Ruhm: Eine Pathographie des Genies.* 4th ed. Munich: Reinhardt, 1956.

Langford, Paul. "Old Whigs, Old Tories and the American Revolution." In *The British Atlantic Empire before the American Revolution,* edited by Peter Marshall and Glyn Williams, 106–29. London: Peter Cass, 1980.

Lanson, Gustave. *Origines et premières manifestations de l'esprit philosophique dans la littérature française de 1675 à 1748.* Reprint. New York: Burt Franklin, 1973.

Laprade, W. T. *Public Opinion and Politics in Eighteenth Century England.* New York: Macmillan, 1936.

Laslett, Peter. "The English Revolution and Locke's *Two Treatises of Government.*" *Cambridge Historical Journal* 12 (1956): 40–56.

————. "John Locke, the Great Recoinage and the Origins of the Board of Trade: 1690–1698." *William and Mary Quarterly* 14 (1957): 370–402.

————. *John Locke: Two Treatises of Government.* Cambridge: Cambridge University Press, 1967.

Lavisse, Ernest, et al. *Histoire de France depuis les origines jusqu'à la Révolution.* 13 vols. Paris: Librairie Hachette, 1910.

Lea, H. C. *A History of Auricular Confession and Indulgences in the Latin Church.* 3 vols. 1896. Reprint. New York: Greenwood Press, 1968.

Lefèvre Pontalis, Germain-Antonin. *John de Witt, Grand Pensionary of Holland.* 2 vols. London: Longmans, 1885.

Leff, Gordon. *Heresy in the Later Middle Ages: The Relation of Heterodoxy to Dissent ca. 1250–ca. 1450.* 2 vols. New York: Barnes and Noble, 1967.

Leith, James A. *The Idea of Art as Propaganda in France, 1750–1799.* Toronto: University of Toronto Press, 1965.

Leng, Heinrich. *Lehrbuch der Gewerbskunde.* Weimar: Ilmenau, 1834.

Lenoble, Robert. *Mersenne, ou la naissance du mécanisme.* Paris: Vrin, 1943.

Levy, Leonard W. *Jefferson and Civil Liberties: The Darker Side.* Cambridge: Harvard University Press, 1963.

Link, Eugene Perry. *Democratic-Republican Societies, 1790–1800.* New York: Octagon Books, 1965.

Looze, Helene Johnson. *Alexander Hamilton and the British Orientation of American Foreign Policy 1783–1803.* The Hague: Mouton, 1969.

Lough, John. *The Encyclopédie.* London: Longmans, 1971.

Lyon, E. Wilson. "The Directory and the United States." *American Historical Review* 43 (1938): 514–32.

————. *Louisiana in French Diplomacy, 1759–1804.* 1934. Reprint. Norman: University of Oklahoma Press, 1974.

Lyons, Sir Henry. *The Royal Society, 1660–1940: A History of Its Administration under Its Charters.* Cambridge: Cambridge University Press, 1944.

Mace, George. *Locke, Hobbes and the Federalist Papers: An Essay on the Genesis of the American Political Heritage.* Carbondale: Southern Illinois University Press, 1979.

McClaughlin, T. "Censorship and Defenders of the Cartesian Faith in Mid-Seventeenth Century France." *Journal of the History of Ideas* 40 (1979): 563–81.

McClelland, Peter D. "The Cost to America of British Imperial Policy." *American Economic Review* 49 (1969): 370–81.

McCoy, Drew. *The Elusive Republic: Political Economy in Jeffersonian America.* Chapel Hill: University of North Carolina Press, 1980.

McDonald, Forrest. *Alexander Hamilton: A Biography.* New York: Norton, 1982.

McGrade, A. S. *The Political Thought of William of Ockham: Personal and Institutional Principles.* Cambridge: Cambridge University Press, 1974.

Mackrell, J. Q. C. *The Attack on "Feudalism" in Eighteenth-Century France.* London: Routledge, 1973.

McNeill, John T. *The History and Character of Calvinism.* New York: Oxford University Press, 1954.

Macpherson, C. B. *The Political Theory of Possessive Individualism: Hobbes to Locke.* Oxford: Oxford University Press, 1962.

Maier, Pauline. *From Resistance to Revolution: Colonial Radicals and the Development of American Opposition to Britain, 1765–1776.* New York: Knopf, 1972.

Main, Jackson Turner. *The Antifederalists: Critics of the Constitution, 1781–1788.* Chapel Hill: University of North Carolina Press, 1961.

Maland, David. *Culture and Society in Seventeenth Century France.* London: B. T. Batsford, 1970.

Malvezin, Theophile. *Histoire du commerce de Bordeaux depuis les origines jusqu'à nos jours.* 4 vols. Bordeaux: A. Bellier et Cie., 1892.

Mandrou, Robert. *Louis XIV et son temps.* Paris: Presses universitaires de France, 1973.

Manning, Brian. "The Godly People." In *Politics, Religion and the English Civil War,* edited by Brian Manning. London: Arnold, 1973.

Mansbridge, Albert. *The Older Universities of England: Oxford and Cambridge.* London: Longmans, Green and Co., 1923.

Mansfield, Harvey C., Jr. *Machiavelli's New Modes and Orders: A Study of the "Discourses on Livy."* Ithaca, N.Y.: Cornell University Press, 1979.

———. *Statesmanship and Party Government.* Chicago: University of Chicago Press, 1965.

Mantoux, Paul. *The Industrial Revolution in the Eighteenth Century: An Outline of the Beginnings of the Modern Factory System.* London: Jonathan Cape, 1961.

Manuel, Frank. *The Eighteenth Century Confronts the Gods.* Cambridge: Harvard University Press, 1959.

———. *Freedom from History and Other Untimely Essays.* New York: New York University Press, 1971.

Martin, D. C. "Sir Robert Moray, F.R.S." In *The Royal Society, Its Origins and Founders,* edited by Harold Hartley. London: Royal Society, 1960.

Martin, V. "Les idées répandues par Marseille de Padove et Occam touchant la constitution de l'Église." *Revue des sciences religieuses* 18 (1937): 261–89.

Masters, Roger D. "Hobbes and Locke." In *Comparing Political Thinkers,* edited by Ross Fitzgerald, 116–40. Sydney: Pergamon, 1980.

———. *The Political Philosophy of Rousseau.* Princeton, N.J.: Princeton University Press, 1968.

Mathias, Peter. *The First Industrial Nation: An Economic History of Britain 1700–1914.* London: Methuen, 1969.

Mathiez, Albert. *Les origines des cultes révolutionnaires, 1789–1792.* Paris: Georges Bellais, 1904.

Meek, Ronald L. *Social Science and the Ignoble Savage.* Cambridge: Cambridge University Press, 1975.

Micheli, Gianni. "Il 'Traité de l'homme' e una supposta crisi della filosofia Cartesiana." *Revista critica de storia della filosofia* 16 (1961): 315–20.

Miller, John C. *Crisis in Freedom: The Alien and Sedition Acts.* Boston: Little, Brown, 1951.

————. *The Federalist Era.* New York: Harper and Row, 1963.

————. *Sam Adams: Pioneer in Propaganda.* Boston: Little, Brown, 1936.

————. *The Wolf by the Ears: Thomas Jefferson and Slavery.* New York: Macmillan, 1977.

Molella, Arthur P., and Reingold, Nathan. "Theorists and Ingenious Mechanics: Joseph Henry Defines Science." *Science Studies* 3 (1973): 323–51.

Mongrédien, Georges. *Colbert 1629–1683.* Paris: Hachette, 1963.

Monk, James Henry. *The Life of Richard Bentley.* 2 vols. 2d ed. rev. 1833. Reprint. Osnabrück, West Germany: Biblio Verlag, 1969.

Morgan, John. "Puritanism and Science: A Reinterpretation." *Historical Journal* 22 (1979): 535–60.

Morley, Iris. *A Thousand Lives: An Account of the English Revolutionary Movement, 1660–1685.* New York: Deutsch, 1954.

Morley, John. *Diderot and the Encyclopédistes.* 2 vols. London: Chapman and Hall, 1978.

Morley, Robert. *Walpole.* London: Macmillan, 1889. Reprint. Westport, Conn.: Greenwood, 1971.

Mornet, Daniel. *Les origines intellectuelles de la révolution française (1715–1787).* 3d ed. Paris: Colin, 1938.

Mossner, Ernest C. *The Life of David Hume.* 2d ed. Oxford: Clarendon Press, 1980.

Mudge, E. T. *The Social Philosophy of John Taylor of Caroline.* New York: Columbia University Press, 1939.

Mulligan, Lotte. "Civil War Politics, Religion and the Royal Society." In *The Intellectual Revolution of the Seventeenth Century,* edited by Charles Webster, 317–46. London: Routledge, 1974.

Murrin, John M. "The Great Inversion, or Court versus Country: A Comparison of Revolution Settlements in England (1688–1721) and America (1776–1816)." In *Three British Revolutions: 1641, 1688, and 1776,* edited by J. G. A. Pocock. Princeton, N.J.: Princeton University Press, 1980.

Musson, A. E., ed. *Science, Technology and Economic Growth in the Eighteenth Century.* London: Methuen, 1972.

Musson, A. E., and Robinson, E. *Science and Technology in the Industrial Revolution.* Manchester, England: University of Manchester Press, 1969.

Neal, Daniel. *The History of the Puritans.* 5 vols. 1732–38. Reprint. London, 1822.

Nef, John U. *Industry and Government in France and England 1540–1640*. New York: Russell and Russell, 1968.

Nicholson, Marjorie Hope. *Pepys' Diary and the New Science*. Charlottesville: University of Virginia Press, 1965.

Nicolet, Claude. *The World of the Citizen in Republican Rome*. London: Batsford, 1980.

Nicolini, G. B. *History of the Jesuits: Their Origin, Progress, and Designs*. London: George Bell, 1893.

Nisbet, Robert. *History of the Idea of Progress*. New York: Basic Books, 1980.

Nordholt, Jan. *The Dutch Republic and American Independence*. Chapel Hill: University of North Carolina Press, 1982.

Nussbaum, Frederick L. *The Triumph of Science and Reason 1660–1685*. New York: Harper, 1953.

Ogg, David. *England in the Reigns of James II and William III*. Oxford: Oxford University Press, 1955.

Ornstein, M. *The Role of Scientific Societies in the Seventeenth Century*. Chicago: University of Chicago Press, 1938.

Owen, John B. *The Rise of the Pelhams*. London: Methuen, 1957.

Ozouf, Mona. *La fête révolutionnaire, 1789–1799*. Paris: Gallimard, 1976.

Padover, Saul K. *The Revolutionary Emperor: Joseph II of Austria*. 2d ed. London: Eyre and Spottiswoode, 1967.

Palmer, R. R. *The Age of Democratic Revolution: A Political History of Europe and America, 1760–1800*. 2 vols. Princeton, N.J.: Princeton University Press, 1959.

Pangle, Thomas. *Montesquieu's Philosophy of Liberalism: A Commentary on "The Spirit of the Laws."* Chicago: University of Chicago Press, 1973.

Parker, Harold T. *The Cult of Antiquity and the French Revolutionaries: A Study in the Development of the Revolutionary Spirit*. Chicago: University of Chicago Press, 1937.

———. *The Cult of Antiquity in the French Revolution*. New York: Octagon, 1965.

Payne, P. L. *British Entrepreneurship in the Nineteenth Century*. London: Macmillan, 1974.

Pennington, Donald, and Thomas, Keith, eds. *Puritans and Revolutionaries: Essays in Seventeenth-Century History Presented to Christopher Hill*. Oxford: Clarendon Press, 1978.

Perkin, Harold. *The Origins of Modern English Society 1780–1880*. Toronto: University of Toronto Press, 1967.

Plum, H. G. *Restoration Puritanism: A Study of the Growth of English Liberty*. 1942. Reprint. New York: Kennikat Press, 1972.

Plumb, J. H. *The Growth of Political Stability in England, 1675–1725*. London: Macmillan, 1967.

———. *Sir Robert Walpole*. 2 vols. 1956–60. Reprint. Clifton, N.J.: Augustus Kelley, 1973.

Pocock, J. G. A. "Cambridge Paradigms and Scotch Philosophers: A Study of the Relations between the Civic Humanist and the Civil Jurisprudential Interpretation of Eighteenth-Century Social Thought." In *The Shaping of Politi-*

cal Economy in the Scottish Enlightenment, edited by Istvan Hont and Michael Ignatieff, 235–52. Cambridge: Cambridge University Press, 1983.

———. *The Machiavellian Moment: Florentine Political Thought and the Atlantic Republican Tradition.* Princeton, N.J.: Princeton University Press, 1975.

———. "The Myth of John Locke and the Obsession with Liberalism." In *John Locke,* edited by J. G. A. Pocock and Richard Ashcraft. Papers read at Clark Memorial Library Seminar, Los Angeles, 1980.

———. *Politics, Language and Time: Essays in Political Thought and History.* London: Methuen, 1972.

Pocock, J. G. A., and Ashcraft, Richard, eds. *John Locke.* Papers read at Clark Memorial Library seminar, 10 December 1977, Los Angeles, 1980.

Pole, J. R. *Political Representation in England and the Origins of the American Republic.* New York: St. Martin's Press, 1966.

Popkin, Richard H. *The History of Skepticism from Erasmus to Spinoza.* 2d ed. rev. Berkeley: University of California Press, 1979.

Price, J. L. *Culture and Society in the Dutch Republic during the Seventeenth Century.* London: Batsford, 1974.

Price, Roger. *The Economic Modernization of France.* London: Croom Helm, 1975.

Proust, Jacques. *Diderot et l'Encyclopédie.* Paris: Vrin, 1962.

Purver, Margery. *The Royal Society: Concept and Creation.* London: Routledge, 1967.

Rabb, T. K. "Puritanism and the Rise of Experimental Science in England." *Journal of World History* 7 (1962).

Rahe, Paul A. "The Primacy of Politics in Ancient Greece." *American Historical Review* 89 (1984): 265–93.

———. *Republics Ancient and Modern: Classical Republicanism and the American Revolution.* In press.

Rambert, Gaston, ed. *Histoire du commerce de Marseille.* 8 vols. Paris: Plon, 1949–59.

Rawson, Elizabeth. *The Spartan Tradition in European Thought.* Oxford: Clarendon Press, 1969.

Redwood, John. *Reason, Ridicule and Religion: The Age of Enlightenment in England, 1660–1750.* London: Thames and Hudson, 1976.

Reik, M. M. *The Golden Lands of Thomas Hobbes.* Detroit: Wayne State University Press, 1977.

Richards, James O. *Party Propaganda under Queen Anne: The General Elections of 1702–13.* Athens: University of Georgia Press, 1972.

Richards, Judith; Mulligan, Lotte; and Graham, John K. "'Property' and 'People': Political Usages of Locke and Some Contemporaries." *Journal of the History of Ideas* 42 (1981): 29–51.

Riezler, Sigmund. *Die literarischen Widersacher der Päpsten zur Zeit Ludwig des Baiers.* Leipzig, 1874. Reprint. New York: Burt Franklin, 1961.

Robbins, Caroline A. *The Eighteenth-Century Commonwealthman: Studies in the Transmission, Development and Circumstances of English Liberal Thought from the Restoration of Charles II until the War with the Thirteen Colonies.* Cambridge: Harvard University Press, 1959.

Robertson, Alexander. *The Life of Sir Robert Moray: Soldier, Statesman and Man of Science (1608–1673).* London: Longmans, Green and Co., 1922.

Robertson, H. M. *Aspects of the Rise of Economic Individualism: A Criticism of Max Weber and His School.* New York: Kelley and Millman, 1959.

Robertson, John M. *Bolingbroke and Walpole.* London: Fisher Unwin, 1919.

Rocquain, Felix. *L'esprit révolutionnaire avant la révolution, 1715–1789.* 1878. Reprint. Geneva: Slatkine Reprints, 1971.

Rolt, L. T. C., and Allen, J. S. *The Steam Engine of Thomas Newcomen.* New York: Science History Publications, 1977.

Ronalds, Francis S. *The Attempted Whig Revolution of 1678–1681.* Urbana: University of Illinois, 1937.

Rosenberg, Nathan. *Inside the Black Box: Technology and Economics.* Cambridge: Cambridge University Press, 1982.

Rossi, Paolo. *Francis Bacon: From Magic to Science.* Chicago: University of Chicago Press, 1968.

Rostovtzeff, M. *Social and Economic History of the Hellenistic World.* 3 vols. Oxford: Oxford University Press, 1941.

Rostow, W. W. *Why the Poor Get Richer and the Rich Slow Down: Essays in the Marshallian Long Period.* Austin: University of Texas Press, 1980.

Rothking, Lionel. *Opposition to Louis XIV: The Political and Social Origins of the French Enlightenment.* Princeton, N.J.: Princeton University Press, 1965.

Rowen, Herbert H. *John de Witt, Grand Pensionary of Holland, 1625–1672.* Princeton, N.J.: Princeton University Press, 1978.

Ruggiero, Guido de. *The History of European Liberalism.* Boston: Beacon Press, 1927.

Rupp, E. G. "Luther and the German Reformation to 1529." In *New Cambridge Modern History.* 2: 70–95. 14 vols. 2d ed. rev. Cambridge: Cambridge University Press, 1967.

Sabine, George H. *A History of Political Philosophy.* 4th ed., revised by T. L. Thorson. Hinsdale, Ill.: Dryden, 1973.

Sachse, W. L. "The Mob and the Revolution of 1688." *Journal of British Studies* 4 (1964): 23–60.

Samuelsson, Kurt. *Religion and Economic Action: The Protestant Ethic, the Rise of Capitalism, and the Abuse of Scholarship.* New York: Basic Books, 1961.

Santillana, Giorgio de. *The Crime of Galileo.* Chicago: University of Chicago Press, 1955.

Saul, S. B. *Technological Change: The United States and Britain in the Nineteenth Century.* London: Methuen, 1970.

Schabert, Tilo. "Diderot." In *Aufklärung und Materialismus in Frankreich des 18. Jahrhunderts,* edited by Arno Baruzzi. Munich: List Verlag, 1968.

Schaefer, David. "The Good, the Beautiful and the Useful: Montaigne's Transvaluation of Values." *American Political Science Review* 73 (1979): 139–54.

————. "Montaigne's Political Skepticism." *Polity* 11 (1979): 514–41.

Schlesinger, Arthur M., Jr., ed. *History of U. S. Political Parties*. Vol. 2. New York: Chelsea House, 1973.

Schofield, Robert E. *The Lunar Society of Birmingham: A Social History of Provincial Science and Industry in Eighteenth-Century England*. Oxford: Clarendon Press, 1973.

Scholz, Richard. *Die Publizistik zur Zeit Philipps des Schönen und Bonifaz VIII: Ein Beitrag zur Geschichte der politischen Anschauungen des Mittelalters*. Stuttgart, 1903.

Schumpeter, J. A. *History of Economic Analysis*. London: Allen and Unwin, 1954.

Seé, Henri. *L'evolution de la pensée politique en France au XVIIIe siècle*. Paris: Giard, 1925.

Seibicke, Wilfried. *Technik: Versuch einer Geschichte der Wortfamilie in Deutschland vom 16. Jahrhunderts bis etwa 1830*. Dusseldorf: VDI-Verlag, 1968.

Shalhope, Robert E. *John Taylor of Caroline: Pastoral Republican*. Columbia: University of South Carolina Press, 1980.

Shapiro, Barbara. *John Wilkins, 1614–1672: An Intellectual Biography*. Berkeley: University of California Press, 1969.

———. "Latitudinarianism and Science in Seventeenth-Century England." In *The Intellectual Revolution of the Seventeenth Century*, edited by Charles Webster, 286–316. London: Routledge, 1974.

Shaw, Peter. *American Patriots and the Rituals of Revolution*. Cambridge: Harvard University Press, 1981.

Singer, Charles, et al., eds. *A History of Technology*. 6 vols. Oxford: Clarendon Press, 1958.

Skinner, A. S., and Wilson, Thomas, eds. *Essays on Adam Smith*. Oxford: Oxford University Press, 1975.

Skinner, Quentin. *Foundations of Modern Political Thought*. 2 vols. Cambridge: Cambridge University Press, 1972.

Smiles, Samuel. *The Huguenots: Their Settlements, Churches and Industries in England and Ireland*. London: Murray, 1867.

———. *Boulton and Watt*. Vol. 4 of *Lives of Engineers*. London: Murray, 1874–99.

Souleyman, Elizabeth V. *The Vision of World Peace in Seventeenth and Eighteenth Century France*. New York: Putnam, 1941.

Sowell, Thomas. *Say's Law: An Historical Analysis*. Princeton, N.J.: Princeton University Press, 1972.

Speck, W. A. "Political Propaganda in Augustan England." *Transactions of the Royal Historical Society* 22 (1972): 17–32.

Spink, John S. *French Free-Thought from Gassendi to Voltaire*. London: Greenwood Press, 1960.

Spivak, Burton. *Jefferson's English Crisis: Commerce, Embargo, and the Republican Revolution*. Charlottesville: University Press of Virginia, 1979.

Spragens, Thomas A. *The Irony of Liberal Reason*. Chicago: University of Chicago Press, 1982.

Spurlin, Paul M. *Montesquieu in America, 1760–1801*. New York: Octagon, 1969.

Stagg, J. C. A. *Mr. Madison's War: Politics, Diplomacy, and Warfare in the Early*

American Republic, 1783–1830. Princeton, N.J.: Princeton University Press, 1983.

Stankiewicz, W. J. *Politics and Religion in Seventeenth-Century France: A Study of Political Ideas from the Monarchomachs to Bayle, as Reflected in the Toleration Controversy.* Berkeley: University of California Press, 1960.

Stevens, David. "Adam Smith and the Colonial Disturbances." In *Essays on Adam Smith,* edited by A. S. Skinner and Thomas Wilson, 202–17. Oxford: Clarendon Press, 1975.

Stevens, David Harrison. *Party Politics and English Journalism 1702–1742.* New York: Russell and Russell, 1967.

Stewart, Larry. "Samuel Clarke, Newtonianism, and the Factions of Post-Revolutionary England." *Journal of the History of Ideas* 41 (1981): 53–72.

Stone, Lawrence. *The Causes of the English Revolution, 1529–1642.* London: Routledge, 1972.

Stourzh, Gerald. *Alexander Hamilton and the Idea of Republican Government.* Stanford, Calif.: Stanford University Press, 1970.

———. *Benjamin Franklin and American Foreign Policy.* 2d ed. Chicago: University of Chicago Press, 1969.

Strassmann, W. Paul, and David, Paul A. *Technical Choice, Innovation, and Economic Growth: Essays on the American and British Experience in the Nineteenth Century.* New York: Cambridge University History, 1975.

Strauss, Gerald, ed. *Manifestations of Discontent in Germany on the Eve of the Reformation: A Collection of Documents.* Bloomington: Indiana University Press, 1971.

Strauss, Leo. *Natural Right and History.* Chicago: University of Chicago Press, 1953.

———. *The Political Philosophy of Hobbes.* Chicago: Free Press, 1963.

Stromberg, Roland M. *Religious Liberalism in Eighteenth-Century England.* London: Oxford University Press, 1954.

Strugnell, Anthony. *Diderot's Politics: A Study of the Evolution of Diderot's Thought after the Encyclopédie.* The Hague: Nijhoff, 1973.

Tann, Jennifer. *The Development of the Factory.* London: Cornmarket, 1970.

Taylor, George V. "Noncapitalist Wealth and the Origins of the French Revolution." *American Historical Review* 72 (1966–67): 469–96.

———. "Revolutionary and Nonrevolutionary Content in the *Cahiers* of 1789: An Interim Report." *French Historical Studies* 7 (1972): 479–502.

Thomas, Keith. *Religion and the Decline of Magic.* New York: Scribner's, 1971.

Thompson, E. P. *The Making of the English Working Class.* New York: Pantheon, 1963.

Thompson, Eric. *Popular Sovereignty and the French Constituent Assembly, 1789–91.* Manchester, England: Manchester University Press, 1952.

Thompson, James Westfall. *Feudal Germany.* Chicago: University of Chicago Press, 1928.

———. *A History of Historical Writing.* 2 vols. New York: Macmillan, 1942.

Thompson, Martyn P. "The Reception of Locke's *Two Treatises of Government* 1690–1705." *Political Studies* 24 (1976): 184–91.

Thorndike, Lynn. *A History of Magic and Experimental Science.* 8 vols. New York: Macmillan, 1923.

Tierney, B. *Foundations of Conciliar Theory.* Cambridge: Cambridge University Press, 1959.

Tiersot, Julien. *Les fêtes et les chants de la Révolution française.* Paris: Hachette, 1908.

Tilley, Arthur. *From Montaigne to Molière, or the Preparation for the Classical Age of French Literature.* London: John Murray, 1908.

Trahard, Pierre. *La sensibilité révolutionnaire (1789–1794).* Paris: Boivin, 1936.

Tranter, N. L. *Population since the Industrial Revolution: The Case of England and Wales.* London: Croom Helm, 1973.

Trevor-Roper, H. R. *Religion, the Reformation and Social Change.* London: Macmillan, 1972.

————. Review of *Intellectual Origins of the English Revolution,* by Christopher Hill. *History and Theory* 5 (1966): 61–82.

Turberville, A. S. *Medieval Heresy and the Inquisition.* 1920. Reprint. London: Archon, 1964.

Turnbull, G. H. *Hartlib, Dury and Comenius: Gleanings from Hartlib's Papers.* London: Hodder and Stoughton, 1947.

Turner, F. M. *Between Science and Religion: The Reaction to Scientific Naturalism in Late Victorian England.* New Haven, Conn.: Yale University Press, 1974.

Turner, Frederick Jackson. "The Policy of France toward the Mississippi Valley in the Period of Washington and Adams." *American Historical Review* 10 (1905): 249–79.

Tyacke, Nicholas. "Science and Religion at Oxford before the Civil War." In *Puritans and Revolutionaries: Essays in Seventeenth-Century History, Presented to Christopher Hill,* edited by Donald Pennington and Keith Thomas, 72–93. Oxford: Clarendon Press, 1978.

Usher, A. P. *The History of the Grain Trade in France, 1400–1710.* Cambridge: Harvard University Press, 1913.

Van Cleve, T. C. *The Emperor Frederick II of Hohenstaufen: Immutator Mundi.* Oxford: Oxford University Press, 1972.

Van der Wee, Herman. "Monetary, Credit and Banking Systems." In *The Cambridge Economic History of Europe,* vol. 5, edited by E. E. Rich and C. H. Wilson. Cambridge: Cambridge University Press, 1977.

Vennes, Paule-Monique. *La ville, la fête, la démocratie: Rousseau et les illusions de la communauté.* Paris: Alcan, 1978.

Vigier, François. *Change and Apathy: Liverpool and Manchester during the Industrial Revolution.* Cambridge: M.I.T. Press, 1970.

Villat, Louis. *La Révolution et l'empire.* Paris: Presses Universitaires de France, 1947.

Wade, Ira O. *The Clandestine Organization and Diffusion of Philosophical Ideas in France from 1700 to 1750.* 1938. Reprint. New York: Octagon Books, 1967.

Wagar, Warren W. *The Idea of Progress since the Renaissance.* New York: Wiley, 1969.

————. "Modern Views of the Origins of the Idea of Progress." *Journal of the History of Ideas* 28 (1967): 55–70.

Ware, Charlotte S. "The Influence of Descartes on John Locke: A Biographical Study." *Revue internationale de philosophie* 4 (1950): 210–30.

Watson, J. Steven. *The Reign of George III, 1760–1815*. Oxford: Clarendon Press, 1960.

Weber, Max. *The Protestant Ethic and the Spirit of Capitalism*. New York: Scribner's, 1958.

Webster, Charles. *The Great Instauration: Science, Medicine and Reform 1626–1660*. London: Duckworth, 1974.

————, ed. *The Intellectual Revolution of the Seventeenth Century*. London: Routledge, 1974.

Weulersse, Georges. *Le mouvement physiocratique en France de 1756 à 1770*. 2 vols. Paris, 1910.

White, A. D. *A History of the Warfare of Science with Theology in Christendom*. 2 vols. 1896. Reprint. Gloucester, Mass.: Peter Smith, 1978.

White, Leonard D. *The Jeffersonians: A Study in Administrative History, 1801–1829*. New York: Macmillan, 1956.

Whitfield, Ernest A. *Gabriel Bonnot de Mably*. London: Routledge, 1930.

Williams, B. R., ed. *Science and Technology in Economic Growth*. New York: Wiley, 1983.

Wilson, Arthur M. *Diderot*. New York: Oxford University Press, 1972.

Wilson, Charles. *Profit and Power: A Study of England and the Dutch Wars*. London: Longmans, 1957.

Wood, Gordon S. *The Creation of the American Republic*. Chapel Hill: University of North Carolina Press, 1969.

————. "Rhetoric and Reality in the American Revolution." In *The Role of Ideology in the American Revolution*, edited by John R. Howe, Jr., 105–21. New York: Holt, Rinehart and Winston, 1970.

Woodbridge, H. E. *Sir William Temple, The Man and His Work*. New York: Modern Language Association, 1940.

Woodbury, Robert S. *Studies in the History of Machine Tools*. Cambridge: M.I.T. Press, 1973.

Wordsworth, Christopher. *Scholae Academicae: Some Account of Studies at the English Universities in the Eighteenth Century*. Cambridge, 1877.

Yates, Frances A. *The Rosicrucian Enlightenment*. London: Paladin, 1975.

Zagorin, Perez. *The Court and the Country: The Beginning of the English Revolution*. London: Routledge, 1969.

Zobel, Hiller. *The Boston Massacre*. New York: Norton, 1970.

Reference Works

Abstract of British Historical Statistics. Edited by B. R. Mitchell and Phyllis Deane. 1962. Reprint. Cambridge: Cambridge University Press, 1976.

America: History and Life. Santa Barbara: ABC-Clio, Inc., 1964–81.

Bibliographical Directory of the American Congress 1774–1961. Washington: U. S. Government Printing Office, 1961.

Catalogue de l'histoire de la révolution française. Edited by A. Martin and G. Walter. 5 vols. Paris: Éditions des Bibliothèques Nationales, 1936.

Clark, G. N. *Guide to English Commercial Statistics 1696–1782.* London: Royal Historical Society, 1938.

European Historical Statistics 1750–1975. Edited by B. R. Mitchell. 2d ed. rev. New York: Facts on File, 1981.

Fueter, Eduard. *Geschichte der neueren Historiographie.* 3d ed. Munich: Oldenbourg, 1936.

Goldsmiths'-Kress Library of Economic Literature: Consolidated Guide to Microfilm Collection. 3 vols. Woodbridge, Conn., 1977.

Handbuch der Kirchen Geschichte. Edited by Hubert Jedin. 3d ed. rev. 7 vols. Freiburg: Herder, 1962. English translation published as *Handbook of Church History* (New York: Seabury Press, 1980).

Harper Encyclopedia of the Modern World. Edited by Richard B. Morris and Graham Irwin. New York: Harper and Row, 1970.

Harrison, John, and Laslett, Peter, eds. *The Library of John Locke.* Oxford: Oxford University Press, 1965.

Harvard Guide to American History. Edited by Frank Freidel. Rev. ed. Cambridge: Belknap Press, 1974.

Histoire parlementaire de la révolution française. Edited by P.-J.-B. Buchez and P.-C. Roux. 40 vols. Paris, 1834–38.

Historical Statistics of the United States: Colonial Times to 1970. Washington: U. S. Government Printing Office, 1975.

Iggers, G. G., and Parker, H. T., eds. *International Handbook of Historical Studies.* London: Methuen, 1980.

International Bibliography of Historical Sciences. 49 vols. Ridgewood, N.J.: K. G. Saur, 1926– .

Langer, William L., ed. *Encyclopedia of World History.* London: Harrap, 1968.

McInnis, R. G., and Scott, J. W. *Social Science Research Handbook.* New York: Harper, 1974.

Mitchell, B. R. *Abstract of British Historical Statistics.* Cambridge: Cambridge University Press, 1962.

Mulhall, Michael. *The Dictionary of Statistics.* 4th rev. ed. London: Routledge, 1899.

The New Cambridge Modern History. 14 vols. 2d ed. rev. Cambridge: Cambridge University Press, 1967.

Research in Economic History: An Annual Compilation of Research. Edited by Paul Uselding and N. F. R. Crafts. Greenwich, Conn.: JAI, 1975– .

Rich, E. E., and Wilson, C., eds. *The Cambridge Economic History of Europe.* 6 vols. Cambridge: Cambridge University Press, 1967.

Richardson, R. C., and Chaloner, W. H. *British Economic and Social History: A Bibliographical Guide.* Manchester, England: Manchester University Press, 1976.

Stephen, Sir Leslie, and Lee, Sir Sidney, eds. *Dictionary of National Biography.* 1885–1901. London: Oxford University Press, 1921–22.

Wilson, Charles, and Parker, Geoffrey. *An Introduction to the Sources of European Economic History, 1500–1800.* Ithaca, N.Y.: Cornell University Press, 1977.

index

Abbé d'Augingac, 103
Abbé de Choisy, 87
Abrégé de la révolution de l'Amérique anglaise, 454
Académie d'architecture, 100
Académie de peinture et de sculpture, 100–102
Académie des sciences, 16, 69, 74, 76, 86, 188, 357, 358, 365, 365n91, 535; activities of, 107–8; founding of, 102–7
Académie française, 100, 104, 361
Accademia de Lincei, 75
Accademia del Cimento, 69, 72, 73, 104, 188
Acquisition, 242, 255. *See also* Interest; Market
Acta eruditorum, 69
Act in Restraint of Appeals to Rome, 131
Act of Supremacy, 131
Acton, J. E. E. D., first baron, 1–2, 204
Adam, 34
Adams, John, 27n16, 453n53, 465n10, 501, 503; *Defense of the Constitution of the United States,* 461; *Discourses on Davila,* 467n11; on political science, 461n3
Adams, Samuel: agitation techniques of, 392–94; amalgamated Old Whig with Court Whig doctrine, 388–89, 389n21; ambition of, 391n24; character of, 394n31; cultivated disaffection, 389; the font of revolution, 388; hostile to commerce, 389–90; used violence, 392–93

Addison, Joseph, 266, 309, 311n47
Adet, P. A., 501
Administration, 88, 92, 93, 164, 232, 234, 382n11, 506
Age of transition, 515–16
Agrarianism, 294, 297–98, 351, 354, 390, 411, 414, 477, 482n28, 484. *See* Physiocracy; Republican party; Virtuous republic
Alba, duke of, 222
Alien and Sedition Acts, 502–3, 503n60
Alquié, Ferdinand, 33n20
Ambition, 44–46, 91, 149, 161n84, 173, 199, 231, 271, 391n24, 448, 466–67, 493. *See also* Greatness
American colonials: British opinion of, 387; myth of British tyranny over, 384–86, 480n25, 489n38; obstructed British administration, 382n11; Whiggism of, 387
American Dream, 381
American Founders, 165, 299, 409, 460, 467
American Philosophical Society, 323
American Revolution, 299, 386, 449, 556; and French Revolution, 452–58
Amerindians, 477–78
Amsterdam Exchange Bank, 246, 248, 263
Anarchy, intellectual, 516–18
Ancien régime, 395, 444, 516–17, 529
Ancient constitution. *See* Constitution, ancient